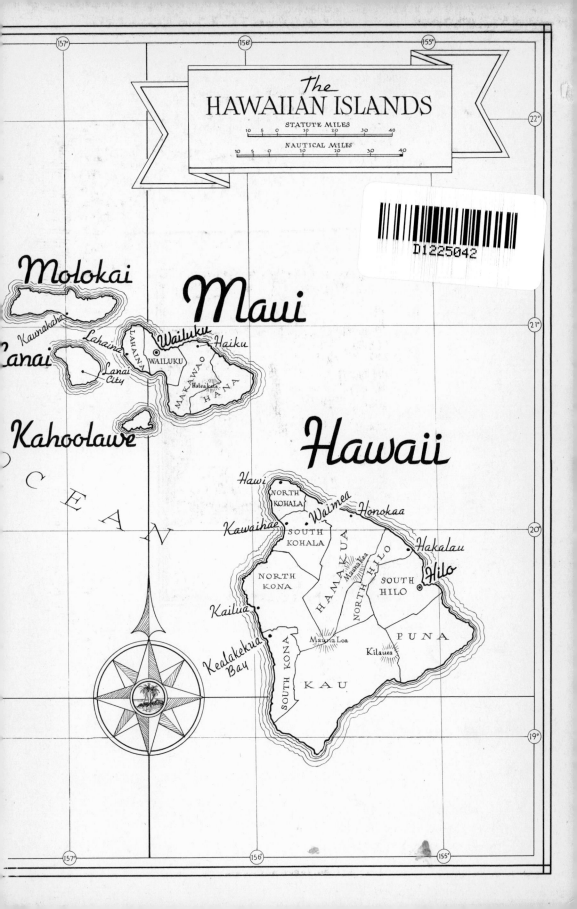

The HAWAIIAN ISLANDS

STATUTE MILES

NAUTICAL MILES

Molokai

Maui

Canai

Kaunakakai

Lahaina

Lanai
City

Lahaina

Wailuku

WAILUKU

Haiku

MAKAWAO

Haleakala

HANA

Kahoolawe

OCEAN

Hawaii

Hawi

NORTH
KOHALA

Waimea

Honokaa

Kawaihae

SOUTH
KOHALA

HAMAKUA

NORTH HILO

Hakalau

NORTH
KONA

Mauna Kea

SOUTH
HILO

Hilo

Kailua

Mauna Loa

PUNA

Kealakekua
Bay

SOUTH KONA

Kilauea

KAU

THE AMERICAN FRONTIER
IN HAWAII

The Pioneers
1789-1843

The
American Frontier
in Hawaii

The Pioneers
1789-1843

BY

HAROLD WHITMAN BRADLEY
Associate Professor of History, Stanford University

STANFORD UNIVERSITY PRESS
STANFORD UNIVERSITY, CALIFORNIA
LONDON: HUMPHREY MILFORD
OXFORD UNIVERSITY PRESS

STANFORD UNIVERSITY PRESS
STANFORD UNIVERSITY, CALIFORNIA

LONDON: HUMPHREY MILFORD
OXFORD UNIVERSITY PRESS

———

THE BAKER AND TAYLOR COMPANY
55 FIFTH AVENUE, NEW YORK

———

COPYRIGHT 1942 BY THE BOARD OF TRUSTEES
OF THE LELAND STANFORD JUNIOR UNIVERSITY

PRINTED AND BOUND IN THE UNITED STATES
OF AMERICA BY STANFORD UNIVERSITY PRESS

First printing, October 1942
Second printing, August 1944

To
MY MOTHER

PREFACE

FEW areas of equal size in this world have been the subject of so many books as have the Hawaiian Islands. For many years the bulk of the printed material relating to the Islands consisted of the accounts of travelers and the reports of missionaries. More recently there have appeared the treatises of scholars who have examined the antiquities of the Hawaiian people, the problems of Hawaiian industry and agriculture, or the social phenomena which have accompanied the development of the complex racial mixture which characterizes the population of the Islands. All of this printed material is grist for the historian. There have been books of history, as well as of travel, and all who embark upon the study of the history of the Islands are under obligation to a distinguished line of predecessors, beginning with David Malo and including the Reverend Sheldon Dibble, James Jackson Jarves, Manley Hopkins, William D. Alexander, William Fremont Blackman, and Ralph S. Kuykendall. Of this group, only Professor Kuykendall has had access to the vast amount of manuscript material located in continental United States and western Europe which bears upon the history of the Islands.

The present and future historian of Hawaii must be indebted not only to the researches and the writings of the men already mentioned but also to the local pride and devotion of innumerable citizens of the territory who have gathered and preserved the material from which the history of their islands can be written. The tangible evidence of their labors is to be seen not only in the territorial archives and in the library and publications of the Hawaiian Historical Society but in various other collections of books and manuscripts, the most important of which is that of the Hawaiian Mission Children's Society in Honolulu. The recognition of historical values exemplified by the care with which the materials of Hawaiian history have been preserved has been matched in part by the activity of the local historians, who have delved into many aspects of Hawaii's storied past. It is with a sense of real appreciation of the labors of those who have preceded me in this field that I venture to add another volume to the already long shelf of Hawaiiana.

This study was begun at Pomona College. It was continued at Stanford University under the ever helpful guidance and encouragement of Professor Edgar E. Robinson. In addition to my debt to this friend and scholar, I am especially grateful for the very valuable suggestions and assistance which were so freely given by the late Bishop Henry B. Restarick of Honolulu, Mr. Albert P. Taylor, late archivist of the Territory of Hawaii, Miss Caroline Green, formerly librarian of the Hawaiian Historical Society, Miss Nellie Pipes of the Oregon Historical Society, and the members of the staff of the library of the Harvard Divinity School. I am also indebted to the Hawaiian Mission Children's Society for permission to use and to quote extensively from the journal of Levi Chamberlain, to Professor Merrill Jensen, editor of the *Pacific Northwest Quarterly*, for permission to incorporate in chapter i sections of an article which was published in the *Quarterly* in July, 1939, and to the late Reverend Akaiko Akana for permission to quote from the tribute to Hiram Bingham which may be found on the walls of the Kawaiahao Church in Honolulu. Above all, I am under the greatest obligations to my mother, who has given freely of time and thought to assist me both in the laborious task of collecting notes and typing manuscript, and in making very helpful suggestions as to content and organization. For financial assistance which made possible much of the research involved and contributed materially toward the publication of the volume, I am indebted to the Council on Research in the Social Sciences of Stanford University and to the University Committee on Publications.

The first citation of each book, article, or manuscript includes the bibliographical data usually desired by the reader. Because the notes are unusually full, there is no formal bibliography. The index, however, contains references to the first citation of each work, published or unpublished, included in the notes.

HAROLD WHITMAN BRADLEY

STANFORD UNIVERSITY
CALIFORNIA

CONTENTS

ABBREVIATIONS

AH ....Archives of Hawaii
F.O. and Ex. ...Foreign Office and Executive
FRUS ....Foreign Relations of the United States
HHS ....Hawaiian Historical Society
NRL ....Naval Records and Library, United States
Department of the Navy
USDS ....United States Department of State

THE PIONEERS

THE history of the United States during the nineteenth century is pre-eminently a story of expansion. All sections of the country and virtually all aspects of American life were affected by the almost universal spirit of optimism and unrest. It was the force that prompted hundreds of thousands of families to seek new homes and better fortune on or near the frontier. It created an industrial society in a region which at the opening of the century had been largely agricultural. It carried American commerce and American influence into every quarter of the globe. Although far removed from the frontier, no section except the West was more affected by the expansive spirit of the age than was New England. The northern half of the frontier from the Mohawk to the Willamette was dotted with communities founded by immigrants from New England. Many an ambitious lad deserted the quiet monotony of New England farm or village life to ship aboard a New England–owned vessel engaged in the carrying trade with distant and little-known ports. In the wake of commerce and to equally remote parts of the world went New England missionaries, intent upon carrying the message of Christianity and determined to inculcate in non-Christian peoples the ideals of the New England churches. The results of this extension of New England commerce and New England theology were nowhere more in evidence than in the Hawaiian Islands.

There has been some doubt as to the identity of the first European to see the Hawaiian Islands, but it remained for Captain James Cook

1

to bring those islands to the attention of Europe and America.[1] Within twenty years of the discovery of the Islands by Cook, there developed a flourishing trans-Pacific trade in furs from the American coast; with that development it required no prophetic genius to foresee that the age-old isolation of the Hawaiian Islands was at an end. Traders who crossed the Pacific from the American coast to China invariably stopped at the Hawaiian Islands for provisions; many vessels, upon leaving the Islands, left behind deserters, who thus became the first European and American residents of the archipelago. In the course of time the foreign population was augmented by merchants and missionaries, and later by planters. With this influx of aliens the most notable feature of Hawaiian development during the nineteenth century was the uninterrupted retreat of the aboriginal civilization before the steady advance of foreign influences. The growing foreign population brought political complications. Until 1893, Hawaiian monarchs continued to reign in their petty kingdom, but before the middle of the century they had ceased to rule. Only the mutual jealousies of the great maritime powers prevented the inclusion of the Hawaiian Islands within the colonial empire of France, Russia, Great Britain, or the United States.

In the rivalry for control of the Islands, Great Britain enjoyed the advantages that accompany priority of discovery; but British

[1] Less than a decade after the visit of Cook to the Islands, the priority of his discovery was disputed and to the present time there has remained some doubt as to whether the great English navigator was the first European to visit them. Cook's confidence that he was the true discoverer of the Islands was not shaken by the finding there of two small pieces of iron, although his associate, Captain James King, believed that the feather capes of the Hawaiian chiefs could be traced to European influence. James Cook and James King, *A Voyage to the Pacific Ocean* (London, 1784), II, 194, 240; III, 137–138.

In support of the assertion that these Islands had been seen by Europeans prior to the visit of Cook there are Hawaiian legends and a series of charts dating from the sixteenth and seventeenth centuries. The legends which form the basis for the argument are described in William Ellis, *Narrative of a Tour through Hawaii* (London, 1826), pp. 371, 417; and in Sheldon Dibble, *History of the Sandwich Islands* (Honolulu, 1909), p. 19. The charts are described in E. W. Dahlgren, *The Discovery of the Hawaiian Islands* (Uppsala, 1917), pp. 151–212. Dahlgren's monograph is the most thoughtful and exhaustive study of the problem, and his rejection of the hypothesis that the Islands had been known to European navigators prior to Cook provides the most convincing answer which this question has yet received. A similar conclusion based on less exhaustive study of the evidence may be found in Henry B. Restarick, *The Discovery of Hawaii* (Honolulu, 1930); John F. G. Stokes, "Hawaii's Discovery by Spaniards," in HHS, *Papers*, No. 20 (Honolulu, 1939), pp. 38–113. The contrary view is concisely presented by Father Reginald Yzendoorn, "A Study in Hawaiian Cartography Prior to Cook's Rediscovery," in HHS, *Twenty-First Annual Report* (Honolulu, 1913), pp. 23–32.

subjects who cherished the hope that the Hawaiian Islands would some day be included within the British Empire were frustrated by the indifference of their government. While England hesitated to seize the prize, American dominance in the economic and political life of the Islands grew apace. At the close of 1842, the administration of President Tyler acknowledged that the extent of American interests in the Islands gave to the government of the United States a special concern for the preservation of Hawaiian independence.[2] The advance of the United States to the Pacific and the continued control of Hawaiian economic institutions by men who were American either by birth or heritage determined the fate of the archipelago. Fully aware of this peaceful conquest, few shrewd observers doubted— after the middle of the century—that the ultimate fate of the proud but vanishing Hawaiians would be to see their beloved kingdom absorbed by the great North American republic. When, in 1900, the Republic of Hawaii was succeeded by a territorial government modeled upon the precedents established by the Northwest Ordinance of 1787, a century of frontier expansion had reached its logical although long-delayed conclusion.[3]

The history of the Hawaiian Islands prior to the visits of Cook is shrouded in considerable doubt despite efforts to identify the characters and to explain the mysteries of Hawaiian antiquity. The similarity between the traditions, social institutions, physical features, and language of the Hawaiian people and of the Polynesians south of the equator clearly indicates that the Hawaiians are a part of the widespread Polynesian race.[4] The ever-tantalizing question as to the original home of the Polynesians has been given so wide a variety

[2] Message of President John Tyler to Congress, December 30, 1842, in James D. Richardson, comp., *Messages and Papers of the Presidents* (Washington, D.C., 1896–1898), IV, 211–214; also Secretary of State Webster to George Brown, Washington, D.C., March 15, 1843, in *Foreign Relations of the United States*, 1894, Appendix II, pp. 60–62.

[3] For a statement of this view of Hawaiian history, see Harold Whitman Bradley, "The American Frontier in Hawaii," in Pacific Coast Branch of the American Historical Association, *Proceedings*, 1930 (Glendale, California, 1931), pp. 135–150.

Cf. Clement Eaton, "The Hawaiian Islands as a Corner of the American Frontier," in *South Atlantic Quarterly*, XXXIII (October 1934), 354–362.

[4] Cook and King, *A Voyage to the Pacific Ocean*, II, 248–251; David Malo, *Hawaiian Antiquities* (Honolulu, 1903), p. 26; James Jackson Jarves, *History of the Hawaiian Islands* (Honolulu, 1847), p. 16; William Fremont Blackman, *The Making of Hawaii* (New York, 1906), p. 3; W. D. Alexander, "The Origin of the Polynesian Race," in HHS, *Seventeenth Annual Report* (Honolulu, 1910), p. 14.

of answers that one American anthropologist observed that "it is easy to find authority for including or excluding the Polynesians in or from all the races of mankind."[5] Competent critics regard the Polynesians as descendants of a primitive Caucasian group which was pushed out of central Asia by the presence of hostile and stronger tribes. Probably these fugitives took their departure by way of India and the Malay Peninsula, turning thence, when the pressure again became too strong to be resisted, eastward to the island archipelagoes of the South Pacific.[6] Less certain is the date when this migration first reached the Hawaiian Islands; but there is evidence that adventurous Polynesians had discovered and colonized the northern archipelago at least ten centuries before the time of Cook.[7]

All Polynesian people cherish traditions of long voyages by their ancestors. Through the medium of such voyages the pioneer Hawaiians for several generations maintained communications with their kinsmen in the islands of the South Pacific; despite danger and interruptions, there were, as late as the fourteenth century, occasional voyages between the Hawaiian Islands and the archipelagoes south of the equator.[8]

The increase of population in the Hawaiian Islands was accompanied by the appearance of the problem of land tenure. The result was the development of a feudal system based upon force and responsive to the need of the average Hawaiian for protection. The land was regarded as the property of the most powerful chief in each district; he apportioned the land among subordinate chiefs who had served him in battle or otherwise merited his favor. The lesser chiefs,

[5] Louis R. Sullivan, "The Status of Physical Anthropology in Polynesia," in *Proceedings of the First Pan-Pacific Scientific Conference* (Honolulu, 1921), p. 63.

[6] S. Percy Smith, *Hawaiki* (1904); Alexander, *loc. cit.*, pp. 14–24; Abraham Fornander, *Fornander Collection of Hawaiian Antiquities and Folk-Lore*, 3d series, in *Memoirs of the Bernice Pauahi Bishop Museum*, VI, No. 2 (Honolulu, 1919), pp. 222–238; Peter H. Buck, *Vikings of the Sunrise* (New York, 1938), pp. 12–25. Dr. Buck (*ibid.*, p. 49) agrees that the probable ancestral home of the Polynesians was in India, but he differs from other students of their migrations in believing that they went

from Indonesia to the central Pacific by way of the Micronesian Islands rather than by the more southerly route through Melanesia.

[7] Abraham Fornander, *An Account of the Polynesian Race* (London, 1878–1885), II, 2; Smith, *Hawaiki*, p. 222.

[8] William Churchill, *Polynesian Wanderings* (Washington, D.C., 1911), p. 180; Fornander, *An Account of the Polynesian Race*, II, 6–7; N. B. Emerson, "The Long Voyages of the Ancient Hawaiians," in HHS, *Papers*, No. 5 (Honolulu, 1893), pp. 1–28; Jarves, *History of the Hawaiian Islands*, p. 16; Malo, *Hawaiian Antiquities*, pp. 25–26.

in turn, permitted the commoners to live upon the land, taking in exchange a substantial portion of the crops raised by their tenants.[9]

The power of the chiefs was absolute, and often that power was exercised in a most arbitrary manner.[10] William Shaler, who visited the Islands early in the nineteenth century, characterized the attitude of the chiefs as "avaricious, cruel, and inhuman in the extreme."[11] Two missionaries, basing their conclusions upon information received from well-informed natives, expressed the belief that the common people had been compelled to see not less than two-thirds of the products of their labors appropriated for the support of the chiefs.[12] An annual tax was systematically collected by agents of the chiefs, while forced labor on public works or for the private benefit of the chiefs was added to the burdens imposed upon the commoners.[13]

The inequalities of Hawaiian feudalism and the uncertainty of land tenure were formidable obstacles to private initiative or sustained industry. Throughout the first half of the nineteenth century, visitors and residents who had come from countries where individual enterprise was highly esteemed viewed the continuance of the ancient feudal polity as an insuperable barrier to all real improvement in the social or economic life of the Hawaiian people.[14] Observers

[9] Sanford B. Dole, "Evolution of Hawaiian Land Tenures," in HHS, *Papers*, No. 3 (Honolulu, 1892), pp. 4–7; Jean Hobbs, *Hawaii: a Pageant of the Soil* (Stanford University, California, 1935), pp. 1–19; William Richards to Charles Wilkes, Lahaina, March 15, 1841, in AH, Richards MSS; "Principles Adopted by the Board of Commissioners to Quiet Land Titles," in Lorrin A. Thurston, comp., *Fundamental Law of Hawaii* (Honolulu, 1904), pp. 140–147; Ellis, *Narrative of a Tour through Hawaii*, pp. 394–398.

[10] Ellis, *op. cit.*, pp. 401–402; Richards to Wilkes, Lahaina, March 15, 1841, in AH, Richards MSS; Cook and King, *A Voyage to the Pacific Ocean*, III, 3; George Dixon, *A Voyage Round the World* (London, 1789), p. 126; Edward Bell, "Log of the Chatham," in *Honolulu Mercury*, I, No. 4 (September 1929), p. 19.

Accounts of the life and customs of the Hawaiian people prior to the arrival of the first Europeans at the Islands may be found in Fornander, *An Account of the Polynesian Race*; Malo, *Hawaiian Antiquities*;

E. H. Bryan, *Ancient Hawaiian Life* (Honolulu, 1938); Handy, Emory, Bryan, Buck, Wise, and others, *Ancient Hawaiian Civilization* [Honolulu, 1933].

[11] [William Shaler], "Journal of a Voyage between China and the North-Western Coast of America," in *American Register*, III (1808), 169.

[12] Dibble, *History of the Sandwich Islands*, p. 74; Richards to Wilkes, Lahaina, March 15, 1841, in AH, Richards MSS.

[13] *Ibid.*

[14] Ellis, *Narrative of a Tour through Hawaii*, pp. 404–405; Gilbert Farquhar Mathison, *Narrative of a Visit to Brazil, Chile, Peru, and the Sandwich Islands* (London, 1825), p. 385; Journal of the Missionaries at Honolulu, February 17, 1821, in *Missionary Herald*, XVIII (July 1822), 207; Asa Thurston and Artemas Bishop to the American Board, Kailua, September 20, 1833, in *ibid.*, XXX (October 1834), 371–372; Letter of John Diell, Honolulu, January 1, 1836, in *Sailor's Magazine*, VIII (July 1836), 339; Joseph G. Clark, *Lights and Shadows of Sailor Life* (Boston, 1848),

accustomed to the emphasis in New England upon thrift and the dignity of labor were disposed to regard the Hawaiians as indolent and vagrant in their habits,[15] although this apparent indolence may have been a by-product of the feudal system or it may have resulted from the inability of the Hawaiian people to adapt themselves to the social upheaval which followed the destruction of the *kapus* (taboos) and the influx of foreigners.[16] Archibald Campbell, who lived on Oahu for thirteen months in 1809 and 1810, declared that the Hawaiians were the most industrious people he had ever known.[17] This opinion, so unlike that expressed by many later observers, was formed before the ancient Polynesian traditions had been undermined by extensive contacts between the Hawaiian people and the outside world.

One notable distinction between Hawaiian and European feudalism had an important influence upon the development of Hawaiian character. The Hawaiian peasant was not bound to the soil. There was nothing, save inertia, to prevent him from wandering from island to island in search of adventure or a happier home.[18] Quite unacquainted with the satisfaction which comes with the ownership of land and accustomed to roaming aimlessly about the Islands, hundreds—and perhaps thousands—of Hawaiians, as late as the middle of the nineteenth century, retained the habits of their ancestors and seemingly without a definite purpose continued to drift from district to district throughout the Islands.[19]

p. 175; William L. Lee, quoted in *The Friend* (Honolulu), March 1866, p. 18.

[15] Journal of Maria S. Loomis (typewritten copy, Hawaiian Mission Children's Society Library, Honolulu), June 21, 1820; Artemas Bishop to the American Board, November 15, 1844, in *Missionary Herald*, XLI (May 1845), 163; George Brown to Secretary of State Upshur, Honolulu, January 16, 1844 (No. 11), in USDS, "Despatches," Sandwich Islands, I; C. E. Hitchcock to Robert C. Wyllie, San Francisco, February 27, 1852, in AH, Miscellaneous Correspondence; Henry T. Cheever, *The Island World of the Pacific* (Glasgow, n.d.), p. 163; Letter of J. F. Munger, Hilo, October 19, 1851, in James F. Munger, *Two Years in the Pacific and Arctic Oceans and China* (Vernon, N.Y., 1852), p. 64.

[16] E. S. Craighill Handy, *Cultural Revolution in Hawaii* (1931), pp. 27–33. A similar view was expressed by Henry T. Cheever (*The Island World of the Pacific*, p. 163) after a visit to the Islands in 1849. Cheever asserted that indolence was the "curse of the whole nation," and added that probably it was more common then than it had been when "the nation was a nation of savages, and the people had to work more for the chiefs, and the women were more occupied than now in making *kapa*."

[17] Archibald Campbell, *A Voyage Round the World, from 1806 to 1812* (Edinburgh, 1816), pp. 162–163.

[18] [Shaler], "Journal," in *American Register*, III (1808), 169; Otto von Kotzebue, *A Voyage of Discovery into the South Sea and Beering's Straits* (London, 1821), III, 246.

[19] Elias Bond to the American Board, [Kohala], June 15, 1846, in *Missionary*

It is apparent that the Hawaiian people had made some progress in agricultural and industrial arts before the coming of the Europeans. Early visitors, including Cook, were favorably impressed by their agricultural methods and products,[20] but it should be added that William Ellis believed that the produce of Hawaiian farms was "less valuable and abundant than in some of the islands both to the west and south."[21] The manufactures also attracted favorable attention. Cook described them as having "an uncommon degree of neatness and ingenuity,"[22] and a quarter of a century later William Shaler noted that the Hawaiians made "excellent white cordage, of all sizes," adding that "for running rigging, there is no better rope."[23]

The Hawaiians were a devout people. So large was the galaxy of deities to whom they paid homage that a recent writer has observed that the "Hawaiian Olympus was overcrowded."[24] In order to assure themselves of a maximum number of favors from their gods they provided wayside shrines where the casual traveler might leave his small contribution to the appeasement of some deity.[25] A more formal expression of piety occurred when, on stated occasions, chiefs and priests retired for several days to more elaborate places of worship, known as *heiaus,* to observe the requirements of their faith.

Herald, XLIII (March 1847), 94; Titus Coan, *Life in Hawaii* (New York, 1882), pp. 58–59; William Richards to Rufus Anderson, Lahaina, December 25, 1834, in Letters to the American Board of Commissioners for Foreign Missions, LXVII, No. 84; The American Mission to Anderson, Honolulu, June 1, 1852, *ibid.,* CCXXXII, No. 40; Journal of Maria S. Loomis, November 4, December 28, 1820.

[20] Cook and King, *A Voyage to the Pacific Ocean,* II, 244; Edward Bell, "Log of the Chatham," in *Honolulu Mercury,* I, No. 4 (September 1929), p. 10; W. F. Wilson, ed., *Hawaii Nei 128 Years Ago, by Archibald Menzies* (Honolulu, 1920), pp. 75–77, 80–81, 105; William Robert Broughton, *A Voyage of Discovery to the North Pacific Ocean* (London, 1804), p. 37; [Shaler], "Journal," in *American Register,* III (1808), 166. A description of early Hawaiian agriculture may be found in Malo, *Hawaiian Antiquities,* pp. 269–273.

[21] William Ellis, *Polynesian Researches* (London, 1831–1832), IV, 25.

[22] Cook and King, *A Voyage to the Pa-*

cific Ocean, II, 237. See also *ibid.,* III, 131; [Shaler], *loc. cit.,* p. 166; Nathaniel Portlock, *A Voyage Round the World* (London, 1789), p. 59; Dixon, *Voyage Round the World,* p. 90; Urey Lisiansky, *A Voyage Round the World* (London, 1814), p. 129; Peter Puget, "A Log of the Proceedings of His Majesty's Armed Tender Chatham" (MS, British Record Office; microfilm copy, University of Washington Library), February 27, 1793.

[23] [Shaler], *loc. cit.,* p. 166. See also Bell, "Log of the Chatham," in *Honolulu Mercury,* I, No. 4 (September 1929), p. 20; G. H. von Langsdorff, *Voyages and Travels in Various Parts of the World* (London, 1813), I, 187.

[24] James Macmillan Brown, *Peoples and Problems of the Pacific* (London, 1927), II, 43. The best account of the religious beliefs of the Polynesians is E. S. Craighill Handy, *Polynesian Religion* (Honolulu, 1927).

[25] Wilson, ed., *Hawaii Nei 128 Years Ago, by Archibald Menzies,* p. 85.

Despite the destruction wrought by time and by the disillusioned natives, the location of more than five hundred of these *heiaus* is now known—an indication of the much greater number which there must have been during the period when the ancient faith still held sway.[26]

No aspect of Hawaiian religious beliefs so closely touched the daily life and thoughts of the people as did the *kapus*, and so competent an authority as E. S. Craighill Handy has characterized the system of *kapus* as "the keystone of the arch that supported the traditional culture of old Hawaii."[27] Temples, idols, sacred localities, and the persons of powerful priests and chiefs received the protection of the *kapu*, and thus were freed from the danger of being polluted by the gaze or the touch of the common people. The *kapu* not only served as an instrument which gave a religious sanction to the caste system, but it also placed the sexes upon a basis of inequality. Women were denied certain foods available for men and were restrained from entering the houses in which men were accustomed to eat or in which they conducted their worship. It seems possible that the *kapus* were observed with as much fidelity in the Hawaiian Islands as in any of the archipelagoes of Polynesia; they were to be, however, the first major institution to disintegrate in the presence of Europeans.

Captain James Cook had completed two extensive voyages of exploration when, in July 1776, he sailed from England upon his last and most notable expedition. Eighteen months later, on January 18, 1778, he sighted two islands not noted upon any of his charts, and on the following day his vessels, the "Resolution" and the "Discovery," anchored in the bay at Waimea, on the southern shore of Kauai. The natives greeted their visitors with amazement which was not unmixed with awe;[28] but their trading instincts were strong and soon they offered hogs and vegetables in exchange for nails and other scraps of iron.[29] Cook may have intended to remain at Kauai for some time, but on the evening of February 1 the "Resolution" was blown to sea. Because of the difficulty of regaining the anchorage, Cook left Kauai and set his course for Alaska.[30]

---

[26] Thomas G. Thrum, "Heiaus (Temples) of Hawaii Nei," in HHS, *Thirty-Second Annual Report* (Honolulu, 1924), p. 15.

[27] Handy, *Cultural Revolution in Hawaii*, p. 3.

[28] Dibble, *History of the Sandwich Islands*, pp. 20–21.

[29] Cook and King, *A Voyage to the Pacific Ocean*, II, 193–194, 199.

[30] *Ibid.*, II, 219–220.

Cook's second visit to the Hawaiian Islands began late in November 1778, when his vessels arrived off the coast of Maui. After cruising among the eastern islands of the group, he brought his vessels to Kealakekua Bay, on the west coast of Hawaii. There, for two weeks, he and his men were treated with the deference due mysterious visitors who clearly were suspected of being more than human. Presently the novelty of entertaining strangers lost its appeal, and the chiefs became solicitous as to when Cook proposed to depart.[31] It must have been with sentiments of relief, therefore, that the Hawaiians watched the "Resolution" and the "Discovery" sail out of the bay on February 4, 1779. Any rejoicing would have been premature; for seven days later, after the "Resolution" had been damaged in a gale, the two vessels returned to Kealakekua Bay.[32]

The reception tendered Cook upon his return was lacking in enthusiasm, and thereafter events moved swiftly to a tragic climax. On the morning of February 14, Cook went ashore with the purpose of luring Kalaniopuu, the king of the island of Hawaii, on board one of the vessels where he could be held as a hostage to insure the return of a cutter which had been stolen during the preceding night. These tactics were defeated when friends of the king persuaded him to decline the invitation of Cook. While Cook argued, news arrived that there had been a skirmish between some Hawaiians and a detachment of British marines. An excited crowd gathered, causing Cook to become alarmed for his own safety. He fired into the crowd and then turned to signal some message to his vessels. While he stood with his back to the crowd, he was struck with a club and stabbed, fell forward into the water, and died.[33]

The visits of Cook brought to a close the era of isolation. Three years later, in 1782, the death of Kalaniopuu plunged the island of Hawaii into a series of civil wars which ultimately spread to all the islands except Kauai and Niihau. By 1791, Kamehameha, a nephew

[31] *Ibid.*, III, 26.

[32] *Ibid.*, III, 30–34; David Samwell, *A Narrative of the Death of Captain James Cook* (HHS, *Reprint*, No. 2, Honolulu, n.d.), pp. 5–6.

[33] Samwell, *op. cit.*, pp. 9–15; Cook and King, *A Voyage to the Pacific Ocean*, III, 41–46; George Gilbert, *The Death of Captain James Cook* (HHS, *Reprint*, No. 5, Honolulu, 1926), pp. 10–12; "Extract from a Pocket Diary by One of the Officers of H.M.S. 'Resolution'," in *Honolulu Mercury*, II (March 1930), 377–378. Hawaiian versions of these events may be found in "Ka Mooolelo Hawaii," trans. in *Hawaiian Spectator*, II (January 1839), 65–66; Ellis, *Narrative of a Tour through Hawaii*, pp. 100–101.

of Kalaniopuu, had emerged as undisputed ruler of the island of Hawaii. He had been unable, however, to dislodge his great rival, Kahekili, from the neighboring island of Maui. After the death of Kahekili, Kamehameha again turned to war, and in 1794 and 1795 he subjugated Maui and Oahu.[34] Not yet satisfied, he twice planned an invasion of Kauai only to be defeated by storm or pestilence. The addition of the leeward islands to his empire had been postponed but not averted. In the winter of 1809–1810, those islands were ceded by negotiation to Kamehameha.[35] By war and the threat of war, Kamehameha had united all of the islands of the archipelago under his rule.

The founder of the new dynasty was endowed with considerable shrewdness and a dominating will. Richard Cleveland, who visited the Islands in 1803, described him as "a perfect savage, but evidently destined by nature, both physically and mentally, to be a chief."[36] It is certain that Kamehameha was respected by his subjects; it is less certain whether that respect was the result of gratitude to a benevolent sovereign or fear of a powerful and autocratic ruler. The mildness of his rule was noted by several visitors, and Archibald Campbell thought that Kamehameha was deservedly popular among his subjects because of the tranquillity and prosperity which accompanied his reign.[37] Less complimentary was the opinion of Hiram Bingham, that the great king was a veritable tyrant whose unquestioned control over his people was made possible primarily by their fear of him.[38]

The reign of Kamehameha was characterized by social and political conservatism. He carefully maintained the absolute power of

[34] For an account of the wars by which Kamehameha established his power, see Ralph S. Kuykendall, *The Hawaiian Kingdom 1778-1854* (Honolulu, 1938), pp. 32-38, 44-47; Jarves, *History of the Hawaiian Islands*, pp. 72-76, 91-92. A popular account of the life of Kamehameha may be found in Herbert H. Gowen, *The Napoleon of the Pacific* (New York, 1919). See also William H. Chickering, *Within the Sound of These Waves* (New York, 1941), pp. 205-295.

[35] John Boit, "The Journal of a Voyage Round the Globe . . . . 1795 & 1796" (MS, Massachusetts Historical Society Library), October 16, 1795; Broughton, *Voyage of*

Discovery, pp. 70-71; Jarves, *History of the Hawaiian Islands*, pp. 92, 96-98.

[36] Richard J. Cleveland, *A Narrative of Voyages and Commercial Enterprises* (Boston, 1850), p. 211.

[37] Campbell, *Voyage Round the World*, pp. 211-212. See also "Extracts from a Journal Kept on Board Ship Atahualpa, Bound on a Voyage from Boston to the N.W. Coast and Sandwich Islands," November 2, 1802, in Massachusetts Historical Society, *Collections*, 1st series, IX (Boston, 1804), 243-244; Alexander Ross, *Adventures of the First Settlers on the Oregon or Columbia River* (London, 1849), p. 46.

[38] Hiram Bingham, *A Residence of Twenty-One Years in the Sandwich Islands*

the monarch, and his influence was sufficient to prevent any weakening of the age-old customs and beliefs of his people. As the first to rule over the entire archipelago, he was compelled to provide for the administration of his kingdom. He allowed the local chiefs to retain a considerable measure of authority in the administration of problems of a purely local character; but the power of each was subject to that of the governor of the island on which he lived. The governors, of whom there was one for each of the major islands except Kauai, were the personal representatives of the King; and within their territory they exercised an authority which was checked only by the pleasure of Kamehameha. There was no legislative body in the kingdom. The King was therefore free to determine and enforce policy without the possibility of interference from any recognized authority. His rule was absolute, but it was not capricious. In practice, he frequently consulted a small group of trusted advisers who had been his friends and constant supporters since the time when he had first entered actively into the political life of the island of Hawaii. The position of these elder statesmen was wholly extralegal; through the policy of Kamehameha they constituted, in fact, an advisory council whose powers were quasi-legislative.

While Kamehameha was occupied with the conquest of an empire, the control of the Pacific passed from Spain to the aggressive traders of Great Britain and the United States. For two centuries Spain had dominated the great ocean from the Philippines to the American coast, and, except for the occasional intrusion of an English or a Dutch buccaneer, the annual galleon from Manila to Mexico had enjoyed an unchallenged monopoly of the commerce of the North Pacific. The first threat to Spanish supremacy in that area came from the Russians who accompanied Vitus Bering upon his voyages eastward from Kamchatka. These voyages stimulated both exploration and trade by revealing that sea otter were to be found along the Aleutian Islands and the Alaskan coast. Until nearly the close of the eighteenth century these trading expeditions were private ventures, and the perils of navigation in dangerous seas or of landing upon islands inhabited by hostile natives restricted this trade to the most

(Hartford, 1847), p. 54. See also John Meares, *Voyages Made in the Years 1788* and *1789, from China to the North West Coast of America* (London, 1790), p. 344.

reckless or the most courageous of the traders. At the close of the eighteenth century they led to the formation of the Russian American Company and to the Russian occupation of Alaska.

Of greater importance to the Hawaiian Islands was the stimulus to trade provided by the voyages of Cook. The official account of his last voyage, published in 1784, noted briefly that the Chinese merchants at Canton had shown more than casual interest in furs gathered along the northwest coast of America.[39] This inference that material gain as well as adventure or the advancement of science might be the reward of seamen who visited the North Pacific was sufficient to prompt merchants in India, China, England, and New England to send vessels to the Pacific to investigate the possibilities of this newest commercial speculation.

The earliest effort to exploit the new fur trade was that of "some Gentlemen in China," who, in 1785, sent Captain James Hanna to the American coast, where he secured a "valuable cargo of Furs." On the return voyage, in the autumn of 1785, Hanna touched at the Hawaiian Islands, thus becoming the first of a long line of traders to take advantage of the convenient location of the archipelago.[40] In the spring of 1786, two English vessels, commanded by Captains Nathaniel Portlock and George Dixon, stopped for twenty days at the Islands on the passage from Cape Horn to the northwest coast. They found the natives at Kealakekua Bay cool to suggestions of trade, but at Oahu they had no difficulty in securing water in exchange for nails and others articles of slight value.[41] While Portlock and Dixon were at the Islands, a French exploring expedition, commanded by the ill-fated La Pérouse, touched briefly at Maui.[42] During the following year, there were at least six vessels in Hawaiian waters—all of them concerned directly or indirectly in the fur trade.[43]

[39] Cook and King, *A Voyage to the Pacific Ocean*, III, 431, 437.

[40] "New Fur Trade," in *The World* (London), October 6, 1788, reprinted in [A. Grove Day and Donald O'Malley, eds.] *White Knight Chapbooks*, Pacific Northwest Series, No. 4 (Menlo Park, California, 1941).

[41] Portlock, *Voyage Round the World*, pp. 58–90; Dixon, *Voyage Round the World*, pp. 50–55.

[42] L. A. Milet-Mureau, ed., *Voyage de la Pérouse Autour du Monde* (Paris, an. V), II, 110–129.

[43] Bernice Judd, *Voyages to Hawaii Before 1860* (Honolulu, 1929), p. 12; Meares, *Voyages from China to the North West Coast of America*, p. xxxix; F. W. Howay, ed., *The Journal of Captain James Colnett aboard the Argonaut from April 26, 1789 to Nov. 3, 1791* (Toronto, 1940), pp. xx–xxi.

With the single exception of the expedition of La Pérouse, all vessels known to have visited the Islands prior to the autumn of 1789 were commanded by British subjects, although one of the vessels sailed under the flag of Austria.[44] The Spanish flag—once seen more frequently on the Pacific than any of its rivals—was first flown in a Hawaiian port in 1791, when Alferez Manuel Quimper, in the "Princess Royal," touched at Hawaii while crossing the Pacific from Mexico to the Orient.[45] The United States was not represented at the Islands by a vessel until the visit of the "Columbia" to Hawaii in August 1789. Within ten years the trans-Pacific fur trade was virtually a monopoly of New England traders and the majority of the vessels which could be found in Hawaiian ports flew the flag of the United States.

The winning of political independence by the United States was followed by a reorientation of its overseas commerce. Independence brought freedom from restrictions which, when enforced, had often proved irksome; it also permitted the British government to erect barriers against American shipping in ports where previously American-owned vessels had enjoyed a lucrative trade. At the close of the Revolution, therefore, American maritime commerce faced a truly critical period, in which it was compelled to seek new markets to replace those which had been lost or were no longer profitable. Confronted by this grim necessity, a number of American merchants turned to the Far East. An experimental voyage to China, in 1784 and 1785, by the "Empress of China," provided information and a moderate return on the investment.[46] Encouraged by the results of this and succeeding voyages, adventurous merchants plunged into the

[44] F. W. Howay, "A List of Trading Vessels in Maritime Fur Trade, 1785–1794," in *Transactions of the Royal Society of Canada*, 3d ser., XXIV (Ottawa, 1930), Sec. II, 115.

[45] Quimper was bound for the Orient, where he was to surrender the "Princess Royal" to representatives of the South Sea Company. Among the incidental objects of Quimper's visit to the Hawaiian Islands were an investigation of the value and extent of their commerce and an effort to gain the good will of the Hawaiian people. Captain James Colnett, who met Quimper at the Islands, declared that he had been informed "by an Officer on board the Princess Royal the Chief errand here to the Sandwich Isles was to discover the properest place to make a settlement." Howay, ed., *Journal of James Colnett*, p. 218; Ralph S. Kuykendall, "James Colnett and the 'Princess Royal'," in *Quarterly of the Oregon Historical Society*, XXV (March 1924), 45.

[46] Josiah Quincy, ed., *The Journals of Major Samuel Shaw* (Boston, 1847), pp. 133–218.

infant trade with China to such an extent that as many as fifteen American vessels were reported to have anchored in the river at Canton during 1789.[47] With but a single exception these vessels had gone to the Far East by way of the Cape of Good Hope and the Indian Ocean; all of them planned to return by that route. These early traders were at a disadvantage in having little that they could offer the Chinese merchants in exchange for tea and nankeens; but the publication of narratives of Cook's last voyage, with its account of the avidity with which Chinese merchants purchased furs collected along the northwest coast of America, suggested an answer to that problem. It was no difficult matter for American merchants to envision a trade which would encircle the globe and would depend largely upon the success with which furs from the American coast could be traded at Canton for a variety of Chinese products in demand in Europe and the United States.

The first American to recognize the possible value of a trans-Pacific trade in furs from the northwest coast was John Ledyard. As a corporal of marines under Cook he had visited Nootka Sound in 1778, and like others who had been with Cook he was later surprised and impressed by the interest of Chinese merchants at Canton in the furs which had been taken on board at Nootka.[48] Following his return to the United States, late in 1782, Ledyard interviewed merchants in several cities in an effort to secure financial backing for a trading voyage to the northwest coast and China. He did succeed in arousing the interest of Robert Morris; but all efforts to charter a vessel for the proposed voyage failed, and in the summer of 1784 Ledyard sailed for Europe in the vain hope of finding there the support which had been lacking in his native country.[49]

The direct participation of American citizens in the Pacific fur trade dates from 1786. In that year, six merchants, five of them residents of Massachusetts, contributed more than fifty thousand dollars

[47] Meares, *Voyages from China to the North West Coast of America*, p. lxxxviii; Robert Gray to Joseph Barrell & Co., Canton, December 18, 1789, "Ship 'Columbia' MSS" (Massachusetts Historical Society Library), and printed in Frederic W. Howay, ed., *Voyages of the "Columbia" to the Northwest Coast* (Massachusetts Historical Society *Collections*, LXXIX, Boston, 1941), pp. 128–130.

[48] John Ledyard, *A Journal of Captain Cook's Last Voyage to the Pacific Ocean* (Hartford, 1783), p. 200.

[49] Jared Sparks, *Memoirs of the Life and Travels of John Ledyard* (London, 1828), pp. 175–183.

to outfit two vessels for a voyage to the northwest coast and China.[50] These vessels, the "Columbia" and the "Lady Washington," were entrusted to the command of two veterans of the sea, Captains John Kendrick and Robert Gray, respectively. They left Boston in September 1787 but failed to reach the west coast of North America until the following summer.[51] After the lapse of another year the two commanders exchanged vessels, following which Gray, in the "Columbia," left the American coast for Hawaii and Canton.[52] In August 1789 Gray reached the island of Hawaii, where he purchased "five Punchions of Pork and . . . . one hundred & fifty live hogs." His brief account of his visit to Hawaii fails to reveal any effort to find a product of the island which might supplement furs in the trading at Canton.[53] He reached China in November 1789, sold there the furs collected along the American coast, and then resumed his voyage westward around the Cape of Good Hope to Boston to become the first of scores of American traders to complete the circumnavigation of the globe.

The course of Kendrick after he assumed command of the "Lady Washington" cannot be traced with complete certainty. He gathered a cargo of furs for Canton and then, in the autumn of 1789, left the coast to follow Gray across the Pacific. There is no conclusive evidence that he visited the Hawaiian Islands during this voyage, but the chronicler of Gray's voyage declared that Kendrick crossed the Pacific "in nearly the same track" as the "Columbia."[54] That he should have done so is a reasonable assumption, for under similar circumstances a few months earlier he had ordered Gray to proceed

[50] Edward G. Porter, "The Ship Columbia and the Discovery of Oregon," in *New England Magazine*, n.s., VI (June 1892), 472–473; Massachusetts Historical Society, *Proceedings*, 1791–1835 (Boston, 1879), 1st ser., I, 25.

[51] Letter of Robert Gray, Nootka Sound, July 13, 1789, "Ship 'Columbia' MSS." This letter and that of Gray dated December 17 cited below were among the letters published by Judge F. W. Howay in *Washington Historical Quarterly*, XII (October 1921), 243–271.

[52] Gray to Joseph Barrell & Co., Canton, December 17, 1789, "Ship 'Columbia' MSS."

[53] Gray to Joseph Barrell & Co., Canton, December 17, 18, 1789, *ibid.*

[54] John Hoskins, "Narrative of a Voyage to the North West Coast of America and China . . . . in the Columbia Rediviva" (MS, Massachusetts Historical Society Library), p. 6, and printed in Howay, ed., *Voyages of the "Columbia,"* p. 164. It may have been on the basis of this evidence that Judge Howay concluded that Kendrick left the American coast for China "by way of the Hawaiian Islands." F. W. Howay, "Voyages of Kendrick and Gray in 1787–90," in *Oregon Historical Quarterly*, XXX (June 1929), 91.

directly to the Hawaiian Islands and thence to continue to China.[55] It is also reasonable to believe that Kendrick was in need of provisions which could be purchased at Hawaii with much less difficulty than at any point along the American coast. The positive references by Hoskins and Ingraham, in 1791, to an earlier visit to the Islands by Kendrick leave little reason to doubt that the "Lady Washington" touched at the Islands in the course of the voyage to China.[56]

Two other American vessels were at the Hawaiian Islands during the winter of 1789–1790. The two were the "Eleanora," commanded by Captain Simon Metcalfe, and the "Fair American," commanded by his son. The "Eleanora" arrived some weeks before the "Fair American," and the elder Metcalfe engaged in desultory trade with the natives while awaiting the arrival of his son. His conduct at the Islands, culminating in the cold-blooded massacre of scores of unoffending natives in retaliation for the theft of a small boat, has given him an unenviable reputation for cruelty. The immediate result was disastrous to his own fortunes. One powerful chief, who had been flogged by order of Metcalfe, avenged the injury by an attack upon the "Fair American." The offended chief secured a full measure of revenge, for but one member of the vessel's crew survived the murderous assault of the natives. The lone survivor was Isaac Davis. He was surrendered to Kamehameha, by whom he was treated kindly but compelled to remain on Hawaii. The elder Metcalfe, meanwhile, was at Kealakekua Bay. Unaware of the tragedy which had overtaken the "Fair American," he permitted John Young, the boatswain of the "Eleanora," to visit a small party of Europeans who resided at Kealakekua. While Young was ashore, Kamehameha placed a *kapu* on all canoes in the bay. The demands of Metcalfe that the *kapu* be lifted to allow Young to return to his vessel were unavailing, and the "Eleanora" sailed from Hawaii with Metcalfe still ignorant of the fate of his son and leaving Davis and Young dependent upon the bounty of Kamehameha.[57]

[55] Gray to Joseph Barrell & Co., Canton, December 17, 1789, "Ship 'Columbia' MSS."

[56] Hoskins, "Narrative," in Howay, ed., *Voyages of the "Columbia,"* p. 210; [Joseph Ingraham], *The Log of the Brig Hope called the Hope's Track among the Sand-wich Islands May 20–Oct. 12, 1791* (HHS, *Reprint*, No. 3, Honolulu, 1918), pp. 10, 18.

[57] There are many nearly contemporary accounts of the visit of the "Eleanora" and the "Fair American" to the Hawaiian Islands. The majority of these accounts are based upon information given by Davis and

Contemporary accounts which have escaped destruction by time or by carelessness provide only an incomplete record of commercial activities in the Pacific prior to 1815.[58] Following the return of Gray to Boston in 1790, American interest in the Pacific fur trade grew rapidly. In 1791 there were not fewer than five—possibly there were as many as seven—American vessels trading along the northwest coast in competition with an equal number of British vessels.[59] Ten years later British vessels had virtually disappeared from the trade; in 1801 there was but a single British trader on the coast to compete with fifteen from the United States.[60]

The colorful and often lucrative commerce which linked Boston,

Young to visitors to the Islands. Among the earliest and most satisfactory of these reports which may be traced to either Davis or Young are those in [Ingraham], *Log of the Brig Hope*, pp. 15–17 (May 26, 1791); George Vancouver, *A Voyage of Discovery to the North Pacific Ocean and Round the World* (London, 1798), II, 136–139; Puget, "Log of the Chatham," February 13, 23, 1793. See also Jarves, *History of the Hawaiian Islands*, pp. 76–77; F. W. Howay, "Captain Simon Metcalfe and the Brig 'Eleanora'," in *Washington Historical Quarterly*, XVI (April 1925), 114–121; *New York Daily Advertiser*, December 17, 1791.

[58] The most complete list of trading voyages along the northwest coast is that compiled by F. W. Howay of New Westminster, B.C., and published in *Transactions of the Royal Society of Canada*, 3d ser., XXIV (1930), Sec. II, pp. 111–134; XXV (1931), Sec. II, pp. 117–149; XXVI (1932), Sec. II, pp. 43–86; XXVII (1933), Sec. II, pp. 119–147; XXVIII (1934), Sec. II, pp. 11–49. With few exceptions the vessels listed by Howay visited the Hawaiian Islands either on the voyage from Cape Horn to the northwest coast or while crossing the Pacific from the American coast to China. Some of them wintered at the Islands as an interlude between two trading seasons along the coast.

The most recent compilation of vessels visiting the Hawaiian Islands during this early period is Bernice Judd, *Voyages to Hawaii Before 1860*. This list is admittedly incomplete, but in conjunction with the extensive list of vessels along the northwest coast it is a very convenient starting point for any more thorough study of the visits of trading vessels to Hawaiian ports.

[59] Howay, "A List of Trading Vessels in Maritime Fur Trade," in *Transactions of the Royal Society of Canada*, 3d ser., XXIV, Sec. II, pp. 120–123; "The Northwest Fur Trade," in *The Merchants' Magazine and Commercial Review* (edited by Freeman Hunt, New York, 1839–1870), XIV (June 1846), 535. In the summer of 1792 Captain George Vancouver reported the presence along the northwest coast of six trading vessels from England, five from the United States, and six owned by British merchants in India or Canton. He also noted the presence of a sloop, built on the coast, which was acting as a tender to the "Columbia" of Boston. Letter of George Vancouver, September 20, 1792, in "Correspondence between the Court of Spain and Great Britain relative to the Settlement of the Nootka Controversy" (typed copy, Provincial Library and Archives, Victoria, B.C.), II, 617.

[60] [William Sturgis], "Examination of the Russian Claims to the Northwest Coast of America," in *North American Review*, XV (October 1822), 372; "The Northwest Fur Trade," in *Merchants' Magazine*, XIV (June 1846), 536; "Solid Men of Boston in the Northwest" (MS in Bancroft Library, University of California), p. 9.

In 1816 Sturgis wrote that he had been "on the Coast in company with 16 American Vessels, employing from 20 to 25 men each, but there are not *usually* so many vessels on the coast at a time." Sturgis to Charles Morris, Boston, August 22, 1816, in USDS, "Miscellaneous Letters."

the northwest coast, and Canton was the product of individual shrewdness and daring. It also required capital, with the result that it was
dominated by a small group of Boston merchants.[61] Those who participated in the trade expected to reap a substantial profit on the
handling of the furs; but the prices brought by the tea and nankeens
which they carried from China to the United States commonly determined the financial success of the entire voyage. In any event, the
trade was highly speculative. Some participants were rewarded with
"large profits";[62] merchants who pursued the trade "systematically
and perseveringly" over a period of years found it generally profitable and even lucrative.[63] Many voyages, however, failed to produce
a return commensurate with the investment in time and cargo, and
not a few voyages were financially disastrous.[64] Rivalry among the
traders was keen, and many did not hesitate to employ every means
at their command to secure a full cargo of furs for the market at
Canton. This hectic competition and the resulting indiscriminate
slaughter of the sea otter along the northwest coast compelled many
traders, after 1805, to remain in the eastern Pacific for more than
one season in order to secure a satisfactory store of furs.

The decline in the number of sea otter along the northwest coast
caused some traders to transfer their activities southward to the coast
of California. Some of those who visited California were content
to secure furs through trade with the residents; others undertook to
capture the otter in the open sea.[65] Because this trade was prohibited
by Spanish law it was conducted in a clandestine manner or under
the pretense of needing provisions or repairs. Occasionally the local
authorities attempted to detain vessels or seamen suspected of engaging in the illicit traffic,[66] but this sporadic enforcement of the law

[61] William Tufts, "Account of the Ves-
sels engaged in the Sea-otter Fur-trade on
the Northwest Coast prior to 1808," in
James G. Swan, *The Northwest Coast* (New
York, 1857), pp. 423–424; "The Northwest
Fur Trade," in *Merchants' Magazine*, XIV
(June 1846), 537.

[62] Timothy Pitkin, *A Statistical View of
the Commerce of the United States of
America* (New York, 1817), p. 249.

[63] "The Northwest Fur Trade," *loc. cit.*,
p. 537.

[64] *Ibid.* In the autumn of 1792, Captain
Charles William Barkley of the "Halcyon"

found "so many Vessells more in this Trade"
than he anticipated, with the prices of furs
high and with "such an extraordinary competition" that he confessed doubts as to
whether the trade was "worth following at
all." Barkley, "Log of the Brig Halcyon"
(MS, Provincial Library and Archives, Victoria, B.C.), November 11, 1792.

[65] An excellent summary of this trade
may be found in Adele Ogden, *The California Sea Otter Trade 1784–1848* (Berkeley, California, 1941), chaps. i–iv.

[66] Cleveland, *Voyages and Commercial
Enterprises*, pp. 196–198; Langsdorff, *Voy-*

does not appear to have interfered seriously with the success of the traders. However excellent may have been the intentions of the officials in California, they were too few in number, if not too incompetent, to police effectively the vast area assigned to their care. At the same time, the missionaries in California—with surprising indifference to the civil authority—openly traded with the visitors.[67] The value and extent of this commerce may be judged by the estimate of one of the most active of the traders, who declared that, in the years immediately after 1800, American vessels annually left in California goods and specie to the value of twenty-five thousand dollars.[68]

The Russians in Alaska did not escape the influence of the ubiquitous traders. The post at Sitka was dependent upon the outside world for supplies,[69] and on at least one occasion Governor Baranov was able to secure an adequate store of provisions only by the purchase of a visiting American vessel and its cargo.[70] In 1808 the Boston firm of J. and T. H. Perkins believed that "some good business" might result from carrying supplies to Sitka;[71] at about the same time their great New York competitor, John Jacob Astor, envisioned the exploitation of the needs of the Russians as a profitable part of his projected monopoly of the trans-Pacific fur trade. Astor's ambitious plans included a division of the fur trade with the Russian American Company and the driving of "transient" traders from the northwest coast.[72] He organized the Pacific Fur Company in 1810, and pro-

ages and Travels, II, 185; Hubert Howe Bancroft, *History of California* (San Francisco, 1886–1890), II, 37–38.

[67] [Shaler], "Journal," in *American Register,* III (1808), 143, 153; Kotzebue, *Voyage of Discovery,* III, 256; "Solid Men of Boston in the Northwest," pp. 19, 53. Shaler thought that the missionaries were "the principal monopolizers" of trade with visiting vessels but added that others took some part in it. H. H. Bancroft quoted the Russian writer Tikhmeneff to the same effect. Bancroft, *History of California,* II, 66 n.

[68] [Shaler], *loc. cit.,* p. 153. In 1803, the "Lelia Byrd" extended the scope of trade along the California coast when it carried four horses from California to the Hawaiian Islands as a present for Kamehameha. From this small beginning, there developed a modest but persistent trade in California horses. Cleveland, *Voyages and Commercial Enterprises,* pp. 204, 205, 208–210.

[69] [Sturgis], "Examination of the Russian Claims to the Northwest Coast of America," in *North American Review,* XV (October 1822), 394; Frank A. Golder, "Proposals for Russian Occupation of the Hawaiian Islands," in Albert P. Taylor and Ralph S. Kuykendall, eds., *Papers Read during the Captain Cook Sesquicentennial Celebration* (Honolulu, 1930), p. 39.

[70] Langsdorff, *Voyages and Travels,* II, 87–89.

[71] Horatio Appleton Lamb, "Notes on Trade with the Northwest Coast, 1790–1810" (MS, Harvard University Library), p. 49; J. and T. H. Perkins to Perkins & Co., Boston, March 29, 1808, in J. and T. H. Perkins Letterbooks (MS, Baker Library, Harvard University School of Business), 1807–1815, p. 121.

[72] Astor to A. B. Bentzon, New York, January 21, 1811, in Kenneth W. Porter,

ceeded with plans for the establishment of a trading post at the mouth of the Columbia River.[73] If we may credit the statement of Washington Irving, Astor cherished "a vague idea" that he might acquire one of the Hawaiian Islands to be used as a base for the vessels which were to carry his furs from the American coast to China.[74]

Many of the American vessels which traded along the coast cruised northward into Alaskan waters and their supercargoes purchased furs from Indians living in territory which the Russian American Company regarded as within its sphere. This brought American traders into a competition which was distasteful to agents of the Company. The situation was not improved by the fact that the Americans sometimes stimulated trade by furnishing firearms to Indians who were unfriendly to the Russians. The unwelcome activities of the New England traders were made the subject of diplomatic protests by the Russian government. Russia did not wish to exclude American

John Jacob Astor (Cambridge, 1931), I, 455–459; Washington Irving, *Astoria, or Anecdotes of an Enterprise beyond the Rocky Mountains* (Philadelphia, 1836), II, 185–186. Alexander Ross believed that Astor had been primarily concerned with the trade with the Russian posts, inasmuch as he reserved for the Russians "the choicest part of all his cargoes" while sending to Astoria "the mere refuse." This, Ross noted, "gave great umbrage to the partners at Astoria; it soured their disposition to see many articles which they stood in need of pass by their door." Ross, *First Settlers on the Oregon*, p. 241.

[73] Porter, *John Jacob Astor*, I, 181–183.

[74] Irving, *Astoria*, I, 68. The Islands were destined to play a minor role in the brief history of the Pacific Fur Company. The annual supply vessels which Astor sent to the Pacific touched at Oahu on their passage to the Columbia, and it was at Honolulu that Astor's agent, W. P. Hunt, secured supplies for Astoria when the third of the annual vessels foundered off the island of Kahoolawe.

The first and best-known of the annual supply ships was the "Tonquin," which in February 1811 stopped at Waikiki, where Astor's agents met Kamehameha. When the "Tonquin" sailed from Oahu it carried twelve Hawaiian laborers who had been persuaded to go to Oregon in the employ

of the Pacific Fur Company. Astor's second annual vessel, the "Beaver," touched at Oahu in 1812 and likewise carried Hawaiian laborers to Oregon. The third of these vessels, the "Lark," encountered a heavy gale shortly before coming in sight of the Hawaiian Islands and was abandoned. The crew succeeded in reaching the island of Kahoolawe, where they were so alarmed by the inhospitable attitude of the natives that the supercargo, Nicholas Ogden, hastened to Hawaii to negotiate with Kamehameha for the relief of the stranded seamen. The King expressed some kindly sentiments but drove a hard bargain. He agreed to furnish the crew of the "Lark" with necessary supplies in return for the right to salvage the vessel and its cargo. Unable to resist these demands, Ogden capitulated, and Astor lost vessel and cargo at a time when both were sorely needed at Astoria. The "Lark" was the last of the vessels sent to the Pacific by the Pacific Fur Company. Irving, *Astoria*, I, 75–79, II, 107, 231, 235–239; Gabriel Franchere, *Narrative of a Voyage to the North West Coast of America* (New York, 1854), pp. 64–66, 81, 84–85, 177, 225–226; Ross, *First Settlers on the Oregon*, pp. 260–262; Elliott Coues, ed., *The Manuscript Journals of Alexander Henry and of David Thompson, 1799–1814* (New York, 1897), II, 763 n.–764 n., 845–847.

vessels from Alaskan waters, and the Russian Foreign Minister assured the representative of the United States that if trade along the Alaskan coast were regulated by treaty guaranties his government would view its increase with satisfaction. This view was elaborated by the Russian chargé d'affaires in the United States, who suggested that if a small group of irresponsible traders were suppressed the trade between responsible merchants and the Russian posts would "daily become firmer and more extensive, whilst subjected to a certain, judicious and prudent regularity."[75] The plan of Astor for the provisioning of Sitka in return for a monopoly of the trade with the Russian posts apparently was in harmony with the professed desires of the Russian government; but neither the vigor of Astor nor the hostility of the Russian American Company sufficed to drive the transient traders from the Alaskan coast.

The Russian post at Sitka was on the periphery of Pacific commerce; the Hawaiian Islands were in the path of vessels bound from the American coast to Canton. The location of the archipelago and the ease with which water, firewood, vegetables, hogs, and salt could be purchased there gave the Islands a very real importance to all who were engaged in the trade of the North Pacific. To these attractions were added the assurance of security of life and property. For fifteen years after the death of Cook, cautious seamen believed it necessary to exercise special care to guard against surprise attacks while at the Hawaiian Islands.[76] The scrupulous protection which Kamehameha

[75] Count Romanzoff to Consul General Harris, St. Petersburg, May 17, 1808, in *American State Papers, Foreign Relations,* V, 439; Daschkoff to Secretary of State Smith, Philadelphia, January 4, 1810, in *ibid.,* V, 438–439; Langsdorff, *Voyages and Travels,* II, 84.

[76] Meares to Captain William Douglas, September 20, 1788, in Meares, *Voyages from China to the North West Coast of America,* Appendix V; C. P. Claret Fleurieu, *Voyage Autour du Monde par Étienne Marchand* (Paris, an. VI–VIII), I, 410; Extracts from instructions to Captain Joseph Ingraham, September 14, 1790, in J. E. C., comp., "Extracts from Letterbooks of J. and T. H. Perkins" (typed MS, Massachusetts Historical Society Library); [Ingraham], *Log of the Brig Hope,* pp. 20–23; Bell, "Log of the Chatham," in *Honolulu*

Mercury, I, No. 4 (September 1929), pp. 19–20; Journal of Bernard Magee (MS, Massachusetts Historical Society Library), March 28, 1793; Boit, "Journal of a Voyage Round the Globe," October 16, 1795; Barkley, "Log of the Brig Halcyon," November 8, 1792.

The seizure of the "Fair American" and the massacre of its crew, in 1790, followed in 1795 by the seizure of the "Jackal" and the "Prince Le Boo," tended to confirm the fears of visiting seamen. One English magazine, in announcing the capture of the "Fair American," referred to the "usual custom of depredation" of the Hawaiians. *Gentleman's Magazine,* LXII, Part I (March 1792), p. 270. In 1791 apparently only the diligence of the watch prevented natives on Oahu from cutting off the "Massachusetts." "A Narrative of Events in the Life

provided for all visiting vessels presently dispelled the fears of visitors while within the territory controlled by the great Hawaiian king.[77] After the extension of his rule to Maui and Oahu, there was no part of the Islands—with the possible exception of Kauai and Niihau[78]—where traders might not anchor with confidence that they were as safe as in any part of the world. It was inevitable, therefore, that virtually every vessel engaged in trade in the northeastern quarter of the Pacific should visit the Hawaiian Islands for provisions or repairs or to allow a weary crew some respite from the dangers and monotony of life at sea.[79] It was with truth that Fleurieu, at the close of the eighteenth century, characterized the Islands as a "great caravansary" on the route from North America to China.[80]

During the early years of the maritime fur trade, masters faced with the necessity of remaining in the eastern Pacific for more than one trading season often wintered at the Hawaiian Islands.[81] Grad-

of John Bartlett of Boston, Massachusetts, in the Years 1790–1793, during Voyages to Canton and the Northwest Coast of North America," in *The Sea, the Ship and the Sailor* (Salem, 1925), p. 311.

[77] The cordial relations which existed between Kamehameha and the officers of Vancouver's expedition during the three visits of Vancouver to Hawaii seem to have played a considerable part in creating confidence in the good intentions of the Hawaiian king. During the second visit of the expedition to Hawaii, Lieutenant Peter Puget noted that "All our former suspicions which the melancholy Fate of Capt Cook had created were now supplanted by others of a far more pleasant sensation." During the same visit Vancouver testified to "the strictest honesty, civility, and friendly attention" with which he had been received at Kealakekua and praised the King as one having a "benevolent, humane, and friendly character." Puget, "Log of the Chatham," February 27, March 1, 1793; Letter of George Vancouver, March 1, 1793, in the *Polynesian* (Honolulu), February 27, 1841.

[78] Captain Broughton, who visited the Islands in 1796, ventured the opinion that any vessel might visit Hawaii with safety; but his experience at Niihau was scarcely reassuring, for at that island two of his crew were murdered by the natives, apparently

without provocation. Broughton, *Voyage of Discovery*, pp. 34, 75–78.

[79] Bell, "Log of the Chatham," in *Honolulu Mercury*, I, No. 4 (September 1929), p. 25; Lisiansky, *Voyage Round the World*, p. 125; Louis Choris, *Voyage Pittoresque Autour du Monde* (Paris, 1822), "Iles Sandwich," p. 8.

[80] Fleurieu, *Voyage Autour du Monde par Étienne Marchand*, I, 410.

[81] Bell, "Log of the Chatham," in *Honolulu Mercury*, I, No. 4 (September 1929), p. 25; Wilson, ed., *Hawaii Nei 128 Years Ago, by Archibald Menzies*, p. 144; Charles Bishop, "Commercial Journal . . . . of the Ship Ruby's Voyage to the Northwest Coast of America and China, 1794–5–6" (MS, Provincial Library and Archives, Victoria, B.C.), p. 81; Langsdorff, *Voyages and Travels*, I, 186. As late as the summer of 1815 a British naval officer reported that American vessels trading along the northwest coast came to the Islands "in the winter months, where they land their skins for the purpose of drying and curing, continuing to go to and from the North West Coast, until they have completed a Cargo for the China Market, which generally takes them two and sometimes three years." T. T. Tucker to Secretary Croker, Portsmouth, June 28, 1815, in *Historical Records of Australia* (Sydney, 1914–), ser. I, VIII, 626.

ually this practice was abandoned and vessels remained on the coast through the winter in order to reopen trading at the earliest possible moment the following spring.[82] Most of the visits of American vessels to Hawaiian ports between 1800 and 1815 were brief stops on the passage from the United States to the northwest coast or from the American coast across the Pacific to China.[83]

The evolution of the wants of the Hawaiian people as revealed by their demands in barter with visiting traders is an interesting commentary upon the spread of civilization among the Hawaiian people. During the earliest years of the fur trade, when the visits of vessels to Hawaiian waters were still a novelty, the naïve and amiable Hawaiians readily parted with their provisions in exchange for nails or scraps of iron.[84] Within a few years, the Hawaiians had become more sophisticated. Visiting vessels ceased to be a source of amazement to the natives and became a source of some profit. In the autumn of 1793 Captain Thomas New of the "Daedulus" found that the increasing trade at Kealakekua had caused a very marked increase in prices at that place within a period of a few months.[85] Shortly thereafter, Peter Puget observed that "Hurry and Commerce" were the prevailing features of life at Kealakekua.[86] The Hawaiians continued to accept nails or iron goods in trade, but they had begun to expect a variety of articles among which the most popular appear to have been cloth and mirrors. The chiefs were more practical; they were engaged in a bitter struggle for the control of the Islands, and

[82] Howay, "A List of Trading Vessels in the Maritime Fur Trade," in *Transactions of the Royal Society of Canada*, 3d ser., XXVI, Sec. II, p. 44.

[83] The courses of the "Caroline" and the "Pearl" appear to have been typical of the experience of trading vessels in the northeastern Pacific. The "Caroline" was at the Hawaiian Islands for twenty days in December 1803 on its outward voyage to the northwest coast, where it remained until June 1805, when it sailed for China. On the passage across the Pacific, it stopped at the Islands for about three weeks. The "Pearl" was at the Islands for eleven days in January 1808, on its voyage from the United States to the northwest coast; it next appeared at the Islands in October 1809 to secure provisions and wood for the voyage to China. Lamb, "Notes on Trade with the Northwest Coast," pp. 41, 43, 47. Cf. Judd, *Voyages to Hawaii Before 1860*, pp. 13–19.

[84] Dixon, *Voyage Round the World*, p. 53; George Mortimer, *Observations and Remarks Made during a Voyage . . . . in the Brig Mercury* (London, 1791), pp. 50, 51; "A Narrative of Events in the Life of John Bartlett," in *The Sea, the Ship and the Sailor*, pp. 308, 313; Fleurieu, *Voyage Autour du Monde par Étienne Marchand*, I, 412.

[85] Thomas New to Mrs. Thomas New, December 16, 1793, MS, Provincial Library and Archives, Victoria, B.C. Captain New asserted that prices "had risen 200 pc." since his previous visit to Kealakekua Bay.

[86] Puget, "Log of the Chatham," January 27, 1794.

they hoped to exploit their monopoly of provisions to secure arms and ammunition with which to carry on their wars.[87] With the return of peace, the chiefs lost interest in the materials of war. By 1804 Kamehameha was reported to have "so great a quantity of small guns, swivels, muskets, and ammunition" that these articles no longer were so eagerly desired, and two Russian visitors discovered that cloth had become a prerequisite for the purchase of provisions.[88] A year later, in 1805, Samuel Patterson noted that the Hawaiians were anxious to secure money in order to buy "European goods"—presumably cloth and other manufactured articles—from vessels which called at the Islands.[89]

The interest of the Hawaiian people in trade no longer reflected the curiosity of the ignorant or the necessities of internecine slaughter, and a few visitors turned to speculations as to the future role of the Islands in the commerce of the Pacific. After a brief visit, in 1804, Dr. George von Langsdorff hazarded the guess that they were "likely to take the lead among the South Sea islands, in becoming a polished and civilized country."[90] Peter Puget was more specific. He believed that the "large and luxurious Growth" of cane on Hawaii "would abundantly repay in Quantity any Labour bestowed on it in Sugar and Rum"; this, if properly developed, might become the basis of "a new Commerce" between the Islands and the Spanish settlements along the American coast or Japan. The results of such a venture were uncertain, because, as he added, the ports of the Spanish settlements were closed to trade, and the possibilities therefore could "only be determined by the Spirit of Commerce which has already so successfully been tried in these Seas."[91]

[87] Vancouver, *Voyage of Discovery*, I, 186–187, II, 110; Thomas Manby, "Journal of Vancouver's Voyage to the Pacific Ocean," in *Honolulu Mercury*, I, No. 1 (June 1929), p. 14; Puget, "Log of the Chatham," February 13, 16, 27, 1793; Journal of Bernard Magee, March 28, 29, 1793, September 22, October 6, 1794; Boit, "Journal of a Voyage Round the Globe," October 14, 16, 1795; Bishop, "Journal of the Ruby," p. 114 (February 20, 1796); Broughton, *Voyage of Discovery*, pp. 68, 73.

[88] Lisiansky, *Voyage Round the World*, pp. 99, 102, 115–116, 125; A. J. von Krusenstern, *A Voyage Round the World, in the Years 1803, 1804, 1805, & 1806* (London, 1813), I, 196–197. Lisiansky observed that iron "is now little regarded, unless in bars. Our rusty hoops, which were deemed so precious on the island of Noocahiva, availed us nothing."

[89] *Narrative of the Adventures and Sufferings of Samuel Patterson* (Palmer, Massachusetts, 1817), p. 66.

[90] Langsdorff, *Voyages and Travels*, I, 186.

[91] Puget, "Log of the Chatham," February 28, 1793. See also Langsdorff, *Voyages and Travels*, I, 188–189, and Lisiansky, *Voyage Round the World*, pp. 128–129.

Speculations of a somewhat different character induced John Turnbull to digress from his narrative of a visit to the Hawaiian Islands, in 1802, to observe:

The Americans carry on in particular a most active trade with these islands, supplying them with property at an easy rate in exchange for provisions, and, unless I am much deceived, will do more than any others to exalt it to a singular degree of civilization. The reader will here pardon me for introducing this remark on American commerce: so far does it exceed all former efforts of former nations, that even the Dutch themselves sink under the comparison. Scarcely is there a part of the world, scarcely an inlet in these most unknown seas, in which this commercial hive has not penetrated. The East-Indies is open to them, and their flags are displayed in the seas of China. And it must be confessed, to their honour, that their success is well merited by their industry.[92]

Until after the turn of the century, the location of the Islands and the abundance of available provisions constituted their claim to notice as a factor in the commerce of the Pacific. Gradually Hawaiian ports gained favor for the ease and convenience with which vessels might be refitted or repaired there. In 1794 two vessels engaged in the fur trade were rebuilt at Honolulu, and in the same year the "Jefferson" was repaired at Kealakekua.[93] The following year, after the "Lady Washington" had been damaged in a typhoon, Captain Kendrick took his ship to the Hawaiian Islands for repairs.[94] Shortly after the opening of the new century, Amasa Delano, an able and experienced seaman, testified that vessels might be repaired at Honolulu "with as much convenience as . . . . at any other place whatever where a vessel lies afloat."[95] For a few years Kealakekua

[92] John Turnbull, *A Voyage Round the World, in the Years 1800, 1801, 1802, 1803, and 1804* (London, 1805), II, 13–14.

[93] Boit, "Journal of a Voyage Round the Globe," October 16, 1795; Journal of Bernard Magee, October 4, 1794.

[94] Howay, "A List of Trading Vessels in the Maritime Fur Trade," in *Transactions of the Royal Society of Canada*, 3d ser., XXV, Sec. II, p. 124. At least one master was less optimistic about the availability of Hawaiian ports for repairs. When the "Ruby" required repairs, in 1796, Captain Charles Bishop felt some alarm, as, in his opinion, there were no harbors at the Hawaiian Islands "where the Ship might lay in smooth water, to careen, and come at these Leaks." Bishop, "Journal of the 'Ruby'," p. 111 (February 9, 1796).

[95] Amasa Delano, *A Narrative of Voyages and Travels in the Northern and Southern Hemispheres* (Boston, 1817), pp. 390–391. The first commercial agent of the United States at the Hawaiian Islands declared more than once that Honolulu had "perhaps one of the safest & most commodious Harbors in the world." John C. Jones to Secretary of State Adams, Oahu, December 31, 1821, in USDS, "Consular Letters," Honolulu, I; Jones to Secretary of State Clay, Oahu, July 1, 1827, *ibid.*

Bay vied with Honolulu in popularity as a port of call,[96] but it could not indefinitely compete with the advantages offered by Honolulu. To Honolulu mariners in distress could safely turn in the expectation of making repairs, recruiting a crew, meeting fellow seamen, or securing a passage to China or to the United States. Shipping, however, had not yet become congested in the harbor at Honolulu; during thirteen months in 1809 and 1810, Archibald Campbell noted the arrival of only twelve vessels, of which nine were owned in the United States.[97]

The resourceful Yankee traders who called at Hawaiian ports could not be indifferent to the possibility of adding Hawaiian products to the cargoes which they carried to China. Less than a year after the first visit to Hawaii of the "Columbia," a few traders had discovered the presence of sandalwood at the islands. The identity of the person who first carried Hawaiian sandalwood to Canton is shrouded in mystery, although tradition has conferred that distinction upon Captain John Kendrick.[98] Kendrick did leave three men at Hawaii late in 1789; but the motives for this action are not certain.[99] The earliest specific mention of sandalwood at the Islands is attributed to Isaac Ridler, a deserter from the "Columbia." Ridler was at Kealakekua Bay in March 1790, during the visit of the "Eleanora"; a year later, he told Captain Joseph Ingraham that while at Kealakekua Captain Metcalfe had been engaged in "taking in sandalwood."[100] Metcalfe may have purchased the sandalwood for use as firewood; it is also possible, if we may credit Ridler's testimony, that he was the first to carry sandalwood from the Hawaiian Islands to China for commercial purposes. A quarter of a century later, Amasa Delano recalled that in 1790 he had seen at Canton "more than thirty tons of what was called sandal wood" which had come from the Hawaiian Islands.[101] Before the close of 1790 Captain William Douglas left

[96] Urey Lisiansky, who touched briefly at Kealakekua Bay in 1804, recorded that eighteen vessels had visited that harbor within a period of twelve months. Lisiansky, *Voyage Round the World*, p. 125.

[97] Campbell, *Voyage Round the World*, p. 153 n. Campbell's statement seems to be substantiated by the most recent compilation of vessels engaged in the Pacific fur trade in 1809 and 1810. Howay, "A List of Vessels in the Maritime Fur Trade, 1805–

1814," in *Transactions of the Royal Society of Canada*, 3d ser., XXVI, Sec. II, pp. 64–71.

[98] Jarves, *History of the Hawaiian Islands*, p. 80; Dibble, *History of the Sandwich Islands*, p. 54.

[99] [Ingraham], *Log of the Brig Hope* (May 23, 1791), p. 10.

[100] *Ibid.* (May 26, 1791), p. 15.

[101] Delano, *A Narrative of Voyages and Travels*, p. 399.

two men at Kauai to gather sandalwood,[102] and in October 1791 Captain Kendrick left three men at the Islands with instructions to collect sandalwood and pearls.[103]

Sandalwood was in great demand in China, but the earliest shipments of the wood from the Hawaiian Islands were of such inferior quality that Chinese merchants refused to purchase them.[104] For twenty years thereafter, cautious traders, perhaps remembering the lack of enthusiasm with which the first Hawaiian sandalwood had been received at Canton, generally ignored its presence at the Islands and continued to regard Hawaiian ports primarily as convenient places at which to secure supplies, to recruit their crews, or to enjoy a brief breathing spell between the long trading season on the coast and the voyage to China. At a time when a few bold mariners were willing to

[102] [Ingraham], *Log of the Brig Hope* (May 26, 1791), pp. 15, 19.

[103] Vancouver, *Voyage of Discovery*, I, 172, 188–189; Barkley, "Log of the Brig Halcyon," November 12, 1792. Kendrick promised to return two years later to secure the anticipated cargo. Some light is thrown upon the casual manner in which he regarded the episode by his failure to mention either the men or the sandalwood in what appears to have been his first report to his employers after leaving the Islands. Kendrick to Joseph Barrell, Macao, March 28, 1792, in *Oregon Historical Quarterly*, XXX (June 1929), 96–98.

Thomas Manby, who was at the Islands on the "Chatham," correctly predicted, in March 1792, that "this piece of speculation will . . . . ill repay the expenses of the Owners." Manby, "Journal of Vancouver's Voyage to the Pacific Ocean," in *Honolulu Mercury*, I, No. 1 (June 1929), p. 24.

Pearls never attained a prominent place in Hawaiian commerce. In 1788 Captain Meares instructed Captain Douglas to ascertain their value, and during the next fifteen years a number of visitors casually noticed the presence of pearls at the Islands, but few if any believed that they had commercial value. In 1816 Kamehameha was reported to have a monopoly of the trade in pearls, but this presumably was a by-product of the royal monopoly of all traffic with visiting vessels. Howay, ed., *Journal of James Colnett*, p. 282; Meares to Douglas, September 20, 1788, in Meares, *Voyages from China to the North West Coast*, Appendix V; Bell, "Log of the Chatham," in *Honolulu Mercury*, I, No. 4 (September 1929), p. 22; Wilson, ed., *Hawaii Nei 128 Years Ago*, pp. 25, 120; *Mémoires du Capitaine Peron* (Paris, 1824), II, 146; Bishop, "Journal of the Ruby" (September 20, 1796), p. 124; Letter of Ebenezer Townsend, Niihau, August 30, 1798, in New Haven Colony Historical Society, *Papers*, IV (1888), 67; Turnbull, *Voyage Round the World*, II, 79; Kotzebue, *Voyage of Discovery*, I, 338; Choris, *Voyage Pittoresque Autour du Monde*, "Iles Sandwich," p. 9.

[104] Delano, *A Narrative of Voyages and Travels*, p. 399. Delano's inference that the first sandalwood shipped from the Hawaiian Islands was not "the real sandalwood" is in harmony with the statement of one Boston merchant that there was a spurious sandalwood at the Islands and with the observation of Vancouver that the Hawaiian sandalwood "seemed but slightly to answer the description given of the yellow sandal wood of India, which is there a very valuable commodity, and is sold by weight." J. and T. H. Perkins *et al.* to Captain Samuel Hill, Boston, June 30, 1815, in Bryant and Sturgis Letterbooks (MS, Baker Library, Harvard University School of Business), 1814–1818, p. 156; Vancouver, *Voyage of Discovery*, I, 188–189.

brave the dangers of trade with the unfriendly natives of the Fiji Islands in order to secure a cargo of the precious wood,[105] Hawaiian sandalwood passed almost unnoticed. The journals of travelers, including a number of active traders, who visited the Hawaiian Islands between 1790 and 1810, are strangely silent concerning sandalwood —impressive evidence that it was not regarded as of commercial importance.[106] It was not altogether forgotten; but available records fail to confirm the statement of Archibald Campbell that Hawaiian sandalwood was "frequently purchased for the China market."[107] As late as the trading season of 1808–1809, less than five thousand piculs of sandalwood was carried to Canton in American vessels.[108] This would scarcely have provided a full cargo for two vessels, and presumably only a part of this total came from the Hawaiian Islands.

[105] Everaad im Thurn and Leonard C. Wharton, eds., *Journal of William Lockerby* ("Works Issued by the Hakluyt Society," 2d ser., LII, London, 1925), pp. 14, 59; *Narrative of the Adventures and Sufferings of Samuel Patterson*, p. 81; Edmund Fanning, *Voyages to the South Seas* (New York, 1838), pp. 60–61, 121–125; James Aickin to Governor King, Sydney, May 13, 1805, in *Historical Records of New South Wales* (Sydney, 1893–1901), V, 621; John Macarthur to Governor King, Parramatta, June 10, 1806, *ibid.*, VI, 92; Proclamation [of Governor King], July 12, 1806, *ibid.*, VI, 109–110.

[106] [John Boit], "Boit's Log of the Columbia, 1790–1792," in Massachusetts Historical Society, *Proceedings*, LIII (Boston, 1920), 261–262; Robert Haswell, "A Voyage on Discoveries In the Ship Columbia Rediviva," in Howay, ed., *Voyages of the "Columbia,"* pp. 357–358; Bishop, "Journal of the Ruby," pp. 111–125 (February 19–28, 1796); *Mémoires du Capitaine Peron*, II, 146–175; Letter of Ebenezer Townsend, Niihau, August 30, 1798, in New Haven Colony Historical Society, *Papers*, IV (1888), 50–78; [Shaler], "Journal," in *American Register*, III (1808), 137–175; Lisiansky, *Voyage Round the World*, pp. 98–137; Cleveland, *Voyages and Commercial Enterprises*, pp. 110–111, 207–213; George Little, *Life on the Ocean* (Aberdeen, 1847), pp. 97–101; *Narrative of the Adventures and Sufferings of Samuel Patterson*, pp. 65–72;

William Martain, "Log of the Ship Hamilton" (MS, Essex Institute, Salem, Mass.), September 27–October 15, 1811; John Ebbets, "Log of the Ship Pearl" (MS, Massachusetts Historical Society Library), September 3–28, 1806; Lamb, "Notes on Trade with the Northwest Coast."

The not always reliable John Myers wrote that the "Jane" "procured a large quantity of Santel wood, and took in a good supply of Hogs and Poultry" at Hawaii in October 1795. It does not follow that the sandalwood was purchased for sale in Canton; it may instead have been used as firewood. During a discussion of the trade carried on by the "Jane," Myers did not mention sandalwood, although he gave considerable attention to the value of furs from the northwest coast. He did note that the "Jane" sailed from Hawaii to Canton "to dispose of the Furs &c. that we had collected on our voyage." Whether or not sandalwood was included in the "&c." does not appear. John Myers, *The Life, Voyages and Travels of Capt. John Myers* (London, 1817), pp. 56–71.

[107] Campbell, *Voyage Round the World*, p. 200. John Turnbull, who visited the Hawaiian Islands in 1802, included sandalwood in his list of Hawaiian products "of high value in the China market." Turnbull, *Voyage Round the World*, II, 79.

[108] Charles Gutzlaff, *Sketch of Chinese History* (London, 1834), II, Appendix IV. A picul contains $133\frac{1}{3}$ pounds.

After about 1805 the possible value of trade with the islands of the Pacific, if carefully exploited, began to attract the interest of a few speculatively minded merchants. In 1807 the influential Boston firm of J. and T. H. Perkins suggested to their Canton correspondents that a trade might be developed in "Tin, Sandal wood &c from Canton to the Islands, & direct back as long as Vessels & Crew's [*sic*] will hold together."[109] It is not clear from the context whether "the Islands" referred to the Hawaiian Islands; but it seems reasonable to assume that they were included within this general term. J. and T. H. Perkins appear to have been the first great trading house to recognize that trade with the islands of the Pacific could be divorced from the fur trade and considered as a separate branch of commerce.[110] It remained for the Winship brothers to prove by actual experience that a profitable voyage could be made from the Hawaiian Islands to Canton with a cargo of sandalwood.

Captains Jonathan and Nathan Winship were already experienced in the trade of the North Pacific when, in the summer of 1809, they left Boston for the northwest coast in command of the "O'Cain" and the "Albatross," respectively.[111] In the following May, the "Albatross" arrived at the mouth of the Columbia. About forty-five miles upstream from Cape Disappointment, Winship attempted to establish a trading post, but a series of misfortunes compelled him to abandon the project. The "Albatross" then traded along the coast until October 1811, when it sailed for Honolulu and Canton with a cargo of furs said to have been valued at more than $157,000. At Honolulu the "Albatross" met the "O'Cain" and the "Isabella," the latter commanded by Captain William Heath Davis. After adding sandal-

[109] J. and T. H. Perkins to Perkins & Co., Boston, May 13, 1807, in J. and T. H. Perkins Letterbooks, 1807–1815, p. 21.

[110] J. and T. H. Perkins to Perkins & Co., Boston, May 13, 22, 1807, March 29, 1808, *ibid.,* pp. 21, 32, 121.

[111] The "O'Cain" left Boston in May 1809; the "Albatross" cleared some time prior to June 21. *Columbian Centinel* (Boston), May 31, June 21, 1809. Jonathan Winship had been to the Pacific on a trading voyage in the "O'Cain" in 1803–1805 and had returned to the Pacific in 1806 as master of that vessel. On the second voyage his brother Nathan had been first mate.

They followed the example of Captain O'Cain by making an agreement with the Russian officials whereby they were permitted to employ more than one hundred and fifty Kodiak Indians in the capture of sea otter off the coast of California. After spending two seasons along the coast and at the Russian settlements they sailed for Canton by way of the Hawaiian Islands in October 1807. They had accumulated furs valued at more than $136,000. They returned to Boston in June 1808 with a cargo of teas, silks, and nankeens. *Ibid.,* June 18, 1808; "Solid Men of Boston in the Northwest," pp. 11, 13–26.

wood to their cargoes, the three vessels sailed for Canton. Almost six months later they again dropped anchor at Honolulu.[112]

Pleased with the results of their venture in sandalwood, the Winships and Davis persuaded Kamehameha to grant them a monopoly of the sandalwood and cotton grown in his kingdom for a period of ten years. In return for this concession the King was to receive, in such form as he might wish, one quarter of the value of the sandalwood and cotton carried from the Islands by the Winships.[113] By one brilliant stroke the Winships appeared to have placed their commercial concerns beyond the perils and annoyances of competition from other traders. In order to devote their attention wholly to their new interests, they withdrew from the trade along the American coast.[114]

In the autumn of 1812 the Winships and Davis began the exploitation of their monopoly when they loaded the "Isabella," the "O'Cain," and three other vessels with sandalwood for Canton.[115] Their enjoyment of the monopoly was brief. At Canton they heard the disturbing news that the United States was at war with Great Britain; when they returned to the Hawaiian Islands, in the summer of 1813, Kamehameha repudiated the sandalwood contract—an action which the Winships and their friends attributed to English influence.[116] After a lapse of nearly three years, however, Kamehameha

[112] "Solid Men of Boston in the Northwest," pp. 29–31, 40–48, 51–60; John S. Tyler to Timothy Dodd, Boston, November 1, 1867, in HHS, *Papers*, No. 8 (Honolulu, 1895), p. 21.

[113] A copy of this agreement, signed by Jonathan and Nathan Winship and William Heath Davis and by the mark of Kamehameha, and dated July 12, 1812, may be found in "Solid Men of Boston in the Northwest," pp. 63–65, and in Massachusetts Historical Society, *Proceedings*, LIV (Boston, 1922), 16.

[114] The Winships withdrew from trade along the coast because they had found a more profitable enterprise. There had been so many vessels on the coast that trade was described as "miserable indeed." The veteran trader, William Sturgis, announced his intention of withdrawing from the trade "as fast as possible," but John Ebbets shrewdly reasoned that "now there are too many ships on the Coast Next Year there will be very few," so that the prospects for the future were encouraging. "Solid Men of Boston in the Northwest," p. 61; Sturgis to Cushing, Boston, March 23, 1812, in Bryant and Sturgis Letterbooks, 1811–1814, p. 51; Ebbets to Astor, Macao, January 11, 1811, in Porter, *John Jacob Astor*, I, 448–453.

[115] F. W. Howay, ed., *The Voyage of the New Hazard . . . . by Stephen Reynolds* (Salem, 1938), pp. 108–109, 111–114 (October 24, November 2–10, 1812). According to Reynolds the five vessels were the "Isabella" (Davis), the "O'Cain" (Winship), the "New Hazard" (Nye), the "Sylph" (La Bell), and the "Lelia Byrd." The master of the "Sylph" was Captain Dubell. The "Lelia Byrd" was owned by Kamehameha.

[116] "Solid Men of Boston in the Northwest," pp. 65–66; [C. Davis], "Sandwich Islands," in *North American Review*, III (May 1816), 52–53; *Boston Daily Advertiser*, quoted in *Niles' Weekly Register*, XVIII (August 12, 1820), 418.

complained that he had not been paid for the sandalwood which he had permitted the Winships and Davis to take from the Islands, and added that they had not returned his vessel, the "Lelia Byrd," in which they had carried sandalwood to Canton.[117]

The effects of the declaration of war by the United States in June 1812 were felt in all parts of the Pacific where American vessels were accustomed to trade. The dangers to American commerce in that ocean were not imaginary, for British men-of-war roamed the Pacific in search of enemy merchantmen. In February 1813 a group of Boston merchants who owned vessels then in the Pacific sent the armed schooner "Tamaahmaah" to the Pacific "to notify the Commanders of those Vessels of the existing war with Great Britain & take down their furs to Canton."[118] In July the "Tamaahmaah" arrived at Honolulu, where it found a number of American vessels taking refuge from the dangers of war and a considerable store of furs awaiting transshipment to China. A part of this valuable cargo was sent to Canton on the "Tamaahmaah";[119] the remainder was cached on the island of Kauai for safety until after the close of the war. Meanwhile a few Americans, marooned in the mid-Pacific by the war, improved the time by trade among the Hawaiian Islands, while others sought to collect sandalwood. One American vessel, the "Atahualpa," was sold to the Russians; another, the "Albatross," was chartered for voyages to the Columbia River and to the Marquesas Islands.[120]

Among the traders who found an asylum on Kauai were the Winships and their partner, Captain Davis. They negotiated with Kaumualii a contract similar to the one they had had with Kamehameha, and, in the spring of 1814, they began the collection of sandalwood.

[117] James W. Snyder, ed., "Voyage of the *Ophelia*," in *New England Quarterly*, X (June 1937), 365.

[118] J. and T. H. Perkins *et al.* to Captain James Bennett, Boston, February 14, 1813, in Bryant and Sturgis Letterbooks, 1811–1814, p. 196.

[119] "Solid Men of Boston in the Northwest," p. 73.

It was reported that the "Tamaahmaah" carried furs valued at $300,000 from the islands to Canton. Coues, ed., *Journals of Alexander Henry and David Thompson*, II, 848.

[120] "Log of the Atahualpa" (MS, Massachusetts Historical Society Library), October 1813—March 1814; F. W. Howay, "Last Days of the Atahualpa," in HHS, *Forty-First Annual Report* (Honolulu, 1933), pp. 70–74; Franchere, *Voyage to the North West Coast*, pp. 177–178; Ross, *First Settlers on the Oregon*, pp. 242, 251.

Alexander Henry observed that had the British man-of-war "Raccoon" visited the Hawaiian Islands "she would have made some valuable prizes." Coues, ed., *Journals of Alexander Henry and David Thompson*, II, 848.

Again they were disappointed. During the following September, the chiefs on Kauai refused to deliver any more wood to Davis or the Winships—a breach of contract which was again attributed by the Winships to the influence of British subjects at the Islands.[121] The Winships considered a bombardment of the village of Waimea as a means of coercing the chiefs; but after twenty-four hours of hesitation they decided to maintain the peace rather than to expose their crews to the danger of retaliation by the natives.[122] With this decision, the Winships ceased to be a force in the sandalwood trade. When American trade in the Pacific revived following the Treaty of Ghent, the exploitation of Hawaiian sandalwood passed into the control of a few powerful commercial houses in Boston and New York.

The increasing number of vessels which touched at Hawaiian ports offered many Hawaiians an opportunity to leave the narrow confines of their native islands to visit distant countries. The earliest of these adventurers embarked as guests or personal servants of the master of the ship.[123] After 1790, a number of vessels added Hawaiians to the crew for a voyage to China or to the American coast; occasionally, as in the case of the "Mercury," in 1795, they were shipped to replace deserters.[124]

121 "Solid Men of Boston in the North-west," p. 68; "Log of the Atahualpa," April 18, 1814; "Journal of an American trader resident at Waimea, Kauai" (MS, bound with "Log of the Atahualpa," Massachusetts Historical Society Library), September 30, 1814.

122 *Ibid.*, September 30, October 1, 1814.

123 The first Hawaiian to leave the Islands was a young woman, who, in 1787, was taken as the personal servant of the wife of the master of the "Imperial Eagle." During the same year the powerful chief, Kaiana, sailed as the guest of Captain Meares and visited China and the northwest coast before returning to the Islands. When the "Columbia" left Hawaii in 1789, it carried a young native of Kauai who reached Boston and returned to the Islands on the "Hope" in 1791. Hawaiians are also reported to have been in Mexico and England as early as 1789. Meares, *Voyages from China to the North West Coast*, pp. xxxix, 4–10, 28, 335–336; Joseph Ingraham, "Journal of the Voyage of the Brigantine 'Hope' from Boston to the North-West Coast of

America 1790 to 1792" (typed MS, Provincial Library and Archives, Victoria, B.C.), p. 2; [Ingraham], *Log of the Brig Hope,* p. 12 (May 24, 1791); Porter, "The Ship Columbia and the Discovery of Oregon," in *New England Magazine,* n.s., VI (June 1892), 478–479; Ralph S. Kuykendall, "An Hawaiian in Mexico, 1789–1790," in HHS, *Thirty-Second Annual Report,* pp. 37–50.

124 Bishop, "Journal of the Ruby," p. 80 (September 1795); Turnbull, *Voyage Round the World,* II, 71; Ebbets, "Log of the Ship Pearl," March 12, 1805; "William Martains book on board the Ship Hamilton . . . . bound from Boston towards the N W Coast of America" (MS, Essex Institute, Salem), October 3, 1809; Franchere, *Voyage to the Northwest Coast,* p. 85; Ross Cox, *Adventures on the Columbia River* (New York, 1832), pp. 50–51; Tucker to Croker, Portsmouth, July 3, 1815, in *Historical Records of Australia,* ser. I, VIII, 627; Camille de Roquefeuil, *Journal d'un Voyage Autour du Monde, pendant les années 1816, 1817, 1818, et 1819* (Paris, 1823), II, 355; Bryant and Sturgis to Captain James Harris, Bos-

The lure of life at sea and the desire to see the strange lands that lay beyond the horizon had a powerful appeal to the Hawaiian imagination. Captain James Colnett, while at the Islands in 1791, believed that thousands of Hawaiian men would be willing to leave their homes in order to experience the excitement of life at sea, and Captain Charles Bishop, in 1796, found "many Islanders" who wished to go to "Beritane," the Hawaiian name for Britain.[125] Eight years later Urey Lisiansky believed that scores of Hawaiians "would have given all they had" for an opportunity to become seamen. He added that Hawaiians had proved "very useful" as seamen on American vessels.[126] Other visitors to the Islands reported that they had met Hawaiians who had been to the northwest coast, had secured enough property to maintain themselves in comparative comfort, and had returned to their native islands to relate to admiring and astonished friends the story of their marvelous adventures.[127]

Among the significant by-products of the growing commerce of the North Pacific was the relatively large number of foreigners who deserted vessels at the Hawaiian Islands to take up residence on shore. In March 1790 there were at least three foreigners living on the island of Hawaii;[128] in that month they were joined by Isaac

ton, July 17, 1820, in Bryant and Sturgis Letterbooks, 1818–1829, p. 144; Bryant and Sturgis to Captain Charles Preble, Boston, October 11, 1820, in *ibid.*, p. 160; Bryant and Sturgis to Captain Daniel Cross, August 14, 1821, in *ibid.*, p. 217. Referring to Hawaiians forcibly added to the crew of the "Mercury," Captain Charles Bishop of the "Ruby" declared that "these fine fellows has [sic] been the guard and protection of the vessel at all places while the others have been employed in the trade." Bishop, "Journal of the Ruby," p. 80.

[125] *Ibid.*, p. 120; Howay, ed., *Journal of James Colnett*, p. 282.

[126] Lisiansky, *Voyage Round the World*, p. 128. See also Langsdorff, *Voyages and Travels*, I, 187, and Franchere, *Voyage to the Northwest Coast*, p. 85.

[127] Turnbull, *Voyage Round the World*, II, 71; Choris, *Voyage Pittoresque Autour du Monde*, "Iles Sandwich," p. 15.

[128] The three residents of Hawaii were S. I. Thomas, John Mackey, and Isaac Ridler. Their presence at Kealakekua Bay in March 1790 is indicated by a letter addressed to them and to John Young by Captain Simon Metcalfe and dated March 22, 1790. Young was a member of the crew of Metcalfe's "Eleanora." The letter is in AH, F.O. and Ex., and was reproduced in HHS, *Twenty-Fifth Annual Report* (Honolulu, 1917), p. 58.

Ridler had been carpenter's mate on the "Columbia," from which he deserted at Hawaii in 1789. Thomas arrived at the Islands on the "Columbia" or the "Lady Washington." Mackey had been surgeon's mate of a trading expedition which visited the northwest coast in 1786. He had been left on the coast, possibly to collect furs, and from there he went to the Hawaiian Islands on the "Imperial Eagle" in 1787. Bruce Cartwright, Jr., "Some Early Foreign Residents of the Hawaiian Islands," *ibid.*, pp. 59–61; "New Fur Trade," in *The World*, October 6, 1788, reprinted in *White Knight Chapbooks*, Pacific Northwest Series, No. 4. Cartwright was in error in supposing that the John Young addressed by Metcalfe was other than the boatswain of

Davis and John Young. In 1790 and 1791, respectively, Captains William Douglas and John Kendrick left men on Kauai to collect sandalwood. By January 1794 the little foreign community on the island of Hawaii numbered at least eleven, and included representatives of six nationalities—English, American, Irish, Portuguese, Genoese, and Chinese. Five years later the population of the Islands included twenty-three foreigners, some of whom were said to have been there for as long as eight years.[129] Despite disillusionment and the call of home, the foreign population of the Islands grew slowly but steadily, until in 1817 and 1818 visitors estimated that there were from one hundred to more than two hundred European and American residents there.[130]

More than one visitor noted that the attractions of a life of ease amid pleasant surroundings was an almost irresistible temptation to seamen, and Dr. George H. von Langsdorff declared that visiting seamen "like so well to revel in a superfluity of the productions of nature without much labour . . . . that a ship scarcely ever touches here without leaving one or more of its sailors behind."[131] These inducements were augmented by the generous welcome commonly extended by the chiefs to foreigners who chose to live with the Hawaiian people. Indeed, the observant Archibald Campbell believed

---

the "Eleanora." A second John Young arrived at the Islands in the summer of 1790. *Log of the Brig Hope*, p. 15 (May 26, 1791).

[129] Bell, "Log of the Chatham," in *Honolulu Mercury*, II (December 1929), 86; Journal of Bernard Magee, October 4, 1794; letter dated August 20, 1798, in *New York Missionary Magazine and Repository of Religious Intelligence*, I (1800), 240.

The personnel of the foreign community at Kealakekua was noted in detail by Peter Puget, who wrote ("Log of the Chatham," January 20, 1794):

"With Boyd came also a Portuguese sailor that had been left by a vessel from Macao and two other People left by Mr. Kendrick for the Recovery of their Health. There were also two other men belonging to Mr. Kendrick's Brig & a Person by the name of Howell who had formerly filled a more respectable office in England than he held on board the Washington . . . .

"There are two other men belonging to

the American Brig Hancock . . . . making in all with our two friends Young and Davis Eleven White People now resident on the Island among which are English, Americans, Irish, Portuguese, Genoese and Chinese and a motley set they are."

Boyd had been mate on the "Lady Washington"; Howell was a former clergyman of the Church of England. For a more extended comment on Howell, see Henry Bond Restarick, *Hawaii 1778–1920 from the Viewpoint of a Bishop* (Honolulu, 1924), pp. 28–31.

[130] Choris, *Voyage Pittoresque Autour du Monde*, "Iles Sandwich," p. 20; "Golovnin's Visit to Hawaii in 1818," in *The Friend*, July 1894, p. 51. A list of foreigners reported to have been living at the Hawaiian Islands at the close of March 1816 may be found in *Columbian Centinel*, November 9, 1816.

[131] Turnbull, *Voyage Round the World*, II, 21–22; Langsdorff, *Voyages and Travels*, I, 187.

that foreigners who conducted themselves "with propriety" not only were entitled to all privileges usually accorded the chiefs but were assured of being supported by the chiefs, who, he declared, were "always anxious to have white people about them."[132]

Only a few of the whites who cast their lot among the Hawaiian people intended to remain at the Islands indefinitely. The majority appear to have been transients seeking to escape for a time from the discipline and the rigors of a trading vessel or to experience for themselves the vaunted pleasures of a tropical archipelago. The increasing number of foreigners at the Hawaiian Islands added to the worries of visiting masters by making desertion more attractive. This evil was remedied in part by the presence throughout the archipelago of a group of experienced seamen, some of whom had tired of idleness or were disillusioned by their experience with native life and were ready to ship for a voyage to the American coast or to China and the United States.[133]

Not all of the foreigners in the Islands were deserters; nor were all of them voluntary exiles. Owners and masters, confronted with the problem of discontented or incompetent seamen, did not hesitate to discharge them there. Thus William Sturgis instructed one of his captains that, should any of the crew desire to leave the ship at the Hawaiian Islands, he was to discharge "as many as possible taking care however to keep sufficient to navigate the Brig down [to Canton] in safety."[134] A few years later the first American commercial agent at Honolulu asserted that unscrupulous masters, apparently preferring Hawaiians to Americans or Europeans as members of their crews, occasionally discharged seamen at the Islands upon trivial pretexts, leaving them stranded and dependent upon the bounty of the chiefs.[135]

Kamehameha was not slow to realize the advantages of attaching

[132] Campbell, *Voyage Round the World*, pp. 165–166. See also Kotzebue, *Voyage of Discovery*, III, 245.

[133] Existing records give little information on this point, but it is evident that there was a steady drift away from the Islands. See Journal of Bernard Magee, October 11, 1794; [Ingraham], *Log of the Brig Hope*, pp. 10, 23 (May 23, 26, 1791); "William Martains book on board the Ship Hamilton," October 9, 1809.

[134] Sturgis to Captain James Bennett, Boston, November 27, 1811, in Bryant and Sturgis Letterbooks, 1811–1814, p. 10. See also "Log of the Atahualpa," March 10, 1812, October 26, 1813; Martain, "Log of the Ship Hamilton," November 25, 1815.

[135] John C. Jones to Secretary of State Adams, Oahu, December 31, 1821, in USDS, "Consular Letters," Honolulu, I.

intelligent and industrious foreigners to his following, and there were numerous witnesses who testified to his kind and often generous treatment of visitors and foreign residents whose conduct merited his approval.[136] In 1795 three foreign artisans—two carpenters and one blacksmith—were in his employ;[137] fifteen years later, he had "a considerable number" of whites in his service, "chiefly carpenters, joiners, masons, blacksmiths, and bricklayers."[138] He withheld his welcome, however, from strangers who came to his shores with the hope of leading an existence more marked by comfort than by labor. Early in the nineteenth century it was reported that he would permit no one to take up residence in the Islands who could not produce "a good character from his captain,"[139] and Gabriel Franchere learned that he despised idlers and drunkards.[140] Kamehameha was more than willing to provide for the comfort of such foreign residents as he admired or found useful, but he did place some restrictions upon their actions which, under his successors, became sources of friction. Thus, he declined to permit foreigners to own land or to build durable houses—privileges which were unknown to his native subjects. The first of these limitations remained effective for more than a quarter of a century after the death of Kamehameha and became the source of ill will within the foreign community and a subject of diplomatic protest by representatives of the great maritime powers. The second restriction was relaxed by Kamehameha's son and successor, Liholiho, when, in 1821, the American missionaries were permitted to erect a frame house at Honolulu.[141] Thereafter frame or stone

[136] Wilson, ed., *Hawaii Nei 128 Years Ago*, p. 73; Bishop, "Journal of the Ruby," pp. 114, 123 (February 21, 28, 1795); [Shaler], "Journal," in *American Register*, III (1808), 171–172; Campbell, *Voyage Round the World*, pp. 122, 145, 150, 160; Ross, *First Settlers on the Oregon*, p. 46; Cox, *Adventures on the Columbia*, p. 40; Peter Corney, *Voyages in the Northern Pacific* (Honolulu, 1896), pp. 36, 47.

[137] Boit, "Journal of a Voyage Round the Globe," October 16, 1795. During the following months "English carpenters" on Oahu built a large boat for Kamehameha—an event which was reported to have "entirely engrossed" the attention of the King.

Broughton, *Voyage of Discovery*, pp. 40, 70.

[138] Campbell, *Voyage Round the World*, p. 166.

[139] Langsdorff, *Voyages and Travels*, I, 187.

[140] Franchere, *Voyage to the North West Coast*, p. 69.

[141] Journal of Maria S. Loomis, February 5, 1821.

As late as November, 1822, there was some prejudice among the natives against permitting foreigners to erect frame houses. The persistence of this prejudice was attributed by one American resident of Honolulu to the fact that the Hawaiians were

houses were commonly built by foreigners who proposed to become residents of the Islands.

The best-known of the early foreigners in the Islands were the two uneducated sailors whom Simon Metcalfe left as involuntary exiles on the west coast of Hawaii in 1790. Little information is available regarding the lives of Isaac Davis and John Young prior to their arrival at the Hawaiian Islands. Both men were natives of England, and both were in middle life when they were stranded on Hawaii.[142] Their uncertain background was not considered a handicap by Kamehameha, and so highly were they regarded by their new sovereign that some precautions were taken to prevent them from leaving the Islands.[143] Within a few years they had become reconciled to their fate and Young frankly told Peter Puget that being "habituated to a Life of Ease and Tranquility, he did not like to launch once more into the Busy World where he was certain that the only Sustenance he could expect must be by hard Labour."[144] The two men adopted the customs, mores, and living conditions of the Hawaiian people, married native wives, and, secure in the confidence of their royal master, advanced in influence and rank until they were the equals of the most powerful chiefs. Davis acted as "co-regent" of Hawaii in 1795, during the absence of Kamehameha, who was then engaged in the conquest of Maui and Oahu.[145] Young served for a time as governor of Hawaii, and later in a similar capacity on Oahu. For many years, visitors to the Islands agreed that Davis and Young used their extraordinary influence and prestige in the conscientious

"quite jealous of the Yankees." J. C. Jones to Marshall and Wildes, Oahu, November 16, 1822, in Massachusetts Historical Society, *Proceedings*, LIV, 44.

[142] Vancouver, *Voyage of Discovery*, II, 140; Puget, "Log of the Chatham," February 13, 1793; Journal of Artemas Bishop, December 14, 1825, in *Missionary Herald*, XXIII (February 1827), 49.

[143] This is indicated by the observation of Peter Puget, who noted that he had asked Kamehameha to permit Davis to visit the "Chatham," and that "after some hesitation & exacting a strict promise that I would not take him off the Island, he consented." Puget, "Log of the Chatham," February 23, 1793.

[144] *Ibid.*, January 14, 1794. Cf. Bell, "Log of the Chatham," in *Honolulu Mercury*, I, No. 6 (November 1929), p. 76; Boit, "Journal of a Voyage Round the Globe," October 16, 1795.

The later recollections of George Goodman Hewett, a surgeon on Vancouver's "Discovery," indicate less enthusiasm on the part of Young. Two marginal comments written by Hewett in his copy of Vancouver's *Voyage of Discovery* (II, 168; III, 65) declare that Young expressed a wish to return to England but was dissuaded by Vancouver. These volumes are now in the Provincial Library and Archives, Victoria, B.C.

[145] Bishop, "Journal of the Ruby," p. 121 (February 20, 1796).

service of Kamehameha and in giving generous assistance to vessels and strangers visiting Hawaiian ports.[146]

Scarcely less important than Davis and Young was Francisco de Paula Marin, whose persistence in various horticultural experiments attracted considerable attention and caused the naturalist of the first Kotzebue expedition to assert that to Marin "the Sandwich islands in general, and Woahoo, his present residence, in particular, lie under great obligations."[147] Two British subjects, Alexander Adams and George Beckley, held responsible positions under Kamehameha—the former as master of the King's most valuable vessel and the latter as commandant of the fort at Honolulu. After the death of Isaac Davis, in 1810, Oliver Holmes, a native of Massachusetts, who had arrived at the Islands in 1793, was regarded as the most influential foreigner on Oahu.[148] He sometimes served as governor of that island, and it was later reported that he had given "good satisfaction" to Kamehameha.[149] Perhaps the most energetic white on Oahu was William Davis, a native of Wales, who became a resident of the Islands about 1800. Of Davis, who was described by Ross Cox as "the king's gardener," Archibald Campbell wrote that he "used to rise every morning at five, and go to his fields, where he commonly remained till the same hour in the evening."[150] Another industrious member of the foreign community on Oahu was Anthony Allen, formerly a slave in New York state. This enterprising Negro arrived at the Islands in 1810, and soon acquired a native wife, a family, land, and livestock. He was one of the most prosperous residents of

[146] Vancouver, *Voyage of Discovery*, III, 65–66; Letter of George Vancouver, March 2, 1794, in AH, F.O. and Ex.; Puget, "Log of the Chatham," "Some General Remarks," March 1793; Boit, "Journal of a Voyage Round the Globe," October 16, 1795; Letter of Ebenezer Townsend, Niihau, August 30, 1798, in New Haven Colony Historical Society, *Papers*, IV (1888), 60; [Shaler], "Journal," in *American Register*, III (1808), 162.

[147] Kotzebue, *Voyage of Discovery*, III, 237. In 1822 Gilbert Mathison observed that Marin's wealth and frugality caused him to be unpopular in the foreign community at Honolulu; four years later, Lieutenant Hiram Paulding believed that Marin owned

"nearly all the cattle on the Island of Oahoo, a number of horses, flocks of goats, sheep, &c. . . . . extensive possessions in land . . . . and a great many houses." Mathison, *Visit to Brazil*, p. 427; Hiram Paulding, *Journal of a Cruise of the United States Schooner Dolphin among the Islands of the Pacific Ocean* (New York, 1831), p. 227.

[148] Cox, *Adventures on the Columbia*, pp. 38–39.

[149] Journal of Stephen Reynolds (MS, Peabody Museum, Salem, Mass.), August 6, 1825.

[150] Cox, *Adventures on the Columbia*, pp. 39, 41–42; Campbell, *Voyage Round the World*, pp. 166–167.

Oahu, and at the time of his death he was described as having been "a pattern of industry and perseverance, and of care for the education of his children."[151] It is unlikely that Allen and Davis were typical of the foreigners on Oahu, and Campbell's observation that Davis' industry "puzzled the natives not a little" is a significant comment upon the habits of many of the whites at the Islands.[152]

The conduct of foreigners in the Islands varied with the character and inclination of each individual. No generalization, therefore, could be just or accurate. It is true that many visitors, using standards prevalent in western Europe or the United States, found much to criticize and even to condemn in the activities and influence of the foreign residents. The comment of Peter Puget, in 1793, concerning the influence of John Shorts, an American living on Maui, was typical of many opinions expressed by later observers. Noting that Shorts was under the protection of Kahekili, Puget wrote:

> This people must imbibe a very imperfect Idea of the manners and Customs of Europeans if they draw their Conclusions from the Conduct of this American, for though he seemed anxious on this occasion to procure some Carpenter's Tools for the Chiefs and other useful articles yet I much fear, that Indolence may be added to his General Character & if any benefit is derived from the Distribution of these Articles among the Natives it will be entirely owing to their own Ingenuity. . . .[153]

A year later, Vancouver believed that the presence on Hawaii of a group of deserters constituted a menace to the peace and welfare of the Hawaiian people.[154] He seems to have been unduly alarmed, although during the ensuing years other visitors noted with concern

---

[151] Letter of John Diell, January 12, 1836, in *Sailor's Magazine*, VIII (June 1836), 323; Bingham, *Sandwich Islands*, p. 106; James Montgomery, comp., *Journal of Voyages and Travels by the Rev. Daniel Tyerman and George Bennet, Esq.* (London, 1831), I, 425–426. In 1812, Ross Cox noted the presence at Oahu of "an American black named Anderson," whom he described as the King's "armourer." In 1828 there died at Honolulu a Negro known locally as "Black Jo," who was said to have been at the Islands for "many years." Cox, *Adventures on the Columbia*, p. 42; Journal of Levi Chamberlain (MS, Hawaiian Mission Children's Society Library, Honolulu; typed copy, Yale University Library), July 8, 1828. See also Kenneth W. Porter, "Notes on Negroes in Early Hawaii," in *Journal of Negro History*, XIX (April 1934), 193–197.

[152] Campbell, *Voyage Round the World*, p. 167. Brief notices of some of the better-known of the pioneer foreign residents of the Islands may be found in Cox, *Adventures on the Columbia*, pp. 38–42; Albert Pierce Taylor, *Under Hawaiian Skies* (Honolulu, 1926), pp. 197–200.

[153] Puget, "Log of the Chatham," March 15, 1793.

[154] Vancouver, *Voyage of Discovery*, III, 66–67. See also Bell, "Log of the Chatham," in *Honolulu Mercury*, II (December 1929), 87.

that the Islands provided a haven for a group of convicts from Botany Bay who were furnishing the natives with an example of idleness and debauchery.[155] Alexander Ross, who was at Oahu for a few days in 1811, later recalled that he had seen there "eight or ten white men comfortably settled; and upwards of thirty others naked and wild among the natives, wretched unprincipled vagabonds, of almost every nation in Europe, without clothing and without either house or home."[156] The American missionaries, who first arrived at the Islands in 1820, held equally unflattering views of the influence and character of many of their fellow foreigners; and these uncomplimentary opinions they perpetuated with their pens.[157] The recollections of Ross and the ungenerous criticisms of the missionaries appear to be confirmed, at least in part, by the comments of Archibald Campbell, who perhaps was in a better position to pass judgment upon the influence of foreigners in the Islands during the first decade of the century. According to Campbell:

> Some of these people are sober and industrious; but this is far from being their general character; on the contrary, many of them are idle and dissolute, getting drunk whenever an opportunity presents itself. They have introduced distillation into the islands; and the evil consequences, both to the natives and whites, are incalculable. It is no uncommon sight to see a party of them broach a small cask of spirits, and sit drinking for days till they see it out.[158]

Against the judgment of Ross and Campbell should be balanced the testimony of John Turnbull, who was at the Islands in 1802.

---

[155] Boit, "Journal of a Voyage Round the Globe," October 16, 1795; Governor King to the Earl of Camden, Sydney, April 30, 1805, in *Historical Records of Australia*, series I, V, 323; Turnbull, *Voyage Round the World*, II, 61–63; Cox, *Adventures on the Columbia*, p. 41.

[156] Ross, *First Settlers on the Oregon*, pp. 46–47.

[157] Typical of the views often expressed by the missionaries were the comments of Sheldon Dibble, who declared that as a result of the "pestilential and deadly influence" of foreigners prior to 1820, a "river of intemperance . . . . connected with the curse of infamous dissipation, made quick work in numbering the unwary people for the grave." In more temperate language, the historian Jarves, who was sympathetic with the mission, expressed a similar judgment upon the influence of the majority of the early foreign residents in the Islands. Dibble, *History of the Sandwich Islands*, pp. 37–38; Jarves, *History of the Hawaiian Islands*, p. 113.

[158] Campbell, *Voyage Round the World*, p. 166. See also Franchere, *Voyage to the North West Coast*, p. 70; Kotzebue, *Voyage of Discovery*, I, 353, and III, 249–250; "Golovnin's Visit to Hawaii in 1818," in *The Friend*, August 1894, p. 61; Bryant and Sturgis to Captain John Roberts, Boston, January 17, 1814, in Bryant and Sturgis Letterbooks, 1811–1814, p. 355; Bryant and Sturgis to Captain Daniel Cross, August 14, 1821, *ibid.*, 1818–1829, p. 217.

Turnbull frankly commended the influence of foreigners he found
there, mentioned "the good conduct hitherto evinced by these strangers, and their consequent good character," and declared that "almost all of them have married in the country, and have a numerous
offspring to whom they are powerfully attached, and have besides renounced all idea of ever returning to their native land."[159]

It is evident that, to a considerable extent, these aliens in an alien
atmosphere adopted the customs and manners of the people among
whom they lived.[160] They could not, however, completely throw off
the habits of a lifetime. The Hawaiian people, therefore, had constantly before them examples of a manner of life quite foreign to
anything previously known in the Islands. The influence of Kamehameha, who welcomed foreigners but shunned some of the revolutionary ideas which they brought, was sufficient to prevent any visible
weakening of the age-old customs and institutions of the Hawaiian
people. The haste with which his former subjects abandoned their
idols and *kapus* after his death suggests that some of his people who
had long been intimately associated with foreigners had begun the
long process of acquiring the outward manners of European civilization while their great king still lived. It also seems to support the
belief of the Rev. William Ellis, an English missionary who lived in
the Islands in 1823 and 1824, that much of the temporal advance
made by the Hawaiians between 1800 and 1820 could be traced to
their acquaintance with foreign residents or visitors.[161]

Neither Kamehameha nor his advisers were disturbed by problems arising from formal relations with other governments. Diplomacy as understood and practiced by the statesmen of Europe and
America was unknown to the simple islanders, whose knowledge of
the world beyond their shores was limited to the confused impressions gathered from chance conversations with visiting seamen. But
Kamehameha and his associates did know that somewhere beyond
the horizon was "Beritane," whence came the ships which had first
broken the isolation of the Islands. After 1790 British vessels visit-

[159] Turnbull, *Voyage Round the World*,
II, 81.

[160] In 1794, Lieutenant Puget met a number of foreigners living in the vicinity of
Kealakekua Bay. Concerning them, he
wrote: "Each has selected his Chief with
whom they live; they adhere to the Religious Customs of the Indians & are, as it
were, become part of their Society." Puget,
"Log of the Chatham," January 20, 1794.

[161] William Ellis, *Polynesian Researches*
(London, 1831–1832), IV, 384.

ing Hawaii were outnumbered by those from the United States, but
the respect for England and things English which had been engendered by the visits of Cook and his countrymen was not soon forgotten by the Hawaiian chiefs. King Kaumualii of Kauai wished
to be called "King George," and in 1804 it was reported that he had
distributed the names of members of the British royal family among
his own relatives.[162] More significant was the attitude of Kamehameha, who shared the respect for Great Britain which was so general among his chiefs. This was not extraordinary. His most satisfactory experiences with foreigners had been his acquaintance with
officers of British men-of-war, and his most trusted advisers included
two British-born seamen.[163]

Not only did the Hawaiian rulers regard England with awe, but
a few imperially minded subjects of Great Britain looked forward to
the inclusion of the Hawaiian Islands within the British Empire. In
1790, John Meares, after having twice visited the Islands, observed
that "Providence, by permitting Great Britain to make a discovery
of the Sandwich Isles, seems to have intended that they should become
a part of herself" and added that the acquisition of the Islands "would
surely add to the grandeur and prosperity of the British Empire."[164]
Three years later, an officer who accompanied Captain George Vancouver to the Pacific thought that it would be profitable for the British
government to encourage the settlement of a few West India planters
at the Hawaiian Islands inasmuch as sugar could be cultivated there
by cheap labor without the necessity of recourse to slavery.[165]

The aspirations of Vancouver were no less imperial. During an
extended voyage in the North Pacific in 1792, 1793, and 1794, he
three times visited the Hawaiian Islands. During the second visit, in
1793, he proposed that Hawaii be placed under the protection of

[162] Vancouver, *Voyage of Discovery*, I,
185; Bell, "Log of the Chatham," in *Honolulu Mercury*, I, No. 4 (September 1929), p.
21; Bishop, "Journal of the Ruby," p. 125
(February 28, 1796); Turnbull, *Voyage
Round the World*, II, 35-37.

[163] Bell, "Log of the Chatham," in *Honolulu Mercury* (October, November, 1929),
I, No. 5, p. 64, and I, No. 6, p. 84; Letter
of Ebenezer Townsend, Niihau, August 30,
1798, in New Haven Colony Historical Society, *Papers*, IV (1888), 74. Townsend

wrote that Kamehameha had "an exalted
opinion of the English from the circum-
stance that their ships, that have stopped
there, have been the king's ships, and in
lieu of bartering as our ships do, they do
all by presents . . . . which is done on a
very liberal scale."

[164] Meares, *Voyages from China to the
North West Coast of America*, p. xcv.

[165] Wilson, ed., *Hawaii Nei 128 Years
Ago, by Archibald Menzies*, p. 79.

Great Britain; but Kamehameha and his chiefs failed to respond.[166] During the third visit, early in 1794, the question was revived with more tangible results. On January 9 Vancouver met Kamehameha at Hilo. After "a little persuasion [*sic*]," the King agreed to accompany Vancouver on a cruise along the coast of Hawaii, during which Vancouver apparently took advantage of the opportunity to urge Kamehameha to establish closer relations between Hawaii and the British Empire, possibly in the form of a cession of the island to Great Britain.[167] They arrived at Kealakekua Bay late in the evening of January 13; on the following day, Kamehameha informed officers of the British expedition that he had summoned his chiefs to convene at Kealakekua.[168] While awaiting the arrival of the chiefs, Vancouver strengthened the bonds of friendship between Kamehameha and himself when he instructed his shipwright to assist three foreigners who were engaged in building a "large boat" for Kamehameha. The vessel, appropriately, was named "Britannia."[169]

Some delay was caused by an estrangement of Kamehameha from his favorite consort;[170] but after the royal pair had been reconciled, Kamehameha and his chiefs were ready to proceed with measures which Vancouver regarded as a formal cession of the island of Hawaii to the British Crown. This was a measure which, if we may believe Vancouver, was "unanimously desired" by the chiefs.[171] The formal ceremonies occurred on February 25, when Kamehameha and his chiefs went on board the "Discovery." Kamehameha acknowledged the benefits to be derived from closer political ties with the most powerful maritime nation of the day, and the chiefs again acquiesced in

[166] *Ibid.*, p. 93; Vancouver, *Voyage of Discovery*, III, 29. Menzies wrote that Vancouver had been "very urgent" in his arguments with Kamehameha; Vancouver merely said that the subject had been "frequently mentioned." Menzies believed the question had been dropped because Kamehameha would not consider it unless Vancouver would promise to leave a man-of-war at the Islands to protect him from his enemies. Vancouver attributed the failure of his arguments to the opposition of the chiefs.

[167] George Vancouver to Philip Stephens, Esq., Kealakekua, February 8, 1794, in "Correspondence Relative to the Nootka Controversy," II, 802.

[168] Puget, "Log of the Chatham," January 14, 1794.

[169] *Ibid.*, January 20, 1794; Vancouver, *Voyage of Discovery*, III, 17–18, 51–52. Puget noted that Kamehameha's "unremitting Attention & Princely Conduct had long demanded some Conspicuous Return. The Boat was thought an excellent subject . . . ."

[170] *Ibid.*, pp. 26–28.

[171] *Ibid.*, pp. 16–17. Puget recorded ("Log of the Chatham," February 6, 1794) that he had been told by the chiefs that they had assembled "to be present at the Grand Council of the Chiefs for the purpose of ceding the Island of Owhyhee and its Dependencies to his Majesty."

a proposal, the implications of which must have been quite obscure to them. There was some discussion concerning the maintenance of inter-island peace, and the formalities were concluded with the firing of a salute from the "Discovery" and the raising of the British flag on the shore of the very bay where, fifteen years before, Cook had lost his life.[172]

Great Britain had obtained a claim to the island of Hawaii which every contemporary would promptly have recognized as valid. But the aspirations of Vancouver were doomed to disappointment, for the serious illness of George III, the occupation of Parliament with matters of greater importance, and his own early death combined to defeat any further assertion of British sovereignty over the Hawaiian Islands. Notwithstanding this inaction, British officials were aware of their grounds for claiming Hawaii, and it is probable that that knowledge influenced British policy toward the Hawaiian kingdom in the early years of the nineteenth century.[173]

From the first, there was some disagreement as to the meaning and purpose of the ceremony by which Kamehameha apparently had ceded his kingdom to Great Britain. That it was a cession in fact as well as in form was believed by Vancouver, who declared that Kamehameha and his chiefs had made "the most solemn cession possible" of the island of Hawaii to Great Britain, and that they had "unanimously acknowledged themselves subject to the British Crown."[174] In the official account of the voyage Vancouver declared that he considered it to be an "incumbent duty" to accept on behalf of the British government "the proffered cession" of Hawaii.[175]

Kamehameha and his advisers seem to have attached less signifi-

[172] Vancouver, *Voyage of Discovery*, III, 54–57; Bell, "Log of the Chatham," in *Honolulu Mercury*, II (January 1930), 127–128. Apparently Vancouver did not hasten to report his action to the Admiralty. Indeed, a communication to the Admiralty dated September 8, 1794, and described by Vancouver as his first letter to them since February 8, did not include any reference to the cession of Hawaii. Vancouver to Philip Stephens, Nootka Sound, September 8, 1794, in "Correspondence Relative to the Nootka Controversy," II, 815–818.

[173] Extract from the instructions to Lord Byron, September 14, 1824, in Hawaiian Historical Commission, *Publications*, I, No. 4 (Honolulu, 1927), pp. 19–20. A notice of the cession of Hawaii, described as "a formal surrender of the sovereignty of these islands," was published in *The Annual Register or a View of the History, Politics, and Literature, for the Year 1816* (London, 1817), p. 476.

[174] Letter signed by Vancouver and dated March 2, 1794 (copy), in AH, F.O. and Ex., and printed in *Polynesian*, February 27, 1841.

[175] Vancouver, *Voyage of Discovery*, III, 31.

cance to the negotiations and to the subsequent ceremony of February 25. In view of their ignorance concerning European practices it is unlikely that any of the chiefs had a just concept of the position assigned to colonies within a great European empire. If later comments of the chiefs are to be accepted, they sought not inclusion within an empire but protection against enemies within the Islands.[176] There is some evidence that Vancouver did assure Kamehameha that soldiers would be sent from England to protect Hawaii against its enemies;[177] such a promise doubtless would have been welcome to Kamehameha and may explain the unanimity with which the chiefs agreed to the "cession." Sixteen years later, in 1810, Kamehameha did acknowledge himself to be a subject of George III;[178] but it is doubtful if he actually believed that Great Britain had any rights of jurisdiction in the Islands. In 1818 the Russian explorer, Vasilii Golovnin, learned that the King explained the cession as merely a confirmation of a defensive alliance and that he was indignant if anyone attributed greater significance to the event.[179]

During the thirty years following the departure of Vancouver few British men-of-war visited the Hawaiian Islands. This absence of attention did not lessen the prestige of Great Britain among the Hawaiian chiefs, nor did it seriously shake the confidence of Kamehameha in the efficacy of the protection which Vancouver had implied he might expect. The lingering affection of Kamehameha and his chiefs for Great Britain seems to be reflected in the evolution of the Hawaiian national ensign. When Vancouver left the Islands at the close of his second visit he gave a British flag to Kamehameha;[180] when he returned ten months later he found "the English Colours"

[176] Jarves, *History of the Hawaiian Islands*, p. 89.

[177] This was the belief of G. G. Hewett, who had been surgeon on the "Discovery" and was at Kealakekua during the negotiations leading to the cession. Hewett's recollections, as revealed by marginal comments in his copy of Vancouver's *Voyage of Discovery*, indicate that Vancouver promised to send some five hundred men to Hawaii and that Kamehameha so understood Vancouver. These comments are to be found in the margins of III, 31, 56, 57, and the volumes are now in the Provincial Library and Archives, Victoria, B.C. Hewett also noted that Vancouver had assured John Young that there would be an English settlement on Hawaii. See comments in margin of II, 168, and III, 65.

[178] Kamehameha to George III, Oahu, August 1810 (copy), in AH, F.O. and Ex., and printed in *Polynesian*, February 27, 1841.

[179] "Golovnin's Visit to Hawaii in 1818," in *The Friend*, July 1894, p. 52.

[180] Bell, "Log of the Chatham," in *Honolulu Mercury*, I, No. 6 (November 1929), p. 82.

flying in front of the King's residence at Waiakea and the canoe in which Kamehameha visited Vancouver's vessels had "an English pennant" at the mast.[181] How frequently or consistently the Hawaiian King employed the British flag is uncertain; but fifteen years after the departure of Vancouver the house in which Kamehameha lived was "distinguished by the British colours."[182] As late as 1818 the British flag was flown on Kauai, where Kaumualii still held nominal sway.[183]

The origin of the design, the identity of the designer, and the date when the Hawaiian flag was first used have been lost in the obscurity which surrounds so much of early Hawaiian history. It is said that during the war between the United States and Great Britain, Kamehameha was warned that the continued use of the British flag might cause complications and that he thereupon determined to provide a new flag for his kingdom.[184] This new flag, which as early as 1816 was flying over the fort at Honolulu, retained the Union Jack in the upper quarter next to the mast, combined with a field of horizontal stripes alternately white, red, and blue.[185] The persistence of English influence was clear, but probably more than one observer noted, as did Gilbert Mathison, that the stripes were "like those of the American flag, in allusion probably to the number of islands."[186] The combination of the distinguishing features of the national emblems of Great Britain and the United States may have been more than a coincidence; whatever its origin, the Hawaiian flag appeared to be a mute symbol of the rising tide of American influence in the Islands. In matters more vital than the design of a flag, England's primacy in the archi-

[181] Bell, *loc. cit.*, II (December 1929), 80–81; Wilson, ed., *Hawaii Nei 128 Years Ago*, p. 138.

[182] Campbell, *Voyage Round the World*, p. 129.

[183] Corney, *Voyages in the Northern Pacific*, p. 88; "Golovnin's Visit to Hawaii in 1818," in *The Friend*, July 1894, p. 51.

[184] W. D. Westervelt, "Kamehameha's Method of Government," in HHS, *Thirtieth Annual Report* (Honolulu, 1922), p. 36.

[185] Kotzebue, *Voyage of Discovery*, I, 321; Choris, *Voyage Pittoresque Autour du Monde*, "Iles Sandwich," plate entitled "Port d'hanarourou." Few visitors to the Islands between 1815 and 1845 left a de-

scription of the Hawaiian flag. Among the descriptions which we have from that early period there is a wide variety of disagreement as to the number of stripes and the order in which they were arranged. Possibly the flag was not standardized before 1845, or these discrepancies may be the result of careless reporting. All agree that there were from seven to nine stripes, and nearly all agree that the stripes were red, white, and blue. The order given in the text is that fixed sometime between 1843 and 1845. Howard M. Ballou, "The Reversal of the Hawaiian Flag," in HHS, *Papers*, No. 12 (Honolulu, 1905), pp. 5–11.

[186] Mathison, *Visit to Brazil*, p. 464 n.

pelago was threatened by England's most formidable commercial rival.

Great Britain might have laid claim to the Islands through priority of discovery or on the basis of the cession of Hawaii to Vancouver. Citizens of the United States, through their virtual monopoly of the trans-Pacific trade, had acquired an active interest in the fate of the Islands. It was the apparent aspirations of the Russian American Company, however, which gave Kamehameha his chief cause for alarm.[187] Officials of the Company and its agents in Alaska were willing to undertake a program of expansion southward along the American coast, and the dependence of Sitka upon the outside world for supplies added to any program of aggrandizement a touch of grim necessity. Although the immediate objective of the Company was the establishment of a post on the coast of California, the most important archipelago of the mid-Pacific could not be beyond the scope of its concern. Two vessels of a Russian exploring expedition stopped briefly at the Hawaiian Islands in 1804.[188] Two years later, Kamehameha informed the Russians that he was willing to send supplies to Sitka each year if the Russians would give him in exchange sea otter skins at a reasonable price.[189] The Russians made no immediate response to this offer, but after the lapse of another two years the chief Russian agent at Sitka, Alexander Baranov, sent the "Neva"

[187] The subject of Russian interests in the Hawaiian Islands during the early years of the nineteenth century is a well-tilled field. The earliest account was written by an American missionary and was based upon traditions common among the natives on the island of Kauai. The first account by a historian was that published by W. D. Alexander at the close of the century. Two papers appeared in 1928, one of which was written by the distinguished student of Russian expansion, Professor Frank A. Golder. The publication in the *Krassnyi Arkhiv* of important documents bearing upon the subject has been the inspiration for another brief article and for the most extended treatment the subject has yet received, the latter by Professor Klaus Mehnert. See Samuel Whitney, "Account of an Alleged Attempt of the Russians to Take Possession of the Island of Kauai," in *Hawaiian Spectator*, I, No. 1 (January 1838), 48–52; W. D. Alexander, "The Proceedings of the Russians on Kauai 1814–1816," in HHS, *Papers*, No. 6 (Honolulu, 1894); Frank A. Golder, "Proposals for Russian Occupation of the Hawaiian Islands," in Taylor and Kuykendall, eds., *Papers Read during the Captain Cook Sesquicentennial Celebration*, pp. 39–49; P. P. Gronskii, "Les Russes aux îles Hawaii au début du XIXᵉ siècle," in *Le Monde Slave*, IV, No. 10 (October 1928), 21–39; Anatole G. Mazour, "Doctor Yegor Scheffer: Dreamer of a Russian Empire in the Pacific," in *Pacific Historical Review*, VI (March 1937), 15–20; Klaus Mehnert, *The Russians in Hawaii 1804–1819* (Honolulu, 1939).

[188] Krusenstern, *Voyage Round the World*, pp. 191–198; Lisiansky, *Voyage Round the World*, pp. 98–137.

[189] Langsdorff, *Voyages and Travels*, I, 187–188.

under Lieutenant Hagemeister to the Hawaiian Islands. Archibald Campbell, who sailed on the "Neva" from Sitka to Honolulu, believed that Hagemeister was instructed to establish a settlement at the Islands.[190] No overt action was taken, however, and Campbell recorded that Hagemeister found little enthusiasm among his men for the proposed colony. Apparently the only constructive result of the voyage of the "Neva" was the purchase by its commander of a cargo of Hawaiian salt.[191]

It may have been the visit of Hagemeister that prompted Kamehameha to seek visible proof of the protection promised by Vancouver fifteen years earlier. In February 1810, thirteen months after the arrival of the "Neva," an English whaler touched at Honolulu. When it departed, early in March, it carried Archibald Campbell, to whom Kamehameha had entrusted a letter to George III. In this letter, the British monarch was reminded of the promises made on his behalf by Vancouver, and he was requested to send a man-of-war to the Hawaiian Islands.[192] In August, Kamehameha addressed a second communication to King George, acknowledging himself to be "a subject of His Most Gracious Majesty," and again requesting some tangible evidence of British protection for his islands.[193] In April 1812 the Foreign Office acknowledged these communications with a reply which was more significant for what it failed to include than for any positive statement of policy. Kamehameha was assured that all British commanders would be instructed to respect vessels belonging to him or to his subjects, and he was informed that the Prince Regent had expressed confidence that "the complete success which He has gained over His enemies in every quarter of the globe will have the effect of securing your Dominions from any attack or

---

[190] Campbell, *Voyage Round the World*, p. 117. Hubert Howe Bancroft stated positively that Hagemeister had instructions to establish a Russian settlement in the Hawaiian Islands. Professor Golder concluded, however, that there was no evidence to substantiate Campbell's assumption that Hagemeister had such instructions. Bancroft, *History of Alaska* (San Francisco, 1886), p. 490; Golder, *loc. cit.*, p. 41. See also Mehnert, *Russians in Hawaii*, p. 20.

[191] Campbell, *Voyage Round the World*, pp. 117, 124–125; Golder, *loc. cit.*, p. 40 n.

[192] Campbell, *Voyage Round the World*, pp. 149–150.

[193] Kamehameha to George III, Oahu, August 1810, in AH, F.O. and Ex.

In 1814 Kamehameha told the commander of a British man-of-war that he regarded himself as a British subject. He is also said to have expressed pleasure when informed that other British men-of-war might be expected to visit the Islands, remarking that he had feared King George had forgotten him. Tucker to Croker, Portsmouth, June 28, 1815, in *Historical Records of Australia*, ser. I, VIII, 625.

molestation on their part." There was no promise of protection and no hint that the Foreign Office considered the Islands a dependency of the British Crown.[194] Although the note fell short of the hopes once entertained by Kamehameha, it apparently was received with some satisfaction and, in 1816, it was shown to a Russian naval officer by John Young as evidence of British interest in and friendship for the Hawaiian kingdom.[195]

Meanwhile the menace of Russian aggression loomed more ominously than before. The principal actor in the Russian intrigues in the Hawaiian Islands was Georg Anton Scheffer, a German physician who chanced to be at Sitka at a time when Baranov wished to send an agent to the Islands to recover the cargo of a vessel which had been wrecked on the coast of Kauai.[196] This mission Baranov entrusted to Scheffer. More than the possession of a salvaged cargo was at stake. It is apparent that from the beginning Baranov hoped to utilize the incident to establish closer relations with the Hawaiian Islands. When Scheffer left Sitka in October 1815 it was agreed that he was to negotiate for the opening of trade between the Islands and the Russian posts, and Baranov proposed to send three Russian vessels to the Islands to assist Scheffer in carrying out his share of these negotiations.[197] An English trader who was then at Sitka later recalled that Baranov had hoped to secure "a footing" in the Hawaiian Islands;[198] but whether Baranov anticipated that Scheffer's mission would produce political as well as commercial ties is not clear.

Scheffer first went to Hawaii and thence to Oahu. At both islands he posed as a scientist and at both, apparently, he was treated with

[194] Earl of Liverpool to Kamehameha, London, April 30, 1812, in AH, F.O. and Ex. This letter was accompanied by presents for Kamehameha consisting of a cocked hat, a uniform, and a considerable quantity of assorted nails and spikes. Letter and presents were sent to the Governor of New South Wales, who was instructed to forward them to Kamehameha at the earliest opportunity. It was not until 1816 that the Governor was able to carry out these instructions. He then entrusted the letter and gifts to Mr. Wilcox, an American trader, who delivered them to Kamehameha. Macquarie to Kamehameha, Sydney, April 12, 1816, *ibid.*; Kotzebue, *Voyage of Discovery*, I, 325. A list of presents sent to Kamehameha may be found in *Historical Records of Australia*, ser. I, VII, 475–476.

[195] Kotzebue, *Voyage of Discovery*, I, 334.

[196] Golder, *loc. cit.*, pp. 41–42.

[197] *Ibid.*, p. 42.

[198] Corney, *Voyages in the Northern Pacific*, p. 46. Corney also wrote that Scheffer had been accompanied by "some settlers for the Sandwich Islands," but inasmuch as Scheffer sailed on the American ship, "Isabella," this is unlikely. The "settlers" sailed later on the vessels which Baranov sent to assist in opening trade.

courtesy and kindness.[199] According to his own report to the directors of the Russian American Company he was granted extensive
tracts of land on Oahu which were suitable for cultivation.[200] While
Scheffer was on Oahu two of the vessels promised by Baranov arrived.
Shortly thereafter Scheffer began the construction of a fort at Honolulu, over which, it is said, he raised the Russian flag. So overt an
act could not pass unchallenged, and John Young, prompted possibly
by instructions from Kamehameha, ordered the Russians to leave the
island. Unable to resist, Scheffer and his men went to Kauai.[201]

The visit to Kauai produced the climax to Scheffer's meteoric
career in the Islands. He quickly gained the goodwill of Kaumualii,
who promised that the salvaged cargo would be returned to its owners. With the nominal object of his mission accomplished, Scheffer
turned to matters of greater import. By the close of May 1816 he
had persuaded Kaumualii to accept a series of agreements by which
the islands of Kauai and Niihau were placed under the protection of
Russia and the Russian American Company was granted a monopoly
of the sandalwood on those islands. The acquiescence of Kaumualii
in these far-reaching arrangements seems to have been secured through
a promise that the Company would furnish men and one or more vessels to support him in a war to wrest Oahu from Kamehameha.[202]
With his imperial program auspiciously launched, Scheffer began
the erection of blockhouses at Waimea and Hanalei.[203] For nearly a
year he was the virtual ruler of Kauai, and as late as April 1817 he
was sufficiently powerful to prevent the officers of a visiting vessel
from having any communication with the shore.[204]

[199] Corney, *Voyages in the Northern Pacific*, p. 48; "A Narrative of the Adventures
of Capt. Charles H. Barnard . . . ." in
The Sea, the Ship and the Sailor, p. 94;
Snyder, ed., "Voyage of the *Ophelia*," in
New England Quarterly, X (June 1937),
366; Kotzebue, *Voyage of Discovery*, I, 303–
304.

[200] Mehnert, *The Russians in Hawaii*, p.
26. Mehnert has included extensive extracts from Scheffer's report to the directors
of the Russian American Company.

[201] *Ibid.*; W. D. Alexander, *loc. cit.*, pp.
10–11; Corney, *Voyages in the Northern
Pacific*, pp. 71–72. There is some confusion

as to the exact sequence of events. Scheffer
may have ordered the construction of the
fort at Honolulu after a visit to Kauai.

[202] The substance of these agreements is
given in Mehnert, *The Russians in Hawaii*,
pp. 27–28, 30; Mazour, *loc. cit.*, pp. 17–18.
See also Alexander, *loc. cit.*, p. 8. This and
other citations from Alexander's paper are
from that part of the paper consisting of a
translation from the history of the Russian
American Company by P. Tikhmeneff and
published at St. Petersburg in 1861.

[203] Mehnert, *The Russians in Hawaii*, p.
29.

[204] Corney, *Voyages in the Northern Pa-

The position of Scheffer was far from secure. American traders who had acted as interpreters in the negotiations between Scheffer and Kaumualii betrayed to Kamehameha the nature of these negotiations; and when the Russian commander, Otto von Kotzebue, visited Hawaii late in 1816, Kamehameha complained of Scheffer's conduct. Kotzebue replied that the actions of Scheffer were not sanctioned by the Czar—an assurance which is said to have pleased Kamehameha. There was thereafter no reason for the King to hesitate to order Kaumualii to expel the unwelcome visitors. It may be that Kaumualii needed no prompting in this matter, for the high-handed policies of Scheffer had aroused suspicion and bitterness among his subjects. Although the Russians converted the blockhouse at Waimea into a fort, they were powerless against a determined attack by the natives and in the spring of 1817 they were driven from Kauai.[205]

From Kauai Scheffer and his men returned to Oahu. There they were received with understandable coolness, and Scheffer soon found it expedient to leave the Islands. Undismayed by the collapse of his plans, he went to St. Petersburg, where he hoped to gain support for his ambition to add the Hawaiian Islands to the Russian empire. It was a vain hope; for before he could reach the Russian capital the Czar, probably influenced by Count Nesselrode, had repudiated the negotiations with Kaumualii. The directors of the Russian American Company were divided as to the wisdom of supporting Scheffer, and the efforts of a group of the directors to reopen the question were defeated by the refusal of the Czar to alter his position.[206]

The unwillingness of the Czar's government to intervene in the Hawaiian Islands may be explained, at least in part, by the realization that Great Britain might claim a special interest in the archipelago.[207] The voyage of Kotzebue to the Pacific from 1815 to 1818 tended to confirm views already held at St. Petersburg. While at the Islands, the naturalist of the expedition noted that any threat to Hawaiian independence would certainly meet with grave obstacles, including the fact that "the secure protection of England, would not

cific, p. 73. Corney was later informed that Scheffer had a dungeon at Waimea in which unruly or dangerous foreigners were confined (*ibid.*, p. 88).

[205] Kotzebue, *Voyage of Discovery*, I, 303–305, and II, 196–197: "Golovnin's Visit

to Hawaii in 1818," in *The Friend*, July 1894, p. 52.

[206] Golder, *loc. cit.*, p. 44; Mehnert, *The Russians in Hawaii*, pp. 36–45.

[207] *Ibid.*, p. 37.

be wanting to frustrate the undertaking."[208] On the same occasion Kotzebue learned that "a very fine ship" was being built at Port Jackson, Australia, to be the gift of the British government to the Hawaiian king.[209] This was far from tangible proof that England would fight to defend her interest in the Islands; but the report of Kotzebue upon his return to Russia must have confirmed Nesselrode in the view that Kauai was not worth the risk involved in antagonizing England.

There is no evidence that the British government was alarmed by the prospect of a Russian advance southward into the Pacific. Therefore there was little reason for any public response to the published suggestion of Alexander M'Konochie, a British naval officer, that a colony be established in the Hawaiian Islands. In support of his proposal M'Konochie argued that the Islands occupied a strategic position for a military base, that an English settlement there would be beneficial to English commerce, and that such a colony would have the effect of offsetting an anticipated extension of Russian settlements along the American and Asiatic coasts.[210] This proposal, if adopted by M'Konochie's superiors, would have placed Great Britain in a position to control the commerce of the North Pacific. The failure of the British government to take advantage of the earlier "cession" of Hawaii already had indicated that it was no more interested in immediate aggrandizement in the Pacific than was the government to which Scheffer appealed.

While the two most powerful nations of the day remained outwardly indifferent to the political fate of the Hawaiian Islands, American traders maintained their control of the commerce which radiated from those islands to all parts of the Pacific. The activities and influence of the fur traders, which might well have seemed transitory to a contemporary observer, were the harbinger of permanent ties to follow. When reinforced by religious and educational institutions, American commerce in the Pacific was destined to create in the Hawaiian Islands an economic and institutional frontier. Against American influence, thus entrenched, no European power could peacefully compete.

[208] Kotzebue, *Voyage of Discovery*, III, 241.

[209] *Ibid.*, I, 325.

[210] The substance of M'Konochie's memorandum was published with the title *Considerations on the Propriety of Establishing a Colony on one of the Sandwich Islands* (Edinburgh, 1816) and is reprinted in HHS, *Fourteenth Annual Report* (Honolulu, 1907), pp. 29–43.

II

THE SANDALWOOD ERA

THE return of peace in 1815 was followed by a spirited revival of trade throughout the Pacific. The establishment of the British-owned North West Company at the mouth of the Columbia did not immediately exclude American ships from the fur trade along the coast.[1] Elsewhere in the North Pacific, American dominance of the great trade routes continued without serious challenge.[2] Important changes occurred, however, in the character and control of this commerce. With the single exception of J. and T. H. Perkins,[3] the power-

[1] Alexander Ross, *The Fur Hunters of the Far West* (London, 1855), I, 41; "The Northwest Fur Trade," *Merchants' Magazine*, XIV (June 1846), 536.

[2] Howay, "A List of Trading Vessels in the Maritime Fur Trade," *Transactions of the Royal Society of Canada*, 3d ser., XXVII, Sec. II, p. 119; Kotzebue, *Voyage of Discovery*, II, 195, and III, 241; "Golovnin's Visit to Hawaii in 1818," in *The Friend*, August 1894, p. 62; De Roquefeuil, *Voyage Autour du Monde*, II, 341 n.; Mathison, *Visit to Brazil*, p. 457; Richard Charlton to George Canning, Oahu, June 10, 1825, in *Correspondence Relative to the Sandwich Islands* [London, 1843], p. 11. In 1824, the commander of the United States naval squadron in the Pacific wrote from Peru that the trade of that region was exclusively in the hands of American and English traders, but during those years English traders seldom appeared at the Hawaiian Islands. In 1827, the commercial agent of the United States at Honolulu, in reporting the arrival of the "Tinmouth," described the vessel as "the first English trader that ever came to these Islands for wood." Isaac Hull to Secretary of the Navy Southard, Callao Bay, October 2, 1824, in *Senate Documents*, 19th Cong., 1st Sess., No. 2, p. 127; John C. Jones to Josiah Marshall, Oahu, July 20, 1827, in Marshall MSS, Harvard University Library.

[3] J. and T. H. Perkins had only an incidental role in the trans-Pacific trade after 1815. They acted as agents for the North West Company and their vessels carried that company's furs from the Columbia to Canton—a subterfuge necessary to evade the monopoly enjoyed by the East India Company. It was reported that in crossing the Pacific these vessels "invariably made Hawaii." *Senate Documents*, 24th Cong., 2d Sess., No. 54, p. 6; "The Northwest Fur Trade," *Merchants' Magazine*, XIV (June, 1846), 538.

ful Boston houses which had been the pioneers in trade along the
northwest coast were no longer represented; in their place there appeared a new but no less energetic group of commercial houses, chief
among which were Bryant and Sturgis, and Marshall and Wildes,
both of Boston, and John Jacob Astor and Son, of New York.

The trans-Pacific trade continued to be a complicated unit, involving the northwest coast, the Russian settlements, Spanish America,
and the islands of the Pacific. From the ports of the United States,
chiefly from Boston, vessels were sent to the Pacific with cargoes
intended for sale in Spanish America or at the Hawaiian Islands. If
the cargo could not readily be sold, it was often landed at Honolulu,
either for later sale at that place or for transshipment to the coast or
to the Russian posts. Having disposed of the cargo brought from the
United States, the vessel either hastened to the coast to secure furs
or took on board a cargo for Canton. The ultimate goal of the Pacific
trade continued to be the market at Canton, where furs, sandalwood,
and miscellaneous products from Spanish America or the South Pacific were exchanged for teas and silks. The success of the entire
enterprise continued to depend upon the profits realized on the goods
carried from Canton to the United States or Europe. Barring acci-
dents, unexpected delays, or violent fluctuations in the markets at
Honolulu, Canton, or Boston, this was a lucrative branch of commerce and one worthy of the daring and ingenuity of the commercial houses which dominated it.

The relation of the Hawaiian Islands to the Pacific trade was
revolutionized by the fact that after 1815 they furnished cargo as
well as provisions to traders crossing the Pacific to Canton. Conservative merchants were slow to recognize the possible value of
Hawaiian sandalwood. Captain Samuel Hill, who sailed from Boston in the summer of 1815 in charge of a venture jointly owned by
three Boston firms, was instructed to secure copper at Valparaiso and
sandalwood at the Ingraham Islands, with the added injunction that
should he be less successful than anticipated the owners "trust finally
upon your success in getting a load of Sandalwood at the Sandwich
Islands." It was not anticipated that there would be difficulty in
securing sandalwood at the Hawaiian Islands, but Hill was informed
that it "would be much inferior in value to Copper" as a cargo for

Canton.[4] A year later Bryant and Sturgis sent their ablest master, Captain John Suter, on a voyage to the northwest coast and China with instructions which contained no mention of sandalwood.[5] Supplementary instructions, forwarded to Suter in October 1817, contained the information that sandalwood had "done better in Canton this season, than was expected," and added that should he be able to secure wood "for any trade you have left it will be an object."[6] The most cautious firm interested in the trans-Pacific trade had become aware of the value of Hawaiian sandalwood, and masters sent to the Pacific in ensuing years were specifically instructed to carry sandalwood as well as furs to Canton.[7]

The organization of Hawaiian politics and the traditional docility with which chiefs and commoners yielded to the wishes of their rulers allowed Kamehameha to monopolize the principal sources of revenue within his kingdom.[8] The most lucrative of the royal monopolies was sandalwood, and traders who wished to include it in a cargo for Canton were compelled to compete for the favor of the King. Kaumualii was permitted to dispose of the sandalwood on Kauai, but elsewhere the chiefs participated in the sandalwood trade only as agents of Kamehameha.[9]

Kamehameha was a shrewd trader and occasionally he reinforced his own caution by refusing to conclude a bargain until assured of its advantages by such trusted advisers as John Young or Kalanimoku.[10] By reserving the sandalwood for his own use, he postponed the time when it would become extinct. Few thoughts of conservation, however, interrupted his own exploitation of the sandalwood forests. His principal desire was to acquire vessels, and traders who visited the Islands between 1815 and 1819 could not long remain

[4] J. and T. H. Perkins, S. G. Perkins & Co., and Bryant and Sturgis to Hill, Boston, June 30, 1815, in Bryant and Sturgis Letterbooks, 1814–1818, pp. 154–159.

[5] Bryant and Sturgis to Suter, Boston, August 6, 1816, *ibid.*, pp. 271–274.

[6] Bryant and Sturgis to Suter, Boston, October 8, 1817, *ibid.*, p. 379.

[7] Bryant and Sturgis to Capt. George Clark, Boston, December 1, 1817, *ibid.*, pp. 402–403; Bryant and Sturgis to Capt. James Hall, Boston, August 31, 1818, *ibid.*, pp. 463–466.

[8] Franchere, *Voyage to the North West Coast*, p. 60; "Solid Men of Boston in the Northwest," pp. 13, 40.

[9] De Roquefeuil, *Voyage Autour du Monde*, II, 360; Kuykendall, *Hawaiian Kingdom*, p. 88.

[10] "A Narrative of the Adventures of Capt. Charles H. Barnard," in *The Sea, the Ship and the Sailor*, p. 94; Corney, *Voyages in the Northern Pacific*, pp. 83a–84a.

in ignorance of that fact. When Captain Hill arrived at Kailua in March 1816, he immediately approached Kamehameha with a proposal to purchase sandalwood, only to learn that the King was indifferent to any trade unless a brig or schooner was involved.[11]

Hill had no vessel with which to tempt Kamehameha. The agents of John Jacob Astor were more successful. Twice during 1816 they sold a vessel to the Hawaiian King, each time taking payment in sandalwood.[12] In September 1817, Captain Andrew Blanchard sold the "Bordeaux Packet" to the Hawaiian chiefs for an unrecorded amount of sandalwood—a transaction which Otto von Kotzebue interpreted as indicating "how dear the Americans are paid in China for sanders-wood."[13] Before his death in May 1819, Kamehameha had given varying amounts of wood for no fewer than six vessels.[14] He also had utilized it to purchase other goods that he needed or desired. In 1818 he gave some four hundred piculs of sandalwood for an assortment of articles, including nails, olive oil, paint oil, brushes, flour, rice, sugar, pitch, Glauber's salt, camp kettles, tea kettles, a baking pan, skittles, and old copper.[15] In March 1819, two months before his death, he bought sixteen kegs of rum, a box of tea, and eight thousand dollars worth of guns and ammunition. For this, he gave 850 piculs of wood.[16]

The discovery that Kamehameha could be persuaded to give large amounts of sandalwood in exchange for vessels opened a new era in Hawaiian commerce. While at the Islands, in 1817, Kotzebue saw many fields which were uncultivated and he was told that the

[11] Snyder, ed., "Voyage of the *Ophelia*," in *New England Quarterly*, X (June 1937), 365. In April when Hill visited Kauai he found that Kaumualii also "seemed indifferent" to trade unless he could secure a vessel in exchange for his sandalwood.

[12] Porter, *John Jacob Astor*, II, 641, 645.

[13] James F. Hunnewell, ed., "Voyage in the Brig Bordeaux Packet . . . . by James Hunnewell," in HHS, *Papers*, No. 8, p. 8; Kotzebue, *Voyage of Discovery*, II, 199.

[14] The six vessels purchased by Kamehameha were the "Albatross," the "Forester," the "Bordeaux Packet," the "Lydia," the "Columbia," and the "Santa Rosa." After purchasing the "Santa Rosa," Kamehameha learned that it had been in the possession of mutineers. He therefore surrendered the vessel, apparently without compensation or complaint, to Captain Hypolito Bouchard of the navy of the revolutionary Republic of La Plata. Porter, *John Jacob Astor*, II, 641, 645, 1149–1150; Journal of James Hunnewell, 1817, in Hunnewell MSS, Harvard University Library; *Columbian Centinel*, April 2, December 6, 1817; Corney, *Voyages in the Northern Pacific*, pp. 71, 83a, 84a, 90, 92, 119.

[15] "Account Book of Ship Sultan, 1815–1819," MS, Massachusetts Historical Society Library.

[16] W. D. Alexander, "Early Trading in Hawaii," in HHS, *Papers*, No. 11 (Honolulu, 1904), p. 23.

inhabitants had been compelled to assist in felling sandalwood trees or in carrying them to the harbor.[17] Several visitors agreed that Hawaiian sandalwood was of poorer quality than that which could be purchased along the coasts of Malabar or Timor;[18] but any inferiority in the quality of the wood from the Hawaiian Islands no longer prevented a profitable disposition of that wood at Canton. Reliable estimates of the value of the sandalwood shipped from the Hawaiian Islands to Canton are lacking; but it seems reasonable to suppose that after 1816 the greater part of the wood sold at Canton by American traders was of Hawaiian origin. The statistics of the sandalwood trade at Canton, therefore, will provide some suggestion as to the ebb and flow of that branch of Hawaiian commerce. In the trading season of 1817–1818, nearly 16,000 piculs of sandalwood were sold at Canton by American merchants; during the next three years, this trade declined until in the season of 1820–1821 only a little more than six thousand piculs were carried to Canton in American vessels.[19] The extravagant years of the sandalwood trade were still in the future, but American traders were said to have received about four hundred thousand dollars for the wood which they carried to Canton during the four years ending in 1821.[20]

Kamehameha hoped to increase his personal fortune not only by trade with visitors but also by active participation in the trade with the Orient. In 1817 he outfitted a vessel, loaded it with a cargo of sandalwood, placed both vessel and cargo in charge of Alexander Adams, and sent them to Canton. This venture was a commercial failure, for Adams was unable to dispose of the cargo at a profit and unanticipated port charges added to the expense of the voyage.[21] Kamehameha, however, was able to turn this experience to advantage; for, having learned that civilized nations were accustomed to

[17] Kotzebue, *Voyage of Discovery*, II, 200.

[18] De Roquefeuil, *Voyage Autour du Monde*, II, 360; Mathison, *Visit to Brazil*, p. 458; F. W. Beechey, *Narrative of a Voyage to the Pacific and Beering's Strait . . . . in the Years 1825, 26, 27, 28* (London, 1831), II, 99.

[19] Gutzlaff, *Sketch of Chinese History*, II, Appendix IV; Hosea Ballou Morse, *The Chronicles of the East India Company Trading to China* (Oxford, 1926), IV, Appendix, 384–385.

[20] Timothy Pitkin, *Statistical View of the Commerce of the United States of America* (New Haven, 1835), p. 304.

[21] Alexander Adams, "Log of the Kaahumanu," in *Hawaiian Almanac and Annual*, 1905, p. 51; *Columbian Centinel*, December 6, 1817; Ellis, *Tour through Hawaii*, p. 398 n; "Golovnin's Visit to Hawaii in 1818," in *The Friend*, July 1894, p. 52.

exact fees from visiting vessels, he determined to adopt the same practice. A pilot was appointed, appropriate fees for this service were fixed, and throughout the remainder of his reign ships anchoring at Honolulu were compelled to pay harbor charges of either forty or sixty dollars—the amount depending upon whether they were outside the reef or in the inner harbor.[22]

The vigor with which Kamehameha turned to commerce and employed every means of increasing his store of specie and of goods was the cause of some unfavorable comment. Samuel Patterson, who met him at Oahu in 1805, described him as "an artful and sagacious man, and extremely avaricious. He wants every thing he sees."[23] In accusing him of avarice, Patterson was not alone,[24] and there were occasional incidents which reflected gravely upon his reputation for generosity to hapless strangers or upon his integrity in business relations.[25] The King, however, did not lack defenders. Archibald Campbell, who became intimately acquainted with Kamehameha during a residence of thirteen months at Honolulu, admitted that he understood "perfectly well how to make a bargain" but added that he was "unjustly accused of wishing to over-reach in his dealings." Emphasizing this defense of his friend, Campbell declared: "I never knew of his taking any undue advantages; on the contrary, he is distinguished for upright and honourable conduct in all his transactions."[26] In his never-ceasing search for added riches Kameha-

[22] "Golovnin's Visit to Hawaii in 1818," *loc. cit.*; Ellis, *Tour through Hawaii*, p. 398. These specific charges were varied from time to time. They were increased during the reign of Liholiho and then, during the visit of the "Blonde" in 1825, they were "considerably reduced." *Ibid.*; Otto von Kotzebue, *A New Voyage Round the World in the Years 1823, 24, 25, and 26* (London, 1830), II, 193; C. S. Stewart, *Private Journal of a Voyage to the Pacific* (New Haven, 1828), p. 124; C. S. Stewart, *Journal of a Residence in the Sandwich Islands* (New York, 1828), p. 97 n.; Journal of Stephen Reynolds, June 6, 1825; [Maria Graham, comp.], *Voyage of H.M.S. Blonde to the Sandwich Islands, in the Years 1824–1825* (London, 1826), pp. 157–159.

[23] *Narrative of the Adventures and Sufferings of Samuel Patterson*, p. 70.

[24] Cf. Ross, *First Settlers on the Oregon*, p. 43; Ellis, *Polynesian Researches*, IV, 385.

[25] His disinclination to be generous is indicated by his anxiety to be relieved of the care of eight Japanese castaways temporarily stranded at Honolulu in 1806. Delano, *Narrative of Voyages and Travels*, pp. 400–401. A better illustration is his attitude toward the crew of the "Lark" in 1813. Irving, *Astoria*, II, 238. More serious charges, involving the good faith of Kamehameha, may be found in Thomas Rutherford Trowbridge, Jr., "History of the Ancient Maritime Interests of New Haven," in New Haven Colony Historical Society, *Papers*, III (1882), 159–160, and F. D. Bennett, *Whaling Voyage Round the Globe* (London, 1840), I, 241 n.

[26] Campbell, *Voyage Round the World*, p. 212.

meha was fortunate. In 1810 Campbell noted that by trading with ships that called at the Islands he had collected "a considerable treasure in dollars, and . . . . a large stock of European articles of every description."[27] With the passing of the years Kamehameha's wealth increased; as his long reign drew to a close, European visitors observed that the trade with visiting mariners had enabled him to amass "immense riches."[28]

The death of Kamehameha in May 1819 marked the end of an era. For more than eight centuries—perhaps for more than twelve— the Hawaiian people had been developing a truly Polynesian civilization. For a quarter of a century that civilization had remained almost impervious to Western customs and ideas. During that period, the guiding hand of Kamehameha controlled so completely the domestic policies of his kingdom that neither the political chaos of the preceding years nor the coming of the foreign traders and residents disturbed the loyalty of his subjects, who, alternately fearing and admiring him, obeyed his slightest wish without question. Whether in the face of the ever-increasing contacts between his own people and the outside world he could long have maintained the ancient religion and customs of his race is doubtful; it is certain that he had been gone from his councils and fields for less than a year before it had become apparent that his successor was unable or unwilling to stay the rising tide of Western influence which threatened to engulf the Hawaiian people.

Kamehameha's twenty-two-year-old son, Liholiho, inherited the throne but not the greatness of his father. Nearly all foreign commentators agreed that the second Kamehameha was a weak and often a reckless sovereign, more interested in his own pleasures and adventures than in the fate of his kingdom or the welfare of his subjects. That he was not without redeeming features is indicated by comments of American missionaries, who certainly were not biased in his favor. When in May 1821 Liholiho attended a banquet, one of the ladies of the mission noted that he was "drest in American fashion and appeared to fine advantage";[29] the Rev. Charles S. Stewart wrote

---

[27] *Ibid.*

[28] Kotzebue, *Voyage of Discovery,* III, 240; De Roquefeuil, *Voyage Autour du Monde,* II, 341 n.

[29] Journal of Maria S. Loomis (MS, Hawaiian Mission Children's Society Library), May 16, 1821. See also Ellis, *Tour through Hawaii,* p. 47.

of Liholiho that, when sober, "his figure is noble . . . . his manners polite and easy and his whole deportment that of a gentleman."[30] He had an active mind; occasionally he showed great interest in learning to read and write; and he was surprisingly well informed on some subjects of general interest, especially geography.[31] These achievements were counterbalanced by addiction to liquor and an unfortunate choice of associates, with the result that contemporary comments concerning the young King were more burdened with criticism than with praise. The same missionary lady whose favorable comment has already been noted described his associates as being "from the very dregs of civilized society";[32] and numerous contemporary accounts contain ample evidence that Liholiho was frequently observed, both in public and in private, under the influence of intoxicants.[33]

The death of Kamehameha removed from Hawaiian commerce all those restrictions with which he had fortified his monopolies. The abundance of sandalwood in the Islands[34] and the permission granted by Liholiho to "some of his more favoured chiefs" to participate in trade[35] provided the incentive needed for the rapid and reckless exploitation of the most available natural resource the Islands afforded. This revolution in Hawaiian commercial policy coincided with a period of financial depression in the United States. The Panic of 1819 increased the difficulty of securing specie for the market at Canton and compelled merchants to rely more generally upon

[30] Stewart, *Private Journal of a Voyage to the Pacific*, p. 101. See also J. Arago, *Promenade Autour du Monde, pendant les années 1817, 1818, 1819 et 1820* (Paris, 1822), II, 144; Ellis, *Tour through Hawaii*, p. 425.

[31] *Ibid.*, pp. 425–426. An interesting defense of the second Kamehameha may be found in Albert Pierce Taylor, "Liholiho: A Revised Estimate of His Character," in HHS, *Papers*, No. 15 (Honolulu, 1928), pp. 21–39.

[32] Journal of Maria S. Loomis, February 7, 1821.

[33] *Ibid.*, January 1, 1822; Thomas Brown to Marshall and Wildes, Oahu, July 6, 1821, in Marshall MSS; Jones to Marshall

and Wildes, Oahu, October 5, 1821, in Massachusetts Historical Society, *Proceedings*, LIV, 35; Journal of James Hunnewell, May 2, 1821, in Hunnewell MSS; Journal of Levi Chamberlain, April 28, May 5, July 6, August 17, 1823; Mathison, *Visit to Brazil*, pp. 364–365; Montgomery, comp., *Journal of Tyerman and Bennet*, I, 471; Stewart, *Private Journal of a Voyage to the Pacific*, p. 91; *Missionary Herald*, XIX (February 1823), 44.

[34] Choris, *Voyage Pittoresque Autour du Monde*, "Iles Sandwich," p. 9; De Roquefeuil, *Voyage Autour du Monde*, II, 360; Mathison, *Visit to Brazil*, p. 458.

[35] Montgomery, comp., *Journal of Tyerman and Bennet*, I, 415.

cargo, including furs and sandalwood, as a medium of exchange in China.[36]

The following three years were featured by the frantic efforts of competing traders to persuade the chiefs to part with their sandalwood in exchange for vessels or manufactured goods for which they had little need and only a vague desire. Competition was often keen and sometimes bitter, with "many different concerns each trying to out do the other."[37] Rival traders vied in offering cloth, blankets, silks, hardware, muskets, powder, wines and spirituous liquors, and "all fancy articles."[38] Marshall and Wildes sent two frame houses to the Islands, the first of which was erected "in an elegant style," much to the joy of Liholiho, who agreed to purchase it.[39]

Still more irresistible to the chiefs were vessels. Unlike Kamehameha, who on at least one occasion refused to purchase a vessel until it had been carefully inspected by his chiefs,[40] Liholiho and his companions were more intrigued by the luxurious furnishings of pleasure craft than by the seaworthiness or commercial value of a vessel. During the summer following the death of Kamehameha, the chiefs purchased at least two vessels, for one of which they gave sandalwood said to have been worth more than fifty thousand dollars.[41] In June, 1820—six months after the death of Kamehameha had become known in the United States[42]—Bryant and Sturgis sent

[36] Samuel Eliot Morison, *Maritime History of Massachusetts* (Boston and New York, 1921), p. 262.

[37] Brown to Josiah Marshall, Oahu, October 8, 1821, in Marshall MSS.

[38] Jones to Secretary of State Adams, Oahu, December 31, 1821, in USDS, "Consular Letters," Honolulu, I. The muskets and powder did not meet with a ready sale, and Jones feared they would be a total loss. Jones to Marshall and Wildes, January 22, 1822, in Marshall MSS. In 1820 James Hunnewell noted that rum was the most salable article of trade, for it would "buy anything this country produces . . . . & it will command more cash than any other article." Journal of James Hunnewell, September 7, 1820, in Hunnewell MSS.

[39] Jones to Marshall and Wildes, Oahu, October 5, 1821, in Marshall MSS.

[40] Corney, *Voyages in the Northern Pacific*, pp. 83a–84a.

[41] Alexander, "Early Trading in Hawaii," in HHS, *Papers*, No. 11, p. 23; *Columbian Centinel*, May 17, 1820. The two vessels were the "Eos" and the "Neo," both of which apparently were sent to the Islands by Josiah Marshall. The "Eos" certainly was Marshall's vessel (*ibid.*, August 19, 1818) and the "Neo" went to the Pacific under the command of Captain William Babcock (*ibid.*, September 19, 1818), who acted as agent for Marshall and Wildes at Honolulu. In 1822 J. C. Jones declared that the chiefs regarded the "Neo" as their "best vessel" and implied that this was one reason why the business affairs of Marshall and Wildes at the Islands were "in as favorable situation as possible." Jones, to Marshall and Wildes, Oahu, October 10, 1822, in Massachusetts Historical Society, *Proceedings*, LIV, 43.

[42] The death of Kamehameha was announced in the *Columbian Centinel*, December 29, 1819.

the "Cleopatra's Barge" to the Islands to be sold for as much as the chiefs could be induced to pay.[43] A month later they forwarded instructions to Captain Suter that it would be *"very desirable* to sell the Barge immediately," as there would be more vessels offered for sale at the Islands than the chiefs would want or could afford.[44] The "Barge" was sold in November 1820 for an amount of sandalwood variously reported to have been from six thousand to eight thousand piculs.[45] The value of the wood given was estimated by later writers to have been between eighty thousand and ninety thousand dollars,[46] estimates which appear to have been much too high in view of the fact that Captain Suter had been instructed not to place a value of more than seven dollars a picul on wood "of good quality."[47] At about the same time the chiefs promised to give Andrew Blanchard eight thousand piculs of sandalwood for the "Thaddeus" and a schooner.[48]

The pleasant business of trading vessels for sandalwood could not continue indefinitely. In May 1821 it was reported that Kaumualii had purchased "a very inferior Brig & Cargo," after which he had bought nearly all the cargo of a second vessel. These transactions presumably added to the profits of Bryant and Sturgis and of Astor, but they placed so severe a strain upon the credit of Kaumualii that an agent of Marshall and Wildes confessed that "our future prospects are very small."[49] Another agent of the same firm wrote from Honolulu that the future of the sandalwood trade was very uncertain,[50] and John C. Jones, also an agent of Marshall and Wildes, declared that although the chiefs were being urged to buy "every merchandize, and vessels more than they know what to do with . . . . they are sick

[43] Bryant and Sturgis to Captain John Suter, Boston, June 20, 1820, Bryant and Sturgis Letterbooks, 1818–1829, pp. 130–131.

[44] Bryant and Sturgis to Suter, Boston, July 18, 1820, in Massachusetts Historical Society, *Proceedings,* LIV, 28.

[45] Jones to Marshall and Wildes, Oahu, October 5, 1821, *ibid.,* p. 36; Journal of Maria S. Loomis, January 4, 1821; William French to Marshall, Canton, September 23, 1821, in Marshall MSS.

[46] Jarves, *History of the Hawaiian Islands,* p. 113; W. D. Alexander, "The Story of the Cleopatra's Barge," in HHS, *Papers,* No. 13 (Honolulu, 1906), p. 29. Two years

earlier, in July 1818, the "Barge" had been sold at auction in the United States for $15,400. *Columbian Centinel,* July 29, 1818.

[47] Bryant and Sturgis to Suter, Boston, June 20, 1820, in Bryant and Sturgis Letterbooks, 1818–1829, p. 131.

[48] James Hunnewell to Sherman Peck, in *The Friend,* January 1867, p. 6. The schooner had been built at Honolulu during the summer of 1820, probably with the intention of selling it to the chiefs.

[49] William Cole to Marshall and Wildes, Kauai, May 25, 1821, in Marshall MSS.

[50] William Babcock to Marshall and Wildes, Oahu, May 3, 1821, *ibid.*

of trading, all their subjects are complaining and endeavoring to influence them to purchase no more."[51] A few weeks earlier, Jones had persuaded Liholiho to purchase a brig and cargo only after "much trouble and difficulty," which included the giving of "handsome presents and . . . . elegant dinners."[52] On Kauai and on Oahu natives were busily occupied in cutting sandalwood to meet the mounting debts of their chiefs,[53] but in July it was reported that the chiefs still owed Captains Suter and Blanchard twelve thousand piculs of wood in addition to that which was due the agents of Marshall and Wildes.[54] With reason, Bryant and Sturgis expressed the fear that with "so many expeditions gone & going to the Islands . . . . there may be some difficulty in keeping the chiefs to their contracts."[55]

Before the close of 1821, Jones suffered the humiliation of being compelled to sell the "Inore," for which he had once refused 4,000 piculs of wood, for 3,760 piculs.[56] He explained that his change of heart was induced by the knowledge that other vessels had been sent to the Islands "to be sold here for what they would fetch."[57] From one of Jones's associates came an acknowledgment that the natives already possessed more ships than they could use[58]—an observation which seems amply confirmed by the report that the Hawaiian rulers owned "Ten large & elegant Brigs, besides a large number of Sloops & Schooners all of which they have purchased from Americans."[59] Although traders did not entirely abandon the hope of persuading the

[51] Jones to Marshall and Wildes, Honolulu, July 6, 1821, in Massachusetts Historical Society, *Proceedings*, LIV, 34.

[52] *Ibid.*, p. 32. Jones reported that he was to receive 7,700 piculs of wood "payable all in one year." One visitor to Honolulu noted that the brig had been sold for sixty thousand dollars' worth of sandalwood. Journal of Nehemiah Haskell (MS, Essex Institute, Salem), June [9], 1821.

[53] Brown to Marshall and Wildes, Oahu, July 6, 1821, in Marshall MSS; Jones to Marshall and Wildes, Honolulu, July 6, 1821, in Massachusetts Historical Society, *Proceedings*, LIV, 33.

[54] Brown to Marshall and Wildes, Oahu, July 6, 1821, in Marshall MSS.

[55] Bryant and Sturgis to Charles B. Bullard, October 12, 1820, in Bryant and Sturgis Letterbooks, 1818–1829, p. 161.

[56] Brown to Marshall, Oahu, December 24, 1821, in Marshall MSS; Jones to Marshall, Oahu, October 2, 1821, *ibid.* A notice of the sale, dated December 26, 1821, may be found in AH, F.O. and Ex. The vessel was purchased by Kalanimoku and Namahana, who agreed to pay 1,360 piculs of wood on demand, 1,200 piculs during 1822, and 1,200 piculs in 1823.

[57] Jones to Marshall and Wildes, Oahu, December 23, 1821, in Massachusetts Historical Society, *Proceedings*, LIV, 37.

[58] Brown to Marshall, Oahu, December 24, 1821, in Marshall MSS.

[59] Jones to Secretary of State Adams, Oahu, December 31, 1821, in USDS, "Consular Letters," Honolulu, I.

chiefs to buy vessels, the natives gradually learned that the acquisition of numerous ships did not bring unalloyed joy. In January 1824 the "Thaddeus," for which the chiefs were still heavily in debt, was reported to have been for two years "a dismantled hulk";[60] and in the following April the "Cleopatra's Barge," which had proved to be notoriously unseaworthy,[61] was wrecked by an incompetent captain on the coast of Kauai.[62] In the autumn of 1824, John Jacob Astor's "Tamaahmaah," described by one observer as "the beautiful brig Tamaahmaah"[63] and by another as "a very beautiful vessel, in some respects superior to the Barge,"[64] failed to find a buyer at Honolulu.[65] The inability of Astor's agents to dispose of the brig should have been no cause for surprise in Honolulu, where for two years it had been recognized that "it would be hard work to sell a vessel to any advantage" and where the chiefs were reported to be wary lest they repeat the error committed in the purchase of the "Thaddeus" and the "Cleopatra's Barge."[66]

The disinclination of the natives to exchange their wood for elegantly furnished vessels reflected the lean years which had overtaken the sandalwood trade. In the autumn of 1821 the Honolulu agents of Marshall and Wildes had complained that their rivals sold goods for prices which made profitable trading difficult;[67] before the close of that year Jones feared that the chiefs, being "now too much enlightened," would "never again make the exertion they have this year."[68] At the close of 1821, it was reported that 30,000 piculs of sandalwood had been sent to China during that year.[69] This appears

[60] James Hunnewell to Charles Thatcher, Oahu, January 12, 1824 (copy), in Hunnewell MSS.

[61] Jones to Marshall and Wildes, Oahu, August 10, 1822, in Massachusetts Historical Society, *Proceedings*, LIV, 41; Mathison, *Visit to Brazil*, p. 463.

[62] Journal of Levi Chamberlain, May 12, 1824; Bingham, *Sandwich Islands*, p. 218.

[63] Stewart, *Private Journal of a Voyage to the Pacific*, p. 313.

[64] Journal of Levi Chamberlain, August 9, 1824. Dixey Wildes, a competitor of Astor, was less enthusiastic, describing the "Tamaahmaah" as "nothing more than common." Wildes to Marshall, Oahu, September 7, 1824, in Marshall MSS.

[65] Porter, *John Jacob Astor*, II, 658.

[66] Jones to Marshall and Wildes, Oahu, August 10, 1822, March 9, May 31, 1823, in Marshall MSS.

[67] Jones to Marshall and Wildes, Oahu, October 5, 1821, *ibid*. Cf. Brown to Marshall, Oahu, November 6, 24, December 24, 1821, *ibid*.

[68] Jones to Marshall and Wildes, Oahu, November 20, December 23, 1821, *ibid*.

[69] Jones to Adams, Oahu, December 31, 1821, in USDS, "Consular Letters," Honolulu, I. Cf. Jones to Marshall and Wildes, Oahu, January 22, 1822, in Marshall MSS; Hunnewell to Blanchard, Honolulu, October 20, 1821, in Hunnewell MSS.

to have been the greatest amount of wood shipped from the Islands in any one year,[70] and there were fears that this avalanche of sandalwood would depress the market at Canton.[71]

The halcyon days of easy profits were indeed past. The sandalwood trade continued its erratic course until the close of the decade; but the triple handicap of a vanishing supply of wood, the indifference of the chiefs, and the specter of burdensome debts incurred during the years of extravagance prevented the return of the carefree trading which had characterized the early years of the reign of Liholiho. In the summer of 1822 John C. Jones found it difficult to estimate the future possibilities of Hawaiian commerce.[72] Three months later he advised his employers never to send "a large cargo . . . . as the market is too uncertain";[73] and in May 1823 he thought that there would always be some trade at Honolulu, but added that "these people do not purchase now as formerly . . . . it is now only as they want to consume that they buy therefore no large sales can be effected at one time."[74] During the ensuing summer, the chiefs, apparently hoping to monopolize the profits of trade, forbade their subjects to make any purchases, and for a time all trade was suspended.[75]

The changed attitude of the chiefs, however novel and annoying it may have seemed to merchants and supercargoes, would scarcely have proved fatal to the profitable continuance of the sandalwood trade. More serious obstacles, however, beset Hawaiian commerce. In the winter of 1822–1823, it was reported that on Kauai and Oahu the once abundant supply of sandalwood was nearing exhaustion.[76] Late in 1823, the agents of Marshall and Wildes found it impossible to secure a full cargo of wood for the "Paragon." The vessel was

[70] Most of the wood was sent from the Islands late in the year and arrived at Canton during the trading season of 1821–1822, or the calendar year of 1822. For estimates of the amount of sandalwood sold at Canton by Americans see Gutzlaff, *Sketch of Chinese History*, Appendix IV, and Pitkin, *Statistical View of the Commerce of the United States* (1835 edition), p. 304.

[71] Jones to Marshall, Oahu, October 2, 1821, in Marshall MSS; Jones to Marshall and Wildes, Oahu, December 23, 1821, January 22, 1822, *ibid.*

[72] Jones to Marshall and Wildes, Oahu, August 10, 1822, *ibid.*

[73] Jones to Marshall and Wildes, Oahu, November 9, 1822, *ibid.*

[74] Jones to Marshall and Wildes, Oahu, May 31, 1823, *ibid.*

[75] Journal of Levi Chamberlain, August 29, 1823; Jones to Marshall and Wildes, Oahu, October 12, 1823, in Marshall MSS; Crocker to Marshall and Wildes, Oahu, October 21, 1823, *ibid.*

[76] Jones to Marshall and Wildes, Oahu, October 10, 1822, January 1823, *ibid.*

detained at the Islands for five months while every effort was made to secure sandalwood for the Canton market,[77] but it eventually sailed with about 3,000 piculs,[78] whereas on a previous voyage it had taken 5,000 piculs to China.[79] The experience of the "Paragon" was typical of the state of Hawaiian commerce.[80] At Canton the imports of sandalwood by American traders declined from more than 20,000 piculs in the season of 1822–1823 to less than 8,500 piculs in 1823–1824.[81]

As the supply of wood approached extinction the quality became noticeably poorer.[82] During the most prosperous period of the trade sandalwood was commonly valued at ten dollars a picul.[83] As the market reacted throughout 1822 to an oversupply of wood as well as to the inferior quality of wood from the Hawaiian Islands, the value of sandalwood steadily declined, until in 1823 it brought only six and a half dollars a picul at Canton.[84] So unpromising was the outlook that some of the traders feared sandalwood could no longer

[77] Jones to Marshall and Wildes, Oahu, October 12, December 3, 1823, *ibid.*; Crocker to Marshall and Wildes, Oahu, October 21, 1823, *ibid.*; Charles Brewer, *Reminiscences* (privately printed, 1884), pp. 20–21.

[78] Jones to Marshall, Canton, February 21, 1824, in Marshall MSS; Pitman and French to Marshall, Canton, March 1, 1824, *ibid.* These reports obviously are in conflict with the statement of Charles Brewer (*Reminiscences*, p. 22) that the "Paragon" left the Islands "with a full cargo of sandal-wood."

[79] Jones to Marshall, Oahu, October 2, 1821, in Marshall MSS; Brown to Marshall, Canton, March 22, 1822, *ibid.*

[80] In 1822 the "Pedler" had some difficulty in securing a full cargo of Hawaiian sandalwood and finally sailed in December with only 2,000 piculs as compared with the 3,000 piculs which it had carried from the Islands in 1821. Porter, *John Jacob Astor*, II, 656–657.

[81] Gutzlaff, *Sketch of Chinese History*, II, Appendix IV.

[82] Jones to Marshall and Wildes, Oahu, January 1823, in Marshall MSS; Pitman and French to Marshall, Canton, January 1, 1823, in *ibid.*; Hunnewell to James P. Sturgis & Co., Oahu, January 9, 1824 (copy), in Hunnewell MSS; Journal of

Stephen Reynolds, July 22, 26, 1824, and June 9, 17, December 30, 1825.

[83] "Golovnin's Visit to Hawaii in 1818," in *The Friend*, July 1894, p. 53; "Account Book of Ship Sultan, 1815–1819"; Perkins & Co. to J. and T. H. Perkins, Canton, January 23, 1820, in Perkins Letterbooks, I, 1; Journal of Maria S. Loomis, January 4, 1821; William French to Marshall, Canton, September 23, 1821, in Marshall MSS; Mathison, *Visit to Brazil*, p. 457. Perkins & Co. reported that Hawaiian sandalwood brought from nine to ten dollars a picul. During the winter of 1821–1822, one of Astor's agents at Canton received tea in exchange for sandalwood at the rate of ten dollars a picul (French to Marshall, Canton, January 4, 1822, in Marshall MSS); and in October 1821, a load of wood was sold at Canton for eight dollars a picul, apparently because the wood was small. Andrew Blanchard to Hunnewell, Canton, October 31, 1821, in Hunnewell MSS.

[84] Mathison, *Visit to Brazil*, p. 458; Pitman and French to Marshall, Canton, October 11, 1822, and January 1, March 2, 1823, in Marshall MSS; French to Marshall, Canton, January 8, 1823, *ibid.*; Bryant and Sturgis to Newell and Hammatt, Boston, October 18, 1823, in Bryant and Sturgis Letterbooks, 1818–1829, p. 293.

be carried profitably from the Islands to China,[85] although at least one of their number predicted a rise in the price of sandalwood at Canton.[86] Time proved his optimism to be justified, for a marked decrease in the amount of sandalwood sent from the Hawaiian Islands during the trading season of 1823–1824[87] was followed by an increase in the price received by the traders.[88]

During 1824 three vessels—the "Lascar," the "Champion," and the "Sultan"—experienced great difficulty in securing cargoes at Hawaiian ports, and the "Lascar" finally sailed with a cargo said to consist chiefly of skins and specie.[89] The export of sandalwood from the Hawaiian Islands continued to decline, and during the trading season of 1825–1826 American traders carried only slightly more than three thousand piculs to China.[90] The value of sandalwood responded to this scarcity by soaring to levels above that of any previous period; during the trading seasons of 1825–1826 and 1826–1827 it sold at Canton for amounts varying from ten and a half dollars to fourteen dollars a picul, depending upon the state of the market and the quality of the wood.[91] Despite this advance in price the sandalwood trade appeared on the verge of collapse.[92] Only the artificial stimulus provided by the desperate efforts of the chiefs

[85] Crocker to Marshall and Wildes, Oahu, December 31, 1823, in Marshall MSS. Cf. Wildes to Marshall, Oahu, July 21, 1824, *ibid.*; Bryant and Sturgis to James P. Sturgis & Co., Boston, October 7, 1823, in Bryant and Sturgis Letterbooks, 1818–1829, p. 291.

[86] Jones to Marshall and Wildes, Oahu, November 9, 1823, in Marshall MSS; Jones to Marshall, Canton, February 19, 1824, *ibid.*

[87] Gutzlaff, *Sketch of Chinese History*, II, Appendix IV. American traders received approximately $59,000 for sandalwood which they carried to Canton during the season of 1823–1824, as compared with more than $134,000 received for sea otter skins. *Senate Documents*, 19th Cong., 1st Sess., No. 31, Appendix G.

[88] Jones to Marshall, Canton, February 19, 1824, in Marshall MSS; Pitman and French to Marshall, Canton, March 1, 1824, *ibid.*; Wildes to Marshall, Oahu, November 5, 1824, *ibid.*; J. B. R. Cooper to Hunnewell, Monterey, August 17, 1824, in Hunnewell MSS.

[89] Wildes to Marshall, Oahu, September 7, November 5, 1824, in Marshall MSS; Journal of Levi Chamberlain, December 2, 1824. Lord Byron, who visited the Islands in 1825, explained the noticeable falling off in trade as a result of "the very high port-charges, and price of provisions of all kinds, laid on by the chiefs, in consequence of the Americans increasing the prices of their articles of trade." Byron to J. W. Croker, Oahu, May 30, 1825, in *Correspondence Relative to the Sandwich Islands*, p. 13.

[90] Gutzlaff, *Sketch of Chinese History*, II, Appendix IV.

[91] Russell & Co. to Marshall, Canton, September 28, 1825, January 19, March 10, 1827, in Marshall MSS; Wildes to Marshall, Canton, March 1826, February 21, 1827, in *ibid.*

[92] Beechey, *Voyage to the Pacific*, II, 99; Paulding, *Cruise of the Dolphin*, p. 232; Bryant and Sturgis to Hammatt, Boston, July 14, 1825, in Bryant and Sturgis Letterbooks, 1818–1829, p. 340.

to liquidate their debts gave sandalwood a renewed importance between 1827 and 1830.

Merchants at Honolulu hoped to reap a substantial profit on goods brought from the United States for sale in the Islands,[93] but competition was keen,[94] and when several vessels had recently arrived from the United States the market was often seriously overstocked, with a consequent depression of prices. The actual realization of profits from the Hawaiian trade was frequently postponed. After two and a half years of the reign of Liholiho, observers noted that the chiefs apparently were more concerned with new purchases than with the liquidation of the debts which had already accumulated, and Jones declared that the King, his queens, and the chiefs, ignoring the mounting tide of debt, were at Oahu "devouring all before them."[95] At the close of 1821, when the aggregate amount for which the chiefs were indebted to traders exceeded 22,000 piculs,[96] Jones reported that "we have got to fight for our pay."[97] Nearly three years later the amount due American citizens was estimated as not far from $300,000.[98] Clearly the chiefs had made no progress toward the reduction of their indebtedness.

As the months lengthened into years and there was no substantial decrease in the debts, pessimism gripped the traders, and the fear was freely expressed that the chiefs would make no serious effort to meet their financial obligations.[99] As late as September 1824

[93] Journal of John N. Colcord (MS in Archives of Hawaii; typed copy Hawaiian Historical Society Library), p. 55; Letter of Rowland Bloxam, September 6, 1825, in *Hawaiian Almanac and Annual*, 1924, p. 68.

[94] Jones to Marshall and Wildes, Oahu, October 5, 1821, in Marshall MSS; Brown to Marshall, Oahu, December 24, 1821, in *ibid.*

[95] Jones to Marshall and Wildes, Honolulu, July 6, 1821, in Massachusetts Historical Society, *Proceedings*, LIV, 33; Journal of James Hunnewell, September 2, 1821, in Hunnewell MSS; Hunnewell to Andrew Blanchard, Oahu, October 12, 1822 (copy), in *ibid.*

[96] Hunnewell to Hall and Thatcher, January 29, 1822 (copy), in *ibid.*

[97] Jones to Marshall and Wildes, Oahu,

December 23, 1821, in Marshall MSS. In the late summer of 1822, Bryant and Sturgis apparently were becoming alarmed lest the chiefs purchase more than they could afford, for they instructed their Honolulu agent that he should investigate "in particular their ability to pay, for they have never shown any reluctance to making purchases." Bryant and Sturgis to Charles H. Hammatt, [September 1822], in Bryant and Sturgis Letterbooks, 1818–1829, p. 265.

[98] Crocker to Adams, Honolulu, September 15, 1824, in USDS, "Consular Letters," Honolulu, I.

[99] Hunnewell to Charles Thatcher, Oahu, January 13, December 29, 1823, in Hunnewell MSS; Jones to Marshall and Wildes, October 12, 24, 1823, in Marshall MSS; Crocker to Marshall and Wildes, Oahu, October 27, 1823, *ibid.*

Dixey Wildes thought that the chiefs intended to pay,[100] but other traders were less sanguine. Earlier in the same year Bryant and Sturgis declared that their "only hope" of securing the wood due them rested upon a visit to the Islands of a United States frigate;[101] in September the acting commercial agent of the United States at the Islands expressed a similar view;[102] and by the summer of 1825 the once optimistic Wildes, after experiencing in person the difficulty of persuading the chiefs to part with the sandalwood, informed his partner that the interests of American commerce at the Islands demanded the intervention of a man-of-war.[103] Twice during the ensuing autumn Wildes urged his partner to make a "strong representation" to the government at Washington, lest without a show of force the debts remain unpaid.[104] A year later the long anticipated man-of-war arrived at Honolulu to investigate the question of the debts.

To the more powerful and more favored chiefs sandalwood was a temporary source of almost fabulous wealth. Neither the cultivation of the trees nor the labor necessary to get the wood to the shore diminished the net profits of the chiefs, for nature had cared for the first and native laborers furnished the second without compensation. The Rev. Charles S. Stewart, who was at the Islands from 1823 to 1825, reported that the sandalwood trade had enriched the chiefs with "considerable wealth in money . . . . and in large quantities of foreign manufacture."[105] In 1827 Captain Beechey found that the chiefs were no longer satisfied with the usual comforts of life but yearned for "its luxuries, and even indulged in its extravagancies." Among the "extravagancies" in the possession of the chiefs Beechey specifically noted chests filled with "the most costly silks of China"

[100] Wildes to Marshall, Oahu, April 29, September 17, 1824, *ibid.*

[101] Bryant and Sturgis to Hammatt, Boston, April 9, 1824, in Bryant and Sturgis Letterbooks, 1818–1829, p. 300. More than a year later, they informed Hammatt that they would "take care in [the] future to put no trust in such faithless People as all the Islanders now appear to be." Bryant and Sturgis to Hammatt, Boston, July 14, 1825, *ibid.*, p. 340.

[102] Crocker to Adams, Honolulu, September 15, 1824, in USDS, "Consular Letters,"

Honolulu, I. In October 1824 there was a rumor in Honolulu that Kalanimoku had declared there was no wood and that he was unable to pay the debts. Journal of Stephen Reynolds, October 12, 1824.

[103] Wildes to Marshall, Oahu, July 18, 1825, in Marshall MSS. See also Grimes to Marshall, Oahu, August 16, 1825, *ibid.*

[104] Wildes to Marshall, Oahu, October 16, December 7, 1825, in *ibid.*

[105] Stewart, *Private Journal of a Voyage to the Pacific*, p. 130.

and several services of plate, including one "of expensively cut glass from Pellatt and Green in London."[106] Liholiho, presumably the principal beneficiary of the sandalwood trade, was said to have received four hundred ready-made garments in a single shipment from Canton.[107] It should be added that the chiefs did not always receive in goods the equivalent of the wood they so readily sold, and the estimate that the sandalwood trade enriched the Islands by more than three million dollars appears to be extravagant.[108] It may readily be believed that the chiefs derived enjoyment and pride from the possessions which their sandalwood made available. It was wealth that came easily, however, and much of it was as easily dissipated.[109]

The commoners were less fortunate. During the years when the trade was at its height the natives were often ordered to go to the mountains to cut sandalwood or to carry it to the shore.[110] It was their labor which made possible the place occupied by sandalwood in the four-cornered trade between the United States, the northwest coast, the Hawaiian Islands, and Canton; and at times they were compelled to neglect their own agricultural pursuits in order to cut sandalwood for their extravagant rulers or the latter's American creditors.[111] The Rev. William Richards, who was familiar with virtually every force influencing the lives of the Hawaiian people, believed that no task imposed by the rulers upon their subjects since the arrival of foreigners had been so burdensome as the forced collection of sandalwood.[112] This view was supported by David Malo, an unusually well-informed native, who asserted that the oppression

[106] Beechey, *Voyage to the Pacific*, II, 97.

[107] Stewart, *Private Journal of a Voyage to the Pacific*, pp. 130–131.

[108] This estimate was made by William D. Blackman in his *Making of Hawaii*, p. 188.

[109] The ablest of the nineteenth-century historians of the Islands declared that the goods secured by the chiefs through the sandalwood trade were "either wasted in riot and debauchery, or destroyed by neglect." James Jackson Jarves, "The Sandwich or Hawaiian Islands," *Merchants' Magazine*, IX (August 1843), 113.

[110] Kotzebue, *Voyage of Discovery*, II, 200; Hunnewell to Hall and Thatcher, Oahu, October 6, 1821 (copy), in Hunnewell MSS; Jones to Marshall and Wildes, Oahu, January 22, 1822, in Massachusetts Historical Society, *Proceedings*, LIV, 39; Mathison, *Visit to Brazil*, p. 451; Montgomery, comp., *Journal of Tyerman and Bennet*, I, 415; Ellis, *Tour through Hawaii*, pp. 275, 338, 370, 375–376; Journal of Levi Chamberlain, July 25, 1823, January 30, 31, 1824.

[111] Kotzebue, *Voyage of Discovery*, II, 200; Journal of the Missionaries at Honolulu, March 19, 1822, in *Missionary Herald*, XIX (June 1823), 184.

[112] Richards to Wilkes, Lahaina, March 15, 1841, in AH, Richards MSS.

of the common people caused by the compulsory collection of wood to meet the debts of the chiefs far exceeded the burdens imposed by the wars of the earlier period.[113] In the spring of 1830, at a time when the weather was bitterly cold, the Rev. Peter J. Gulick found a number of natives in the mountains of Kauai collecting sandalwood and "often driven by hunger to eat wild and bitter herbs, moss, &c."[114] Nine years later Malo declared that many had died while in the mountains in search of sandalwood, although the debts still were not fully paid.[115]

It is evident that the common people had little cause to regret the decline of the sandalwood trade. It is unlikely that any regret would have been expressed by Jacques Arago, who was at the Islands in 1819 and whose obvious fondness for a cleverly turned phrase prompted him to provide his contemporaries with an amusing picture of the frenzied quest for Hawaiian sandalwood. According to Arago:

Commerce has attracted to Oahu some Americans, who, in the hope of speedily making their fortunes, established themselves here some years ago. . . . . In the morning, they take to the Governor a half dozen bottles of wine . . . . they make presents to the principal chiefs of some axes, or two or three muskets, and all the rest of the population is at the disposal of these gentlemen. Some strong, active men are sent into the mountains; the forests are examined, the sandalwood is felled; and for two yards of European cloth, twenty women carry it at night to the shore, where it is embarked on a vessel always stationed in the harbor. When spring comes, their correspondents on the northwest coast of America come here, laden with furs, to secure provisions, to augment their valuable stocks with all the acquisitions of their partners; and, certain of an immense profit, they hasten to Macao or to Canton, to sell their cargoes to the lazy Chinese for cash, sugar or silks, which they know how to forward quickly to Europe. This type of commerce, however lucrative it may be, has its drawbacks, and I do not know how the perilous activity of some, and the long solitude of others is alluring so many to that place.[116]

---

[113] Malo, "On the Decrease of Population on the Hawaiian Islands," translated by L. Andrews, in *Hawaiian Spectator*, II (April 1839), 126–127.

[114] Journal of P. J. Gulick, April 13, 1830, in *Missionary Herald*, XXVII (December 1831), 382.

[115] Malo, *loc. cit.*, pp. 126–127. See also *Ka Mooolelo Hawaii*, translated in *Poly-*

nesian, August 1, 1840. Many years later, Robert C. Wyllie aptly described the labor imposed upon the commoners to satisfy the insistent creditors of the chiefs as "the hard penalties which the superior civilization exacts of the inferior." *Report of the Minister of Foreign Relations*, 1855, p. 4.

[116] Arago, *Promenade Autour du Monde*, II, 199–200.

Furs, which had dominated the trans-Pacific trade in the early years of the century, occupied a subordinate role in that commerce after 1815. In place of the fur trade which had flourished between 1790 and 1812 there developed a highly diversified trade in which sandalwood was more important than furs. This new commerce found its logical center at Honolulu. Cargoes from the United States intended for distribution throughout the Pacific were landed at Honolulu; from that port traders took their departure in search of markets or cargoes at the Russian settlements, along the American coast, or in the islands of the South Pacific.[117] Thus favored by the traders,

[117] In 1829 John C. Jones divided American vessels touching at Hawaiian ports into five groups: vessels from the United States bound for Manila or Canton which stopped to secure sandalwood; vessels engaged in trade along the northwest coast which visited the Islands on their passages to or from the United States or while crossing the Pacific to or from China; vessels which touched at the Islands while crossing the Pacific from the American coast to China, visiting Hawaiian ports "for recruits or repairs, to obtain freight, or dispose of what small cargoes they may have left"; vessels owned by Americans resident in the Islands and engaged in trade with various parts of the Pacific; and vessels engaged in whaling off the coast of Japan. Jones to Captain W. C. B. Finch, Honolulu, October 30, 1829, in *Senate Documents*, 21st Cong., 2d Sess., No. 1, pp. 203–204, and in C. S. Stewart, *A Visit to the South Seas, in the U.S. Ship Vincennes, during the Years 1829 and 1830* (New York, 1831), II, 214.

An impressive statistical survey of the extent to which vessels from virtually every maritime country visited the Islands may be found in *The Friend*, May 1, 1844, p. 49. Other indications of the extent and variety of the trade which centered at Honolulu may be found in Porter, *John Jacob Astor*, II, chap. xiii, and in "Index to N. W. C. & Sand. Isles Voyages 1820–1829," in Marshall MSS. Specific examples include the voyages of Astor's brig, the "Pedler," between 1820 and 1823. During that three-year period the "Pedler" successively visited Honolulu, New Archangel, Kamchatka, the Hawaiian Islands, Canton, the Hawaiian Islands, the American coast, the

Hawaiian Islands, Canton, the Russian settlements, the Hawaiian Islands, and Canton, finally leaving from Canton in 1823 on the homeward voyage to New York. Porter, *John Jacob Astor*, II, 654–657. Typical of trading voyages to the Pacific as contemplated by American merchants were the instructions of Bryant and Sturgis to Captain George Newell, who left Boston in the summer of 1822. Newell was informed that the "principal objects of the voyage now entrusted to your care, are, to dispose of a part of the cargo at the Sandwich Islands, to supply our Brigs Lascar & Rob Roy, now on the North West Coast, & to procure as many furs as you can obtain in the course of one season without paying too high a price." Newell was further informed that he was to be followed to the Pacific by the schooner "Ann," which was "intended to be used at the Sandwich Islands in collecting wood &c as long as wanted, & then sold." Bryant and Sturgis to Newell, Boston, June 25, 1822, in Bryant and Sturgis Letterbooks, 1818–1829, p. 245. Three months later, Bryant and Sturgis varied the usual procedure by sending the "Champion" to Gibraltar and thence around Cape Horn to the Pacific. Bryant and Sturgis to Captain Charles Preble, Boston, September 29, 1822, *ibid.*, p. 260. One further example of the extent to which Honolulu had become the crossroads of the Pacific may be taken from the correspondence of Henry A. Peirce in the spring of 1832. Within a few weeks, according to Peirce, the "Diana" had sailed for China, the "Ivanhoe" for San Blas, the "Bolivar" for the northwest coast, and the "Crusader" for Norfolk Sound. The "Volunteer" and the "Eagle" were in port, destined for

and possessing a harbor which was said to be "the only safe and commodious harbor in these seas to which ships can resort to be repaired, hove out, coppered &c,"[118] Honolulu emerged as the foremost seaport of the eastern Pacific—a community in which Polynesian traditions and New England practices were curiously blended.

Although furs had ceased to occupy the principal place in the commerce of the Pacific, they continued to be the most important objective of traders visiting the northwest coast. The direct trade between Oregon and the Hawaiian Islands was somewhat diversified by the sale at Honolulu of lumber and salmon from the northwest coast. As early as 1822 the missionaries at Honolulu purchased "some logs & spars from the N. W. Coast,"[119] but lumber and salmon were monopolies of the Hudson's Bay Company and they were seldom available as cargoes for American vessels. Every merchant engaged in the sandalwood trade was interested also in the maritime fur trade, and the most experienced masters often commanded ships which left Honolulu in the spring to cruise along the coast and returned to Honolulu in the late autumn to transship such furs as they had been able to purchase.

The success of vessels trading along the northwest coast was subject to considerable fluctuation. Competition was keen, and the

South America and the Columbia, respectively. The "Marcus" had recently arrived from the Marquesas Islands, the "Harriett Blanchard" from the South Pacific, and the "Sir George Murray" from New Zealand. The "Dhaulle" was expected soon from Tahiti via Manila. Several other vessels were said to be in port. Peirce to Hunnewell, Oahu, April 10, 1832, in Hunnewell MSS.

[118] Jones to Secretary of State McLane, Oahu, December 31, 1834, in USDS, "Consular Letters," Honolulu, I.

[119] The American Mission to Jeremiah Evarts, Oahu, December 28, 1822, in Letters to the American Board, IX, 130. For some years, Honolulu was the most important market for the lumber of Oregon. It was, however, a very small and uncertain market. Letters of George Simpson, [October 1828], July 10, 1830, in Frederick Merk, ed., *Fur Trade and Empire* (Cambridge, Massachusetts, 1931), pp. 298, 327;

Richard Charlton to John McLoughlin, Oahu, November 7, 1829, in *ibid.*, p. 319; Letters of John McLoughlin, August 5, 1829, March 16, 1831, in E. E. Rich, ed., *The Letters of John McLoughlin*, 1st ser. 1825–38 (Toronto, 1941), pp. 76–77, 226.

Honolulu also provided the principal market for salmon from the northwest coast. As in the case of lumber, the commerce in salmon was dominated by the Hudson's Bay Company, but occasionally an American vessel carried one or more casks of salmon from the coast, and in 1830–1831 Captain John Dominis carried a few barrels of salmon from the Columbia to Boston in the "Owyhee." Apparently this was the first salmon to reach Boston from Oregon. See Merk, *op. cit.*, p. 121 n.; Journal of Levi Chamberlain, October 20, 1827; William H. Bordman, Jr., to Seth Barker, Boston, October 7, 1831, in Bordman Letterbook (MS, Baker Library, Harvard University School of Business), p. 96.

profits from the fur trade were uniformly less than they had been prior to 1810.[120] In 1821 the usually well-informed partners of Bryant and Sturgis recognized the probability that there would be "more vessels on the coast in 1822 than can be profitably employed."[121] The situation was not materially improved in 1823, when six vessels cruising along the coast collected about 350 furs each—a collection which was fairly described as "hardly a saving business."[122] A year later there was some optimism among the traders. Bryant and Sturgis predicted that trade along the northwest coast would be "better . . . . than for years past";[123] and from Honolulu Captain Eliab Grimes reported that the "rage for the N West runs high."[124] This was but a temporary revival of the maritime fur trade. By 1828 that once lucrative branch of commerce had clearly passed its zenith and a few competent observers predicted that it had come to a close.[125] In July 1829 an employee of the Hudson's Bay Company reported that the Indians along the coast were demanding as much for a single beaver as they had for five beavers in earlier years;[126] and at the close of the year James Hunnewell wrote that the northwest coast had been completely abandoned by American vessels.[127]

[120] Ross, *Fur Hunters of the Far West*, I, 41; Howay, "A List of Trading Vessels in the Maritime Fur Trade," in *Transactions of the Royal Society of Canada*, 3d ser., XXVII, Sec. II, p. 120, and XXVIII, Sec. II, p. 13. It is impossible to determine the exact number of vessels trading along the coast. In 1822 William Sturgis declared that there were fourteen American vessels employed in trade in the eastern Pacific; but it is clear that in no year after 1815 were there as many vessels actively engaged in the fur trade. The results of the thorough research on this subject by Judge Howay indicate that during the eleven years from 1815 through 1825 there were from seven to ten vessels on the coast each year. A number of vessels cleared from eastern ports for the northwest coast but failed to reach that destination. Some of the vessels were sold at the Hawaiian Islands while on the passage from the United States to the coast. [Sturgis], "Examination of the Russian Claims to the Northwest Coast of America," in *North American Review*, XV (October 1822), 372; Howay, *loc. cit.*, XXVII, Sec. II, pp. 123–147, and XXVIII, Sec. II, pp. 16–45.

[121] Bryant and Sturgis to Charles Preble, February 17, 1821, Bryant and Sturgis Letterbooks, 1818–1829, p. 181.

[122] Bryant and Sturgis to James Bennett, Boston, March 16, 1824, *ibid.*, p. 300.

[123] Bryant and Sturgis to C. H. Hammatt, Boston, April 9, 1824, *ibid.*, p. 301.

[124] Grimes to Marshall, Oahu, November 5, 1824, in Marshall MSS.

[125] Jones to Marshall, Oahu, October 30, 1827, *ibid.*; A. Duhaut-Cilly, *Voyage Autour du Monde* (Paris, 1834–1835), II, 319–320.

[126] William Todd to Edward Ermatinger, York Factory, July 15, 1829, in *Washington Historical Quarterly*, I (July 1907), 258. See also Jones to Marshall, Oahu, October 30, 1827, in Marshall MSS, and Charles Taylor to Marshall, Oahu, April 15, 1828, *ibid.*

[127] Hunnewell to Bryant and Sturgis, Oahu, December 15, 1829 (copy), in Hunnewell MSS.

Occasionally after 1829 an American vessel made a successful voyage along the coast.[128] In 1829–1830 Josiah Marshall's "Owhyhee" remained there for eighteen months in competition with agents of the Hudson's Bay Company. After leaving the coast, the "Owhyhee" carried its cargo of beaver and "a large number of lesser furs" to Boston by way of Honolulu, thus avoiding the depressed prices at Canton. Innovation, however, could not save the maritime fur trade and Marshall was ready to withdraw from it.[129] To the general rise in the price of furs along the coast was added the hostility of the Hudson's Bay Company, whose agents were frankly desirous of driving American traders from the coast.[130] The death blow to the maritime fur trade was dealt by changing fashions—the substitution after 1830 of "cheap furs & other articles," principally silk, in the manufacture of hats.[131] Against such an adversary it was futile for the traders to struggle.

Meanwhile the revolutions in Mexico and South America removed many of the obstacles which once had made trade with those countries a precarious occupation. New opportunities brought increased interest. Late in 1821 Eliab Grimes returned to Honolulu from a very brief voyage to California with sea otter skins and cash aggregating in value nearly five thousand dollars, which he had received in exchange for goods that had cost him less than two thousand dollars.[132] As Grimes prepared to leave again for California upon an extended trading cruise, his associate, John C. Jones, predicted that there would be "many to contend with in that part of the

[128] James Lambert to Hunnewell, Tumgass, September 11, 1830, *ibid.*; Henry A. Peirce to Hunnewell, Honolulu, September 25, 1831, *ibid.*; W. K. Lamb, in Rich, ed., *Letters of John McLoughlin*, p. lxxx.

[129] William H. Bordman, Jr., to Seth Barker, Boston, June 7, 1831, Bordman Letterbook, p. 89.

[130] Dominis to Marshall, Chinook, March 4, 1829, Kigarney, June 14, 1829, in Marshall MSS; D. W. Thompson to Marshall, Columbia River, March 26, 1829, *ibid.*; Bordman to Barker, Boston, October 7, 1831, in Bordman Letterbook, p. 97. George Simpson to John McLoughlin, July 10, 1830, in Merk, ed., *Fur Trade and Empire*, p. 326. The views of agents of the company may

be inferred from the complaint of Dr. McLoughlin, in August 1830, that an American vessel trading along the coast had caused "an immensity of trouble." John McLoughlin to John Rowland, Fort Vancouver, August 3, 1830, in *ibid.*, p. 327.

[131] Bordman to Barker, Boston, September 8, 1832, in Bordman Letterbook, p. 122.

[132] Grimes to Marshall and Wildes, in Massachusetts Historical Society, *Proceedings*, LIV, 40. Neither the printed portion of this letter nor the manuscript copy of the original in the Josiah Marshall Letterbooks contains any date. References to contemporary incidents, including the anticipated sailing of the "Pedler," indicate that it was written in December 1821.

world."[133] His prediction was confirmed by his report ten months later, in October 1822, that the large number of vessels trading along the California coast precluded any one of them from reaping large profits.[134]

Throughout the decade the Honolulu-California trade continued to attract the resident merchants in the Islands. In 1825 Honolulu was described as "a depot" for goods which Americans intended to smuggle into Mexico or Colombia;[135] three years later it was reported that all goods were in demand in California;[136] and in 1831 three Honolulu merchants found the California trade so lucrative that they planned to send to the United States for a vessel and "a large cargo" which they might devote to that trade.[137] At the same time the British Consul in Honolulu conceded that the commerce between the Islands and "the new States in America" was "almost entirely in the hands of citizens of the United States."[138] Cargoes carried to California and to the west coast of South America seem to have included manufactured goods of all kinds from the United States, together with selections of goods from China. From California, merchants at Honolulu received horses,[139] beef,[140] sea otter furs, and cash.[141]

Less important than the northwest coast or California to American traders were the Russian settlements at Sitka and Kamchatka. As had been true prior to 1812, Astor appears to have been more consistently interested in trade with the Russians than were his competitors. His brig, the "Forester," sailing under British colors, visited the Russian settlements during the Anglo-American war, spent the

[133] Jones to Marshall and Wildes, Oahu, December 23, 1821, in Marshall MSS.

[134] Jones to Marshall and Wildes, Oahu, October 10, 1822, *ibid.*

[135] Charlton to Canning, Oahu, June 10, 1825, in *Correspondence Relative to the Sandwich Islands*, p. 11. See also Ogden, *California Sea Otter Trade*, pp. 86–94.

[136] Jones to Marshall, Oahu, November 1828, in Marshall MSS.

[137] Peirce to Hunnewell, Oahu, September 25, 1831, in Hunnewell MSS. Only a few vessels were employed in the Hawaiian-California trade. Of approximately one hundred vessels listed by H. H. Bancroft as having been at California ports during the five years from 1826 through 1830,

eleven took part in the trade with the Hawaiian Islands. Bancroft, *History of California*, III, 145–149.

[138] Charlton to Aberdeen, Oahu, December 1, 1831, in *Correspondence Relative to the Sandwich Islands*, p. 25.

[139] Journal of Levi Chamberlain, August 5, 1823, and August 25, 1827; Journal of Stephen Reynolds, July 26, 1827; Beechey, *Voyage to the Pacific*, II, 68; Thompson to Marshall, Oahu, November 19, 1830, in Marshall MSS.

[140] Jones to Marshall and Wildes, Oahu, October 10, 1822, in Massachusetts Historical Society, *Proceedings*, LIV, 42.

[141] Grimes to Marshall and Wildes, *ibid.*, p. 40.

summer of 1815 at Norfolk Sound and Kamchatka, and left Kamchatka in November 1815 with a cargo for California and the Hawaiian Islands.[142] Until the withdrawal of Astor from the Pacific trade, about 1827, his vessels commonly included the Russian posts among their ports of call.[143] His rivals, although less systematic in their exploitation of trade with the Russians, did not entirely overlook it. Occasionally vessels were sent to the Pacific with cargoes intended particularly for sale at the Russian posts;[144] more often the visits of traders at Sitka or Kamchatka were but incidents in extensive trading voyages that included every available market in the North Pacific.

The Russians continued to be dependent upon the outside world for foodstuffs and manufactured goods. Their needs, in part, were met by imports from Russia or from the Russian post in California; and these imports were supplemented by purchases from transient traders who called at Sitka or Kamchatka. When there was any interruption in the regular means of supply, the Russians in Alaska were compelled to turn either to visiting traders or to the American merchants at Honolulu to secure foodstuffs desperately needed to prevent a famine.[145] As Honolulu emerged as the focal point in American commerce in the eastern Pacific, the management of the trade with the Russian settlements, like that with California and Oregon, passed largely into the hands of the merchants on Oahu. The latter had a considerable variety of goods from which to choose cargoes for the Russian posts, but there seems to have been little to distinguish a cargo for Sitka from one intended for California. Vessels from Honolulu bound for Sitka or Kamchatka carried provisions, manufactured articles, and the products of China.[146] In 1821 a group of the Hawaiian chiefs entered the trade with Kamchatka with a voyage which the missionaries at Honolulu hailed as "this

[142] Porter, *John Jacob Astor*, II, 641.

[143] *Ibid.*, II, chapter xiii.

[144] Bryant and Sturgis to Suter, Boston, August 6, 1816, in Bryant and Sturgis Letterbooks, 1814–1818, pp. 271–274; Bryant and Sturgis to Captain Peter Allen, Boston, September 25, 1827, *ibid.*, 1818–1829; Bryant and Sturgis and Paschal P.

Pope to Captain William H. Hammatt, Boston, July 29, 1828, *ibid.*

[145] Bancroft, *History of Alaska*, pp. 537–539.

[146] Jones to Marshall and Wildes, Oahu, August 10, 1822, in Massachusetts Historical Society, *Proceedings*, LIV, 41; Jones to Marshall and Wildes, Oahu, January 22, 1822, in Marshall MSS; Wildes to Marshall, Oahu, July 18, 1825, *ibid.*

commencement of commerce with a foreign country."[147] On its northward voyage, the "Thaddeus," owned by the chiefs and commanded
by Captain William Sumner, carried salt; it returned with a cargo
of cordage, canvas, axes, and dried fish.[148]

American trade with the Russian settlements was threatened with
extinction by the Czar's ukase of September 16, 1821, issued at the
instance of the Russian American Company, which closed the coast
north of the fifty-first degree to traders and prohibited any foreign
vessel from approaching within one hundred Italian miles of the
shore. For a time Russian men-of-war patrolled the forbidden area,[149]
and American merchants were alarmed lest they lose permanently the
right to trade along the coast from Vancouver Island to Sitka.[150] The
tension was relieved when the Czar yielded to pressure from Great
Britain and the United States and permitted the signing, in April
1824, of a treaty which restored to a large extent the opportunity
for trade along the entire coast.[151]

The reopening of the coast north of the fifty-first parallel was
followed by a brief flurry of interest in trade with the Russian settlements.[152] The most experienced of the agents at Honolulu hazarded
the prediction, in 1827, that the Russians at Sitka and Kamchatka

[147] Journal of the Missionaries at Honolulu, July 12, 1821, in *Missionary Herald*,
XVIII (September 1822), 273–274.

[148] Jones to Marshall and Wildes, Oahu,
November 5, 1821, in Massachusetts Historical Society, *Proceedings*, LIV, 37; Jones
to Marshall and Wildes, Oahu, November
20, 1821, in Marshall MSS; Jones to Secretary of State Adams, Oahu, December 31,
1821, in USDS, "Consular Letters," Honolulu, I.

[149] Jones to Adams, Oahu, December 20,
1822, September 1, 1823, *ibid.* It may have
been the presence of Russian men-of-war
off the coast of Alaska and Siberia that
led Jones to assert that an American naval
vessel was "much wanted" to protect the
increasingly important commerce of the
Hawaiian Islands and the North Pacific.
Jones to Adams, Oahu, December 31, 1822,
ibid.

[150] Bryant and Sturgis to Daniel Cross
and William Bryant, Boston, October 18,
1823, in Bryant and Sturgis Letterbooks,
1818–1829, p. 292.

[151] The treaty may be found in William
M. Malloy, comp., *Treaties, Conventions,
International Acts, Protocols and Agree-
ments between the United States of Amer-
ica and Other Powers* (Washington, 1910),
II, 1512–1514.

[152] Among the commercial houses which
were interested in trade with the Russian
settlements were Bryant and Sturgis and
Marshall and Wildes. The interest of Bryant
and Sturgis is reflected in the instructions
which they gave to masters of their vessels
in the Pacific trade. See Bryant and Sturgis
to Captain William Bryant, [Boston, August 1826], in Bryant and Sturgis Letterbooks, 1818–1829, pp. 368–369; Bryant
and Sturgis to Captain Peter Allen, Boston, September 25, 1827, *ibid.*; Bryant and
Sturgis and Paschal P. Pope to Captain
William H. Hammatt, Boston, July 29, 1828,
ibid. For voyages to the Russian posts by
vessels belonging to Marshall and Wildes,
see "Index to N. W. C. & Sand. Isles Voyages, 1820–1829," in Marshall MSS.

would be "always in want of certain articles for which they will pay a good profit."[153] This trade might be profitable; it could not become extensive. It appears to have declined during the ten years that it was protected by the Treaty of 1824. In 1838 the Russian Foreign Minister, seeking to justify the withdrawal of the privileges of trade along the coasts of Alaska and Kamchatka, declared that "never more than four American vessels arrived in the course of a whole year, and that even this number . . . . diminished in proportion as enterprises on the northwest coast offered fewer chances of success."[154] The implication that the visits of American traders to the Russian posts were auxiliary to the maritime fur trade is a fair summary of the rise and decline of American commerce with Sitka and Kamchatka.

The extension of whaling into the western Pacific after 1820 added a new element to the maritime interests which radiated from Hawaiian ports. The history of American whaling in the Pacific is nearly as old as the story of American navigation in that ocean. The first whaler to leave the United States for the Pacific was the "Beaver," which left Nantucket in August 1791.[155] Other vessels quickly followed this example. With the exception of 1796, one or more whalers left New England each year from 1792 to the outbreak of the war with England.[156] The return of peace brought a prompt revival in the whaling industry, and in the years immediately thereafter American whalers were frequently reported at the islands of the South Pacific or along the west coast of South America.[157] There is no evidence, however, that any whaling vessel from the United States visited the Hawaiian Islands prior to 1820.

The emergence of Honolulu as the rendezvous of the whaling fleets of the Pacific followed the discovery of important whaling grounds off the coast of Japan. The policy of exclusion by which

[153] Jones to Marshall, Oahu, October 30, 1827, *ibid.*

[154] Count Nesselrode to George M. Dallas, St. Petersburg, March 9, 1838, in *Senate Documents*, 25th Cong., 3d Sess., No. 1, p. 70.

[155] Obed Macy, *History of Nantucket* (Boston, 1835), p. 141; Alexander Starbuck, *History of the American Whale Fishery* (Waltham, 1876), pp. 186–187.

[156] *Ibid.*, pp. 186–215.

[157] *Columbian Centinel*, March 3, October 2, 9, 20; November 6, 1819; and December 30, 1820. A communication signed "Pacificus" (*ibid.*, October 20, 1819) estimated that seventy-one whalers from the three Massachusetts ports of New Bedford, Nantucket, and Martha's Vineyard were in the Pacific or on their way to that ocean.

the ports of Japan were closed to the commerce of the world compelled the masters of whaling vessels to look elsewhere for harbors
where they could secure supplies or transship their oil to the United
States. In convenience of location and in facilities offered to shipping, no port frequented by American vessels in the Pacific surpassed
Honolulu. The identity of the first whaler to visit the western Pacific
is uncertain, but tradition has assigned that role to the "Maro" of
Nantucket, commanded by Captain Joseph Allen.[158] The "Maro"
left Nantucket late in October 1819, touched at Maui briefly in the
following May, and then sailed for the western Pacific, where it is
said to have enjoyed "singular success." It returned to the mid-
Pacific during the autumn, and in November touched at Honolulu
for twenty-four hours.[159] It had followed a course destined to become
routine for hundreds of American whalers during the ensuing forty
years.

After 1820 the number of whalers which visited Honolulu increased steadily. In the summer of 1822 John C. Jones reported that
the harbor at Honolulu had been "crowded with whale ships, not
less say than sixty";[160] less than four years later, he informed the
State Department that Hawaiian ports were "almost indispensable"
to vessels engaged in whaling in the western Pacific.[161] In 1825 excessive port charges at Honolulu and the high price of provisions on
Oahu drove many of the whalers to the roadstead at Lahaina, on the
west side of Maui.[162] In the following year the majority of the whalers
again called at Honolulu, and from that time until after 1840 Honolulu retained its primacy as a port of call for the whaling fleets of
the Pacific. Lahaina, however, was not completely deserted, and
after 1828 the number of whaling ships which dropped anchor there
steadily increased.[163] A third port, Hilo, played a minor role in

[158] Starbuck, *History of the American Whale Fishery*, p. 96; Bingham, *Sandwich Islands*, p. 134.

[159] Journal of the Missionaries at Honolulu, November 1, 1820, in *Missionary Herald*, XVII (September 1821), 280.

[160] Jones to Marshall and Wildes, Oahu,
August 10, 1822, in Massachusetts Historical Society, *Proceedings*, LIV, 41.

[161] Jones to Secretary of State Clay, Oahu,

May 8, 1826, and July 1, 1827, in USDS,
"Consular Letters," Honolulu, I.

[162] Charlton to Canning, Oahu, June 10,
1825, in *Correspondence Relative to the
Sandwich Islands*, p. 11. Charlton wrote
that Honolulu had been "almost abandoned" by the whalers.

[163] It is difficult to tell how dependable
are the available statistics which indicate
the number of whalers visiting Honolulu

furnishing supplies or in catering to the whims of visiting whalers.[164]

At least one and often two visits to Hawaiian ports were a part of the annual routine of virtually every whaler in the North Pacific. Twice each year—in March or April, and again in the autumn— Hawaiian merchants welcomed these wanderers of the sea who came in search of provisions, recruits, recreation, and often of repairs. The semiannual visits of whalers varied in length from a few days spent in the outer harbor to extended stays of six weeks. The remainder of the year was devoted to the arduous business which had brought vessel and crew to the Pacific. The summer commonly was spent on the whaling grounds in the western Pacific, while during the winter months most vessels cruised along the coast of California or south of Hawaii in the vicinity of the equator.[165] Not every ship followed this routine, and indeed there commonly were more whalers in Hawaiian waters during the autumn months than in the spring; but for forty years the semiannual visits of the whaling fleet regularly brought new life to Hawaiian ports and the hope of increased sales to local merchants. Only after 1860 did the plantation supplant the whaler as the cornerstone of Hawaiian prosperity.

The advent of the whaler in the economic life of the Islands coincided with the bonanza years of the sandalwood trade and for a time was overshadowed by the extravagance of that trade. Its true importance in Hawaiian economic life may be judged by the report of the American commercial agent, in 1827, that during the visits of the whaling ships there were usually not less than six hundred

and Lahaina in the 'twenties and 'thirties. Probably the best available figures for Honolulu are those compiled from records kept by Stephen Reynolds and which were printed by Robert C. Wyllie in *The Friend*, May 1, 1844, p. 49. The statistics for Lahaina were compiled by members of the American mission there and were included in a letter from the Rev. William Richards and the Rev. Ephraim Spaulding, dated Lahaina, December 7, 1833, in *Sailor's Magazine*, VI (August 1834), 358. These figures indicate 107 visits of whalers at Honolulu in 1826, 82 in 1827, 112 in 1828, 109 in 1829, 94 in 1830, 81 in 1831, and 118 in 1832. Beginning in 1828, the number of whalers touching at Lahaina rose steadily, with 45 in 1828, 62 in 1829, and 80 in 1832.

[164] Finch to Secretary of the Navy, October 10, 1829, in NRL, "Capt. Finch's Cruise of the U.S.S. Vincennes"; *Missionary Herald*, XXVI (April 1830), 110. Finch believed that Hilo attracted principally whalers which were "homeward bound."

[165] Jones to Secretary of State Clay, Oahu, July 1, 1827, in USDS, "Consular Letters," Honolulu, I. An indication of the wide variation in the length of the stay of a whaler at Honolulu is suggested by the cruise of the "Ontario" in 1825 and 1826, when on three visits to Oahu the vessel remained there seventy-five hours, thirty-six days, and twenty-one days, respectively. Journal of Alex. D. Bunker (MS, Harvard University Library), April 5-8, 1825, April 14, September 25, 1826.

seamen in port at one time.[166] It may be safely assumed that the majority of the seamen could easily be induced to leave a large share of their wages in Honolulu, to which could be added the amount spent by the ships' officers for supplies and repairs.

The development of Honolulu as a commercial center was accompanied by notable changes in the character of the foreign community. Lieutenant Hiram Paulding, after a visit of sixteen weeks in 1826, estimated that there were between fifty and one hundred foreigners at Honolulu. This was a conservative estimate; later in the year, Captain Thomas ap Catesby Jones placed the number at about two hundred.[167] Since 1820 there had been at Honolulu a few missionary families—the most influential addition to the foreign population during the period. Although relatively few in number, they were destined, by precept and by example, to mold the character and habits of thousands of Hawaiians, and to play a major role in the evolution of the political and social institutions of the Islands. Another new element in the community was a small group of resident traders, who occasionally acted in the dual role of retail merchant and agent of one of the American firms engaged in the sandalwood trade. In contrast to the missionaries, few if any of the merchants proposed to remain permanently in the Islands, although some of their number were so prone to postpone their departure that they became in effect permanent residents of the little kingdom. Because they regarded themselves as transients whose sole concern was the prosecution of their trade, they were generally indifferent to local problems and to the welfare of the native population.

Missionary and merchant alike gave an appearance of stability to the hitherto unstable foreign community. They did not constitute the whole number of foreigners at the Islands. In 1823, Charles S. Stewart found some fifteen or twenty whites who had "dropped all connexion with their native countries" and had acquired "plantations and other property, under the king and various chiefs."[168] Quite

---

[166] Jones to Clay, Oahu, July 1, 1827, in USDS, "Consular Letters," Honolulu, I. The Secretary of the Navy reported that during 1826 more than two thousand American seamen had visited Honolulu. Report of the Secretary of the Navy, December 1, 1827, in *House Executive Documents*, 20th Cong., 1st Sess., No. 2, p. 200.

[167] Paulding, *Cruise of the Dolphin*, p. 226; NRL, Jones, "Report of the Peacock's Cruise to the Sandwich, Society and other Islands in the Pacific Ocean performed in the years 1826 and 27," pp. 19–20.

[168] Stewart, *Private Journal of a Voyage to the Pacific*, p. 155.

different in character was a fluctuating group of transients who, many observers agreed, constituted a menace to the peace and morals of the community.[169] In 1822 John C. Jones reported that Honolulu was filled with deserters whose baneful influence was converting that pleasant port into "one of the vilest places on the globe."[170] Four years later he characterized these transients as "lost to every sense of justice, honor, and integrity."[171] In the same year, Hiram Paulding saw at Honolulu some of the "most abandoned members of society," among whom he included those who earned a livelihood "by keeping tippling shops for sailors, and practising such chicaneries as are suggested by opportunities and the absence of law."[172] This army of purposeless drifters, if we may believe Jones, consisted of "from fifty to one hundred lawless seamen of every nation."[173]

The first published law of the Hawaiian kingdom prohibited desertion from visiting vessels and forebade the leaving of seamen at the Islands without the permission of the governor of the island.[174] This salutary law was reaffirmed as part of the port regulations adopted during the visit of Lord Byron in 1825,[175] but apparently it was poorly enforced.[176] In addition to the ever-present deserters, there were also at Honolulu a varying number of disabled seamen who had been discharged from their vessels and left at the Islands dependent upon such care as might be provided by the American

[169] See *ibid.*, pp. 156–157; Kotzebue, *New Voyage Round the World*, II, 217; Paulding, *Cruise of the Dolphin*, pp. 225–226; Beechey, *Voyage to the Pacific*, II, 117–118; Charlton to Canning, Oahu, October 4, 1826, in *Correspondence Relative to the Sandwich Islands*, p. 15; Duhaut-Cilly, *Voyage Autour du Monde*, II, 319; Journal of Maria S. Loomis, September 23, 1822; Martin Brewster to Marshall and Wildes, Oahu, October 11, 1822, in Massachusetts Historical Society, *Proceedings*, LIV, 43.

[170] Jones to Marshall and Wildes, Oahu, November 16, 1822, *ibid.*, p. 44.

[171] Jones to Isaac Hull, quoted in Charles Oscar Paullin, *Diplomatic Negotiations of American Naval Officers* (Baltimore, 1912), p. 336.

[172] Paulding, *Cruise of the Dolphin*, p. 226. See also the comment of a Catholic missionary at Honolulu, in 1828, that nearly

all foreigners at Honolulu were deserters or adventurers whose influence was to be seen in the love of liquor and gambling which prevailed among the chiefs. Quoted by Francis Furey in *Records of the American Catholic Historical Society*, XLV (March 1934), 68.

[173] Jones to Clay, Oahu, July 1, 1827, in USDS, "Consular Letters," Honolulu, I.

[174] This law was dated March 8, 1822. A facsimile may be found in Ralph S. Kuykendall and Herbert E. Gregory, *A History of Hawaii* (New York, 1928), p. 128.

[175] *Regulations for the Port of Honolulu, Oahu*, in Hunnewell MSS. These regulations were dated Oahu, June 2, 1825. They are printed in [Graham, comp.], *Voyage of H.M.S. Blonde*, p. 159.

[176] Charlton to Canning, Oahu, October 4, 1826, in *Correspondence Relative to the Sandwich Islands*, p. 15.

commercial agent. The number thus discharged was reported by Jones to have been "very large."[177] Whatever alarm may have been felt in the community by the presence of a considerable group of restless and often unscrupulous seamen must have been greatly intensified during the semiannual visits of the whaling fleet at Honolulu and Lahaina. To many seamen the islands of the Pacific were a haven where law and morality were superfluous and where all restraints might be cast aside, and only the fear of discipline on board ship averted serious rioting or bloodshed in a remote part of the world where the native authorities would have found it difficult to control unruly visitors.

The earliest retail business at Honolulu seems to have been that conducted by James Hunnewell and a Mr. Dorr in 1817 and 1818. After the sale of the "Bordeaux Packet," upon which they had come to the Islands as officers, the two men remained at Honolulu to dispose of the rest of the cargo brought to the Pacific by that vessel.[178] This mercantile venture was necessarily transient. During a residence of less than ten months at the Islands, Hunnewell and Dorr apparently disposed of most, if not all, of their goods, and in September 1818 they left for Canton and the United States.[179] Nearly thirty years later Hunnewell remembered that during this time "there was only one other trading establishment besides ours" at Honolulu.[180] He did not reveal the identity of the other concern. Contemporary accounts indicate that there were transient traders at Honolulu between 1818 and 1820, but it is difficult to determine the exact nature of their activities. The available evidence indicates that they were men who had come to the Islands as officers of trading vessels and that often they were in the employ of Boston or New York merchants. If, as seems probable, they continued in the employ of those merchants during their residence at Honolulu, these ob-

---

[177] Jones to Clay, Boston, November 5, 1825, in USDS, "Consular Letters," Honolulu, I; Jones to Secretary of State Livingston, Oahu, February 8, 1834, *ibid.*

[178] Journal of James Hunnewell, December 8, 1817, in Hunnewell MSS; Hunnewell to S. Peck, in *The Friend*, January 1867, p. 6.

[179] An account of Hunnewell's experiences, taken largely from his journal, may be found in Hunnewell, ed., "Voyage in the Brig Bordeaux Packet . . . . and Residence in Honolulu, 1817–1818," in HHS, *Papers*, No. 8, pp. 8–17.

[180] Hunnewell to J. F. B. Marshall, Charlestown, Mass., December 12, 1845 (copy), in Hunnewell MSS.

scure traders were the pioneer agents at the Islands of the great New England and New York houses which dominated the trade of the Pacific.[181] There was but little money in the Islands, and most of the trade was in the form of barter; in ten months Hunnewell received only a little more than one hundred dollars in cash, nearly all of which came from the master of one English vessel.[182]

Retail trade at Honolulu had its origin in efforts to dispose of specific cargoes. By 1821 this random trading had been largely superseded by the feverish competition of semipermanent mercantile establishments managed by the agents of great American houses and seeking the patronage of chiefs, foreign residents, and visiting mariners. The development of whaling in the western Pacific greatly increased the number of vessels calling at Hawaiian ports and consequently increased the opportunities for the sale of American and European goods at the Islands. Meanwhile, natives living near Honolulu were becoming increasingly aware of such ordinary articles of trade as clothing, ornaments, hardware, and dishes, as well as such exotic luxuries as carriages and billiard tables. Few Hawaiians

---

[181] Captain William Pigot, who had come to the Pacific as master of Astor's "Forester," was at Honolulu from 1818 to 1820. The most recent and satisfactory biography of Astor suggests that during the time Pigot was at Honolulu he was "probably doing some business for himself." It is possible that he may have regarded himself as still in the employ of Astor, as he had been primarily concerned with Astor's interests until the time of his arrival at Honolulu. In 1820 he acted as agent for Astor's "Pedler" and later sailed to the American coast on that vessel. Meanwhile, he had purchased the "San Martin," perhaps entirely on his own account, and had sent the vessel on a trading voyage to the Far East. Porter, *John Jacob Astor*, II, 641–642, 654.

Another early trader at Honolulu was Captain William Babcock, who went to the Pacific in command of the "Neo." The "Neo," which left Boston in September 1818, was sent to the Pacific by Josiah Marshall. It was sold at the Hawaiian Islands in 1819, and Babcock remained there for some time. He is mentioned casually in contemporary accounts as engaged in trade or as possessing, late in 1821, a store close to the harbor.

Early in 1821 he was acting as agent for Marshall and Wildes, and it is reasonable to suppose that he had been continuously in the employ of Marshall, or of the expanded firm, from the time that he left Boston. *Columbian Centinel*, September 19, 1818; Journal of James Hunnewell, May 18, 25, July 11, 1820, in Hunnewell MSS; Journal of Maria S. Loomis, January 1, 1821; Journal of the Missionaries, November 12, 1821, in *Missionary Herald*, XVIII (September 1822), 279; Babcock to Marshall and Wildes, Oahu, May 3, 1821, in Marshall MSS. In January 1822 John C. Jones informed Marshall and Wildes that "Capt. Babcock and myself remain as your agents." Jones to Marshall and Wildes, Oahu, January 22, 1822, in Massachusetts Historical Society, *Proceedings*, LIV, 40.

[182] Hunnewell to J. F. B. Marshall, Charlestown, December 12, 1845 (copy), in Hunnewell MSS; James Hunnewell, *Journal of the Voyage of the "Missionary Packet," Boston to Honolulu, 1826* (Charlestown, 1880), p. xiii; Louis de Freycinet, *Voyage Autour du Monde, Historique*, II, Pt. 2 (Paris, 1839), p. 617.

could aspire to the ownership of luxuries, but many of them found less expensive manufactured articles within their means.

In 1826 Hiram Paulding estimated that the natives received "thousands of dollars" for the provisions which they sold to whalers. This money, he observed, passed into the hands of the merchants in exchange for "silk, cotton, calicoes, cloth &c."[183] The results were apparent to visitors, and in 1825 Kotzebue concluded that even the poorest natives at Honolulu had acquired "some article of European clothing." Hawaiian women, like the members of their sex the world around, had "set their hearts upon the most fashionable mode of dress"; on Sunday scores of Hawaiians of both sexes appeared at church "in full dress to be admired," with results which Kotzebue characterized as "sufficiently comic."[184] Three years later, in 1828, it was reported that the ladies of a newly arrived missionary company were chagrined when they discovered that they were less well dressed than some of the Hawaiian women.[185] A small but not unimportant retail trade in American and European manufactures had developed. In response to the combined demands of the domestic market and the needs of the whalers, there were at Honolulu, in 1826, retail stores "well stocked with a great variety of goods," whose proprietors, it was thought, were rewarded with "handsome profits."[186]

A wide variety of imported goods passed over the counters of the stores at Honolulu. In January 1823, when business conditions at Honolulu were said to be dull, John C. Jones wrote to his Boston employers that an ideal cargo for Honolulu would include superfine cloths, calicoes, ready-made clothes, shoes, hats, rum, wine, lumber, copper, paints, rigging, tables, cheap writing desks, trunks covered with red leather, pumps, and an assorted collection of vehicles, including wheelbarrows, handcarts, and carriages. At the same time he reported that the King and Kalanimoku probably could be persuaded to pay any price for a steamboat, and that the former was said to be anxious to acquire a billiard table.[187] Six months later

---

[183] Paulding, *Cruise of the Dolphin*, p. 232.

[184] Kotzebue, *New Voyage Round the World*, II, 221–222.

[185] Journal of Stephen Reynolds, May 20, 1828.

[186] Paulding, *Cruise of the Dolphin*, p. 232.

[187] Jones to Marshall and Wildes, Oahu, January 1823, in Massachusetts Historical Society, *Proceedings*, LIV, 45. See also Jones to Marshall and Wildes, Oahu, March 9, 1823, *ibid.*, p. 46.

Jones summarized a cargo suitable for the retail trade at Honolulu as one which was "in short a sample of every thing in Boston."[188] This advice he qualified with the observation that everything should be "new and elegant," as the Hawaiians demanded the best that could be obtained.[189]

So varied were the goods offered for sale in Honolulu that one British visitor believed that the merchants of that community were able to provide their patrons with every necessary article of American manufacture, with the products of China, or with equipment for vessels.[190] These conclusions appear to be confirmed by the invoices of cargoes consigned to James Hunnewell at Honolulu between 1826 and 1830. Among the goods sent to Hunnewell, or listed by him as sold, were cotton goods, fancy goods, stationery, shoes, umbrellas, table covers, towels, cutlery, hatchets, fishhooks, brass and steel pocket pistols, scissors, files, jackknives, razors, crockery, gilt finger rings, handkerchiefs, Calcutta twine, tea, sugar, coffee, chocolate, spices, vinegar, salt pork, champagne, rum, castor oil, soap, blankets, jelly, ink powder, medicine, smoked beef, perfumery, old and new pantaloons, card tables, pearl buttons, chairs, Dutch pipes, prints, and pictures.[191]

The Rev. Charles S. Stewart, who arrived at the Islands in 1823, found at Honolulu four retail stores conducted by agents of great American business houses. Of them, he wrote:

> Their storehouses are abundantly furnished with goods in demand by the Islanders; and, at them, most articles contained in common retail shops and groceries in America, may be purchased. The whole trade of the four, probably, amounts to one hundred thousand dollars a year:—sandalwood, principally, and specie, being the returns for imported manufactures. Each of these trading houses, usually, has a ship or brig in the harbour, or at some one of the Islands; besides others that touch to make repairs, and obtain refreshments, in their voyages between the North-west Mexican and South American coasts and China.[192]

[188] Jones to Marshall, Oahu, June 16, 1823, in Marshall MSS.

[189] Jones to Marshall and Wildes, Oahu, May 31, 1823, in Massachusetts Historical Society, *Proceedings*, LIV, 47.

[190] Beechey, *Voyage to the Pacific*, II, 97.

[191] Hunnewell to B. Pitman, Oahu, October 15, 1830, in Hunnewell MSS; "Invoice of case of merchandise shipped by Gardner Brewer on board Sch. Missionary Packet," Boston, January 5, 1826, *ibid.*; "Invoice of goods shipped by owners of the Griffon," February 1, 1828, *ibid.*; "Invoice of goods belonging to L. Barker," Honolulu, February 3, 1828, *ibid.*; Statement of James Hunnewell, Boston, January 12, 1826, *ibid.*

[192] Stewart, *Private Journal of a Voyage to the Pacific*, p. 154.

Stewart did not identify any of the firms represented at Honolulu, but it is clear that they must have included the agencies of John Jacob Astor,[193] of Marshall and Wildes,[194] and of Bryant and Sturgis.[195] According to Stewart the fourth agency represented a Rhode Island firm, which would seem to identify it as the agency of De Wolf and Smith of Bristol.[196]

Further evidence of the growing importance of Honolulu as a commercial center may be found in the success of the firm of James Robinson and Company, established there in 1822 and originally confined to the building and repairing of vessels.[197] There also were increased facilities for the comfort and entertainment of transient visitors. In 1822 it was reported that there were no less than seventeen grog shops at Honolulu owned by foreigners;[198] four years later Captain Beechey saw there "two hotels, at which a person might board respectably for a dollar a day; two billiard rooms . . . . and ten or a dozen public houses for retailing spirits."[199] To Beechey nothing in Honolulu seemed more indicative of advancing civilization than "the number of wooden houses, the regularity of the town laid out in squares, intersected by streets properly fenced in, and the many notices which appeared right and left, on pieces of board, on which we read 'An Ordinary at one o'clock, Billiards, the Britannia, the Jolly Tar, the Good Woman,' &c."[200]

Foreign residents found that living in Honolulu was "much more

---

[193] Porter, *John Jacob Astor*, II, 659–660.

[194] The most important of the Honolulu agents of Marshall and Wildes was John C. Jones, but during the decade of the sandalwood trade several other men were either associated with Jones or acted as agent in his absence.

[195] From 1823 to 1825, Charles H. Hammatt acted as agent of Bryant and Sturgis; from 1826 to 1830, the agent was James Hunnewell. NRL, "Court Martial Records," XXIII, 1830, No. 531, p. 205; Letter of James Hunnewell, in *The Friend*, March 1867, p. 20; Bryant and Sturgis to Hunnewell, Boston, January 14, 1826, in Bryant and Sturgis Letterbooks, 1818–1829, p. 354.

[196] De Wolf and Smith played but a minor role in the trade of the North Pacific. In 1823 a shrewd rival prophesied that De

Wolf would lose so heavily on a current venture that he would withdraw from the trade, but three years later the firm still maintained an agent at Honolulu. Grimes to Marshall and Wildes, Oahu, October 25, 1823, in Marshall MSS; Testimony of John W. Spurr, in NRL, "Court Martial Records," XXIII, 1830, No. 531, p. 147.

[197] *Pacific Commercial Advertiser* (Honolulu), September 19, 1868; Gorham D. Gilman, "Streets of Honolulu in the Early Forties," in *Hawaiian Almanac and Annual*, 1904, p. 81.

[198] Jones to Marshall and Wildes, Oahu, November 16, 1822, in Massachusetts Historical Society, *Proceedings*, LIV, 44.

[199] Beechey, *Voyage to the Pacific*, II, 97.

[200] *Ibid.*, I, 317.

expensive than in Boston."[201] Judged by the caustic comments made by Dixey Wildes, their life was not exhausting, for he observed that they "divide the 24 hours into three parts, Drinking, Gambling and Sleeping."[202] Doubtless life at Honolulu was less strenuous than in Boston; but it was not free from vexation. Intracommunity feuds arising from the frantic competition of rival traders divided the mercantile community into hostile camps.[203] More apparent was the antagonism between merchants and missionaries, which seems to have arisen, in part, from the belief that missionaries had increased the hazards of the traders by warning the chiefs against paying excessive prices for inferior goods.[204] Whatever justification may have existed for this suspicion, it seems certain that the native rulers were becoming increasingly cautious in their dealings with the merchants.[205]

The most influential of the resident traders was John C. Jones, who added to his duties as agent for Marshall and Wildes the responsibilities of commercial agent of the United States. Although his government had not intended that he should enjoy the power usually possessed by a consul, the remoteness of Honolulu and the weakness of the native government afforded him ample opportunity not only to usurp the normal duties of a consul but also to assume powers generally reserved for those assigned to diplomatic posts. He consistently, although erroneously, designated himself as United States Consul when signing official documents,[206] and many contemporary

---

[201] Jones to Marshall and Wildes, Oahu, October 10, 1822, in Marshall MSS.

[202] Wildes to Marshall, Canton, March 27, 1825, *ibid.* In a similar vein William Sturgis referred to the mercantile community at Honolulu as "a society where indolence, intemperance, debauchery and gambling are so fashionable." Bryant and Sturgis to Hammatt, [September 1822], in Bryant and Sturgis Letterbooks, 1818–1829, p. 267.

[203] Jones to Marshall and Wildes, Honolulu, July 6, 1821, in Massachusetts Historical Society, *Proceedings*, LIV, 33–34. Jones's associate at Honolulu, Thomas Brown, reported that there was "so much underhand work going on, lying, cheating, stealing that it is almost impossible for honesty to live."

Brown to Marshall and Wildes, Oahu, July 6, 1821, in Marshall MSS.

[204] Jones to Marshall and Wildes, Oahu, December 23, 1821, March 9, 1823, in Massachusetts Historical Society, *Proceedings*, LIV, 38, 46.

[205] Jones to Marshall and Wildes, Oahu, May 31, 1823, in Marshall MSS.

[206] Documents containing Jones's signature as United States Consul include Jones to Adams [Kuakini], Oahu, April 10, 1823, in AH, F.O. and Ex.; three certificates and debentures, dated October 29, 1828, October 8, 1829, and October 9, 1832, in Letters to the American Board, CXCI; and miscellaneous notes and certificates dated December 3, 1831; September 30, 1832; April 28, 1834; December 26, 1834; and January 14,

observers commonly accepted his representation that he was indeed the Consul of the United States.[207]

Jones was a resident of Massachusetts, and he was in Boston when, in October 1820, he accepted the appointment as commercial agent of the United States at the Hawaiian Islands. He had previously visited the Islands and, if we may accept his own statement, he was "considerably acquainted with the language, customs and resources of the natives."[208] He received the appointment through the influence of Marshall and Wildes. For that reason the appointment was greeted with understandable coolness by Bryant and Sturgis, who promptly instructed their agents in the Pacific to treat the new commercial agent with civility but to have as little business with him as was possible.[209] A few years later, however, they conceded that Jones was one of the few honest men in Honolulu.[210]

During the greater part of his residence at Honolulu Jones was more active in commercial pursuits than in the performance of his official duties. This was inevitable. The agent of Marshall and Wildes was almost constantly confronted with problems arising from com-

---

1839, in Hunnewell MSS. As early as 1824 Jones used an official seal on which appeared the words "American Consulate Sandwich Islands." The earliest use of the term in his correspondence with the Department of State was on May 8, 1826, when he announced that he had returned to the Islands and had entered again upon "the duties of the Consulate." Jones to Secretary of State Clay, Oahu, May 8, 1826, in USDS, "Consular Letters," Honolulu, I.

[207] Montgomery, comp., *Journal of Tyerman and Bennet*, I, 468; Mathison, *Visit to Brazil*, pp. 363, 388, 436; Journal of the Missionaries at Honolulu, June 14, 1821, and January 24, 1823, in *Missionary Herald*, XVIII, 211, XIX, 319 (July 1822; October 1823); William French to Marshall, Canton, September 23, 1821, in Marshall MSS; Journal of Levi Chamberlain, May 21, 1826; Chamberlain to Evarts, Honolulu, September 11, 1826, in Letters to the American Board, XXXI, No. 65; [William Torrey], *Torrey's Narrative* (Boston, 1848), p. 179.

[208] Jones to Secretary of State Adams, Boston, October 2, 1820, in USDS, "Consular Letters," Honolulu, I. Jones was the son of a prominent Boston merchant and local politician. The elder Jones had served in the state Legislature, and had been speaker of the Massachusetts House of Representatives during the session of 1802. During the same session, John Quincy Adams was a member of the State Senate. Alden Bradford, "Commercial Sketch of Boston," in *Merchants' Magazine*, I (August 1839), 131; Charles Francis Adams, ed., *Memoirs of John Quincy Adams* (Philadelphia, 1874–1877), I, 251.

[209] Bryant and Sturgis to Captain Robert Turner, Boston, October 12, 1820, in Bryant and Sturgis Letterbooks, 1818–1829, p. 161; Bryant and Sturgis to Charles Bullard, Boston, October 12, 1820, *ibid.*, p. 162; Bryant and Sturgis to Captain Lemuel Porter, October 12, 1820, *ibid.*, p. 163; Bryant and Sturgis to Captain John Suter, October 12, 1820, *ibid.*, p. 166; Bryant and Sturgis to Turner, August 14, 1821, *ibid.*, p. 220.

[210] Bryant and Sturgis to Captain Henry Bancroft, Boston, March 12, 1827, *ibid.*

petition with many merchants for a share in the retail trade at Honolulu, but the duties of the United States commercial agent were far
from arduous. Competition in the business community was keen,
and Jones—like many of his rivals—was not overscrupulous in the
methods by which he sought to promote sales. Thus, in the autumn
of 1822, when there were rumors that the illness of Liholiho might
lead to a revolution intended to place Kaumualii on the throne, Jones
assured his employers that he was endeavoring to persuade the natives that a revolt was imminent "in order that we may sell our
powder and muskets."[211] This preoccupation with trade did not add
dignity or prestige to the position of Jones as the representative of a
great maritime power; neither did it give him any real sympathy with
the problems and aspirations of the hundreds of seamen who annually
came within his jurisdiction.[212] Captain Thomas ap Catesby Jones,
commander of the U.S.S. "Peacock," who was at Honolulu in the
autumn of 1826, was said to have been convinced that there were
"many abuses which ought to be remedied" in the representation of
the United States at Honolulu.[213] This view was shared by Captain
William C. B. Finch. After a brief visit to Honolulu, in 1829, Finch
came to the conclusion that the government should send to the Islands "salaried Consuls, or a Charge des Affaires . . . . restricting
them from all participation in business," and noted that "whilst such
official personages are still merchants, their influence is comparatively small or nothing."[214]

This summary of the unsatisfactory condition of American representation in the Pacific was not an overstatement in so far as it
concerned Honolulu. The situation was open to further criticism
during the occasional absences of Jones from Honolulu. When in

[211] Jones to Marshall and Wildes, Oahu, December 1822, in Massachusetts Histori-cal Society, *Proceedings*, LIV, 45.

[212] Journal of John N. Colcord, p. 57; *Torrey's Narrative*, pp. 178–179. Colcord, a former seaman who became a resident of Honolulu and for a time owned a small retail store, asserted that it was useless for him to apply to Jones for protection, inas-much as he had never known Jones "to do anything for a poor sailor." Torrey re-ported that "for some slight difficulty" on board an American vessel, Jones had pun-ished four seamen by placing them in irons and ordering a daily fare of six lashes and hard labor as long as their ship remained at Honolulu. From this position they were rescued by the arrival of Commodore Downes, who, according to Torrey, "most severely" reprimanded Jones.

[213] Journal of Stephen Reynolds, Novem-ber 25, 1826.

[214] Finch to the Secretary of the Navy, December 1, 1829, in NRL, "Capt. Finch's Cruise of the U.S.S. Vincennes," and in Stewart, *Visit to the South Seas*, II, 276.

January 1824 he left for a visit to the United States, he entrusted his official functions and his mercantile interests to Thomas Crocker, concerning whom he confessed that "a more improper and unfit person" could not have been chosen.[215] It is difficult to explain the action of Jones in entrusting his responsibilities to a man whom he held in so low repute. It may be that the only explanation is to be found in the experience of Crocker, who, when about to leave for the United States, was unable to induce any reputable American resident to assume the duties of commercial agent. The disinclination to act as commercial agent, according to Crocker, arose in part from "the very frequent & troublesome calls" upon that officer and, in part, from the fact that Honolulu was "a place destitute of all law as regards the whites."[216] During subsequent absences from Honolulu Jones transferred his official functions to his friend and fellow-merchant, Stephen Reynolds, a man of some ability but of erratic temperament and not universally popular among the visiting seamen with whom he was compelled to conduct the greater part of his official business.

The trials and tribulations which, according to Crocker, harassed the American commercial agent seem to have left Jones unperturbed. If we may believe his own statement he was, in 1826, on "the best of terms with all the authorities of the land."[217] He was, however, distinctly out of sympathy with the American missionaries at the Islands, and after 1826 through his hostility to the mission he was often forced into conflict with the native rulers. Other foreigners shared his antipathy for the mission, but no one frankly avowed a dislike for missionary policies and influence as early as did Jones. In December 1821 he complained that there were "plenty of canting, hypocritical missionaries" who were ready to inform the chiefs concerning the true value of the goods offered by the traders;[218] fourteen months later, he accused the missionaries of "telling the King and Chiefs that the . . . . traders are cheating and imposing on them, consequently [they] have depreciated the value of most articles."[219] This

215 Jones to Marshall and Wildes, Canton, February 21, [1824], in Marshall MSS; Jones to Marshall, Canton, March 1, [1824], *ibid.*

216 Crocker to Secretary of State Clay, Boston, November 9, 1825, in USDS, "Consular Letters," Honolulu, I.

217 Jones to Marshall, Oahu, June 18, 1826, in Marshall MSS.

218 Jones to Marshall and Wildes, Oahu, December 23, 1821, in Massachusetts Historical Society, *Proceedings*, LIV, 38.

219 Jones to Marshall and Wildes, Oahu, March 9, 1823, *ibid.*, p. 46.

belief that the influence of the mission was an obstacle to profitable trade he retained for some years. In June 1826 he made the curious accusation that the missionaries had determined "to oppose every thing like enterprise or exertion,"[220] and four years later he informed his employers that the chiefs were "bigoted and superstitious" persons "who having been converted to *christianity* conceive that honesty and integrity are not essential requisites to form the character of a good man. Such are the good effects of missions."[221] The belief that the friendship between the missionaries and the chiefs was a peril to profitable trade must be accounted one of the explanations of the bitterness manifested by Jones and other merchants toward the American missionaries.

The efforts of the native rulers, after 1826, to establish and enforce a policy of moral reforms in conformity with the views of the missionaries intensified the antipathy of Jones toward the mission and brought him directly into open opposition to the government. In defiance of the known wishes of the majority of the powerful chiefs Jones defended and encouraged the pioneer Catholic missionaries, who arrived at Honolulu in 1827. He supported their efforts to return to the Islands after 1836, and from 1836 to 1840 he was an avowed supporter and a frequent contributor to two Honolulu newspapers which vigorously attacked the American mission and the Hawaiian government. At the close of the period he was described by Alexander Simpson as "a man of reckless private conduct and atheistical opinions," who had been "long the bitterest, ablest, and most determined opponent of the [American] missionaries."[222]

The absence of trustworthy statistics and the constant shifting of the personnel of the foreign community make it impossible to determine what proportion of the foreigners at the Islands were from the United States. Archibald Campbell estimated that not more than one-third of the sixty foreigners on Oahu in 1810 were Americans; the others, he believed, were "almost all English," some of whom were escaped convicts from New South Wales.[223] It may be doubted

---

[220] Jones to Marshall, Oahu, June 18, 1826, in Marshall MSS. See also Jones to Marshall, Oahu, May 5, 25, 1826, *ibid.*

[221] Jones to Marshall, Oahu, October 4, 1830, *ibid.*

[222] Alexander Simpson, *The Sandwich Islands: Progress of Events since their Discovery* (London, 1843), p. 33 n.

[223] Campbell, *Voyage Round the World*, p. 165.

if Americans constituted a majority of the foreigners living at the Hawaiian Islands at any time prior to the settlement of missionary families throughout the archipelago. From an early date, however, they were the most aggressive national group at Honolulu.

In no way was the latent nationalism of Americans in the Hawaiian Islands more strikingly illustrated than in the enthusiasm with which they annually greeted the anniversary of American independence. In 1814 the American residents of Oahu celebrated the Fourth of July with a banquet, at which they were hosts to John Young, Marin, Liholiho, and the great Kamehameha.[224] Two years later the day was observed at Honolulu with the firing of salutes, and the Americans at that place provided a dinner to which they invited the foreign residents and officers of vessels in the harbor.[225] Extant records reveal that there were celebrations of the holiday in 1818 and 1820;[226] thereafter the observance of the day became an annual affair and commonly included a public dinner and the firing of salutes.[227] The festive spirit of these occasions was not confined to Americans. In 1823 "all the principal chiefs in the village" were present at the dinner in honor of the day.[228] A year earlier the gathering had been more cosmopolitan, and dinner had been served to "Americans, English, Sandwich Islanders, Africans, and Spaniards from the colonies,"[229] many of whom may neither have understood nor appreciated the significance of the day they celebrated but into the observance of which they seem to have entered with some spirit.

The celebration of the great day was not restricted to Honolulu.

[224] *Pacific Commercial Advertiser*, July 10, 1856. The account in the *Advertiser* is based upon the recollections of Alexander Adams, who was present at the event and who, in 1856, was living near Honolulu. The statement that Kamehameha provided the banquet upon that occasion seems to have been an error.

[225] *Niles' Register*, XII (April 5, 1817), 96.

[226] Journal of James Hunnewell, July 4, 1818, in Hunnewell MSS; Journal of the Missionaries at Honolulu, July 4, 1820, in *Missionary Herald*, XVII (June 1821), 172.

[227] Journal of Maria S. Loomis, July 4, 1821; Journal of Nehemiah Haskell, July 4, 1821; Jones to Marshall and Wildes, Honolulu, July 6, 1821, in Massachusetts Historical Society, *Proceedings*, LIV, 35; Montgomery, comp., *Journal of Tyerman and Bennet*, I, 468–469; Mathison, *Visit to Brazil*, pp. 388–390; Journal of Levi Chamberlain, July 4, 1823, July 5, 1824, July 4, 1825; Journal of Stephen Reynolds, July 4, 1825. In 1825, according to Reynolds, the American residents "spent the day in mirth and glee."

[228] Journal of Levi Chamberlain, July 4, 1823.

[229] Montgomery, comp., *Journal of Tyerman and Bennet*, I, 468–469. The Africans to whom Tyerman and Bennet referred probably were Negroes from the United States.

In 1813 a group of American masters at Kawaihae, Hawaii, observed the anniversary of American independence with a dinner, the firing of salutes at noon and at sunset, and the playing of patriotic music.[230] A year later, Americans, temporarily stranded by war at Waimea, Kauai, celebrated the Fourth of July with the customary dinner, following which they drank thirteen "patriotic toasts" in "good old Madera" furnished by Jonathan Winship.[231] Waimea was again the scene of an observance of the holiday, in 1821, when two American masters were hosts at dinner.[232] Two years later, July 4, 1823, the anniversary of American independence was observed at Kailua, Hawaii, with salutes and by a public entertainment which was provided by Governor Kuakini.[233]

The annual celebrations of the Fourth of July were the expressions of the enthusiasm of a small group of traders, but for timid chiefs and jealous rivals they held a more ominous portent. The economic dominance of Americans in the Hawaiian Islands was very real, and rumors were not lacking that commerce would be followed by the flag. In 1816 the naturalist of the Kotzebue expedition noted "the jealous vigilance of the Americans, who possess the almost exclusive commerce of these seas";[234] and boastful American visitors had informed the credulous chiefs that the United States would sometime seize the Islands.[235] The fear of possible American aggrandizement, said to have been assiduously propagated by influential British residents of the Islands,[236] probably antedated the coming of the pioneer missionaries. When in April 1820 the first group of missionaries asked for permission to reside at Honolulu, Liholiho hesitated, asserting that he had been told the Americans were a dangerous people,[237] and members of the mission believed that he placed

---

[230] Howay, ed., *The Voyage of the New Hazard . . . . by Stephen Reynolds*, pp. 143–144 (July 4, 5, 1813).

[231] "Log of the Atahualpa," July 3, 1814.

[232] Ethel Damon, "First Mission Settlement on Kauai," in *The Friend*, October 1925, p. 226.

[233] Ellis, *Tour through Hawaii*, p. 35.

[234] Kotzebue, *Voyage of Discovery*, III, 241.

[235] Journal of the Missionaries at Honolulu, April 8, 1820, in *Missionary Herald*, XVII (April 1821), 118; Montgomery, comp., *Journal of Tyerman and Bennet*, I, 471.

[236] Hunnewell to William Ellis, Charlestown, Massachusetts, January 20, 1833 (copy), in Hunnewell MSS.

[237] Holman to the American Board, Kauai, November 21, 1820, in Letters to the American Board, IX, No. 231.

some faith in the statements that Americans coveted possession of Oahu.[238] In the following month, when "some bad minded Englishmen" spread reports that Americans sought to secure possession of the Islands, "a great deal of trouble and noise" ensued, which culminated in the caning of two of the offending Englishmen.[239]

Early in August 1820 the foreign community in Honolulu was disturbed by rumors of approaching trouble;[240] a few days later, Jean Rives, the King's companion and secretary, ordered all foreigners on Oahu to assemble and then read to them an order, said to have emanated from the King, that unless they "belonged" to Kalanimoku or Liholiho they must leave the Islands immediately.[241] For a few weeks efforts actually were made to deport foreigners from the Islands;[242] but apparently the chiefs lost interest in this measure, for many who would seem to have been affected by the order remained unmolested at Honolulu. The fears of the King continued to trouble him, and in February 1821 he anxiously inquired of a native of Kauai, who had visited the United States, if that nation would send a frigate to take Oahu.[243] Whether or not the reply that the United States was so rich as to have no desire to possess Oahu lessened the King's worries does not appear. The disquieting reports continued unabated and in the summer of 1822 two English visitors believed that Liholiho was "manifestly uneasy on account of these rumours" and that he would welcome "the substantial protection of British sailors and soldiers to secure his fief against the encroachments of any other Christian power."[244]

Liholiho clearly was worried, but he cherished the hope that Great Britain might afford him some protection against his enemies. This hope was not entirely without foundation, for the British government had indicated its friendly interest in the welfare of the native dynasty

---

[238] Holman to the American Board, *loc. cit.*, Journal of the Missionaries, April 8, 1820, in *Missionary Herald*, XVII (April 1821), 118.

[239] Journal of James Hunnewell, May 11, 1820, in Hunnewell MSS.

[240] *Ibid.*, August 2, 1820. Among the rumors was one that all foreigners were to be driven from the Islands, and another that two British residents were trying to persuade the chiefs to expel all Americans.

[241] *Ibid.*, August 8, 1820; Journal of Maria S. Loomis, August 8, 1820.

[242] Journal of James Hunnewell, September 13, 21, 1820, in Hunnewell MSS.

[243] Journal of Maria S. Loomis, February 9, 1821; Journal of the Missionaries at Honolulu, February 7, 1821, in *Missionary Herald*, XVIII (July 1822), 206.

[244] Montgomery, comp., *Journal of Tyerman and Bennet*, I, 471–472.

by the presentation to the King, in the spring of 1822, of a schooner built at Port Jackson for that purpose. The young King appeared to be "extremely gratified" by this gesture of good will, and it was reported that he was willing to become a vassal of King George if that would help him to win a promise of British protection of his Islands. When, on May 1, he took formal possession of the schooner, he made no secret of his pleasure nor of his admiration for England.[245] A few weeks later he informed one visitor that while the British government had given him a fine vessel, American traders had imposed upon him by selling him worthless ones.[246] The incident seems to have strengthened his conviction that England was friendly, and in informal conversation he declared that the Islands belonged to Great Britain as a result of the cession of Hawaii to Vancouver.[247] In August 1822, in a personal letter to King George, he acknowledged the arrival of the vessel, and added that he wished to place his kingdom "under the protection of Your most Excellent Majesty, wishing to observe peace with all Nations, and be thought worthy of the confidence I place in Your Majesty's wisdom and Judgment."[248]

The climax of Liholiho's fears and hopes was as daring as it was unexpected. When, early in November 1823, there were rumors that the King would soon leave for England, they were discounted by so competent an observer as John C. Jones with the comment that the departure of the King "would cause great difficulty here."[249] Apparently some of the chiefs shared the same view; but Liholiho was not the person to be deterred by the apprehension of his associates.[250] On November 27 he embarked on the English whaler, "L'Aigle," accompanied by a few intimate friends and his favorite queen. His

[245] *Ibid.*, I, 351, 392, 435–436. The schooner was one which the British government had ordered built in response to the importunate requests of Kamehameha to a visiting naval officer. The order for the construction of the vessel had been sent to the Governor of New South Wales in the summer of 1815; apparently construction of the vessel was begun in 1816, but unforeseen delays prevented the earlier delivery of the schooner. Tucker to Croker, Portsmouth, June 28, 1815, in *Historical Records of Australia*, ser. I, VIII, 625; Earl Bathurst to Macquarie, London, July 27, 1815, *ibid.*, p. 624; Sir Thomas Brisbane to Earl Bathurst, Sydney, February 18, 1823, *ibid.*, XI, 22; Macquarie to Kamehameha, Sydney, April 12, 1816, in AH, F.O. and Ex.

[246] Mathison, *Visit to Brazil*, p. 463.

[247] *Ibid.*, pp. 366–367, 441.

[248] Kamehameha II to George IV, Oahu, August 21, 1822, in *Historical Records of Australia*, ser. I, XI, 22–23.

[249] Jones to Marshall and Wildes, Oahu, November 9, 1823, in Marshall MSS. See also Journal of Levi Chamberlain, November 8, 9, 1823.

[250] Bingham, *Sandwich Islands*, p. 202.

departure, reported Jones, was "sudden & his object not known."[251]
His destination was England.

Many factors may have led Liholiho to undertake his fateful
voyage. He was naturally a restless individual, and such a venture
was in harmony with his impetuous character.[252] More specific reasons, however, have been advanced to explain his determination to
visit London. Throughout 1823 Jones reported that the rivalries and
ambitions of the chiefs together with the weakness of the King constituted a threat of imminent revolution; in November he declared
that Liholiho had "lost all authority and command, and has become
very unpopular" and reiterated his belief that "a revolution is soon
to take place."[253] Kotzebue, who was at Honolulu shortly after the
departure of the royal party, was told that the King had not been
popular and that the trip was planned in the hope that the dissatisfaction would subside while Liholiho was abroad.[254] More flattering
to the young King were the comments of two missionaries, who believed that the motives for his visit to England included curiosity, a
desire to gain information concerning the governments and the commerce of foreign nations, and a hope that it would increase his own
prestige, power, and wealth.[255]

Liholiho may have toyed with the idea of including a visit to the
United States in his foreign itinerary.[256] If so, this was little more
than a passing thought. England was accepted by the King and his
advisers as the traditional friend and protector of the Hawaiian kingdom. No such political considerations bound them to the United States.
Despite assurances that the United States did not covet his Islands,
Liholiho does not appear to have been wholly convinced that there
was no danger; and the fears aroused by the growing influence of

[251] Jones to Secretary of State Adams,
Oahu, December 31, 1823, in USDS, "Consular Letters," Honolulu, I.

[252] Cf. Jones to Marshall and Wildes,
Oahu, October 5, 1821, in Massachusetts
Historical Society, *Proceedings*, LIV, 35;
Hunnewell to Hall and Thatcher, Oahu,
October 6, 1821 (copy), in Hunnewell MSS;
Hunnewell to Charles Thatcher, Oahu, Au-
gust 28, 1823 (copy), in *ibid.*; Journal of
Maria S. Loomis, February 3, 14, 1821;
Journal of Levi Chamberlain, August 5,
1823.

[253] Jones to Marshall and Wildes, Oahu,
January, May 31, October 12, 24, November 16, 1823, in Marshall MSS.

[254] Kotzebue, *New Voyage Round the
World*, II, 203–204, 229.

[255] Bingham to Evarts, Honolulu, Novem-
ber 21, 1823, in Letters to the American
Board, IX, No. 176; Ellis, *Tour through
Hawaii*, p. 427.

[256] Asa Thurston to the American Board,
Kailua, November 4, [1823], in *Missionary
Herald*, XXI (April 1825), 97; Bingham,
Sandwich Islands, p. 202.

Americans at Honolulu may have played a part in Liholiho's determination to embark upon the long voyage to England. In support of this view there is evidence that both the King and his intimate adviser, Boki, declared that the purpose of the visit to England was to discuss the possibility of placing the Islands under the protection of Great Britain.[257]

The journey which began with such high hopes ended in tragedy. Shortly after the arrival of the royal party in London, in the summer of 1824, Queen Kamamalu was stricken with illness and a few days later she was dead. Within a week she was followed in death by her husband. In announcing to King George the passing of the Hawaiian King, George Canning took the opportunity to suggest the advisability of assigning a man-of-war to convey the bodies of Liholiho and his consort to their native land. This, argued Canning, would be an act of courtesy; it would also be, as he noted, "an Attention perhaps the more advisable as the Governments both of Russia and the United States of America are known to have their Eyes upon those Islands."[258] This suggestion was accepted by King George, and shortly thereafter the "Blonde" was selected for this delicate mission.

Before embarking upon the "Blonde," the surviving members of Liholiho's party were received by King George, who assured them that Great Britain would protect the Islands from external aggression. This subject, it was later recalled, had been "the chief topic" discussed on that occasion.[259] The same subject was discussed in the instructions given Lord Byron, the commander of the "Blonde." These instructions informed Byron of the cession of Hawaii to Vancouver, but added that the British government did not wish to press this claim

[257] This evidence includes the testimony of a missionary then resident in Honolulu, of a British officer at Rio de Janeiro, a port visited by Liholiho on the voyage to England, and a statement made many years later by Kekuanaoa, who had accompanied the King on the visit to England. Ellis, *Tour through Hawaii*, p. 427; George Eyre to Croker, Rio de Janeiro, March 5, 1824, in *Correspondence Relative to the Sandwich Islands*, p. 2; *The Friend*, January 1, 1855, p. 7; MS, dated February 28, 1850, and endorsed "Extract from a Manuscript in the handwriting of the late Mr. Richards, found among his papers . . . . by Mr. Wyllie," in AH, F.O. and Ex.

[258] Canning to George IV, July 14, 1824, in Hawaiian Historical Commission, *Publications*, I, No. 2 (Honolulu, 1925), p. 33.

[259] [Graham, comp.], *Voyage of H.M.S. Blonde*, pp. 73, 153; J. Y. Kanehoa to R. C. Wyllie, January 31, 1851, in *Polynesian*, October 11, 1851; MS dated February 28, 1850, in AH, F.O. and Ex.; Frederick Byng to Planta, March 4, 1826, cited in Jean Ingram Brookes, *International Rivalry in the Pacific Islands* (Berkeley, California, 1941), p. 50.

"in opposition to, or in controul of, any native Authority . . . . in order to avoid any difference of Sentiment on an occasion so peculiar as your present Mission to those Islands." This self-denying policy was to be abandoned if it appeared that any power had designs upon the Islands. If necessary, Byron was ordered "to assert the prior rights of His Majesty" or to extend British protection to the native rulers and "to deny the right of any other Power to assume any Sovereignty, or to make any exclusive settlement in any of that group."[260] These instructions were eminently pacific. They reflected only in part the belief, held in some quarters, that either Russia or the United States might attempt to seize the Islands, and that to insure British interests in the Pacific against such an eventuality "it was of some importance to grant the protection the king had come to seek, for our own sake as well as for his."[261]

The "Blonde" left Portsmouth on September 29, 1824. After brief visits at Madeira and at several South American ports, it arrived at Lahaina on May 4, 1825. Two days later it dropped anchor at Honolulu, where it remained for a month.[262] During that time Byron frequently conferred with the chiefs concerning "new regulations, laws, etc."[263] In contrast to the expectations of residents of Honolulu,[264] he consistently refused to furnish the chiefs with a code of laws or to intervene in the political life of the Islands.[265] Early in June, just prior to his departure from Honolulu, he met with a few of the principal chiefs to discuss the future of the island kingdom. On that occasion Byron expressed some apprehension that the influence of the American missionaries might retard the commercial and political development of the Islands. He seems to have been satisfied,

[260] Secret Instructions to Lord Byron, September 14, 1824, in Hawaiian Historical Commission, *Publications*, I, No. 4, pp. 19–20.

[261] [Graham, comp.], *Voyage of H.M.S. Blonde*, p. 72.

[262] *Diary of Andrew Bloxam* (Honolulu, 1925), pp. 23–49; [Graham, comp.], *Voyage of H.M.S. Blonde*, pp. 103–161. The news of the death of the King and Queen had preceded the "Blonde" to the Pacific. Journal of Levi Chamberlain, March 9, 1825; Journal of the Missionaries at Honolulu, March 9, 1825, in *Missionary Herald*, XXII (April 1826), 109; William H. McNeil to Marshall, Honolulu, March 21, 1825, in Marshall MSS.

[263] Letter of Rowland Bloxam, September 6, 1825, in *Hawaiian Almanac and Annual*, 1924, p. 71.

[264] Eliab Grimes to Marshall, Oahu, June 7, 1825, in Marshall MSS.

[265] Byron to Croker, Oahu, May 30, 1825, in *Correspondence Relative to the Sandwich Islands*, p. 13; Letter of Rowland Bloxam, September 6, 1825, in *Hawaiian Almanac and Annual*, 1924, p. 71.

however, by the assurances of missionaries who were present that their sole purpose was to propagate their faith, and that their instructions specifically prohibited any interference in political affairs.[266] He then addressed the chiefs, and at the conclusion of the meeting he handed them a memorandum containing suggestions for the conduct of their government. Among the suggestions were proposals for a system of taxation, a limitation of the power to inflict capital punishment, the establishment of the right of children of chiefs to inherit the lands held by their parents, and the support of the King as the head of the nation.[267] The following day the "Blonde" left Honolulu.

The circumstances of the visit of the "Blonde" to the Hawaiian Islands might well have been utilized by the British government to strengthen its position in those islands. A spokesman for the American Board conceded, in 1828, that "things are now tending toward the occupation of these islands by a foreign power"—a result that he regarded as inevitable unless the Hawaiians "should become so far civilized, as to institute an efficient police, and cause their rights to be respected."[268] No other power possessed a claim to the Islands comparable to that which could be advanced by Great Britain, and the instructions to Byron reveal clearly that the Cabinet, at least, would not willingly have seen any other power secure possession of the archipelago. In contrast to the activities of American traders and missionaries, British concern with the Hawaiian Islands was largely passive, and the determination of the British government to protect and possibly to encourage British interests in the mid-Pacific through the appointment of a consul at Honolulu was not sufficient to check the steady advance of American influence there.

The first British consul at Honolulu was Richard Charlton, who earlier had visited the Islands as master of the trading vessel, "Active."[269] He arrived at Honolulu on April 16, 1825, and entered

[266] Journal of Levi Chamberlain, June 6, 1825; Journal of the Missionaries at Honolulu, June 6, 1825, in *Missionary Herald*, XXII (March 1826), 72.

[267] [Graham, comp.], *Voyage of H.M.S. Blonde*, pp. 154–157. The missionaries merely noted in their journal that Byron handed to the chiefs "a paper for their perusal at their leisure containing his

friendly advice." Journal of the Missionaries at Honolulu, June 6, 1825, in *Missionary Herald*, XXII (March 1826), 72.

[268] [Jeremiah Evarts], "American Missionaries at the Sandwich Islands," in *North American Review*, XXVI (January 1828), 68.

[269] Judd, *Voyages to Hawaii Before 1860*, pp. 23, 49.

immediately upon his official duties.[270]   He was destined to have a
long but stormy tenure of office.   On the very day that he arrived at
Honolulu, one suspicious American resident expressed the fear that
"everything is to be under the English."[271]   This impression may have
been gained as a result of conversation with Charlton, for the new
consul was an ardent nationalist, sensitive as to the position and rights
of his country and quick to resent any injustice suffered by one of
his countrymen.   One French visitor, in 1828, found Charlton friendly
to strangers and devoted to the interests of his country,[272] but few of
his contemporaries were so charitable in their judgments.   Native
rulers, American merchants and missionaries, and some of his own
countrymen at Honolulu incurred his displeasure and shared the belief that he was very poorly qualified for the office he held.

Honolulu was not a happy location for Charlton, for he was everywhere surrounded by indisputable evidence of the growing power
and influence of the United States throughout the eastern Pacific.
Early in his consular career, there was a report that he would soon
be superseded,[273] but until 1843 he withstood all efforts to secure his
removal from office.   After 1826 he made no effort to disguise his
hostility to the American missionaries.   Whether this opposition was
prompted by the rigid tenets and comprehensive policies of the mission or was actuated by a desire to minimize all forms of American
influence in the Islands is a matter of question.[274]   John C. Jones, who
was well acquainted with Charlton, scarcely exaggerated the prevailing opinion of Americans in the Islands when he described the
British consul as an unprincipled man who was "most bitter against
the Americans."[275]   Whatever may have been the extent of Charl-

[270] Charlton to Canning, Oahu, June 9,
1825, in *Correspondence Relative to the
Sandwich Islands*, p. 9.

[271] Journal of Stephen Reynolds, April
16, 1825.

[272] Duhaut-Cilly, *Voyage Autour du
Monde*, II, 306.

[273] Journal of Levi Chamberlain, June 3,
1828.

[274] Cf. the American Mission to Evarts,
Lahaina, December 18, 1826, in Letters to
the American Board, XXXII, No. 250;
Chamberlain to Anderson, Honolulu, Feb-

ruary 13, 1827, in *ibid.*, XXXI, No. 66;
Jarves, *History of the Hawaiian Islands*,
p. 136.

[275] Jones to Wildes, Oahu, September 30,
1827, in Marshall MSS.   James Jackson
Jarves, whose personal differences with
Charlton undoubtedly colored his testimony,
wrote that the British consul had "zeal-
ously lent himself to the injury" of the
Hawaiian nation, "opposing all that they
favored, and nourishing every case which
could generate discord or involve the rulers."
Jarves, *History of the Hawaiian Islands*,
p. 167.

ton's endeavors to counteract American influence in the Islands, his success in those efforts was meager. It would be inaccurate, as well as ungenerous, to ascribe to Charlton the failure of British prestige in the Islands to keep pace with the rapidly expanding interests of the United States. All that can be said fairly is that the British consul, with his blustering manners and his indifference to the sensibilities of the native rulers, was powerless to delay the inevitable substitution of American for British dominance in the political life of the Hawaiian kingdom.

The belief that Great Britain might claim or attempt to gain a privileged position in the Hawaiian Islands persisted for many years. One English visitor to Honolulu in 1831 was quoted as believing that radical changes were imperative in the political control of the Islands and that the initiative for such changes must come from Great Britain.[276] Another English visitor returned to England to publish an open letter in which he condemned the activities of the American missionaries in the Islands and urged the British government to establish a colony upon one or more of the Islands, in order that "such a valuable group should become as soon as possible, substantially a British Possession."[277] According to the author of this letter, T. Horton James, nearly all the foreigners in the Islands, with the exception of the missionaries, would welcome the substitution of British rule for that of Kamehameha III. It may be questioned whether the American residents would have been pleased to have British rule extended to the Hawaiian Islands, but it is certain that James was justified in anticipating that there would be opposition from the American missionaries. In the summer of 1831, while James was still at the Islands, Hiram Bingham expressed the fear that Great Britain might secure political control of the Hawaiian kingdom;[278] in May 1833, he characterized the letter of James as "the ill natured and ill advised pamphlet," and said that he had shown it to the young King.[279]

Meanwhile, a series of visits to the Islands by American men-of-war served to strengthen the bonds by which Hawaiian interests

[276] Peirce to Hunnewell, Honolulu, July 7-22, 1831, in Hunnewell MSS.

[277] This letter, dated London, August 22, 1832, is in HHS, *Fifteenth Annual Report* (Honolulu, 1908), pp. 36-47.

[278] Bingham to Evarts, Honolulu, September 8, 1831, in Letters to the American Board, LXVII, No. 3.

[279] Bingham to Anderson, Oahu, May 7, 1833, *ibid.*, LXVII, No. 17.

were being made increasingly dependent upon the United States. The first American naval vessel to visit the Islands was the "Dolphin," commanded by Lieutenant John Percival. Percival had been charged with the pursuit and capture of a group of notorious mutineers; he also had been instructed to visit the Hawaiian Islands, if practicable, to inquire "whether the present king or individuals of the islands, who owe American citizens, have the means and disposition to pay their debts."[280] He arrived at Honolulu early in January 1826. Less than a week later, Wildes reported that "we have since been waiting to represent to him our business here."[281] Percival appeared willing to use his influence to secure the payment of the sandalwood due American merchants,[282] but the extent to which this question entered into his discussions with the native rulers is uncertain. In May, shortly before the departure of the "Dolphin," John C. Jones declared that Percival had rendered "essential service to American concerns in this place";[283] and to the Secretary of State he reported that the debts "have been in Council, acknowledged to be public debts and assurances given of their speedy adjustment."[284] In his own account of his achievements while at Honolulu, Percival made no mention of the problem of the debts.[285] Some hopes undoubtedly were raised, and between March and September some wood was cut;[286] but the situation was not materially improved. At the close of the

[280] Hull to Percival, Chorillos, August 14, 1825, in *House Reports*, 22d Cong., 2d Sess., No. 86, pp. 3–5.

[281] Wildes to Marshall, Oahu, January 10–12, 1826, in Marshall MSS. Wildes and his associate, Captain Eliab Grimes, had been among the first to greet Percival upon his arrival at Honolulu and to extend hospitality to him. Journal of Stephen Reynolds, January 14, 1826. A month later, Levi Chamberlain, usually an accurate representative of the views of the American missionaries in Honolulu, expressed the hope that the visit of the "Dolphin" would result in a settlement of the claims against the government—one of the rare occasions in that decade when the mission and the mercantile community were in agreement on a matter of public policy. Chamberlain to Anderson, Lahaina, February 7, 1826, in Letters to the American Board, XXXI, No. 60.

[282] A. B. Thompson to Marshall, Oahu, January 26, March 6, 1826, in Marshall MSS. At least one of the creditors apparently entertained some doubts as to how promptly Percival would act. When Percival addressed a note to several traders asking for information concerning the debts, Stephen Reynolds observed laconically that the information "will be acted on by & by." Journal of Stephen Reynolds, January 24, 1826.

[283] Jones to Marshall, Oahu, May 5, 1826, in Marshall MSS.

[284] Jones to Clay, Oahu, May 8, 1826, in USDS, "Consular Letters," Honolulu, I.

[285] Percival to John Anderson, West Barnstable [Massachusetts], January 17, 1833, in *House Reports*, 22d Cong., 2d Sess., No. 86, pp. 5–6.

[286] Thompson to Marshall, Oahu, March 6, 1826, in Marshall MSS; Wildes to Marshall, Oahu, September 18, 1826, *ibid.*

summer, Jones was willing to do no more than to predict that "eventually all the debts will be paid."[287] Four days later his associate, Dixey Wildes, wrote that he was anxiously looking forward to the anticipated visit of the U.S.S. "Peacock," adding, "We depend on her for our debts."[288]

The dispatch of the "Peacock" to the Hawaiian Islands was in response to reports that the lives and property of American citizens there were in grave danger. In December 1824 one hundred and thirty-seven persons interested in the whaling fleets in the Pacific united in urging President Monroe to station a naval force in that ocean to prevent the repetition of such sensational mutinies as had recently occurred on board the "Globe."[289] Four months later a memorial from Nantucket informed President Adams that at the Hawaiian Islands there were "over one hundred and fifty seamen . . . . prowling about the country, naked and destitute, associating themselves with the natives, assuming their habits and acquiring their vices," with the consequent danger that "necessity would induce those lawless deserters to commit some act of a piratical nature." In view of these deplorable conditions, the existence of which they did not appear to doubt, the memorialists warned the President that the Islands might "soon become a nest of pirates and murderers" unless an adequate naval force should be stationed in the vicinity.[290] It was in response to these memorials from the center of the American whaling interests that Secretary of the Navy Samuel L. Southard, in May 1825, sent instructions to Commodore Hull, commanding the United States squadron in the Pacific, ordering him to visit the Hawaiian Islands. After instructing Hull to secure information concerning American commerce at the Islands, Southard added:

> You will afford to our citizens, vessels, and commerce, the protection which may be found to be necessary, and to which they may be lawfully

[287] Jones to Marshall, Oahu, September 29, 1826, *ibid*.

[288] Wildes to Marshall, Oahu, October 3, 1826, *ibid*.

[289] William Coffin *et al.* to President Monroe, Nantucket, December 1824, in *House Reports*, 28th Cong., 2d Sess., No. 92, pp. 9–10.

[290] Aaron Mitchell *et al.* to President Adams, Nantucket, April 5, 1825, in *ibid.*, p. 11. The acting commercial agent of the United States in Honolulu in September 1824 urged his government to send a man-of-war to Honolulu to check the frequent desertions from American whalers. Crocker to Secretary of State Adams, Honolulu, September 15, 1824, in USDS, "Consular Letters," Honolulu, I.

entitled. *You will everywhere encourage the best feelings towards our government, nation, and interests; manifesting, on all occasions, that kindness, moderation, and decision, which becomes your own character, and that of the government you represent.*

One of the definite objects of your visit is to make a proper disposition of the seamen at the Sandwich Islands, which are mentioned in the memorial . . . . And the safety of our commerce, as well as the peace and good order of these islands, requires that they should . . . . be removed from the scenes of the mischief they are promoting and perpetuating.[291]

Hull entrusted this mission to Captain Thomas ap Catesby Jones, commander of the U.S.S. "Peacock." The instructions by which Jones was to be guided left much to his discretion, but it appears that he was expected to investigate the "claims for property" which had been agitating American traders at Honolulu.[292] Jones left Callao on May 30, 1826; after brief visits to the Marquesas Islands and Tahiti, he arrived at Honolulu on the tenth of the following October.[293] News of the impending visit of the "Peacock" had preceded it to Honolulu, and for five months traders at that port had looked forward to its arrival with confidence that the presence of an American man-of-war would hasten the collection of the troublesome debts.[294] When at length the "Peacock" arrived, the commercial agent of the United States reported that he and other traders "hope now to be able to make arrangements in regard to our debts, that they may actually be discharged."[295]

Captain Jones could not be hurried into a discussion of the debts. In order to gain time in which to study the situation at the Islands and to familiarize himself with the character and disposition of the Hawaiian people, he approached the business of his voyage with caution and without haste.[296] His first message to the chiefs was dated

[291] Southard to Hull, Navy Department, May 24, 1825, in *House Reports*, 28th Cong., 2d Sess., No. 92, p. 8.

[292] Hull to Jones, Callao Bay, May 25, 1826, in *ibid.*, p. 13. For a biography of Captain Jones, see Udolpho Theodore Bradley, "The Contentious Commodore, Thomas ap Catesby Jones," unpublished Ph.D. dissertation, Cornell University, 1933.

[293] Jones to Southard, Guayaquil, June 24, 1826, in NRL, "Letters from Masters Commandant," 1826, I; NRL, Thomas ap Catesby Jones, "Report of the Peacock's Cruise to the Sandwich, Society and other Islands in the Pacific Ocean performed in the years 1826 and 27," p. 18.

[294] J. C. Jones to Marshall, Oahu, May 5, 1826, in Marshall MSS; Wildes to Marshall, Oahu, September 18, 1826, *ibid.*

[295] J. C. Jones to Marshall, Oahu, October 13, 1826, *ibid.*

[296] NRL, Jones, "Report of the Peacock's Cruise," p. 23.

October 17, 1826; two more followed before the close of the month, all three dealing with the vexatious problem of desertions from American whalers.[297]   In his communication of the seventeenth, after informing the King of his intention to check desertion from whalers, Jones wrote that the President earnestly desired to encourage "the most friendly intercourse between the citizens of the United States, and your Majesty's people, so long as it can be maintained upon principles of perfect reciprocity." Six days after he had conveyed to the King this generous expression of goodwill for a feeble nation, Jones returned to the question of the deserters, declaring that the regulations already adopted by the chiefs were inadequate. In order to strengthen these regulations, Jones suggested additional provisions, including a fine of thirty dollars for every master of a vessel failing to report seamen absent from his ship, and drastic restrictions upon the granting of licenses for the maintenance of boardinghouses or saloons. On November 1, at the house of the American commercial agent and in the presence of Governor Boki, Captain Jones met "a large concourse of runaway sailors." After a rigid questioning of those present, all who were suspected of desertion and who were without visible means of support, together with "all other foreigners who did not support a good character," were given their choice of shipping on board the "Peacock" or on one of the whalers in the harbor. By this means, according to Jones, nearly thirty Americans were removed from "the scenes of their iniquity."[298]   On the same day, Jones reported to the Secretary of the Navy that "the evil of desertion, so loudly complained of in the New Bedford memorial, existed to an alarming degree at the time of my arrival here."[299]

[297] *Ibid.;* Jones to Kauikeaouli, Oahu, October 17, 23, 31, 1826 (copies), in NRL, "Cruises of the Cyane, Franklin, Ontario, Peacock, and United States."

[298] NRL, Jones, "Report of the Peacock's Cruise," pp. 24–25; Journal of John N. Colcord, p. 67. This statement appears to be confirmed by a journal kept by Thomas J. Harris, a seaman on the "Peacock." On November 15, Harris noted that ten men arrived on the "Peacock," having been "sent on board by Capt. Jones." These men, according to Harris, "were Americans, who had resided on the Islands for some time,

and whom we brought on board for the purpose of carrying them to the U. States." Journal of Thomas J. Harris (MS, Library of Congress), October 23, 1826—January 4, 1827, *passim.*

[299] Jones to Southard, Oahu, November 1, 1826 (copy), in NRL, "Cruises of the Cyane, Franklin, Ontario, Peacock, and United States." The strenuous measures adopted by Jones could not provide any permanent solution for the ever-present problem of desertion. When Captain Finch arrived at Honolulu, in October 1829, he was requested by five masters of American vessels to do

Two further matters of official business remained to occupy the attention of Jones while at Honolulu. On November 4 he submitted to the King a list of claims preferred by American citizens against the government, declaring that these were debts "of long standing, and for value received," which the United States "has the *will*, as well as the power to enforce, when other, and more pacific measures are disregarded."[300] Jones apparently had little fear that the chiefs would refuse any reasonable settlement which he might propose, for he had already informed Secretary of the Navy Southard that they were "exerting every nerve to comply with their contract."[301] He was aware that they preferred to proceed with deliberation,[302] and for nearly six weeks he did not press the matter.

Meanwhile Jones introduced the last important business of his visit when, on November 13, he submitted to the King the draft of a proposed treaty. This move was beyond the authority conferred in his instructions, but he was too aggressive and self-confident to be daunted by the lack of specific instructions. Apparently upon no better authority than his own concept of what constituted desirable policy, he informed the King that the proposed articles were not designed to give the United States any exclusive privileges at the Islands and that all his country either asked or expected was "equal privileges with the *most favoured* in time of peace, and *strict neutrality*, in case of war."[303] Again anxious not to press the chiefs, Jones waited a month for their decision.

The traders were possessed of less patience. When the first week

---

what he could toward the suppression of desertion at the Islands. Faced with this problem, Finch assured the American commercial agent that he was instructed to reclaim all deserters at the Islands and "to induce this government . . . . to discountenance the practice." Three days before leaving Honolulu, Finch called the attention of the King to the desirability of preventing desertion and offered some suggestions as to how this might be accomplished. Henry Gifford *et al.* to Finch, Lahaina, October 1829, in NRL, "Capt. Finch's Cruise of the U.S.S. Vincennes"; Finch to Jones, Honolulu, October 19, 1829, *ibid.*; Finch to Kauikeaouli, November 21, 1829, in AH, F.O. and Ex.

[300] Jones to Kauikeaouli, Oahu, November 4, 1826 (copy), in NRL, "Cruises of the Cyane, Franklin, Ontario, Peacock, and United States."

[301] Jones to Southard, Oahu, November 1, 1826 (copy), *ibid.* See also Wildes to Marshall, Oahu, November 4, 1826, in Marshall MSS.

[302] NRL, Jones, "Report of the Peacock's Cruise," p. 26.

[303] Jones to Kauikeaouli, Oahu, November 13, 1826 (copy), in NRL, "Cruises of the Cyane, Franklin, Ontario, Peacock, and United States."

of December passed without any move by the government to pay its debts, the creditors again addressed Jones, declaring that there was no prospect that their claims would be satisfactorily adjusted "without the interference of power," and urging him to use his influence to secure a liquidation of the debts.[304] On December 14, Jones called upon the chiefs to discuss the pending problems;[305] but evidently they had failed to consider seriously his earlier communications, for he found them unprepared to discuss the issues which he raised.[306] Thereafter negotiations proceeded more rapidly. On December 23, 1826, Jones and representatives of the regency signed the first treaty to which the Hawaiian kingdom had been a party; and four days later the government adopted measures for the settlement of the claims of the traders.[307] Jones later declared that as a result of his intervention American claimants had received more than half a million dollars;[308] but this was a gross exaggeration. Before presenting the claims, Jones had estimated that the debts amounted to more than two hundred thousand dollars;[309] but when acknowledged by the chiefs on December 27 the total was fixed at fifteen thousand piculs of sandalwood, the value of which has been variously estimated at from $120,000 to $160,000.[310] With the hope that his negotiations had accomplished "in some degree" the main object of the cruise, Jones left Honolulu on January 6, 1827.[311]

[304] J. C. Jones, Dixey Wildes, Stephen Reynolds, Thomas Meek, John Ebbets, and James Hunnewell to Captain Jones, Oahu, December 10, 1826 (copy), *ibid.;* Journal of Stephen Reynolds, December 11, 1826.

[305] Journal of Stephen Reynolds, December 14, 1826.

[306] Journal of Levi Chamberlain, December 14, 1826.

[307] NRL, Jones, "Report of the Peacock's Cruise," p. 25.

[308] Jones to Ogden Hoffman, Washington, D.C., May 3, 1838, in *House Reports*, 28th Cong., 2d Sess., No. 92, p. 22.

[309] Jones to Southard, Oahu, November 1, 1826 (copy), in NRL, "Cruises of the Cyane, Franklin, Ontario, Peacock, and United States."

[310] J. C. Jones and Thomas Meek to Captain W. C. B. Finch, Oahu, October 28, 1829, in NRL, "Capt. Finch's Cruise of the U.S.S. Vincennes." A tax law of December 1826 set the value of sandalwood at

eight dollars a picul. Professor Kuykendall has concluded, therefore, that the real value of the debts was $120,000. But well-informed contemporaries, presumably basing their estimates upon some other valuation of the wood, set a somewhat higher figure. In March 1827 Hiram Bingham spoke of the debts as amounting to about $160,000; and nearly three years later two of the creditors declared that the aggregate of the debts acknowledged by the chiefs was $150,000. Kuykendall, *Hawaiian Kingdom*, pp. 434-436; Bingham to Evarts, Oahu, March 4, 1827, in Letters to the American Board, XXXI, No. 10; Jones and Meek to Finch, Oahu, October 28, 1829, in NRL, "Capt. Finch's Cruise of the U.S.S. Vincennes."

[311] Captain Jones to Southard, Honolulu, December 25, 1826 (copy), in NRL, "Cruises of the Cyane, Franklin, Ontario, Peacock, and United States"; Journal of Stephen Reynolds, January 6, 1827.

The traders had cause to be satisfied with the results of the negotiations, and at least one of their number—Dixey Wildes—believed
that the treaty signed by Jones and the chiefs would be "of great
service" to American commerce at the Islands.[312] It was true that, if
scrupulously observed, the treaty provided a legal basis for the protection of the persons and property of Americans engaged in trade
at the Islands. It guaranteed to citizens of the United States the privileges extended to nationals of the most-favored nation. It likewise
obligated the Hawaiian authorities to suppress desertion and to assist in salvaging shipwrecked American vessels.[313] Although well
calculated to protect American interests at the Islands, it was ignored
by the government at Washington—perhaps because any official acknowledgment of the treaty would have implied a recognition of
Hawaiian independence. It was not submitted to the Senate, and
therefore never became binding upon the signatory countries. As
late as 1837, however, Americans in Honolulu, including the commercial agent of the United States, seem to have regarded the treaty
as valid, while the bewildered Hawaiian rulers feared to risk the displeasure of the United States by ignoring its provisions.[314]

[312] Wildes to Marshall, Oahu, January 2, 1827, in Marshall MSS.

[313] An original copy of the treaty is in NRL, "Cruises of the Cyane, Franklin, Ontario, Peacock, and United States." It has been printed in various places, including *House Reports*, 28th Cong., 2d Sess., No. 92, pp. 19–20; FRUS, 1894, Appendix II, pp. 35–36; Hunter Miller, ed., *Treaties and Other International Acts of the United States of America*, III (Washington, D.C., 1933), 269–272.

[314] In October 1836 Commodore Kennedy, in an oral interview with the King and in a written communication to him, referred to the treaty as though it were binding upon the Hawaiian government; and in the following May, John C. Jones urged the King to respect the provisions of the treaty. In December 1837, Kinau, whose authority in the Hawaiian government was next to that of the King, discussed the treaty in a letter to the President of the United States with apparent confidence that it was valid; but in August 1838 the Rev. William Richards, the principal adviser of the King, wrote to the Attorney General of the United States, Benjamin F. Butler, calling attention to the negotiations in 1826, with the admission that "whether those articles were ever noticed by the President is not known." Finally, in December 1842, Richards, while on a mission to the United States, officially inquired of Secretary of State Webster as to the status of the treaty, adding that the Hawaiian rulers had always conformed to its provisions. Two Honolulu editors, one in 1836 and the other in 1841, appeared to believe that the articles of 1826 constituted a valid treaty. Journal of Levi Chamberlain, October 7, 1836; Kennedy to Kauikeaouli, Honolulu, October 7, 1836, in AH, F.O. and Ex.; Jones to Kamehameha III, May 23, 1837, in *ibid.*; Kinau to the President of the United States, Honolulu, December 2, 1837, in *ibid.*; Richards to Butler, Lahaina, August 21, 1838, in USDS, "Miscellaneous Letters," January – April, 1839; Richards and Haalilio to Webster, Washington, D.C., December 14, 1842, in FRUS, 1894, Appendix II, pp. 41–42; *Sandwich Island Gazette*, November 19, 1836; *Polynesian*, May 15, 1841.

More interesting to the impatient traders was the announcement by the chiefs, on January 2, 1827, of the imposition of taxes designed to secure money and wood with which to liquidate the long-standing debts.[315] Missionaries and traders alike seem to have been favorably impressed by the promptness with which the government acted, and some of the creditors hoped that the debts would be settled before the close of the year.[316] The chiefs showed considerable energy in the collection of sandalwood;[317] from January until the middle of summer interested observers reported the absence of many natives from their homes.[318] The absentees were in the mountains in search of sandalwood.

The result of all this activity fell short of satisfying the creditors. Spring turned to summer before James Hunnewell received a picul of wood,[319] and in September John C. Jones reported that the natives had returned from the mountains and that their future policy was uncertain.[320] By that time four thousand piculs had been divided among the creditors. Jones obviously was worried. He complained that the chiefs had failed to co-operate with the traders and asserted that force would be useful in persuading them to act more promptly.[321] At the end of January 1828 nearly seven thousand piculs had been delivered

[315] This decree, dated December 27, 1826, imposed upon every adult male Hawaiian a tax of one-half picul of sandalwood or four Spanish dollars. Every female above the age of thirteen was to pay one Spanish dollar or to contribute a mat or kapa of equal value. Copies of the decree may be found in *House Reports*, 28th Cong., 2d Sess., No. 92, pp. 18–19; *Report of the Minister of Foreign Relations [Hawaiian Islands]*, 1855, pp. 3–4.

[316] Levi Chamberlain to Evarts, Honolulu, March 2, 1827, in Letters to the American Board, XXXI, No. 68; Wildes to Marshall, Oahu, January 2, 1827, in Marshall MSS; Jones to Marshall, Oahu, January 4, March 6, July 20, 1827, ibid. Chamberlain commended the efforts of the chiefs to provide for the payment of the debts as "highly creditable."

[317] Jones to Marshall, Oahu, June 29, 1827, ibid.; Jones to Wildes, Oahu, July 20, 1827, ibid. To Secretary of State Clay, Jones reported that the arrangement made by the government for the discharge of its debts was in full operation. Jones to Clay, Oahu, July 1, 1827, in USDS, "Consular Letters," Honolulu, I.

[318] Journal of Stephen Reynolds, January 22, 23, 1827; Journal of Levi Chamberlain, January 28, March 1, April 19, 1827; Jones to Marshall, Oahu, March 6, June 29, July 20, 1827, in Marshall MSS; Jones to Wildes, Oahu, July 20, 1827, in ibid.; Chamberlain to Evarts, Honolulu, February 22, March 2, 1827, in Letters to the American Board, XXXI, Nos. 67, 68; Bingham to Evarts, Oahu, March 4, 1827, ibid., XXXI, No. 10.

[319] James Hunnewell to Joseph Hunnewell, Oahu, June 29, 1827, in Hunnewell MSS.

[320] Jones to Wildes, Oahu, September 30, 1827, in Marshall MSS.

[321] Ibid.; Jones to Marshall, Oahu, September 30, 1827, in ibid.

to the creditors in payment of the debts,[322] but this was less than half of the amount acknowledged as due during the visit of the "Peacock." Thereafter the zeal of the chiefs for the liquidation of the debts waned. At the close of 1828 a French missionary at Honolulu thought it unlikely that the chiefs would be able to pay the debts because of the ever-mounting interest,[323] and in August 1829 Jones was compelled to inform his employers that "not a stick of wood has been paid since the Parthian sailed, nor is there any prospect there ever will be."[324] The "Parthian" had sailed for Canton in October 1828.[325]

The failure of the Hawaiian rulers to discharge their debts more rapidly could not be explained by any lack of resources, for the taxes imposed in January 1827 had yielded about eight thousand dollars and more than 25,000 piculs of sandalwood. Of this amount, only ten thousand piculs of wood and none of the money had been utilized to settle the claims of the traders. The remainder, according to report, had been retained "by the different chiefs for their own use."[326]

[322] "Account of Tax Wood paid in by the native government to be divided equally between Stephen Reynolds, John C. Jones, Jr., Don Marin, and James Hunnewell," in Hunnewell MSS.

[323] Letter of Alexis Bachelot quoted by Francis Furey, in *Records of the American Catholic Historical Society*, XLV (March 1934), 85.

[324] Jones to Marshall, Oahu, August 13, 1829, in Marshall MSS.

[325] "Index to N.W.C. & Sand. Isles Voyages 1820-1829," in *ibid.*

[326] The difference between the total collected and the amount paid to the government's creditors represented, at least in part, the personal exigencies of Governor Boki. Following the death of Kalanimoku in 1827, the task of supervising the payment of the national debt passed to Boki, who apparently assumed this responsibility in good faith. In October 1827 John C. Jones wrote that Boki and the young King were "making great exertions to pay all they can this season," and some months later Boki himself complained—probably with considerable justice—that no other chief was making any effort to reduce the debt of the government. Jones to Wildes, Honolulu, October 30, 1827, in Marshall MSS; Journal of Stephen Reynolds, June

13, 1828. Boki's attention presently wandered from the settlement of the debts. He was politically ambitious, but the payment of the traders was more seriously affected by his interest in a series of business ventures which included the manufacture of sugar, the ownership of a hotel in Honolulu, and the financing of trading voyages to the American coast and to the South Pacific. Bingham, *Sandwich Islands*, pp. 339, 341-342, 343; Beechey, *Voyage to the Pacific*, II, 112-113; Stewart, *Visit to the South Seas*, II, 20-21, 115; R. S. Kuykendall, "Some Early Commercial Adventurers of Hawaii," in HHS, *Thirty-Seventh Annual Report* (Honolulu, 1929), 19-21; Grimes to Marshall, Oahu, July 20, 1828, in Marshall MSS. See also an agreement between Boki and Thomas Meek and George Marini, dated June 9, 1828 (AH, Historical and Miscellaneous MSS), whereby Boki agreed to pay the expense of a trading voyage to the northwest coast, entrusting the management to Meek and Marini, who were to receive half the proceeds of the voyage.

According to Beechey, Boki's mills had been "for some time past . . . . a subject of annoyance to him, in consequence of the expense incurred by their continually breaking." In the summer of 1827 Boki purchased the cargo of the "Tinmouth," which

The situation appeared desperate from the standpoint of the traders, and Jones expressed the reasonable belief that no action could be secured until the anticipated arrival of the U.S.S. "Vincennes."[327] It must have been with high hopes that the creditors saw the "Vincennes" round Diamond Head on October 13, 1829; but it was not until the end of the month that they officially brought their claims to the attention of Captain William C. B. Finch, the commander of the vessel.[328] On November 2 Finch conferred with the chiefs and advised them to liquidate their obligations as quickly as possible.[329] The King, Boki, and four powerful chiefs thereupon signed a note acknowledging their indebtedness to John C. Jones and Thomas Meek to the amount of 4,700 piculs of sandalwood—the unpaid balance of the debts acknowledged at the time of the visit of the "Peacock."[330] At the same time the chiefs signed a second note, agreeing to pay 2,165 piculs of wood, which represented the balance due from their purchase of a vessel in February 1828.[331] Finch had received instructions "to cultivate the most friendly relations" with the chiefs;[332] at the close of the negotiations he reported that he had carefully refrained from any possible threats, and had appealed to the "magnanimity and sense of justice" of the chiefs and to their own interests.[333]

he proposed to sell at retail in Honolulu. It is significant that one trader, commenting upon the purchase, remarked that "how Poki [Boki] is to pay for this Cargo is hard to determine." Jones to Wildes, Oahu, July 20, 1827, in Marshall MSS. It is unlikely that these commercial speculations did more than increase Boki's personal indebtedness to foreigners in Honolulu—an indebtedness which was also augmented by his fondness for luxuries sold by the merchants and by losses in games of chance. Beechey, *Voyage to the Pacific*, II, 97; Journal of Stephen Reynolds, February 28, July 26, 1827, June 23, 26, 1828. Thus tempted, Boki appropriated for his own use some of the wood which he had collected for the payment of the national debt. Stewart, *Visit to the South Seas*, II, 212; Bingham, *Sandwich Islands*, p. 341.

[327] Jones to Marshall, Oahu, August 13, 1829, in Marshall MSS.

[328] John Ebbets to Finch, Oahu, October 26, 1829, in Porter, *John Jacob Astor*, II, 1195–1196; John C. Jones and Thomas Meek to Finch, Oahu, October 28, 1829, in NRL, "Capt. Finch's Cruise of the U.S.S. Vincennes."

[329] Journal of Levi Chamberlain, November 2, 1829.

[330] The original of this note is in AH, F.O. and Ex. A copy may be found in NRL, "Capt. Finch's Cruise of the U.S.S. Vincennes."

[331] A copy of this note may be found in *ibid.* It is printed in Porter, *John Jacob Astor*, II, 1197. Apparently Finch pressed the claims of only three of the creditors— Jones, Meek, and John Ebbets—and ignored other claims because they were too small. This policy is said to have been the result of the influence of Jones. Journal of Stephen Reynolds, November 2, 1829.

[332] An extract from these instructions, dated January 20, 1829, is in FRUS, 1894, Appendix II, p. 36.

[333] Finch to Secretary of the Navy Branch, Honolulu, November 22, 1829, in NRL, "Capt. Finch's Cruise of the U.S.S. Vincennes."

The negotiations so deftly conducted by Finch did not prove to be the final solution of the problem. The question of the debts was complicated by the willingness of the chiefs to incur new debts while neglecting the old and by the readiness with which the traders, who complained bitterly of the failure of the chiefs to pay their debts, extended credit in order to stimulate new sales.[334] It was further complicated by the disappearance of Governor Boki, who left Honolulu in December 1829 on a voyage to the South Pacific from which he never returned. His creditors insisted that the government should assume the responsibility for his debts; but this was blocked by the opposition of the Queen Regent.[335] In August 1832 the question was reopened during the visit to Honolulu of the U.S.S. "Potomac." Captain John Downes urged the chiefs to make some provision for the prompt payment of their debts, including those contracted by Boki, but all that he gained was a promise that the government would pay for goods actually used by the government or by the King.[336] Not until the visit of Captain Edmund Kennedy, in 1836, were the obligations incurred by Boki added to the public debt.[337]

Meanwhile the government made little progress toward the liquidation of its debts. In October 1830 John C. Jones complained that all the chiefs upon whom the traders had relied for the settlement of their claims were gone.[338] A year later a pessimistic missionary reported that the chiefs had neither sandalwood nor money with which to satisfy their creditors, and he warned that conditions pointed to "the seizure

[334] Artemas Bishop to Rufus Anderson, Kailua, November 22, 1831, in Letters to the American Board, LXVII, No. 93; P. J. Gulick to Evarts, Waimea, Kauai, February 18, 1830, *ibid.*, XXXII, No. 178. Another missionary, the Rev. Samuel Whitney, complained of "the cupidity of those whose interests are suffered to be promoted by involving the rulers in debt." Whitney to the American Board, Waimea, Kauai, September 9, 1833, in *Missionary Herald*, XXX (December 1834), 449.

[335] Charlton to Kamehameha III, Honolulu, August 11, 1830, in AH, F.O. and Ex.; Journal of Levi Chamberlain, October 25, 1831.

[336] Downes to Secretary of the Navy Woodbury, Valparaiso, October 26, 1832, in NRL, "Captains' Letters"; Journal of Levi Chamberlain, August 14, 1832; Journal of Stephen Reynolds, August 14, 1832. Downes later informed Congress that in order to cultivate friendly relations with the chiefs —and presumably to put them into a mood favorable to the payment of the debts—he had presented the King with swords for "a troop of cavalry," together with other articles "of considerable value" both to the King and to others in authority. See *House Reports*, 23d Cong., 2d Sess., No. 102, pp. 1–2.

[337] Journal of Stephen Reynolds, October 6, 1836.

[338] Jones to Marshall, Oahu, October 4, 1830, in Marshall MSS.

[of the Islands] by some foreign power."[339] The situation was not quite so desperate. The creditors were American citizens, and they did expect the assistance of American naval officers in the collection of the debts; but there was little probability that any American officer would be so indiscreet as to seize an important archipelago in the mid-Pacific in order to appease a small group of traders. In the absence of a responsible government in the Islands this meant that the individual chiefs might safely neglect the payment of the debts.

The chiefs who had taken the most active part in the sandalwood trade and who had received the major share of whatever benefits it had brought to the Islands were dead. It is not surprising that the survivors were less than enthusiastic about the liquidation of the debts of their late associates. The result of this lack of enthusiasm is revealed in the estimates of the amount of the debt. In 1829, during the visit of the "Vincennes," it was estimated that the government owed the traders about $50,000.[340] More than three years later Henry A. Peirce believed that the total indebtedness of the chiefs was not far from $40,000.[341] When the debts contracted by Boki were added to the total, even this slight reduction in the national debt was wiped out. Among the claims presented on behalf of the traders by Captain Edmund Kennedy, in 1836, was one for $50,000, said to be due "on Boki's account."[342]

With the exception of the traders themselves, no group in the Islands followed the question of the sandalwood debts with more concern than did the American missionaries. Coming from a predominantly New England background, the missionaries shared the horror of debt which was so nearly universal in that section of the United States. Being concerned with the temporal as well as the spiritual prosperity of the Hawaiians, they viewed the sandalwood debts with particular misgivings, and on at least one occasion—during the visit

339 Bishop to Anderson, Kailua, November 22, 1831, in Letters to the American Board, LXVII, No. 93.

340 Finch to Secretary of the Navy Branch, Honolulu, November 22, 1829, in NRL, "Capt. Finch's Cruise of the U.S.S. Vincennes"; Stewart, *Visit to the South Seas*, II, 212.

341 Peirce to Hunnewell, Honolulu, March 11, 1833, in Hunnewell MSS.

342 The Mission to Anderson, Lahaina, June 20, 1838, in Letters to the American Board, CXXXIV, No. 10.

During the years between 1836 and 1840, the chiefs seem to have made greater progress in the payment of the debts, for in March 1840 William Richards declared that only one of "the old debts" remained unpaid. Richards to Hunnewell, Honolulu, March 22, 1840, in Hunnewell MSS.

of Downes—a spokesman for the mission challenged the validity of some of the claims presented by the traders.[343] On other occasions, missionaries expressed the opinion that the debts were "a hindrance to the mental improvement of the people," or that they rested "like an incubus on the energies of the nation."[344]

Each Hawaiian who went to the mountains in 1827 to cut sandalwood for the government was given the privilege of cutting a half picul of wood for his own private speculation. Many took advantage of this opportunity, and in October Jones reported that much of the wood cut during the preceding months was the property of commoners.[345] The dual stimulus of the partial payment of the debts and the inroads of private speculators in the sandalwood forests revived temporarily the lagging commerce in Hawaiian sandalwood. Thirteen thousand piculs of wood were sent to Canton from Hawaiian ports during the season of 1827–1828,[346] and at least an equal amount was shipped from the Islands during the following twelve months.[347] The market value of sandalwood at Canton quickly reflected the influence of the increased imports. In November 1827 a cargo of Hawaiian sandalwood was sold at Canton for thirteen dollars a picul;[348] early in the following year its value had dropped to ten dollars.[349] Thereafter the decline continued unchecked. Throughout 1829 prices quoted at Canton fluctuated from six to seven and a half dollars a picul;[350] during the following two years the value of Hawaiian san-

[343] Journal of Stephen Reynolds, August 14, 1832.

[344] Mrs. Hiram Bingham to Jeremiah Evarts, Waimea, Hawaii, September 17, 1830, in Letters to the American Board, LXVII, No. 1; Samuel Whitney to the American Board, Waimea, Kauai, September 9, 1833, in *Missionary Herald*, XXX (December 1834), 449; The Mission to Anderson, Lahaina, June 20, 1838, in Letters to the American Board, CXXXIV, No. 10.

[345] Jones to Marshall, Oahu, October 30, 1827, in Marshall MSS.

[346] Jones to Marshall, Oahu, November 30, 1827, in *ibid.*; Gutzlaff, *Sketch of Chinese History*, II, Appendix IV.

[347] Sturgis & Co. to Marshall and Wildes, Canton, December 12, 1828, in Marshall MSS; Gutzlaff, *op. cit.*, II, Appendix IV.

[348] Sturgis & Co. to Marshall and Wildes, Canton, December 26, 1827, in Marshall MSS.

[349] Sturgis & Co. to Marshall and Wildes, Canton, January 20, 1828, *ibid.*; Sturgis & Co. to Hunnewell, Canton, March 13, 1828, in Hunnewell MSS.

[350] Sturgis & Co. to Marshall and Wildes, Canton, December 12, 1828, January 9, 1829, in Marshall MSS; Peter Allen to Hunnewell, Canton River, March 18, 1829, in Hunnewell MSS. At Honolulu, in the winter of 1829–1830 sandalwood was valued at from seven to seven and a half dollars a picul. Hunnewell to Sturgis & Co., Oahu, December 18, 1829 (copy), in *ibid.*; bills from W. J. Hammatt to James Hunnewell, Dr., receipted December 1, 2, 1829, in *ibid.*

dalwood declined steadily, until at the close of 1831 it was almost worthless at Canton, where it sold for a dollar and a half a picul.[351]

The collapse of the sandalwood market may be explained in part by the heavy importations of wood from the islands of the Pacific and from the shores of the Indian Ocean. A contributing factor was the increasingly unsatisfactory quality of Hawaiian sandalwood, which in 1827 was described as "small and crooked, and only fit for the use of the Jos houses in China."[352] Thereafter competent critics generally agreed that it was small and of inferior quality,[353] and merchants who once had shared in the profits of the sandalwood trade planned to withdraw from the commerce of the Pacific or cautioned their agents not to invest in Hawaiian sandalwood.[354]

After 1825 trade at Honolulu was often described as being dull or slow.[355] These reports suggest that trade in the Pacific responded to the same cycles of frenzied buying and stagnant markets as in other parts of the world. They were balanced by a persistent confidence that there would always be "*something* doing here sufficient to employ a small capital to a good advantage and profit."[356] It was because there seemed to be opportunity for only "a small capital" that the agencies of the great American firms of Astor, Marshall and

[351] Mathews Green to Hunnewell, Canton, February 10, 1830, *ibid.*; O. H. Gordon to Hunnewell, Canton, April 19, 1830, *ibid.*; Peirce to Hunnewell, June 10, July 7, 1831, *ibid.*; Benjamin Pitman to Hunnewell, Canton, December 29, 1831, *ibid.* In October 1830 John C. Jones reported that three trading voyages to the Islands had lost heavily during the preceding year. Two of them he estimated would lose fifty per cent, the other he declared "must make a most ruinous voyage." Jones to Marshall, Oahu, October 4, 1830, in Marshall MSS.

[352] Beechey, *Voyage to the Pacific,* II, 99.

[353] Journal of Stephen Reynolds, May 26, 1827; Jones to Marshall, Oahu, September 8, 1828, September 16, 1829, October 4, 1830, in Marshall MSS; Hunnewell to Sturgis & Co., Oahu, December 18, 1829 (copy), in Hunnewell MSS; Peirce to Hunnewell, December 26, 1830, July 7, 1831, March 11, 1833, in *ibid.*; O. H. Gordon to Hunnewell, Canton, April 19, 1830, in *ibid.*; *Chinese Repository,* II (February 1834),

469; Jarves, "The Sandwich or Hawaiian Islands," in *Merchants' Magazine,* IX (August 1843), 118 n.

[354] Sturgis & Co. to Hunnewell, Canton, May 19, 1830, in Hunnewell MSS; Marshall to Jones, Boston, April 26, December 21, 1832, in Marshall MSS; Bordman to Seth Barker, Boston, June 7, 1831, in Bordman Letterbook, p. 89.

[355] Sturgis & Co. to Marshall, Canton, December 15, 1826, in Marshall MSS; Grimes to Marshall, Oahu, July 20, 1828, in *ibid.*; Hunnewell to Bryant and Sturgis, Oahu, December 15, 1829 (copy), in Hunnewell MSS; Hunnewell to Joseph Barker and Son, Oahu, March 16, 1830, in *ibid.*; Jones to Marshall, Oahu, October 4, 1830, in Marshall MSS; Stephen D. Macintosh to Hunnewell, Honolulu, August 1833, in Hunnewell MSS; Peirce and Hinckley to Hunnewell, Honolulu, June 20, 1834, in *ibid.*

[356] Peirce to Hunnewell, Honolulu, July 7–22, 1831, *ibid.*

Wildes, and Bryant and Sturgis were discontinued. In their place there appeared an ever-changing group of resident merchants.

The withdrawal from Hawaiian trade of the great Boston and New York houses which so long had controlled it wrought a minor revolution in the economic life of the Islands. It did not seriously disturb the dominance of American citizens in the commerce which continued to radiate from Honolulu. In the summer of 1831 there were nine mercantile establishments at Honolulu, the most important of which seems to have been the partnership of James Hunnewell and Henry A. Peirce. Other prominent retail merchants included John C. Jones, Stephen Reynolds, William French, and Eliab Grimes.[357] Each was from the United States; with the exception of Peirce, each had taken a prominent part in the sandalwood trade of the preceding decade. With so little change in the personnel of the mercantile community, it is not surprising that the annual celebration of the anniversary of American independence continued with apparently unabated enthusiasm.[358]

Further evidence that the ties between the Islands and the United States had grown stronger may be found in the attitude of the Hawaiian chiefs, although there are only casual incidents to indicate that the Hawaiian rulers who had looked so long to Great Britain for protection and possible guidance had become aware of the North American republic. In October 1826 the regent Kalanimoku referred to the President of the United States as "our chief in America."[359] Five months earlier the chiefs had asked William Sturgis to accept an appointment as Hawaiian commercial agent in the United States, alleging that it was desired to have someone there to defend their interests should occasion require.[360] Sturgis declined this appoint-

[357] Peirce to Hunnewell, Honolulu, July 7–22, 1831, in Hunnewell MSS.

[358] Journal of Stephen Reynolds, July 4, 1827, July 4, 1828, July 4, 1829; Journal of Levi Chamberlain, July 4, 1827, July 4, 1828, July 4, 1829, July 4, 1830, July 2, 1831, July 4, 1832. In 1832 Chamberlain observed that "Chinese, Bengalese, Englishmen and natives of other countries" took part in the festivities of the day.

When, in December 1826, the news reached Honolulu that John Adams and Thomas Jefferson were dead, the "resi-

dents and masters of shipping" agreed to hoist their flags at half-mast and to wear crepe on their left arms for six days. In addition to these marks of respect, Americans in Honolulu met to honor the memory of the ex-presidents and to listen to an appropriate sermon by the Rev. Hiram Bingham. Journal of Stephen Reynolds, December 16, 21, 1826.

[359] Kalanimoku to Hiram Bingham, Honolulu, October 28, 1826, in *Missionary Herald*, XXIII (August 1827), 243.

[360] Kalanimoku and Boki to Sturgis,

ment,[361] and for twenty years the Hawaiian government remained un-represented in the United States. This lack of representation was unimportant, for it was through the unofficial agencies of missionary and merchant that the bonds which united the two nations were strengthened.

The fears of Liholiho that the designs of the restless traders who visited his kingdom included political as well as commercial supremacy were without foundation. There was little danger that the reins of government would be seized by the men who visited Honolulu in search of sandalwood and whose most cherished ambition was to acquire financial competence and to return to their native land. The sandalwood trade was the foundation of the earliest noticeable American influence in the Hawaiian Islands, but it can scarcely be said to have contributed to the eventual extinction of the Hawaiian monarchy. It added liberally to the number of transient foreigners in the Islands; but of the men who first visited Hawaiian ports in search of the precious wood few became permanent residents, fewer established successful mercantile houses there, and only one attained a commanding position, official or otherwise, in the political life of the nation.[362]

The sandalwood trade was a picturesque and passing incident. Economically it contributed little to the Hawaiian chiefs or to their subjects except the destruction of the sandalwood forests; socially it was nearly as barren of result. Through this trade the chiefs acquired a varying degree of fondness for clothing, carriages, frame houses, billiard tables, chinaware, and numerous other articles of comfort or luxury; but only as it imposed upon the common people forced labor in the mountains or as it weakened their loyalty to the religious faith of their ancestors did the commerce in sandalwood

Oahu, May 3, 1826, in NRL, "Court Martial Records," XXIII, 1830, No. 531, Appendix 39. A copy of the commission sent Sturgis may be found in *ibid.*, Appendix 41.

[361] Testimony of William Sturgis, *ibid.*, pp. 328–329.

[362] The single exception was Henry A. Peirce, who served as clerk in the Honolulu store of James Hunnewell until the departure of the latter for the United States in 1830, and thereafter was a partner of Hunnewell and a successful Honolulu merchant for a number of years. In 1869, Peirce was appointed United States Minister Resident to the Hawaiian kingdom by President Grant, and served in that post for eight years. His influence in Honolulu probably exceeded that of any other diplomatic representative of the United States to the Islands, and he was partly responsible for the successful negotiation of the reciprocity treaty of 1875.

directly affect the placid lives of the mass of the Hawaiian people.
Superficially it appears as a highly colorful but transient episode
in Hawaiian history; in reality it represented the beginning of American interest in the Islands and of American concern for the fate of
the archipelago. Among small but influential groups in the United
States it advertised the location, inhabitants, and commercial advantages of the Hawaiian Islands. To pious and philanthropic New
Englanders it brought the challenge of caring for the temporal and
eternal welfare of one hundred thousand Hawaiians exposed to the
mixed blessings and evils of commerce. It was the prominence of
Honolulu in this trade that prompted the State Department to send
a commercial agent to the Islands, and it was the tribulations of the
sandalwood traders as well as the presence at Honolulu of numerous deserters that provided the motives for sending the first American
man-of-war to the Islands. Alone, the sandalwood trade contributed
but little to the reorientation of Hawaiian life or to the determination
of the future of the Islands; it was followed by great missionary and
agricultural enterprises which were to reshape the economic and
social fabric of the archipelago and to decide the political fate of
the Hawaiian kingdom. In the meantime, as the center of the sandalwood trade and later as the rendezvous for the whaling fleets of the
Pacific, Honolulu had become the metropolis of the eastern Pacific.
This position it proudly maintained until after the American occupation of California.

III

THE RELIGIOUS REVOLUTION

THE dawn of the nineteenth century found New England prosperous and perplexed. Commerce was the lifeblood of that section, and every New England port hummed with activity; but in the midst of this prosperity New England conservatives were thoroughly alarmed. Throughout Christendom there was unrest and change; everywhere the ideals and institutions which men had cherished for generations were being challenged, and New England itself—long regarded by New Englanders as a haven of virtuous thought in a wicked world—seemed to be in danger of being engulfed by the leveling and impious tendencies which were sweeping the Western world.

Unfortunately for the mental peace of the conservatives, New England was being threatened from within as well as from without. The election of Thomas Jefferson to the presidency was interpreted in New England as the triumph of political and religious heresy; merchants and ministers joined in fearing that the victorious Republicans would proceed to destroy commerce and good government and to undermine morals and revealed religion. More serious to the New England churches than the politics of Thomas Jefferson was the schism caused by the growing number of ministers and laymen who dissented from the Calvinist position upon such central theological problems as the Trinity and the nature of man. The strength that these dissidents could muster was demonstrated in 1805 when a professed Unitarian was appointed to the Hollis Professorship of Divinity at Harvard College. With Jefferson in the White House and the

121

Unitarians in Harvard, the conservatives were indeed on the defensive, but they were not dismayed.

Confronted by such danger, the New England churches could not remain passive. Minor doctrinal differences which hitherto had caused divisions among the orthodox were submerged. One symbol of the unity of Calvinists in the face of the enemy was an ambitious missionary program, formally launched in 1810 with the organization of the American Board of Commissioners for Foreign Missions. Many factors gave strength to the rising tide of missionary interest in the New England churches. The example of the London Missionary Society which had established missions in the South Pacific and the increased information concerning non-Christian lands brought back by hundreds of traders had not been without effect. In its beginning, however, the history of New England missionary enterprise was the story of a few young college students who were deeply stirred by the contemplation of the temporal and eternal fate of millions of dark-skinned heathen whose lives were passed in ignorance of the Christian gospel.[1]

The attention of the American Board was early called to the Ha-

[1] The background of the missionary movement in New England may be found in Oliver Wendell Elsbree, *The Rise of the Missionary Spirit in America, 1790–1815* (Williamsport, Pennsylvania, 1928). For the American Board, see Joseph Tracy, *History of the American Board of Commissioners for Foreign Missions* (New York, 1842) and [Rufus Anderson], *Memorial Volume of the First Fifty Years of the American Board of Commissioners for Foreign Missions* (Boston, 1861).

There is a vast store of material relating to the history of the mission to the Hawaiian Islands. The volume that may be regarded as an official history is Rufus Anderson, *History of the Mission to the Sandwich Islands* (Boston, 1874), written by a man who had been secretary of the American Board for more than forty years. In 1869 the Board published, in pamphlet form, a very brief account of the mission written by Professor S. C. Bartlett, with the title *Historical Sketch of the Hawaiian Mission and the Missions to Micronesia and the*

Marquesas Islands. A revised edition of this little work is S. C. Bartlett and C. M. Hyde, *Historical Sketch of the Hawaiian Mission* (Boston, 1893).

An extensive account of the first twenty years of the mission to the Hawaiian Islands, written by the most influential of the pioneer missionaries, may be found in Hiram Bingham, *A Residence of Twenty-One Years in the Sandwich Islands* (Hartford, 1847). Numerous extracts from the letters and journals of the missionaries are included in the Rev. and Mrs. Orramel Hinckley Gulick, *The Pilgrims of Hawaii* (New York and Chicago, 1918). See also Sheldon Dibble, *History and General Views of the Sandwich Islands' Mission* (New York, 1839) and Andrew P. Peabody, *The Hawaiian Islands, as Developed by Missionary Labors* (Boston, 1865). The former was based upon lectures given in the United States by a missionary who had lived in the Islands. The latter was written as a review article for the *Boston Review* of May 1865.

waiian Islands. The importance of those Islands to commerce in the Pacific and the consequent publicity which both the Islands and their inhabitants had received were enough to explain the interest of the Board in the evangelization of the Hawaiian people.[2] That interest was reinforced by sentiment. In 1809 a friendless young Hawaiian named Opukahaia wandered to the campus at Yale College, where he was found by the Rev. E. W. Dwight. Dwight immediately took an interest in the stranger and undertook to care for him and to give him some instruction. Before the close of the year Opukahaia attracted the attention of Samuel J. Mills, who was a leader in the movement to establish foreign missions. Under the influence of Mills, Opukahaia accepted Christianity and expressed a wish to return to his native land to teach his fellow-Hawaiians the great truths he had learned. The presence of Opukahaia in New England was a constant reminder to friends of foreign missions that one hundred thousand Hawaiians lived in utter ignorance of Christian doctrines and ideals; his death in 1818 was interpreted by some as a challenge to the American Board to organize a mission for the Hawaiian Islands as quickly as possible.[3] This had been suggested as early as 1816,[4] but formal announcement that a mission was to be established in the Hawaiian Islands was deferred until the late summer of 1819.[5] Two members of the graduating class at Andover Theological Seminary, Hiram Bingham and Asa Thurston, had already volunteered for this mission. To this nucleus the Board added two teachers, one physician, one printer, and one farmer.[6] Accompanied by their wives and by three Hawaiians—who were described as "bright and promising . . . . and . . . . qualified to instruct their countrymen"[7]—the first

[2] Before 1800, an ardent German friend of missionary activities suggested the establishment of a mission in the Hawaiian Islands, and in 1799 officers of the London Missionary Society agreed that the Islands, being "very large and populous, furnish, in many respects, a noble field for missionary labours." The Society, however, was fully occupied with missionary endeavors elsewhere and was compelled to neglect this opportunity to introduce Christian institutions among the Hawaiian people. Fifth Annual Report, 1799, in *Reports of the Missionary Society, from Its Formation in the Year 1795, to 1814, Inclusive,* I, 98–99.

[3] Anderson, *History of the Mission to the Sandwich Islands,* pp. 10–12; Bingham, *Sandwich Islands,* pp. 57–59; [E. W. Dwight], *Memoir of Henry Obookiah* (Elizabethtown, N.J., 1819).

[4] Bingham, *Sandwich Islands,* p. 58.

[5] *Panoplist and Missionary Herald,* XV (September 1819), 428–430; *Columbian Centinel,* September 15, 1819.

[6] Bingham, *Sandwich Islands,* pp. 59, 61.

[7] *Columbian Centinel,* October 16, 1819.

missionaries to the Hawaiian Islands embarked upon the "Thaddeus" on October 23, 1819.[8]

The objectives of the mission were comprehensive and exacting, reflecting its Calvinist and New England origins. The missionaries carried to the mid-Pacific the doctrines of original sin, election, and the sufficiency of the Scriptures; they carried also such New England ideals as the strict observance of the Sabbath, the value of education and of industry, and the rigid moral codes of their Puritan forebears. Their instructions gave more than a hint of the breadth of their program, for they were urged "to aim at nothing short of covering those Islands with fruitful fields and pleasant dwellings and schools and churches; of raising up the whole people to an elevated state of Christian civilization; of bringing or preparing the means of bringing thousands and millions of the present and succeeding generations to the mansions of eternal blessedness."[9] The presence of a farmer and two teachers among the pioneer missionaries was evidence of the hope of the Board that the mission would confer material as well as spiritual benefits upon the Hawaiian people.[10]

A more propitious time for the launching of this venture could scarcely have been chosen, for the death of the first Kamehameha,

[8] *Columbian Centinel*, October 27, 1819; *Panoplist and Missionary Herald*, XV (November 1819), 528.

The three Hawaiian converts were designated by the Board as native assistants. They had been educated at the mission school at Cornwall, Connecticut, and they had become professed Christians. It was hoped that they would be of considerable service in persuading their fellow countrymen to give a respectful hearing to the message of the missionaries. The missionaries were accompanied by a fourth Hawaiian, George Kaumualii, who returned to his island home after a residence of some years in the United States. Although friendly with the missionaries, he was not officially a member of their party.

The general policy of the Board was to expect men entering its service as missionaries to be married. In order to satisfy the Board in this matter, several of the men who went to the Hawaiian Islands as members of the American mission sought and found wives interested in missionary enterprises and willing to devote their lives to missionary work. Lucy G. Thurston, *Life and Times of Mrs. Lucy G. Thurston* (Honolulu, 1921), pp. 3–6; Mrs. Titus Coan, *Life of Mrs. Sybil Moseley Bingham* (n.p., n.d.), pp. 5–6; Henry M. Lyman, *Hawaiian Yesterdays* (Chicago, 1906), pp. 2–3.

[9] A copy of part of these instructions may be found in AH, F.O. and Ex. They are printed, in part, in *Life and Times of Lucy G. Thurston*, pp. 14–16.

[10] The farmer attached to the mission was Daniel Chamberlain, of Brookfield, Massachusetts. He was described as "a farmer in the prime of life, who, by his own industry and good management, was placed in very eligible worldly circumstances." *Panoplist and Missionary Herald*, XVI (December 1820), 569; *Report of the American Board of Commissioners for Foreign Missions*, 1820, p. 60.

in 1819, had brought to a close the period when the oppressive *kapus* of the past could command the respect of the Hawaiian people. For thirty years, foreigners had lived in the Islands in almost complete disregard of the injunctions considered sacred by generations of natives, but no injury had followed their impiety. During the same period many natives had traveled abroad and had suffered no ill effects from their neglect of the native gods. More devastating to the ancient beliefs was the introduction of intoxicants, for while under the influence of liquor high chiefs had often violated the most sacred and revered *kapus* of their ancestors. The absence of any consequent divine anger must have added to the growing skepticism of the Hawaiians, and apparently it was only the steadfast adherence of Kamehameha to the customs and beliefs of the past that prevented a general disregard of the old religion during the early years of the nineteenth century.[11]

With the death of Kamehameha the last barrier to the abandonment of the ancient religion was gone. Although Liholiho hesitated for a time, the opposition to the *kapus* by powerful female chiefs, who resented the added restrictions imposed upon their sex, could not long be ignored. In August 1819 the King and a group of his chiefs publicly violated one of the most important of the *kapus* by eating at the same table with women.[12] As the news of this bold event spread rapidly throughout the kingdom, the once sacred *kapus* and idols were abandoned by chiefs, priests, and commoners, with a haste which was indicative of the disrepute into which the ancient religion had fallen. Only a brief and unsuccessful rebellion against the reforming King suggested that the deserted idols and ideas still claimed the loyalty of any part of the Hawaiian people. The old faith did not completely disappear as a result of this repudiation, and travelers in

[11] A discussion of the causes of this sentiment may be found in Bingham, *Sandwich Islands*, pp. 77–79; Montgomery, comp., *Journal of Tyerman and Bennet*, I, 442–444; Jarves, *History of the Hawaiian Islands*, pp. 106–107; Dibble, *History of the Sandwich Islands*, pp. 122–125; and in an unsigned book review written by R. H. Dana, Jr., in *North American Review*, LV (July 1842), 192–193.

[12] Ellis, *Tour through Hawaii*, pp. 95–97; Dibble, *History of the Sandwich Islands*, pp. 125–130; Jarves, *History of the Hawaiian Islands*, pp. 107–109; Bishop to Evarts, Kailua, November 30, 1826, in Letters to the American Board, XXXI, No. 102; W. D. Alexander, "Overthrow of the Ancient Tabu System in the Hawaiian Islands," in HHS, *Twenty-Fifth Annual Report*, pp. 37–45.

isolated regions found ample evidence that some of the ancient beliefs and practices had not been entirely abandoned.[13]

Unaware of the political and social changes which so recently had occurred in the Islands, the pioneer missionaries arrived at Kailua, Hawaii, on March 30, 1820. There they learned that Kamehameha was dead, that Liholiho had succeeded him, and that the ancient religious practices of the Hawaiians had been abandoned. Two days later they were visited by Kalanimoku, who promised to bring to the attention of Liholiho their wish to reside in the Islands and to be allowed to preach their message. Some delay ensued; and it was apparent that the foreigners at Kailua, including John Young,[14] had used their influence to defeat the wishes of the missionaries. Reports were circulated that the newcomers intended to interfere in Hawaiian politics and to monopolize Hawaiian commerce and that the British government would be displeased if the chiefs permitted American missionaries to reside in the Islands. To Liholiho, who feared possible American aggression and who wished to retain the good will of Great Britain, these were powerful arguments. Not until he had been assured that he need not permit the missionaries to remain indefinitely did he agree that they might reside in his Islands for a year. After further hesitation he acquiesced in the proposal of the missionaries that some of their number should proceed to Honolulu while the others took up residence at Kailua. When the "Thaddeus" left for Honolulu, Thurston, Dr. Thomas Holman, their wives, and two Hawaiians who had come from the United States remained at Kailua to inaugurate the work of the mission at that place.[15]

[13] Cf. Ellis, *Tour through Hawaii,* pp. 204–206, 236, 276–281, 305–306, 324–325.

[14] The belief that Young opposed the landing of the missionaries rests upon the testimony of James Hunnewell, who was a mate on the "Thaddeus" and a friend of the missionaries. Hunnewell to William Ellis, Charlestown, Massachusetts, January 20, 1833 (copy), in Hunnewell MSS; Letter of James Hunnewell, Boston, June 24, 1863, in *The Friend,* January 1864, p. 5. Despite the positive statements of this eyewitness, a belief has persisted that Young favored the admission of the missionaries and exerted his great influence on their behalf. Stewart, *Private Journal of a Voyage*

to the Pacific, p. 158; Dibble, *History of the Sandwich Islands,* pp. 137–138; George Simpson, *Journey Round the World* (London, 1847), II, 156; *Sandwich Island News* (Honolulu), February 24, 1847; Restarick, *Hawaii from the Viewpoint of a Bishop,* pp. 42–43.

[15] Journal of the Missionaries, March 30–April 11, 1820, in *Missionary Herald,* XVII (April 1821), 114–120; Bingham, *Sandwich Islands,* pp. 69–70, 81–92; Louise Loomis Christison, ed., "From a Missionary Journal," by Samuel and Nancy Ruggles, in *Atlantic Monthly,* CXXXIV (November 1924), 650–651.

Among the natives who returned to the Islands in the company of the missionaries was George Kaumualii, a son of the titular king of Kauai. Being anxious to be reunited with his father, he left Oahu for Kauai early in May, accompanied by Samuel Whitney and Samuel Ruggles, the two teachers attached to the mission.[16] They were cordially welcomed by the elder Kaumualii, who urged them to remain and to instruct his people.[17] Impressed by the evident good will of this important chief, Whitney and Ruggles returned to Oahu to consult their colleagues. The decision was soon made. The missionaries could not afford to ignore the interest of Kaumualii, who was the only chief who had promised to assist them in their labors. Before the close of July, Whitney and Ruggles returned to Kauai to establish a mission station at Waimea.[18]

Kaumualii was one of the most intelligent and popular of the chiefs.[19] For twenty years prior to the arrival of the missionaries his career had been marked by worry, turmoil, and disappointment.[20] He therefore must have experienced real pleasure in welcoming the men who had befriended his son and whose sole purpose, as he was assured, was to labor for the temporal and eternal welfare of his people. At Waimea, with his approval and probably with his assistance, the missionaries soon gathered a group of pupils, to whom they taught the rudiments of reading and writing in English. Perhaps because of the interest shown by its royal patron, who himself submitted to the instruction of the missionaries, this school was distinguished by its discipline[21]—a unique feature in the history of early Hawaiian education. The zeal of the King, once enlisted in support of his missionary friends, soon involved more than attendance at

[16] Journal of Maria S. Loomis, May 12, 1820; Bingham, *Sandwich Islands*, pp. 97–98.

[17] *Ibid.*, p. 98; Journal of the Missionaries, June 28, 1820, in *Missionary Herald*, XVII (June 1821), 169–170; The American Mission to the American Board, Honolulu, July 23, 1820, *ibid.*, XVII (April 1821), 112; Christison, ed., "From a Missionary Journal," in *Atlantic Monthly*, CXXXIV (November 1924), 652–655.

[18] Bingham, *Sandwich Islands*, pp. 98–99.

[19] Cf. Turnbull, *Voyage Round the World*, II, 33, 42, 48–51. According to Turnbull, Kaumualii was "by far the most intelligent native of these seas," and far superior to Kamehameha in character.

[20] John M. Lydgate, "Ka-umu-alii, The Last King of Kauai," in HHS, *Twenty-Fourth Annual Report* (Honolulu, 1916), pp. 21–36.

[21] Bingham, *Sandwich Islands*, p. 114; W. D. Westervelt, "The First Twenty Years of Education in the Hawaiian Islands," in HHS, *Nineteenth Annual Report* (Honolulu, 1912), p. 17.

school. Early in 1821 he agreed to enforce a strict observance of the Sabbath,[22] and it was reported that so great was his affection for his teachers that he had promised to refrain from the use of intoxicants.[23]

The missionaries were to enjoy the fruits of their influence over him for but a short time. In September, Liholiho visited Kauai and by a ruse compelled Kaumualii to return to Oahu with him. Until his death in 1824 the former king of Kauai was detained on Oahu as the guest of Liholiho and as the husband of the imperious Kaahumanu.[24] This bloodless revolution deprived the missionaries on Kauai of a valued friend; but it did not disturb seriously their position. The new governor of Kauai, the high chief Keeamoku, was regarded as friendly to the missionaries,[25] and they were able to turn to the mastery of the Hawaiian language and to the extension of their schools with the assurance that there was no barrier to prevent the preaching and teaching of their doctrines in all parts of the island.

From the establishment of the mission its most important post was the one at Honolulu, and the missionaries at that place occupied a pre-eminent position among their brethren. This resulted, in part, from their location at the very heart of the Hawaiian kingdom, in a great seaport through which passed the commerce of the North Pacific. They were much less isolated from the rest of the world than were their colleagues on other islands; they daily met other foreigners, and occasionally they were hosts at dinner or tea to some of the foreign residents or to officers of visiting vessels. While thus re-

[22] Whitney and Ruggles to Worcester, Kauai, February 1821, in *Missionary Herald*, XVIII (June 1822), 190; Journal of the Missionaries, February 1821, in *ibid.*, XVIII (July 1822), 206.

[23] Lydgate, "Ka-umu-alii, The Last King of Kauai," in HHS, *Twenty-Fourth Annual Report*, p. 35.

[24] Bingham, *Sandwich Islands*, pp. 146, 148; Stewart, *Private Journal of a Voyage to the Pacific*, pp. 97-98. After his forcible removal to Oahu, Kaumualii continued to be friendly with the missionaries. Following his death, the former King of Kauai was described by one missionary as having been "more civilized—more dignified—more

like a Christian, than any of his fellows; and I can, with the strictest veracity, say of him that which I can hardly do of any other in the nation—that I have never heard from him a word, nor witnessed in him a look or action, unbecoming a prince —or what is far more important—inconsistent with the character of a professedly pious man." *Ibid.*, p. 290. See also Bingham, *Sandwich Islands*, pp. 158, 216; Bingham, Whitney, *et al.* to Evarts, Oahu, September 17, 1824, in Letters to the American Board, XXXII, No. 230.

[25] Bingham, Whitney, and Ruggles to Worcester, Kauai, October 11, 1821, *ibid.*, IX, No. 116; *Missionary Herald*, XVIII (May 1822), 145.

taining some of the social pleasures they had known in their native land, they were so placed that their character and conduct was open to the scrutiny and criticism of hundreds of their countrymen; and many casual visitors to Honolulu returned to the United States to praise or to censure the missionaries in the Hawaiian Islands on the basis of information they had received at that port. Because of the central location of Honolulu on the route from Kauai to the windward islands, the missionaries located there traveled more extensively than did those in remote localities and became more familiar with conditions throughout the archipelago. It was natural, therefore, for them to assume positions of leadership in the councils of the mission. This leadership, early gained, was jealously guarded by the senior missionary at Honolulu, Hiram Bingham.

In many ways Bingham was admirably qualified to be the guiding force in a pioneer enterprise. He was determined to the point of stubbornness and courageous to the point of belligerency; he was skillful and persistent in argument; he was never slow to take up his pen in defense of the mission; and he never conceded that the missionaries might be in error or that their critics might be justified. His location at Honolulu and his unswerving devotion to the rigid tenets of New England Calvinism caused him to be a convenient target for the foes of the mission. In turn he became recognized as the leading spokesman for the missionaries and the principal defender of their policies. His position of leadership was unofficial. It never was recognized by the American Board, and apparently it was privately resented by some of his colleagues.[26] Certainly there were occasions during his twenty years in the Islands when his brethren were restive under his lengthy disquisitions and his domineering manners. His courage and devotion, however, were beyond question; and, moved either by discretion or by respect for his great services in establishing the mission on a firm foundation, his associates never openly questioned his unofficial primacy.

From the time of their arrival in the Islands, the missionaries conducted public worship each Sunday. At the first public service in

[26] Lucy Thurston to Mrs. G. P. Judd, March 20, 1847, in AH, "Historical and Miscellaneous Documents"; Sereno Edwards Bishop, *Reminiscences of Old Hawaii* (Honolulu, 1916), p. 51; Anderson, *Mission to the Sandwich Islands*, pp. 232–234.

Honolulu, Bingham preached to a congregation that included thirty foreigners in addition to a crowd of curious Hawaiians.[27] For many months attendance at public worship was small, and for at least a year it was held in one room of a native house occupied by the mission.[28] In April 1821 James Hunnewell observed that few Hawaiians attended the services at the mission, although groups of natives "frequently assemble round the fence & are quite noisey."[29] Hiram Bingham conceded that it had been with difficulty that the missionaries had persuaded the natives to attend public worship during his first two years at Honolulu.[30] Occasionally large congregations assembled to listen to the missionaries;[31] but these infrequent occurrences apparently were to be ascribed to the caprice or the curiosity of the natives.[32] The foreign residents were as indifferent to the claims of religion as were the Hawaiians, and but few of the hundreds of seamen who annually visited Honolulu could have been found on Sunday at the mission.[33] The missionaries, however, enjoyed friendly social intercourse with many officers of visiting vessels;[34] and in the summer of 1821, when a new meetinghouse was planned, residents and visitors subscribed "nearly three hundred dollars for the building of a church for the worship of Almighty God."[35] With this financial assistance, the missionaries dedicated the first church edifice on Oahu on September 15, 1821.[36]

The missionaries believed that public worship and preaching were the most effective means of winning the confidence of the natives and of inculcating Christian doctrines.[37] True to their New England background, they regarded education as an important auxiliary in the spread of religious truths; and they promptly organized a school at Honolulu for native and half-caste children. They were encour-

[27] Journal of Maria S. Loomis, April 23, 1820.

[28] Bingham, *Sandwich Islands*, pp. 117, 133.

[29] Journal of James Hunnewell, April 29, 1821, in Hunnewell MSS.

[30] Bingham, *Sandwich Islands*, pp. 156–157.

[31] *Ibid.*, pp. 132, 157–159.

[32] Mathison, *Visit to Brazil*, pp. 378, 432.

[33] Journal of James Hunnewell, April 8, 15, 1821, in Hunnewell MSS.

[34] Journal of Maria S. Loomis, 1820–1821, *passim*; Bingham, *Sandwich Islands*, p. 134.

[35] William H. Davis to Bingham, July 2, [1821], in *Missionary Herald*, XVIII (September 1822), 273.

[36] Journal of Maria S. Loomis, September 15, 1821.

[37] Dibble, *History of the Sandwich Islands*, pp. 235–242; The Mission to Evarts, Honolulu, January 11, 1823, in Letters to the American Board, IX, Nos. 131–132.

aged in this project by some of the foreign residents who had acquired families and who were pleased that their offspring were to have an opportunity to escape illiteracy.[38] The school was opened in May 1820.[39] Before the close of June there were twenty students in attendance; by September the number had doubled and included children and adults.[40] Residents and visitors indicated their approval of the school by liberal contributions toward its support,[41] and on at least one occasion a number of foreigners were present at the quarterly examination of the pupils.[42]

The school was under the direction of Mrs. Bingham. Instruction was necessarily in English, a language with which the pupils had very little acquaintance. The curriculum was limited to elementary instruction in reading and composition, and the lessons were planned to convey a maximum of religious instruction.[43] The missionaries were pleased with the influence of the school. One of their number observed that the pupils passed on to their associates the religious ideas learned in school, thus spreading "some of the first principles of Christianity" beyond the immediate circle around the mission.[44] After a year of instruction, more than one-half of the pupils could read portions of the Bible and many of them had learned Watts's catechism.[45] The missionaries could not forget, however, that the spiritual welfare of the Hawaiian people was their first responsibility, and as they became more familiar with the Hawaiian language they were increasingly occupied with the religious instruction of interested natives. They therefore abandoned the school for half-caste children.[46] This decision enabled them to give all their time to the primary object of their mission; but by it they surrendered an important means of retaining the friendly interest of their fellow countrymen at Honolulu.

[38] Bingham, *Sandwich Islands*, pp. 105–106. Among the residents interested in the establishment of the school were Francisco de Paula Marin, Oliver Holmes, and Captain George Beckley.

[39] *Ibid.*, p. 105.

[40] Journal of Maria S. Loomis, June 21, 1820; Journal of the Missionaries at Honolulu, September 14, 1820, in *Missionary Herald*, XVII (August 1821), 244.

[41] Journal of the Missionaries at Honolulu, December 26, 1820, *ibid.*, XVIII (July 1822), 204.

[42] Journal of Maria S. Loomis, December 14, 1820.

[43] Bingham, *Sandwich Islands*, pp. 103, 106–107.

[44] Journal of Maria S. Loomis, September 14, 1820.

[45] *Ibid.*, June 9, 1821.

[46] John Diell, "Oahu Charity School," in *Hawaiian Spectator*, I, No. 1 (January 1838), p. 23.

The mission at Kailua had a brief and checkered history. The Thurstons established there a school for chiefs, which numbered among its pupils the King, his queens, his seven-year-old brother and heir-apparent, and several powerful chiefs. As at Honolulu, it was necessary to rely upon English as the medium of instruction; but despite this handicap a few of the royal pupils attended regularly and appeared to learn rapidly. For a time the King struggled with the alphabet and with the mysteries of a foreign language, and at the close of the summer he was able to read a few passages from the New Testament. Meanwhile some of the other pupils advanced to "the easy reading lessons of Webster's spelling book."[47] In a short time Liholiho tired of his studies, but being desirous of testing further the efficacy of a written language, he selected two young companions to receive in his stead the advantages of missionary instruction.[48] By this whim of a king the missionaries were privileged to guide the earliest formal education of John Ii, who was destined to rise to the most influential positions in the Hawaiian government and in the mission churches that were open to commoners and laymen.[49]

Liholiho and Kaumualii were not alone among the chiefs in exhibiting an interest in the new educational opportunities. In response to an invitation from Kalanimoku, whose influence and prestige was second only to that of the King, Elisha Loomis, the printer of the mission, left Honolulu in the summer of 1820 to give religious instruction to the chief and to five or six "favorite boys" at Kawaihae.[50] But disaster awaited the mission on Hawaii. Its forces were depleted by desertion,[51] and before the close of 1820 the decision of Liholiho

[47] *Journal of Lucia Ruggles Holman* (Honolulu, 1931), p. 30 (June 24, 1820); Bingham, *Sandwich Islands*, p. 104.

[48] *Life and Times of Lucy G. Thurston*, pp. 42–43.

[49] Ii, who became an Associate Justice of the Supreme Court of Hawaii, was regarded by the missionaries as one of the most consistently faithful and exemplary of their converts. Bingham to the American Board, Honolulu, December 15, 1827, in *Missionary Herald*, XXIV (July 1828), 212; Armstrong to Anderson, Honolulu, September 23–October 15, 1841, October 10, 1847, June 8, 1852 (private), in Letters to the American Board, CXXXVI, No. 80,

CCXXXIII, No. 85, and CCXXXIII, No. 112; Frederick J. Teggart, ed., *Around the Horn to the Sandwich Islands and California . . . . by Chester S. Lyman* (New Haven, 1924), pp. 93–94.

[50] Journal of Maria S. Loomis, July 25, 1820; Journal of the Missionaries, August 9, 1820, in *Missionary Herald*, XVII (August 1821), 242–243; *Report of the American Board*, 1821, p. 82.

[51] The most serious defection from the ranks of the pioneer missionaries was that of Dr. and Mrs. Holman, who declared that the unfriendly attitude of Bingham and Thurston justified them in leaving the mission. Their conduct met with the disap-

to transfer his capital to Honolulu was followed by an invitation—virtually a command—to the Thurstons to accompany him to Oahu. They had no alternative, and in November they left Kailua for Honolulu.[52] In the same month Loomis returned to Honolulu with five of the "favorite boys," whose education he proposed to continue.[53]

The abandonment of the station at Kailua was a major disappointment to the missionaries. For more than two years thereafter their influence was confined to the islands of Oahu and Kauai. Although thus restricted, they could take comfort from the apparent stability of the missions at Honolulu and Waimea. Of the two, the mission on Kauai was in the stronger position because it enjoyed the favor of powerful chiefs. The missionaries at Honolulu had no such advantage; but at the close of 1821 John C. Jones reported that their labors had been "crowned with success."[54] The proof of their triumph he found in the fact that at Honolulu "the true God is worshipped in a house consecrated to his service." This definition of success would not have been acceptable to the missionaries. From two hundred to three hundred Hawaiians commonly attended the preaching services at Honolulu; but the missionaries informed friendly visitors that there was "small appearance of the gospel having taken root even in a few hearts."[55] Sincere Calvinists, deeply concerned with the problem of original sin and the necessity for repentance, were not likely to believe that their labors thus far had been crowned with success.

Among the early activities of the missionaries, none was more vital to their future program than was the reduction of the Hawaiian language to writing. The missionaries were convinced that it would be impolitic as well as impractical to give instruction in English to

proval of their former associates, who waited eight months while the Holmans wandered from island to island, and then expelled them from the fellowship of the mission church. *Missionary Herald*, XVII (July, December 1821), 217, 397; Whitney to Worcester, Oahu, July 20, 1820, in Letters to the American Board, IX, No. 203; Daniel Chamberlain to Worcester, Kauai, November 14, 1820, *ibid.*, IX, No. 218; Bingham and Thurston to Worcester, Oahu, February 15, 1821, *ibid.*, IX, Nos. 235-263; Bingham to Evarts, Oahu, January 31, 1821, *ibid.*, IX, No. 156; Holman to Worcester, Kauai, November 21, 1820, *ibid.*, IX, Nos. 231-234. Holman did not leave the Islands until October 1821. Holman to Hunnewell, Oahu, October 2, 1821, in Hunnewell MSS.

[52] *Life and Times of Lucy G. Thurston*, p. 51.

[53] Journal of Maria S. Loomis, November 10, 14, 1820.

[54] Jones to Secretary of State Adams, Oahu, December 31, 1821, in USDS, "Consular Letters," Honolulu, I.

[55] Montgomery, comp., *Journal of Tyerman and Bennet*, I, 393.

the mass of the natives.[56] They were equally convinced of the importance of the printed page in any program of religious instruction. They had no alternative, therefore, but to create a body of literature in the Hawaiian language. This was a pioneer work. Hawaiian place names had appeared in print, and a few visitors had compiled brief vocabularies of Hawaiian words; but there was no general agreement as to the spelling of these words and no understanding of the construction of the language. It was these problems which the missionaries first were compelled to consider.

In the summer of 1821 the missionaries were actively engaged in the creation of a Hawaiian alphabet. From a mass of contradictory evidence supplied by the natives, they arbitrarily selected twelve letters, five vowels and seven consonants, as the basis of the written language. In this, they were guided primarily by their desire to use an alphabet which would be simple enough to be learned easily and comprehensive enough to express all the sounds used by the Hawaiians. They likewise hoped to create an alphabet similar to that already adopted in Tahiti and "so near to that of the English as not

[56] Bingham, *Sandwich Islands*, pp. 102–103. Many years later, Mrs. Gerrit P. Judd recalled that it had been "a maxim with the Mission that in order to preserve the nation, they must preserve its speech." In what appears to have been a tacit defense of the policies of his brethren, Amos Cooke wrote, in 1841, that he discouraged instruction in English for "many reasons," among which were the facts that the people spoke only one dialect, that there were many books translated into Hawaiian, and that most of the people were able to read their own language. Laura Fish Judd, *Honolulu: Sketches of Life Social, Political, and Religious, in the Hawaiian Islands from 1828 to 1861* (Honolulu, 1928), p. 62; Amos Cooke to the Rev. A. F. Waller, Honolulu, March 15, 1841, MS, Oregon Historical Society Library.

In later years, the missionaries were subjected to considerable criticism because of their insistence upon making Hawaiian rather than English the medium of instruction. Much of this criticism came from men who were generally hostile to the mission, but occasionally there was adverse comment from visitors who were otherwise

sympathetic with its policies. For instances of such criticism see Simpson, *Journey Round the World*, II, 30; A Haole [G. W. Bates], *Sandwich Island Notes* (New York, 1854), pp. 422–424; S. S. Hill, *Travels in the Sandwich and Society Islands* (London, 1856), p. 142; Manley Hopkins, *Hawaii: the Past, Present, and Future of Its Island-Kingdom* (New York, 1869), p. 390; communication signed "Politicus," in *Sandwich Island Gazette* (Honolulu), October 8, 1836; communication signed "Peregrine," in *Daily Alta California* (San Francisco), April 13, 1851; *Polynesian*, 1856–1862, passim.

Berthold Seamann and J. G. Vassar, who were at Honolulu in 1849 and 1851, respectively, observed that there was criticism of the continued use of Hawaiian rather than English in the mission schools. Seamann characterized this criticism as "absurd," adding that the substitution of one language for another "must be the work of ages." Berthold Seamann, *Narrative of the H.M.S. Herald during the Years 1845–51* (London, 1853), II, 89–90; John Guy Vassar, *Twenty Years Around the World* (New York, 1862), p. 240.

greatly to embarrass the young Owhyhean [Hawaiian] in acquiring the English, or the American in reading this language."[57]

The first test of this labor came early in 1822 when the missionaries printed a limited number of copies of an elementary speller and reader, using only words whose spelling was regarded as fixed. On January 7, 1822, a few copies of this speller were run off the mission press at Honolulu—a truly memorable event, which marked the inauguration of printing in the Hawaiian language.[58]

The novelty of the printed page aroused the curiosity of chiefs and commoners. Liholiho promptly insisted that he should be the first to receive instruction, and in the summer of 1822 he began the study of reading and writing in his own language. His restless spirit and his indolent habits, however, frequently proved stronger than his will to learn.[59] He did encourage his chiefs and friends to study, and with his approval the most important personages of the kingdom were soon engaged in learning to read and to write.[60] There was reason to anticipate that this enthusiasm might presently wane.[61] Meanwhile, the example of the rulers of the nation bending over their books and slates was not lost upon the commoners, many of whom freely admitted that they would follow the lead of their chiefs in accepting or rejecting the religious counsel of the mission.[62] The

[57] The Mission to Worcester, Oahu, July 6, 1821, in *Missionary Herald*, XVIII (March 1822), 91; Journal of Hiram Bingham, July 14, 1821, *ibid.*, XVIII (August 1822), 242; Journal of the Missionaries at Honolulu, January 1, 1822, *ibid.*, XIX (February 1823), 42; Bingham, *Sandwich Islands*, pp. 152–156; Thomas Marshall Spaulding, "The Adoption of the Hawaiian Alphabet," in HHS, *Papers*, No. 17 (Honolulu, 1930), pp. 28–33.

[58] Journal of Maria S. Loomis, January 7, 1822; Journal of the Missionaries at Honolulu, January 7, 1822, in *Missionary Herald*, XIX (February 1823), 42; Bingham, *Sandwich Islands*, p. 156. A month later, Mr. Bingham and Governor Kuakini exchanged letters written in Hawaiian—an event which may be considered as the beginning of written communication in that language. Journal of the Missionaries at Honolulu, February 8, 1822, in *Missionary Herald*, XIX (June 1823), 183.

[59] Journal of the Missionaries at Hono-

lulu, August 11, 1822, *ibid.*, XIX (September 1823), 283; Montgomery, comp., *Journal of Tyerman and Bennet*, I, 464, 475–476; Tyerman and Bennet to London Missionary Society, Honolulu, August 10, 1822, *ibid.*, I, 405; Mathison, *Visit to Brazil*, pp. 428–429.

[60] *Ibid.*, p. 429; *Life and Times of Lucy G. Thurston*, p. 66; The Mission to Evarts, Oahu, August 9, 1822, in *Missionary Herald*, XIX (April 1823), 100–101.

[61] Mathison, *Visit to Brazil*, p. 429.

[62] As reported by the Rev. Asa Thurston, the natives commented that when "the king becomes good, we will be good; but if he does bad, then we shall do bad likewise." Thurston to Worcester, Oahu, May 4, 1821, in *Missionary Herald*, XVIII (June 1822), 190. See also Mathison, *Visit to Brazil*, pp. 372, 422–423; Ellis, *Tour through Hawaii*, p. 57; Tyerman and Bennet to London Missionary Society, Honolulu, August 10, 1822, in Montgomery, comp., *Journal of Tyerman and Bennet*, I, 404–405.

missionaries soon were besieged by scores of eager Hawaiians, attracted by the example of their superiors and by the novelty of the new learning. As rapidly as possible the missionaries made provisions for the instruction of the natives. Their progress was slow, and, in January 1823, they could report only that there were "more than 200 pupils" in the schools and that they anticipated the early establishment of at least two schools on Kauai.[63]

Adequate facilities for giving instruction to hundreds of pupils were lacking. The principal product of the mission press was school texts, but these were elementary in character and limited in quantity.[64] More serious was the fact that many of the schools were necessarily entrusted to poorly trained natives whose sole qualification consisted of some acquaintance with the rudiments of reading and composition. With teachers so inadequately prepared, eager students quickly equaled their instructors in learning and could advance no further because there was no one to teach them. A few of the schools were under the direct supervision of a missionary, and an effort was made to raise the level of instruction in the other schools by encouraging the native teachers to visit schools taught by some member of the mission, after which they were expected to return to their own schools to impart to their pupils their added learning. As an additional stimulus to study, the missionaries on Oahu resorted to a device—later common in the mission schools on the other islands—of a public examination of pupils from all the schools of a district. In these examinations chiefs and commoners alike were given an opportunity to display their attainments in reading and in composition for the edification of friends and of interested foreigners.[65]

The establishment of schools on Oahu and Kauai was a notable advance in the general program of the mission. The limited resources

---

[63] Bingham, *Sandwich Islands*, p. 160; The Mission to the American Board, Honolulu, January 11, 1823, in *Missionary Herald*, XIX (August 1823), 272.

[64] Howard M. Ballou and George R. Carter, "The History of the Hawaiian Mission Press, with a Bibliography of the Earlier Publications," in HHS, *Papers*, No. 14 (Honolulu, 1908), pp. 9–44.

[65] The Mission to the American Board,

Honolulu, January 11, 1823, in *Missionary Herald*, XIX (August 1823), 272; Whitney to the American Board, Kauai, January 1824, *ibid.*, XX (October 1824), 317; *Report of the American Board*, 1823, p. 111; Edwin O. Hall, "Condition of Common Schools at the Sandwich Islands," in *Hawaiian Spectator*, I (October 1838), 352; Westervelt, "The First Twenty Years of Education in the Hawaiian Islands," in HHS, *Nineteenth Annual Report*, p. 20.

of the mission precluded the immediate extension of the schools to the other islands—a situation which was partially remedied during 1823 by an increase in the number of missionaries in the Islands. In February the mission was strengthened by the temporary accession of an English missionary, the Rev. William Ellis.[66] A more important reinforcement occurred in May, when the missionaries at Honolulu welcomed the arrival from the United States of eighteen new associates. Included in this company were three clergymen, two teachers, a physician, and an experienced merchant who was to be responsible for the secular concerns of the mission. It is significant that the farmer and mechanics whom the Board had intended to include in this reinforcement were missing.[67] At the close of the year, the Board confessed that its former belief that "agriculture and the mechanical arts" should occupy a prominent place in the program of the mission no longer appeared expedient.[68] This reversal of a major policy was reflected in the instructions by which the missionaries were to be guided. The pioneer missionaries in 1819 had been urged to cover the Islands with "fruitful fields, pleasant dwellings, schools, and churches";[69] three years later, members of the reinforcement were informed that they were expected to inculcate "the duties of justice,

[66] Ellis had been at Honolulu, in 1822, in the company of two representatives of the London Missionary Society. When the party was about to leave the Islands, a group of the chiefs at Honolulu joined in inviting Ellis to return to become actively associated with the American missionaries at that place. This invitation was endorsed by the American missionaries. It was in response to this invitation and with the approval of his superiors in the London Missionary Society that Ellis returned to Honolulu in February 1823. Ellis to Evarts, Oahu, March 10, 1823, in Letters to the American Board, IX, Nos. 307–308; Montgomery, comp., *Journal of Tyerman and Bennet*, I, 446–447; Ellis, *Tour through Hawaii*; Tyerman and Bennet to the American Board, Oahu, August 9, 1822, in *Missionary Herald*, XIX (April 1823), 102–104; Bingham, *Sandwich Islands*, pp. 161, 167, 181.

[67] Anderson, *History of the Mission to the Sandwich Islands*, p. 18.

[68] *Report of the American Board*, 1823, p. 107. The reversal of policy appeared more marked because of the departure from the Islands of Daniel Chamberlain, the farmer who had been a member of the pioneer missionary company. His return to the United States was caused primarily by failing health, but it was generally recognized that his efforts to improve the knowledge and skill of Hawaiian farmers had failed to produce tangible results. The Board had hoped that the Hawaiian farmers "might profit immediately by such improvements in tillage, as an American farmer would be able to introduce." It was apparent, however, that American methods of agriculture were not easily applied to conditions in the Hawaiian Islands, and consequently this part of an ambitious program for the transfer of New England culture to the mid-Pacific was abandoned. *Ibid.*, pp. 107–108; Bingham, *Sandwich Islands*, p. 182.

[69] *Life and Times of Lucy G. Thurston*, p. 15.

moderation, forbearance, truth, and universal kindness," and to strive
"to make men of every class good, wise and happy."[70]

Following the arrival of the reinforcement, the missionaries
turned promptly to plans for the extension of their work to Maui and
Hawaii. They quickly agreed that missionaries should be located at
Lahaina, the most populous community on Maui, and they assigned
the Rev. Charles S. Stewart and the Rev. William Richards to that
place.[71] Further expansion was postponed until they could secure
more information concerning the geography and the distribution of
population of the island of Hawaii.

Lahaina was the second port of the kingdom and was becoming
increasingly important as a port of call for whalers. Missionaries
resident there might anticipate the criticism and perhaps the hostility
of visiting seamen should the policies of the mission interfere with
the freedom which seamen traditionally expected in the islands of
the Pacific. Lahaina was also the home of Queen Keopuolani, the
mother of Liholiho and by birth the ranking chief of the kingdom,
who was known to be interested in the revolutionary ideas introduced
by the missionaries. The interest of the most respected chief in the
Islands was worthy of encouragement and probably explains the
immediate assignment of two ordained missionaries to Lahaina.
Stewart and Richards were welcomed to Lahaina by Keopuolani and
Kalanimoku, who appeared anxious to provide for their comfort and
to afford the newcomers every opportunity to teach their doctrines.[72]
They found in Keopuolani a receptive pupil, who quickly gladdened
her New England teachers by her anxiety to learn more about God
and His plans for the salvation of mankind and by her serious speculation upon the fate of ignorant or indifferent persons who died
without accepting the Christian gospel.[73] A few weeks later, when
she lay at the point of death, the missionaries acceded to her insistent
request and administered the sacrament of baptism.[74] The dying

[70] "Instructions of the Prudential Committee to the Missionaries about to embark
for the Sandwich Islands," November 18,
1822, in *Missionary Herald*, XIX (April
1823), 108.

[71] Stewart, *Private Journal of a Voyage
to the Pacific*, p. 168; Bingham, *Sandwich
Islands*, p. 190.

[72] *Ibid.*, pp. 190–191; Journal of William
Richards and C. S. Stewart, May 31, June
1–3, 1823, in *Missionary Herald*, XXI (February 1825), 39–41.

[73] Ellis, *Tour through Hawaii*, pp. 50,
53–54.

[74] *Memoir of Keopuolani, Late Queen of
the Sandwich Islands* (Boston, 1825), p. 36;

Queen Mother thus became the first of a long line of Hawaiian converts to receive baptism at the hands of the American missionaries.

In July and August 1823, a deputation of four missionaries visited the island of Hawaii in search of information that would prove useful in deciding the location of additional stations of the mission.[75] As a result of this tour the mission, in October, agreed to resume its work at Kailua and to establish a post at Hilo on the east coast of Hawaii.[76] No such imperative reason motivated the missionaries in selecting Kailua and Hilo as had dictated the choice of Lahaina; but both Kailua and Hilo were at the center of populous districts, and from the two communities missionary work could be expanded to include nearly the entire island. Sentiment indicated that Thurston should be returned to Kailua, and the missionaries named the Rev. Artemas Bishop as his associate. They enjoyed the official patronage of Governor Kuakini, although that chief failed to give any convincing evidence of personal piety. He had earlier ordered his people to erect a building for use in public worship,[77] and there Thurston preached each Sunday to congregations numbering from six hundred to one thousand persons, who were said to listen "with a good degree of seriousness."[78]

The return of missionaries to Kailua was followed by an unanticipated extension of missionary activity to Kaawaloa—sixteen miles south of Kailua. For more than a year Naihe and his wife, Kapiolani—the most powerful chiefs at Kaawaloa—had been "very solicitous" to have some missionary assigned to their village, and they had expressed dissatisfaction that Hilo had been favored while Kaawaloa was neglected. With the re-establishment of the mission at Kailua, an effort was made to satisfy the Kaawaloa chiefs by an occasional visit to that district by one of the missionaries at Kailua. Kapiolani, however, could not be placated so easily. Early in 1824,

The Mission to the American Board, Honolulu, October 23, 1823, in *Missionary Herald*, XX (June 1824), 183–184.

[75] An account of the experiences and observations of this deputation may be found in Ellis, *Tour through Hawaii*, and in his *Polynesian Researches*, IV.

[76] Journal of Levi Chamberlain, October 10, 1823; The Mission to the American

Board, Honolulu, October 23, 1823, in *Missionary Herald*, XX (June 1824), 184.

[77] Ellis, *Tour through Hawaii*, pp. 383–384; Journal of Levi Chamberlain, February 4, 1824.

[78] Thurston to the American Board, Kailua, February 5, 1824, in *Missionary Herald*, XXI (April 1825), 98.

the visit to Kaawaloa of James Ely, one of the recently arrived missionaries, led to the suggestion from Naihe and Kapiolani that he be permanently assigned to their community. As evidence of their sincerity and good faith, they erected a church building, which was dedicated at the close of March. In the following month their persistence was rewarded when Ely returned to Kaawaloa as a resident missionary.[79]

Greater difficulty attended the inauguration of missionary work at Hilo. No powerful chief resided in that district, and for a time the people showed little interest in learning to read.[80] In July 1824 a visiting missionary expressed doubts as to the future usefulness of the Hilo mission;[81] and the situation of the missionaries at that place was further embarrassed by the difficulty of securing adequate supplies.[82] Before the close of the year, prospects were somewhat brighter. The church was sometimes crowded on Sunday morning, a school for girls had been established, and the missionaries hoped that the people of Hilo had become more amenable to instruction.[83] In the following February, Levi Chamberlain found there a school with one hundred pupils, a Sunday congregation of between two hundred and three hundred persons, and "a new and increased attention of the people to instruction."[84] This was not a spectacular showing, but it was a sufficient guaranty that the mission at Hilo would not be abandoned.

By the summer of 1824 the mission had passed through its pioneer period and—barring some unexpected reverse—it was firmly established. The missionaries themselves seem to have been in an optimistic mood, and Levi Chamberlain believed that the people were "in a waiting posture."[85] The position of the mission was immeasurably strengthened by the friendly attitude of some of the most powerful chiefs. In May 1823 Chamberlain reported that twenty-four

[79] Bingham, *Sandwich Islands*, pp. 209–211; Stewart, *Private Journal of a Voyage to the Pacific*, p. 262; Rufus Anderson, *Kapiolani, the Heroine of Hawaii* (New York, 1866); Journal of Levi Chamberlain, October 11, 1823, and February 16, 1824.

[80] Journal of Levi Chamberlain, February 19, 1824.

[81] *Ibid.*, July 1, 1824.

[82] *Ibid.*, February 19 and September 25, 1824.

[83] *Ibid.*, November 26, 1824; Chamberlain to Hill, Honolulu, November 27, 1824, in Letters to the American Board, CXCI.

[84] Journal of Levi Chamberlain, February 3, 4, 6, 13, 20, 1825.

[85] Chamberlain to Hill, Honolulu, October 25, 1823, in Letters to the American Board, CXCI, No. 5.

chiefs on Oahu, including the King, "favor our objects, attend religious worship, and are desirous of receiving instruction;—and many of them, of having a teacher particularly attached to them."[86] In 1824 it was reported that some of the principal chiefs held family worship and asked a blessing at meals.[87] At least three chiefs, including the dowager Queen Kaahumanu, expressed a desire to be baptized,[88] although they could have had but little understanding of the significance of that sacrament. Governor Kuakini often attended church services at Kailua,[89] and on at least one occasion he ordered his people to refrain from work or play on Sunday.[90] Queen Kamamalu was receptive to the influence of the missionaries, and it was said that she had commended their teachings to her personal servants.[91] The most spectacular demonstration of faith was provided by Kapiolani, who defied Pele, the dreaded goddess of Kilauea. Accompanied by a missionary and several of her servants, she visited the volcano, descended into its crater, and there sang hymns and contemptuously ate berries hitherto sacred to Pele while daring the goddess to harm her.[92] Less convincing but more significant was the evidence that the mission enjoyed the good will and sympathy of Kalanimoku, whose power in shaping public policy exceeded that of any other chief and whose influence was regarded as the principal bulwark of internal peace during and immediately after the reign of Liholiho.[93] Following the death of Keopuolani, he requested the

[86] Chamberlain to Hill, Oahu, May 17, 1823, *ibid.*, CXCI, No. 1.

[87] Journal of the Missionaries at Honolulu, April 14, 1824, in *Missionary Herald*, XXI (July 1825), 211; [James Hunnewell] to Evarts, Oahu, November 1824 (copy), in Hunnewell MSS.

[88] Journal of Levi Chamberlain, September 27, 1823, and April 3, 15, 1824.

[89] *Ibid.*, February 4, 1824.

[90] Ellis, *Tour through Hawaii*, pp. 383–384.

[91] Ellis, *Polynesian Researches*, IV, 452–453.

[92] Chamberlain to the American Board, Honolulu, March 26, 1825, in *Missionary Herald*, XXII (February 1826), 41; Richards to Anderson, Lahaina, January 31–March 17, 1825, in Letters to the American Board, XXXI, No. 128; Ely to Evarts, Kaawaloa, May 1, 1825, *ibid.*, XXXI, No. 113; Bingham, *Sandwich Islands*, pp. 254–256; W. D. Alexander, *Brief History of the Hawaiian People* (New York, 1899), pp. 188–190.

[93] Kotzebue, *New Voyage Round the World*, II, 229–230. More than any other chief, Kalanimoku enjoyed the confidence and good will of the merchants and other foreigners in the Islands. He was generally entrusted with the management of all business involving foreign residents or visitors. In July 1821 John C. Jones wrote that Kalanimoku and Kaahumanu did "most of the business"; later in the same year he characterized them as "the only persons we put any dependence on," and added that they had "some sense of propriety and integrity." Jones to Marshall and Wildes, July 6, October 5, 1821, in Massachusetts Historical Society, *Proceedings*, LIV, 33,

missionaries to visit him daily and to give him instruction;[94] and late in 1824 he boasted to a visitor that he was a Christian and that he could read and write.[95]

Of the powerful chiefs, Liholiho alone appeared unresponsive to the teachings of the missionaries. He urged his followers to attend school and to study faithfully, and occasionally he attended public worship. His restless nature, however, was ill adapted to rigid moral codes, and as often as he pleased the missionaries by indications of friendship or interest he disappointed them by relapsing into conduct which they could not condone. To the time of his departure from the Islands he must have been a puzzle to the missionaries, and they could report nothing more than that there was no evidence that "Christianity exerted any decisive influence on his heart."[96] They might well have questioned whether Christianity had yet exerted a decisive influence on the personal conduct or social outlook of any great chief. Their friend, James Hunnewell, whose testimony was certainly unbiased and was based upon actual observation, believed that the adoption of the outward forms of Christianity by the rulers represented nothing more substantial than a desire to please their missionary friends.[97]

Liholiho left the Islands for England in November 1823. Upon his departure he entrusted the government to the two most powerful chiefs, Kalanimoku and Kaahumanu. The death of Liholiho in July 1824 resulted in a continuance of the regency of these two chiefs during the minority of Kauikeaouli, Liholiho's eleven-year-old brother and heir.[98] The failure of Liholiho to designate the respective powers

---

36. Gilbert Mathison (*Visit to Brazil*, p. 424) learned in 1822 that "no business . . . . can be transacted, unless Krimakoo [Kalanimoku] is made acquainted with it, and favourably inclined towards the persons interested or the object in view." In 1825, the British Consul attributed the "present peaceable state of the islands" to the mild rule of Kalanimoku. Charlton to Canning, Oahu, June 10, 1825, in *Correspondence Relative to the Sandwich Islands*, pp. 10–11.

[94] Richards and Stewart to the American Board, Lahaina, December 1, 1824 [1823],

in *Missionary Herald*, XXI (April 1825), 101.

[95] Kotzebue, *New Voyage Round the World*, II, 230.

[96] Ellis, *Polynesian Researches*, IV, 447.

[97] [Hunnewell] to Evarts, Oahu, November 1824 (copy), in Hunnewell MSS. See also Kotzebue, *New Voyage Round the World*, II, 208–209.

[98] Bingham, *Sandwich Islands*, p. 203; Letter of Elisha Loomis, Utica, N.Y., August 7, 1827, in Letters to the American Board, XXXII, No. 190; Kotzebue, *New Voyage Round the World*, II, 204, 254.

of the two regents has led to considerable dispute as to whether he intended that either of them should occupy a superior position in the government or whether they were to rule as equals.[99] Fortunately for the peace of the kingdom, no disagreement as to public policy marred the relations of the two regents, who in fact if not in theory ruled the kingdom jointly and in harmony until the death of Kalanimoku in 1827.

The missionaries soon learned that the new King was no more dependable than his predecessor. He was uniformly friendly in his relations with the missionaries, and occasionally he urged his subjects to accept the religious and educational ideals of the mission. His consistent support would have been of incalculable value. This was recognized by Mrs. Bingham, who wrote that "with his accepting or rejecting the offers of salvation may be closely connected the future . . . . condition of a multitude."[100] The influence of the foreign community was stronger than that of the missionaries. The King frequently was present at public worship, but it was evident that he found more pleasure in billiards, horses, and rum than in prayers and sermons.

The missionaries could take some comfort, however, from the fact that the King was a minor and that the government was in the hands of chiefs known to be friendly to the mission. The significance

[99] There was a wide divergence of opinion among contemporaries as to the relative rank of Kalanimoku and Kaahumanu, and in some instances the same authority held varying views upon different occasions. After the death of Kalanimoku, the missionaries were especially anxious to strengthen the position of Kaahumanu and they and their friends have tended to maintain that Kaahumanu was the actual regent while Kalanimoku was her minister. For a statement of such views, see Bingham to Evarts, Oahu, September 14, 1829, in Letters to the American Board, XXXI, No. 25; Dibble, *History of the Sandwich Islands,* p. 168; Jarves, *History of the Hawaiian Islands,* p. 131; and R. C. Wyllie to Richard Armstrong, Honolulu, March 11, 1847, in AH, "Foreign Office Letter Book," XIII, 90. Captain Jones evidently held a similar view in 1826, for he described Kaahumanu as the person "in whom the Government of the Islands rests." NRL,

"Report of the Peacock's Cruise," p. 24. Kalanimoku was then seriously ill. For statements indicating that the two were equal in power, see Kotzebue, *New Voyage Round the World,* II, 204, 254; [Graham, comp.], *Voyage of H.M.S. Blonde,* pp. 54, 103; Bingham, *Sandwich Islands,* p. 203; Charlton to Canning, Oahu, June 10, 1825, in *Correspondence Relative to the Sandwich Islands,* pp. 10–11; and Journal of Levi Chamberlain, November 22, 1826. Beechey (*Voyage to the Pacific,* II, 96) spoke of Kalanimoku as regent without mentioning Kaahumanu. William Ellis (*Tour through Hawaii,* p. 428) described the regency as including Kalanimoku "and the other chiefs" chosen by the King.

[100] Mrs. Bingham to Evarts, September 17, 1830, in Letters to the American Board, LXVII, No. 1; Journal of Levi Chamberlain, August 18, December 26, 27, 1825, and 1827–1829 *passim*; Bingham, *Sandwich Islands,* pp. 346–347, 403–404.

of this political situation was soon apparent. Between December 1823 and June 1824 the residents of Honolulu, Lahaina, and the islands of Kauai and Niihau were informed by public proclamation that all unnecessary work on the first day of the week was thereafter forbidden.[101] In April a group of chiefs, including the two regents, met at Honolulu, listened to addresses by Bingham and the Rev. William Ellis, and agreed to encourage their people to attend school. At the same meeting, the regents publicly announced their intention to follow the precepts and injunctions of the missionaries. In explaining this decision, Kalanimoku confessed that some of the chiefs would have adopted similar resolutions at an earlier date had they not been deterred by fear of offending Liholiho.[102] In June, while at Lahaina, Kaahumanu promulgated a series of decrees which prohibited murder, theft, and fighting, enjoined the observance of the Sabbath as "the sacred day of Jehovah," and announced that all her subjects must attend schools as soon as they should be established.[103] On Kauai and Niihau and in the district of Kaawaloa, the local chiefs carried the reforms still further when they prohibited drunkenness[104] —a step which was publicly commended by Kaahumanu, who urged the chiefs of other districts to take similar action.[105]

Meanwhile the mission made tangible progress in other directions. In the summer of 1825 two Hawaiians were admitted to mem-

[101] Journal of Levi Chamberlain, December 21, 1823; Journal of the Missionaries at Honolulu, December 21, 1823, in *Missionary Herald*, XXI (June 1825), 173; Richards to the American Board, Lahaina, August 13, 1824, *ibid.*, XXII (August 1826), 240; Whitney to the American Board, Kauai, January, 1824, *ibid.*, XX (October 1824), 317. During the summer of 1824 the missionaries at Honolulu, upon learning that natives were working on Sunday, personally visited the offenders in order to persuade them to leave their labors until the following day. Journal of Levi Chamberlain, June 27, August 1, 15, 22, 29, and November 21, 1824.

[102] Journal of the Missionaries at Honolulu, April 13, 1824, in *Missionary Herald*, XXI (July 1825), 210–211; Chamberlain to Hill, Honolulu, April 12, 1824, in Letters to the American Board, CXCI, No.

9; Journal of Maria S. Loomis, April 13, 1824.

[103] Stewart, *Private Journal of a Voyage to the Pacific*, p. 319; Richards to the American Board, Lahaina, August 13, 1824, in *Missionary Herald*, XXII (August 1826), 240. In September, Kaahumanu instructed the chiefs of eastern Maui to erect school buildings and to order their people to give attention to the *palapala* and the *pule*—that is, to learning and religion. C. S. Stewart to the American Board, Honolulu, November 15, 1824, *ibid.*, XXII (February 1826), 38.

[104] Whitney to the American Board, Kauai, January 1824, *ibid.*, XX (October 1824), 317; Journal of James Ely, September 7, 1824, *ibid.*, XXI (October 1825), 319.

[105] [Graham, comp.], *Voyage of H.M.S. Blonde*, p. 154; Bingham, *Sandwich Islands*, p. 269.

bership in the church at Lahaina[106]—the first converts to be thus formally recognized. In the following December, eight Hawaiian converts, including Kaahumanu and Kalanimoku, were admitted to the communion of the church at Honolulu.[107] The action of the churches at Lahaina and Honolulu gained significance from the value which the missionaries attached to the privilege of church membership. It was impossible for the missionaries to establish inflexible standards by which the qualifications of candidates for admission to the church could be judged. In general, they required a profession of belief in the principal tenets of their faith, together with evidence that the candidate proposed to mold his life in accordance with the strict moral code of Puritanism. As good Calvinists the missionaries also looked for some evidence that the convert had become convinced of his depraved condition as a sinner and recognized that his only hope of eternal bliss rested in the mercy of a just God. Too much was not to be expected of simple Polynesian folk, unaccustomed to the consideration of abstruse philosophical questions. The theological and psychological problems involved in the doctrines of original sin and redemption were not always understood by the Hawaiian converts, and often the missionaries were called upon to mourn the hardness of the human heart in its refusal to bow to a conviction of sin.

The missionaries hoped that the example and authority of their distinguished converts would enhance the influence of the mission.[108] In this they were not disappointed. Kalanimoku was in poor health and was compelled to conserve his energy; but until his death in February 1827 he remained "the uniform friend of the missionaries."[109]

[106] Richards to the American Board [Lahaina, August 9, 1825], in *Missionary Herald*, XXII (June 1826), 176. One of the Hawaiians admitted to the church at Lahaina was the blind Puaaiki, who had been interested in the teachings of the missionaries since 1821. Following his admission to the church he was active in assisting the missionaries. Late in life he was licensed to preach, and in February 1843—shortly before his death—he was ordained as an evangelist and given charge of a small church at Honuaula. E. W. Clark to Anderson, Wailuku, November 1, 1843, in Letters to the American Board, CXXXV, No. 194; Anderson, *History of the Mission to the Sandwich Islands*, pp. 209–219.

[107] Journal of Levi Chamberlain, December 4, 1825; Chamberlain to the American Board, Honolulu, December 8, 1825, in *Missionary Herald*, XXII (October 1826), 309; Bingham, *Sandwich Islands*, p. 277.

[108] Journal of Levi Chamberlain, November 25, 1825.

[109] Letter of Elisha Loomis, Utica, August 7, 1827, in Letters to the American Board, XXXII, No. 190.

He was less active than Kaahumanu in public demonstrations of his loyalty to the faith he had embraced. The Queen Regent, whose will was described by one visitor as "a perfect law" to her subjects,[110] did not hesitate to use her great power to promote the educational and religious program of the mission. She was frequently in the company of the missionaries, and as she traveled through her kingdom she often urged the people to study and to attend public worship.[111]

To thousands of Hawaiians, long accustomed to obeying the slightest hint from their chiefs, the counsel of Kaahumanu and other chiefs was irresistible, and throughout the Islands attendance at public worship showed a marked increase. The experience of the church at Honolulu appears to have been typical. In 1824 the congregations there were described as small but attentive.[112] Late in 1825 they had greatly increased in number and occasionally included "at least 3000 people."[113] From that time until after the death of Kaahumanu in 1832 the church at Honolulu frequently was thronged on Sunday morning by congregations numbering from three thousand to four thousand Hawaiians. A "large proportion" of these thousands of worshipers were residents of Honolulu who attended regularly; but there were also "less constant hearers from neighboring villages . . . . occasional hearers from all parts of the island, and strangers from other islands."[114] Sympathetic observers, in the spring of 1832, found the congregation at Honolulu as quiet and attentive as many congregations in the United States.[115] Similar reports came from missionaries in many parts of the Islands. At Kailua, it was said that the

110 Letter of Rowland Bloxam, September 6, 1825, in *Hawaiian Almanac and Annual*, 1924, p. 73.

111 Bingham, *Sandwich Islands*, pp. 294–297, 371, 373, 381, 426; Chamberlain to Hill, Honolulu, July 26, 1826, in Letters to the American Board, CXCI.

112 Journal of Levi Chamberlain, August 29, September 5, 19, October 3, 10, 1824.

113 *Ibid.*, November 20, 1825; Chamberlain to Hill, Honolulu, October 26, 1825, in Letters to the American Board, CXCI.

114 Bingham, Clark, *et al.* to the American Board, Oahu, March 20, 1830, in *Mis-*sionary Herald, XXVII (April 1831), 117; Journal of Levi Chamberlain, February 14, 1830; Journal of John S. Emerson, May 21, [1832], in Oliver Pomeroy Emerson, *Pioneer Days in Hawaii* (Garden City, N.Y., 1928), p. 48; Journal of W. P. Alexander, May 20, [1832], in Mary Charlotte Alexander, *William Patterson Alexander in Kentucky, the Marquesas, Hawaii* (Honolulu, 1934), p. 73.

115 Journal of Dr. and Mrs. Alonzo Chapin (MS, Hawaiian Mission Children's Society Library), II, 30, and III, 14–15 (May 20, 28, 1832); Journal of John S. Emerson, May 21, [1832], in Emerson, *Pioneer Days in Hawaii*, p. 48.

congregation often filled the "spacious church to overflowing." At Kaawaloa, Lahaina, and Wailuku, congregations numbering from two thousand to thirty-seven hundred were regularly in attendance at public worship; and more than two thousand worshipers—a number equal to one-fifth of the inhabitants of the island—greeted Hiram Bingham when he occupied the pulpit at Waimea, Kauai, in November 1832.[116]

Among the thousands who each week crowded the churches, the missionaries found an increasing number of candidates for church membership. Despite the caution with which the missionaries continued to guard admission to that privilege, nearly six hundred Hawaiian converts convinced their spiritual advisers of the sincerity of their religious professions and were admitted to the communion of the churches in the seven years ending in June 1832.[117] The greatest number of converts was at Honolulu, where the indomitable Hiram Bingham was compelled to compete with all the distractions of a Polynesian seaport.

No part of the work of the missionaries prospered more generally during the years of the regency than did the mission schools. The decision of the chiefs in April 1824 to encourage education was followed by "numerous applications" for books printed by the mission, "very many new scholars" asked for instruction, and some new schools were opened.[118] At Honolulu the effect of this impetus was only temporary;[119] but elsewhere throughout the archipelago educational statistics reflected the growing appeal and influence of the mission schools. This expansion was facilitated by the active support of powerful chiefs. The governors of Kauai, Maui, and Hawaii encouraged or commanded their people to attend the schools and to study.[120]

[116] Thurston and Bishop to the American Board, Kailua, December 10, 1828, May 13, 1830, in *Missionary Herald*, XXV (October 1829), 317, and XXVII (May 1831), 146; Richards, Andrews, Tinker, and Shepherd to the American Board, November 29, 1831, *ibid.*, XXVIII (August 1832), 250; Bingham, *Sandwich Islands*, p. 442.

[117] General Letter of the Mission, June 23, 1832, in *Missionary Herald*, XXIX (May 1833), 163.

[118] Journal of Levi Chamberlain, April 14, 1824; Journal of Maria S. Loomis, April 14, 1824.

[119] Journal of Levi Chamberlain, June 11, 1824; Chamberlain to Anderson, Honolulu, November 14, 1824, in Letters to the American Board, XXXI, No. 47.

[120] Levi Chamberlain reported that Governor Hoapili of Maui had threatened all who refused to study with banishment from that island, and that Governor Kuakini of Hawaii had encouraged respect for education among his people by becoming for a

From every mission center there radiated an ever widening circle of schools, whose increase was retarded only by the absence of competent teachers and by the lack of an adequate supply of books.[121] Before the close of 1826 the missionaries had extended their schools to "every district throughout the whole group of islands"; and so rapidly had the number of pupils increased that it had become virtually impossible to keep an accurate record of the numbers enrolled.[122]

Varied motives brought the native pupils to the schools. Some attended because they wished to please or to obey powerful chiefs; others were attracted for a time by the novelty rather than by the value of the written page; a few expected to acquire some magic art which would enable them to wax prosperous without labor; and an indeterminate number apparently attended because of their personal affection for the missionary who urged them to do so. Teachers more experienced and competent than the ill-equipped natives who presided over the common schools of the Hawaiian Islands might well have been awed by the task of giving instruction to classes which included pupils of both sexes, of all ages, and of varying degrees of desire and capacity to learn. Only meager opportunities were offered to the heterogeneous groups of students that gathered around native teachers who were scarcely more advanced in learning than their primitive pupils. The quality of instruction was further weakened by the lack of textbooks and slates, and in many schools from two to five persons were compelled to follow the teacher from a single book.[123] Teaching methods necessarily were adapted to the inexperience of the teachers and the absence of adequate facilities. Visitors to Honolulu found that a Hawaiian school was a noisy institution

time a teacher. See Chamberlain to Anderson, Honolulu, November 14, 1824, in Letters to the American Board, XXXI, No. 47; Journal of Levi Chamberlain, November 13, 1824, September 8, 1825.

[121] *Ibid.*, December 28, 1824; Thurston and Bishop to the American Board, Kailua, February 17, 1825, in *Missionary Herald*, XXII (May 1826), 141.

[122] *Missionary Herald*, XXIV (April 1828), 104. In the summer of 1826 Levi Chamberlain reported that there were about four thousand persons in the schools on Oahu, of whom about two-thirds were "acquainted with the letters" and might be expected soon to be able to read. Chamberlain to Hill, Honolulu, July 26, 1826, in Letters to the American Board, CXCI.

[123] Richards to the American Board, Lahaina, April 14, 1828, in *Missionary Herald*, XXV (February 1829), 55; Bingham, *Sandwich Islands*, p. 257. Bingham wrote that one school on Oahu "was taught from a single copy of elementary lessons in spelling and reading."

where the teacher pronounced a letter or a word, which was then repeated by all the pupils present—sometimes in unison and sometimes individually. It is not difficult to understand the comment of Otto von Kotzebue, who declared that in Honolulu the schools could be "easily recognized afar off."[124] Despite the failings of the teachers, the popularity of the schools grew apace. In 1829 at least forty-five thousand Hawaiians were receiving instruction in some seven hundred schools.[125] Three years later, just prior to the death of Kaahumanu, the number of schools had increased to eleven hundred and there were more than fifty thousand natives enrolled as pupils.[126]

The population of the Islands in 1832 was reported to be slightly more than 130,000. If this figure was approximately accurate, nearly forty per cent of all Hawaiians were at least nominally enrolled in the mission schools, although the attendance of many was irregular and there probably was no general enthusiasm for learning. A considerable proportion of the pupils were adults. In 1829 it was said that scarcely one-tenth of those who attended the schools on Oahu were children,[127] and Hiram Bingham later declared that the pupils were "mostly above the years of childhood, and . . . . were generally supposed to be willing to receive instruction from God's word."[128] To what extent this willingness to receive instruction was prompted by a hint or a command from some chief does not appear.

The proportion of adults in the schools provided the missionaries with an unusual opportunity to influence the thinking of mature men and women and to prepare them to read their own Bibles. It was viewed with less satisfaction by critics of the mission. Captain Beechey thought that the "praiseworthy purpose" of the missionaries had failed of accomplishment because the adult students had been compelled to devote an unreasonable amount of time to their books while neglecting other interests.[129] Captain Kotzebue was more

---

[124] Kotzebue, *New Voyage Round the World*, II, 258. See also *Wanderings and Adventures of Reuben Delano* (Worcester, 1846), p. 23.

[125] *Missionary Herald*, XXV (June 1829), 182; General Letter of the Mission, February 20, 1830, *ibid.*, XXVI (October 1830), 311–312.

[126] *Missionary Herald*, XXIX (January 1833), 19.

[127] *Report of the American Board*, 1831, p. 50.

[128] Bingham, *Sandwich Islands*, p. 324.

[129] Beechey, *Voyage to the Pacific*, II, 101–102.

severe in his comments. He characterized the persistence of Kaahumanu in compelling adults to learn to read as "tyranny," and predicted that compulsory attendance of adults at the schools would
cause such general neglect of agriculture as to create the danger of
famine.[130] Nearly two years later Captain Duhaut-Cilly found farms
overrun with weeds, irrigation canals in disrepair, and kalo patches
abandoned—a sad state which he attributed to the preoccupation of
the men with education.[131] Beechey was less explicit, being content
to observe that the disproportionate amount of time devoted to the
schools had been productive of "much mischief."[132]

It would be easy to overestimate the popularity or the achievements of the schools. It seems certain that thousands of natives made
the effort to learn to read only because of the positive command or
implied wishes of some chief, and the missionaries confessed that
statistics were misleading, inasmuch as many "attend our schools
occasionally, and are enrolled as scholars, who give very little evidence of deriving material benefit."[133] Of the thousands who were
counted as pupils of the common schools, perhaps one-half could
read—with greater difficulty than success—elementary books and
pamphlets printed in their own language.[134] The great object of training a nation of men and women to read their own Bibles was not immediately realized. The presence of thousands of Hawaiians in the
mission schools, however, was a matter of great significance to the
missionaries, for it gave them an unparalleled opportunity to mold
public opinion. We may well accept the verdict of Hiram Bingham
that the schools, with their many weaknesses, were indispensable to
the success of the mission.[135]

The missionaries were aware of the unsatisfactory instruction,
which lessened materially the value of their schools. In 1825 a general meeting of the mission recommended that particular attention

[130] Kotzebue, *New Voyage Round the World*, II, 261–262.

[131] Duhaut - Cilly, *Voyage Autour du Monde*, II, 283–284.

[132] Beechey, *Voyage to the Pacific*, II, 102.

[133] General Letter to the Mission, June 23, 1832, in *Missionary Herald*, XXIX (May 1833), 161.

[134] *Ibid.*, XXV (June 1829), 182; XXVII (May, June, 1831), 144, 182. One mission-ary declared that not more than one-fifth of the persons in his district who were con-sidered able to read could do so with fa-cility and understanding. Lorenzo Lyons to Anderson, Waimea, Hawaii, September 6, 1833, in Letters to the American Board, LXVIII, No. 43.

[135] Bingham, *Sandwich Islands*, p. 457.

be given at each church to the training of teachers;[136] and two years later it was proposed that committees should visit the schools once in every two months.[137] Apparently neither proposal was put into effect, and the incompetence of the teachers continued to be a source of concern to the missionaries.[138] Perhaps the most effective expedient was the suggestion that the mission provide special schools for the training of prospective teachers[139]—a suggestion which was partially realized in the establishment of the mission seminary at Lahainaluna in 1831.

In all parts of the Islands the supervision of the schools was re-garded as one of the most important duties of the missionaries, and educational as well as evangelical motives caused many missionaries to make periodic tours of their districts, preaching to congregations of natives, ministering to the sick, inspecting the schools, and ex-horting teachers and pupils alike to be faithful and diligent. In some districts, and notably upon the island of Oahu, the missionaries for many years held public examinations of the pupils from the common schools—a device which served to stimulate both teachers and pupils to greater exertion than could have been produced by the more prosaic method of daily recitations alone.

The earliest examination of schools at Honolulu seems to have included only pupils from that community or the near vicinity.[140] In

---

[136] Journal of Levi Chamberlain, May 24, 1825; "Minutes of the General Meeting of the Sandwich Island Mission" (MS, Hawaiian Mission Children's Society Library), May 24, 1825.

[137] Journal of Levi Chamberlain, July 24, 25, 27, and 30, 1827.

[138] Letter of the Missionaries on Oahu, September 20, 1830, in *Missionary Herald*, XXVII (May 1831), 144; Thurston and Bishop to the American Board, Kailua, October 15, 1831, *ibid.*, XXVIII (July 1832), 223. Describing the teachers on Maui, William Richards wrote: "In each district there is one or more teachers with whom I am particularly acquainted and who superin-tends all the schools. These teachers are nearly all of them young men who . . . . are well acquainted with all the books published in their language. Most of them have learnt to calculate a little by figures.

They can repeat the multiplication table, and add and subtract a little. They are considered as persons of established moral character, and some of them are hopefully pious . . . . The under teachers are many of them extremely ignorant, though all of them are able to read and most of them have the spelling book committed to mem-ory. There are many of them however, that do not read new books with facility, al-though they will find them out after con-siderable study." Richards to the Ameri-can Board, Lahaina, April 14, 1828, *ibid.*, XXV (February 1829), 54.

[139] Letter of the Missionaries on Oahu, September 20, 1830, *ibid.*, XXVII (May 1831), 144; *Report of the American Board*, 1830, p. 67.

[140] Journal of Levi Chamberlain, July 21, November 23, 1825.

the spring of 1826, the missionaries invited pupils from all parts of the island to attend an examination at Honolulu. On that occasion, some five hundred or more persons—approximately one-fifth of the number examined—had come from rural Oahu beyond the district of Honolulu.[141] Thereafter examinations which called to Honolulu pupils from all parts of Oahu seem to have been held with some regularity.[142] The Rev. Charles S. Stewart, who witnessed such an examination in October 1829, described it as consisting, "like all others of a similar kind, of specimens in reading and writing, exercises in arithmetic, &c. &c., concluding, at the end of an hour or more, with a hymn and short prayer."[143]

The examination which Stewart observed probably was purposely brief in order not to tire distinguished visitors who were present; normally several days were required to complete the examination of all the pupils who presented themselves for the approval of the mission. In January 1827 Stephen Reynolds observed that the examinations were attended by many persons who came from remote districts of the island and who were compelled to be absent from their homes for as long as a week, during which time they often were without adequate food or shelter.[144] Notwithstanding these hardships, thousands of Hawaiians regularly undertook the long journey and accepted any privations which were necessary in order to visit the metropolis whenever the missionaries announced a general examination of the schools on Oahu.[145]

The importance of the school system could not be measured fairly by its meager curriculum. According to so competent an authority as Hiram Bingham, the missionaries always attempted to associate "the

[141] Journal of Levi Chamberlain, April 19, 20, 1826.

[142] *Ibid.*, July 21, 1826, April 19, 20, 21, 1830, April 19, 22, 1831; Journal of Stephen Reynolds, January 16, 18, 19, 20, 1827, April 19, 23, 1832; Stewart, *Visit to the South Seas*, II, 176–181.   [143] *Ibid.*, II, 180.

[144] Journal of Stephen Reynolds, January 16, 18, 19, 20, 1827.

[145] The device of general examinations of the schools, in which large numbers of pupils would be brought together for a demonstration of their achievements, was also em-

ployed on Hawaii and Maui, although apparently no missionary there attempted the ambitious project of examining representatives of schools from all parts of an island at one time and place. Journal of Levi Chamberlain, September 17, 1828; Letter of William Richards, October 2, 1830, in Samuel Williston, *William Richards* (Cambridge, Massachusetts, 1938), pp. 24–25; Journal of Dr. and Mrs. Alonzo Chapin, IV, 10 (December 4, 1832); Thurston and Bishop to the American Board, Kailua, October 15, 1831, in *Missionary Herald*, XXVIII (July 1832), 222–223.

elements of morals and religion" with instruction in reading and writing.[146] On Maui, William Richards instructed the more capable and trusted teachers "to assemble the people on the Sabbath, and spend the time in attention to the catechism, commandments, and scripture tracts, and conclude with prayer."[147] Despite the undoubted incompetence of most of the teachers, and the occasional misconduct of some, the missionaries believed that attendance at their schools tended to diminish crime and vice by absorbing the attention of the young people during a part of the day when otherwise they would have had much leisure. The influence of the schools, therefore, was moral as well as literary.[148]

The beginnings of the mission schools were modest and the limitations of those schools were apparent to all observers. The missionaries, however, could look beyond the present problems of keeping the schools open and the students interested and could hope that ultimately those schools might play a major part in the life of the nation. Indeed, they more than once expressed the hope that influences flowing from the schools would prove the salvation of the little kingdom. In an article published in 1838, E. O. Hall declared that the schools were "the only *sure* foundation on which to build up this nation," and added that by "imparting knowledge to this people, they will be raised up to take their place among the enlightened nations of the earth, civilized, Christianized, saved."[149] In a similar

[146] Bingham, *Sandwich Islands*, p. 103.

[147] Richards to the American Board, Lahaina, April 14, 1828, in *Missionary Herald*, XXV (February 1829), 54.

[148] Alexander to Anderson, Waioli, January 5, 1837, in Letters to the American Board, LXVIII, No. 51; Bingham to Miller, Honolulu, September 26, 1831 (copy), *ibid.*, LXVII, No. 8; Journal of Levi Chamberlain, May 22, 1827; *Missionary Herald*, XXXII (August 1836), 306–307; Ellis, *Tour through Hawaii*, p. 172; Blackman, *Making of Hawaii*, pp. 167–168. In October 1826 the missionaries, in a spirited defense of their policies, challenged their critics with the question: "Is it nothing that thousands who formerly devoted their time to gaming, quarreling, and the practice of iniquity

in all its varied forms; and the thousands who wasted their days in idleness, should now be assembled in schools, and spend their leisure time in reading scripture tracts and listening to instruction?" (MS statement by the missionaries, Sandwich Islands, October 3, 1826, in AH, "Historical and Miscellaneous Documents"). A century later one careful student thought that the common schools had been "the salvation of the younger generation, and the stepping stones which enabled the Hawaiians of character and intelligence . . . . to emerge from the critical period, stable and sound." Handy, *Cultural Revolution in Hawaii*, pp. 31–32.

[149] Hall, "Condition of Common Schools at the Sandwich Islands," in *Hawaiian Spectator*, I (October 1838), 360.

vein Levi Chamberlain explained to James Hunnewell the importance which the missionaries attached to their schools. Writing in November 1832, Chamberlain declared:

. . . . we feel a strong inclination to make a great effort to preserve the people from coming under the power of other governments, by imparting to them the ability, so far as we are able, to govern themselves; and this we believe we can most effectually do, by teaching them arts, imparting to them a taste for knowledge, and inspiring them with a feeling of self respect by raising their characters.[150]

Closely associated with the educational program of the mission was the work of its press. With the increasing popularity of the schools early in 1824, the supply of books was unequal to the demands of the Hawaiians.[151] To enable the missionaries to respond to the requests for printed material, the mission press in 1825 printed more than seventy thousand copies of pamphlets and books, with an aggregate of more than one and a quarter million pages,[152] but this was insufficient to supply the ever increasing demand. By 1829 the annual output of the press had increased to 114,000 copies of books and tracts, with a total of nearly four and one-half million pages.[153] During the eight years from January 1822 to March 1830 nearly four hundred thousand copies of twenty-eight different books and tracts were issued by the mission.[154] Apparently the supply had not yet exceeded the demand. From Kauai, Peter J. Gulick wrote that books were still much desired,[155] and in 1832 one missionary observed that the Hawaiians not only were "eager to receive instruction" but were ready to perform "any service, however menial, for a book."[156] In 1834 an English writer noted that "school-books and religious publications . . . . were so numerous and well-diffused

[150] Chamberlain to Hunnewell, Honolulu, November 12, 1832, in Hunnewell MSS.

[151] Journal of Levi Chamberlain, March 24, 1824.

[152] The American Mission to the American Board, Oahu, March 10, 1826, in *Missionary Herald*, XXII (December 1826), 370.

[153] General Letter of the Mission, February 20, 1830, in *ibid.*, XXVI (October 1830), 311.

[154] The Mission on Oahu to the American Board, Honolulu, March 20, 1830, in *ibid.*, XXVII (April 1831), 115.

[155] Letter of P. J. Gulick, Waimea, October 1830, in Ethel M. Damon, *Koamalu* (Honolulu, 1931), I, 275.

[156] Journal of Dr. and Mrs. Alonzo Chapin, III, 18 (May 29, 1832); Mrs. Chapin to Thomas Tenney, Honolulu, June 19, 1832, *ibid.*, II, 66–67. Cf. Gulick to the American Board, February 18, [1830], in *Missionary Herald*, XXVI (September 1830), 284.

as to be seen in almost every peasant's hut."[157] Every book in the Hawaiian language had been translated or prepared by members of the mission and had been published by the mission press; through the monopoly of the printed page the missionaries possessed a powerful agency for molding the thoughts and lives of the Hawaiian people.

The almost universal poverty of the Hawaiians, combined with their insistence that books be furnished them, provided the missionaries with a delicate problem. For a time they hesitated to accept money from the natives, and until after 1832 goods or produce—sometimes of doubtful value—were commonly accepted in exchange for books.[158] Those who came empty-handed often were given books,[159] although the missionaries hoped that efforts to secure the purchase price would encourage habits of thrift and industry among the Hawaiian people.[160]

Foremost among the literary achievements of the missionaries was their translation of the Bible into Hawaiian. This formidable undertaking was begun in October 1824; it was concluded in March 1839, after more than fourteen years of careful work in which many of the missionaries had shared.[161]

The tangible evidence of the influence of the mission was not confined to statistical triumphs. One inescapable proof of their influence was the quiet observance of Sunday, which they boasted was "almost universal" throughout the Islands.[162] This, like the efforts to promote

[157] Bennett, *Whaling Voyage Round the Globe*, I, 226.

[158] Richards to the American Board, Lahaina, April 14, 1828, in *Missionary Herald*, XXV (February 1829), 55; Chamberlain to Anderson, Honolulu, June 19, 1826, in Letters to the American Board, XXXI, No. 63; Chamberlain to Evarts, Honolulu, November 19, 1830, *ibid.*, LXVIII, No. 151; Chamberlain to Hill, Honolulu, February 13, 1832, *ibid.*, CXCI; Chamberlain and Judd to Anderson, Honolulu, December 11, 1832, *ibid.*, "Sandwich Islands, 1831–1837," Part I, No. 37.

[159] Chamberlain to Hill, Honolulu, February 13, 1832, *ibid.*, CXCI.

[160] Hall, "Condition of Common Schools at the Sandwich Islands," in *Hawaiian Spectator*, I (October 1838), 354; Journal of Mrs. John S. Emerson, September 16,

[1832], in Emerson, *Pioneer Days in Hawaii*, p. 61.

[161] Journal of the Missionaries at Honolulu, October 21, 1824, in *Missionary Herald*, XXI (September 1825), 275; Bingham to the American Board, Honolulu, April 19, 1839, *ibid.*, XXXVI (May 1840), 188; Journal of Levi Chamberlain, March 26, 1839; A. Bishop, "A Brief History of the Translation of the Holy Scripture into the Hawaiian Language," in *The Friend*, August 1, 1844, pp. 74–75.

[162] Manuscript statement by the missionaries, Sandwich Islands, October 3, 1826, in AH, "Miscellaneous Documents." In 1829 the Rev. Peter J. Gulick declared that he had never lived in any part of the United States "in which the external observance of the Sabbath appeared to be so carefully maintained" as it was at Waimea,

temperance and chastity, had been largely the product of decrees by powerful chiefs friendly to the mission. There was evidence also of a more spontaneous response to the teachings of the missionaries. In Honolulu hundreds of persons learned a verse of Scripture each day,[163] and elsewhere in hundreds of native homes private worship was a regular feature of the daily routine.[164] Under the insistent persuasion of the missionaries many natives discarded the convivial habits of their ancestors and attempted to regulate their lives by the strict standards of New England Puritans. In some churches the missionaries organized groups of natives whose character and conduct were believed to be above reproach. Membership in those groups was said to be highly prized, and the missionaries hoped they would become instruments for making morality a requisite for social acceptance.[165] At Honolulu the missionaries organized a society for the suppression of intemperance.[166] At Lahaina a movement initiated to discourage the use of tobacco met with a surprisingly favorable response. Within a short time no less than twenty-five hundred persons had promised to discontinue the habit of smoking, described by one missionary as "a *great evil*"; and many brought their formerly cherished pipes to the missionaries as mute testimony that, however weak their will might soon prove to be, their intentions were sincere.[167]

When Otto von Kotzebue visited Honolulu in September 1825 he found that there had been "an entire change" in the daily life and habits of the Hawaiian people[168]—a development which he regarded as principally the result of missionary influence. It is clear that this change was not pleasing to Kotzebue, for he complained:

Kauai. Gulick to the American Board, May 13, 1829, in *Missionary Herald*, XXVI (April 1830), 107–108.

[163] Journal of Dr. and Mrs. Alonzo Chapin, II, 35–36 (May 27, 1832).

[164] Ephraim Spaulding to the American Board, Lahaina, October 23, 1832 (copy), in Letters to the American Board, LXVIII, No. 73; Letter of J. S. Emerson, August 20, [1832], in Emerson, *Pioneer Days in Hawaii*, pp. 59–60.

[165] Bingham, Clark, *et al.* to the American Board, March 20, 1830, in *Missionary Herald*, XXVII (April 1831), 117; Rich-

ards and Green to the American Board, Lahaina, October 2, 1830, *ibid.*, XXVII (June 1831), 180–181; Thurston and Bishop to the American Board, Kailua, May 13, 1830, *ibid.*, XXVII (May 1831), 145; Dibble, *History of the Sandwich Islands*, pp. 222–223.

[166] Journal of Levi Chamberlain, April 5, 6, 1831.

[167] Letter of Ephraim Spaulding, undated, in Letters to the American Board, LXVIII, No. 71.

[168] Kotzebue, *New Voyage Round the World*, II, 254–255.

The inhabitants of every house or hut in Hanaruro [Honolulu] are compelled by authority to an almost endless routine of prayers; and even the often dishonest intentions of the foreign settlers must be concealed under the veil of devotion. The streets, formerly so full of life and animation, are now deserted; games of all kinds, even the most innocent, are sternly prohibited; singing is a punishable offence; and the consummate profligacy of attempting to dance would certainly find no mercy. On Sundays, no cooking is permitted, nor must even a fire be kindled: nothing, in short, must be done; the whole day is devoted to prayer, with how much real piety may be easily imagined.[169]

Other visitors to the Islands joined Kotzebue in this criticism of missionary policy as unreasonable.[170] The missionaries, however, found little that was commendable and much that seemed evil in the traditional games, dances, and songs of the Islands. The Rev. William Richards conceded that some of the ancient songs and poetry possessed real literary merit, but he declared that a "great majority of their songs, are of the most immoral character, and have exerted the worst possible influence." For that reason he felt obliged to condemn the ancient songs, although the effect was to discourage literary efforts.[171] Sheldon Dibble declared that many of the pastimes formerly popular among the Hawaiians had been accompanied by gambling or lewdness and therefore could not be condoned by the mission.[172] There were many variations of the native dances. The missionaries were convinced of "the folly and vanity" of the least objectionable of the dances;[173] others they regarded as "very revolting."[174] In either event they preferred to see the Hawaiians engaged in more serious and profitable exercises. Apparently there were no

[169] *Ibid.*, II, 256–257.

[170] Beechey, *Voyage to the Pacific*, II, 101–103; Duhaut-Cilly, *Voyage Autour du Monde*, II, 290–291; Letter of William Miller, September 25, 1831, in AH, F.O. and Ex. See also a review article entitled "Sandwich Islanders," in *Quarterly Review*, XXXV (March 1827), 438–441, and *Remarks on the "Tour Around Hawaii,"* by the Missionaries, Messrs. Ellis, Thurston, Bishop, and Goodrich (Salem, Massachusetts, 1848). A defense of the missionaries may be found in [Jeremiah Evarts], "The American Missionaries at the Sandwich Islands," in *North American Review*, XXVI (January 1828), 59–111, and in *An Examination of Charges against the American Missionaries at the Sandwich Islands, as alleged in the Voyage of the Ship Blonde, and in the London Quarterly Review* (Cambridge, Massachusetts, 1827).

[171] Letter of William Richards, in *Missionary Herald*, XXV (December 1829), 372.

[172] Dibble, *History of the Sandwich Islands*, pp. 101–102.

[173] Damon, "First Mission Settlement on Kauai," in *The Friend*, September 1925, p. 208. Cf. Journal of Maria S. Loomis, January 30, 1821; Ellis, *Tour through Hawaii*, pp. 48–49.

[174] Dibble, *History of the Sandwich Islands*, p. 100.

decrees expressly prohibiting the ancient games and dances, but as the powerful chiefs came under the influence of the mission they discouraged sports and dancing among their followers. The result was as effective as any legislation could have been. Only during the infrequent periods of revolt against missionary influence were the ancient games or the *hula* to be seen in Honolulu. Elsewhere, except in remote areas, they were generally discontinued.

The missionaries encountered greater difficulty in their efforts to impose upon the Hawaiian people the standards of sexual morality prevalent in New England. This required a major reorientation of the social philosophy of the Hawaiian people. Family ties had hitherto been so unstable that one of the best-informed missionaries concluded that there had been "nothing among the Hawaiians that was worthy, or could even bear the name of domestic happiness in a civilized community."[175] It was not difficult for the missionaries to secure promises from friendly natives who agreed to alter their mode of life; but the example of many foreigners and the mores bequeathed by generations which had known no such strict codes were difficult to overcome. An important step toward popularizing the Christian ideal of marriage was taken in October 1823 when William Richards united two powerful chiefs—Hoapili and Kalakua—in marriage.[176] Gradually the ideal of monogamous marriage, solemnized by a religious ceremony, was accepted by the natives. By 1830 hundreds of couples annually sought the benediction of the mission for their unions, and the missionaries could report that there were few couples living within a convenient distance of the home of a missionary who had not been formally united in marriage. It is difficult to credit the added statement that there appeared to be few violations of the marriage vow.[177]

The duties of a missionary were numerous and varied; often they were as perplexing as they were arduous. To many natives, includ-

[175] Richards to Charles Wilkes, Lahaina, March 15, 1841, in AH, Richards MSS.

[176] Richards and Stewart to the American Board, Lahaina, December 1, 1824 [1823], in *Missionary Herald*, XXI (April 1825), 103.

[177] Richards to the American Board, Lahaina, April 14, 1828, *ibid.*, XXV (February 1829), 53–54; Journal of Artemas Bishop, August 29–September 8, 1828, *ibid.*, XXV (May 1829), 147–151; General Letter of the Mission, February 20, 1830, *ibid.*, XXVI (October 1830), 312; General Letter of the Mission, June 28, 1831, *ibid.*, XXVIII (March 1832), 74; Journal of Mrs. G. P. Judd, [April 1828], in Judd, *Honolulu*, p. 14.

ing some of the most powerful chiefs, he was preacher, teacher, counselor, and social monitor; and in rural districts he was compelled to
assume the role of physician. He conducted a series of regular devo-
tional and preaching services each week, superintended the schools
in his district, conversed with the natives upon a variety of subjects
vital to their spiritual and temporal welfare, shared in the translation
of the Bible or prepared other books and tracts for the press, and
occasionally made an extended tour of neighboring areas in which no
missionary resided. To as great an extent as time and the state of
her health permitted, his wife combined the direction of her household
with the care of a school and with the religious and moral instruction
of the women of the community.

With so imposing an array of duties confronting them daily, it is
not surprising that the missionaries persistently urged the American
Board to strengthen the mission by generous additions to its personnel.
Nor were they without justification in their fear that failure to send
more missionaries to the Islands would postpone indefinitely the
eagerly anticipated day when the Hawaiian kingdom might be regarded as a Christian nation. Within ten years after the establishment of the mission, illness or a loss of enthusiasm caused six missionary families to return to the United States. The American Board
did not permit the withdrawal of individuals to impair permanently
the strength of the mission. In 1822, 1827, 1830, and frequently
thereafter the Board sent reinforcements to the Islands; and the Hawaiian mission, which consisted of but fourteen adults in 1819, numbered more than fifty men and women in 1832. Thus strengthened,
it established an academy for the training of teachers, founded
churches in rural areas hitherto seldom visited by missionaries, and
planned the organization of a mission to the Washington Islands.

Notable among the men sent to the Hawaiian Islands between
1823 and 1832 were: William Richards, destined to become the most
trusted counselor of the chiefs and the pioneer Hawaiian diplomat;[178]
Levi Chamberlain, who abandoned a successful business career to
participate directly in the spread of Christian missions;[179] Dr. Gerrit

---

[178] R. S. K[uykendall], "William Richards," in *Dictionary of American Biography*,
XV, 560–561; Williston, *William Richards*.
[179] Levi Chamberlain was born in Ver-

mont in 1792. He was trained for a career
as a merchant and in 1817 entered a partnership to carry on trade with the Far East.
Although he was successful in this busi-

P. Judd, who was to become for more than a decade the most influential adviser and spokesman of Kamehameha III;[180] Lorrin Andrews, educator and lexicographer;[181] Jonathan S. Green, fiery apostle of righteousness and patient experimenter with products of Hawaiian soil; and Sheldon Dibble, future historian of the Islands.

The mission was compelled to rely heavily upon the assistance of natives. Not only did Hawaiians serve as teachers in all parts of the Islands but occasionally in the absence of a missionary some native would assume responsibility for the Sunday services or the midweek lecture.[182] Three Hawaiian converts, educated in the United States at the expense of the American Board, accompanied the pioneer missionaries to the Hawaiian Islands. Other Hawaiians, similarly trained, followed in later years. The hope that these native helpers would prove of considerable assistance to the missionaries was only partially realized. In 1849 five of the six survivors of this group were in good standing in some mission church, but it was reported that each at times had been "wayward and unstable."[183] Some of

ness, he early became interested in foreign missions. He therefore gave up his career as a merchant and offered his services to the American Board, by whom he was assigned to the mission to the Hawaiian Islands. He accompanied the reinforcement which the Board sent to the Islands in 1822. He served as secular agent of the mission until his death in 1849. His singular devotion to the work of the mission and his consistent refusal to become involved in the political disputes which constantly threatened to enmesh the mission or to distract the attention of its members, together with the advantages gained from his experience as a merchant, enabled him to win the confidence and respect of his brethren and of the foreign community to an extent achieved by few, if any, other members of the mission. T. J. Farnham, who met him on a voyage from Honolulu to California in 1841, described him as "a man of fine mind and unpretending goodness." T. J. Farnham, *Life, Adventures, and Travels in California* (New York, 1849), p. 46. For comments typical of the views of the missionaries, see Reuben Tinker to Anderson, Honolulu, May 3, 1836, in Letters to the American Board, LXVIII, No. 27; Cochran Forbes to the

American Board, November 8, 1834, *ibid.*, LXVIII, No. 102; and Anderson, *History of the Mission to the Sandwich Islands*, pp. 237–239. Other brief accounts of the career and influence of Chamberlain may be found in *Polynesian*, August 4, 1849, and *Honolulu Star-Bulletin*, April 12, 1920, p. 33. Chamberlain declared that he was devoted to his labors as a missionary and would not exchange his position "for that of the most prosperous merchant in the United States." Chamberlain to Anderson, Honolulu, March 22, 1836, in Letters to the American Board, LXVIII, No. 177; Chamberlain to Henry J. Holbrook, Honolulu, November 14, 1837, *ibid.*, CXXXV, No. 110½.

[180] R. S. K[uykendall], "Gerrit Parmele Judd," in *Dictionary of American Biography*, X, 229–230.

[181] J. C. A[rcher], "Lorrin Andrews," *ibid.*, I, 295–296.

[182] Journal of Levi Chamberlain, August 24, 31, 1823, January 22, 29, October 22, November 5, 1826, and August 24, 27, 1828; Journal of Stephen Reynolds, May 30, 1824.

[183] Henry T. Cheever, *Life in the Sandwich Islands* (New York, 1851), p. 55.

them had been useful as teachers or in subordinate capacities,[184] but none of them had become a leader in the schools or churches and as a group they had disappointed the missionaries by their inability to adapt themselves to steady employment in the schools.

More important in the extension of the influence of the mission were the converts and teachers who went into districts seldom visited by a missionary and urged their countrymen to believe in Jehovah and to obey His commandments. Judged solely by their efficacy in the exposition of Christian doctrines, these exhortations of uneducated Hawaiians must have been more confusing than enlightening to their ignorant hearers. Some such misgivings evidently assailed the missionaries, and it was reported that on Maui the natives who conducted religious services in remote communities confined themselves

[184] The best-known and evidently most active of these Hawaiian assistants was Thomas Hopu, one of the natives who accompanied the pioneer missionaries to the Islands. Prior to his departure, it was reported in Boston that he was well qualified to act as a catechist or teacher, and it was as a teacher that he most frequently appears in contemporary accounts. From 1822 to 1825 he was actively engaged in teaching and religious work on Hawaii, first at Kailua, and, following the establishment of a mission station at Kaawaloa, as an assistant at that place. By the missionaries at Kaawaloa it was reported that his "indefatigable and assiduous labor" entitled him to "the remembrance and esteem of the church." After 1825 he appears only infrequently in the reports of the missionaries, but apparently he continued to be identified with the mission schools and churches. He resided at Kailua, where, in 1839, he was a teacher in one of the schools. Nine years later, he was one of the deacons in the church at Kailua. *Columbian Centinel*, September 15, 1819; Journal of Maria S. Loomis, December 21, 1820, August 15, 1821, November 9, 1822; Hopu to the Rev. Herman Daggett, October 6, 1821, December 22, 1823, in *Missionary Herald*, XVIII (May 1822), 145–146, XX (November 1824), 366; James Ely to Evarts, [Kaawaloa, May 1, 1825], *ibid.*, XXII (June 1826), 178; Journal of Peter J. Gulick, December 12, 1831, in *ibid.*, XXVIII (October 1832), 330; S. L. An-

drews to the American Board, Kailua, May 12, 1838, *ibid.*, XXXV (May 1839), 166; Journal of Levi Chamberlain, February 4, 1824; Bingham, Thurston, *et al.* to Evarts, Oahu, December 28, 1822, in Letters to the American Board, IX, No. 130; Journal of Dr. and Mrs. Alonzo Chapin, IV, 15–16 (December 20, 21, 1832); Hopu to Kamehameha III, Kailua, May 21, 1838, in AH, "Historical and Miscellaneous Documents"; Teggart, ed., *Around the Horn to the Sandwich Islands*, p. 133; Rufus Anderson, *The Hawaiian Islands: their Progress and Condition under Missionary Labors* (Boston, 1865), p. 49 n.

Other Hawaiians, trained in the United States, who rendered some service to the mission over a period of years, included Robert Haia, who was "a most valuable teacher to the princess and her school" at Lahaina; John Honolii, who was active in teaching and in leading private and sometimes public devotions; and Richard Kalaaialulu, who was employed by the mission press. Report of the Missionaries at Lahaina, October 15, 1828, *ibid.*, XXV (July 1829), 212; Mathison, *Visit to Brazil*, pp. 433–434; Journal of Levi Chamberlain, November 16, December 7, 1823, March 3, 1824, March 17, September 20, 1825, February 25, 1835; [W. J. Hooker], "A Brief Memoir of the Life of Mr. David Douglas, with extracts from his letters," in *Companion to the Botanical Magazine* (London, 1835–1836), II, 171–172, and in *Hawaiian Spectator*, II (October 1839), 417.

to reading "the various Scripture tracts and other books," after which they concluded with prayer.[185]

Almost from the time of the establishment of the mission in the Hawaiian Islands, both the missionaries and the American Board looked beyond the narrow boundaries of eight small islands in search of larger fields as yet unoccupied by Christian missions. The opportunities for missionary expansion in the central and eastern Pacific were limited. South of the equator English Protestant missions had been attempted or were planned in each of the principal archipelagoes, although the failure of the mission to the Marquesas Islands led the American Board later to contemplate a mission to those islands.

Along the American coast only Oregon remained open to Protestantism. The frequent visits to Honolulu of traders familiar with the northwest coast, some of whom were entertained at the homes of the missionaries, were a constant reminder that the aborigines of that region were still beyond the pale of the gospel. Little was known of the willingness of the Indians to receive religious instruction, but there was much to point to Oregon as the logical site for American missionary enterprise. American traders regularly visited the coast and through them missionaries in Oregon might expect to maintain communication with Honolulu and Boston. The Anglo-American convention of 1818 gave to the United States and its citizens the right of "joint occupation" of the vast Oregon territory and appeared to foreshadow the time when the United States would gain complete sovereignty over much of the region north of California. A few sanguine patriots, impressed by the irresistible march westward of American population, predicted that it would not be stayed until it had crossed plains and mountains and reached the valley of the Columbia. To missionaries and friends of the American Board it seemed imperative that Protestant institutions should be firmly established in Oregon in advance of the tide of settlement.[186]

[185] Report of the Missionaries at Lahaina, October 15, 1828, in *Missionary Herald*, XXV (July 1829), 209–210.

[186] *Ibid.*, XXIII (December 1827), 396–397: "It is by no means improbable, that the first mission which shall be fitted out for this region will be accompanied by a little colony; which, though distinct in its organization, and in some sense secular as to its object, will be formed and sent forth with the same views, and for the accomplishment of the same great end; viz. the planting of Christian institutions on the shores of the Pacific.

"The tide of emigration is rolling westward so rapidly, that it must speedily surmount every barrier, till it reaches all the habitable parts of this continent. . . . .

In October 1820 the missionaries at Honolulu—after talking with two captains who had just returned from the coast—wrote that the "Gospel can be propagated on the N.W. coast. It *must be*; it *will be*."[187] A few weeks later, they sent a letter to "the head chief of the most important tribe on the North-West Coast," assuring him that missionaries would be sent to his people and suggesting that meanwhile he might send one or two of his own children to Honolulu to be instructed by the missionaries.[188] Evidently the responsibilities and problems of the immediate task thereafter absorbed all their energy, for only occasionally did the northwest coast appear in their correspondence and journals. The Board, however, did not forget Oregon. In July 1827 they announced that "a *mission to the North-West Coast* will soon be expedient; and . . . . it had better be attempted, probably, by some of the missionaries from the Sandwich Islands."[189] When, later that year, a third company of missionaries was sent to the Hawaiian Islands, the Rev. J. S. Green was instructed to visit the coast to secure such information as would indicate if a mission could be established there.[190] Green's report was unfavorable to the proposed mission,[191] and the Board temporarily dropped the matter.

How noble an object is here; and how worthy of American enterprise;—to convey the inestimable treasure of divine truth to pagan tribes, scattered over a vast extent of territory, and to prepare the way for future settlers from the Atlantic coast and the valley of the Mississippi. In this manner, early provision will be made for the religious wants of the adventurous voyager and the fearless man of the woods, who shall meet in these remote regions; and thus will a foundation be laid for churches, schools and colleges, and all that bright array of moral influences, which accompany Christian institutions, and form a well organized civil community. In a word, thus may be sent forth another Plymouth Colony, which shall extend its beneficent influences over millions of intelligent, enlightened and happy men, through successive ages to the end of the world . . . ."

[187] Journal of the Missionaries at Honolulu, October 24, 1820, *ibid.*, XVII (September 1821), 280.

[188] Journal of the Missionaries at Honolulu, January 8, 1821, *ibid.*, XVIII (July 1822), 204.

[189] Readers of the *Missionary Herald* were told that "a *mission to the North-West Coast* will soon be expedient; and that whenever it is expedient, it had better be attempted, probably, by some of the missionaries from the Sandwich Islands. From those islands access to the coast will be easy, and may be frequent; and for some of the missionaries, such an enterprise may furnish a desirable change of climate. The mission on the N. W. Coast might be regarded as a Branch of the Sandwich Island mission, and labors and laborers might be interchanged, as should be deemed expedient: and the expense of the new mission, thus undertaken, and thus conducted, would be considerably less, than it must be, if sent originally from this country.

"In view of this not improbable state of things, it becomes still more important, that the present necessities of the mission at the islands be supplied with a liberal hand." *Missionary Herald*, XXIII (July 1827), 228.

[190] *Ibid.*, XXIII (December 1827), 397.

[191] *Ibid.*, XXVI, 343–345, 369–373, XXVII, 33–39, 75–79, 105–107 (November, Decem-

When it was revived, the Oregon mission was organized as an independent enterprise rather than as an extension of the mission in the Hawaiian Islands.

Ten years after the arrival of the pioneer missionaries their influence was apparent in nearly all parts of the Islands. Throughout the archipelago the traveler could find churches, schools, a growing body of religious literature, large congregations at public worship, and many homes in which private worship was conducted with considerable regularity. It did not follow that these outward proofs of missionary influence had been accompanied by revolutionary changes in the thinking of any considerable number of Hawaiians. With some plausibility, critics stressed their belief that the mission had been only superficially successful. One trader declared, in 1828, that the natives were *"over* religious" and disgustingly adept at dissimulation,[192] and John C. Jones reported that religion was "the order of the day" to which all other interests were subordinated. With the obvious bias of a creditor unable to collect the money due him, Jones added that neither industry nor integrity was a part of that religion.[193]

The missionaries were aware of the unpleasant implications raised by these doubts. In the midst of their apparent triumphs there were temporary reverses, and the specter of uncertainty tempered the confidence and optimism of the realists in the mission. The most serious reaction against the rigid tenets of the mission occurred at Honolulu in February 1827. Early in that month, Stephen Reynolds —one of the most persistent and caustic critics of the mission— recorded that never before had he seen "so much immorality among the court circle" as he had recently witnessed.[194] Prominent natives who had been consistent attendants at church services absented themselves from public worship on Sunday morning. The tranquillity of the Sabbath was disturbed after a period of many months in which its observance had been enforced by the decrees and wishes of the

ber 1830, and February–April 1831) and reprinted in Archer Butler Hulbert and Dorothy Printup Hulbert, eds., *The Oregon Crusade: Across Land and Sea to Oregon* (Denver, 1935), pp. 45–83.

[192] Letter of Marcus T. Peirce, Waimea Bay [Kauai], February 7, 1828, in Hunnewell MSS.

[193] Jones to Marshall, Oahu, September 16, 1829, in Marshall MSS.

[194] Journal of Stephen Reynolds, February 5–8, 1827; Journal of Levi Chamberlain, February 8, 9, 10, 12, 1827; Chamberlain to Anderson, Honolulu, February 13, 1827, in Letters to the American Board, XXXI, No. 66.

chiefs.[195] Hundreds of natives discarded their recently acquired inhibitions, and the missionaries were chagrined when cards, dice, rum, and the *hula* again commanded the attention of the changeable Hawaiians.[196] At the close of the month, Levi Chamberlain confessed that the immediate prospects of the mission were "in some respects dark, owing to the prevalence of sin around us . . . . & the almost total suspension of the schools."[197]

More serious than temporary lapses from public morality and private piety was the danger that the outward evidences of religious devotion manifested by so many Hawaiian converts would prove illusory. It is evident that the concern of prospective converts for their own spiritual welfare was often little more than a passing fancy, induced by the example of their neighbors or by the exhortations of some chief. Early in 1832, when large numbers of natives were visiting the missionaries at Honolulu and declaring their purpose to become Christians, Levi Chamberlain was unable to observe "much evidence of deep conviction of sin" in any of his visitors[198]—a sad failure in the opinion of a Calvinist missionary. That Chamberlain's fears were shared by other missionaries besieged by hundreds of self-announced converts is indicated by the caution with which natives were admitted to the responsibilities and privileges of church membership.[199] It was hope and confidence, however, rather than doubts and fears that dominated the thinking of the missionaries during the fateful years of the regency. Many of their number undoubtedly were overconfident—an error easily produced by the active co-operation of nearly every important chief and by the flattering number of natives who visited their homes, studied in their schools, or flocked each Sunday to listen to their preaching.

[195] Journal of Stephen Reynolds, February 18, 1827.

[196] Chamberlain to Anderson, Honolulu, February 13, 1827, in Letters to the American Board, XXXI, No. 66; Beechey, *Voyage to the Pacific*, II, 102–103.

[197] Journal of Levi Chamberlain, March 1, 1827.

[198] *Ibid.*, February 9, 1832. See also Chamberlain to Samuel Ruggles, May 20, 1831, quoted in Kuykendall, *Hawaiian Kingdom*, p. 114.

[199] For statements of skepticism from the missionaries, see Chamberlain to Evarts, Honolulu, February 22, 1827, in Letters to the American Board, XXXI, No. 67; Sheldon Dibble, "A Review of the letters of the Revd. C. S. Stewart," *ibid.*, LXVIII, No. 31; Thurston and Bishop to the American Board, Kailua, October 15, 1831, in *Missionary Herald*, XXVIII (July 1832), 220–222; Richards, Andrews, *et al.* to the American Board, November 29, 1831, *ibid.*, XXVIII (August 1832), 249–250.

It was no small achievement that the missionaries had been able to persuade the proud and despotic chiefs to accept the teachings of a faith which flourished in a democratically controlled church and state and which was noted for the rigid restrictions which it imposed upon the power and pleasures of its adherents. The story of the acceptance of Puritan ideas by the Hawaiian rulers can be traced without difficulty. It is less easily explained.

The Hawaiians were a religious people, and the abandonment of the ancient beliefs undoubtedly left a void in the lives of thousands of natives. In that respect fortune favored the pioneer missionaries. More significant was the almost universal admiration of the Hawaiians for foreigners and for the new standards of living which the foreigners had introduced. It is not surprising that they were interested in the religion of the outside world as well as in its material conveniences, nor is it strange that they were impressed by the apparently intimate knowledge of the missionaries concerning the purposes and mandates of the creator of a universe whose size and wonders the Hawaiians were beginning dimly to realize. The rigorous theology of Calvinism raised few questions in the minds of the natives, who generally failed to grasp its implications and who understood only that a powerful and distant being called Jehovah created the universe and retained an active interest in the conduct of His creatures. The missionaries brought not only new and convincing religious ideas but also the miraculous art of writing. The multiple shortcomings of the schools were a source of constant worry to the missionaries, but few doubts assailed the self-satisfaction of the thousands of Hawaiians who were given an inadequate introduction to the intricacies of the printed page. The position of the mission was strengthened by the favor of the chiefs, some of whom at least must have regarded the insistence of the missionaries upon a strict observance of the Sabbath as less burdensome than the equally insistent demands of the merchants that the old debts be paid more promptly.

No explanation of the success of the mission would be complete without a recognition of the character, the perseverance, and the confidence of its leaders. Most of them were graduates of recognized American colleges, and all of them were fully convinced of the supreme importance of their work. Too serious to waste time or energy in frivolous pursuits, the missionaries won their dominant position by force of character and tenacity of purpose, against which the early indifference of the Hawaiians and the latent hostility of the foreign community could not prevail. Tenacity was fortified by confidence. In the midst of the reaction against the mission, in February 1827, Levi Chamberlain was sure of the future, declaring that "God has begun a good work, which he will carry on till righteousness shall fill the land."[200] Secure in the unshakable faith that God would reward their labors, the missionaries never relaxed their efforts to transfer the religious and social ideals of New England to the Hawaiian Islands.

[200] Chamberlain to Evarts, Honolulu, February 22, 1827, in Letters to the American Board, XXXI, No. 67. Chamberlain maintained this confidence despite the danger that the recent death of Kalanimoku would weaken the position of chiefs friendly to the mission while enhancing the power of Boki, who was believed to be opposed to its program.

IV

PURITANISM AND PUBLIC POLICY

THE American missionaries in the Hawaiian Islands were spiritual heirs of New England Puritanism. They had been reared in a church founded by great Puritan leaders and in a region which counted Winthrop, Cotton, and the Mathers among its heroes. With such a background, they could scarcely have been content with the abstract task of rescuing Hawaiian souls from the horrors of future punishment or with the comparatively tranquil efforts to teach the natives to read and write. In keeping with the traditions of Puritanism, they were convinced that the introduction of Christianity into the Hawaiian Islands could not be fully successful until there had been a reformation in the private lives of the Hawaiian people. They therefore encouraged the chiefs to adopt a program of moral legislation designed to substitute the ideals of rural New England for the folkways of a Polynesian archipelago.

The entrance of the mission into the controversial field of public policy was fraught with danger to the success of its educational and religious projects. Positive instructions from the American Board warned the missionaries that they must "abstain from all interference with the local and political views of the people," and that it was particularly incumbent upon a missionary "to stand aloof from the private and transient interests of chiefs and rulers."[1] After the forma-

---

[1] "Instructions of the Prudential Committee to the Missionaries about to embark for the Sandwich Islands," November 18, 1822, in *Missionary Herald*, XIX (April 1823), 106–110. The quotation will be found on p. 108.

tion of the regency it became difficult to observe either the letter or the spirit of these instructions, for the rulers showed a distinct willingness to lend the prestige and power of their great offices to the enforcement of a series of moral reforms. Missionaries imbued with Puritan traditions were not likely to be daunted by quibbles as to the appropriate relation of church and state. Certainly no such scruples disturbed Hiram Bingham as he counseled the chiefs or as he defended the community of interests between the mission and the regency with the affirmation that the "rulers of a state ought doubtless to understand God's will, and to encourage the inculcation of just principles, and to restrain blasphemy against God and trespass against men."[2]

The acceptance of the rigid moral standards of New England was basic in the thinking of the missionaries. The majority of the foreign residents held quite different views. With more than a little basis in fact, Levi Chamberlain reported, in 1825, the prevalence of "gross . . . . vices, in which most of the foreigners, far removed from the restraints of law and civilized society, shamelessly degrade themselves."[3] Serious-minded Calvinists were not likely to regard their fellow-citizens, thus presumably lost to honor and virtue, with respect or sympathy. It was equally unlikely that the whites in Honolulu would acquiesce quietly in policies which threatened to interfere with their pleasures or their liberty. The missionaries must have been aware that an effort to restrict the freedom of the foreign residents would be resisted vigorously, but they chose to ignore the danger and to press forward with their efforts to induce the chiefs to impose by law the strict moral codes of New England.

There were other sources of disagreement which tended to estrange the missionaries from other foreigners at Honolulu. The

[2] Bingham, *Sandwich Islands*, p. 279. This view was frankly stated by the missionaries in a public defense of their policies addressed to the foreign community of Honolulu in 1826. A manuscript copy, dated October 3, 1826, may be found in the file of "Historical and Miscellaneous Documents" in the Archives of Hawaii.

[3] Chamberlain to Hill, Honolulu, December 8, 1825, in Letters to the American Board, CXCI. Cf. Journal of Levi Chamberlain, August 7, 1825; Stewart to Hunne-

well, Lahaina, November 10, 1823, in Hunnewell MSS; Bingham to Evarts, Oahu, September 14, 1829, in Letters to the American Board, XXXI, No. 25; Journal of Dr. and Mrs. Alonzo Chapin, II, 34 (May 22, 1832). In contrast to these unfavorable reports was the statement of the Rev. E. W. Clark that the majority of the foreign residents were "probably not so degraded & lost to all shame as our friends suppose." Clark to Evarts, Honolulu, September 14, 1833, in Letters to the American Board, LXVII, No. 140.

traders were interested primarily in the accumulation of profits and were only mildly concerned with the welfare of the Hawaiian people among whom they lived. The missionaries, in contrast, felt so strong an interest in the happiness and prosperity of the Hawaiians that they could not remain neutral in the event of a conflict of interests between the natives and the traders. This was soon recognized by some of the merchants. In 1823 John C. Jones accused the missionaries of "living like lords in this luxurious land" while engaged in fruitless and hypocritical labors. At the same time, he furnished a clue to his antipathy for the missionaries by declaring that they had warned the chiefs of the danger of being cheated by the merchants, thus compelling the latter to lower their prices.[4] Three years later, he declared that the missionaries were "determined to oppose every thing like enterprise or exertion."[5] Two other merchants interested in the sandalwood trade agreed that the influence of the missionaries had not been advantageous to business at Honolulu.[6] This was contradicted by James Hunnewell, who declared that in spite of competition his own sales had increased.[7] The implications of Hunnewell's statement may have been correct, but it is evident that the belief that the presence of the missionaries at Honolulu had interfered with the profits to which traders were accustomed explains much of the bitterness which divided the foreign community at Honolulu into two hostile camps.

The mutual suspicion which, after 1825, effectively separated missionary and merchant developed slowly. Some of the foreigners at Honolulu greeted the pioneer missionaries with apparent cordiality and hastened to make some provision for their comfort.[8] There were occasional social contacts between the mission and the foreign community, and a few residents were consistently friendly with the mis-

[4] Jones to Marshall and Wildes, Oahu, March 9, 1823, in Massachusetts Historical Society, *Proceedings,* LIV, 46.

[5] Jones to Marshall, Oahu, June 18, 1826, in Marshall MSS. For other statements that the influence of the mission had been detrimental to trade or industry, see Jones to Marshall, Oahu, May 5, 25, September 21, 1826, January 4, 1827, September 16, 1829, October 4, 1830, *ibid.*; Kotzebue, *New Voyage Round the World,* II, 254–262.

[6] Crocker to Marshall and Wildes, Oahu, December 3, 1823, in Marshall MSS; Testimony of William Sturgis in NRL, "Court Martial Records," XXIII, 1830, No. 531, p. 330.

[7] Hunnewell to Warren Fay, Oahu, April 1828 (copy), in Hunnewell MSS.

[8] Journal of Maria S. Loomis, April 18, 1820; Bingham, *Sandwich Islands,* p. 95.

sionaries. The Rev. Charles S. Stewart wrote that some residents "of every class are warmly and decidedly our friends," and added that others, who were known for their determined hostility to the mission, "treat us personally with respect; and, often, with great kindness."[9] Officers from visiting vessels frequently called at the homes of the missionaries, where they were cordially welcomed and entertained with tea, conversation, and the singing of hymns.[10] Only rarely could the residents have been found there. For a few weeks in the summer of 1824, there was a friendly interchange of social calls between the mission and the foreign community. Two of the merchants, Stephen Reynolds and Thomas Crocker, visited the missionaries with some regularity,[11] and on one occasion the missionaries were entertained at dinner by Captain John Ebbets.[12] A few days later some twelve or fifteen foreigners were guests at the home of the missionaries. Although Stephen Reynolds and Levi Chamberlain agreed that the evening had passed "very agreeably,"[13] the experiment was seldom if ever repeated.

Each week the missionaries held preaching services in English for the benefit of a congregation which continually fluctuated in size. One well-informed missionary reported, in 1833, that some foreigners appeared "to wish us & our cause well,"[14] but with the exception of a few faithful attendants the mercantile community was sparsely represented at public worship. When the congregation was augmented by worshipers not connected with the mission, the visitors usually were devout or curious officers and seamen from ships in the harbor.[15] The evident sincerity and piety of a few of their visitors was a source of great satisfaction to the missionaries, who were accustomed to hearing their activities slighted or maligned; and one such visitor returned to his native land to publish an account of his voyage in which

[9] Stewart, *Private Journal of a Voyage to the Pacific*, pp. 160–161.

[10] Journal of Maria S. Loomis, 1820–1821, *passim*; Journal of Levi Chamberlain, 1823–1830, *passim*; Bingham, *Sandwich Islands*, p. 134.

[11] Journal of Stephen Reynolds, July 4, 11, 18, August 25, 1824.

[12] *Ibid.*, July 16, 1824.

[13] *Ibid.*, July 19, 1824; Journal of Levi Chamberlain, July 21, 1824.

[14] E. W. Clark to Evarts, Honolulu, September 14, 1833, in Letters to the American Board, LXVII, No. 140.

[15] Journal of Levi Chamberlain, 1823–1830, *passim*. In 1829 it was estimated that not more than one person in twenty among the foreigners in Honolulu attended public worship. Journal of Stephen Reynolds, February 15, 1829.

he warmly defended the missionaries as "the benefactors, not of the natives merely, but of the human race."[16] Among the influential merchants of the community, only James Hunnewell was consistent in attendance at public worship, and he alone appeared to covet the society and approval of the missionaries.[17] Indeed, so strong was the prejudice against the missionaries that some foreigners refused to call at their homes or to speak to them on the streets, and one missionary reported that visitors exposed only to the bias of the foreign community left the Islands to spread throughout the world "the most erroneous impression of our influence here, and, not unfrequently, the lowest slanders of our character."[18] Nevertheless, some of the most outspoken critics of the mission occasionally forgot their prejudices, and the reports of Levi Chamberlain to the Treasurer of the American Board annually listed as contributors to the mission men whose opposition to its policies was a matter of notoriety.[19]

By the summer of 1825 foreigners at Honolulu were confronted with ample evidence that the mission could rely upon the co-operation of the regency in any effort to effect a moral reformation throughout the Islands. During the preceding year unnecessary work on Sunday had been prohibited by local proclamations at Honolulu, Lahaina, and on the islands of Kauai and Niihau.[20] There seems to have been

[16] Benjamin Morrell, *A Narrative of Four Voyages* (New York, 1832), p. 157.

[17] In 1829 Hunnewell and two English ladies in Honolulu were said to be "the most constant attendants" at public worship. Journal of Levi Chamberlain, April 19, 1829. As early as 1820 the missionaries had characterized Hunnewell as "our constant friend"; four years later, Chamberlain wrote that his "kind attentions & his uniformly correct deportment have secured him the esteem of the missionaries." When, in 1830, Hunnewell left the Islands for the last time, Chamberlain again praised his conduct, declaring that he had shown himself "worthy of our esteem and he returns to America with an unblemished character." Journal of the Missionaries, December 26, 1820, in *Missionary Herald*, XVIII (July 1822), 204; Journal of Maria S. Loomis, December 14, 1820; Chamberlain to Evarts, Honolulu, December 14, 1824, November 19, 1830, in Letters to the American Board,

XXXI, No. 48, and LXVIII, No. 151. Cf. American Mission to Evarts, Oahu, December 28, 1822, *ibid.*, IX, No. 130; *Missionary Herald*, XXV (January 1829), 22 n.

[18] Stewart, *Private Journal of a Voyage to the Pacific*, p. 160.

[19] See the annual reports of Levi Chamberlain, from 1824 to 1831 inclusive, addressed to Henry Hill, Treasurer of the American Board, in Letters to the American Board, CXCI. Among the residents who made substantial gifts of money or goods to the mission were James Hunnewell, Stephen Reynolds, John C. Jones, Thomas Meek, and John Ebbets.

[20] Journal of the Missionaries at Honolulu, December 21, 1823, in *Missionary Herald*, XXI (June 1825), 173; Richards to the American Board, Lahaina, August 13, 1824, *ibid.*, XXII (August 1826), 240; Whitney to the American Board, Kauai, January 1824, *ibid.*, XX (October 1824), 317.

no substantial opposition to the enforcement of these decrees, and this lack of opposition doubtless emboldened the missionaries to hope that more far-reaching reforms might be instituted. They were also encouraged when two groups of visiting officers expressed the wish that vice and intemperance could be suppressed among the crews of vessels visiting Hawaiian ports.[21] In the meantime the missionaries, according to the recollections of Hiram Bingham, were making "great efforts . . . . to enlighten the public mind and particularly the minds of the rulers respecting the claims of the revealed word of God."[22] The death of Liholiho and the consequent continuation of the regency during the minority of Kamehameha III gave the missionaries the assurance that any program of moral reform which they might propose would receive sympathetic consideration. The views of Kalanimoku upon this question are uncertain, but he was personally friendly to the missionaries and he made no effort to thwart their wishes. The co-regent, the imperious Kaahumanu, was more positive in her support of the mission and its policies. In June 1824 she ordered the people at Lahaina to observe the sanctity of the Sabbath and to refrain from fighting, gambling, and murder.[23] A year later, in publicly commending the action of the chiefs at Kaawaloa, who had prohibited drunkenness in their district, she urged the other chiefs to enforce similar regulations.[24]

The increasing evidence that the Queen Regent was responsive to the views of the missionaries on controversial matters doubtless explains the growing apprehension in the foreign community and among some visitors. In June 1825 Lord Byron stated that he had been told that the missionaries proposed to submit a code for adoption by the chiefs,[25] and Eliab Grimes, a prominent trader, reported that the missionaries wished the chiefs to enact "a Code of laws . . . .

[21] Journal of Levi Chamberlain, March 27, 29, 1824; Journal of the Missionaries, March 29, November 6, 17, 1824, in *Missionary Herald*, XXI (July 1825), 210, XXII (January 1826), 15.

[22] Bingham to Evarts, Oahu, September 14, 1829, in Letters to the American Board, XXXI, No. 25. In February 1825 Levi Chamberlain and William Richards visited Governor Hoapili of Maui to discuss the evils arising from prostitution at the port of Lahaina. Other chiefs were present, and they agreed to do all in their power to put a stop to the practice. Journal of Levi Chamberlain, February 25, 1825.

[23] Richards to the American Board, Lahaina, August 13, 1824, in *Missionary Herald*, XXII (August 1826), 240.

[24] Bingham, *Sandwich Islands*, p. 269.

[25] [Graham, comp.], *Voyage of H.M.S. Blonde*, p. 155.

similar to the old Connecticut blue laws."[26] Bingham's vigorous denial of any intent to interfere in the political life of the nation apparently satisfied Byron; but it was soon evident that the missionaries had not renounced the intention of securing the support of the government for the sweeping moral reforms which they favored. At the close of June the chiefs agreed to suppress vice, intoxication, theft, and violations of the Sabbath.[27] In August public criers announced the determination of the chiefs that their subjects must attend school, observe the Sabbath, and attend public worship, and that gambling and adultery were forbidden.[28] This edict Bingham described as "a general prohibition of lewdness in the Sandwich Islands," and such it evidently was intended to be.[29] With reason, Levi Chamberlain commented that should this drastic decree be enforced "the indignation of the dissolute foreigners, which is beginning to kindle, will burst into a flame."[30]

The efforts of the mission and the regency to impose upon the community a rigid code of moral conduct served to emphasize the differences which separated missionary and merchant. When in August 1825 the new laws were announced, it seemed evident to the foreign residents that the missionaries had gained so great an ascendancy over the chiefs as to be able to dictate public policy.[31] Criticisms of the mission's political influence were said to have been "almost universal" among the merchants,[32] and some of the foreign residents complained that the mission had injured their business and that it had condoned dishonesty by admitting to membership in the church the chiefs who had refused to pay the sandalwood debts.[33] Residents and visitors alike recognized that the influence of the mission had become so great as to constitute a virtual union of church and state; and the missionary historian—Sheldon Dibble—conceded

[26] Grimes to Marshall, Oahu, June 7, 1825, in Marshall MSS.

[27] Journal of Levi Chamberlain, June 28, 1825.

[28] *Ibid.*, August 20, 1825.

[29] Bingham to Evarts, Oahu, September 14, 1829, in Letters to the American Board, XXXI, No. 25.

[30] Chamberlain to Evarts, Honolulu, August 27, 1825, in *ibid.*, XXXI, No. 55.

[31] Grimes to Marshall, Oahu, August 16, 1825, in Marshall MSS; Journal of Stephen Reynolds, August 27, 1825.

[32] Testimony of Charles H. Hammatt, in NRL, "Court Martial Records," XXIII, 1830, No. 531, p. 207.

[33] Journal of Levi Chamberlain, December 12, 1825.

that such a union "did exist to a very considerable extent, notwith-standing the constant endeavors of missionaries to prevent it."[34]

The growing hostility of the merchants toward the mission is suggested by the experience of Stephen Reynolds. Reynolds had become a resident of Honolulu in 1823. Throughout 1824 he was fre-quently present at public worship, and during the summer he occa-sionally called socially at the homes of the missionaries. The follow-ing year he could have been found less often at church, and his journal reveals an increasing irritation with the efforts of the missionaries to secure moral reforms through political action.[35] By the close of 1825 Reynolds was thoroughly suspicious of the motives and influence of the missionaries, and thereafter he was counted among the irreconcil-able opponents of the mission. The alienation of Reynolds virtually completed the isolation of the missionaries from their fellow country-men in the Islands.

Opponents of the mission's policies centered their attacks upon Hiram Bingham, and some of the residents circulated a petition ask-ing the King to expel him.[36] It was obvious to all interested persons that Bingham was the most trusted counselor of Kaahumanu and by many it was believed that he was principally responsible for the moral legislation sponsored by the regency. His conduct appeared to be in conflict with the instructions from the American Board, which re-quired him to avoid interference in the political life of the kindom, but he was too firmly convinced that it was the duty of government to foster education, religion, and private virtue to be overscrupulous

[34] Dibble, *History of the Sandwich Is-lands*, p. 78. This view is in contrast with that of Dibble's colleague, Hiram Bingham, who emphatically declared that "against the *union of church and state* the missionaries have, from the beginning, carefully and suc-cessfully guarded." Bingham, *Sandwich Is-lands*, p. 278.

[35] Journal of Stephen Reynolds, 1824–1825, *passim*.

[36] Journal of Levi Chamberlain, Septem-ber 5, 1826; Chamberlain to Evarts, Hono-lulu, September 11, 1826, in Letters to the American Board, XXXI, No. 65. This let-ter is printed in part, without identifica-tion of the author or of the critics of Bing-ham, in *Missionary Herald*, XXIII (July 1827), 203. Not all of the missionaries were as unpopular in the foreign community as was Bingham. Kotzebue, who was severe in his strictures upon the conduct and influ-ence of Bingham, described the Rev. C. S. Stewart as "a judicious and well-informed man" who had been unable to use his tal-ents effectively because of the dominance of Bingham and who therefore proposed to leave the Islands. Kotzebue, *New Voyage Round the World*, II, 256. When Stewart left Honolulu, in October 1825, foreigners gave him "many valuable presents," said to have been worth more than one hundred dollars. Journal of Levi Chamberlain, Oc-tober 17, 1825.

concerning the dangers of ecclesiastical domination.[37] So great was Bingham's influence with his colleagues and with the chiefs that some foreigners, perhaps with unintentional irony, sometimes referred to that staunch Congregationalist as "Bishop."[38] Less reasonable were the accusations that personal ambition outweighed his missionary zeal,[39] or that his aspirations did not stop short of the throne itself.[40]

The problems raised by the program of moral reform were complicated when the chiefs at Honolulu and Lahaina extended the decree against adultery to include a prohibition of the visits of women to vessels for purposes of prostitution. Few of the residents could have been directly affected by this interpretation of the law, although the merchants could complain that the new policy would reduce the amount of money in circulation in the Islands and hence would reduce the volume of retail sales. No such practical consideration was needed, however, to cause alarm in the foreign community. It was assumed that the chiefs had acted with the approval of the missionaries and that the latter had been responsible for the decision to prohibit prostitution. No other argument was required to insure the sympathy of many of the residents for any seamen who might protest against the loss of a privilege which they so long had enjoyed at all Hawaiian ports.

The protests were not lacking when the whalers returned from their summer cruising in the western Pacific. At Lahaina, in October, the crew of the "Daniel" resorted to threats of violence in a futile effort to secure a relaxation of the unpopular law.[41] At Honolulu, a group of twenty seamen visited Hiram Bingham and Kaahumanu to seek a modification of the government's policy. The explanation by Kaahumanu that the chiefs had become acquainted with the word of God and had learned that prostitution was sinful did not placate the seamen, who replied that they proposed to secure women and would

[37] Bingham, *Sandwich Islands*, pp. 278–282.

[38] Grimes to Marshall, Oahu, August 16, 1825, in Marshall MSS.

[39] Kotzebue, *New Voyage Round the World*, II, 255.

[40] Chamberlain to Hill, Honolulu, August 30, 1826, in Letters to the American Board, CXCI.

[41] The Mission to the American Board, Oahu, October 15, 1825, in *Missionary Herald*, XXII (July 1826), 208; Journal of William Richards, October 1825, *ibid.*, XXIII (February 1827), 40–42. Richards also noted that the decree against prostitution had not alienated all seamen visiting Lahaina, writing that "a considerable number of American whalers visited us, and were as polite and kind as usual."

use force if necessary.[42] The situation had become critical. Levi Chamberlain declared that "a virulent spirit existed against the mission," and the government assigned an armed guard to protect the homes of the missionaries.[43] There was no violence, possibly because the seamen were able to secure their objective without a resort to force. Competent witnesses differed widely as to the efficacy of the decree at Honolulu, but apparently it was enforced less rigidly there than at Lahaina. A number of Americans who had been in Honolulu late in 1825 or early in 1826 testified under oath at a naval court-martial that despite the decree women had openly visited ships in the harbor at Honolulu.[44] Three witnesses maintained that they knew of few or no instances in which the decree had been violated prior to its abrogation in February 1826.[45]

The question of reform legislation was revived at the close of 1825. On December 4 the regents were admitted to membership in the church at Honolulu; six days later it was reported that Bingham was in conference with them, "trying to have laws of his own put in force."[46] The following Sunday, Bingham "preached hard" against the chiefs who presumably were blocking his proposals,[47] and at the close of the service Kalanimoku arose and announced that the chiefs would convene on the following day to consider the adoption of new laws.[48] When the chiefs assembled, foreign residents and missionaries were present. That the missionaries favored the enactment of laws based upon the Decalogue admits of no doubt. Hiram Bingham had already shown a copy of the Commandments to Kalanimoku,

[42] Journal of Levi Chamberlain, October 4, 1825; The Mission to the American Board, Oahu, October 15, 1825, in *Missionary Herald*, XXII (June 1826), 208.

[43] Chamberlain to Hill, Honolulu, December 8, 1825, in Letters to the American Board, CXCI.

[44] Testimony of Thomas Dyer, in NRL, "Court Martial Records," XXIII, 1830, No. 531, p. 68; testimony of James D. Grover, in *ibid.*, pp. 70, 78, 81; testimony of Samuel B. Gibbs, in *ibid.*, p. 169; testimony of Benjamin Pickens, in *ibid.*, p. 202; testimony of Charles H. Hammatt, in *ibid.*, p. 207; testimony of Dixey Wildes, in *ibid.*, p. 212; testimony of Daniel Williams, in

ibid., pp. 223, 225; testimony of Thomas Spooner, in *ibid.*, pp. 230–231; testimony of Hiram Paulding, in *ibid.*, p. 321; testimony of Arthur Lewis, in *ibid.*, p. 343; testimony of Charles H. Davis, in *ibid.*, pp. 347–348; testimony of Nathaniel C. Lawrence, in *ibid.*, pp. 354–355.

[45] Testimony of Elisha Loomis, in *ibid.*, p. 118; testimony of Peleg Stetson, in *ibid.*, p. 145; deposition of William H. Haskins, in *ibid.*, Appendix No. 68.

[46] Journal of Stephen Reynolds, December 10, 1825.

[47] *Ibid.*, December 11, 1825.

[48] Journal of Levi Chamberlain, December 11, 1825.

with the pertinent comment that they were the laws of God, and during the deliberations of the chiefs he reminded them that Boki and others who had been in England had been told by King George that the word of God was worthy of respect and obedience. The regents would have been willing to accept this advice from their spiritual counselor, but the opposition of foreigners and of Governor Boki prevailed.[49] The council adjourned without taking action. On the following day, the mission published the Decalogue, with added advice on Christian living.[50]

The excitement occasioned by the debate on the proposed code had scarcely subsided when the community was plunged into fresh controversy and turmoil. In January 1826 the U.S.S. "Dolphin" arrived at Honolulu. From the moment that the "Dolphin" dropped anchor in the harbor, relations between the visitors and the missionaries were strained. Officers of the vessel were reported to have been surprised and perhaps offended when the missionaries failed to join their fellow countrymen at the waterfront to welcome the visitors.[51] The missionaries, in turn, were displeased when Lieutenant John Percival, the commander of the "Dolphin," insisted upon firing the customary salutes of courtesy on Sunday, disregarding the expressed wish of the native authorities to postpone that ceremony until the following day.[52]

Percival seems to have been willing to cultivate friendly relations with the missionaries, for he attended public worship and advised the chiefs to give attention to the instructions of the missionaries.[53] Being anxious to conclude agreements with the government concerning desertion and debts, he was more than willing to establish cordial relations with the chiefs. To this end, he provided "a course of liberal entertainments" for them.[54] His efforts to create good will were offset by his attempts to persuade the chiefs to modify the decree outlawing prostitution. In this he acted to appease a portion of his crew who

[49] Journal of Levi Chamberlain, December 12, 1825; testimony of Dixey Wildes, in NRL, "Court Martial Records," XXIII, 1830, No. 531, pp. 211–214; Bingham, *Sandwich Islands,* p. 282.

[50] Journal of Levi Chamberlain, December 13, 1825.

[51] Paulding, *Cruise of the Dolphin,* pp. 196–197.

[52] Bingham, *Sandwich Islands,* p. 284.

[53] Journal of Levi Chamberlain, February 19, 22, 1826.

[54] Percival to John Anderson, West Barnstable, [Massachusetts], January 17, 1833, in *House Reports,* 22d Cong., 2d Sess., No. 86, p. 6.

had become increasingly restless because of the refusal of the government to allow women to visit the "Dolphin."

Percival first sought an interview with the chiefs to urge them to make some concessions to his men.[55] Kaahumanu opposed any relaxation of the law,[56] and the chiefs sought to evade responsibility by asking the missionaries to advise them as to what answer should be made to Percival. It was the turn of the missionaries to be embarrassed. They could not conscientiously advise compliance with Percival's request, and they thought it inexpedient to take too firm a stand in opposition to it. Consequently they too evaded the issue by referring the chiefs to appropriate passages of Scripture.[57] The chiefs may have found comfort in this reply, but the seamen were less easily satisfied. On the following Sunday, February 26, a group from the "Dolphin"—probably augmented by men from other ships in the harbor and numbering altogether about fifty—attacked the homes of Kalanimoku and Bingham and assaulted the latter, whom they regarded as primarily responsible for their disappointments. A crowd of natives quickly assembled and more serious consequences were averted only when Percival intervened to restore order.[58] It was apparent that Percival was not wholly unsympathetic with his men,[59] and that same evening he visited Governor Boki to urge again the repeal of the decree against prostitution. This time Boki—who never had wholeheartedly favored its enforcement—complied, and women were again free to visit vessels at Honolulu.[60]

If the residents believed that the relaxation of the decree against

[55] Journal of Levi Chamberlain, February 22, 1826; Journal of Stephen Reynolds, February 22, 1826; Bingham and Chamberlain to Evarts, Oahu, June 12, 1828, in Letters to the American Board, XXXI, No. 76; Bingham, *Sandwich Islands*, pp. 284–286. According to Chamberlain, Percival "conversed very mildly" with the chiefs.

[56] Bingham, *Sandwich Islands*, pp. 285–286.

[57] Journal of Levi Chamberlain, February 23, 1826.

[58] *Ibid.*, February 26, 1826; Journal of John N. Colcord, pp. 66–67; The Mission to the American Board, Oahu, March 10, 1826, in *Missionary Herald*, XXII (December 1826), 370; Mrs. Bingham to the Rev.

and Mrs. Osgood, March 1, 1826, in Coan, *Life of Mrs. Sybil Moseley Bingham*, pp. 38–42; Bingham, *Sandwich Islands*, pp. 286–288; affidavit of Hiram Bingham, Honolulu, August 19, 1829, in Letters to the American Board, XXXI, No. 26. In a brief paragraph, Hiram Paulding, who was an officer on the "Dolphin," described this "most unpleasant occurrence," which he asserted "was afterwards unjustly and most ungenerously ascribed to the officers of the Dolphin." Paulding, *Cruise of the Dolphin*, pp. 225–226.

[59] Journal of Levi Chamberlain, February 26, 1826; testimony of Hiram Paulding, in NRL, "Court Martial Records," XXIII, 1830, No. 531, p. 303.

[60] Bingham, *Sandwich Islands*, p. 288.

prostitution represented the end of the reforms, they were soon disillusioned; for on April 1, while the "Dolphin" was still at Honolulu, the community was informed that the decree would again be enforced.[61] Three months later the campaign to establish the Decalogue as the basis of Hawaiian law was renewed when Bingham and Kaahumanu toured Oahu in an effort to win public favor for the proposal.[62] It was obvious that the missionaries would not be easily discouraged. They were concerned, however, lest the opposition of the foreign community result in a misrepresentation of their position.

At their general meeting in Honolulu in September, the missionaries appointed a committee to deliberate upon problems arising from the strained relations with the other foreigners in the Islands. In a lengthy report the committee declared that missionaries should abstain from all interference in the political life of the nation but qualified this statement by asserting that, however attached to their vices the Hawaiians might be, "we are not to cease lifting up our voices against them as destroyers both of temporal peace and eternal happiness." Explaining their position, the committee added that it was entirely proper for members of the mission to furnish "information and advice" about the arts or institutions of civilized states, to use their influence "to discountenance every vice, and encourage every virtue," that they should not be "indifferent to the kind and nature of the laws about to be promulgated," and that, should the chiefs desire to model their own statutes in accordance with divine requirements, it would become the duty of the mission "to make known to them the laws of God, as well as the nature of those codes of laws that are adopted by Christian nations." Adding a further note of warning that the missionaries should never assume to dictate to the chiefs in problems of legislation, the committee declared that they should not conceal that it was their purpose "to produce an entire change in the former state of things in these islands and to aim at nothing short of raising up the whole people to an elevated state of Christian civilization."[63]

[61] Journal of Levi Chamberlain, April 1, 1826.

[62] Chamberlain to Evarts, Honolulu, July 26, 1826, in Letters to the American Board, XXXI, No. 64, and in *Missionary Herald*, XXIII (July 1827), 206; Bingham, *Sandwich Islands*, pp. 294–297.

[63] Minutes of the General Meeting of the Sandwich Island Mission, September 27, 1826.

A month later the missionaries assumed a bold position in a circular letter, intended as a defense of their own course and a challenge to critical foreigners to investigate the activities of the mission or to prove that the missionaries had interfered improperly in political or commercial matters.[64] The challenge did not pass unnoticed. A group of the most persistent critics of the mission—including John C. Jones, Richard Charlton, Eliab Grimes, Stephen Reynolds, John Meek, John Dominis, and Dixey Wildes—suggested that the presence of the U.S.S. "Peacock" provided an opportunity for the investigation which the circular letter had invited.[65] More than a month intervened before the rival parties gathered to present charges and explanations. The correspondence which passed between the mission and its critics indicates that the missionaries hoped to compel the hostile residents to present formally as accusations the charges which were circulated freely in the foreign community on Oahu. The residents refused to act either as accusers or as investigators, declaring that they wished merely to have "a candid hearing" in which the missionaries might have an opportunity to defend their program for "correcting the evils which exist in this heathen land."[66]

Finally, on the morning of December 8, with Captain Jones of the "Peacock" and a crowd of curious spectators present, a delegation from the mission met a group of the foreign residents to discuss openly the charges which for several years had been told and retold throughout the foreign community and to credulous strangers. The stage was set for a dramatic interchange of accusations, but any among the spectators who had come to be entertained must have been disappointed. Charlton did express himself freely, declaring that he was very dissatisfied with the conduct and policies of the mission.

[64] A manuscript copy of this letter may be found in the file of "Historical and Miscellaneous Documents" in the Archives of Hawaii. It was printed in *Missionary Herald*, XXIII (August 1827), 240–242, and, in part, in Bingham, *Sandwich Islands*, pp. 300–301. It was dated October 3, 1826, but it was not publicly circulated until October 26. Stephen Reynolds noted (Journal of Stephen Reynolds, October 27, 1826), that it was sent to "all the residents and masters of vessels"; Levi Chamberlain observed that it caused "considerable excite-ment." Journal of Levi Chamberlain, October 26, 27, 1826.

[65] The original of this reply, undated, is in AH, "Historical and Miscellaneous Documents."

[66] Copies of all the correspondence are in Richards, Bingham, *et al.* to Evarts, Lahaina, December 18, 1826, in Letters to the American Board, XXXII, No. 250. A part of this correspondence may be found in AH, "Historical and Miscellaneous Documents."

Otherwise, the proceedings were very prosaic. Both groups appeared anxious that the other should bear the burden of proof. When the critics of the mission declined to reduce their charges to writing or to produce witnesses, Captain Jones chided them upon their failure to substantiate accusations which they had helped to circulate throughout the commercial world, and the meeting adjourned.[67] The missionaries regarded the entire episode as a vindication of their character and program, and Captain Jones wrote that the meeting had resulted in the "most perfect, full, complete, and triumphant victory for the missionaries that could have been asked by their most devoted friends."[68]

The verdict of Jones may be questioned, for no discussion had occurred and the missionaries had made no effort to defend themselves against the general charges advanced by Charlton. The advantage undoubtedly rested with the missionaries, who had unexpectedly won the confidence and sympathy of an important officer of the United States Navy. It was believed that strenuous efforts had been made to prejudice Jones against the missionaries.[69] His official report of his visit to Honolulu, however, described Bingham and his associates as "humble servants of the Lord," who were "scoffed at, reviled and calumniated by many English and Americans, who occasionally visit the scene of their operations, and all forsooth because they preach and teach against Idolatry, Adultery, Sabbath breaking, and all other vices incompatible to a moral well regulated Society."[70] The partiality of Jones for the missionaries did not pass unnoticed in Honolulu, and Stephen Reynolds recorded in his journal the discomfiting information that the captain was "very much . . . . in favor of Bingham," and had said that the latter "must and ought to have the lead."[71]

On January 6 Jones left Honolulu.[72] Four days earlier, in a letter

[67] Richards, Bingham, *et al.* to Evarts, Lahaina, December 18, 1826, in Letters to the American Board, XXXII, No. 250; Journal of Levi Chamberlain, December 8, 1826; Journal of Stephen Reynolds, December 8, 1826; Bingham, *Sandwich Islands*, p. 302.

[68] *Ibid.*, p. 303.

[69] Loomis to Evarts, Baltimore, June 24, 1827, in Letters to the American Board, XXXII, No. 188.

[70] NRL, "Report of the Peacock's Cruise to the Sandwich, Society and other Islands in the Pacific Ocean performed in the years 1826 and 27." This report was dated May 14, 1827.

[71] Journal of Stephen Reynolds, January 4, 1827.

[72] *Ibid.*, January 6, 1827.

marked by its cordiality and friendship, he had warned the missionaries of the danger of attempting too rapid a reform of Hawaiian
life, with the timely admonition that "coercive measures for . . . . the
repression of certain immoralities, seldom produce the desired effect."[73] This was pertinent advice and might well have been recalled
later by Bingham and his colleagues. At the time the letter was written, plans for further reforms were in abeyance while missionaries
and traders alike awaited with anxiety lest the serious illness of Kalanimoku should have a fatal termination.

As it became increasingly evident that the death of the co-regent
could not long be postponed, the hopes and fears of the missionaries
and of their critics turned to Kaahumanu and Boki. The Queen
Regent was generally unpopular with the foreign residents, who had
ample cause to fear that she would be subservient to the missionaries
and indifferent to the payment of the sandalwood debt. Opponents of
Kaahumanu found a willing and pliable aspirant for the regency in
the person of Boki. He was a brother of Kalanimoku and he had
been an intimate friend of Liholiho. Thus fortunately placed, he
had risen to the responsible post of Governor of Oahu. He had accompanied Liholiho to England, whence he had returned enhanced
in prestige and experience and, presumably, richer in knowledge and
wisdom.

For a time, Boki had appeared friendly to the missionaries; but
by the summer of 1826 the relations of the Governor and the mission
were seriously strained. The missionaries believed that he had played
an important part in blocking the adoption by the chiefs of a comprehensive program of moral reforms. In November, covert suspicion
became open hostility after the missionaries at Honolulu had publicly
condemned gambling—a pastime to which Boki was much addicted.
In reply he accused the missionaries of having vilified his character.
Three days later, accompanied by the King, Charlton, J. C. Jones,
and other foreigners, he went to Manoa Valley, where these critics of
the mission compared their grievances.[74] In December it was reported in Honolulu that Boki was planning a rebellion which would

[73] Jones to the Sandwich Island Mission, Oahu, January 2, 1827 (copy), in Letters to the American Board, XXXII, No. 199.

[74] Chamberlain to Evarts, Honolulu, February 22, 1827, *ibid.*, XXXI, No. 67; Journal of Levi Chamberlain, November 11–16, 1826.

drive Kaahumanu from the regency,[75] and one friendly visitor declared that the Governor had assembled troops at the fort.[76] Whatever may have been Boki's intentions, he was, as usual, timid. When, in February, news reached Honolulu that Kalanimoku was dead, the tidings had been so long expected that they caused no disturbance.[77] Boki immediately acknowledged the supremacy of Kaahumanu,[78] and Levi Chamberlain reported that from all appearances "peace and order are likely to prevail."[79]

In the following July a new element was introduced into the complex politics of Honolulu by the arrival of a group of French missionaries and artisans, who were intended to form the nucleus of a French colony in the Hawaiian Islands and perhaps a center from which French influence might radiate throughout the central Pacific.[80] The little colony was the result of the activities of Jean Rives.[81] Rives had been a companion of Liholiho, whom he had accompanied to England. Following the death of the King, Rives crossed the Channel to his native France, where he represented himself as a person of great influence with the Hawaiian government. He succeeded in interesting a group of speculators in a commercial colony which he proposed to establish in the Hawaiian Islands. His impositions were equally successful in official circles, where influential subordinates in the Bureau of Commerce and Colonies and in

[75] Journal of Levi Chamberlain, December 20, 1826.

[76] Beechey, *Voyage to the Pacific*, II, 110.

[77] Jones to Marshall, Oahu, March 6, 1827, in Marshall MSS.

[78] Journal of Levi Chamberlain, February 13, 1827. Evidently Boki's submission to Kaahumanu was not generally known in Honolulu, for at the close of February Richard Charlton wrote that "Boki has succeeded to the Regency, and appears likely to govern with justice and moderation." Charlton to Planta, Oahu, February 27, 1827, in *Correspondence Relative to the Sandwich Islands*, p. 18. The uncertainty surrounding the actual composition of the Hawaiian government is illustrated by the fact that two visitors to Honolulu, one in 1826–1827 and the other in 1828, believed that Boki was in fact the regent. Beechey, *Voyage to the Pacific*, II, 113; Duhaut-Cilly, *Voyage Autour du Monde*, II, 261, 263–264.

[79] Chamberlain to Evarts, Honolulu, February 22, 1827, in Letters to the American Board, XXXI, No. 67.

[80] George Verne Blue, "The Project for a French Settlement in the Hawaiian Islands, 1824–1842," in *Pacific Historical Review*, II (March 1933), 85–89.

[81] Jean Rives arrived at the Hawaiian Islands "about 1804" (Taylor, *Under Hawaiian Skies*, p. 199), but until the accession of Liholiho to the throne he remained in obscurity. His later claims of extraordinary influence in the Hawaiian government probably were based upon his intimacy with Liholiho. John C. Jones wrote that Rives "is the King's right hand man, and whatever he says is law." Jones to Marshall and Wildes, Honolulu, July 6, 1821, in Massachusetts Historical Society, *Proceedings*, LIV, 33.

the Ministry of Foreign Affairs embraced the opportunity for planting a French colony in the mid-Pacific. The religious order of the
Society of Picpus provided priests, who it was hoped would serve in
the dual capacity of confessors for the colonists and missionaries to
the Hawaiian people.[82]

The little group of missionaries and colonists was dogged by disappointment. When they arrived at Honolulu, Rives was not there
to greet them, nor did he ever again set foot on Hawaiian soil. The
failure of Rives to meet them at Honolulu left the newcomers in a
precarious position. They were without resources or friends, and
their presence was unwelcome to the powerful American missionaries,
who could not view with equanimity the establishment of a French
Catholic colony in a country where Protestantism seemed to be on
the eve of triumph. They were without land which the agriculturists
could cultivate and without the means of selling the cargo which they
had brought from France. Their situation was somewhat improved
when Boki assured them that they should enjoy his protection,[83] but
it was far from secure. They evaded hearing an order to leave the
Islands only because they "prudently neglected to answer" a sum-
mons from Kaahumanu,[84] and they escaped deportation because the
master of the vessel on which they had come to the Islands refused to
carry them away.[85]

Their continued presence at Honolulu was in defiance of the
known will of the Queen Regent. They had the tacit support of Boki,
who redeemed his early promise of friendship by granting them as
much land as they were able to cultivate.[86] They also had the sympathy of some of the foreign residents who disliked the American
mission, and three of the residents—John C. Jones, Stephen Reynolds,
and John Ebbets—presented their children to the priests for baptism, a gesture indicative of their antipathy against the American

[82] Duhaut - Cilly, *Voyage Autour du
Monde*, I, Introduction; Blue, *loc. cit.*, pp.
86–89; Reginald Yzendoorn, *History of the
Catholic Mission in Hawaii* (Honolulu,
1927), pp. 28–31; *Annales de la Propagation de la Foi*, VIII (July 1835), 6. The
three priests were Fathers Alexis Bachelot,
Abraham Armand, and Patrick Short.
Bachelot was designated as Apostolic Pre-
fect.

[83] *Suppliment to the Sandwich Island
Mirror*, January 15, 1840, pp. 7–8.

[84] Yzendoorn, *History of the Catholic
Mission in Hawaii*, p. 36.

[85] Journal of Levi Chamberlain, July 17,
23, 1827; Journal of Stephen Reynolds,
July 17, 1827.

[86] *Ibid.*, July 30, 1827.

missionaries.[87] Until the end of 1827 the priests generally remained in seclusion in order not to attract unfavorable attention from the chiefs, but the lay members of the colony were active in their several trades.[88] There were occasional rumors that the chiefs were contemplating some action against the priests;[89] but more than three years passed before the government made a serious effort to remove them from Honolulu. While free from any overt interference by the chiefs, the little colony was weakened by the departure of some of its number. Within six months after their arrival, the superintendent and two of the artisans left the Islands; and during 1829 the colony lost one priest and one lay member.[90]

Gradually the priests attracted the attention of curious natives to whom the ornaments and habits of the missionaries were a matter of novelty and interest. In January 1828 they opened a small chapel, and by the close of the year they had baptized seventeen persons, only five of whom were adults. The following year they were more successful, with eighty-two baptisms during the first seven months of 1829. Thereafter the number declined noticeably—a development attributed by the historian of the Catholic mission to "the acute persecution" of 1830 and 1831. During the four years from the arrival of the priests at Honolulu in 1827 to their expulsion from the Islands at the close of 1831, they found only thirty-five adult men in good health who desired to receive baptism.[91] Barring some turn of fortune which might end the regency of Kaahumanu, it was apparent that the Catholic mission could not immediately become a formidable competitor of the well-established American mission.[92]

[87] Journal of Stephen Reynolds, December 25, 1827, September 14, 1828; Duhaut-Cilly, *Voyage Autour du Monde,* II, 305.

[88] Chamberlain to Anderson, Honolulu, September 14, 1827, in Letters to the American Board, XXXI, No. 70.

[89] Journal of Stephen Reynolds, May 17, 1828; Blue, *loc. cit.,* p. 93.

[90] *Ibid.,* pp. 92, 93, 95.

[91] Yzendoorn, *History of the Catholic Mission in Hawaii,* pp. 41–43, 59, 72.

[92] Apparently Hiram Bingham took some comfort in this belief, for he assured a former colleague that the influence of Kaahumanu would deter all but the boldest of her subjects from embracing Catholicism.

Bingham to the Rev. Charles Stewart, Oahu, September 29, 1828, in "Missionary Letters" (typed manuscript, Hawaiian Mission Children's Society Library, Honolulu), II, 355.

One friend of the Catholic mission believed that the great opportunity for the priests would come with the death of Kaahumanu, and that should they win the favor of the young King they might anticipate an easy triumph over their American rivals; should they fail to gain the approval of the King, then both they and the American missionaries might be expelled. Duhaut-Cilly, *Voyage Autour du Monde,* II, 288–289.

With the settlement of Catholic missionaries in the Islands the American mission was confronted with a delicate problem. The American missionaries had inherited in full measure the distrust of "papists" which was traditional in New England and among Calvinists everywhere. They regarded the priests at Honolulu as "dangerous to the civil government of these islands . . . . as exerting a deadly influence in drawing away souls from God's word; as hinderers of the progress of the people in civilization and literature; as enemies of sound morality, and as enemies of the Religion of Jesus Christ."[93] They did not doubt that it was their duty to adopt effective measures to nullify the influence of their Catholic rivals; but they were without specific instructions from the American Board, and some of their number would have been pleased to avoid a policy which might be condemned as savoring of persecution.

Upon learning that Catholic missionaries were on the way to the Islands, Hiram Bingham had asked the Board for instructions as to how this unwelcome competition should be met.[94] Until an answer was received from Boston, the missionaries in the Islands were compelled to formulate their own policies. A few gestures of friendship toward the newcomers may have been indicative of the hesitancy with which Bingham and his associates embarked upon an openly anti-Catholic policy.[95] When these offers of friendship were rebuffed, some of the American missionaries adopted more aggressive tactics. Sermons were utilized to condemn idolatry or to outline the history of the primitive church in such a manner as to expose the alleged departure of the church at Rome from the paths of truth, and the mission press published a geography contrasting the unhappy conditions existing in Catholic countries with the progress and prosperity of Protestant nations.[96] These measures were approved by the American Board, whose policy was well summarized in a resolution, adopted in 1840, declaring that it had been the obligation of its

---

[93] *Minutes of a General Meeting of the Sandwich Island Mission*, 1830, p. 32. Hiram Bingham characterized Catholicism as "a foreign superstition" which was "subversive of the Gospel." Bingham, *Sandwich Islands*, pp. 311, 414.

[94] Bingham to Evarts, Oahu, June 29, 1827, in Letters to the American Board, XXXI, No. 12.

[95] Yzendoorn, *History of the Catholic Mission in Hawaii*, pp. 36–37.

[96] Bingham to Anderson, Honolulu, May 15, 1839, in Letters to the American Board, CXXXV, No. 9.

missionaries as "faithful protestant ministers and teachers" to warn the people against "the great and leading errors" of Catholicism.[97]

Meanwhile a series of trivial incidents involving William Richards and the influence of the missionaries at Lahaina had revived the latent hostility between the mission and the foreign community. Like many of his colleagues, Richards frequently offered the natives cloth or other articles of trade in exchange for produce or labor. For this he was criticized on the ground that he had interfered with the normal course of trade at Lahaina.[98] He also encountered criticism when he sold potatoes and firewood to visiting vessels. The prices which he set for his potatoes and wood became the standard prices asked and received by the chiefs at that port, and friends of Richards defended his action as having enabled the chiefs to obtain a fair return for their produce. So greatly did rumor distort the situation that nearly a quarter of a century later seamen visiting Lahaina heard reports that the missionaries there had reaped huge profits through the sale of wood.[99]

Still further criticism of Richards followed a clash between the crew of the "John Palmer" and the authorities at Lahaina, caused by the unsuccessful attempt of Governor Hoapili to prevent native women from visiting the vessel.[100] News of this incident reached Honolulu late in October 1827; the following day Levi Chamberlain noted the existence of considerable resentment in the foreign community.[101] The difficulties of the "John Palmer" were soon obscured by a more serious charge against Richards.

In August, foreigners at Honolulu had been startled to find in an issue of the *New York Observer* an account of the almost forgotten difficulties of the "Daniel" at Lahaina.[102] This version of the episode, which many in Honolulu professed to regard as unjust to Captain Buckle, was attributed to Richards; and when Buckle returned to

[97] *Report of the American Board*, 1840, pp. 35–37.

[98] Journal of Stephen Reynolds, April 17, 1827; Journal of Levi Chamberlain, May 20, 1827.

[99] *Ibid.*, March 28, 1827; Dwight Baldwin to Anderson, Honolulu, April 21, 1849, in Letters to the American Board, CCXXXIII, No. 183.

[100] For accounts of this incident, see Richards to the American Board, Honolulu, December 6, 1827, *ibid.*, XXXII, No. 138; Hoapili to Kaahumanu, Lahaina, October 24, 1827, in *Missionary Herald*, XXIV (September 1828), 276–277; Bingham, *Sandwich Islands*, pp. 313–314.

[101] Journal of Levi Chamberlain, October 25, 26, 1827.

[102] Journal of Stephen Reynolds, August 4, 1827.

Honolulu, late in October 1827, he threatened to go to Lahaina to secure redress from Richards.[103] Kaahumanu thereupon summoned Richards and the principal chiefs to Honolulu.[104] The little community was soon filled with rumors and speculations as to the purposes of the Regent in convening a council. Stephen Reynolds heard a report that Richards was to be "tried by his countrymen," and some of the natives gave credence to a story that the accused missionary faced banishment or death.[105] Few outside of the mission were aware that more than a hearing of the charges against Richards was involved.

The "trial" of Richards was little short of a farce, and after some hesitation the chiefs agreed that the charges against him should be dropped.[106] Their decision did not improve the relations between the mission and the foreign community, nor did it remove the immediate cause of the complaints of the residents. For a number of years thereafter, the publication in American journals of articles written by missionaries and reflecting upon the character or conduct of foreigners in the Islands was a source of continued discord in Honolulu and a principal item in the list of grievances from which traders and visitors claimed they suffered.[107]

The presence in Honolulu of the principal chiefs was utilized by Kaahumanu to secure a consideration of policies which she and her missionary advisers were anxious to have incorporated in the law of the land. Her intentions were not unknown to the missionaries; and early in November, when the chiefs were being summoned to hear the charges against Richards, Levi Chamberlain was aware that other "very important business" would also be discussed.[108] The foreign residents, in general, were not so well informed, and apparently they viewed the assembling of the chiefs without alarm.[109] Within a week their complacency was shaken. On the first of December the chiefs

---

[103] Journal of Levi Chamberlain, October 27, 1827.

[104] *Ibid.*, November 3, 1827; Bingham, *Sandwich Islands*, p. 317.

[105] Journal of Stephen Reynolds, November 6, 1827; Journal of Levi Chamberlain, November 1, 5, 1827.

[106] *Ibid.*, November 26, 1827; Richards to the American Board, Honolulu, December 6, 1827, in Letters to the American Board, XXXII, No. 138; *Missionary Her-*

ald, XXIV (September 1828), 279–280; Bingham, *Sandwich Islands*, pp. 318–319.

[107] Journal of Levi Chamberlain, May 5, December 9, 1828, June 1, 1829; Journal of Stephen Reynolds, May 31, June 1, 1829, March 18, 1833.

[108] Journal of Levi Chamberlain, November 3, 1827.

[109] John C. Jones, usually one of the best-informed of the foreign residents, reported casually the day before the meeting

debated the enactment of "some general laws" proposed by Kaahumanu. Hiram Bingham was present by invitation to give his opinion
as to whether or not the laws were in conformity with Biblical precepts,[110] a fact which was sufficient to cause concern in the foreign
community. No action was taken at this meeting; but six days later
the chiefs agreed to prohibit murder, theft, adultery, prostitution,
gambling, and the sale of spirituous liquors.[111] When the decision of
the chiefs was publicly announced on December 14, only the prohibitions of murder, theft, and adultery were proclaimed as law. Opposition from foreigners in Honolulu had compelled Kaahumanu to
postpone the enforcement of other parts of the new code. It was announced, however, that after the other laws had been explained to
the people they might be enforced, and Hiram Bingham took comfort
from the knowledge that many of the chiefs wished "to suppress the
dram shops, and to put a stop to drunkenness, as well as to the evils
connected with horse-racing, billiards, cards, &c."[112] Nearly fifteen
months elapsed before the regency announced its determination to
enforce, in modified form, the remainder of the code of December
1827.[113]

of the chiefs that the impending council
would consider "some changes" in the government and would discuss the debts; but
there is no indication that Jones realized
the significance of the changes which were
being proposed. Jones to Marshall, Oahu,
November 30, 1827, in Marshall MSS.

[110] Journal of Levi Chamberlain, December 1, 1827.

[111] *Ibid.*, December 7, 1827. Boki objected to the adoption of these laws without consulting the British government
(*ibid.*, December 8, 1827), an objection
which may have been suggested by Charlton, who is reported to have told the chiefs
that they should pass no laws until after
they had consulted King George. David
Malo to Elisha Loomis, Honolulu, December 11, 1827, in Letters to the American
Board, XXXII, No. 204.

[112] Bingham to the American Board,
Honolulu, December 15, 1827, in *Missionary
Herald*, XXIV (July 1828), 209–210; Journal of Stephen Reynolds, December 14,
1827; Journal of Levi Chamberlain, December 14, 1827. The exact form of the

laws of December 1827 is open to question,
as printed copies of those laws now extant
differ slightly. Their meaning is identical.
Murder was declared to be a capital crime;
those guilty of theft were to be placed in
irons; imprisonment was prescribed for
those guilty of selling liquor or of gambling; and prostitution was punishable by
a fine. Printed copies of this early code
may be found in the file of the laws in the
Archives of Hawaii. The missionaries described these decrees as "the first regular
laws that ever existed on the Sandwich Islands." *Missionary Herald*, XXV (June
1829), 181. A year later, in December 1828,
a Catholic missionary noted that there were
some five or six published laws but regarded them as unimportant—for, as he
said, the wish of a chief was more effective than any possible code might be. Letter of the Rev. Alexis Bachelot, quoted by
Francis Furey in *Records of the American
Catholic Historical Society*, XLV (March
1934), 88.

[113] The revised laws, as proclaimed in
March 1829, prohibited intoxication and

The new decrees as proclaimed and enforced did not directly affect the placid lives of the foreign residents. The latter, however, could not be indifferent to governmental policies which threatened to curtail sales or to reduce the amount of money in circulation. They therefore viewed with misgivings the enforcement of the laws prohibiting intoxication and prostitution, but the fear that those laws might injure merchants already established in the retail trade was not confirmed by the experience of those whose business consisted chiefly in the sale of spirituous liquors. At the close of 1829 the British Consul reported that the number of saloons in Honolulu had "greatly increased." Among the owners of saloons he listed the young King and Governor Boki.[114]

The success of Kaahumanu in enforcing her policies was dependent to a very considerable extent upon her ability to persuade Boki to acquiesce in a program with which he was not in sympathy. In this, the Regent faced no easy task. Boki was restless and ambitious, and he coveted the good will of the foreign residents. He was the only chief to whom opponents of Kaahumanu's policies could turn with any reasonable hope that the will of the Regent could be thwarted; and his open friendship with avowed enemies of the regency kept Honolulu in a mild state of excitement, which occasionally was enlivened by threats of violence.[115] Such a situation developed early in April 1829, when there were visible preparations for armed conflict[116] and a few excitable foreigners "talked of immediate war, and of their readiness to take arms."[117] There were rumors that an effort would be made—presumably by friends of Kaahumanu—to depose the King and to elevate his half-sister, Kinau, or her son to the throne; and Boki added to the general confusion and alarm by confiding to his friends in the foreign community that there was constant

prostitution. Journal of Levi Chamberlain, March 2, 1829; Journal of Stephen Reynolds, March 2, 1829.

[114] Charlton to Aberdeen, Oahu, November 28, 1829, in *Correspondence Relative to the Sandwich Islands*, p. 23.

[115] In July 1828 there were reports that Charlton had threatened to kill Kaahumanu and had declared that all foreigners on Oahu would join him. This vain boast was properly estimated by Stephen Reynolds, who commented that Charlton "may be ready to take up arms against the chiefs, but few, if any, I believe, would follow him or join him." Journal of Stephen Reynolds, July 13, 1828.

[116] Journal of Levi Chamberlain, April 4, 1829.

[117] Bingham, *Sandwich Islands*, p. 343.

danger that all foreigners would be massacred.[118] Had Boki been more resolute, or had his support been more general, civil war could have been avoided only with difficulty. The threatened hostilities never materialized. The excited boasts of a few foreigners and the passive sympathy of many others constituted the strength of Boki's cause, for nearly all the influential chiefs were known to be friendly to Kaahumanu.

Boki seems to have recognized the weakness of his position, and he offered no opposition when Hiram Bingham sought to arrange a reconciliation with the Regent. In an atmosphere of dramatic simplicity the two contenders for the control of the government met at the home of Hiram Bingham to sing hymns and to consider their problems. Bingham, in recounting this historic meeting, made no mention of any discussion of the political problems that so vitally concerned the two chiefs. He asserted merely that as a result of his intervention Boki "proposed to attend again to instruction" and "concurred with Kaahumanu and the people connected with my station in the erection of a church."[119] Kaahumanu was still supreme in the government of the Islands. Boki retained his dual position as Governor of Oahu and guardian of the youthful King, but he exercised little influence in the determination of Hawaiian policy. Before the close of the year he left the Islands, never to return.

The submission of Boki left Kaahumanu free to embark upon bolder policies than any which hitherto had been expedient. In August she gave a pointed hint of her attitude toward the Catholic mission when she ordered the priests to discontinue public worship.[120] The anti-Catholic program remained in abeyance, however, while the government, under the leadership of the Regent, attempted to impose its will upon foreigners within its jurisdiction. The first indication of so radical a departure in public policy came late in September 1829, when the chiefs ordered all couples not properly married to separate and announced that this edict must be obeyed by foreigners as well as by natives.[121] Before the foreign residents could protest

[118] Journal of Levi Chamberlain, April 4, 1829; Journal of Stephen Reynolds, April 1, 1829.

[119] Bingham, *Sandwich Islands*, p. 343.

[120] Journal of Levi Chamberlain, August 8, 10, 1829; Journal of Stephen Reynolds, August 9, 1829.

[121] This edict, dated September 21, 1829, may be found in the file of the laws in the Archives of Hawaii.

this unexpected invasion of their personal liberties, the whole problem of Hawaiian jurisdiction over foreigners in the Islands was precipitated by a petty dispute concerning a cow.

The cow was the property of a foreign resident. It had been killed by a native who resented the freedom with which the animal invaded his fields, and this seemingly minor incident so enraged Charlton and John C. Jones that they undertook to punish the offending native with unusual severity.[122] So flagrant a disregard of constituted authority could not fail to arouse resentment among friends of the Regent. Their displeasure was not abated when Charlton and those who agreed with him addressed a lengthy memorial to the King, protesting that the killing of a cow indicated that their property and indeed their lives were in jeopardy.[123] In reply, the government published a declaration signed by the King, Kaahumanu, and ten of the principal chiefs, condemning the infliction of injury upon the native by private persons without trial. This declaration contained two statements not calculated to conciliate the opponents of the government. All laws, it asserted, applied equally to natives and to foreign residents; more offensive to some was a repetition of the recently promulgated order that all couples who did not regard themselves as married must immediately separate.[124]

On October 13, six days after the government had issued this reply to the memorialists, the U.S.S. "Vincennes," commanded by Captain W. C. B. Finch, dropped anchor outside the harbor at Honolulu.[125] The following day, Finch was formally received by the King, to whom he read an official communication signed by the Secretary of the Navy, Samuel L. Southard. The Rev. Charles S. Stewart, who was present, reported that both the King and Kaahumanu were visibly affected by the cordial expressions of good will which this letter

[122] Kauikeaouli *et al.* to Finch, Honolulu, October 30, 1829, in NRL, "Capt. Finch's Cruise of the U.S.S. Vincennes," and printed in Stewart, *Visit to the South Seas,* II, 196–198. See also *ibid.,* II, 150–152, and Bingham, *Sandwich Islands,* p. 350.

[123] *Ibid.;* Stewart, *Visit to the South Seas,* II, 152.

[124] Printed copies of this declaration, dated Oahu, October 7, 1829, may be found filed with the laws in the Archives of Hawaii, and it is printed in Bingham, *Sandwich Islands,* pp. 351–352; Stewart, *Visit to the South Seas,* II, 153–156; *British and Foreign State Papers,* XVII (London, 1832), 1248–1249. According to a rumor, credited by Stephen Reynolds, the declaration of the chiefs had been dictated by Hiram Bingham. Journal of Stephen Reynolds, October 8, 1829.

[125] Stewart, *Visit to the South Seas,* II, 114.

contained.[126] They might well have been satisfied, for Secretary Southard wrote that the President of the United States

has heard with admiration and interest of the rapid progress which has been made by your people in acquiring a knowledge of letters and of the True Religion—the Religion of the Christian's Bible. These are the best and the only means, by which the prosperity and happiness of Nations can be advanced and continued, and the President and all men everywhere, who wish well to yourself and your people, earnestly hope that you will continue to cultivate them, and to protect and encourage those by whom they are brought to you.

The President also anxiously hopes that peace, and kindness, and justice will prevail between your people and those Citizens of the United States who visit your Islands, and that the regulations of your Government will be such as to enforce them upon all.

Our Citizens who violate your laws, or interfere with your regulations, violate at the same time their duty to their own Government and Country, and merit censure and punishment. We have heard with pain that this has sometimes been the case, and we have sought to know and to punish those who are guilty. Captain Finch is commanded diligently to enquire into the conduct of our Citizens, whom he may find at the Islands, and as far as he has the authority to insure proper conduct and deportment from them.[127]

The assurance that Americans who violated Hawaiian laws merited "censure and punishment" and that Finch was instructed "to insure proper conduct and deportment" by American citizens in the Islands was accepted too literally by the native rulers. They addressed a communication to Finch, complaining of the conduct of John C. Jones and William French, and requesting him to "bring them to a full account here" or to inform the chiefs as to "the proper course that we are to take."[128] Finch could only advise the King to refer any such complaints to the President,[129] but apparently the

[126] Stewart, *Visit to the South Seas*, II, 125–130.

[127] Southard to Kamehameha III, Washington, January 20, 1829, in AH, F.O. and Ex. This letter has been printed many times, and may be found in whole or in part in *British and Foreign State Papers*, XVII, 1249–1250; *Appendix to the Report of the Minister of Foreign Relations* [Hawaiian Islands], 1851, p. 127; *Polynesian*, December 13, 1845; Bingham, *Sandwich Islands*, pp. 355–356; Stewart, *Visit to the South Seas*, II, 127–129. A list of the presents which Finch brought from the United States to be distributed among the principal chiefs may be found in *Niles' Register*, XXXV (February 14, 1829), 403.

[128] Kauikeaouli *et al.* to Finch, Honolulu, October 30, 1829, in NRL, "Capt. Finch's Cruise of the U.S.S. Vincennes." A copy may be found in AH, F.O. and Ex., and it is printed in Stewart, *Visit to the South Seas*, II, 196–198.

[129] Finch to Kauikeaouli, Honolulu, November 3, 1829 (copy), in NRL, "Capt.

chiefs were satisfied with this answer. Before the "Vincennes" left Oahu, the King addressed a letter to the President, expressing gratitude for the presents which had been sent, declaring that he recalled his interview with Finch with pleasure, and expressing the hope that the relations of the two nations might be marked by perpetual peace and mutual justice and prosperity.[130]

The American missionaries likewise had reason to be pleased with the results of the visit of Finch. Although Charlton and Jones had criticized the mission in the presence of the officers from the "Vincennes,"[131] Finch had been on the most cordial terms with the missionaries at Honolulu.[132] In his official report he defended both the native authorities and the American missionaries, declaring that he was "at a loss to decide wherein the foreign residents have just cause to complain of or contemn the government of the Sandwich Islands." Continuing, he reported that the "constant complaining against the missionaries is irksome in the extreme," and that although the missionaries were perhaps too literal in their efforts to transfer the Mosaic commandments to the mid-Pacific, "the evil will ultimately correct itself, by the very tuition which they afford the inhabitants, more certainly and effectually than by the denunciation and declamation of foreigners, who are interested and temporary sojourners, without other than monied transactions to engage the confidence of the natives."[133]

This report was written after Finch left Honolulu. Its contents would have offended the foreign residents could they have read it. It is unlikely that they would have been surprised, for already they had characterized the visit of the "Vincennes" as a "missionary visit."[134] They had not accepted their discomfiture without a protest. In a communication to the government at Washington, a representative group

Finch's Cruise of the U.S.S. Vincennes." It is printed in Stewart, *Visit to the South Seas*, II, 198–200.

[130] Kamehameha III to the President of the United States, November 23, 1829, in Bingham, *Sandwich Islands*, pp. 359–360.

[131] Memorandum of C. S. Stewart, August 12, 1830, in Letters to the American Board, XXXII, No. 151.

[132] Journal of Levi Chamberlain, October 17, 19, 30, 31, November 3, 1829; General Letter of the Mission, February 20, 1830, in *Missionary Herald*, XXVI (October 1830), 312–313.

[133] Finch to Secretary of the Navy Branch, December 1, 1829, in NRL, "Capt. Finch's Cruise of the U.S.S. Vincennes." This letter is printed in Stewart, *Visit to the South Seas*, II, 268–280.

[134] Finch to Branch, Honolulu, November 22, 1829, in NRL, "Capt. Finch's Cruise of the U.S.S. Vincennes."

of foreigners at Honolulu attacked the spirit and contents of the letter from Secretary Southard. They declared that the statement that American citizens were subject to Hawaiian law would give the chiefs an undue sense of power and authority and might encourage them to enact measures displeasing to foreigners. They condemned the praise of the missionaries as the disseminators of the "true religion," as that might cause the chiefs to penalize or exclude other faiths and thus deprive foreigners of the opportunity of worshiping as they chose. Finally, they insisted that officers of American men-of-war should confine their activities to the protection of American commerce and refrain from any action calculated to promote the interests of any religious faith or group.[135]

The echo of the parting salutes had scarcely died before Boki was again in the midst of ill-fated schemes for personal aggrandizement. In November 1829 a vessel from New South Wales touched at Honolulu and the members of its crew spread the interesting and agreeable rumor that the New Hebrides Islands abounded in valuable sandalwood. To Boki, who was heavily indebted to the merchants of Honolulu, the prospect of exploiting this new source of income was attractive. In the hope of recouping his waning fortunes, and perhaps of forgetting his political embarrassment, Boki left Oahu in December 1829 upon a venture which was destined to be fatal to him and to nearly all of those who accompanied him.[136]

Upon Boki's departure from the Islands, his wife, Liliha, succeeded to his position as Governor of Oahu. She inherited also his feud with Kaahumanu and his ambition to supplant the dowager Queen in the regency. She was believed to have considerable influence with the King,[137] and she may have received some sympathy

[135] John Ebbets, William French, Stephen Reynolds, A. B. Thompson, William B. Blanchard, John Meek, N. Spear, William R. Warren, and Charles R. Smith to the Secretary of State of the United States, Honolulu, November 10, 1829, *ibid.*

[136] Chamberlain to the American Board, Honolulu, August 16, 1830, in *Missionary Herald*, XXVII (April 1831), 121–122; Bingham, *Sandwich Islands*, pp. 361–362. The fate of Boki has never been definitely known. Boki's expedition consisted of two vessels. After touching at one of the Fiji Islands, the two vessels separated, and the one on which Boki sailed disappeared without leaving any clue as to its fate. It has been suggested that he may have reached some island of the South Pacific and have chosen to remain there (Yzendoorn, *History of the Catholic Mission in Hawaii*, p. 52), but this appears to be unlikely and it is probable that he and all who were on the vessel with him were lost at sea.

[137] Journal of Levi Chamberlain, June 1, 1830.

from him in her ambition to overthrow Kaahumanu.[138] A contract, now in the Archives of Hawaii, bears her signature as "Regent of the Sandwich Islands," and on the same contract—apparently in tacit approval—is the signature of the King. The American missionaries were no more friendly toward her than they had been toward her husband, and she in turn was equally unsympathetic with the reform policies which they so ardently championed. The mutual antipathy between Liliha and the missionaries, together with the belief that she would pay the debts contracted by Boki more readily than would other chiefs, secured for her the approval of most of the foreign residents.[139] Although they were said to be "generally warm friends" of Liliha, their friendship availed her little, for they were not willing to espouse her aspirations openly in opposition to Kaahumanu and the majority of the ranking chiefs.[140]

Late in January 1831 a report reached Honolulu that Kaahumanu intended to remove Liliha from her post as Governor of Oahu. This news caused considerable excitement. Liliha declared she would not surrender her position unless ordered to do so by the King. Natives friendly to her came to Honolulu from all parts of the island, bringing arms and ammunition with which to resist the Regent should she actually attempt to depose Liliha.[141] Throughout February the tension continued, and at the close of the month Liliha had five hundred well armed men in each of the forts at Honolulu.[142] The King, Kaahumanu, and many of the most influential chiefs were at Lahaina when they learned of these warlike preparations. They determined to oppose war with peaceable negotiations. For the delicate task of placating Liliha and then persuading her to resign her position, the chiefs chose Liliha's father, Governor Hoapili. His mission met with unexpected success. He arrived at Honolulu on March 2; on the following day he conferred with Liliha, who agreed to surrender and to return with him to Lahaina.[143]

[138] Peirce to Hunnewell, Oahu, January 31, 1831, in Hunnewell MSS; Chamberlain to Evarts, Honolulu, December 5, 1831, in Letters to the American Board, LXVIII, No. 158.

[139] *Ibid.*

[140] Clark to Evarts, Honolulu, September 14, 1831, *ibid.*, LXVII, No. 140.

[141] Peirce to Hunnewell, Oahu, January 30, 31, 1831, in Hunnewell MSS.

[142] Journal of Levi Chamberlain, February 22, 1831.

[143] *Ibid.*, March 2, 3, 1831; Peirce to Hunnewell, Honolulu, March 8, 1831, in Hunnewell MSS; Bingham, *Sandwich Islands*, p. 406.

With the submission of Liliha, the undisputed control of Oahu passed for the first time into the hands of Kaahumanu. She quickly indicated her particular interest in that island by appointing as its governor her brother, Kuakini, who had already gained considerable experience while occupying a similar position on Hawaii.[144] The arrival of Kuakini at Honolulu marked the close of the period when foreigners or natives on Oahu might ignore the decrees of the government with the assurance that they would suffer no inconvenience for their temerity. To some the new Governor was interesting solely because of the extreme difficulty with which he conveyed his four hundred pounds about the community; but Kuakini was noted for his mental energy and determination, mixed with a considerable degree of shrewdness, rather than for his extraordinary weight. In a desire for knowledge, no chief exceeded him. He had become the first of his race to read English, and he later won a like distinction in mastering the written form of his own language. On the island of Hawaii he was noted for the building of roads and for marked success in mercantile pursuits. In 1828 he joined the Protestant church at Kailua. Thereafter he was generally regular in his attendance at public worship and consistently friendly with the missionaries, although he was never noted for piety or for any unusual display of devotion to the mission.

From the beginning of his administration, Kuakini exercised more determination than tact. Upon assuming office he undertook the enforcement of the moral legislation sponsored by Kaahumanu but generally ignored by Boki and Liliha. On the first day of April the residents of Honolulu met to hear the will of their new Governor. After an announcement by Kaahumanu that the Ten Commandments were to be the basis of law in the future, Kuakini informed the assembly that no more licenses for the sale of liquor would be issued and that gambling and the retailing of liquor would thereafter be rigidly prohibited. In defense of this policy he adverted to the fact that this was not a new law but merely the enforcement of a decree which had been announced previously but never observed.[145] Some of the resi-

[144] Journal of Stephen Reynolds, March 24, 1831.

[145] Journal of Levi Chamberlain, April 1,

1831; Peirce to Hunnewell, Honolulu, April 14, 1831, in Hunnewell MSS; Bingham to Evarts, Oahu, November 23, 1831, in Letters to the American Board, LXVII, No. 4.

dents were reported to be "exceedingly angry" as a result of this startling announcement;[146] and Henry A. Peirce, the partner of Hunnewell, believed that, although the new policy was justified, it had been announced so unexpectedly that it had made stocks of liquor in the possession of merchants virtually worthless, and that "upwards of two hundred white men" had been deprived of employment.[147]

The vigorous policy of Kuakini was not wholly satisfactory to any party. Levi Chamberlain reported that the Governor was making a "commendable effort" to "reform the morals" of the inhabitants of Honolulu, for which purpose an armed force was "called out daily to perambulate the village; which has of course given great offence to those whose pursuits are pleasure or gain."[148] Peirce was less sanguine. In a letter to Hunnewell he declared that many "vile & arbitrary acts" had been committed by the "unprincipled & uncontrouled soldiery."[149] Foreign residents, who regarded the restrictive legislation as already obsolete, undoubtedly received an unpleasant surprise. The police stopped residents found riding for recreation on Sunday, and, in some instances, deprived them of their horses;[150] they entered the home of one foreigner while dinner was being served and ordered the host to remove liquor from the table;[151] and on another occasion the local authorities invaded a private residence to interrupt a billiard game, apparently because it was believed that the players were gambling.[152] When the police found several persons "rolling ninepins," they interrupted the game and confiscated the balls and pins— an action which was sustained by the Governor despite the assertion of the King that he had given permission for the game to be played.[153]

It was not to be expected that the foreigners in Honolulu would submit quietly to this interference with their personal pleasures. Apparently there was much criticism of the missionaries, who were

[146] Journal of Levi Chamberlain, April 2, 1831.

[147] Peirce to Hunnewell, Honolulu, April 14, 1831, in Hunnewell MSS.

[148] Chamberlain to Evarts, Honolulu, April 20, December 5, 1831, in Letters to the American Board, LXVIII, Nos. 153, 158.

[149] Peirce to Hunnewell, Honolulu, April 14, 1831, in Hunnewell MSS.

[150] *Ibid.*; Journal of Levi Chamberlain,

April 17, 1831; Clark to Evarts, Honolulu, September 14, 1831, in Letters to the American Board, LXVII, No. 140.

[151] Peirce to Hunnewell, Honolulu, April 14, 1831, in Hunnewell MSS.

[152] Bingham to Evarts, Oahu, November 23, 1831, in Letters to the American Board, LXVII, No. 4.

[153] Journal of Stephen Reynolds, April 29, 1831.

regarded as responsible for the new order;[154] but the most effective means of protest was a remonstrance signed by many of the residents and addressed to the chiefs. The protestants received no reply, but the policies of which they had complained were greatly modified. Liquor was again sold in Honolulu, although the Governor refused to issue permits for its sale.[155] Dr. G. P. Judd conceded that nearly as much liquor was consumed in Honolulu as formerly had been the case, but he hazarded the incomprehensible opinion that "intemperance has received a check which it will not soon get over."[156] Chamberlain later declared that the patronage of saloons had come chiefly from foreigners;[157] and Ephraim Spaulding wrote that of the approximately three hundred foreigners on Oahu only six could be induced to join a temperance society.[158] These statistics are an eloquent explanation of the difficulties which Kuakini encountered in seeking to prevent the sale of intoxicants on that island. On the other islands, where there were fewer foreign residents to interpose objections or to resist the will of the local authorities, the efforts to enforce the moral legislation met with greater success. On Maui and Kauai and along the populous west coast of Hawaii missionaries observed with obvious satisfaction that the laws prohibiting the sale of intoxicants were enforced and that instances of drunkenness in public were almost unknown.[159]

The missionaries at Honolulu found some cause for satisfaction in the results of Kuakini's attempts to secure the tranquillity of the Sabbath. Foreigners accustomed to riding on that day for recreation or exercise were compelled to forego that pleasure.[160] Peirce reported

---

[154] Journal of Levi Chamberlain, April 9, 1831; Bingham to Evarts, Oahu, November 23, 1831, in Letters to the American Board, LXVII, No. 4; Chamberlain to Evarts, Honolulu, December 5, 1831, *ibid.*, LXVIII, No. 158.

[155] *Ibid.*; Peirce to Hunnewell, Honolulu, July 7, 1831, in Hunnewell MSS.

[156] Judd to Hunnewell, Honolulu, October 29, 1832, in *ibid.*

[157] Chamberlain to Anderson, Honolulu, March 26, 1833, in Letters to the American Board, LXVIII, No. 163.

[158] Undated letter of Ephraim Spaulding, *ibid.*, LXVIII, No. 71.

[159] Gulick to Evarts, Waimea, Kauai,

August 15, 1828, in Letters to the American Board, XXXI, No. 38; Journal of P. J. Gulick, March 17, 1830, in *Missionary Herald*, XXVII (December 1831), 381; Thurston and Bishop to the American Board, Kailua, October 15, 1831, in *ibid.*, XXVIII (July 1832), 221; undated letter of Ephraim Spaulding, in Letters to the American Board, LXVIII, No. 71; Spaulding to Greenleaf, Lahaina, November 24, 1835, in *Sailor's Magazine*, VIII (June 1836), 313.

[160] Clark to Evarts, Honolulu, September 14, 1831, in Letters to the American Board, LXVII, No. 140; Chamberlain to Evarts, Honolulu, December 5, 1831, *ibid.*, LXVIII, No. 158.

that on Sunday there was "universal silence";[161] and a year later a
visitor found that "the sacred repose of the Sabbath seemed to rest
upon the whole place."[162] Apparently the first day of the week was
observed with as much formality and with as many restrictions in the
principal port of the eastern Pacific as in the hamlets of rural New
England.

The careful observance of the Sabbath was the only substantial
result of Kuakini's vigorous campaign to enforce the codes of 1827
and 1829. It was sufficient to keep alive the bitterness which followed
his early efforts to compel conformity with the entire program of the
regency. Peirce condemned Kuakini as a "stupid & obstinate" ruler
who combined ambition with avarice and "so taxed and oppressed"
the people that they bitterly disliked him.[163] The missionaries were
inclined to view his rule with more equanimity, but at the close of
1831 one of their number, Artemas Bishop, gloomily predicted:

> The determined unyielding spirit of opposition manifested by foreign
> residents and the numerous ships that touch here, the unwearied pains that
> are taken to prejudice all strangers against the rulers, the heedless manner
> also in which the government transact their affairs, the impositions & insults
> continually heaped upon the chiefs . . . . seem to indicate a crisis, perhaps a
> bloody crisis not far distant.[164]

The bloody crisis anticipated by Bishop did not materialize.
Kuakini's methods and purposes, however, did widen the breach between the missionaries and the other foreigners in Honolulu. When
his intentions became evident, in April 1831, some of the foreigners
in Honolulu hoped that Bingham would be willing and able to persuade the Governor to desist from his interference with their amusements. This Bingham refused to do.[165] This refusal was followed
by a voluminous correspondence[166] between Bingham and the protesting residents, featured by a series of charges and countercharges—
sometimes more ridiculous than reasonable—rather than by a serious
effort to obtain an amicable solution of the problems which vexed

[161] Peirce to Hunnewell, Honolulu, July 7, 1831, in Hunnewell MSS.

[162] Francis Warriner, *Cruise of the United States Frigate Potomac* (New York, 1835), p. 221.

[163] Peirce to Hunnewell, Honolulu, July 7–22, 1831, in Hunnewell MSS.

[164] Bishop to Anderson, Kailua, November 22, 1831, in Letters to the American Board, LXVII, No. 93.

[165] Bingham to Evarts, Oahu, November 23, 1831, in *ibid.*, LXVII, No. 4.

[166] *Ibid.*

the entire community. This acrimonious exchange of letters served chiefly to confirm the correspondents in the views which each already held. In September, Levi Chamberlain defended the strenuous measures adopted by Kuakini as having been in behalf of policies which were "laudable and most praiseworthy, and should have the hearty cooperation of every friend of Civilization & Christianity."[167] Few persons outside the ranks of the missionaries shared this opinion, and from General William Miller came a sweeping criticism of the attempted reforms.

General Miller was an English soldier who had gained distinction in the Peruvian wars for independence. During a visit to the Islands in 1831 he seems to have been friendly with the chiefs and missionaries,[168] but before leaving he penned a memorandum which contained a condemnation of the reforms as "despotic and vexatious," arising "rather from sectarian enthusiasm, not to say intolerance, than from justice or sound policy." With respect to the part played by the missionaries, Miller declared:

> Great however as is the praise due these well deserving Teachers of the gospel, it is, I think, to be regretted that their evangelical zeal sometimes carries them to extremes by enacting, or by their influence causing to be enacted, certain restrictions on society which I conceive ought to be attributed rather to over-righteous opinions peculiar to their sect than to true religion. The natives had formerly numerous games such as running, wrestling, throwing the spear &c., but these have either been prohibited or discountenanced so efficaciously as to cause their prohibition by the missionaries under the pretext of being too nearly allied to idolatry, as an excitement to gambling, or as time ill spent which ought to be employed in religion.[169]

So severe an indictment of the policies of the mission and of the native government was not likely to pass unnoticed by Hiram Bingham, who replied that the members of the mission were not responsible for either the accomplishments or the errors of the government

[167] Chamberlain to Hunnewell, Honolulu, September 27, 1831, in Hunnewell MSS.

[168] General Letter of the Mission, Honolulu, January 17, 1832, in *Missionary Herald*, XXVIII (November 1832), 351–352.

[169] Memorandum of William Miller, September 25, 1831, in AH, F.O. and Ex. A copy may be found as an enclosure in Bingham to Evarts, Oahu, December 13, 1831, in Letters to the American Board, LXVII,

Nos. 7–8. Ten years later another distinguished British visitor, Sir George Simpson, wrote that, although the missionaries were anxious to promote the welfare of the Hawaiian people, they had "counselled the enactment of some very strange and unusual laws which foreigners find irksome and vexatious." Simpson to J. H. Pelly, Honolulu, March 10, 1842, in *American Historical Review*, XIV (October 1908), 91.

except as those arose from the teaching of the truths of the Christian religion.[170] This rationalization would have convinced few of the foreign residents. Henry A. Peirce admitted that the motives of the missionaries were commendable, but he believed that "Hiram Bingham & Co. govern . . . . they are the jugglers behind the curtain, by whom the government persons or puppets are set in motion."[171] Two years later, after the death of Kaahumanu, Peirce reported that the missionaries had enjoyed "unbounded influence" over the Regent, who in turn had ruled her subjects with a firm hand. The result, according to Peirce, had been "ecclesiastical tyranny."[172]

The supremacy of Kaahumanu was disastrous to the Catholic mission. From spiritual counselors whose judgment she trusted implicitly the Regent learned that Catholicism inculcated serious religious error and that its influence was a menace to the temporal and eternal prosperity of her subjects. Her distrust of the Catholic missionaries doubtless was increased by the friendly relations which existed between them and Governor Boki.[173] So long as Boki remained a power in Hawaiian politics, that very friendship was the most significant guaranty that the Regent would not attack the Catholic mission. In the summer of 1829, when Boki had been reduced to virtual impotence in the public life of the nation, Kaahumanu was at last free to embark upon a program designed ultimately to drive Catholicism from the Islands.

Before taking any definite action she consulted the King, Governor Hoapili, Hiram Bingham, and William Richards. Then, in spite of a warning from the two missionaries that she would encounter

[170] Bingham to Miller, Honolulu, September 26, 1831 (copy), in Letters to the American Board, LXVII, No. 8.

[171] Peirce to Hunnewell, Honolulu, July 7, 1831, in Hunnewell MSS.

[172] Peirce to Hunnewell, Honolulu, August 10, 1833, *ibid.*

[173] The Governor frequently was present at worship at the Catholic mission, and it was said that he urged his friends to follow his example. Eight years later one of the priests recalled that he and his colleagues had gathered "a small congregation . . . . under the protection of Boki."

The authorized historian of the Catholic mission has observed that the influence of Boki provided an uncertain degree of protection, presumably because his undisguised friendship with the priests blocked any overt effort to remove them from the islands. P[atrick] Short to Edward Belcher, Honolulu, July 8, 1837, in *Suppliment to the Sandwich Island Mirror*, January 15, 1840, pp. 39–40; Yzendoorn, *History of the Catholic Mission in Hawaii*, pp. 20, 41; Bingham to Anderson, Honolulu, May 15, 1839, in Letters to the American Board, CXXXV, No. 9; Richards and Haalilio to Guizot, Paris, May 1, 1843 (copy), in AH, F.O. and Ex.

determined opposition, she ordered the priests to discontinue public worship. On the following day, August 9, 1829, she posted guards at the homes of the priests and of Francisco de Paula Marin to insure the enforcement of this edict.[174] With the connivance of Boki the priests did resume public worship for a time late in 1829,[175] but they were soon deprived of his protection. He sailed from Honolulu on December 2, 1829; within a month, Kaahumanu had again warned the priests that they must not open their chapel to natives.[176]

The priests did not again attempt any public exercise of their office, but some of their neophytes braved the anger of the chiefs to attend mass or to confer with their spiritual advisers.[177] It was quickly evident that the government was determined to crush Catholicism in the Islands. Throughout 1830 it sought to checkmate the priests by forcing their converts to apostatize. Some were called before the chiefs and admonished, some were sentenced to manual labor, and others were imprisoned.[178] With few exceptions, the small group of Hawaiian converts whom the priests had gathered were tenacious in their adherence to their faith.[179] Not even the personal admonitions of the King could shake their loyalty, and on one occasion they defied his expressed wish that they renounce Catholicism by openly seeking proselytes among his subjects.[180] This brazen indifference to the requests of the King was scarcely reassuring to the chiefs, some of whom undoubtedly shared the fears of Kaahumanu that the presence of the priests carried the threat of sedition and perhaps of revolt.

On Oahu, where Liliha was believed to have the sympathy of the French colonists in her aspirations to become regent,[181] the uncertain

---

[174] Journal of Levi Chamberlain, August 8, 10, 1829; Journal of Stephen Reynolds, August 9, 1829.

[175] *Suppliment to the Sandwich Island Mirror*, January 15, 1840, pp. 11–12.

[176] *Ibid.*, pp. 12–13. Stephen Reynolds noted in his journal (December 25, 1829) that Kekuanaoa, the acting Governor of Oahu, had told the priests that they must leave the Islands. Probably this was only a warning of what was to come. If intended as a definite order it was premature, for the chiefs were not yet sufficiently united on the measure to warrant an attempt by Kaahumanu to deport the priests.

[177] Charlton to Aberdeen, Oahu, December 20, 1831, in *Correspondence Relative to the Sandwich Islands*, p. 26; *Suppliment to the Sandwich Island Mirror*, January 15, 1840, p. 13.

[178] *Ibid.*, pp. 13–16; Journal of Levi Chamberlain, June 17, 18, July 30, September 20, 21, and October 18, 1830; Yzendoorn, *History of the Catholic Mission in Hawaii*, pp. 53–58.

[179] Journal of Levi Chamberlain, September 20, 1830.

[180] Chamberlain to Hunnewell, Honolulu, November 12, 1832, in Hunnewell MSS.

[181] Dibble, *History of the Sandwich Islands*, p. 327.

political situation gave the chiefs some cause for alarm. Early in January 1831 they met to consider the policy of the government with reference to the Catholic mission and its converts. With the exception of Liliha every important chief was present, and the council agreed that the priests must be expelled from the kingdom.[182] Not until April —after the removal of Liliha from the governorship—were the priests officially informed of this decision.[183] Three months were allowed them in which to make the necessary arrangements,[184] but the summer passed and they were still in Honolulu. By September it was apparent that the priests did not propose to depart voluntarily, and the chiefs determined to force the issue by using one of their own vessels for the purpose of removing them.[185] That vessel, the "Waverly," was placed under the command of Captain William Sumner, and in December the priests were ordered to embark upon it. Although they expressed a wish to be permitted to remain at Honolulu to celebrate Christmas Day with their converts, Kaahumanu was in no mood to make concessions, and on December 24 Bachelot and Short were compelled to embark upon the "Waverly."[186] Two artisans, one carpenter and one mason, remained in Honolulu[187]—the feeble remnant of the colony which had been launched five years before by speculators and bureaucrats in France.

[182] A copy of this decree may be found in AH, F.O. and Ex. It is printed in Yzendoorn, *History of the Catholic Mission in Hawaii*, p. 60.

[183] *Ibid.*, pp. 60–63; Journal of Stephen Reynolds, April 2, 1831; Journal of Levi Chamberlain, April 2, 1831.

[184] Peirce to Hunnewell, Honolulu, April 14–18, 1831, in Hunnewell MSS; Bingham to Anderson, Oahu, April 21, 1831, in Letters to the American Board, LXVII, No. 2. According to Stephen Reynolds, the priests were informed that should they fail to leave within the specified time, their property would be confiscated, and that should they still be in the Islands at the end of four months they would be taken to the Fort and placed in chains. Journal of Stephen Reynolds, April 2, 1831.

[185] Journal of Levi Chamberlain, September 8, 1831.

[186] Yzendoorn, *History of the Catholic*

Mission in Hawaii, pp. 69–74; The Mission at Honolulu to the American Board, January 17, 1832, in *Missionary Herald*, XXVIII (November 1832), 352; Journal of Hiram Bingham, December 21, 23, 24, 1831, in Letters to the American Board, LXVII, No. 6. Some force was necessary to persuade the priests to depart, even when it had become apparent that they could not long resist the will of the determined Queen Regent. On December 23 they refused to leave their home, although native officers with orders to effect their removal visited the priests and were ready to assist in carrying their luggage to the wharf. On the following day Kekuanaoa went in person to the home of the priests and "forced the doors of the French missionaries & took Mr. Bachelot and Mr. Short & forced them on board [the] Waverly." Journal of Stephen Reynolds, December 23, 24, 1831.

[187] The Mission at Honolulu to the American Board, January 17, 1832, in *Missionary Herald*, XXVIII (November 1832), 352.

Sumner's instructions ordered him to carry the exiles to some place along the California coast where they would be certain to find sustenance and safety.[188] The priests were aware of their destination and were satisfied. They were assured of a welcome at the Catholic missions in California, and from that place they might return to the Hawaiian Islands whenever the occasion seemed propitious.[189] Desiring to evade the payment of port charges, Sumner landed his passengers at San Pedro. Lurid tales of the hardships suffered by the priests have been perpetuated by many writers, who have insisted that they were forcibly landed on a barren shore far from any human habitation, "without food, without water, and without arms to defend themselves against the wild beasts."[190] In contrast, Sumner declared that he had provided carefully for the welfare of his passengers upon their arrival at San Pedro. He sent two of his crew in quest of aid for the priests, and on the following morning the men returned with a farmer who was ready to help them. Shortly thereafter the priests left the "Waverly," and their baggage—said to consist of six boxes and a cask of salmon—was sent ashore. During the following night Sumner departed for Santa Barbara, where he hoped to secure provisions and perhaps a profitable cargo.[191] The missionaries at San Gabriel immediately offered an asylum to the exiles, and three days after leaving the "Waverly" Bachelot and Short were at the mission of San Gabriel.

[188] A copy of these instructions may be found in AH, F.O. and Ex. They are printed in Bingham, *Sandwich Islands*, p. 418. Four days before the forced departure of Bachelot and Short, Richard Charlton reported that Kaahumanu apparently was providing carefully for their physical comfort by "amply providing the vessel with necessaries of every description for the voyage." Charlton to Aberdeen, Oahu, December 20, 1831, in *Correspondence Relative to the Sandwich Islands*, p. 26.

[189] Statement of F. Girand, January 3, 1832, in AH, F.O. and Ex.; Yzendoorn, *History of the Catholic Mission in Hawaii*, p. 71; Chamberlain to Anderson, Honolulu, February 6, 1832, in Letters to the American Board, LXVIII, No. 159.

[190] Adolphe Barrot, "Les Iles Sandwich," in *Revue des Deux Mondes*, 4th ser., XIX (August 15, 1839), 529; [Alfred Robinson], *Life in California* (New York, 1846), pp. 122–123; *Suppliment to the Sandwich Island Mirror*, January 15, 1840, p. 21; J. C. Jones to Kamehameha III, Honolulu, June 16, 1837, in AH, F.O. and Ex.; J. M. Guinn, "Historic Seaports of Los Angeles," in Historical Society of Southern California, *Annual Publications*, V (1900), 65; Rev. Father Stephen, "Brief History of the Catholic Church in Hawaii," in *Father Bachelot Memorial Review* (Honolulu, n.d.), p. 5; Simpson, *Journey Round the World*, II, 107; J. N. Reynolds, *Voyage of the Potomac* (New York, 1835), p. 418.

[191] Captain Sumner's account of the arrival and landing of the priests is in his journal for January 21, 22, 1832, in *Sandwich Island Gazette*, November 24, 1838. See also Yzendoorn, *History of the Catholic Mission in Hawaii*, pp. 76–77.

A variety of motives induced the chiefs to expel the priests and to attempt to eradicate all traces of Catholic influence in the Islands. The anti-Catholic policy of the regency was not wholly divorced from politics, and there were some who believed that political apprehensions dictated the decision of the chiefs.[192] The priests had carefully refrained from any action which might appear aggressive or domineering, but they could not entirely escape the political forces which disturbed Honolulu between 1826 and 1831. Thus they regarded Boki as their especial friend and protector, and many of their followers were known as partisans of Boki and Liliha. Their presence seemed to be a threat of future civil strife, for there was the danger that should any important chief be converted to Catholicism his followers would be arrayed against the regency.[193] In 1831, however, the political influence of the priests was negligible, and political expediency is scarcely sufficient to explain the persistence of Kaahumanu in her opposition to the Catholic mission.

Friends and defenders of the exiled priests have insisted that the American missionaries were largely, if not solely, responsible for the action of the chiefs.[194] There is much evidence to support this view. In November 1830 Levi Chamberlain frankly declared that he and his colleagues were much annoyed by the presence of the priests and hoped that "the Lord would open the way for their removal."[195] One month later two missionaries encouraged Kapule, the widow of Kaumualii, to support any effort by the chiefs to remove the Catholics.[196] The American missionaries had already debated this delicate problem during their annual meeting in 1830. Apparently there was no unanimity of opinion among their number.[197]

[192] Clark to Anderson, Waialua, September 6, 1832, in Letters to the American Board, LXVII, No. 141.

[193] Cf. Samuel Whitney to David Greene, Kauai, October 25, 1830, *ibid.*, LXVII, No. 54. Whitney wrote that should the priests "succeed in gaining some of the influencial chiefs to their party, a conflict will doubtless ensue which will shake the Sand[wich] Isl[ands] to the center."

[194] *Suppliment to the Sandwich Island Mirror*, January 15, 1840, p. 19; *Annals of the Propagation of the Faith*, I (1840), 356 n. Some Catholic writers have been more specific, placing the blame for the expulsion of the priests solely upon Hiram Bingham. *Annales de la Propagation de la Foi*, XII (May 1840), 240, 242 n.; Yzendoorn, *History of the Catholic Mission in Hawaii*, p. 80.

[195] Chamberlain to Greene, Honolulu, November 6, 1830, in Letters to the American Board, LXVIII, No. 150.

[196] Journal of Levi Chamberlain, December 10, 1830.

[197] According to Hiram Bingham, one member of the mission had told Governor Kuakini that the government should make

They did, however, adopt a formal resolution expressing the view that if questioned by the chiefs they should reply that rulers had a legal right to remove from their country any foreigners whose presence they found objectionable, with the added admonition that it would be improper to deprive the priests of the right to preach or teach as long as they were permitted to remain in the Islands.[198] This resolution, which was a transparent compromise between the desire of the mission to avoid the appearance of religious persecution and its desire to be relieved of the menace of Catholicism, seems to have represented fairly the policy which most of the missionaries regarded as just and wise.

The American missionaries did not disguise their approval of the decision to expel the priests. In their annual meeting in 1831 they asserted that they fully approved the course adopted by the chiefs, and added the somewhat equivocal resolution that "we caution them against adopting any measures which can rationally be interpreted as persecution for conscience sake; that they also be forbearing, but still decided and energetic."[199] In the following November the missionaries at Honolulu "observed a season of fasting and prayer" to beseech divine guidance in facilitating the removal of the Catholic missionaries.[200] These prayers were soon answered, for on the same day the King signed the commission instructing Captain Sumner to take command of the "Waverly" and to carry Bachelot and Short from the Islands. Throughout the four years that the priests had been in Honolulu, Bingham had enjoyed the complete confidence of Kaahumanu. The chiefs did not fail to keep him and his associates informed of the development of their policy toward the Catholic mission, and during the critical month of December 1831, when the expulsion of the priests was imminent, the Regent often sought his counsel.[201]

---

no effort to expel the priests, while another missionary had informed the Governor that the chiefs might deport them if they were unwelcome or dangerous to the peace of the Islands. Bingham to Anderson, Honolulu, May 15, 1839, in Letters to the American Board, CXXXV, No. 9.

[198] *Minutes of the General Meeting of the Sandwich Island Mission*, 1830, pp. 32–33.

[199] *Ibid.*, 1831, pp. 15–16.

[200] Bingham to Evarts, Oahu, February 6, 1832, in Letters to the American Board, LXVII, No. 9; Journal of Levi Chamberlain, November 5, 1831.

[201] Journal of Hiram Bingham, December 7, 12, 13, 21, and 24, 1831, in Letters to the American Board, LXVII, No. 6.

Following the expulsion of the Catholic missionaries Hiram Bingham and Levi Chamberlain expressed some alarm lest the action of the government cause unfavorable comment in the United States and Europe.[202] Their colleague, the Rev. E. W. Clark, was more confident, believing that the conduct of the mission would not be condemned by "candid Protestants."[203] However Protestants generally may have viewed the failure of the American missionaries to protect their rivals from the attack of the government, no criticism was forthcoming from the American Board, the Prudential Committee of which had already evaded the issue by advising caution and by recalling the historical precedent of the New England pioneers who had exercised the right "of excluding heretical & dangerous men from their community."[204]

It is clear that the American missionaries encouraged the chiefs to persevere in their decision to remove the priests from the Islands. It does not follow that they approved the punishments inflicted upon Hawaiian Catholics. In their annual meeting in 1830 they sought to distinguish between the legal right of a government to deport aliens and the moral wrong involved in punishing its own subjects for their religious convictions.[205] In July 1830 Levi Chamberlain advised Kekuanaoa that persecution was not warranted by the Bible and suggested that kindness rather than harsh treatment would be effective in convincing native Catholics of their errors. But Chamberlain confided to his journal that he was perplexed as to the proper means "to counteract & prevent the evils which the introduction of the Catholic sentiments is calculated to produce."[206] Obviously his perplexity was shared by many of his colleagues, who were conscientiously opposed to persecution but who regarded the presence of Catholicism as injurious to the progress of truth and morality among the Hawaiian people. Thus disturbed by conflicting beliefs and emotions the missionaries commonly sought to evade the issue and were content to tell

[202] Bingham to Anderson, Oahu, February 16, 1832, in *ibid.*, LXVII, No. 6; Chamberlain to Hunnewell, Honolulu, November 12, 1832, in Hunnewell MSS.

[203] Clark to Anderson, Waialua, September 6, 1832, in Letters to the American Board, LXVII, No. 141.

[204] R. A[nderson] to the Missionaries at the Sandwich Islands, Boston, November 16, 1831, in Letters from the American Board, Foreign, VI (1827–1832), 375–376.

[205] *Minutes of the General Meeting of the Sandwich Island Mission*, 1830, pp. 32–33.

[206] Journal of Levi Chamberlain, July 29, 1830.

the chiefs that the treatment of native Catholics was a problem which must be solved by the political authorities.[207]

When it became known that the departure of Bachelot and Short was imminent, a group of foreign residents visited them to express sympathy and to bid them farewell.[208] To what extent the sentiments of this group was indicative of feeling in the foreign community is uncertain. Levi Chamberlain noted that some foreigners believed that the action of the government was very unjust.[209] Stephen Reynolds feared that the expulsion of the priests would be a precedent for the removal of other foreigners—a fear evidently shared by John C. Jones, although he was quoted as saying that he hated Catholics.[210] Aside from two half-hearted protests from Richard Charlton there was no effort by the foreign community to interfere with the plans of the chiefs. In November 1831, and again in the following month, Charlton protested the expulsion of Short, who was a British subject;[211] but when he was pressed by the government to state whether or not it had the right to deport unwelcome aliens, he refused to comment.[212] Other foreigners in the Islands acquiesced quietly in the decision of the government, while a few openly approved it. Two English visitors advised the chiefs that the government was acting in accordance with its recognized prerogatives in expelling unwanted aliens,[213] and one of the visitors advised the Catholic missionaries to leave the Islands so that the Hawaiian people might not become con-

[207] Journal of Levi Chamberlain, September 20, 1830. When, in September 1830, the question of the punishment of native Catholics was raised during a conversation with the King and other powerful chiefs, the missionaries, as usual, were at a loss for an answer, and, according to Mrs. Bingham, "Not knowing what to say, no remarks were made on that point, in our conversation, this morning." Mrs. Bingham to Evarts, Waimea, Hawaii, September 17–29, 1830, in Letters to the American Board, LXVII, No. 1. This cautious policy, as Chamberlain observed, allowed the missionaries to disclaim "any agency as a church in any measure that savours of persecution." Journal of Levi Chamberlain, September 21, 1830.

[208] Yzendoorn, *History of the Catholic Mission in Hawaii*, p. 74.

[209] Chamberlain to Anderson, Honolulu, February 6, 1832, in Letters to the American Board, LXVIII, No. 159.

[210] Journal of Stephen Reynolds, April 2, 1831; Journal of Hiram Bingham, December 24, 1831, in Letters to the American Board, LXVII, No. 6.

[211] Kaahumanu to Charlton, November 16, 1831, in AH, F.O. and Ex.; Charlton to Kaahumanu, Honolulu, December 10, 1831, in *ibid.*; Journal of Hiram Bingham, December 12, 1831, in Letters to the American Board, LXVII, No. 6.

[212] Journal of Hiram Bingham, December 8, 1831, in *ibid.*

[213] Journal of Levi Chamberlain, December 13, 1831.

fused by the claims of rival faiths.[214] Henry A. Peirce was said to
have believed that the action of the government had been politically
expedient, and John N. Colcord, always friendly with the American
missionaries, openly approved the course adopted by the chiefs.[215]

The year which was drawing to a close when Bachelot and Short
left Honolulu had been one of considerable anxiety for Kaahumanu.
As she went to listen to the preaching of Hiram Bingham on Christmas
morning she may well have reflected that the humiliation of Liliha
and the deportation of the priests had left her position in the Islands
apparently impregnable. She was not destined long to enjoy her
triumphs. Early in 1832 she visited the islands of Hawaii and
Maui, but soon after her return to Oahu she became ill and retired to
her home in Manoa Valley, northeast of the village of Honolulu. As
her strength waned, she turned more completely to the spiritual assurances of her missionary teachers. The friends who gathered to
comfort her in the closing days of her life engaged in prayer or read
passages from the New Testament; and on June 5, apparently cheered
by the presence at her side of her favorite teacher and counselor,
Hiram Bingham, she quietly passed away.[216] Six days later, Henry A.
Peirce, who long had been skeptical as to the genuineness of her
faith, conceded that the scenes in Manoa Valley had convinced him
that "she really believed in & practiced the principles of the Christian
religion."[217]

The regency of Kaahumanu was in reality a continuance of the
absolutism of her late consort, Kamehameha. Although faced with
more serious obstacles and lacking the prestige of a conqueror, she
achieved a dominance in Hawaiian politics which was unquestioned
by the chiefs, and Henry A. Peirce recalled that she had ruled her
subjects with a rod of iron.[218] Her attempts to enforce more rigid
reform measures than foreigners in Honolulu would accept was an

[214] The Mission at Honolulu to the American Board, January 17, 1832, in *Missionary Herald*, XXVIII (November 1832), 351.

[215] Journal of John N. Colcord, pp. 70–
71; Journal of Hiram Bingham, December 24, 1831, in Letters to the American
Board, LXVII, No. 6; William Miller to
Bingham, Callao, May 1, 1832, in *ibid.*,
"Sandwich Islands, 1831–1837," Part I, No.
17.

[216] Journal of Dr. and Mrs. Alonzo
Chapin, II, 34–35 (May 27, 1832). Bingham, *Sandwich Islands*, pp. 433–434; Bingham to the American Board, [June 8, 1832],
in *Missionary Herald*, XXIX (April 1833),
166–167.

[217] Peirce to Hunnewell, Oahu, June 11,
1832, in Hunnewell MSS.

[218] Peirce to Hunnewell, Honolulu, August 10, 1833, in *ibid.*

error in judgment but one which arose naturally from her acceptance of the teachings and advice of the missionaries. Alexis Bachelot described Kaahumanu as a woman of considerable force of character and a "friend of law and order," whose friendship with the American missionaries resulted partly from their mutual aversion to disorder.[219] At the beginning of the regency, while Kalanimoku still lived, one British visitor declared that Kaahumanu possessed "the most peaceful influence throughout the island";[220] and near the close of her career General Miller asserted that she was the "fittest person" in the Islands for the responsibilities of government.[221] Her attachment to the American mission and her unwavering support of its program was a constant source of joy and hope to the missionaries, to whom she was the "new and good Kaahumanu."[222]

The troubled years of Kaahumanu's regency were marked by the first indications of the decay of the political absolutism bequeathed by generations of Hawaiian kings. After the death of Kalanimoku, in 1827, no influential Hawaiian openly questioned the position of Kaahumanu as active head of the state and no chief persisted in refusing to obey her commands or to accept the policies she sponsored. The periodic threats of insubordination from two successive governors of Oahu and the evident hostility of many of the foreign residents compelled her to proceed cautiously. She often was guided and at times she was restrained by a small group of powerful chiefs, some of whom had been friends and counselors of Kamehameha. The unwavering support which Kaahumanu received from these great

[219] Letter of Alexis Bachelot, Honolulu, December 1828, in *Annales de la Propagation de la Foi*, IV, 294.

[220] Letter of Rowland Bloxam, September 6, 1825, in *Hawaiian Almanac and Annual*, 1924, p. 67.

[221] Memorandum of William Miller, September 25, 1831, in AH, F.O. and Ex.

[222] Jarves, *History of the Hawaiian Islands*, p. 125; *Quarterly Review*, XCIV (December 1853), 87. Discussing her character, Jarves, the most impartial of the early historians of the Islands, asserted: "After her conversion, her violent passions were checked; the cold and contemptuous behavior gave way before the strong, natu-

ral flow of affection. To the missionaries she became warmly attached; and among her own people, and even foreigners, her character was so entirely altered, her deportment so consistent with the principles of her faith, that none could doubt its sincerity. 'The new and good Kaahumanu,' passed into a proverb."

Twelve years after her death, one missionary described her as having been a "noble, energetic, pious woman, whose terrible eye flashed dread upon natives and foreigners," and added that the missionaries had "never seen her like among the rulers of the Islands." Dwight Baldwin to the American Board, December 10, 1844, in *Missionary Herald*, XLI (September 1845), 313.

chiefs was the real bulwark of her authority throughout the kingdom. The price of their support was a voice in the determination of public policy. In so far as there was any theoretical organization of the government apart from the actual practice of the rulers, Hawaii under Kaahumanu was still an absolute monarchy. It was, in fact, an oligarchy, with the Regent the most powerful of a group of influential chiefs.

Kaahumanu was a woman of determination and of considerable strength of character. It was only as a matter of political expediency that she had modified the ancient absolutism. The power which thus passed to the chiefs they jealously guarded; but within a few years they followed Kaahumanu in death and the government passed into the control of young and inexperienced chiefs who were unable to retain more than the outward symbols of power. All unwittingly, Kaahumanu and the chiefs who counseled her had taken the first step on the long road from an absolute monarchy to a responsible government—a development in which first the King and then the chiefs were to be submerged by the rising tide of American commerce, democratic institutions, and a growing concern for the interests of the commoners.

V

THE COMMERCIAL FRONTIER

THE death of Kaahumanu was symbolic of the passing of an era. The far-reaching modifications which characterized Hawaiian life after 1832 were as apparent in the realm of commerce as in politics. The wealth of the sandalwood forests had been dissipated and the once lucrative sandalwood trade had ceased to be a factor in the commerce of the Pacific. With the disappearance of sandalwood, the Hawaiian Islands produced little for export except the provisions required by the scores of whalers which annually visited Hawaiian harbors. Under more favorable circumstances the development of such staple crops as sugar, tobacco, coffee, cotton, or indigo might have furnished an export to balance the increasing importation of European and American manufactures. Lack of capital, however, and the archaic land laws discouraged all but the boldest adventurers. The economic prospects of the Islands were further depressed by the collapse of the trans-Pacific trade in furs. The depletion of the supply of sandalwood and the diminishing number of sea otter along the American coast left traders without cargoes which could be sent to Canton to exchange for teas and nankeens. With reason, the partners of the great business houses which had dominated the trade in furs and sandalwood thought so little of the prospects of Pacific commerce that they curtailed their activities in that ocean and generally discontinued their agencies at Honolulu. The business of that community thus passed into the hands of a small group of American and European residents on Oahu. It was a highly speculative trade, but one which Henry A. Peirce was confident would "employ a small capital to a good advantage and profit."[1]

For forty years, from 1790 to 1830, the commercial importance of the Hawaiian Islands depended upon their role in supplying provisions or sandalwood to vessels engaged in the maritime fur trade. During the thirty years from the decline of that trade to the outbreak of the Civil War in the United States, the ever fluctuating prosperity of Hawaiian merchants was in almost direct proportion to the demands of visiting whalers for provisions or repairs.[2] The long reign of Kamehameha III, which closed with his death in December 1854, coincided with the period of the greatest expansion in the American whale fishery. The number of American vessels engaged in whaling increased from almost two hundred in 1829 to more than four hundred in 1834 and to more than seven hundred in 1846.[3] More important to all who were interested in trade at Honolulu was the cruise of the "Ganges," of Nantucket, which in 1835 opened a new chapter in the Pacific whale fishery when it took whales along the coast of Alaska.[4] During the ensuing ten years, which were characterized by Alexander Starbuck as the "Golden Age" of American whaling,[5] nearly all American whalers went around Cape Horn to the Pacific in search of their prey.[6] There were three principal whaling areas in the Pacific. One was in the western Pacific in the vicinity of Japan; the second was south of the Hawaiian Islands along the equator; and the third and most important was off the coasts of Alaska and Kamchatka.[7]

---

[1] Peirce to Hunnewell, Honolulu, July 7–22, 1831, November 13, 1832, in Hunnewell MSS.

[2] For statements concerning the period from 1830 to 1843, see Rufus Newburgh, "A Narrative of Voyage &c.," August 21, 1835, in AH, F.O. and Ex.; Barrot, "Les Iles Sandwich," in *Revue des Deux Mondes*, 4th ser., XIX (August 15, 1839), 538; George Simpson to J. H. Pelly, Honolulu, March 10, 1842, in *American Historical Review*, XIV (October 1908), 90; Jarves, "The Sandwich or Hawaiian Islands," in *Merchants' Magazine*, IX (August 1843), 119; Robert C. Wyllie, in *The Friend*, July 1, 1844, p. 61. Wyllie estimated that visiting whalers left from $800 to $1,500 each

in the Islands to pay for supplies, repairs, or the pleasures of the crew.

[3] Pitkin, *Statistical View of the Commerce of the United States of America* (1835 ed.), p. 42; *Merchants' Magazine*, XVI (January 1847), 99; *Daily National Intelligencer* (Washington), March 13, 1846.

[4] Starbuck, *History of the American Whale Fishery*, p. 98.

[5] *Ibid.*

[6] Walter S. Tower, *History of the American Whale Fishery* (Philadelphia, 1907), p. 59.

[7] Simpson, *Journey Round the World*, II, 137.

Whalers cruising in the North Pacific almost inevitably touched at the Hawaiian Islands. The Islands were within easy reach of each of the great whaling grounds of the Pacific; and at Hawaiian ports, whalers in the midst of a cruise could secure repairs, recruits, or recreation, or could transship oil to the United States. The facilities and advantages offered by Honolulu and Lahaina were scarcely less vital to the success of the whalers than was the patronage of the whaling fleet to the prosperity of merchants at those ports. There was little or no exaggeration in the report of the United States Commercial Agent at Honolulu that if the whalers were deprived of free access to Hawaiian ports whaling in the western Pacific would be seriously crippled.[8]

The expansion of American whaling fleets after 1830 was not immediately reflected in the statistics kept at Honolulu and Lahaina. On the contrary, from 1833 through 1840, there was an almost uninterrupted decline in the number of whalers which called at those ports. In 1832 there were some two hundred visits by whalers at the two ports—the greatest total recorded in any year up to that time.[9] The following year a reaction set in. By 1837 the aggregate number of visits by whalers to Honolulu and Lahaina had decreased to one hundred and thirty; three years later, in 1840, that total had fallen below ninety. In the same year fewer than fifty whalers touched at Honolulu—the smallest number in any year since 1825.[10] Not until the whaling industry had recovered from the depression which followed the Panic of 1837 was there a substantial increase in the number of whalers which visited Hawaiian ports each spring and autumn.

There was no lack of harbors in the Islands. Two major ports

[8] Brinsmade to Secretary of State Webster, Washington, D.C., April 8, 1842, in USDS, "Consular Letters," Honolulu, I. Cf. Jones to Clay, Oahu, July 1, 1827, in *ibid.*

[9] Available records are confined to statistical statements, without detail. These indicate that there were at least 118 visits of whalers to Honolulu during 1832 and at least eighty to Lahaina during the same year. It is possible that, in a few instances, the same vessel touched at both places. A very few whalers called at other Hawaiian ports. *The Friend*, May 1, 1844, p. 49; Letter of William Richards and Ephraim

Spaulding, Lahaina, December 7, 1833, in *Sailor's Magazine*, VI (August 1834), 358.

[10] Statistics dealing with the number of whalers visiting Honolulu during these years may be found in *The Friend*, May 1, 1844, p. 49. Similar information concerning visits of whalers to Lahaina from 1837 to 1843 may be found in *ibid.*, December 2, 1844, p. 113. Estimates of the number of whalers at Lahaina during 1835 and the last six months of 1836 may be found in Spaulding to Jonathan Greenleaf, Lahaina, November 24, 1835, April 26, 1837, in *Sailor's Magazine*, VIII (June 1836), 311–312; IX (August 1837), 366.

and at least half a dozen lesser ones offered a wide variety of advantages and conveniences to the whaling fleet. Masters who preferred to touch at some less frequented harbor, either to avoid high port charges or to purchase provisions for less than the prevailing price on Oahu, could call at Hilo or Kealakekua on Hawaii, at Waimea, Koloa, or Waioli on Kauai, or at the island of Niihau.[11] Only a very few vessels could have been seen at any of these places in the course of a year, and the overwhelming majority of the whalers called either at Honolulu or at Lahaina.

The eight lean years culminating in 1840 witnessed a continuation of the rivalry between Honolulu and Lahaina. In this competition, Honolulu possessed certain obvious advantages, which led an American naval officer to the conclusion that "no place in the Pacific affords equal advantages to it, as a place of Rendezvous for our whale fishery."[12] Chief among the attractions at Honolulu was a well-protected harbor—a contrast to the open roadstead in which vessels calling at Lahaina were compelled to anchor. At Honolulu there were a greater number of stores, a wider variety of manufactured goods for sale, and facilities for the repair of vessels superior to similar conveniences in any other port of the North Pacific.[13] Against these obvious advantages it was necessary to balance the high port charges which drove an increasing number of whalers from Honolulu to Lahaina or to one of the harbors on Hawaii or Kauai.[14] Provisions of the best quality could be purchased at Lahaina as readily and often

[11] Jarves, "The Sandwich or Hawaiian Islands," in *Merchants' Magazine*, IX (August 1843), 115; *Polynesian*, May 22, 1841; R. C. Wyllie, in *The Friend*, December 2, 1844, p. 115. Captain Charles Wilkes, who was at the Islands in 1840 and 1841, was told that only two or three whalers called at Kealakekua in the course of a year to "take in a few provisions and wood." Wyllie, however, reported that during 1843 twenty-two vessels, "mostly whalers," visited Kealakekua. Charles Wilkes, *Narrative of the United States Exploring Expedition* (Philadelphia, 1845), IV, 97; Wyllie, *loc. cit.*

[12] C. K. Stribling to Secretary of State Forsyth, New York, September 27, 1839, in USDS, "Miscellaneous Letters." A similar view was expressed editorially by the *Sandwich Island Gazette*, December 10, 1836.

[13] On October 17, 1840, the *Polynesian* modestly admitted that Honolulu offered opportunities for the repair of ships "not to be surpassed in any other portion of the Pacific." This observation was supported by the testimony of men actually engaged in trade. D. W. Thompson to Marshall, Oahu, November 19, 1830, in *Oregon Historical Quarterly*, XXVIII (June 1927), 128; Jones to Secretary of State McLane, Oahu, December 31, 1834, in USDS, "Consular Letters," Honolulu, I; Letter of Peirce and Brewer, September 23, 1840, in *Polynesian*, October 3, 1840.

[14] Edward Belcher, *Narrative of a Voyage Round the World* (London, 1843), I, 63.

at a lower cost than at Honolulu.[15] But to some masters the principal attraction at Lahaina was the order commonly prevailing in that community—a fact which was ascribed to the conscientious enforcement of the laws regulating the sale of intoxicants. The absence of saloons presumably gave Lahaina no added charm to thousands of seamen, but the masters and owners were often pleased to purchase provisions at a port which was described by Captain Wilkes as the most orderly of its size in Polynesia.[16] It was not until 1841, however, that whaling vessels called more frequently at Lahaina than at Honolulu.[17] In the following spring the American commercial agent at the Islands took official cognizance of the importance of Lahaina to American shipping by appointing Captain John Stetson vice commercial agent of the United States for that port.[18]

The overwhelming majority of the whalers which called at Hawaiian ports were owned in the United States. Approximately five out of every six whalers which visited Honolulu during that period flew the American flag, and at Lahaina the proportion of American ships in the whaling fleet passed 90 per cent. With few exceptions the other whalers which called at the Islands were owned in Great Britain.[19] The merchants at Honolulu were content to share indirectly in the profits of the whaling industry. Although James J. Jarves believed that the opportunities for local participation in the whale fishery were "great, and worthy the attention" of Honolulu merchants, capital was scarce in the Islands and competent officers were not always available to assume command of a whaling voyage.[20] Only rarely before the middle of the century was any Honolulu-owned vessel sent to the sea in search of whales. The first of these infrequent

[15] *Sailor's Magazine*, V (July 1833), 322 n.; Letter of Dwight Baldwin, Lahaina, January 4, 1839, *ibid.*, XI (July 1839), 353; Robert C. Wyllie, in *The Friend*, September 4, 1844, p. 78; James J. Jarves, *Scenes and Scenery in the Sandwich Islands* (Boston, 1843), pp. 170–171.

[16] Wilkes, *United States Exploring Expedition*, IV, 267; Letter dated Lahaina, November 1832, quoted in *Sailor's Magazine*, V (July 1833), 322–323. See also a memorial signed by eighteen officers of whalers and dated Lahaina, November 17, 1835, in Bingham, *Sandwich Islands*, p. 478;

W. S. W. Ruschenberger, *A Voyage Round the World* (Philadelphia, 1838), p. 457.

[17] *The Friend*, May 1, 1844, p. 49, December 2, 1844, p. 113.

[18] Hooper to Secretary of State Webster, Sandwich Islands, June 10, 1842, in USDS, "Consular Letters," Honolulu, I.

[19] *The Friend*, May 1, 1844, p. 49, December 2, 1844, p. 113.

[20] Jarves, "The Sandwich or Hawaiian Islands," in *Merchants' Magazine*, IX (August 1843), 118 n.

voyages was planned by Henry A. Peirce and Captain G. W. Cole. Peirce withdrew, however, and when the "Denmark Hill" put to sea in November 1831 it was chartered to Cole. It is said that the vessel returned with one thousand barrels of oil; but this result was not so attractive as to encourage similar ventures.[21]

During the spring and autumn when the whalers arrived at the Islands for the semiannual visits, merchants at Honolulu experienced their most active seasons. At no time, however, did the prosperity of Honolulu depend exclusively upon the whaling fleet, and the oft-repeated assertion that the whalers "made" Honolulu is an exaggeration. Despite the disappearance of Hawaiian sandalwood and the decline in trans-Pacific trade, Honolulu continued to be the center from which radiated the principal trade routes of the eastern and central Pacific. The position of the Islands and the growing importance of trade in the eastern Pacific prompted the editor of the *Sandwich Island Gazette* to predict, in 1837, that the Hawaiian Islands were destined to become "the West Indies of the Pacific."[22] Three years later a representative of the prominent Honolulu firm of Peirce and Brewer estimated that one-half of the goods of American or European origin which were landed at Honolulu were re-exported to California, the Russian settlements, or the islands of the South Pacific.[23]

The region which was commercially tributary to Honolulu was one of more promise than activity. No great markets existed or were likely to exist in the other island groups of the Pacific, and the population along the coast of North America was too sparse or too poor to support more than a very limited trade. The editor of the *Hawaiian Spectator*, in introducing his journal to an unexcited world in 1838, truthfully asserted that the west coast of the neighboring continent was attracting the attention of "civilized colonists and Christian philanthropists" and that its "hitherto unappreciated" agricultural potentialities were at length being recognized,[24] but the realization of

[21] Peirce to Hunnewell, Oahu, February 16, [1832], in Hunnewell MSS; Journal of Levi Chamberlain, November 29, 1831; T. G. Thrum, "Honolulu's Share in the Pacific Whaling Industry of By-Gone Days," in *Hawaiian Almanac and Annual*, 1913, pp. 47–48.

[22] *Sandwich Island Gazette*, March 18, 1837.

[23] *Polynesian*, September 12, 1840.

[24] [Peter A. Brinsmade], "Introductory Observations," in *Hawaiian Spectator*, I, No. 1 (January 1838), p. 2. Similar views were expressed by James Jackson Jarves

those prospects was postponed until after the occupation of California by the United States. It was, therefore, a quiet and generally uneventful commerce which found its natural center at Honolulu. Compared with the scores of whalers which annually called at Hawaiian ports, the number of merchant vessels engaged in the trade of the eastern and central Pacific was not large. During the twelve months from July 1, 1836, to July 1, 1837—the last full year before this trade was adversely affected by the Panic of 1837—only thirty-four merchantmen arrived at Honolulu from ports outside the Hawaiian archipelago. They came from the United States, Great Britain, and virtually every part of the Pacific. They departed for destinations equally varied and remote. It is significant that more than one-half of the arrivals and departures were of vessels engaged in direct trade between Honolulu and the west coast of North America.[25]

No feature of the commerce of the Pacific between 1830 and 1840 testified more convincingly to the changes which had overtaken trade in that ocean than did the lessened significance of the northwest coast in the itineraries of American traders. The vast territory which stretched from California to the Bering Sea was dominated by two powerful trading companies, each of which coveted a monopoly of trade within its own sphere of activity. The position of the Russian American Company was convincingly demonstrated in 1834, when the government of Russia took advantage of the expiration of the fourth article of the Treaty of 1824 to exclude American traders from a considerable part of the Alaskan coast.[26] This action, presumably

in an editorial in the first issue of the *Polynesian,* June 6, 1840. On that occasion, Jarves described the Hawaiian Islands as "a beautiful Archipelago, fast developing its great natural resources, and . . . . surrounded by islands and countries springing, almost Minerva like, into the ranks of civilized nations."

[25] Information concerning the origin, cargoes, and destination of shipping which called at Honolulu may be found in the marine news of the *Sandwich Island Gazette,* July 30, 1836—July 27, 1839, and as enclosures in the reports of the United States commercial agent at Honolulu, in USDS, "Consular Letters," Honolulu, I. For unofficial statistics of the port of

Honolulu during part or all of the period from 1834 to 1841, see Jarves, "The Sandwich or Hawaiian Islands," in *Merchants' Magazine,* IX (August 1843), 114–115; *Sailor's Magazine,* XIII (July 1841), 333; Letters of John Diell, Oahu, January 1835, Honolulu, January 1, 1836, and January 1, 1838, in *ibid.,* VIII (September 1835), 22; VIII (July 1836), 338; XI (May 1839), 265; Diell to Greenleaf, Honolulu, January 1, 1837, in *ibid.,* X (October 1837), 41–42.

[26] The first notice that Russia would take advantage of the expiration of the fourth article to prohibit American vessels from trading along the coast came shortly after the date of expiration when the governor of

instigated by officials of the company, was explained by Count Nesselrode as having been motivated in part by a desire to secure for the
company a monopoly of trade north of the fifty-fourth parallel and in
part by a determination to prevent the sale to the Indians of firearms
and intoxicants—two articles in the cargoes of many of the northwest
traders. Nesselrode further explained that the action of his government would cause no undue hardship to American commerce because
so few vessels had taken part in the forbidden traffic; but from Honolulu John C. Jones informed the State Department that "a profitable
and long enjoyed commerce" had been lost to citizens of the United
States.[27] The new Russian policy did not interfere immediately with
trade at the settlements in Alaska, and in the ensuing years American
merchants at Honolulu occasionally sent vessels to Sitka or Kamchatka with manufactured goods and provisions.[28] Even this small
traffic was imperiled in 1840, when the Russian American Company
leased a large tract of land to the Hudson's Bay Company in an
agreement whereby the latter was to furnish the Russian posts with
all agricultural and manufactured products they might require.[29]

South of fifty-four forty the situation was more complicated. The
Hudson's Bay Company was no less anxious to monopolize the fur
trade than was its neighbor to the north. It was compelled, however,
to adopt different methods to secure that monopoly. The "joint occupation" of Oregon provided by the Anglo-American convention of
1818 precluded any possibility that the company could look to the
government in London for assistance in excluding its American rivals
from the northwest coast. The principal weapon at its command was a

the Russian American Company, Baron
Wrangel, warned two American masters
that the privileges of trade along the Alaskan coast had been withdrawn. Subsequently this policy was approved in St.
Petersburg and was formally communicated to the government in Washington.
Baron Krudener to Acting Secretary of
State Dickins, Washington, May 31, 1835,
in *Senate Documents*, 25th Cong., 3d Sess.,
No. 1, p. 25.

[27] Nesselrode to George M. Dallas, St.
Petersburg, March 9, 1838, in *ibid.*, pp.
69–70; Jones to Secretary of State Forsyth,
Honolulu, November 30, 1836, *ibid.*, p. 34.

[28] See enclosures in the semiannual reports of the United States commercial
agent at Honolulu, in USDS, "Consular
Letters," Honolulu, I. See also *Sandwich
Island Gazette*, August 6, 1836, May 6, 13,
1837; Stephen Reynolds to James Hunnewell, Oahu, January 1, 1837, in Hunnewell
MSS; Finlayson to McLoughlin, September 29, 1836, in Rich, ed., *Letters of John
McLoughlin*, p. 334; Charlton to Palmerston, February 9, 1840, in *Correspondence
Relative to the Sandwich Islands*, p. 69.

[29] Roderick Finlayson, "History of Vancouver Island and the Northwest Coast"
(typed manuscript, University of Washington Library), pp. 7, 11–12.

competition so intense that no rival could hope to make a profitable voyage along any part of the coast occupied by the company. In 1831 the company's agents in Oregon embarked upon a policy of establishing permanent posts along the coast, apparently for the purpose of securing a monopoly of the maritime fur trade.[30] Whenever possible rivals appeared, the company's agents offered the Indians more for furs than the visitors could afford, and on occasion offered prices which would have been ruinous if long continued. It was a policy fraught with some danger, for the Indians were prone to hold their furs until a vessel hove in sight in the hope of capitalizing upon the competition which followed;[31] but it served the great and immediate purpose of compelling competitors to abandon the voyage or to incur loss. Despite the great resources of the company and the shrewdness of its agents, this was not a simple operation. The Yankee masters who visited the coast were resourceful and not easily intimidated; perhaps quite as important was the fact that their vessels commonly carried adequate stocks of liquor—a commodity greatly in demand among the natives.[32]

Gradually American vessels disappeared from the northwest fur trade. In the summer of 1836, two American traders offered "a very keen competition" to John Work, the agent at Fort Simpson;[33] a year later, "no Yankee Opponents" appeared to annoy Work, who reported that he had made "such arrangements that should they come again they would get so little that they would not be induced to return and that we would get rid of them altogether."[34] Within a few years, the Hudson's Bay Company, co-operating with the Russian American Company, had gained "entire control" of the maritime fur trade

[30] Alexander Caulfield Anderson, "History of the Northwest Coast" (typed manuscript, Provincial Library and Archives, Victoria, B.C.), p. 5. For other notices of the efforts of the Hudson's Bay Company to drive American competitors from the fur trade, see Finlayson, "History of Vancouver Island and the Northwest Coast," pp. 14, 19; Hall J. Kelley to Caleb Cushing, Boston, January 31, 1839, in *House Reports*, 25th Cong., 3d Sess., No. 101, pp. 57–58; William A. Slacum to Secretary of State Forsyth, San Blas, March 26, 1837, *ibid.*, pp. 34–35.

[31] Hubert Howe Bancroft, *History of the Northwest Coast* (San Francisco, 1886), II, 641.

[32] Finlayson, "History of Vancouver Island and the Northwest Coast," p. 13.

[33] Work to Edward Ermatinger, Fort Simpson, February 15, 1837, in *Washington Historical Quarterly*, II (April 1908), 258.

[34] Work to Ermatinger, N.W. Coast of America, February 10, 1838, in Work MSS, Provincial Library and Archives, Victoria, B.C.

along the northwest coast.[35] To what extent the decision of American masters to abandon the fur trade is to be explained by the tactics of the Hudson's Bay Company is not easy to determine. Doubtless other factors, including the scarcity of sea otter and the declining demand for furs, discouraged some who otherwise would have defied the efforts of the company to drive them from the coast.

One logical result of the company's dominance of Oregon was its participation in the trade between the northwest coast and the Hawaiian Islands. This development was mutually beneficial to the Islands and to the company, as each gained an extension of the limited markets for some of its products. From Oregon the company sent fish, lumber, and flour to the Hawaiian Islands; in exchange, it received sugar, molasses, coffee, rice, and salt. For a time the company's business at the Islands was entrusted to Richard Charlton, but "the frequent intercourse" between the Columbia and Honolulu caused officials of the company, in 1833, to send a full-time agent to Honolulu.[36] A year later, in August 1834, George Pelly arrived at Honolulu to assume charge of the Hawaiian interests of the company.[37] It was only a small trade which was thus stimulated, but it was one which was profitable to the company. As a center for the production and export of grain and lumber, Fort Vancouver, on the Columbia, became "a place of considerable importance," and the market for those products was presently extended to include China, South America, and the Russian posts in Alaska.[38] Until after the settlement of an agricultural population in Oregon, the company enjoyed an unchallenged monopoly of the fish, lumber, and grain of that country. It was able to send its products to its agency at Honolulu in its own ships, and thus it was in a position to dominate the trade between the northwest coast and the Hawaiian Islands. The editor of the *Polynesian* recognized an inevitable result when, in May 1841, he lamented the fact that trade along the northwest coast, once so

[35] Finlayson, "History of Vancouver Island and the Northwest Coast," p. 19.

[36] Merk, ed., *Fur Trade and Empire*, p. 319 n.; John Pelly to Palmerston, November 13, 1833, in *Correspondence Relative to the Sandwich Islands*, pp. 34–35.

[37] Journal of Levi Chamberlain, August 7, 1834. For accounts of Pelly's career see Rich, ed., *Letters of John McLoughlin*, p. 353; Duncan Finlayson to James Hargrave, February 29, 1836, in G. P. de T. Glazebrook, ed., *The Hargrave Correspondence* (Toronto, 1938), p. 230.

[38] Finlayson, "History of Vancouver Island and the Northwest Coast," p. 58.

important to American shipping, had passed "entirely into the hands of a rival nation."[39] The company, however, seems to have been more anxious to extend the market for its products than to enjoy the advantages of monopoly in the Hawaiian trade, and Honolulu merchants who were in competition with the company's agency occasionally were able to advertise for sale salmon or lumber recently received from the company's territories in Oregon.[40]

The influx of American settlers into Oregon after 1840 opened new opportunities for all who were concerned with the commerce of the North Pacific. The same movement effectively destroyed any danger that the Hudson's Bay Company might gain a permanent monopoly of the Oregon-Hawaiian trade. As elsewhere throughout the Pacific, an increase of trade followed closely upon settlement. Among the principal beneficiaries of this expanded commerce were the merchants at Honolulu, for vessels bound from the United States to the Columbia usually stopped at Honolulu on both the outward and the return voyages. At Oahu these vessels added provisions necessary for the voyage and engaged in a varied trade. Those bound for the Columbia added to their cargoes either typically Hawaiian products such as sugar and coffee or "other commodities" of English, American, or Chinese origin. Returning from the coast, these traders brought the products of Oregon, which they endeavored to sell at Honolulu, where they sometimes invested their profits in sugar or hides for the United States.[41]

The virtual exclusion of American vessels from the maritime fur trade compelled American traders along the west coast of North

[39] *Polynesian*, May 22, 1841.

[40] See, for example, the advertisements of William French, in *Sandwich Island Gazette*, July 30, December 31, 1836.

[41] E[lijah] White to Secretary of War Porter, Willamette, November 4, 1844, in *Senate Documents*, 29th Cong., 1st Sess., No. 1, p. 623. The instructions given to Captain John Couch of the "Chenamus" before he left Massachusetts for Honolulu and Oregon in 1841 and again in 1843 indicate the emphasis which some traders placed upon a return cargo to be purchased at Honolulu. On the outward voyage the "Chenamus" carried a cargo intended to be sold in part at Honolulu and in part in Oregon. On both occasions Couch was ordered to go directly to Honolulu, to dispose of a part of his cargo there, and then to proceed to Oregon. The profits from the sales at Honolulu were to be invested in goods or produce which could be sold at a profit in the United States. The instructions of 1843 mentioned arrowroot and "Good California Cow Hides" as articles which would sell well in the United States and which could be purchased at Honolulu. John Cushing to Captain John Couch, Newburyport, October 7, 1841, September 15, 1843, in Elkanah Walker MSS, Huntington Library.

America to shift their interests southward to the Mexican ports from Monterey to San Blas. The most active of the traders along the California coast were the agents of the Boston firm of Bryant and Sturgis, who first became interested in the commerce of California as an auxiliary of their participation in the maritime fur trade. The most important exports of California were hides and tallow, and after the dissolution of the competing firm of McCulloch, Hartnell, and Company in 1828 Bryant and Sturgis controlled the major share of the California hide trade. Lacking serious competition from any merchants in the United States, they continued to dominate California trade until their withdrawal from business in 1841.[42] They were not alone in their interest in the slowly expanding commerce of California. Their most active and resourceful rivals were the American-born merchants who had established mercantile houses at Honolulu, including such prominent Honolulu traders as Peirce and Brewer, John C. Jones, William French, and Eliab Grimes and Company.[43] Indeed, if we may trust the statistics of H. H. Bancroft, vessels from the Hawaiian Islands outnumbered those from Boston in the California trade.[44] Vessels from the Islands were regarded with suspicion by Mexican officials, who recognized that they were inclined to engage in smuggling on a generous scale. For some reason, supercargoes and masters of vessels from the United States acquired no such unenviable reputation, perhaps because they found more subtle means of evading a part of the heavy duties imposed by Mexican law.[45]

There was no market in the Islands for California hides, as hides

[42] Adele Ogden, "Boston Hide Droghers along California Shores," in *California Historical Society Quarterly*, VIII (December 1929), 289–296.

[43] *Ibid.*, p. 299.

[44] Bancroft, *History of California*, III, 381, IV, 104–106.
The peculiar interest of American merchants at Honolulu in the trade with California was indicated when twenty-nine American residents of that community signed a memorial to Captain Edmund Kennedy of the U.S.S. "Peacock," urging him to visit California to investigate injustices alleged to have been suffered on that coast by American traders resident at Honolulu. Commenting upon the memorial, the editor of the *Sandwich Island Gazette* described California as "a country where so much American property is at stake" as to require the protection of the proper authorities. It is evident that a part of that property was the shipping owned by Americans at Honolulu. *Sandwich Island Gazette*, September 17, 1836. The memorial may be found as an enclosure in Kennedy to Secretary of the Navy Dickerson, Mazatlan, November 14, 1836, in NRL, "Captain's Letters, Nov. 1836," No. 38; it is printed in Ruschenberger, *Voyage Round the World*, pp. 489–491.

[45] Bancroft, *History of California*, III, 368, IV, 81–82; Ogden, *loc. cit.*, p. 304.

ranked high among Hawaiian exports,[46] and those which were carried from California to Honolulu were intended for reshipment to the United States. Bancroft believed that at the beginning of this trade Honolulu merchants were more interested in "skins and horses" than in hides[47]—the skins evidently being those of the sea otter. In 1833 it was reported that sea otter along the California coast were rapidly disappearing because of the "piratical manner" in which ships from the Hawaiian Islands took their prey.[48] In later years, however, otter skins were often included with land furs, soap, lumber, beans, horses, hides, and tallow among the products which California sent to Honolulu.[49] During this period, only the United States surpassed California in the aggregate value of the products which it shipped to the Islands.[50] Competent observers noticed the reciprocal commercial importance of California and the Hawaiian kingdom. The French explorer Duflot de Mofras described the Islands as an appendage of California, and predicted that the nation which gained possession of one would also control the other.[51] His prediction was to be fulfilled; but in characterizing the Islands as an appendage of California he had underestimated the real importance of Hawaiian ports to the trade of the Pacific. A British contemporary, Sir George Simpson, was nearer to an appreciation of the economic role of the Islands when he wrote:

> But, after all, it is not to their internal resources that these islands, as a whole, must look for prosperity. Their position alone has, in a great measure, made their fortune;—a position which is equally admirable, whether viewed in connexion with the length or with the breadth of the surrounding ocean.
>
> For all practical purposes, the Sandwich Islanders are on the direct route from Cape Horn to all the coasts of the Northern Pacific. With respect to Kamschatka and the Sea of Ochotsk, this is evident at a glance . . . . with respect to California and the northwest coast, the apparently inconvenient

[46] Jarves, "The Sandwich or Hawaiian Islands," in *Merchants' Magazine*, IX (August 1843), 118.

[47] Bancroft, *History of California*, III, 132.

[48] John B. R. Cooper to Hunnewell, Monterey, April 22, 1833, in Hunnewell MSS. About two years later, Alexander Forbes declared that the trade in otter furs had "dwindled into insignificance." Alexander Forbes, *California: A History of Upper and Lower California* (London, 1839), p. 284.

[49] *Polynesian*, September 12, 1840; Jarves, "The Sandwich or Hawaiian Islands," in *Merchants' Magazine*, IX (August 1843), 116; Ogden, *California Sea Otter Trade*, p. 147.

[50] Jarves, *loc. cit.*, pp. 116–117.

[51] Duflot de Mofras, *Exploration du Territoire de l'Orégon* (Paris, 1844), II, 73–74. A similar view was expressed by Captain Charles Wilkes. See Wilkes, *United States Exploring Expedition*, V, 279.

deviation to the left is rendered not only expedient, but almost necessary, by the prevailing breezes. . . . .

But the group as naturally connects the east and the west, as the south and the north. Lying in the very latitude of San Blas and Macao, with an open sea in either direction, it crosses the shortest road from Mexico to China; while . . . . it may . . . . be regarded as a stepping-stone from the whole of the American coast to the Celestial Empire. . . . .

. . . . Already have the Sandwich Islands begun to be a common centre of traffic for some of the countries, which they serve to link together. Even now, their exports comprise a larger proportion of foreign commodities than of native productions, such as hides and sea-otters, from California, silver from Mexico, teas and manufactures from China. . . . . In this respect, the tendencies of nature have, to some extent, been strengthened by the capricious administration of the impolitic laws of Mexico. In that republic, the duties . . . . are collected, according to whim or necessity, with greater or less strictness, each port, as well as each week, having its own peculiar mode of reducing the theory to practice; so that, when a vessel finds the authorities in a troublesome or extortionate humour, she runs for it to Honolulu, there disposing of her cargo at better prices, or at least depositing it for better times. As an instance of this, the "Joseph Peabody" . . . . was indeed from Mazatlan . . . . but had actually brought most of her goods by that circuitous route from China.[52]

As had been true during the period of the fur trade, the maritime activities which centered at Honolulu after 1830 resulted in a steady flow of Hawaiian men away from their native land. Many of them were of an adventurous nature, and they were only too pleased to have an opportunity to experience life at sea or to visit some foreign country. They retained their early reputation as excellent sailors, and they were commonly regarded as satisfactory laborers when employed at simple tasks on shore. They were generally amiable and docile and they were willing to work for very moderate wages. In consequence, they were much in demand as seamen or as laborers at various points along the American coast. Captain Wilkes enlisted some fifty Hawaiians as members of the crew of the United States Exploring Expedition to replace seamen whose term of enlistment had expired; and Sir George Simpson, after a visit to the Islands in 1842, asserted that approximately one thousand men "in the very prime of life" annually left the Islands to seek employment or adventure elsewhere. It was estimated in 1844 that there were from three hundred

[52] Simpson, *Journey Round the World,* II, 132–135. See also Jarves, *Scenes and* *Scenery in the Sandwich Islands,* pp. 42–43.

to four hundred Hawaiians in Oregon, principally in the service of the Hudson's Bay Company; and the Rev. Gustavus Hines, who had an opportunity to observe the work of many of these expatriated Hawaiians, declared that they were "much better adapted" than the Indians for such labors. Both Hines and Simpson agreed that many of the men who thus left the Islands never returned to their homeland.[53]

The growth of Honolulu and Lahaina as bases for the whaling fleet, the presence of American families on each of the principal islands, and the changing standards of living among the native population created an ever expanding domestic market for many commodities considered necessary for comfort in the United States and for some of the luxuries familiar to Americans and Europeans of the period. Merchant vessels, therefore, brought to Honolulu a wide variety of imports intended for domestic consumption or for transshipment to the American coast or to the South Pacific. On their departure they sometimes carried a cargo of hides, salt, or other products of the Islands. More often their outward cargo was listed as general merchandise—evidently goods brought to the Islands from the United States and destined for ultimate consumption along the American coast; occasionally it was specie or nothing more profitable than ballast. Ships bound direct for the United States frequently carried whale oil or California hides which had been sent to the Islands for transshipment.[54]

Available records of imports and exports at Honolulu during the decade following 1830 are complicated by numerous discrepancies. From this statistical confusion some generalizations may safely be drawn. Throughout that period Hawaiian economic life suffered from an apparently adverse balance of trade, but the effects were mitigated by the fact that a "large portion" of the goods listed as imports were intended for reshipment to other parts of the Pacific.[55]

[53] Wilkes, *United States Exploring Expedition*, III, 386; Simpson, *Journey Round the World*, II, 15; Gustavus Hines, *Oregon: Its History, Condition and Prospects* (Auburn and Buffalo, 1851), p. 413; *Senate Documents*, 25th Cong., 2d Sess., No. 470, p. 8; Robert C. Wyllie, in *The Friend*, September 4, 1844, p. 79.

[54] Much important statistical information concerning the number, identity, cargoes, and destination of American merchant ships touching at Honolulu may be found in the semiannual reports of the United States commercial agent at Honolulu, in USDS, "Consular Letters," Honolulu, I.

[55] Jarves, "The Sandwich or Hawaiian Islands," in *Merchants' Magazine*, IX (August 1843), 117–118.

Supplies to whalers constituted from one-third to one-half of all the exports from the Islands; and apparently only the ever fluctuating demands of the whaling fleet prevented a serious deflation of the retail trade so laboriously created by merchants at Honolulu. The poverty of Hawaiian exports is strikingly demonstrated by the fact that until after 1839 the vanishing sandalwood was ranked next to provisions in the list of Hawaiian exports. Other products of the Islands sent abroad in sufficiently large quantities to attract the attention of the statisticians included hides, sugar, molasses, salt, goat skins, tobacco, arrowroot, and kukui oil.[56] Contemporary estimates of the value of Hawaiian commerce must be regarded as subject to considerable suspicion, but judged from available records the years from 1834 through 1838 constituted a period of steady decline in exports, the value of which fell from more than $150,000 in 1834 to $73,000 in 1836, and to $67,000 in 1838.[57] In 1839 the value of the exports rose to $94,000, and thereafter there was a steady increase in the annual value of the cargoes shipped from Hawaiian ports.

The history of imports at Honolulu shows a more complicated and apparently a more erratic course. During the two years 1834 and 1835 the aggregate value of imports at Honolulu was about $575,000.[58] In the year 1836 it increased to $413,000, but thereafter dropped until in 1838 the value of imports was only $207,000.[59]

---

[56] *Ibid.*, p. 118; *Polynesian*, September 12, 1840; *Niles' Register*, L (August 27, 1836), 440. Two visitors to Honolulu in 1834 and 1835 respectively believed that salt and hides, both in small quantities, were the most important exports aside from provisions. In 1836, the *Sandwich Island Gazette* listed more than twenty-five exports of the Islands, including salt, tobacco, cotton, sugar, coffee, indigo, and leather. None of these was produced in large quantities in 1836, and many of them seem to have been potential rather than actual exports. By 1843 the course of agricultural development had become somewhat more definite, and the acting commercial agent of the United States reported that sugar was the only export "worthy of note." It was shipped from the Islands to Sydney and the west coast of America. Bennett, *Whaling Voyage Round the Globe*, I, 237; Newburgh, "A Narrative of Voyage

&c.," in AH, F.O. and Ex.; *Sandwich Island Gazette*, October 22, 1836; William Hooper to the Secretary of State, Sandwich Islands, July 26, 1843, in USDS, "Consular Letters," Honolulu, II.

[57] For 1834, see statistics furnished by a Honolulu merchant, printed in *Boston Mercantile Journal* and reprinted in *Niles' Register*, L (August 27, 1836), 440, and in *Sailor's Magazine*, IX (January 1837), 153–154. For the period from 1836 to 1840, see Jarves, "The Sandwich or Hawaiian Islands," in *Merchants' Magazine*, IX (August 1843), 118.

[58] Ruschenberger, *Voyage Round the World*, p. 488. The figures cited by Ruschenberger were furnished by Henry A. Peirce.

[59] Jarves, "The Sandwich or Hawaiian Islands," in *Merchants' Magazine*, IX (August 1843), 117; *The Friend*, June 1, 1844, p. 58.

It then rose again sharply until during the twelve months from August 1840 to August 1841 the total value of the imports was $455,000.[60] These statistics included a considerable amount of manufactured goods which later were shipped to the American coast or elsewhere. It is impossible therefore to make any accurate comparison of the value of exports and imports; but after all necessary deductions from the import statistics, it seems probable that the value of imports destined for consumption in the Islands was not less than three times the value of the domestic exports including provisions to whalers.

These imports represented a wide variety of commodities. In the summer of 1844 the indefatigable Robert C. Wyllie listed more than two hundred separate articles which had been landed at Honolulu during the preceding year and which had come from the United States, Great Britain, and the principal areas bordering upon the Pacific.[61] Included in the long list of products which the Islands received from the United States were cotton cloth, hardware, copper, cordage, naval stores, flour, bread, liquor, soap, shoes, books, furniture, and many other less useful or less prominent articles. From California came hides and otter skins, together with lesser quantities of wine, tallow, soap, and horses. Mexico furnished specie and bullion; China sent nankeens, tea, silk, rice, and British manufactures; Manila supplied the Islanders with cigars, rope, and coffee; the northwest coast of America sent lumber, spars, and salmon; and England furnished—either directly or through some Pacific port where cargoes were transshipped—manufactured products similar to those which came from the United States.[62]

Despite frequent reports, especially after 1835, that business at Honolulu was slow and that the prospects for profitable trade were discouraging,[63] the economic life of the community became steadily

60 *Polynesian*, September 4, 1841.

61 *The Friend*, June 1, 1844, pp. 56–57.

62 *Ibid.*, p. 58; *Polynesian*, September 12, 1840; Charlton to Palmerston, Oahu, February 9, 1840, in *Correspondence Relative to the Sandwich Islands*, p. 69.

63 Reynolds to Hunnewell, Oahu, November 14, 1836, January 1, 1837, in Hunnewell MSS; Peirce and Brewer to Hun-

newell, October 5–November 10, 1838, in *ibid.*; Reynolds to Thomas O. Larkin, Oahu, January 21, June 6, 1840, October 17, 1841, July 3, 31, November 3, 1842, in Thomas O. Larkin MSS (Bancroft Library, University of California), I, Nos. 32, 63, 182, 285, 299, 353; Marshall and Johnson to Larkin, Honolulu, October 13, December 9, 1841, *ibid.*, I, Nos. 177, 197; E. and H. Grimes to Larkin, Honolulu, De-

more complex. There was a motley foreign population at Honolulu, one which, in 1831, included ten merchants, fifteen missionaries, three physicians, and a continually fluctuating number of artisans and discharged seamen.[64] In the same year Henry A. Peirce reported that there were at Honolulu nine mercantile houses, most of which were "well stocked with goods."[65] Three years later, an English visitor judged that supplies "of almost every description" could be purchased on Oahu with as much ease as at "a second-rate sea port in England."[66] The first number of the *Sandwich Island Gazette*, published July 30, 1836, contained the advertisements of six Honolulu firms dealing in general merchandise, one firm which sold naval stores, one shipwright, one sailmaker, one auctioneer, one barber, one physician, one maker of saddles and harness, and one artisan who described himself as a mason, bricklayer, and plasterer. Several of these advertisements quickly disappeared, and no new advertising appeared in the *Gazette* until after the first of the following year.

That the needs and whims of the small community were adequately met is indicated by a lengthy article in the *Polynesian* in the autumn of 1840 in which the author listed the number of firms and artisans at Honolulu. The truly impressive roster included twenty retail and four wholesale houses, two hotels, two taverns, twelve boarding-houses for seamen, two billiard rooms, seven bowling alleys, the shops of two cabinet makers, two provision stores, three vegetable markets, one copper foundry, one paint-oil factory, one lumber yard, one bakery, four blacksmith shops, two barber shops, two apothecary shops, fourteen ship carpenters, five house carpenters, and one or more physicians, masons, tailors, sailmakers, calkers, shoemakers, saddle makers, butchers, cigar makers, auctioneers, engravers,

cember 7, 1841, *ibid.*, I, No. 194; Marshall to Larkin, Honolulu, November 1, 1842, *ibid.*, I, No. 351; John Couch to John Cushing, Oahu, April 10, 1842, in Walker MSS.

[64] Bingham to Evarts, Oahu, November 25, 1831, in Letters to the American Board, LXVII, No. 5. The three physicians noted by Bingham seem to have been Dr. G. P. Judd, who was attached to the American mission; Dr. John Pelham, who arrived at Honolulu in May 1827; and Dr. T. C. B. Rooke, a native of England,

who arrived at Honolulu before 1830. Journal of Levi Chamberlain, May 8, 1827; *Polynesian*, December 11, 1858. In 1832 a fourth physician, Dr. T. K. Thomas, arrived from the United States. Journal of Dr. and Mrs. Alonzo Chapin, III, 54 (September 25, 1832); J. K. Townshend, *Sporting Excursions in the Rocky Mountains* (London, 1840), II, 30.

[65] Peirce to Hunnewell, Honolulu, July 7, 1831, in Hunnewell MSS.

[66] Bennett, *Whaling Voyage Round the Globe*, I, 208.

printers, and tinkers.[67] This list appears to be confirmation of statements that every important trade and every learned profession except the law was represented by practitioners at Honolulu.[68] Notwithstanding the number and variety of stores and artisans, produce and wearing apparel cost much more in Honolulu than in the United States.[69]

With few exceptions the principal mercantile houses in the Islands were owned by Americans resident there. The most important exception was the agency at Honolulu of the Hudson's Bay Company. The dominance of that company in the commerce of Oregon and the subsequent establishment of agencies at Honolulu and San Francisco caused some American observers to fear that the company had embarked upon a sinister plot to monopolize the trade of the northeastern Pacific. At least two American merchants at Honolulu subscribed to this view, and one of them warned Senator Lewis F. Linn that the company would attempt to "drive off" American traders from that vast area.[70] James J. Jarves expressed the belief that the company wished to control the politics of the little kingdom,[71] and the master of a vessel engaged in trade along the northwest coast informed a Congressional committee that the company planned to secure control of Oregon, California, and the Hawaiian Islands.[72]

These fears were greatly exaggerated. The agency at Honolulu served as a distributing point for the products of Oregon, including lumber, salmon, and flour, which were either sold in the Islands or reshipped to other parts of the world.[73] This was far removed from a monopoly of the commerce of the single port of Honolulu, and there is no evidence that the company ever sought to embarrass the Hawaiian government or to infringe upon the prerogatives of the native

[67] *Polynesian*, October 17, 1840.

[68] Peirce to Hunnewell, August 13, 1837, in Hunnewell MSS; Wilkes, *United States Exploring Expedition*, III, 411.

[69] S. N. Castle to Anderson, Honolulu, February 4, 1840, in Letters to the American Board, CXXXVII, No. 137; Francis Allyn Olmstead, *Incidents of a Whaling Voyage* (New York, 1841), p. 213.

[70] Henry A. Peirce to Linn, Boston, May 1, 1842, in *House Reports*, 27th Cong., 3d Sess., No. 31, p. 62, and reprinted in *Niles' Register*, LXIII (December 17, 1842), 242–

243; Francis Johnson to Thomas O. Larkin, Honolulu, August 31, 1840, in Larkin MSS, I, No. 83.

[71] Jarves, *History of the Hawaiian Islands* (1843 edition), p. 367.

[72] Journal of Captain Josiah Spalding, in *House Reports*, 27th Cong., 3d Sess., No. 31, p. 60.

[73] Belcher, *Voyage Round the World*, I, 295–296; N. J. Wyeth to Caleb Cushing, Cambridge, February 4, 1839, in *House Reports*, 25th Cong., 3d Sess., No. 101, p. 12.

rulers. In 1842 it furnished the money to finance a Hawaiian diplomatic mission which visited the great maritime powers to plead for a recognition of Hawaiian independence; and in 1859, after the announcement that the agency at Honolulu was to be abandoned, the government-owned *Polynesian* expressed the appreciation of the Hawaiian government for the "uniform, unwavering kindly feeling ever manifested by the Company and its Agents towards this Government, and that at times of its greatest trouble and necessity."[74]

Sir George Simpson, while visiting the Islands in 1842, found six mercantile houses at Honolulu engaged in trade on a sufficiently large scale to include consignments from abroad as well as the usual importations on their own account. Two of these stores were owned by British subjects; the other four were the property of citizens of the United States.[75]

[74] *Polynesian,* November 26, 1859.

[75] Simpson to the Hudson's Bay Company, Honolulu, March 1, 1842, in *Correspondence Relative to the Sandwich Islands,* p. 94.

The six stores noted by Simpson were those owned by Henry Skinner, Jules Dudoit, Peirce and Brewer, E. and H. Grimes, Ladd and Company, and William French and Company. There were a number of smaller retail stores in Honolulu, including those owned by Stephen Reynolds, Thomas Cummins, Milo Calkin, L. H. Anthon, E. Espener, and John N. Colcord, and by the firms of Marshall and Johnson, Henry Paty and Company, and E. and H. Boardman. The advertisements of a bakery owned by two Chinese, Sam and Mow, appeared regularly in the *Polynesian* during 1840 and 1841.

Eliab Grimes was a native of Massachusetts. He had served on a privateer during the War of 1812, and was said to have acquired "a little fortune" as a result of that service. He came to the Pacific as the master of one of the vessels owned by Marshall and Wildes. He remained at Honolulu in their employ, being particularly concerned with trade between Honolulu and California. After the withdrawal of Marshall and Wildes from Pacific trade Grimes opened his own store at Honolulu, but apparently the trade with California and the quest for sea otter off the California coast continued to absorb much of his

interest. He seems to have been successful, for he was remembered as a wealthy merchant. He became a resident of California in 1842. His partner at Honolulu was his nephew, Hiram Grimes. Bancroft, *History of California,* III, 767; William Heath Davis, *Seventy-five Years in California* (San Francisco, 1929), pp. 102, 157.

Henry Paty, also a native of Massachusetts, was one of three brothers who were prominent in the trade of the eastern Pacific after 1834. The Honolulu firm consisted of Henry, William, and John Paty, and Eli Southworth. Henry Paty died at sea in 1841, and the business at Honolulu, including trade with California, was continued by the surviving partners. Bancroft, *History of California,* IV, 769.

Stephen Reynolds, an erratic and irascible person, was a native of Massachusetts who had resided continuously in the Islands since 1823. He was a man of simple habits, intensely loyal to his native country, and greatly concerned about the education and training of the offspring of foreigners in Honolulu. His store was described as notable chiefly for the "indescribable confusion" in which his goods were to be seen on the shelves and counters; but he seems to have been a successful merchant, and he was described by contemporary observers as a wealthy and highly respected resident of Honolulu. Gilman, "Streets of Honolulu in the Early Forties," in *Hawaiian Almanac and Annual,* 1904, pp. 79–80;

Two of these firms merit more extended consideration. The influential house of Peirce and Brewer traced its origin to October 1826, when James Hunnewell purchased a plot of ground in Honolulu and offered for sale the small cargo he had brought from the United States for that purpose.[76] He was successful beyond his own expectations; when he left the Islands four years later he had accumulated "a very pretty fortune."[77] Throughout his residence in the Islands he enjoyed the friendship and the confidence of the American missionaries—an achievement of which few of the traders at Honolulu could have boasted and which few of them even cared to attain. When, in October 1830, Hunnewell took his departure from Honolulu, Levi Chamberlain declared that he had shown himself "worthy

---

A. J. Allen, comp., *Ten Years in Oregon* (Ithaca, N.Y., 1850), p. 43; Davis, *Seventy-five Years in California*, p. 293.

William French was a native of New England who arrived at Honolulu in 1825 after a brief experience as a merchant at Canton. He soon opened a store in Honolulu and continued in business there until 1842. He was described by one visitor as "one of the most thriving merchants of the town." In 1840 French had two stores on the island of Hawaii, the one at Kawaihae serving as "the depot of all goods shipped from this part of the island, as well as for goods destined for the interior." Testimony of William French, March 24, 1845 (enclosure in Wyllie to United States Secretary of State, Honolulu, May 10, 1845), in AH, F.O. and Ex.; Townshend, *Sporting Excursions in the Rocky Mountains*, II, 30; Olmstead, *Incidents of a Whaling Voyage*, p. 228.

John Colcord was from Maine, and had spent many years in the Islands as an artisan before opening a store, probably in the winter of 1834–1835. The Seamen's Chaplain at Honolulu described him as a practicing Christian, a man of "unblemished moral character" and "a pattern of industry, perseverance & frugality." Because he sold no intoxicants Colcord enjoyed the sympathy of the American missionaries, but this may not have added to his sales. When Colcord left Honolulu in 1844 he was said to have accumulated some $20,000. Colcord to Hunnewell, Oahu, December 22, 1835, March 15, 1837, in Hun-

newell MSS; John Diell to Hunnewell, Oahu, January 13, 1836, in *ibid.*; Richard Armstrong to Reuben Chapman, Honolulu, November 19, 1844, in Richard Armstrong MSS, Library of Congress.

J. F. B. Marshall was a native of Charlestown, Massachusetts, who left his studies at Harvard College because of failing eyesight and went to the Islands in 1838, apparently with the intention of pursuing a mercantile career. W[alter] L. W[right], Jr., "James Fowle Baldwin Marshall," in *Dictionary of American Biography*, XII, 312.

Francis Johnson arrived at Honolulu late in 1839. Soon thereafter he became bookkeeper for Peirce and Brewer (Johnson to Hunnewell, Honolulu, December 28, 1839, in Francis Johnson MSS, Huntington Library); but in May 1841 he and Marshall formed a partnership to engage in business on their own account. In April 1841 they had informed Thomas O. Larkin, a merchant at Monterey, that they hoped to be able to supply him with goods. Marshall and Johnson to Larkin, Honolulu, April 8, 1841, in Larkin MSS, I, No. 127; *Polynesian*, May 29, 1841.

[76] Journal of Levi Chamberlain, October 25, 1826.

[77] *Ibid.*, November 20, 1830. During four years in the Islands, Hunnewell had been able to expand an original investment of five thousand dollars into nearly seventy thousand dollars. Josephine Sullivan, *History of C. Brewer and Company, Ltd.* (Boston, 1926), p. 29.

of our esteem and he returns to America with an unblemished character."[78]

Hunnewell planned to return to the Islands and presumably to resume the active direction of his business interests.[79] Before leaving the Islands he formed a partnership with Henry A. Peirce, who had served as his clerk during the preceding two years.[80] By the close of 1833 it was apparent that Hunnewell would not return to the Islands, and the partnership with Peirce was dissolved. On the following day, January 1, 1834, Peirce entered into partnership with Thomas D. Hinckley.[81] Peirce was but twenty-four years old when he became the senior partner in a firm which was said by one observer to have "the largest retail trade" in Honolulu and by another to be "the most correct and most profitable" business on Oahu.[82] In the new firm Peirce was the dominant personality. With the restraining influence of Hunnewell removed, Peirce and Hinckley expanded their interests beyond a mere passive share in the retail business at Honolulu, and— as an indication of the new policy—they chartered a vessel and sent it on a voyage to Kamchatka and Canton.[83] Because of the ill health of Hinckley, the new firm was short-lived, being dissolved before the close of 1834.[84] More than a year passed before Peirce again entered into a partnership. Finally, on February 1, 1836, Peirce and Charles Brewer established the firm of Peirce and Brewer.[85] Thereafter Peirce spent much of his time either in the United States or in active direction of the trade along the American coast. The control of the business at Honolulu therefore passed largely into the hands of

[78] Journal of Maria S. Loomis, December 14, 1820; Journal of Levi Chamberlain, December 14, 1824; *Missionary Herald*, XXV (January 1829), 22 n.; The Mission to Evarts, Oahu, December 28, 1822, in Letters to the American Board, IX, No. 130; Chamberlain to Evarts, Honolulu, December 14, 1824, November 19, 1830, in *ibid.*, XXXI, No. 48, LXVIII, No. 151.

[79] Hunnewell to Peirce, Honolulu, January 1, 1830 (copy), in Hunnewell MSS.

[80] Sullivan, *History of C. Brewer and Company, Ltd.*, p. 23.

For brief sketches of the career of Peirce, see W[alter] L. W[right], Jr., "Henry Augustus Peirce," in *Dictionary of American Biography*, XIV, 404–405; *Biography of*

Henry Augustus Peirce (San Francisco, 1880); Bancroft, *History of California*, IV, 771.

[81] Peirce to Hunnewell, January 26, 1834, in Hunnewell MSS.

[82] Thomas O. Larkin to Hunnewell, Monterey, June 1, 1833, in *ibid.*; C[harles] Taylor to Hunnewell, Honolulu, May 2, 1834, *ibid.*

[83] Peirce to Hunnewell, January 26, 1834, *ibid.*

[84] Peirce to Hunnewell, Honolulu, October 15, November 2, 1834, *ibid.*

[85] Peirce to Hunnewell, Honolulu, December 18, 1835, *ibid.*

Brewer, and in 1843 Peirce withdrew from the partnership and from active participation in the trade of the Islands. During fifteen years as clerk and merchant he had amassed a fortune estimated at about one hundred thousand dollars.[86]

The second of the commercial houses at Honolulu to merit individual notice was the ill-fated firm of Ladd and Company. The three partners—Peter A. Brinsmade, William Ladd, and William Hooper —were young men from New England, and the partnership agreement had been signed in Boston in December 1832.[87] They arrived at Honolulu late in July 1833[88] and within two days Brinsmade had rented space for a store.[89] Brinsmade had studied for the ministry at two of the best-known theological schools in New England,[90] and he and his partners were generally regarded as pious men who were in sympathy with the aspirations of the American missionaries. The missionaries therefore welcomed the arrival of the three partners, and Levi Chamberlain hoped that "this new accession to the number who are in favor of religion will prove a blessing to the place."[91] The friendship between the missionaries and the newcomers did not increase the prestige of the latter in the foreign community, nor did it gain for them the confidence or the good will of their fellow merchants. Henry A. Peirce already had expressed the fear that the missionaries had formed a "deep laid plan" to increase their own influence and power by encouraging the settlement in the Islands of merchants who would favor the objects of the mission;[92] and after the arrival of the partners he repeatedly described them, with ill-concealed contempt, as the "pious traders."[93]

The ties of sympathy between the mission and the new firm ap-

[86] *Biography of Henry Augustus Peirce,* p. 8.

[87] Arthur C. Alexander, *Koloa Plantation 1835–1935* (Honolulu, 1937), p. 4. Brinsmade and Ladd were from Hallowell, Maine; Hooper was from Boston. At the time of their arrival in the Islands, Brinsmade was twenty-eight years old, Ladd was twenty-six, and Hooper was twenty-four. *Ibid.,* pp. 2–3.

[88] Journal of Levi Chamberlain, July 27, 1833.

[89] Journal of Stephen Reynolds, July 29, 1833.

[90] *General Catalogue of the Theological Seminary, Andover, Massachusetts, 1808–1908* (Boston, n.d.), p. 108; *Eighth General Catalogue of the Yale Divinity School* (New Haven, 1922), p. 8.

[91] Journal of Levi Chamberlain, July 27, 1833.

[92] Peirce to Hunnewell, Honolulu, May 6, 1833, in Hunnewell MSS.

[93] Peirce to Hunnewell, August 10, 16, October 4, December 1, 1833, January 26, May 6, 1834, in *ibid.*

peared to be strengthened when Brinsmade undertook the care of "a respectable Bible Class,"[94] and opponents of the mission concluded that he was especially favored by the missionaries.[95] The current of rumors that swept Honolulu and carried truth and absurdity alike to all parts of the foreign community gave rise to a report that the new firm had been launched with the assistance of capital furnished by the American Board.[96] This was untrue, but there is no cause to question the later observation of Alexander Simpson that "the missionary influence was strongly exercised in favour of this house."[97] Fourteen years later Brinsmade admitted that the establishment of the firm of Ladd and Company had received the approval of "several persons connected with the direction of missionary operations" who had hoped that thereby "valuable aid would be indirectly afforded to the philanthropic and christian objects of the mission." He denied that there had been any connection between the mission and the company other than a mutual "sympathy and affection."[98]

The firm of Ladd and Company was destined to have a checkered and disastrous career. For several years it secured a large share of the trade with visiting whalers. Rival merchants, however, professed to be unconcerned and declared that the newcomers were unlikely to profit from their apparent success.[99] Their capital was small;[100] but in February 1835 Levi Chamberlain declared that they appeared "to

[94] Bingham to Anderson, Honolulu, March 27, 1836, in Letters to the American Board, LXVII, No. 43.
Mrs. Asa Thurston described Brinsmade as "one of the pious merchants who has lately come out from America to reside at the Islands." Mrs. Thurston to William and Abigail Goodell, Kailua, October 24, 1834 (copy), in *ibid.*, LXVII, No. 53. In contrast to this favorable view of the new firm was the opinion of the Rev. Jonathan S. Green, always one of the most critical members of the mission. Writing to the American Board in December 1834 to urge the settlement in the Islands of a pious and dependable family "in whom you and the christian public have confidence," Green spoke of the disappointment of the missionaries "in the case of Messrs. Ladd and Brinsmade." Green to Anderson, Wailuku, December 16, 1834, *ibid.*, LXVII, No. 119.

Cf. Chamberlain to Hill, Honolulu, February 17, 1835, *ibid.*, CXCI.

[95] *Sandwich Island Gazette*, June 24, 1837.

[96] Simpson, *Sandwich Islands*, p. 33.

[97] *Ibid.*

[98] Brinsmade to John Ii, Pauoa, July 1, 1847, in *Sandwich Island News* (Honolulu), July 7, 1847. Cf. Brinsmade to Ii, July 9, 1847, in *ibid.*, July 14, 1847.

[99] Peirce and Hinckley to Hunnewell, Honolulu, May 6, 1834, in Hunnewell MSS; Peirce to Hunnewell, Honolulu, November 2, 1834, *ibid.*; Reynolds to Hunnewell, Oahu, February 5, 1835, *ibid.*; Bingham to Hunnewell, Honolulu, December 11, 1835, *ibid.*

[100] Peirce to Hunnewell, Honolulu, February 9, 1835, *ibid.*

be doing well for themselves."[101] A few months later, they discarded caution and turned their principal energies and interests away from the retail trade at Honolulu to engage in an ambitious project for the cultivation and manufacture of sugar.

It was with good reason that conservative merchants had preferred the fluctuations of an ever changing market at Honolulu to the uncertainties of Hawaiian agriculture. The scarcity of capital and labor and the lack of accessible markets would have sufficed to delay the development of large-scale agricultural ventures in the Islands. More annoying to prospective planters was the unwillingness of the government to modify the ancient principles which governed the tenure of land. Visitors might argue that only the insecurity of land tenure and the lack of an adequate labor supply prevented Hawaiian agriculture from enjoying considerable prosperity,[102] but political considerations made immediate or revolutionary changes in land policy inexpedient. Fear or jealousy of foreigners doubtless played some part in the determination of the government to keep complete control of its land.[103] This was to be seen especially in the belief of the chiefs and of the missionaries that if the right to own and to dispose of land without restriction were granted to foreigners there would be an influx of speculators whose influence would be inimical to the stability of the government and to the rigid moral reforms advocated by the mission.

In the face of a rising tide of pressure in the foreign community, the chiefs did make a series of concessions which failed to satisfy all the demands of the foreign residents but did open the way for some agricultural ventures. From the early years of the century, foreigners had been in actual possession of plots of land in many parts of the Islands. The title to this land remained with the King or chiefs, and the tenant was subject to eviction at the pleasure of the chief from whom he held it. Only rarely had a foreigner been dispossessed of land he had occupied, but to persons born in a country where the right of private property was considered fundamental to the well-being of

[101] Chamberlain to Hill, Honolulu, February 17, 1835, in Letters to the American Board, CXCI.

[102] For example, see Newburgh, "A Narrative of Voyage &c.," in AH, F.O. and Ex.

and Ruschenberger, *Voyage Round the World*, p. 488.

[103] Journal of John N. Colcord, p. 112; Bennett, *Whaling Voyage Round the Globe*, I, 238.

society the precarious land tenure in the Islands appeared to be particularly obnoxious. With few exceptions, it served as an effective barrier against experimentation with staple crops.[104]

The first important step in the liberalization of Hawaiian land policy as it affected foreigners occurred in 1835, when the government leased a valuable tract of land on Kauai to Ladd and Company for a period of fifty years.[105] It does not follow that the chiefs intended to abandon the old order. Ladd and Company enjoyed the favor of the American missionaries and through the missionaries they had won the confidence of the government. The lease, therefore, may be regarded as little more than a special privilege extended to a favored group of capitalists whose operations were expected to provide employment for some natives and to serve as an example of industry to others.

Whatever may have been the purpose of the chiefs, the lease to Ladd and Company had established a precedent. This first reversal of the land policies was followed by other developments which weakened still further the determination of the government to maintain the ancient system. The question of land tenure was raised during successive visits to Oahu, in 1836 and 1837, of three men-of-war, with the result that foreigners at Honolulu believed their own property was more secure.[106] The inevitable liberalization of Hawaiian land policy had begun. By 1840, land was leased to the highest bidder for a term of twenty-five years;[107] and in 1841 the Hawaiian legislature authorized the governors of the several islands to lease land to foreigners for terms of fifty years.[108]

Meanwhile foreigners with a limited capital and expansive ambitions were increasingly tempted to turn to agriculture in order to

[104] Jarves, *History of the Hawaiian Islands*, p. 154; Hobbs, *Hawaii: A Pageant of the Soil*, pp. 17–27.

[105] The lease is printed in *Report of the Proceedings and Evidence in the Arbitration between the King and Government of the Hawaiian Islands and Messrs. Ladd & Co.* (Honolulu, 1846), Appendix, pp. 15–16.

[106] Peirce to Hunnewell, Honolulu, August 6, 1837, in Hunnewell MSS.

[107] J. S. Emerson to Anderson, Waialua,

July 27, 1840, in Letters to the American Board, CXXXVI, No. 108.

[108] *Polynesian*, June 19, 1841. A copy of this law as proclaimed by the King may be found in AH, F.O. and Ex. John N. Colcord, long a resident of Honolulu but never an influential member of the foreign community, wrote that the leases granted prior to 1844 were invariably given to men of power or wealth, while poor or uninfluential foreigners were unable to secure land on such generous terms. Journal of John N. Colcord, pp. 112–113.

escape the competition in the mercantile community at Honolulu. In 1836 Stephen Reynolds noted "a strong inclination" among foreign residents to invest in agricultural enterprises, while the editor of the *Sandwich Island Gazette* heard rumors of contemplated plantations and ventured the belief that "the attention of the majority" was turning toward the advantages of agriculture.[109] Four years later it was reported on Oahu that plantations and herds of cattle were "multiplying in various directions,"[110] and in 1842 Peter A. Brinsmade asserted that "general attention" was being given to the cultivation of staple crops.[111] There was an element of exaggeration in these reports. In a small way and against great obstacles, a few pioneers were laying the foundations of the great plantations of the late nineteenth century.

Sugar and silk received the greatest degree of attention from planters and interested observers. There were significant experiments with other crops, and James J. Jarves asserted that experience indicated that cotton, indigo, coffee, and wheat flourished in the Islands. Only capital and attention, he wrote, were required to convert those crops into "profitable exports."[112] Tobacco "of great perfection" had been raised by the natives,[113] and there was general agreement that a fine quality of coffee could be raised in many parts of the archipelago.[114] Cotton and indigo grew indigenously throughout the

[109] Reynolds to Hunnewell, Oahu, November 14, 1836, in Hunnewell MSS; *Sandwich Island Gazette*, September 3, 1836.

[110] Emerson to Anderson, Waialua, July 27, 1840, in Letters to the American Board, CXXXVI, No. 108. See also G. P. Judd, Lowell Smith, and S. N. Castle to Anderson, Honolulu, July 20, 1840, in *ibid.*, CXXXVII, No. 79; Letter of W. P. Alexander, July 1840, in Alexander, *William Patterson Alexander in Kentucky, the Marquesas, Hawaii*, pp. 241–242.

[111] Brinsmade to Webster, Washington, D.C., April 8, 1842, in USDS, "Consular Letters," Honolulu, I. Among the staple crops cultivated in the Islands Brinsmade listed sugar, coffee, indigo, silk, and wheat. In 1836 the *Sandwich Island Gazette* included sugar, tobacco, cotton, coffee, and indigo among the productions of the Islands. Sir George Simpson listed the products as sugar, silk, tobacco, cotton, coffee, arrowroot, indigo, rice, and ginger—the

last two of little or no commercial value at the time of his visit to the Islands in 1842. *Sandwich Island Gazette*, October 22, 1836; Simpson, *Journey Round the World*, II, 124–127.

[112] Jarves, "The Sandwich or Hawaiian Islands," in *Merchants' Magazine*, IX (August 1843), 119. For a brief description of the status of agriculture in the Hawaiian Islands in 1842, see *ibid.*, pp. 119–123; Simpson, *Journey Round the World*, II, 121–130.

[113] Bennett, *Whaling Voyage Round the Globe*, I, 255; *Sandwich Island Gazette*, October 22, 1836; Jarves, "The Sandwich or Hawaiian Islands," in *Merchants' Magazine*, IX (August 1843), 118 n. According to the *Gazette*, "considerable quantities" of tobacco had already been exported from the Islands.

[114] The earliest recorded attempt to raise coffee in the Islands was that of Francisco de Paula Marin in 1817. Eight years later

Islands,[115] but they were neglected by prospective planters; and Captain Wilkes added that the manufacture of indigo was poorly understood there.[116] There were efforts to cultivate various cereals; and, in 1841, it was reported that the natives were "engaging quite extensively in the cultivation of wheat."[117] Potatoes of excellent quality were grown on East Maui,[118] and on several of the Islands there were dairy farms, catering either to the local market or to the trade with whalers.[119] On Hawaii, John Parker, a native of Massachusetts, took

John Wilkinson planted coffee in the Manoa Valley, near Honolulu. From that time until 1842 there were occasional efforts to grow coffee, although not always for commercial purposes. About 1830 two missionaries, Samuel Ruggles and Joseph Goodrich, planted coffee in the districts of Kona and Hilo, respectively. A visitor to the Islands in 1834 was shown samples of coffee grown near Honolulu which appeared to justify the hope that it could be grown successfully in the Islands. The *Sandwich Island Gazette* in 1836 noted that the coffee grown in the Islands had been called "first rate," and in 1840 there were at least two plantations of "several thousand trees" near Hilo, one of which was owned by a Mr. Castle, who was also a carpenter. In 1844 the usually well-informed Robert C. Wyllie listed coffee as one of the exports from Hilo. T. G. Thrum, "Notes on the History of Coffee Culture in the Hawaiian Islands," in *Hawaiian Almanac and Annual*, 1876, pp. 46–47; Thurston and Bishop to the American Board, Kailua, October 15, 1831, in *Missionary Herald*, XXVIII (July 1832), 222; Bennett, *Whaling Voyage Round the Globe*, I, 256; *Sandwich Island Gazette*, October 22, 1836; Jarves, "Sketches of Kauai," in *Hawaiian Spectator*, I, No. 1 (January 1838), p. 70; William Ladd, "Remarks upon the Natural Resources of the Sandwich Islands," *ibid.*, I, No. 2 (April 1838), p. 77; Wilkes, *United States Exploring Expedition*, IV, 220; *Polynesian*, August 22, 1840; R. C. Wyllie, in *The Friend*, December 2, 1844, p. 115.

[115] In 1825 Richard Charlton predicted that cotton "of a very superior quality" would eventually become one of the exports of the Islands. In 1832 Levi Chamberlain noted that William French and a Mr. Reid had planned to raise cotton at Ewa but had been disappointed in not being able to secure land. An edict issued in 1839 and reaffirmed in November 1840 provided that cotton should be accepted in payment of taxes, as also might other products of the soil at the discretion of the tax collectors. Charlton to Canning, June 10, 1825 (No. 7), in *Correspondence Relative to the Sandwich Islands*, p. 11; Journal of Levi Chamberlain, February 3, 1832; Thurston, comp., *Fundamental Law of Hawaii*, pp. 25–26.

In 1836, the *Sandwich Island Gazette* observed that cotton could be grown at the Islands, and added that "some exertions are progressing, which will soon open the door to this staple." Two years later James J. Jarves wrote that experiments were in progress "in the raising of coffee and cotton"—presumably on the island of Kauai. Neither the *Gazette* nor Jarves gave any hint as to the identity of the experimenters, and apparently the only direct reference to the cultivation of cotton during that period was the statement of Henry A. Peirce that Charles R. Smith had become "a planter of *cotton at Maui.*" *Sandwich Island Gazette*, October 22, 1836, February 25, 1837; Jarves, "Sketches of Kauai," in *Hawaiian Spectator*, I, No. 1 (January 1838), p. 70; Peirce to Hunnewell, August 13, 1837, in Hunnewell MSS.

[116] Bennett, *Whaling Voyage Round the Globe*, I, 256; Wilkes, *United States Exploring Expedition*, IV, 76, 302; Simpson, *Journey Round the World*, II, 126; *Sandwich Island Gazette*, October 22, 1836.

[117] *Polynesian*, February 6, 1841.

[118] *Ibid.*, May 8, 1841; Wilkes, *United States Exploring Expedition*, IV, 270.

[119] One of the best known of the early dairy farms was conducted at Ewa, Oahu,

advantage of the large number of wild cattle on that island to develop a prosperous cattle ranch;[120] at Waimea, on the same island, there was a small settlement of foreigners engaged in trades subsidiary to the cattle industry, including the curing of hides and the production of tallow and leather.[121] Nearly all varieties of "foreign fruits and vegetables" also had been introduced into the Islands, and with few exceptions they had flourished.[122]

Sugar, which was destined to exert a greater influence upon the fate of the island kingdom than any other economic force, was indigenous to the Islands. The presence of sugar was noted by a number of early visitors, one of whom predicted that Hawaiian sugar would ultimately supply the needs of Kamchatka and all Siberia.[123] Little is known of the first efforts to convert Hawaiian cane into sugar. There is a persistent tradition that, as early as 1802, a Chinese resident on Lanai was so engaged;[124] and nine years later, a visitor at Oahu saw a "cane mill and boiler" owned by the King.[125]

The first serious attempt to grow Hawaiian sugar for export purposes is to be credited to John Wilkinson, a middle-aged British subject, who arrived at the Islands on the "Blonde" and who remained in the hope of recouping his personal fortune and restoring his failing

by the Rev. Artemas Bishop, the Protestant missionary at that place. A more ambitious dairy and cattle farm was that owned by Richard Charlton and operated by a tenant near Hanalei, Kauai. Captain Edward Belcher reported that Charlton's tenant "feeds cattle, makes butter, cheese, and farms to great advantage." Three years later, in 1840, it was said that Charlton owned "upwards of one hundred" head of cattle. Belcher, *Voyage Round the World*, I, 67; Wilkes, *United States Exploring Expedition*, IV, 79.

120 For a brief notice of Parker's career at the Islands, see *Hawaiian Club Papers* (Boston), October 1868, pp. 50–51.

121 *Sandwich Island Gazette*, September 24, 1836; Wilkes, *United States Exploring Expedition*, IV, 232–233; Olmstead, *Incidents of a Whaling Voyage*, p. 233; [Lorenzo Lyons], "Report of Waimea Station on Hawaii, from April 1839 to April 1840," in Letters to the American Board, CXXXVI, No. 158. Lyons wrote that there were "some 60 or 70 foreigners" in the vicinity of

Waimea, among whom were "beef catchers, sugar manufacturers, shoe makers, merchants, tanners, sawyers, carpenters, blacksmiths, combmakers, masons, doctors, farmers & what not."

122 Wilkes, *United States Exploring Expedition*, IV, 302.

123 Cook and King, *Voyage to the Pacific Ocean*, II, 244; Dixon, *Voyage Round the World*, pp. 92, 110; Turnbull, *Voyage Round the World*, II, 69; Campbell, *Voyage Round the World*, p. 183; Franchere, *Voyage to the Northwest Coast*, p. 70; Ross, *First Settlers on the Oregon*, p. 38; Lisiansky, *Voyage Round the World*, pp. 128–129; Langsdorff, *Voyages and Travels*, I, 188–190.

124 Thomas G. Thrum, "Notes on the Sugar Industry of the Hawaiian Islands," in *Hawaiian Almanac and Annual*, 1875, p. 34.

125 Howay, ed., *Journal of the New Hazard by Stephen Reynolds*, p. 8 (March 5, 1811).

health. He obtained permission to cultivate a tract of land in the Manoa Valley, and there he planted sugar, corn, potatoes, bananas, and other crops.[126] In February 1826 Wilkinson hoped to harvest sufficient cane to make twenty thousand pounds of sugar,[127] and in the following summer he was employing some forty Hawaiians on his land.[128] He actually began the grinding of the cane,[129] but he died before he could realize the reward of his enterprise and his plantation passed into the control of Governor Boki.[130] For a time, Boki continued the project energetically. Late in 1826 he was manufacturing sugar "on a pretty large scale,"[131] apparently expecting to send some of it to California.[132] For some unexplained cause—perhaps the complicated politics of the kingdom or his own financial stringency—Boki leased his plantation to William French, who in turn transferred it to a Dr. Seriere.[133] Seriere, who had arrived at the Islands in May 1828, was described as "a man of much information" who had traveled extensively. During the following winter he undertook the manufacture of sugar and rum, and Stephen Reynolds believed that he had "some prospects of success."[134] The attempt to manufacture rum was displeasing to the missionaries, who saw in intoxicants only a curse that would degrade the natives. This feeling they communicated to Kaahumanu, and after Seriere had abandoned his project the Regent ordered the cane destroyed and replaced by potatoes.[135]

In 1835 the interest in the cultivation and manufacture of sugar was revived by two ambitious projects for the establishment of sugar plantations. The first was that of William French, who brought a sugar mill and laborers from China. He was unable to secure land for a plantation, but he did set up his mill at Waimea, Kauai, where for two years he ground cane on shares for Governor Kaikioewa. He failed ultimately because he could not compete with the plantation

[126] Paulding, *Cruise of the Dolphin*, pp. 220-222.

[127] Journal of Levi Chamberlain, February 24, 1826.

[128] *Ibid.*, August 3, 1826.

[129] *Ibid.*, August 10, 1826.

[130] *Ibid.*, November 30, 1826.

[131] NRL, Jones, "Report of the Peacock's Cruise," p. 28; Journal of Stephen Reynolds, March 2, July 4, 1827.

[132] Beechey, *Voyage to the Pacific*, II, 100.

[133] Journal of Levi Chamberlain, December 31, 1828.

[134] Journal of Stephen Reynolds, May 19, 1828, February 21, 24, March 4, 1829.

[135] Bingham, *Sandwich Islands*, p. 340.

and mill which Ladd and Company had established in the neighboring district of Koloa.[136]

The decision of Ladd and Company to shift their major interests from trade to agriculture had the approval and the co-operation of the missionaries and chiefs. In June 1835 Ladd went to Kauai to select a site suitable for a plantation;[137] at the close of the following month, he and his partners secured a fifty-year lease of nearly one thousand acres at Koloa.[138] This tract of land was described as one of the finest in the Islands, and on it Ladd and Company proposed to grow and to manufacture sugar and molasses for export to California, South America, and the Russian settlements.[139] Rum was not included among the anticipated products of this venture. By mutual consent, the lease contained a provision prohibiting the manufacture or consumption of intoxicants upon the property.

To William Hooper, the youngest of the partners, was assigned the duty of managing the Koloa Plantation. He began work at Koloa in September 1835, when he selected twelve acres on which cane was to be grown. More serious labor came the following spring, when the cane was planted and work was begun on a mill. At the end of a year Hooper noted in his journal that he had completed the erection of a dam and mill, had planted twenty-five acres to cane, and had set out thousands of coffee trees.[140] For a young man who had come to Kauai quite unacquainted with the island, the climate, the language, the habits of the natives, or even with the cultivation of sugar,[141] and who had been compelled to build from nothing, this was no small accomplishment. The methods adopted by Hooper were necessarily

[136] Kuykendall, *Hawaiian Kingdom*, p. 175.

[137] Journal of Stephen Reynolds, June 5, 1835.

[138] A copy of the lease may be found in *Report of the Proceedings and Evidence in the Arbitration between the King and Government of the Hawaiian Islands and Messrs. Ladd & Co.*, Appendix, pp. 15–16.

A brief account of Koloa during the early years of the Koloa Plantation may be found in Bernice Judd, "Koloa: A Sketch of Its Development," in HHS, *Forty-fourth Annual Report* (Honolulu, 1936), pp. 51–80.

[139] Peirce to Hunnewell, Honolulu, July 30, 1835, in Hunnewell MSS.

James J. Jarves, who was familiar with the locality, described the land as being "rich, and watered by a fine stream, which affords sufficient water power for the necessary mills." Jarves, "Sketches of Kauai," in *Hawaiian Spectator*, I, No. 1 (January 1838), p. 70.

[140] Alexander, *Koloa Plantation*, pp. 6–7. Extracts from the journal kept by Hooper during his first year on Kauai may be found in "The First Plantation on the Hawaiian Group," in *San Francisco Chronicle*, February 16, 1896, p. 9.

[141] Alexander, *Koloa Plantation*, p. 5.

crude, and the quality of sugar produced at Koloa during the early years was such as would have been "scarcely merchantable" in 1850.[142] There were observers who could foresee only disaster for the experiment.[143] These predictions of failure were balanced by reports that the plantation at Koloa appeared to be flourishing,[144] and a visiting American naval officer recommended it to Kinau as a model of what should be encouraged in other parts of the Islands.[145]

The friendly relations between Ladd and Company and the mission led some to hope that the plantation at Koloa would furnish a clue to possible means of encouraging industry or of raising the standard of living among the natives. The Koloa Plantation, therefore, was more than a commercial speculation. It was an experiment with broad social implications. It provided employment for a number of natives, said at the close of 1838 to be as many as four hundred.[146] The company also encouraged natives in the vicinity to grow cane on their own land and to bring it to the company's mill, where it was either purchased or ground on shares.[147]

When employed by the company, native laborers received the standard wage of twelve and one-half cents a day. In addition they enjoyed certain perquisites, including freedom from taxation, free housing, and a supply of their basic foods—fish and poi.[148] The wages were paid in paper currency, redeemable only at the company's store at Koloa. For that reason and because the price of goods at the Islands was commonly double the price in the United States, Captain Wilkes estimated that the natives received in reality only the

[142] R. W. Wood, "The Manufacture of Sugar," in *Transactions of the Royal Hawaiian Agricultural Society*, I, No. 1 (1850), pp. 67–68.

[143] *Ibid.*

[144] Peirce to Hunnewell, August 13, 1837, in Hunnewell MSS; Letter of John Diell, Oahu, October 19, 1837, in *Sailor's Magazine*, X (July 1838), 454; Wilkes, *United States Exploring Expedition*, IV, 64. Wilkes was told that the plantation was "doing a good business," and had sold sugar in the United States at a profit.

[145] C. K. Stribling to Kinau, Honolulu, October 1836, in Ruschenberger, *Voyage Round the World*, pp. 500–502.

[146] Hooper to Ladd & Co., December 7, 1838, in Alexander, *Koloa Plantation*, p. 26.

[147] Wilkes, *United States Exploring Expedition*, IV, 64.

By 1842 there was such an extension of small-scale farming in the vicinity of Koloa that Ladd and Company abandoned the cultivation of cane and concentrated upon the manufacture of sugar. Despite this move, the company's mill was said to be "entirely inadequate" to care for all the cane grown near by. See letter of Ladd and Company, quoted in Simpson, *Journey Round the World*, II, 124.

[148] Charles Burnham to Levi Chamberlain, July 23, 1841, in Alexander, *Koloa Plantation*, p. 37.

equivalent of six and one-quarter cents a day.[149] The company, however, could point to the substantial advantages enjoyed by its employees, and Charles Burnham, the successor of Hooper at Koloa, believed that when the value of these advantages was added to the actual wages the native employees received the equivalent of twenty-five cents a day.[150] However low real wages at Koloa may have been, the managers of the plantation were satisfied that they were making a contribution to the welfare of the natives. At the close of his first year at Koloa, Hooper asserted that if the system introduced there were continued by other foreigners, it would ultimately "emancipate the natives from the miserable system of chief labor."[151] His successor asserted that in no sugar-producing country in the world were wages higher than at Koloa.[152]

The example of one of the most prominent of the Honolulu business houses investing heavily in the cultivation and manufacture of sugar stimulated a wave of interest in the possibilities of Hawaiian agriculture. The publicity which accompanied the Koloa experiment attracted to the region other foreigners, some of whom presently embarked upon ambitious projects for the cultivation of sugar or silk. Others were content to grow sugar to be ground at the mill of Ladd and Company under an agreement whereby the company retained half of the product in payment.[153] This new interest in sugar was not confined to the single island of Kauai. In various parts of the Islands, in 1838, no less than twenty mills were either completed or in the process of construction.[154] Nearly all of these mills were small and crude and were operated by animal power. Several missionaries built small mills,[155] and at least four of the principal chiefs, including

[149] Wilkes, *United States Exploring Expedition*, IV, 64.

[150] Charles Burnham to Levi Chamberlain, July 23, 1841, in Alexander, *Koloa Plantation*, p. 37. In 1843 Hooper reported that the "usual rate of wages" on Hawaiian sugar plantations was eighteen cents a day. Hooper to Webster, Sandwich Islands, July 26, 1843, in USDS, "Consular Letters," Honolulu, II.

[151] Quoted in "The First Plantation on the Hawaiian Group," in *San Francisco Chronicle*, February 16, 1896, p. 9.

[152] Burnham to Chamberlain, July 23, 1841, in Alexander, *Koloa Plantation*, p. 37.

[153] Among the foreigners who cultivated cane to be ground at the mill at Koloa were Charles Tobey, Dr. R. W. Wood, and two former missionaries, Dr. Thomas Lafon and the Rev. Reuben Tinker. Alexander, *op. cit.*, pp. 35–36.

[154] Ladd, "Remarks upon the Natural Resources of the Sandwich Islands," in *Hawaiian Spectator*, I, No. 2 (April 1838), p. 77.

[155] *Sandwich Island Mirror*, May 15, June 15, 1840, cited in Kuykendall, *Hawaiian Kingdom*, p. 180.

the King, were actively interested in the manufacture of sugar.[156] In this, as in virtually every aspect of the economic development of the Islands, citizens of the United States took the lead, and nearly all of the "plantations" were the property of men born in that country.[157] With sugar being grown in "large quantities" on each of the principal islands,[158] the amount exported rose from 4,200 pounds in 1837 to 420,000 pounds during the twenty months from January 1840 through August 1841.[159] The value of the exported sugar rose during the same period from $300 to approximately $25,000.[160]

Despite optimistic reports and superficially encouraging statistics, the cultivation of Hawaiian sugar was a precarious occupation. The sugar was of an inferior quality, and the price fell to two cents a pound and then fluctuated from two to four cents a pound. There were other obstacles which confronted the planters if they hoped to develop the manufacture of sugar for purposes of export. Among those obstacles were the necessity of importing machinery from the United States or England, the distance of the Islands from potential markets, and the difficulty of securing an adequate supply of cheap labor.[161] With these problems to be solved, many persons doubted, in 1843, whether the production of sugar in the Hawaiian Islands would be profitable.[162]

[156] The King owned a mill at Wailuku, Maui, which he had placed under the management of a Chinese superintendent. James J. Jarves thought it was the best of the mills at that place, and Captain Wilkes believed that "with proper attention" the mill could become a profitable venture. Jarves, *Scenes and Scenery in the Sandwich Islands*, p. 174; Wilkes, *United States Exploring Expedition*, IV, 259. Kekuanaoa owned the sugar mill at Ewa, Oahu, which was partially destroyed by fire in April 1841. *Polynesian*, April 10, 1841; Report of Dr. G. P. Judd, in 1840–1841, in Letters to the American Board, CXXXVII, No. 91. Governor Kuakini of Hawaii, who was interested in several business ventures, planted nearly one hundred acres of cane, which he leased to a Chinese tenant. He likewise built a mill which, in 1840, was managed by "two or three Chinamen." The plantation is said to have flourished; but Captain Wilkes found the mill in "a wretched condition." Thrum, "Notes on the History of the Sugar Industry of the Hawaiian Islands," in *Hawaiian Almanac and Annual*, 1875, p. 36; Wilkes, *op. cit.*, IV, 223. The fourth chief was Kapiolani, who had ordered a mill to be built at Kealakekua, hoping to encourage her people to cultivate sugar and thereby acquire habits of industry. *Ibid.*, IV, 98.

[157] Hooper to Webster, Sandwich Islands, July 26, 1843, in USDS, "Consular Letters," Honolulu, II.

[158] Charlton to Palmerston, Oahu, February 9, 1840, in *Correspondence Relative to the Sandwich Islands*, p. 69.

[159] *Polynesian*, September 12, 1840, September 4, 1841.

[160] Jarves, "The Sandwich or Hawaiian Islands," in *Merchants' Magazine*, IX (August 1843), 118.

[161] *Ibid.*, pp. 120–121.

[162] Jarves, *Scenes and Scenery in the Sandwich Islands*, p. 99.

For a few years silk vied with sugar for the favor of planters, particularly on the island of Kauai. The earliest efforts to adapt silk culture to Hawaiian conditions occurred in 1837. One of these attempts was that of Charles R. Smith, on Maui, which attracted little attention and met with less success.[163] In the same year three American citizens—James J. Jarves, Sherman Peck, and Charles Titcomb—entered into a partnership under the name of Sherman Peck and Company and leased a tract of land near Koloa from Ladd and Company. Jarves was an inactive partner, leaving the management of the project to Peck and Titcomb. In 1838 Peck went to the United States to secure machinery and eggs and to employ a family to superintend the reeling of the silk. At that time the prospects of the venture were so favorable that Jarves believed the partners could have disposed of their investment at a profit of 200 per cent. There were unexpected delays and disappointments, caused principally by the difficulty of acclimating either the American or the Chinese worms to conditions at Koloa. Finally, in the spring of 1840, there followed a season of drought, pests, and storms, which destroyed many of the mulberry trees.[164] Titcomb, who seems to have been the most active of the partners, withdrew in June 1840;[165] four months later Captain Wilkes learned that the failure was attributed in part to climatic conditions at Koloa and in part to an initial investment so great as to preclude an adequate return.[166] After further disappointments Peck returned his lease to Ladd and Company in March 1841.[167] At the close of

---

[163] Journal of Levi Chamberlain, March 6, 1837; Richard Armstrong to Anderson, Wailuku, August 4, 1838, in Letters to the American Board, CXXXVI, No. 72.

[164] Jarves, *Scenes and Scenery in the Sandwich Islands*, pp. 105–112. In October 1837 a missionary at Koloa described Peck's prospects as "bright"; three years later the same missionary reported that there were four "silk plantations" on the island of Kauai, with "a prospect that they will increase." He did not identify any of the four plantations. Letters of William P. Alexander, October 27, 1837, July 1840, in Alexander, *William Patterson Alexander*, pp. 225, 242. In the spring of 1840 the condition of the plantation owned by Peck, Titcomb, and Jarves was so promising that the British consul and the American com-

mercial agent agreed that silk would soon become an important article of export from the Islands. Charlton to Palmerston, Oahu, February 9, 1840, in *Correspondence Relative to the Sandwich Islands*, p. 69; Brinsmade to Secretary of State Forsyth, Sandwich Islands, July 1, 1840, in USDS, "Consular Letters," Honolulu, I.

[165] See contract between Charles Titcomb and Ladd and Company, June 25, 1840, in *Arbitration between the . . . . Government of the Hawaiian Islands and Messrs. Ladd & Co.*, Appendix, pp. 23–24.

[166] Wilkes, *United States Exploring Expedition*, IV, 63–64.

[167] See contract between Sherman Peck and Ladd and Company, March 23, 1841, in *Arbitration between the . . . . Govern-*

that year the Rev. Peter J. Gulick reported that efforts to cultivate silkworms in the vicinity of Koloa had been abandoned.[168]

With the collapse of the silk experiment at Koloa, the firm of Peck and Company was dissolved. The hope that the production of silk could be made profitable upon Kauai did not so easily disappear. When, in 1840, Titcomb withdrew from Peck and Company, he transferred his movable property across the mountains to a tract of land which he had previously leased in "a fertile and sheltered valley" in the district of Hanalei. Shortly thereafter it was reported that he had eighty acres of mulberry trees and would soon be prepared to feed half a million worms.[169] At the close of the year, the *Polynesian*, edited by his former partner, James J. Jarves, declared that the Hanalei plantation was in a "flourishing state," and predicted that silk would soon be second in importance to no other product of the Islands.[170] The King added his approval to the experiment and urged the people of the vicinity to seek employment on Titcomb's plantation. Native women were employed to reel the silk, and small amounts were produced for export; but the returns were so slow or so meager that Titcomb became discouraged. Sometime in 1844 or 1845 he abandoned silk and turned to the cultivation of coffee.[171] About two

ment of the Hawaiian Islands and Messrs. Ladd & Co., Appendix, p. 24.

[168] Gulick to Anderson, Koloa, December 24, 1841, in Letters to the American Board, CXXXVI, No. 9.

In 1839, at a time when it appeared that the experiment of Peck and Company would be successful, a second group of foreign residents entered the field of silk culture at Koloa. In June, three residents—John Stetson, Asa Rogers, and James Lindsey—formed a partnership with Ladd and Company and then under the name of Stetson and Company leased about 150 acres near Koloa. This venture suffered from the same series of drought and pests that ruined the trees of Peck and Company, and at the close of 1842 the land was returned to Ladd and Company. The contract, lease, and surrender of the lease by Stetson are in *Arbitration between the . . . . Government of the Hawaiian Islands and Messrs. Ladd & Co.*, Appendix, pp. 19–22.

Captain John Stetson, who seems to have been the most active of the partners,

had several times visited the Islands as master of a vessel. He returned to Honolulu from the United States in the company of Peter A. Brinsmade in 1839. Like the partners of Ladd and Company, Stetson was regarded by the missionaries as "an enterprising, industrious, enlightened and pious man." It was said by one of their number that he had invested his money "for the benefit of *the nation* as well as for his own interest." Richards to Anderson, Honolulu, July 28, 1840, in Letters to the American Board, CXXXV, No. 89.

[169] *Polynesian*, August 29, 1840.

[170] *Ibid.*, December 19, 1840. Captain Wilkes, who was at Honolulu in the autumn of 1840, "understood" that Titcomb had been successful in the production of silk. Wilkes, *United States Exploring Expedition*, IV, 76.

[171] Jarves, "The Sandwich or Hawaiian Islands," in *Merchants' Magazine*, IX (August 1843), 122; Jarves, *Scenes and Scenery in the Sandwich Islands*, pp. 164–169; Damon, *Koamalu*, I, 332–333.

years later, in April 1847, he told a visitor that he had lost fifteen thousand dollars in his unsuccessful efforts to introduce silk culture into the Hawaiian Islands.[172]

The missionaries watched the establishment of plantations and the construction of sugar mills with mingled hope and anxiety. The advance of Hawaiian agriculture was welcome to the missionaries, a majority of whom believed that only through such an advance could the means be provided whereby the Hawaiian people would acquire habits of industry or find the employment necessary if their standard of living was to be raised. There was the danger that this development would be controlled largely by men indifferent to the welfare of the Hawaiian people and contemptuous of the religious and educational policies of the mission. Thus the great aspirations would be imperiled if not defeated.

Recognizing the dilemma in which they were placed, the missionaries, in July 1836, prepared a memorial to the American Board. They emphasized their belief that it was imperative that the imminent expansion of Hawaiian agriculture should be directed by men friendly to the objects of the mission. To assure this great end they urged the Board either to send agriculturists to the Islands or to form a separate organization for that purpose. They asked specifically that at least seven men be sent to the Islands. These seven included a general superintendent to advise the chiefs on matters of law and politics, a merchant to transact necessary mercantile business, a man familiar with the manufacture of cotton to assume charge of a proposed cotton factory, and four farmers, each of whom should supervise the cultivation of cotton and sugar on one of the principal islands. They also suggested that pious artisans be employed as assistants, and recommended that all men sent to the Islands should be prepared to instruct the natives in some trade. They believed that this ambitious enterprise, if successfully placed in operation, would raise the general standard of living among the natives by offering to some an opportunity to learn a trade and by providing others with steady employment. In more general terms, they expressed the hope that these proposals, if adopted, would "secure permanently the blessings of

[172] Teggart, ed., *Around the Horn to the Sandwich Islands and California 1845–1850*   (Journal of Chester S. Lyman, April 3, 1847), p. 173.

civilization and Christianity" to the Hawaiian people and would contribute to "the morality, intelligence and piety" of future generations.[173]

These recommendations were too revolutionary in character to be acceptable to the American Board, by whom they were quickly rejected. The development of Hawaiian agriculture therefore continued to be wholly under secular control. The missionaries were left with nothing more tangible than a hope that some of the planters would be sympathetic with the objects of the mission and that the new interest in agriculture, when directed by benevolent foreigners, would encourage habits of industry, stimulate ambition, and improve living conditions among the Hawaiian people. These hopes were but partially realized. The new enterprises furnished employment for a few natives. Even on a limited scale this was an innovation in Hawaiian economy. The results were observed with considerable interest by missionaries and visitors, some of whom reported that in the vicinity of the plantations and mills there was an increased circulation of money, a more general use of European clothing, a spread of "the conveniences of life," or the appearance of a class of native artisans.[174] There was another side to the story. After three years at Koloa, William Hooper was convinced of "the complete worthlessness of Sandwich Islanders as laborers on a farm";[175] and from Waimea, Hawaii—the center of the cattle industry and of related interests—the Rev. Lorenzo Lyons complained that the "moral influence" of many of the foreigners was unfortunate, as they lived "without God" and indulged in "a variety of sins," chief among which was intemperance.[176]

The early efforts to exploit Hawaiian agriculture were necessarily speculative. Thousands of unused acres capable of producing

[173] The memorial, signed by Hiram Bingham, William Richards, Lorrin Andrews, and Levi Chamberlain as a committee for the mission, may be found in Letters to the American Board, CXXXIV, No. 3.

[174] Wilkes, *United States Exploring Expedition*, IV, 69, 82; Peter J. Gulick to Anderson, Koloa, October 3, 1840, in Letters to the American Board, CXXXVI, No. 7; Edwin Locke to Anderson, Waialua, March 1841, in *ibid.*, CXXXVII, No. 159;

Titus Coan to the American Board, Hilo, May 1, 1840, February 20, 1843, in *Missionary Herald*, XXXVII (May 1841), 199, XXXIX (November 1843), 441.

[175] Hooper to William Ladd, November 28, 1838, quoted in Alexander, *Koloa Plantation*, p. 22.

[176] [Lorenzo Lyons], "Report of Waimea Station on Hawaii, from April 1839 to April 1840," in Letters to the American Board, CXXXVI, No. 158.

sugar, cotton, wheat, or coffee were a constant reminder to residents and visitors that the true wealth of the Islands was to be found in the soil. Markets, labor, and capital, however, were undependable. Of these deficiencies the most serious was the scarcity of capital, and more than one planter believed that if sufficient capital could be raised the other obstacles could be surmounted. This capital could be supplied only by American or European investors, and Hawaiian speculators with enlarged ambitions were compelled to turn to the United States or to Europe if they hoped to secure financial assistance for the development of plantations.

Apparently the belief that American or European capital could be attracted to Hawaiian plantations originated with Milo Calkin, who from June 1837 to January 1842 was chief clerk for Ladd and Company. In the winter of 1839–1840 Calkin sought to lease an extensive tract of land on Kauai. If successful in this, he proposed "to interest the capitalists in the United States to invest their funds in getting up a joint-stock company for the cultivation of those lands, and for carrying on agricultural pursuits." William Richards, a former missionary and a trusted adviser of the chiefs, is said to have favored the project, hoping that it would provide employment for the natives and revenues for the government. He explained the project to the King and presumably expressed his approval of it; but while the lease was under consideration Calkin suddenly relinquished his plans to avoid conflict with a similar plan being formulated by his employers.[177]

The proposals of Calkin were certain to be congenial to the partners of Ladd and Company. Brinsmade, Ladd, and Hooper seem to have been promoters rather than planters. Not content with their sugar plantation and mill at Koloa, they became involved in a series of speculative enterprises beginning in 1839. In that year, they agreed to contribute five thousand dollars to promote an experiment in the production of silk.[178] Two years later, they formed a partnership with D. H. Goodale to manufacture oil from kukui and other

[177] Testimony of Milo Calkin, October 5, 1846, in *Arbitration between the* . . . . *Government of the Hawaiian Islands and Messrs. Ladd & Co.*, pp. 183–186.

[178] See "Co-partnership agreement between Ladd & Company and Stetson & Company," June 14, 1839, *ibid.*, Appendix, pp. 21–22.

nuts.[179] Although the company was in debt,[180] Brinsmade continued to think in terms of expansion. He was still securely entrenched in the confidence of the mission and of the government, and through that favored position he was able to secure a lease permitting the company to occupy and to cultivate all "unoccupied and unimproved" land in the Islands.[181]

It was evident that only with funds from abroad could Ladd and Company hope to exploit this extraordinary concession. Five years later William Richards testified that the description of the lands to be leased was left vague at the suggestion of Brinsmade, who believed that such a definition would be useful in persuading American or European capitalists to invest funds in the development of the land.[182] For a time Brinsmade contemplated the sale of privileges under the lease to individual investors. This proposal was opposed by Richards, who feared that the government would experience great difficulty in regulating the activities of a number of individual capitalists. Brinsmade therefore decided to attempt the formation of a joint stock company to develop the land available to Ladd and Company.[183] Toward the consummation of this project Brinsmade hoped that American or European speculators could be persuaded to furnish the funds, while Ladd and Company provided the land and the Hawaiian people the labor. Shortly after the negotiation of the lease, Brinsmade sailed for the United States in search of unwary investors. The failure of his mission doomed Ladd and Company to bankruptcy, although not until he and his grandiose schemes had played a leading role in the efforts of the Hawaiian government to secure a recognition of its position as an independent nation.

Amidst the excitement of the semiannual visits of the whaling fleet and the development of an agricultural hinterland, Honolulu

---

[179] See "Co-partnership agreement between D. H. Goodale and Ladd & Company," June 23, 1841, *ibid.*, Appendix, pp. 22–23.

[180] Chamberlain to Hill, Honolulu, November 10, 1841, in Letters to the American Board, CXCI.

[181] A copy of this agreement, dated November 24, 1841, may be found in *Arbitration between the . . . . Government of the Hawaiian Islands and Messrs. Ladd & Co.*, Appendix, pp. 30–32.

[182] Testimony of William Richards, September 3, 1846, in *ibid.*, p. 146. Two days earlier Richards had declared (p. 104) that he had assumed that it was understood that Ladd and Company would establish one plantation on each of the principal islands, with perhaps two on Hawaii, but that the amount of land from which the company could select was limited.

[183] Testimony of William Richards, August 27, 1846, in *ibid.*, pp. 72–73.

remained the social and commercial metropolis of the archipelago. Visitors commented favorably upon the "spirit of enterprise" found there,[184] and there can be no reason to question the verdict of Captain Wilkes that Honolulu appeared to be more advanced in civilization than any other town in Polynesia.[185] It was a city of contrasts. Everywhere the old and the new were side by side, but to careful observers it was apparent that the new was in the ascendancy and that the old was being submerged. Trade was conducted wholly with specie, the coins being chiefly those of the American republics,[186] while articles which a few years before had been regarded as luxuries became accepted as necessities.[187] Slowly but steadily the thatched buildings gave way to frame or stone churches, warehouses, stores, or dwellings.[188] The houses of many of the foreigners were "built after the European manner," but they were marked by a wide range of architecture and comfort. The homes of the missionaries were comfortable but not pretentious, and one visitor condescendingly admitted that they "would not disgrace any of the villages of Western New York."[189] In the homes of the chiefs and of the more successful merchants there was a greater degree of luxury, and in some of those homes "elegant furniture" could have been found.[190]

The transformation of Honolulu from a sleepy Polynesian village to a busy commercial center was accompanied by an increase in the number of foreign residents and visitors on Oahu. A local census, taken in the autumn of 1831, indicated that there were about 180 foreigners residing at Honolulu; and a few years later, between 1836 and 1839, the number of foreigners in the community was estimated at approximately three hundred.[191] In 1843 the usually well-

184 Newburgh, "A Narrative of Voyage &c.," in AH, F.O. and Ex.; Wilkes, *United States Exploring Expedition*, III, 394.

185 *Ibid.*, III, 393.

186 Bennett, *Whaling Voyage Round the Globe*, I, 237; Bishop, *Reminiscences of Old Hawaii*, p. 29; Dugald Mactavish to Hargrave, April 2, 1842, in Glazebrook, ed., *Hargrave Correspondence*, p. 384.

187 Newburgh, "A Narrative of Voyage &c.," in AH, F.O. and Ex.

188 Townshend, *Sporting Excursions in the Rocky Mountains*, II, 30–31; Belcher, *Voyage Round the World*, I, 63; *Poly-*

nesian, May 15, 1841; Journal of Mrs. Gorham Nye (Manuscript, Archives of Hawaii), January 12, 1843; Jarves, "The Sandwich or Hawaiian Islands," in *Merchants' Magazine*, IX (August 1843), 124.

189 Hines, *Oregon: Its History, Condition and Prospects*, p. 214.

190 Olmstead, *Incidents of a Whaling Voyage*, p. 200.

191 Journal of Hiram Bingham, December 13, 1831, in Letters to the American Board, LXVII, No. 6. Samuel Parker, *Journal of an Exploring Tour Beyond the Rocky Mountains* (Ithaca, 1842), p. 364; John Diell, "Sketch of Honolulu, Oahu,"

informed James J. Jarves declared that there were between five hundred and six hundred whites in Honolulu—a figure which may have included a number of transients.[192] The increasingly cosmopolitan nature of the little seaport was suggested by the boast of the *Polynesian* that in few places could there be found "so great a proportion of travelers, voyagers, or those whose business has led them over so much of the earth's surface."[193]

The increase of the foreign population in Honolulu brought added activity to the limited social circles of the city. In 1833 there were weekly receptions, given alternately by the ladies of the foreign community;[194] and in the same year Henry A. Peirce reported that foreigners in Honolulu might be invited to tea or to a dinner party nearly every week.[195] When, in 1836, John Butler opened an "ordinary," his house was crowded with "the fashion and ton of Honolulu."[196] In the following year, the *Sandwich Island Gazette* carried notices of "a delightful ball" at a local hotel and of the King's Band which had been marching through the streets of Honolulu "decked in gorgeous caparisons" and playing music which the *Gazette* slyly remarked "was not the worst in the world."[197] The customary recreations of visitors included bowling, billiards, riding, or visiting.[198] Occasionally there were amateur theatricals,[199] or concerts by local talent.[200] Visitors or residents who sought more serious entertainment might have recourse to a museum or to a public library which contained from three hundred to four hundred volumes.[201] At least one secret fraternal order, the Masons, had a chapter in Honolulu by 1843.[202]

The ever growing number of women in the foreign community

in *Hawaiian Spectator*, I, No. 2 (April 1838), p. 84; M. [Cyrille Pierre Théodore] Laplace, *Compagne de Circumnavigation de la frégate l'Artémise* (Paris, 1841–1854), V, 448.

[192] Jarves, "The Sandwich or Hawaiian Islands," in *Merchants' Magazine*, IX (August 1843), 124.

[193] *Polynesian*, June 6, 1840.

[194] W. S. Hinckley to Hunnewell, Honolulu, November 26, 1833, in Hunnewell MSS.

[195] Peirce to Hunnewell, Honolulu, October 4–8, 1833, in *ibid.*

[196] *Sandwich Island Gazette*, September 17, 1836.

[197] *Ibid.*, February 4, 1837.

[198] Wilkes, *United States Exploring Expedition*, IV, 62.

[199] Bennett, *Whaling Voyage Round the Globe*, I, 208; *Sandwich Island Gazette*, November 19, 1836.

[200] Olmstead, *Incidents of a Whaling Voyage*, p. 200.

[201] *Polynesian*, October 17, 1840.

[202] Journal of Mrs. Gorham Nye, April 8, 1843.

gave added zest to social life; and when, in 1837, Honolulu society
was "considerably augmented" by the addition of four or five young
ladies from the United States, there were many entertainments in
their honor.[203] The hospitality of the foreign residents made Honolulu
appear especially attractive to many visitors, and in this the missionaries with their "quiet, orderly tea-parties" equaled their compatriots.[204] One visitor after being entertained at the homes of the
missionaries declared he could have believed he was again in New
England;[205] another asserted that when among the foreign residents
of the community he could imagine himself "in the heart of civilization, instead of being amongst the poor heathen";[206] and a third
described Honolulu as "by far the most agreeable town in the Pacific."[207]

Not all was peace in this tropical Eden. Visitors to Honolulu
found discord as well as hospitality in the little foreign community.
The oldest and most embittered of the divisions which rent Honolulu
society was the division between the missionaries and the mercantile
community. In the controversial issues of the decade from 1829 to
1839, missionary and merchant almost invariably had been arrayed
upon opposing sides, with a consequent increase in mutual suspicion
and ill will. The criticism, first voiced about 1824, that the missionaries coveted political or economic power was occasionally revived,[208]
and visitors from Great Britain found additional cause for alarm in
the fear that the admittedly great influence of the mission would be
exerted to injure the interests of British subjects at the Islands.[209]
A few of the more determined critics of the mission were said to have
"cursed the 'American missionary' at all times, and for all things"[210]
—an observation apparently supported by the comments of Alexander Simpson. Simpson was a friend of Richard Charlton, with

[203] Townshend, *Sporting Excursions in the Rocky Mountains*, II, 162.

[204] R. C. Wyllie, in *The Friend*, October 9, 1844, p. 91; Hines, *Oregon*, pp. 230–231.

[205] Warriner, *Cruise of the Potomac*, p. 224.

[206] Journal of Avery Sylvester (MS, Oregon Historical Society Library), p. 2.

[207] William Maxwell Wood, *Wandering Sketches of People and Things in South America, Polynesia, California and Other Places* (Philadelphia, 1849), p. 190.

[208] Peirce to Hunnewell, Honolulu, October 2, 1831, in Hunnewell MSS; Abel Du Petit-Thouars, *Voyage Autour du Monde sur la Frégate La Vénus* (Paris, 1840), I, 346–347; Edward Russell to Commodore Mason, February 3, 1837, in *Correspondence Relative to the Sandwich Islands*, p. 46.

[209] *Ibid.*; George Simpson to J. H. Pelly, Honolulu, March 10, 1842, in *American Historical Review*, XIV (October 1908), 91.

[210] Journal of John N. Colcord, p. 82.

whom he shared the ambition to convert the Islands into a British colony. He cannot be accused of undue tenderness for the American missionaries, but he did recognize the extremes to which some of the residents had carried their hostility to the mission. In a summary of the efforts to counteract the influence of the mission, Simpson wrote:

The residents accused the missionaries . . . . of having a design to prevent the natives from advancing in civilization, and from profitably employing their industry, in order to retain and increase their own influence and power,—of causing the enactment of laws which, for trivial offences, ordained severe punishments,—and of counselling the chiefs to continue their oppressive system of government. They viewed every action of the missionaries, however innocent or well meant, with suspicion; they called them—and by frequently calling them so, came to believe them to be—hypocrites even in religion; they were wroth with such visitors as would not re-echo their attacks; they established and maintained, at a very heavy expense, a school, on the principle of teaching the English language to the half-caste children, merely because the missionaries considered it best that the native language only should be taught; they supported, for several years, a newspaper, the chief aim of which was to attack the missionaries, and throw doubt and discredit on missionary reports and efforts. . . . .[211]

The missionaries were not always more charitable in their judgment of the foreign residents. The Rev. Samuel Parker informed the American public that he had "never witnessed direct enmity to every thing morally good, in so much bitterness and power, as in Oahu."[212] From the interior of the island of Hawaii—far removed from the influence of any seaport—the Rev. Lorenzo Lyons described the majority of the foreigners in that district as "bitter enemies" of the mission, whose moral influence was greatly to be deplored, and whose sins included not only the familiar one of intemperance but also "quarreling, fighting, devouring."[213] Officers of visiting vessels, both at Honolulu and at Lahaina, often were on friendly terms with the missionaries and occasionally accepted invitations to social gatherings at their homes.[214] Very few of the foreign residents, before

[211] Simpson, *Sandwich Islands*, pp. 17–18.

[212] Parker, *Exploring Tour Beyond the Rocky Mountains*, pp. 375–376.

[213] [Lorenzo Lyons], "Report of Waimea Station on Hawaii, from April 1839 to April 1840," in Letters to the American Board, CXXXVI, No. 158.

[214] Letter of D[wight] Baldwin, Lahaina, December 17, 1841, in *Sailor's Magazine*, XIV (August 1842), 371–372; [C. W.

1840, were entertained by the missionaries at Honolulu, if we may judge from the journal of Levi Chamberlain;[215] still fewer of the foreigners in the Islands were regarded as devout or exemplary Christians.[216]

The slow but steady increase in the number of merchants and planters at the Islands, some of whom were accompanied by their wives, modified the character of the foreign population. Among the newcomers were some who were quite willing to be friendly with the missionaries and a few who were openly sympathetic with their policies and aspirations. This subtle change in the attitude of the foreign population was grudgingly conceded by Richard Armstrong, who wrote that of twelve or fifteen foreigners living in the vicinity of Wailuku, Maui, none were "open opposers of religion."[217] Hiram Bingham was more generous and doubtless equally accurate when, in 1833, he assured a correspondent in the United States that the merchants and mechanics of Honolulu were not to be regarded as differing in character or conduct from those of other cities "who make no pretentions to religion of any kind, and whose objects are gain and pleasure."[218] As the decade progressed, missionaries and their friends observed the shifting population of Honolulu with satisfac-

---

Gelett], *A Life on the Ocean* (Honolulu, 1917), pp. 33, 47; Journal of Levi Chamberlain, November 28, 29, 1832, February 2, November 8, 22, 1833, April 26, 1834, September 24, 1835, November 1, 1837, February 4, December 11, 1840.

[215] From 1832 to 1839, Chamberlain noted the presence socially at the homes of the missionaries one or more times of William Ladd, Dr. Thomas, P. A. Brinsmade, Captain Dominis, Henry Skinner, and several ladies, the wives or other relatives of foreign residents. *Ibid.*, August 29, September 29, 1832, September 24, 1835, November 1, 1837, February 26, 1839. This record is probably far from complete, but its very brevity indicates the lack of any cordial or steady social contacts between the missionaries and the resident foreigners.

[216] In March 1834, John N. Colcord and Peter Anderson "made a public profession of religion" in the church at Honolulu and became members of that church. Peter

A. Brinsmade attended religious meetings of the mission, conducted "a respectable Bible class," and was active at the Seamen's Chapel at Honolulu. *The Friend*, January 1, 1845, p. 5; Journal of Levi Chamberlain, November 4, 1833, March 3, 1834; Chamberlain to Hill, Honolulu, February 17, 1835, in Letters to the American Board, CXCI; Bingham to Anderson, Honolulu, March 27, 1836, in *ibid.*, LXVII, No. 43; Letters of John Diell, January 1835, January 1, 1836, in *Sailor's Magazine*, VIII (September 1835, July 1836), 22, 340. There were other and less prominent residents of Honolulu whose piety the missionaries recognized and approved.

[217] Armstrong to Anderson, Wailuku, January 23, 1839, in Letters to the American Board, CXXXVI, No. 74.

[218] Bingham to Joseph Brown, Oahu, May 8, 1833, in *Sailor's Magazine*, VI (February 1834), 186.

tion. In 1836, Dr. W. S. W. Ruschenberger believed that it included "comparatively few disreputable people";[219] two years later the missionaries agreed that the trade of Honolulu was in the hands of merchants who conducted their business "on principles, honorable, we think, to that class of the community, and favorable to the prosperity of the country."[220] William Richards was able to detect "a very favorable state of feeling" on the part of influential foreigners toward the mission and the government,[221] and in 1843 the Seamen's Chaplain reported that the "tone of moral feeling is rising. Former practices would not now be tolerated."[222]

When Captain Wilkes was at Honolulu in 1840 he was surprised to discover that, with few exceptions, missionaries and merchants were less embittered than he had anticipated. He heard little or no abuse of the missionaries, and he was led to hope that the two groups would develop a mutual feeling of good will to which, as he observed, "they had long been strangers."[223] This hope was only partially realized. The disappearance of older political issues and the increasing division of sentiment in Honolulu along national lines tended to soften old antagonisms and occasionally created a temporary community of interests between the missionaries and their fellow countrymen on Oahu. There did not develop, however, any real cordiality between the two groups, and in 1842 a distinguished British visitor believed that the missionaries and merchants were "on barely decent terms with each other."[224]

Meanwhile national jealousies and commercial rivalries had created new social divisions within the little community. Sir George Simpson, who sought to be friendly with various groups at Honolulu, found that among the merchants at that place there was "no imaginable limitation of the sources of discord," and with what appears to have been only a slight exaggeration he declared that "one half of all

[219] Ruschenberger, *Voyage Round the World*, p. 477.

[220] General Letter of the Mission, June 20, 1838, in *Missionary Herald*, XXXV (April 1839), 147.

[221] Richards to Anderson, Honolulu, July 27, 1840, in Letters to the American Board, CXXXV, No. 88. Among the friendly residents named by Richards were Brinsmade,

Ladd, Jarves, Francis Johnson, Dr. R. W. Wood, Sherman Peck, Milo Calkin, and Captain John Stetson.

[222] S. C. Damon to Anderson, Honolulu, April 5, 1843, *ibid.*, CXXXVII, No. 209.

[223] Wilkes, *United States Exploring Expedition*, III, 415.

[224] Simpson, *Journey Round the World*, II, 156.

the strangers in this strange land are not on speaking terms with the other."[225]

The position of Honolulu as a center for the distribution of goods to all parts of the northeastern Pacific encouraged American merchants at that place to consider the possible advantages to be gained from the establishment of a newspaper on Oahu. Such a paper presumably would be devoted primarily to the interests of the mercantile community and it might expect to receive support not only from the residents of the Islands but also from English-speaking merchants in every port of the Pacific. As early as 1833 Henry A. Peirce declared that there were enough interested persons at Honolulu to support a small newspaper "if judiciously managed."[226] Three years later, in July 1836, the first number of the weekly *Sandwich Island Gazette* was published at Honolulu—the first newspaper in English west of the Rocky Mountains.

The origin of the *Gazette* is obscure, and whether or not it was launched with the purpose of becoming the organ of any faction in the community cannot be ascertained. The publishers were Stephen D. Mackintosh and Nelson Hall, two citizens of the United States. Mackintosh was a local merchant without editorial experience. He continued his mercantile interests, and for a time he acted as editor, merchant, and auctioneer.[227] Hall was a printer by trade, and apparently he had come to Oahu at the invitation of Mackintosh to become printer of the *Gazette*.[228] He rented a room at the home of Melchior Bondu, a lay member of the Catholic mission, and he and

[225] Simpson, *Journey Round the World*, II, 157–158.

[226] Peirce to Hunnewell, Honolulu, April 8, 1833, in Hunnewell MSS.

[227] Mackintosh may have lived in Boston, as an editorial comment in the *Gazette*, August 27, 1836, stated that "our first acquaintance with Dictionary and grammar" was in a school in Boston taught by the well-known Oregon adventurer, Hall J. Kelley. In the opening number of the *Gazette* Mackintosh confessed that he was not familiar with "the duties of an editor." The same issue carried an advertisement in which he offered for sale at his store "a variety of Merchandise." The issue of November 12, 1836, carried an announcement of an auction, with Mackintosh listed as auctioneer. The *Gazette* of January 7, 1837, contained a notice of the formation of a co-partnership by Mackintosh, Nelson Hall, and Samuel A. Cushing, with the firm name of Mackintosh & Co. The partners published the *Gazette* throughout 1837 and 1838, and continued Mackintosh's business as auctioneer.

[228] Journal of Melchior Bondu, May 30, 1836, quoted in Reginald Yzendoorn, "Establishment of the First English Newspaper in the Hawaiian Islands," in HHS, *Twenty-Second Annual Report* (Honolulu, 1914), pp. 17–18. Hall was a native of Concord, New Hampshire. *The Friend*, February 15, 1845, p. 32.

Mackintosh proposed to publish their paper on the premises occupied by Bondu. This association aroused suspicion in the minds of some of the chiefs, and may explain the disfavor with which Kinau viewed the application of Mackintosh and Hall to be allowed to establish a newspaper.[229] Not until after the King had intervened to grant the necessary permission could plans for the publication of the *Gazette* go forward.[230]

The first number of the new journal appeared on July 30, 1836. Scarcely two months had passed before the editors provided a clue as to their attitude toward the American mission. On October 1 they announced that they had rejected a communication describing religious services on the U.S.S. "Peacock" written in "a well known hand"—presumably that of Hiram Bingham. In the same number, they bemoaned the lack of items from their correspondents. Two weeks later they indulged in implied criticism of the Calvinist missionaries when they praised the character and virtues of William Ellery Channing and expressed the wish that "all who wear the cloth could—did—resemble this great divine."[231] The *Gazette*, however, pursued a cautious policy for nine months, during which the editors generally avoided issues which would cause dissension in Honolulu. This policy was abandoned in April 1837, when they published a communication bitterly attacking the American mission. Accompanying this communication was the comment of the editors that controversial items would no longer be excluded from the columns of their paper.[232] Although the *Gazette* presumably opened its columns to all views, few communications appeared which could be regarded as friendly to the mission, and after April 1837 the editorial policy of the paper and the opinions expressed by its correspondents were consistently and often bitterly hostile to the mission and to the Hawaiian government.

After two and a half years Mackintosh left the editorship of the *Gazette* and was succeeded by a committee of the foreign residents. The American missionaries believed that the editorial policy of the paper was largely formulated by a Catholic priest, the Rev. Robert A.

[229] Yzendoorn, *loc. cit.*; Journal of Stephen Reynolds, June 14, 1836.

[230] *Ibid.*, July 16, 1836.

[231] *Sandwich Island Gazette*, October 1, 15, 1836.

[232] *Ibid.*, April 15, 1837.

Walsh.[233] The *Gazette* was supported primarily by the mercantile community and its editors displayed a considerable concern for the news of the commercial world, but their editorial policy was a constant reminder that they were the spokesmen of a single faction in Honolulu. They persistently advocated that the foreign residents be granted the right to own real estate, defended the efforts of Catholic missionaries to secure admission to the Hawaiian kingdom, fought the reforms favored by the American missionaries, and belittled the value of the mission's achievements.[234]

It is impossible to estimate the influence of the *Gazette* either in the Hawaiian Islands or in other parts of the world, but it is unlikely that it molded the opinion of any considerable number of persons. Mackintosh sent a file of his paper to a number of American and British periodicals, many of which noticed in their columns—sometimes with complimentary remarks—the existence of the *Sandwich Island Gazette*. The extracts which they reprinted from its pages were largely confined to such innocuous news as the activities of the royal family, the visits of men-of-war, the Oahu Charity School, or notes on the commerce or products of the island kingdom.[235] At least three American newspapers reprinted some of the comments of the *Gazette* on the conduct of the American mission and the alleged perse-

[233] Chamberlain to Anderson, Honolulu, February 11, 1839, in Letters to the American Board, CXXXV, No. 120.

[234] For illustrations of the editorial policy of the *Gazette* see especially the issues of August 26, September 23, October 21, 28, 1837, January 6, July 28, 1838, March 2, May 25, July 27, 1839. James J. Jarves, who arrived at the Islands during the brief career of the *Gazette*, wrote that it "became an organ of virulent abuse of the government, missionaries, and their patrons. . . . . By its misstatements numbers of benevolent individuals abroad were led to suppose that . . . . the government set at defiance all international law. Hence their sympathies were unintentionally enlisted against a much wronged people." Jarves, *History of the Hawaiian Islands*, p. 156. H. L. Sheldon, another pioneer journalist at Honolulu, declared that the *Gazette* "was coarsely and violently opposed to the government of the day, and abused the American mis-

sionaries without stint." H. L. Sheldon, "Historical Sketch of the Press of Honolulu," in *Hawaiian Almanac and Annual*, 1876, p. 41. It is not surprising, therefore, that one of the missionaries described the *Gazette* as "one of the most contemptible publications that I ever read." Lowell Smith to Anderson, Honolulu, November 20, 1837, in Letters to the American Board, CXXXVII, No. 21.

[235] *Bunker Hill Aurora*, January 28, 1837; *Nantucket Inquirer*, June 3, 1837; *Chinese Repository* (Canton), V (February 1837), 478; *Portland* (Maine) *Advertiser*, April 28, 1838; *British Packet and Argentine News* (Buenos Aires), September 9, 1839; *Evening Chronicle* (London), January 25, 1837; *Journal du Havre*, June 24, 1837; *Canton Press*, April 8, 1837; *Hampshire Telegraph*, May 15, 1837; *New Bedford Mercury*, November 3, 1837; *Sydney Herald*, August 14, 1837; *Daily National Intelligencer*, May 6, 1837.

cution of Catholics at Honolulu, and one of these—the *Boston Pilot*—confined its quotations largely to articles concerning the relations of the American missionaries and their Catholic rivals.[236]

The circulation of the *Gazette* is said to have been about one hundred copies, and within the kingdom it aroused considerable opposition by its implacable antagonism to the mission and the government. It remained in existence for three years and in July 1839 came to a little-mourned end—probably because of lack of support. It was followed by a monthly journal, known as the *Sandwich Island Mirror and Commercial Gazette,* which was controlled by the same group that had guided the destinies of the *Gazette,* and the editorial columns of the *Mirror* reflected the same hostility to missionary activities that had been displayed by its predecessor. After a year it also suspended publication.[237]

Before the *Mirror* ceased publication, a vigorous rival—the *Polynesian,* edited by James Jackson Jarves[238]—was in the field. In the first issue, which appeared June 6, 1840, Jarves assured readers that the *Polynesian* would be "the organ of no sect or party"—a promise that must have been welcome to the American missionaries. The Rev. William Richards, formerly a prominent member of the mission and in 1840 the principal adviser of the chiefs, frankly wished the *Polynesian* success in order to forestall the danger that another anti-missionary journal might be undertaken.[239] Jarves, who had come from Boston in 1837 "in pursuit of health and recreation,"[240] was a nephew of the Rev. Reuben Tinker, and the columns of the *Polynesian* reflected the friendly attitude of its editor toward both the mission and the government. Although its news columns were of more general interest than those of its predecessors, the *Polynesian* encountered financial storms. In December 1840 Jarves confessed that his expenses were heavy while the circulation of his paper

[236] *Boston Pilot,* April 13, May 4, June 29, 1839; *New York Evening Star,* June 30, 1837; *Louisiana Advertiser,* April 23, 1839.

[237] Riley H. Allen, "Hawaii's Pioneers in Journalism," in HHS, *Thirty-Seventh Annual Report* (Honolulu, 1929), p. 79.

[238] For a sketch of the life of Jarves, see T[heodore] S[izer], "James Jackson Jarves," in *Dictionary of American Biography,* IX, 618–620. See also Sizer, "James Jackson Jarves, A Forgotten New Englander," in *New England Quarterly,* VI (June 1933), 328–352.

[239] Richards to Hunnewell, Honolulu, July 31, 1840, in Hunnewell MSS.

[240] Jarves, *History of the Hawaiian Islands,* p. 8.

was "very limited";[241] a year later, with the issue of December 4, 1841, Jarves surrendered the *Polynesian*. A week later it appeared under the editorial guidance of James F. B. Marshall, but "for want of a printer" publication was suspended after only one issue had appeared.[242] With this one feeble effort to keep it alive, the *Polynesian* was engulfed in the fate that already had overtaken the *Gazette* and the *Mirror*. Its disappearance from the stores and homes of Honolulu was not permanent. In the spring of 1844 Jarves returned to the Islands from a visit to the United States, and in May a revived *Polynesian* once again brought the news of the Pacific area and the comments of its youthful editor to the English-speaking population of the Islands.

There was one other early entrant in the field of Hawaiian journalism. This was the *Hawaiian Spectator*, a quarterly journal edited by "an association of gentlemen," of whom Peter A. Brinsmade seems to have been the most active and influential.[243] This quarterly, the first issue of which appeared in January 1838, was chiefly devoted to articles on the history, people, and contemporary conditions of the Hawaiian Islands, but contained some notices of intellectual and political problems of more general interest. Although its brief span of existence covered but two years,[244] the eight numbers of the

[241] Jarves to Larkin, Honolulu, December 8, 1840, in Larkin MSS, I, No. 107. There were seven subscribers to the *Polynesian* at Monterey. Jarves to Larkin, Honolulu, April 3, 1841, *ibid.*, I, No. 166.

[242] Marshall to Hunnewell, Honolulu, December 18, 1841, in Hunnewell MSS.

[243] The group that sponsored the publication of the *Hawaiian Spectator* seems to have been composed largely of members of the "Sandwich Island Institute," which was organized in November 1837. Pledged by its constitution to promote the intellectual improvement of its members and to gather and preserve information concerning the islands of Polynesia and the west coast of America, the Institute was the result of the earliest interest shown by foreigners in the Hawaiian Islands in philosophical or scientific problems. The Institute maintained a circulating library and enrolled thirty-one resident members. Its president was Peter A. Brinsmade, and

included in its membership were representatives of the American mission as well as of that portion of the community which disliked many of the policies of the missionaries. Henry B. Restarick, "Intellectual Life Led by Hawaii a Century Ago," in *Honolulu Star-Bulletin*, October 26, 1929; Letter of John Diell, Honolulu, January 1, 1838, in *Sailor's Magazine*, XI (May 1839), 267.

[244] Following the publication in the *Spectator* of a controversial article dealing with the visit of Captain Laplace to Honolulu in July 1839, Brinsmade retired as editor, possibly after the French and British consuls had urged him to do so. Inasmuch as Brinsmade had been principally responsible for the financial support of the quarterly, its continuation proved impossible, although the Rev. Reuben Tinker was selected as editor and hopes were entertained by some of the missionaries that the *Spectator* could be kept alive or later revived. Bingham to

Spectator remain a storehouse of information concerning the Hawaiian Islands in the early part of the nineteenth century. Unlike the *Gazette* and the *Mirror*, it was distinctly friendly to the American missionaries, printed articles by representatives of that group, and defended them against the accusations of their detractors.[245]

The statistical superiority of the United States in the commerce of Honolulu was less decisive than it had been during the first thirty years of the century. Only about one-half of the merchant vessels which called at the Islands were owned in the United States,[246] and less than 50 per cent of the value of the cargoes landed at that port was represented by goods from the United States.[247] After the Panic of 1837 the American maritime trade underwent a marked decline for a few years—a development clearly reflected in the commercial statistics at Honolulu. English traders were the beneficiaries, and in 1841 one English trader at Honolulu jubilantly reported that the value of British commerce with the Islands had increased over six hundred per cent within three years, until it surpassed the value of American and French trade combined.[248]

The losses suffered by American commerce with the Islands after 1837 were but temporary, and the statistics which appeared to show a lessening in American control of the economic life of the Islands

Anderson, Honolulu, November 18, 1839, in Letters to the American Board, CXXXV, No. 11; Chamberlain to Anderson, Honolulu, January 13, 1840, in *ibid.*, CXXXV, No. 126.

[245] The *Spectator* was printed by the mission press. It was anticipated that the missionaries would be the principal contributors, and it was suggested that they could make the new journal "almost what they wish." The Rev. Artemas Bishop declared that the missionaries had "long felt the need of such a publication as a vehicle of presenting such facts before the world as the resources of Polynesia afford." E. O. Hall to Anderson, Honolulu, October 18, 1837, in Letters to the American Board, CXXXVII, No. 116; Artemas Bishop to Anderson, Ewa, October 20, 1837, in *ibid.*, CXXXV, No. 65.

[246] Jarves, "The Sandwich or Hawaiian Islands," in *Merchants' Magazine*, IX (Au-

gust 1843), 114–115; Letters of John Diell, January 1835, January 1, 1836, January 1, 1838, in *Sailor's Magazine*, VIII (September 1835, July 1836), 22, 338, XI (May 1839), 265; Diell to Greenleaf, Honolulu, January 1, 1837, *ibid.*, X (October 1837), 41–42; *ibid.*, XIII (July 1841), 333. Official lists of American vessels calling at Honolulu from 1836 through 1840 may be found in the semi-annual reports of the United States commercial agent at that port, in USDS, "Consular Letters," Honolulu, I.

[247] *The Friend*, June 1, 1844, p. 58; *Polynesian*, September 12, 1840; Jarves, "The Sandwich or Hawaiian Islands," in *Merchants' Magazine*, IX (August 1843), 116–117.

[248] Henry Skinner to Captain Jenkin Jones, Honolulu, October 11, 1841, in *Correspondence Relative to the Sandwich Islands*, p. 120; Jones to Rear Admiral Ross, Monterey, November 6, 1841, in *ibid.*, p. 99.

were misleading. Most of the important and successful merchants at Honolulu were Americans. Nearly all of the experiments with agriculture were carried on by natives of the United States, and the ultimate prosperity of the Islands depended upon the semiannual visits of American whalers in the Pacific. Americans seem to have outnumbered all other foreigners in Honolulu,[249] and English and French visitors agreed that nearly all of the influential aliens in the community were from the United States.[250]

The predominance of Americans was more pronounced in other parts of the archipelago. A census taken in 1840 on the island of Kauai revealed that among seventy-five foreigners then resident on that island sixty had come from the United States.[251] The proportionately large number of Americans on Kauai may have been the result of the plantations established on that island by American capital, together with its lack of attractions for deserters or mechanics. There are no equally satisfactory figures for the foreign population of Maui or Hawaii. In view of the distribution of American missionaries throughout the Islands it is likely that Americans formed the largest body of foreigners in virtually every district of the archipelago. In the spring of 1841 the *Polynesian* declared that there were sixty American families in the Islands, including the missionary families, and added that the "whole number of Americans here cannot be much short of six hundred, or at least several hundred more than those of all other foreigners of whatever nation."[252] Two years later a census taken under the direction of the acting commercial agent of the United States revealed only 404 Americans resident

[249] George M. Colvocoresses, *Four Years in the Government Exploring Expedition* (New York, 1853), p. 185; Journal of Henry Bridgman Brewer, April 16, [1840], in *Oregon Historical Quarterly*, XXIX (December 1928), 349; [J. Henshaw Belcher], *Around the World. A Narrative of a Voyage in the East India Squadron* (New York, 1840), II, 310; Diell, "Sketch of Honolulu, Oahu," in *Hawaiian Spectator*, I, No. 2 (April 1838), p. 84; Jarves, *Scenes and Scenery in the Sandwich Islands*, p. 38. Alexander Simpson (*Sandwich Islands*, p. 107) offered statistics to indicate that in 1842 there were 147 British subjects in Honolulu and only 144 Americans, but he

failed to include the members of the American mission.

[250] Barrot, "Les Iles Sandwich," in *Revue des Deux Mondes*, 4th ser., XIX (August 1, 1839), 315; *Extracts from the Letters and Journal of Daniel Wheeler* (Philadelphia, 1840), p. 169. Barrot believed that the majority of laborers and mechanics in Honolulu were natives of Great Britain.

[251] *Polynesian*, August 15, 1840.

[252] *Ibid.*, May 22, 1841. Cf. Jarves, "The Sandwich or Hawaiian Islands," in *Merchants' Magazine*, IX (August 1843), 123. Among the aliens in the Islands were about forty Chinese. Simpson, *Journey Round the World*, II, 151.

in the Islands. Of this number, "a large proportion" were said to be "more or less interested in landed property."[253]

Additional evidence of the commanding position of Americans in the Islands may be found in the distribution of property among residents of Honolulu. In 1832 and in 1836 two observers agreed that the total value of buildings and merchandise owned by aliens in Honolulu was about five hundred thousand dollars, of which four-fifths belonged to citizens of the United States.[254] A number of the merchants at Honolulu owned vessels which they sent on trading voyages to various parts of the Pacific. The number of locally owned vessels fluctuated, but all reports indicated that a majority of the vessels owned by foreigners in the Islands belonged to Americans.[255] In 1841 the *Polynesian* estimated the value of all property owned by Americans at the Islands, exclusive of shipping, was not less than one million dollars,[256] and Peter A. Brinsmade informed Secretary of State Webster that "the whole amount of American capital" invested in commerce or agriculture by Americans in the Islands was not less than $1,500,000.[257] Estimates of the value of property owned by British subjects in the Islands are not available, but it is improbable that it approached, much less equaled, the value of American-owned property there.

In view of this marked superiority of Americans in the commercial life of the Hawaiian kingdom it is not surprising that Honolulu was said to show "many evidences of their enterprise" or that their homes and stores could be described as "the largest and handsomest in the place."[258] These same Americans—voluntary exiles from the land of their birth—retained a strong affection for their native country. This was demonstrated in many ways, but never more enthusiastically than on the annual return of the anniversary of American

[253] Hooper to Secretary of State Webster, Oahu, March 7, 1843, in USDS, "Consular Letters," Honolulu, I.

In April 1843 *The Friend* (April 7, 1843, p. 18) reported that there were 400 Americans in the Islands, of whom 257 were adults and 143 were children. One hundred and ninety-eight, or nearly one-half of the total, were members of missionary families.

[254] *Niles' Register*, LI (October 29, 1836), 130; Ruschenberger, *Voyage Round the World*, p. 488.

[255] *Niles' Register*, XLIII (September 8, 1832), 22; *Polynesian*, September 12, 1840, September 4, 1841.

[256] *Ibid.*, May 22, 1841.

[257] Brinsmade to Webster, Washington, D.C., April 8, 1842, in USDS, "Consular Letters," Honolulu, I.

[258] Colvocoresses, *Four Years in the Government Exploring Expedition*, p. 185.

independence. The observance of the day was not confined to Americans, for Hawaiian chiefs often participated in the festivities. Many
of Honolulu's stores were closed in honor of the day; the American
children emulated their cousins in the United States by employing
noise-making devices of various descriptions; the government fired
salutes as a mark of courtesy; and a variety of social events brought
the great day to a happy close. With some reason, James J. Jarves
declared that nowhere was the day observed with more enthusiasm
than in Honolulu.[259]

By 1840 Honolulu had assumed many of the aspects of a great
seaport, and the presence there of hundreds of transient visitors added
to the problems which taxed the ingenuity of the native authorities
and their advisers. It is not easy to evaluate the influence of visitors
and residents from alien shores, although it is evident that the foreign
community of Honolulu, like that of all busy ports, was composed of
men from all classes of society and of widely varying interests and
ambitions. Twice a year, when the vessels of the whaling fleet called
to purchase supplies or to allow their crews a short respite from the
strenuous life at sea, Honolulu was almost literally overrun with
visiting seamen. These were often a source of embarrassment to the
government, and at times there was a serious danger of conflict between the often irresponsible sailors and the usually indiscreet native
constables. Partly to minimize the likelihood of such a conflict, and
partly in the hope of diminishing prostitution among the native
women, the government adopted legislation requiring all seamen to
return to their ships by eight o'clock each night. This regulation was
vexing to the sailors,[260] and the conduct of the police added to their
resentment. A dangerous situation was narrowly averted on the
evening of November 17, 1842, when "nearly two hundred sailors"
from vessels in the harbor paraded in protest against the unpopular
law.[261] Despite the absence of violence on this occasion, Governor

[259] Jarves, *Scenes and Scenery in the Sandwich Islands*, p. 38. See also Olm-stead, *Incidents of a Whaling Voyage*, pp. 216–217; Journal of Levi Chamberlain, July 5, 1841; *Polynesian*, July 10, 1841.

[260] Goble *et al.* to Kekuanaoa, Honolulu, November 22, 1842, in AH, F.O. and Ex.; Smith *et al.* to Kekuanaoa, Honolulu, No-vember 22, 1842, in *ibid.* In April 1843 the Hawaiian legislature modified this regula-tion by passing a new law permitting sea-men to remain on shore until 9:30 each evening. A copy of this law may be found filed with the laws in the Archives of Ha-waii.

[261] Journal of Mrs. Gorham Nye, Novem-ber 17, 1842.

Kekuanaoa ordered all constables to carry arms at night[262]—an order which was ill calculated to allay the friction between the seamen and the police.[263] Although the presence of hundreds of sailors intent on forgetting the long months of labor at sea and free to enjoy the questionable pleasures of Honolulu saloons created a problem which was always a menace to the peace of the community, serious rioting did not occur until after 1850.

In 1820, when the sandalwood trade entered upon its most lucrative period, few Americans could have realized that a small but enterprising group of their countrymen were establishing an economic frontier in the mid-Pacific. Twenty years later it was apparent to all well-informed persons that citizens of the United States, led by merchants and missionaries, were actively engaged in extending their influence and control over virtually every phase of Hawaiian life. The Hawaiian people were but passive and uncomprehending spectators of the struggle for control of Hawaiian commerce and resources. Several of the surviving chiefs were financially interested in trade or in the manufacture of sugar, but in neither did they take the initiative. The submergence of the Hawaiian people before the irresistible advance of commerce and agriculture was apparent to every intelligent observer, and neither philanthropy nor education could delay the economic conquest of the Islands.

The probability that the Hawaiian people would always play a minor role in the exploitation of their own archipelago was made a virtual certainty by the continued decrease in their numbers. While the American and English population increased in numbers, wealth, and political influence, the sinister forces of depopulation wreaked havoc among the natives. Two estimates of the population, one in 1832 and the other in 1836, told graphically the pathetic story of the disappearance of a nation. During those four years the population

[262] The order, signed by Kekuanaoa, Honolulu, November 18, 1842, may be found in AH, F.O. and Ex.

[263] Statement of Robert Oglie, dated November 23, 1842, in *ibid.* According to Oglie, Stephen Reynolds, who was then acting as pilot at Honolulu, openly sympathized with the seamen in their feud with the local authorities, and on one occasion advised a group of sailors to give the constables "a good hiding." During the previous year Governor Kekuanaoa had complained to Brinsmade that the captains of American whalers had sent men ashore contrary to the laws of the kingdom and on one occasion had aided a man confined in the prison to escape. Kekuanaoa to Brinsmade, July 13, 1840, in *ibid.*

of the Islands decreased from 130,000 to less than 109,000[264]—a decline of approximately sixteen per cent. No epidemic or great natural disaster explained this rapid loss in numbers. A high death rate and a low birth rate had become common phenomena among the Hawaiian people. Commenting upon the decreasing population of the Islands, Henry A. Peirce predicted that within twenty years only a remnant of the Hawaiian people would be left,[265] and the Rev. Lowell Smith bemoaned the fact that "the millennium of the Hawaiian nation" had passed.[266] Both believed that the Islands were passing rapidly into the hands of foreigners.

It was less certain what nation would be the ultimate beneficiary of the passing of the Hawaiian people. The visits of French men-of-war to the Pacific and the activity of Catholic missionaries, who looked to France for protection, were evidence that the government of Louis Philippe might have imperial ambitions. Great Britain showed less immediate concern with the Pacific, but its commercial interests in the Hawaiian Islands were second only to those of the United States. Informed observers, however, were aware that the position of the United States in that remote archipelago—doubly fortified by the success of merchants and missionaries—could not be successfully challenged short of a resort to force. The supremacy of American interests in the Islands was the principal reason to expect that France and Great Britain would make no effort to secure possession of the archipelago. For the future, that same supremacy embodied the ominous threat that commerce and the mission would be followed by the flag.

---

[264] Jarves, *History of the Hawaiian Islands*, p. 237.

[265] Peirce to Hunnewell, August 13, 1837, in Hunnewell MSS.

[266] Smith to David Leslie, Honolulu, March 21, 1844, MS, Oregon Historical Society Library.

VI

THE TURBULENT 'THIRTIES

THE death of Kaahumanu, on June 5, 1832, left Hawaiian politics in confusion. Six days later, Henry A. Peirce wrote that Kinau had succeeded to the regency and that the King would continue "under Kinau as he did under Kaahumanu."[1] Friends of the late Regent, including the American missionaries, were desirous that her position and authority should be inherited by Kinau—who was a daughter of Kamehameha and one of the widows of Liholiho. Such a development could scarcely have been pleasing to the strongly vocal groups which had disliked the rule of Kaahumanu, for Kinau was friendly to the American missionaries and might be expected to favor the rigid moral reforms which the regency had imposed. Whatever uncertainty may have existed as to the succession was dispelled on July 5, after a council of the chiefs, when two proclamations—one by the King and one by Kinau—informed the public that henceforth Kauikeaouli would be king in fact as well as in name. His power, however, was to be limited by the revival of the unique office of *kuhina nui,* which was to be filled by Kinau.[2]

According to accepted tradition, the position of *kuhina nui* had been created by Kamehameha, who distrusted the qualifications of Liholiho as a ruler and who therefore wished to provide some check

[1] Peirce to Hunnewell, Oahu, June 11, 1832, in Hunnewell MSS.
[2] Journal of Levi Chamberlain, July 5, 1832. The proclamations may be found in AH, F.O. and Ex. They are printed in *Arbitration between the . . . . Government of the Hawaiian Islands and Messrs. Ladd & Co.,* pp. 231–232.

upon the anticipated capriciousness of his successor. The power of
the *kuhina nui* was very great, for in accordance with the supposed
will of Kamehameha, all actions of the King required the consent of
his *kuhina nui* in order to be effective.[3] With the departure of Liholiho for England in 1823, the office had been allowed to lapse. The
revival of the office, nine years later, apparently was designed to provide a method of compromise between the partisans of Kauikeaouli
and of Kinau.

Proclamations could not determine the relative influence of the
two rivals for control of the government. One visitor, friendly to
Kinau, described her as "wholly unacquainted with the affairs of government" and as either very timid or lacking in energy.[4] She was
possessed of more force of character than the King, and she could
rely upon the advice and influence of the powerful missionaries; but
her position was imperiled by the rising tide of protest against the
moral reforms sponsored by Kaahumanu. The King was believed to
be in sympathy with the obvious wishes of the foreign residents, who
in turn hoped to see him freed from the limitations placed upon his
power by the elevation of Kinau. For eight months there was grave
uncertainty as to the ability of the King and the *Kuhina Nui* to co-
operate in the conduct of public business.

Early in 1833 the situation moved rapidly to a crisis. In February, the King was reported to be drinking heavily and to have countenanced the revival of the suppressed *hula,* possibly in the hope that he
might thereby increase his own popularity.[5] He was obviously restless, and for a time his closest associates were chosen from a group
of young men notoriously hostile to the policies advocated by the missionaries.[6] On March 9 a public announcement that all laws except
those prohibiting murder and theft were repealed indicated that the
party opposed to the mission was at least temporarily in control of
the government.[7] With reason, the missionaries were alarmed. Some
of their number feared that the King would seek to restore the abso-

[3] Jarves, *History of the Hawaiian Islands,*
p. 108; Alexander, *Brief History,* p. 166;
Kuykendall, *Hawaiian Kingdom,* p. 64;
Constitution of 1840, in Thurston, comp.,
Fundamental Law of Hawaii, p. 4.

[4] Warriner, *Cruise of the Potomac,* p. 239.

[5] Journal of Levi Chamberlain, February 8, 14, 15, 17, 18, 21, 23, 28, 1833.

[6] Bingham, *Sandwich Islands,* p. 447.

[7] Journal of Levi Chamberlain, March 9,
1833.

lute monarchy,[8] and there were rumors that Kinau was to be assassinated or deposed.[9]

The elder chiefs who had been counselors of Kamehameha and Kaahumanu were no better pleased than the missionaries by the threat of a return to absolutism.[10] When news of the confusion at Honolulu reached the other islands, two of the chiefs hastened to Honolulu to counsel the King against the adoption of rash measures.[11] After conferences between the King and the chiefs, the people in Honolulu were summoned, on March 15, to listen to the will of their rulers. The King addressed the assembly, reiterating his intention to assume the royal prerogatives. Then, after a moment of apparent hesitation, he announced that the enforcement of the laws would be committed to Kinau.[12] His statements were somewhat ambiguous, and it was uncertain whether or not he proposed to relegate Kinau to a subordinate position in the government. Observers well acquainted with the King, including two missionaries, believed that he hoped to concentrate in his own hands all power of legislation.[13] This may have been his purpose, but he was too vacillating to make any persistent effort to establish himself as the dominant force in his government, and on March 19 he told Governor Hoapili that he proposed to restore to Kinau the legislative powers of the crown.[14] Meanwhile he had assured Hiram Bingham that the disorders which alarmed the missionaries would be suppressed.[15]

The decision of the King to allow Kinau to exercise a major share in the determination of public policy enabled him to avoid an immediate conflict with the elder chiefs. It did not so readily dispose of all causes of friction. The announced division of power was not wholly satisfactory to any of the groups interested in Hawaiian politics. Missionaries and chiefs were disturbed lest Kauikeaouli persist in his

[8] Bingham to Anderson, Oahu, March 20, 1833, in Letters to the American Board, LXVII, No. 25.

[9] Journal of Levi Chamberlain, March 3, 1833.

[10] Chamberlain to Anderson, Honolulu, March 26, 1833, in Letters to the American Board, LXVIII, No. 163.

[11] Journal of Levi Chamberlain, March 11, 14, 1833; Bingham, *Sandwich Islands,* pp. 447–448.

[12] *Ibid.,* p. 448; Journal of Levi Chamberlain, March 15, 1833.

[13] *Ibid.,* March 17, 1833; Bingham to Anderson, Oahu, March 20–April 9, 1833, in Letters to the American Board, LXVII, No. 25; Peirce to Hunnewell, Honolulu, April 8, 1833, in Hunnewell MSS.

[14] Journal of Levi Chamberlain, March 19, 1833.

[15] *Ibid.,* March 16, 1833.

announced determination to be king in fact as well as in name. Opponents of the mission were chagrined that Kinau was continued in power.[16] The situation was further complicated by the lack of cordiality between the two principals. Incidents were not wanting to indicate the suspicion with which each viewed the other. In May the King expressed a desire that Kekuanaoa, the husband of Kinau, resign his post as commander of the royal guards.[17] A month later, the chiefs sought to induce the King to go to Lahaina, where he would be less susceptible to the influence of foreigners and therefore more amenable to the wishes of the chiefs. With obvious reluctance the King agreed, but before he could embark he was waited upon by a group of foreigners who persuaded him to remain in Honolulu.[18] The uncertainty and ill will which thus clouded Hawaiian politics continued for two years; that it did not culminate in violence probably is to be explained by the character of the King. In March 1833 the British consul predicted that the King would "eventually be obliged to have recourse to arms" if he intended to reduce Kinau to an inferior position in the government.[19] Such a step would have required a strength of will foreign to the King.

Kauikeaouli, henceforth known as Kamehameha III, seems to have been not wholly unlike his brother Liholiho in character. Vacillating and amiable, he brought to his exalted position a desire to please bulwarked by good intentions but unsupported either by experience or by strength of character. After he had been proclaimed titular King in 1825 his education had become the cause of concern to all the conflicting elements which hoped through him to advance personal fortunes or to shape the destiny of his petty kingdom. His guardians were successively the impetuous Boki and the pious Kaahumanu. The influence of Boki was stronger, but it was broken by the tragic voyage to the South Pacific; and the efforts of Kaahumanu to induce her royal charge to adopt the ideas and ideals of the mis-

[16] Chamberlain to Anderson, Honolulu, March 26, 1833, in Letters to the American Board, LXVIII, No. 163; Journal of Stephen Reynolds, March 15, 1833; Charlton to Palmerston, Oahu, March 19, 1833, in *Correspondence Relative to the Sandwich Islands*, pp. 33–34.

[17] Journal of Levi Chamberlain, May 29, 30, 1833.

[18] *Ibid.*, June 23, 24, 1833; Journal of Dr. and Mrs. Alonzo Chapin, IV, 69–70 (June 23, 24, 1833).

[19] Charlton to Palmerston, Oahu, March 19, 1833, in *Correspondence Relative to the Sandwich Islands*, pp. 33–34.

sionaries failed to overcome his natural conviviality and dislike of restraints. For many years he retained an easy familiarity with many of the foreigners in Honolulu, and his personal associates were drawn from all classes of his subjects. Representatives of all the contending groups in Honolulu had ample opportunity to enjoy his friendship and to secure his confidence; with a characteristic desire to please everyone, he might play billiards with traders or seamen in the afternoon and sing hymns with the missionaries in the evening. The missionaries feared that "interested foreigners" had considerable influence with the King;[20] but however the residents may have sought to prejudice him against the mission, they did not prevent him from remaining on friendly terms with many of the missionaries. His divided affections were well characterized twenty years later by Friederich Gerstaecker, who described him as "entirely conquered by the spirit—partly that of religion through the missionaries, and partly that of cognac through the French."[21]

On formal occasions the King appeared dignified and at ease amidst the pomp and splendor of his court, but usually he was surrounded with little of the formality commonly regarded as inseparable from royalty. He was fond of outdoor sports and was adept at billiards, and often he might have been found playing billiards or bowling with some of the foreign residents or visiting seamen. On such occasions all pretense of ceremony was cast aside and one visitor to Honolulu observed, in 1836, that the young King was on the most friendly terms with the "commonest skippers that visit the port," who did not hesitate to address him by name or put their arms about his neck.[22] The qualities which commended him to foreigners and to

[20] Chamberlain to Anderson, March 26, 1833, in Letters to the American Board, LXVIII, No. 163. See also Warriner, *Cruise of the Potomac*, p. 238; Ruschenberger, *Voyage Round the World*, p. 460. In 1834 an English visitor was told by foreign residents "best acquainted with the character" of the King, that the associates of the young monarch were such as "to suppress his better and to foster his less favourable feelings." Two years later an English Quaker learned from Kuakini that foreigners had supplied the King "with money,

and every other thing" he wished and thus had him "so completely in their hands" as to be able to persuade him "to allow the free use of spirits." Bennett, *Whaling Voyage Round the Globe*, I, 231; *Extracts from Letters and Journal of Daniel Wheeler*, pp. 169–170.

[21] F. Gerstaecker, *Narrative of a Journey Round the World* (New York, 1853), p. 280.

[22] Ruschenberger, *Voyage Round the World*, p. 459.

subjects alike were well summarized by the naval officer who declared that he was "frank, kind and generous."[23]

The King was only mildly interested in the details of official business, and he seldom sought to mold the policies which were pursued in his name. In February 1834 he adopted a son born to Kinau and Kekuanaoa, an action which was commonly interpreted as indicating a reconciliation between the King and the *Kuhina Nui*.[24] Later in the same year, the King and chiefs adopted a code of criminal law based upon laws and decrees issued by the chiefs during the preceding decade. The new code was divided into five chapters, dealing with murder, theft, adultery, perjury, drunkenness, and similar misdeeds. It was proclaimed publicly by the King on January 5, 1835, at which time the enforcement of the laws was committed to Kinau. Levi Chamberlain reported that, in accordance with a prior decision of the council of chiefs, Kinau was also named as governor of Oahu.[25] She did not actively serve in that post, being content to allow her husband, Kekuanaoa, to perform the duties of that important office. With the King generally indifferent to affairs of state and with the administration of the most important island safely within the circle of her own family, the dominance of Kinau was not seriously challenged, and competent observers united in acknowledging that the real administrative control of the government was in her hands.

The friendship of Kinau with the missionaries at Honolulu was open and beyond question; and critics believed, with some cause, that her public actions were often determined by the opinions and wishes of her missionary friends.[26] There is every reason to assume that she listened attentively to their advice, and it is reported that on one occasion Dr. and Mrs. Judd dissuaded her from an announced intention of retiring from public life.[27] The policy of the government,

---

[23] Colvocoresses, *Four Years in the Government Exploring Expedition*, p. 216. Cf. Townshend, *Sporting Excursions in the Rocky Mountains*, II, 55–57.

[24] Judd, *Honolulu*, p. 47.

[25] Journal of Levi Chamberlain, January 5, 1835; W. D. Westervelt, "Hawaiian Printed Laws before the Constitution," in HHS, *Sixteenth Annual Report*, pp. 48–49.

[26] Charlton to Palmerston, Oahu, November 23, 1836, in *Correspondence Relative to the Sandwich Islands*, p. 44; Newburgh, "A Narrative of Voyage &c.," in AH, F.O. and Ex.; Barrot, "Les Iles Sandwich," in *Revue des Deux Mondes*, 4th ser., XIX (August 1, 1839), 307; Belcher, *Voyage Round the World*, I, 53; Laplace, *Campagne de Circumnavigation de la frégate l'Artémise*, V, 432, 437.

[27] Judd, *Honolulu*, p. 41.

however, was determined not by the missionaries but by a small group of elder chiefs who had been the advisers of Kaahumanu and who had given Kinau indispensable support during the uncertain months following the death of the Regent. All of these chiefs were friendly to the mission; some of them were outspoken champions of its program. It is possible that they would have been willing to re-enact the moral legislation of earlier years, but expediency dictated a policy of caution and delay. Meanwhile, as during the regency, the Hawaiian kingdom was ruled by an oligarchy rather than by an absolute monarch.

Kinau retained the position of *kuhina nui* until her death in April 1839. During the last four years of her life she was the dominant personality in Hawaiian politics and, in effect, the administrative head of the government. Her position was not challenged by any of her subjects and the King acquiesced in the policies which she and the chiefs adopted. Her relations with foreigners in the Islands were less tranquil, and apparently she did little to reconcile the foreign community to her or to her government. By a missionary friend she was described as "a little haughty" in her attitude toward strangers,[28] and there is evidence that she was even more stubborn when her views were disputed by foreign residents or visitors.

The lack of cordiality between Kinau and the foreign community increased the opportunity for misunderstanding and ill will at a time when there were many issues awaiting an amicable settlement. During the four-year period when Kinau was responsible for the decisions of the government, she was confronted with at least six major problems of policy. These included the tenure of land by foreigners, the proposed revival of the moral legislation, the treatment of native Catholics, the insistence of Catholic missionaries that they be allowed to propagate their faith in the Islands, efforts to secure the recall of the commercial agent of the United States, and the selection of some competent person to act as adviser to the chiefs and to guide them in the organization of a constitutional government.

The foreign residents were not indifferent to the issues involved in any of these questions. As a group they were most vitally concerned over the reluctance of the government to modify the ancient

[28] *Ibid.*, p. 39.

land policy. Feudal tenure, with the title of all land nominally vested in the King, continued to be the only recognized method of holding land. In effect, the tenure of land was less precarious than it had been a half-century earlier. There had been no general redistribution of land since the reign of the first Kamehameha, and the advice of Lord Byron, in 1825, that chiefs and commoners alike should be given a reasonable assurance that they would not be dispossessed of the land they occupied, had been generally respected by the government.[29] This negative policy fell far short of satisfying aggressive foreigners, who demanded the right to buy, sell, or bequeath land in the Islands without restriction.

Since early in the reign of Kamehameha, foreign residents had been allowed to occupy land which they had used for buildings or for agriculture. Their use of the land had been subject to the same limitations as were imposed upon native tenants. Only rarely had a foreigner been deprived of land which he had used; but the uncertainty of tenure remained to annoy the tenant. The situation was further complicated by the misgivings with which the chiefs viewed the increasing activity and wealth of foreigners in the Islands.[30] When these fears were translated into a basis for possible public policy, they became a matter of grave concern to the foreign residents.

As a corollary of the feudal tenure of land, as well as from their meager understanding of international law, the Hawaiian rulers insisted that they might deny the privilege of residence to anyone whom they disliked. These pretensions were disputed in the foreign community. The residents found an argument in the fifth article of the treaty negotiated by Captain Jones in 1826, for that article contained a clause guaranteeing to American citizens engaged in commerce, "whether resident or transient," protection "in their lawful pursuits." This was sufficiently vague to admit of varying interpretations. It was argued by the residents that the clause guaranteed to American citizens the right to reside in the Islands whether or not such residence was agreeable to the native rulers.[31] The chiefs rejected this interpre-

[29] Hobbs, *Hawaii: A Pageant of the Soil*, pp. 26–27.

[30] Bennett, *Whaling Voyage Round the Globe*, I, 238; Jarves, *Scenes and Scenery in the Sandwich Islands*, p. 96; Journal of John N. Colcord, p. 112.

[31] Bingham to Evarts, Oahu, December 13, 1831, in Letters to the American Board, LXVII, No. 7.

tation, but neither chiefs nor residents seem to have been disturbed by the fact that the treaty to which the latter appealed had not been rati-fied by the Senate of the United States.

The dual problem of land tenure and residence presented impli-cations of more than casual concern to the missionaries. In this, as in all political matters, the position of the mission was most forcefully stated by the missionaries at Honolulu and particularly by Hiram Bingham. His stubbornly held views appear to have been dictated by his anxiety to protect the natives against encroachments by un-scrupulous whites. He opposed any move which would limit the power of the Hawaiian government over foreigners within its domain or which would increase the influence of foreigners generally in the agricultural or industrial life of the Islands. Against the assertion that American citizens had been guaranteed the right freely to reside in the Islands, Bingham argued that "so long as no foreigner owned a foot of land on the Sandwich Islands, the owners of the soil most certainly have a right, if they choose to exercise it, to object to any foreigner's gaining a residence in their country."[32] He viewed with misgivings the efforts of an increasing number of foreigners to acquire land for large-scale agricultural enterprises. Many years later Peter A. Brinsmade recalled that Bingham had held the "decided opinion" that the introduction of foreign capital on a large scale would prove disastrous to the native population. In contrast to opinion in the foreign community, he believed that the natural resources of the Islands could be developed safely only by men who would employ their funds and energies "disinterestedly for the common good of the people" in a spirit of benevolence comparable to that which had prompted the establishment of the mission.[33] In common with many of his colleagues he feared that the undeveloped resources of the Islands would attract speculators who would exploit not only the soil but also the people. A warning which he addressed to the American Board in 1833 was reiterated in the well-known memorial addressed to the Board by the mission in July 1836. In that memorial, endorsed by virtually the entire missionary group, four of the ablest and best informed of the missionaries declared:

[32] *Ibid.*
[33] Brinsmade to John Ii, Pauoa, July 16,   1847, in *Sandwich Island News*, July 21, 1847.

. . . . foreign speculators may be expected to seize on the advantages which the country affords for agriculture, manufactures and commerce; and an inevitable influx of foreign population, induced only by the love of pleasure or gain, would doubtless hasten the waste of the aborigines, and at no distant period the mere mouldering remnants of the nation only could be pointed out to the voyager.[34]

The missionaries who signed this memorial were among the trusted advisers of Kinau and the chiefs; presumably they did not neglect to express their apprehensions in informal conversations with the rulers of the nation. These warnings must have added to the disinclination of the chiefs to modify the established land policy or to grant additional privileges to aliens. The opponents of that policy could not have failed to recognize that unsupported appeals to the chiefs would bring no relaxation of the land laws. They did have greater faith that assistance might come from the visits of men-of-war.

In January 1835 a group of residents urged John C. Jones to request the dispatch of an American naval vessel to Honolulu to "settle the affairs of this country,"[35] among which they included the vexing questions of residence and land tenure. When, in September 1836, an American squadron under the command of Captain Edmund Kennedy arrived at Honolulu, the principal item in the list of grievances presented by American residents was the refusal of the government to allow foreigners to sell or to transfer land at will.[36] On October 4 Kennedy, accompanied by a number of foreign residents, called upon the chiefs to discuss various questions that concerned Americans at Honolulu. The principal subject for discussion was the desire of foreigners to be allowed to own and to transfer land. For four days the discussions continued, during which Kennedy is said to have assumed a "very imperious" manner.[37] His efforts were

[34] Bingham to Anderson, March 20–April 9, 1833, in Letters to the American Board, LXVII, No. 25; Memorial of the Mission, signed by Hiram Bingham, William Richards, Lorrin Andrews, and Levi Chamberlain, July 1836, in *ibid.*, CXXXIV, No. 3.

[35] Journal of Stephen Reynolds, January 23, 1835.

[36] Kennedy to Kauikeaouli, Honolulu, October 7, 1836, in Ruschenberger, *Voyage Round the World*, pp. 498–500.

[37] Journal of Levi Chamberlain, October

4, 7, 1836; Journal of Stephen Reynolds, October 4–7, 1836; Samuel Parker to David Greene, Honolulu, November 14, 1836, in Letters to the American Board, LXXI, No. 192. Commenting upon these conferences, the *Sandwich Island Gazette* noted editorially: "The rights of proprietorship of foreigner's estates,—estates of which they have become the legal possessors, were discussed;—the rights of the King and chiefs to expel foreigners from the Sandwich Islands, were talked about. The policy of leasing land to strangers, was upon the

in vain. The King agreed that there was some merit in a proposal to lease land to industrious foreigners, but he stubbornly declined to agree to any modification of existing policy—a refusal that was attributed by at least one observer to the influence of the American missionaries.[38] On the final day of the conferences Kennedy threatened to inform the President that the Hawaiian government had failed to observe its treaty obligations;[39] but the chiefs were adamant. With reason, Americans in Honolulu complained that the visit of Kennedy had done very little to advance the economic interests of Americans in the Islands.[40]

Six weeks later, the question of the ownership of land was reopened by the visit of the British man-of-war "Acteon," commanded by Lord Edward Russell. Russell presented to the chiefs the draft of a proposed treaty which would grant to British subjects more extensive privileges than they previously had enjoyed. His manner was described as "wholly dictatorial";[41] and he and Charlton plainly implied that should the King reject the proposed articles the "Acteon" would fire upon the town.[42] The King thereupon agreed to the treaty, but he insisted that the clause guaranteeing to British subjects the right to reside in the Islands and to erect houses should be modified to make that privilege dependent upon the consent of the King.[43] Stephen Reynolds thought that by the treaty British residents had

tapis. The treatment of prisoners, confined by the Sandwich Island Government, was treated upon. Debts against the Government, in favour of Americans, were brought forward." *Sandwich Island Gazette*, October 15, 1836.

[38] Barrot, "Les Iles Sandwich," in *Revue des Deux Mondes*, 4th ser., XIX (August 15, 1839), 545.

[39] Journal of Stephen Reynolds, October 7, 1836.

[40] *Sandwich Island Gazette*, October 15, 1836; Reynolds to Hunnewell, Oahu, November 14, 1836, January 1, 1837, in Hunnewell MSS. The *Gazette* commented editorially: "Now we attended the meetings alluded to, until we got out of patience with the tedious prolixity of the measures, which were, finally, *not taken;* and we could neither ascertain, that the Commodore . . . . nor any other person, or per-

sons, could bring to pass any thing which would be promising to the afflicted."

[41] Parker to Greene, Honolulu, November 14, 1836, in Letters to the American Board, LXXI, No. 192.

[42] Journal of Levi Chamberlain, November 15, 1836; Parker, *Journal of an Exploring Tour Beyond the Rocky Mountains*, p. 374; Kamehameha III to William IV, Honolulu, November 16, 1836, in AH, F.O. and Ex.

[43] The text of the treaty may be found in FRUS, 1894, Appendix II, p. 37. According to Hiram Bingham, the King and the chiefs and missionaries who were present at the signing of the treaty agreed that the government had not surrendered its right to exclude from the Islands any person whom it found obnoxious. Bingham to Anderson, Honolulu, May 15, 1839, in Letters to the American Board, CXXXV, No. 9.

gained "the privilege of buying and selling their premises, [and] buildings";[44] and the *Sandwich Island Gazette* announced the conclusion of the treaty under the heading, "The Happy Day has come!"[45] It was easy to exaggerate the importance of the treaty. In conversation in Honolulu, Richard Charlton declared that it granted British subjects the right of residence in the Hawaiian Islands,[46] but in transmitting a copy to the British Foreign Office he merely commented that it would have "a beneficial tendency" for British subjects in the Islands and would protect the Hawaiian people, inasmuch as it decreased the danger that the native rulers would become embroiled with some great power.[47] He, too, had overestimated the importance of the Russell treaty. The government in London judged it at more nearly its true value, believing it to be, in the words of Alexander Simpson, the "promises of good behaviour made by the petty chief of a distant and almost unknown archipelago, whose affairs it knew or cared very little about."[48]

The problems raised by the hope of the missionaries that the rigid moral legislation of the regency could be revived were less significant economically, but they were charged with a higher emotional content than was the dispute as to land tenure. After the death of Kaahumanu the fate of the reform laws had been dependent upon the attitude of the governors of the several islands. On Maui, Governor Hoapili continued to suppress the sale of intoxicants,[49] and apparently he adhered to this policy even after the King had announced the repeal of those laws. A similar situation existed on Hawaii and Kauai. On Oahu the nominal prohibition of the sale of intoxicants was ignored between the time of the death of Kaahumanu and the formal abrogation of the law in March 1833. Critics of the restrictive legislation received encouragement during the visit to Honolulu of the U.S.S. "Potomac" in July and August, 1832. From Captain Downes the missionaries received "very polite attentions,"[50] but the

44 Journal of Stephen Reynolds, November 16, 1836; Reynolds to Hunnewell, Oahu, January 1, 1837, in Hunnewell MSS.

45 *Sandwich Island Gazette*, November 19, 1836.

46 Bingham to Anderson, Honolulu, May 15, 1839, in Letters to the American Board, CXXXV, No. 9.

47 Charlton to Palmerston, Oahu, November 22, 1836, in *Correspondence Relative to the Sandwich Islands*, p. 43.

48 Simpson, *Sandwich Islands*, p. 21.

49 *Sailor's Magazine*, V (July 1833), 322–323.

50 Chamberlain to Hill, Honolulu, August 7, 1832, in Letters to the American

political advantage rested with their opponents. In discussions with the chiefs Downes condemned the attempts to impose moral reforms by law, declared specifically that the Decalogue was not a satisfactory basis for civil law, and requested that those who had sold liquor to the crew of the "Potomac" should not be punished.[51]

The advice of Downes coincided with the personal inclinations of the King. The consequences were soon apparent. In October 1832 there were said to be thirty places in or near Honolulu where the forbidden beverages were sold openly.[52] In the following April, Hiram Bingham reported that for two months there had been "unusual confusion" at Honolulu accompanied by "an obvious increase of drunkenness, gambling and debauchery."[53] In March the King formally rescinded the moral legislation of the regency; and soon thereafter, in defiance of the wishes of many of the elder chiefs, he granted licenses for the sale of liquor in Honolulu.[54] Three American merchants declined to sell intoxicants,[55] but their example was lost upon the community.

For two years advocates of temperance found little cause for encouragement at Honolulu.[56] Gradually, however, as Kinau gained in political experience and confidence, the missionaries turned their attention again to moral reforms. In 1835 they devoted a large part of their annual meeting to a discussion of the means of arousing support for temperance among the Hawaiian people. Unhampered by any dissenting opinion as to the desirability of their purpose, they planned to hold quarterly meetings throughout the Islands to extol

Board, CXCI; Journal of Mrs. W. P. Alexander, [August 6, 1832], in Alexander, *William Patterson Alexander*, p. 85; Judd, *Honolulu*, p. 40; Journal of Levi Chamberlain, August 15, 1832.

[51] *Ibid.*, August 13, 1832; Bingham to Anderson, Oahu, March 20–April 9, 1833, in Letters to the American Board, LXVII, No. 25; Chamberlain to Anderson, Honolulu, March 26, 1833, in *ibid.*, LXVIII, No. 163.

[52] Armstrong to Anderson, Honolulu, October 22, 1832, in *ibid.*, LXVIII, No. 89. William Torrey, who was at Honolulu in 1833 and 1834, wrote—perhaps with some exaggeration—that along the road from Honolulu to Waikiki there were "at inter-

vals of only a few rods . . . . refreshment stations . . . . well supplied with billiard and card tables and every means of dissipation." Saloons also were "very frequent." *Torrey's Narrative*, p. 178.

[53] Bingham to Anderson, Oahu, March 20–April 9, 1833, in Letters to the American Board, LXVII, No. 25.

[54] Bingham to Hunnewell, Oahu, April 2, 1833, in Hunnewell MSS.

[55] *Ibid.*; Bingham to Anderson, Oahu, March 20–April 9, 1833, in Letters to the American Board, LXVII, No. 25. The three merchants were Henry A. Peirce, Henry Paty, and Captain Gorham Nye.

[56] John Diell to Hunnewell, Oahu, April 13, 1835, in Hunnewell MSS.

the virtues and advantages of sobriety. More significant was their agreement that "by moral suasion" they would exert their influence to prevent "the making, vending, and use" of liquor, and to that end they would "converse with the chiefs and principal men of the nation, and endeavor to enlist them on the side of entire abstinence."[57] Before the close of the year this renewed interest in the restriction of the sale of intoxicants had borne fruit when "a great popular temperance meeting" was held at Honolulu and a petition, signed by more than twenty-seven hundred natives, including Kinau, Kekauluohi, and Governor Kekuanaoa, was sent to the King, urging him to prohibit the manufacture or sale of spirituous liquors.[58] More significant, as well as probably more spontaneous, were two memorials on the same subject from masters and officers of vessels calling at Hawaiian ports. One memorial, signed by eighteen officers of American vessels, requested that legislation prohibiting the sale of liquor at Lahaina be enforced.[59] The other alleged that the memorialists had suffered "great inconvenience and frequently serious disadvantages" because of the unrestricted sale of liquor at Honolulu. To this statement of fact, they added the threat that should the conditions then existing continue they would be compelled to omit Honolulu as a port of call and go to some port "where ardent spirits are not afforded."[60]

These petitions had little immediate effect upon the situation at Honolulu, although it was believed that Kinau was ready to prohibit the importation or sale of intoxicants.[61] The King was less amenable, possibly because he was the owner of three distilleries and of one or more of the "public-houses" frequented by seamen at Honolulu.[62] In the summer of 1836 a delegation from the mission called upon him to urge him to sign a decree, said to have been prepared by the missionaries, which would have closed saloons and outlawed the sale of

[57] *Minutes of the General Meeting of the Sandwich Island Mission,* 1835, p. 22.

[58] A copy of this petition, dated November 26, 1835, may be found in Bingham, *Sandwich Islands,* p. 479.

[59] Bingham to Hunnewell, Honolulu, December 11, 1835, in Hunnewell MSS. A copy of the memorial, dated November 17, 1835, may be found in Bingham, *Sandwich Islands,* p. 478.

[60] This memorial, dated Honolulu, November 20, 1835, may be found in AH, F.O. and Ex.

[61] *Extracts from the Letters and Journal of Daniel Wheeler,* p. 179.

[62] General Letter of the Mission, [July 7, 1836], in *Missionary Herald,* XXXIII, 277 (July 1837); Charlton to Palmerston, Oahu, November 23, 1836, in *Correspondence Relative to the Sandwich Islands,* p. 45.

intoxicants.[63] This appeal was without effect, and there was no indication during the remainder of the year that the sale of liquor at Honolulu was likely to be restricted either by public opinion or by law. At the close of the year the Seamen's Chaplain hoped that the "principles of temperance" were gaining support in Honolulu,[64] but there is no evidence that they were being more extensively observed in the foreign community or by visiting seamen.[65] Through the influence of the King, licenses for the sale of liquor were again granted in the spring of 1837.[66] Elsewhere throughout the archipelago, the civil authorities enforced with a fair degree of success decrees prohibiting the sale of intoxicants.[67]

With the support of a few foreign residents and some masters of visiting vessels,[68] the missionaries continued to press their efforts to reduce the amount of liquor sold in Honolulu. In January 1838 it was said that the government intended to suppress saloons entirely or to limit their number to one or two, which would be allowed to exist only under severe restrictions.[69] For once the rumors were correct, and on March 13 the King issued a notice that at the expiration of the licenses already granted for the sale of liquor only two would be renewed.[70] A week later the King signed a decree regulating the sale of liquor by licensed shops, ordering their closing at ten o'clock each night and all day on Sunday, and providing penalties to be imposed upon merchants who permitted their patrons to become intoxicated on the premises.[71] These developments led Hiram Bingham to hope

[63] Journal of Stephen Reynolds, June 17, 1836.

[64] Diell to J. Greenleaf, Honolulu, January 1, 1837, in *Sailor's Magazine*, X (October 1837), 44.

[65] Cf. General Letter of the Mission, [July 7, 1836], in *Missionary Herald*, XXXIII (July 1837), 277. The missionaries reported that "the deluge of intemperance still rolls on."

[66] Journal of Levi Chamberlain, April 3, 1837.

[67] W. P. Alexander and Levi Chamberlain to "Merchants, Ship-owners, and Ship-masters," Honolulu, June 15, 1836, in *Sailor's Magazine*, X (December 1837), 112; General Letter of the Mission, [July 7, 1836],

in *Missionary Herald*, XXXIII (July 1837), 277.

[68] *Hawaiian Spectator*, I (October 1838), 389–390; Jarves, *History of the Hawaiian Islands*, p. 163.

[69] Letter of John Diell, Honolulu, January 1, 1838, in *Sailor's Magazine*, XI (May 1839), 266.

[70] This notice, signed by the King at Lahaina, March 13, 1838, and countersigned by Kinau at Waikiki, March 15, 1838, is filed with the laws in the Archives of Hawaii.

[71] *Hawaiian Spectator*, I (July 1838), 335–336; Thurston, comp., *Fundamental Law of Hawaii*, pp. 107–108. This decree, signed by the King at Lahaina, March 20, 1838, is filed with the laws in the Archives of Hawaii.

that the King intended to bring about gradually the exclusion of liquor from his kingdom.[72]

There was some complaint that unlicensed places persisted in the sale of liquor,[73] but it is not likely that this was the result of any indifference on the part of the chiefs. The willingness of the King to restrict so greatly the sale of liquor at Honolulu indicated that again the views of the missionaries were beginning to prevail. The sequel followed quickly. In August the chiefs promulgated a law, to become effective on January 1, 1839, forbidding the sale, manufacture, or importation of rum, brandy, gin, alcohol, or distilled spirits. Wines might be imported; but they must be submitted to the harbor master for inspection and the payment of a duty of fifty cents per gallon, and a heavy fine was fixed as the penalty for any evasion of the provisions of the law. In approving the measure Kinau addressed a naïve appeal to "Foreign Consuls, philanthropists, and all friends of order . . . . to lend their aid to enforce the above wholesome and important regulations."[74]

The return of prohibition to Honolulu was received with mixed emotions in the foreign community. There were merchants, including the partners of the influential house of Peirce and Brewer, who approved the measure,[75] and ten masters of whalers wrote from Lahaina that they had heard with satisfaction of the new regulations.[76] These expressions of approval indicated the views of a minority. More typical of the reaction of the majority was the protest forwarded to the British consul by a group of dissidents who alleged that they would suffer "extreme hardships" if the prohibitory laws were enforced.[77] Protests were unavailing. The cycle had run its course and the influence of the missionaries was again as great as it had been during the regency. For six months the sale of intoxicants was generally suppressed at Honolulu. The result was eminently satisfactory to the missionaries, and the *Polynesian* commented that drunkenness

---

[72] Bingham to Anderson, Honolulu, April 26, 1838, in Letters to the American Board, CXXXV, No. 6.

[73] George Bush to Kekuanaoa, October 15, 1838, in AH, F.O. and Ex.

[74] *Hawaiian Spectator*, I (October 1838), 389–392. The proclamation is filed with the laws in the Archives of Hawaii.

[75] Richards to Hunnewell, Lahaina, August 25, 1838, in Hunnewell MSS.

[76] This letter, addressed to Kauikeaouli and dated Lahaina, December 1, 1838, is in AH, F.O. and Ex.

[77] This memorial, addressed to Richard Charlton and dated Honolulu, April 3, 1838, may be found in *ibid.*

and "its attendant miseries were unknown, or practiced only in secret."[78] How long this condition might have continued had there been no interference from outside is uncertain. The satisfaction of the missionaries was doomed to an early shock when a commercial treaty, imposed upon the government by a French naval commander in July 1839, contained a provision compelling the government to permit the importation of French wines and brandies. In consequence the prohibitory laws, although not specifically repealed, became unenforceable.

The influence of the missionaries upon public policy was no less apparent in the renewed opposition of the government to Catholicism. The death of Kaahumanu removed the central figure in the attack upon the Catholic mission, and the political uncertainty of the ensuing years prevented the government from pursuing the anti-Catholic program of the regency. During the months of confusion the cause of the native Catholics was championed by influential persons. In August 1832 Captain Downes interceded with the King on behalf of a group of Catholics who were imprisoned or assigned to hard labor.[79] When the suggestions of Downes brought no tangible results, Charlton intervened on behalf of the prisoners, who were soon released.[80] During the following three years, Catholics in the Islands enjoyed a period of comparative peace and security. When the anti-Catholic policy was revived, it appears to have been motivated more by fear of Catholic missionaries who had come to the Islands than by any definite desire to punish or suppress the small group of Hawaiians who had clung to that faith.

The absence of a strong administrative force in the Hawaiian government after 1832 led some observers to believe that the two exiled Catholic missionaries, Fathers Bachelot and Short, would be able to return to the Islands without molestation. Opponents as well as friends of the priests were aware of this possibility, and Hiram Bingham frankly feared that the political turmoil in the Islands would open the way for a resumption of the Catholic mission. He consoled

[78] *Polynesian*, May 15, 1841; Letter of Samuel N. Castle, in *ibid.*, September 5, 1840; Richard Armstrong to George Paulet, Honolulu, March 14, 1843, in AH, "British Commission Documents."

[79] Reynolds, *Voyage of the Potomac*, pp. 418–419.

[80] Journal of Stephen Reynolds, September 2, 1832; *Annales de la Propagation de la Foi*, XII (May 1840), 244–245.

himself with the hope that Kinau, the King, and the chiefs would join in opposing such a move. From their refuge in California, Bachelot and Short kept in as close touch with the situation at Honolulu as distance would permit; and from the reports of one of the French artisans who had remained on Oahu they were encouraged to believe that the King would acquiesce in their return to the Islands.[81] This opinion appeared to be confirmed by the observations of Columba Murphy, who visited Honolulu in 1835.[82] So confident was Murphy that the priests would be permitted to reside in the Islands that he arranged for their passage to Oahu,[83] but circumstances delayed their attempt to return until 1837.

On September 30, 1836, another Catholic missionary, the Rev. Robert A. Walsh, arrived at Honolulu only to discover that Kinau and her advisers were unwilling for him to reside in the Islands.[84] The commanders of two men-of-war—one French and one British— intervened to prevent his expulsion. The permission to remain in the Islands which Walsh thus secured was modified by a stipulation that he was not to teach or to minister to natives.[85] Shortly after the departure of the men-of-war the King signed a communication to Walsh specifically repeating the injunction against the propagation of Catholicism and apparently enlarging the scope of the prohibition to include ministering to Europeans as well as to Hawaiians.[86]

[81] Yzendoorn, *History of the Catholic Mission in Hawaii*, pp. 78, 87; Bingham to Anderson, Oahu, March 20–April 9, 1833, in Letters to the American Board, LXVII, No. 25; Journal of Levi Chamberlain, March 19, 1833. Dr. W. S. W. Ruschenberger, who was at Monterey on board the U.S.S. "Peacock" in July 1836, noted that Bachelot and Short were then at Monterey and "anxious to obtain a passage to Oahu, in the hope of finding there an opportunity of proceeding to the Gambier Islands, where there is a Catholic mission." Ruschenberger, *Voyage Round the World*, p. 512.

[82] Yzendoorn, *History of the Catholic Mission in Hawaii*, pp. 87–88; Columba Murphy to the Bishop of Nilopolis, in *Annales de la Propagation de la Foi*, IX (November 1836), 189–191.

[83] Yzendoorn, *History of the Catholic Mission in Hawaii*, p. 88.

[84] *Sandwich Island Gazette*, October 8, 1836; *Suppliment to the Sandwich Island Mirror*, January 15, 1840, p. 25.

[85] Yzendoorn, *History of the Catholic Mission in Hawaii*, pp. 95–96; Jarves, *History of the Hawaiian Islands*, p. 153. Prior to the arrival of the two men-of-war, Walsh had been protected by the British consul. Parker to Greene, Honolulu, November 14, 1836, in Letters to the American Board, LXXI, No. 192; *Suppliment to the Sandwich Island Mirror*, January 15, 1840, p. 25.

[86] Kamehameha III to Walsh, Honolulu, December 5, 1836, in AH, F.O. and Ex. The King's message contained the ominous threat that any infraction of the injunction would result in the expulsion of Walsh; but on the same day the latter answered a question as to when he intended to depart by the statement that he did not expect to leave the Islands. Journal of Stephen

The most dramatic episode in the efforts of the government to exclude Catholic missionaries followed the reappearance of Bachelot and Short at Honolulu. They arrived on April 17, 1837, on the brig "Clementine," fully aware that they might not be welcome and having already conceded that in "all probability we shall be treated as enemies."[87] Their fears were soon realized. When their presence in Honolulu became known to the authorities they were ordered to leave the Islands upon the vessel upon which they had come—an order which was repeated almost daily for a month.[88] Kinau hurried to Honolulu,[89] and the King signed a statement of policy which contained the assertion that "all who shall be encouraging the Papal

---

Reynolds, December 5, 1836; *Suppliment to the Sandwich Island Mirror*, January 15, 1840, p. 29.

Walsh continued in a clandestine manner to provide both instruction and baptism to any Hawaiians who came to his house, and the missionaries were aware that he was "secretly using his influence to promote Popish ends." He was interested in the notoriously anti-missionary *Sandwich Island Gazette*, of which he was said to be "a chief supporter." Letter of G. P. Judd, Honolulu, October 7, 1838, in Letters to the American Board, CXXXVII, No. 77; Bingham to Anderson, Honolulu, July 26, 1839, in *ibid.*, CXXXV, No. 10; Yzendoorn, *History of the Catholic Mission in Hawaii*, p. 97. A contemporary apologist asserted, perhaps truthfully, that Walsh "never opened his church, except for members of his household." *Suppliment to the Sandwich Island Mirror*, January 15, 1840, p. 29.

[87] Letter of Alexis Bachelot, November 3, 1836, quoted in *Annales de la Propagation de la Foi*, XII (May 1840), 256, and in Yzendoorn, *History of the Catholic Mission in Hawaii*, p. 98.

Bachelot and Short hoped that the interviews and negotiations of naval commanders at Honolulu had paved the way for their return. Short based his hopes on the treaty negotiated by Lord Russell in the autumn of 1836, although his interpretation of its provisions was not accepted by the chiefs. Bachelot apparently believed that a French commander, Captain Vaillant,

had secured promises from Kamehameha III that the priests would be permitted to return. By a writer sympathetic with the Catholic missionaries it was later declared that there was "the most incontrovertible proof" that such a promise had been made. *Suppliment to the Sandwich Island Mirror*, January 15, 1840, p. 27. The King believed that Vaillant had conceded the right of the Hawaiian government to exclude Catholic missionaries if they were unwelcome. Bingham to Anderson, Honolulu, May 15, 1839, in Letters to the American Board, CXXXV, No. 9; Bingham, *Sandwich Islands*, p. 506.

[88] Journal of Stephen Reynolds, April 18, 1837. A copy of an order to Bachelot and Short to leave the Islands, signed by Kekuanaoa and dated April 19, 1837, may be found in AH, F.O. and Ex.

Accounts of the arrival of the priests and of the events of the following month, culminating in the forced embarkation of Bachelot and Short upon the "Clementine," may be found in *Suppliment to the Sandwich Island Mirror*, January 15, 1840, pp. 29–37; Short to the Archbishop of Chalcedon, in *Annales de la Propagation de la Foi*, XII (May 1840), 257–261; Kaahumanu II [Kinau] *et al.* to the President of the United States, Honolulu, December 2, 1837, in AH, F.O. and Ex.; Kamehameha III to William IV, Honolulu, October 23, 1837, in *ibid.* See also Bingham, *Sandwich Islands*, pp. 505–507.

[89] *Sandwich Island Gazette*, May 6, 1837.

missionaries, I shall regard as enemies to me, to my counsellors, to my Chiefs, to my people, and to my kingdom."[90]

Kinau and her advisers were determined to compel Bachelot and Short to leave the Islands whenever the "Clementine" sailed for a foreign port. On May 20, two days before the scheduled departure of that vessel, native officers were sent to the home of the priests to inform them that they must leave immediately. In its report of ensuing events the *Sandwich Island Gazette* asserted that Bachelot and Short had been "dragged from their peaceful dwelling" and "led through the streets like public malefactors" to the water front.[91] Commenting upon the resort of the government to violence, Stephen Reynolds declared that the situation was "alarming" and that soon the foreign residents would "have to unite to defend their property, if not their lives."[92]

Following the forced return of the priests to the "Clementine," the owner of the vessel, Jules Dudoit, hauled down the British flag and abandoned his ship, claiming that it had been seized by the Hawaiian government.[93] For six weeks Bachelot and Short remained as prisoners on the "Clementine," while animosities in Honolulu became steadily more embittered and accusations followed one another in quick succession. It was Richard Charlton who foresaw correctly the eventual outcome of the problem, when in urging the King to release his clerical prisoners he predicted that soon "it will be too late, and must be settled by the Admiral and Commodore."[94]

On July 8 the British man-of-war "Sulphur," commanded by Captain Edward Belcher, arrived at Honolulu. Two days later, Belcher visited Charlton and J. C. Jones, from whom he learned of the plight of the priests. A visit to Kinau followed; but the request of Belcher and Charlton that the prisoners be released was met with an insistent demand that Bachelot and Short leave the Islands. Before further action could be taken, the French frigate, "La Vénus," commanded by Captain Abel Du Petit-Thouars, dropped anchor at

[90] The original of this proclamation is in AH, F.O. and Ex. It is reprinted in Jarves, *History of the Hawaiian Islands*, p. 155 n.; Yzendoorn, *History of the Catholic Mission in Hawaii*, p. 100; Bingham, *Sandwich Islands*, pp. 505–506; *Sandwich Island Gazette*, June 24, 1837.

[91] *Ibid.*, May 27, 1837.
[92] Reynolds to Hunnewell, Oahu, May 26, 1837, in Hunnewell MSS.
[93] Kinau to Kauikeaouli, Honolulu, May 23, 1837, in AH, F.O. and Ex.
[94] Charlton to Kauikeaouli, Honolulu, May 31, 1837, in *ibid.*

Honolulu. After another conference, attended by Kinau, Charlton, Jones, and both naval commanders, had failed to bring any concessions from Kinau, Belcher ordered his marines to seize the "Clementine" and to liberate the priests.[95]

On July 20, the King, who had been at Lahaina, returned to Honolulu. On the following day he was visited by Belcher, Du Petit-Thouars, Charlton, and Jones, who came to discuss the issues raised by the liberation of Bachelot and Short. After approximately four hours of discussion the group agreed upon a compromise suggested by Lorrin Andrews. As a result, the King granted permission to Bachelot and Short to remain on shore until they could secure passage to some part of the civilized world.[96] Upon the insistence of the King, Belcher and Du Petit-Thouars signed guaranties that the two priests would not engage in preaching while they remained at the Islands.[97]

Du Petit-Thouars was anxious to have France placed upon an equal footing with Great Britain in her relations with the Hawaiian kingdom. Upon his arrival at Honolulu he addressed a note to the

[95] Manuscript account of Captain Belcher's proceedings, by Kaahumanu II [Kinau] and Kekuanaoa, October 23, 1837, in *ibid.*; Belcher, *Voyage Round the World*, I, 52–55; Du Petit-Thouars, *Voyage Autour du Monde*, I, 327–329; Bingham, *Sandwich Islands*, pp. 507–508; *Sandwich Island Gazette*, July 15, 1837; *Suppliment to the Sandwich Island Mirror*, January 15, 1840, pp. 38–41.

An interesting feature of these conferences and one which throws some light upon Hawaiian politics and foreign relations was the part played by Hiram Bingham. He acted as interpreter at the first conference, where he defended the course of the chiefs and expressed his disapproval of Belcher's intention to seize the "Clementine," predicting that it would result in bloodshed. Belcher replied by threatening to hold him responsible should any of the crew be injured while liberating the priests. *Ibid.*, p. 40; Bingham, *Sandwich Islands*, p. 508; Belcher, *Voyage Round the World*, I, 54; manuscript account of Captain Belcher's proceedings, by Kaahumanu II and Kekuanaoa, in AH, F.O. and Ex.

At a later conference both Belcher and Du Petit-Thouars requested the exclusion of Bingham, but this the chiefs declined to grant. The missionary, however, was restrained from his usual avocation of defending and advising the chiefs by what Belcher described as "the sharp glances of some of the officers of both ships" and "something very much allied to menace from one of the Lieutenants of the Venus." Belcher, *Voyage Round the World*, I, 57–58; Bingham, *Sandwich Islands*, pp. 508–509; Journal of Levi Chamberlain, July 10, 1837.

[96] Lorrin Andrews to Robert C. Wyllie, no date, in AH, F.O. and Ex.; "The Statement of Lorrin Andrews concerning the interviews between Kamehameha III and Captains Belcher and Du Petit-Thouars," in *ibid.*; Belcher, *Voyage Round the World*, I, 57–58; Du Petit-Thouars, *Voyage Autour du Monde*, I, 337–339.

[97] *Ibid.*, I, 344–345; Bingham, *Sandwich Islands*, pp. 510–511. Belcher's written guaranty contained the promise that Short would not transgress any of the laws of the Hawaiian kingdom, but Du Petit-Thouars confined his statement to a stipulation that Bachelot would not preach.

King, demanding the negotiation of a treaty similar to that which had been secured by Lord Edward Russell.[98] The chiefs were not anxious to make any agreement which might obligate them to admit all foreigners, and the King obviously was cool to the proposal. Du Petit-Thouars was persistent, and on July 24, during his last interview with the chiefs, he secured the consent of the King to a brief convention of four articles, guaranteeing to French subjects in the Hawaiian Islands privileges equal to those enjoyed by nationals of the most-favored nation. In the discussion which preceded the signing of this treaty Du Petit-Thouars made a final concession when he agreed that the proposed treaty would not compel the Hawaiian government to admit Catholic missionaries into the Islands.[99] Before leaving Honolulu he made one further arrangement for the protection of French interests by naming Jules Dudoit, a British subject of French descent, consular agent of France.[100]

In November 1837 two more Catholic priests arrived in Honolulu. In accordance with the policy of the government, the Rev. Louis Maigret was not permitted to land. His companion, the Rev. Columba Murphy, had been recently and secretly ordained—a fact not known to the local authorities. He was permitted to take up residence on shore after Charlton had assured the chiefs that he was not a priest. Shortly thereafter Maigret left Honolulu for the South Pacific. He was accompanied by Bachelot, who died at sea on December 5, 1837.[101] Short had already departed for Chile,[102] and only two Catholic priests, the Rev. Fathers Walsh and Murphy, remained at the Islands. Their position at best was precarious. It was not improved when, on December 18, 1837, the King signed a proclamation reaffirming the well-known policies of the government and designed to

[98] Du Petit-Thouars to Kamehameha III, Honolulu, July 15, 1837, in AH, F.O. and Ex.

[99] Du Petit-Thouars, *Voyage Autour du Monde*, I, 345–347; Andrews to Wyllie, no date, in AH, F.O. and Ex. A copy of the treaty may be found in *ibid.* It is printed in Bingham, *Sandwich Islands*, p. 511; Du Petit-Thouars, *Voyage Autour du Monde*, I, 347–348.

[100] *Ibid.*, p. 348; Laplace, *Campagne de Circumnavigation*, V, 438.

[101] Manuscript account of a conference between Kinau and Jules Dudoit, November 3, 1837, in AH, F.O. and Ex.; Dudoit to Kinau, Honolulu, November 7, 10, 13, 1837, in *ibid.*; Kinau to Dudoit, Honolulu, November 8, 14, 1837, in *ibid.*; Samuel N. Castle, in *Polynesian*, November 6, 1841; Bingham, *Sandwich Islands*, pp. 511–514; Yzendoorn, *History of the Catholic Mission in Hawaii*, pp. 113–117.

[102] *Suppliment to the Sandwich Island Mirror*, January 15, 1840, pp. 45–46; Bingham, *Sandwich Islands*, p. 513.

prevent the teaching of Catholic doctrines or the residence of Catholic missionaries in any part of the Islands.[103]

The government already had resumed, somewhat sporadically, the punishment of native Catholics. This does not appear to have been either a sustained or systematic persecution, but during the years from June 1835 to the summer of 1838 some eight or ten native Catholics had been subjected to varying punishments for what the chiefs called idolatry.[104] In June 1838, when the power of Kinau was at its height, six Catholics were arrested. Three days later they were sentenced to imprisonment as idolaters—a charge resulting from the inability of the native authorities to distinguish between Catholic forms of worship and the abandoned rites of the ancient Hawaiians.[105] During the ensuing year men and women who were unwilling to surrender their faith at the behest of their temporal superiors were compelled to labor upon public projects or were confined in prison in the same manner as were ordinary criminals. The vivid reports of cruelties said to have been inflicted upon these prisoners may have been exaggerated; but the Hawaiian penal system was not distinguished by gentleness, and severe or cruel punishments commonly were the lot of native malefactors or luckless deserters who were apprehended by the authorities.[106] The chiefs were in no mood to give special favor

[103] *Sandwich Island Gazette*, January 6, 1838. An original printed copy of this ordinance, entitled "Rejecting the Catholic Religion," signed by Kamehameha III and dated Lahaina, December 18, 1837, is filed with the laws in the Archives of Hawaii.

[104] *Annales de la Propagation de la Foi*, XII (May 1840), 248; Journal of Stephen Reynolds, August 7, 1835; Letter of G. P. Judd, Honolulu, October 7, 1838, in Letters to the American Board, CXXXVII, No. 77.

[105] Yzendoorn, *History of the Catholic Mission in Hawaii*, pp. 124–125. Dr. G. P. Judd, a close friend of Kinau, denied that she was unable to distinguish between Catholicism and the abandoned idolatry of primitive Hawaii, and declared that the chiefs were disturbed because the Catholics "gathered persons disposed to return to idolatry, and that those persons . . . . practiced R. Catholic ceremonies with the same notions they had previously cherished."

Letter of G. P. Judd, Honolulu, October 7, 1838, in Letters to the American Board, CXXXVII, No. 77.

In defense of her policies Kinau declared: "And when the Roman Catholic priests came they sought out the ignorant, those who despised learning, and those who secretly favored idolatry, and found them ready to join their party. They suspended their images about their necks and practiced foolish things. We sent [to them] to turn back but their hearts were rebellious and they would not hear. There was therefore no alternative in our opinion but to punish them. So we have done with all cases of persons using idolatrous practices, and such is the law of the land." Kaahumanu II to Elliott, Honolulu, October 1, 1838, in AH, F.O. and Ex.

[106] Cf. The White Slaves in the Wahoo Fort to T. C. B. Rooke, August 24, 1835, in AH, "Historical and Miscellaneous Documents"; Journal of Stephen Reynolds, De-

to the Catholics, for the misdeeds of the latter were a repeated and deliberate defiance of the will of the King—a very serious offense in the eyes of Hawaiian chiefs.

Kinau died on April 4, 1839. For a few weeks her successor, the dowager Queen Kekauluohi, continued the anti-Catholic policy with vigor. Sixty or more natives were arrested in the district of Waianae, on Oahu, for having persisted in their attachment to Catholicism. Although the prisoners were brought to Honolulu, only thirteen were punished.[107] This was the last time that the government inflicted a penalty upon Catholics because of their religious beliefs. To what extent there was an official change of policy is uncertain. Competent contemporary observers have asserted that the King, on June 17, 1839, issued a decree forbidding the further use of force or threats against native Catholics;[108] but there is no copy of the supposed decree extant today, and it may be that the reputed edict of toleration was a verbal one. A month later a treaty negotiated by a French naval commander brought to a definite conclusion the long struggle of the chiefs to exclude Catholicism from the Hawaiian Islands.

It is impossible to determine the number of Hawaiians who were directly affected by the anti-Catholic policy of Kaahumanu and her successors. Samuel N. Castle declared that twenty-eight persons had "at different times been punished for the practice and propagation of the Roman Catholic religion," and he admitted that the penalty usually had been "a short imprisonment and labor for a period of about four months."[109] The government had arrested and questioned

---

cember 14, 1828; Journal of Dr. and Mrs. Alonzo Chapin, IV, 67 (May 25, 1833); Journal of John N. Colcord, p. 81; Simpson, *Sandwich Islands,* pp. 40–42.

[107] *Sandwich Island Gazette,* June 22, 1839.

[108] S. N. Castle, "An Account of the Visit of the l'Artemise," in *Hawaiian Spectator,* II (October 1839), 469; Jarves, *History of the Hawaiian Islands,* p. 159. Cf. Alexander, *Brief History of the Hawaiian People,* p. 223; Kuykendall, *Hawaiian Kingdom,* pp. 163–164. On June 18 Kekauluohi informed Bingham that the punishment of Catholic converts had been "brought to an end" and that in the future "it will, doubt-

less, be the rule to admonish." Kekauluohi to Bingham, June 18, 1839, in Bingham, *Sandwich Islands,* p. 535. Opponents of the government's policy asserted that the decree either had not been issued or had not been enforced. *Suppliment to the Sandwich Island Mirror,* January 15, 1840, p. 58.

[109] Castle, "An Account of the Visit of the l'Artemise," in *Hawaiian Spectator,* II (October 1839), 469. The statistics used by Castle had been "carefully collected" by Dr. G. P. Judd. It was possible, Castle admitted, that they were "not entirely accurate." Castle to Anderson, Honolulu, February 4, 1840, in Letters to the American Board, CXXXVII, No. 137.

many more than twenty-eight Catholics, but it is possible that no more had been imprisoned or forced to labor because of religious convictions.

No policy of the Hawaiian government has been the subject of so much adverse criticism as its uncompromising hostility to Catholicism during the decade following the departure of Boki for the South Pacific. Kinau defended the policy of the government on the ground that the use of images by Catholics constituted a violation of the established law against idolatry.[110] Less naïve was the defense offered by the Rev. William Richards, missionary and diplomat, who went to the United States and Europe in 1842–1844 to secure the recognition of Hawaiian independence. In an effort to convince the French Foreign Office that the policy of his government had not been based entirely upon caprice and intolerance, Richards ascribed the action of the chiefs to political as well as religious motives. He recalled that some of Boki's followers had shown an interest in Catholicism—a fact which had alarmed the chiefs loyal to Kaahumanu lest Catholicism and rebellion should be united. When the suspects were called before the chiefs, some of them were noncommittal and others appeared sullen. This, declared Richards, had caused the chiefs anxiety and they had inflicted punishments "which the government does not pretend to justify, but to palliate."[111] This statement did not remove the doubts of M. Guizot, nor did it afford a complete explanation of the penalties and embarrassments to which Hawaiian Catholics had been subjected.

Friends of the exiled priests and critics of the American mission joined in attributing the discomfiture of the Catholic missionaries to the influence and intolerance of their Protestant rivals. Bachelot and Short professed to believe that Hiram Bingham had been the principal instigator of the anti-Catholic policy of the government.[112] An anonymous contributor to the *Sandwich Island Mirror*, believed to have been John C. Jones, accused the American missionaries of using "every stratagem, which the ingenuity of man could invent . . . .

[110] Kaahumanu II to Captain R. Elliott, Honolulu, October 1, 1838, in AH, F.O. and Ex.

[111] Richards and Haalilio to Guizot, Paris, May 1, 1843, in *ibid.*

[112] *Annals of the Propagation of the Faith*, I (1840), 368; Short to the Archbishop of Chalcedon, in *Annales de la Propagation de la Foi*, XII (May 1840), 259, 261.

every means . . . . which illiberality and a spirit of exclusiveness could suggest" in their determination to prevent Catholicism from gaining a foothold in the Islands.[113] The editors of the *Sandwich Island Gazette* asserted that there could be no appeal from the conclusion that the measures adopted by the government "must always be laid at the door of the American missionaries, by every candid observer, and by every scrupulous investigator."[114] The judgments of Bachelot, Short, Jones, and the editors of the *Gazette* could fairly be regarded as the product of prejudice. The opinion of Henry A. Peirce could not be dismissed so easily. Peirce was less disturbed about the exclusion of the priests, but he declared that the persecution of native Catholics could not fail to arouse indignation, and, pointing an accusing finger toward the missionaries, he declared that they were "digging a grave beneath their feet which will one day or other swallow them up."[115]

The position of the American mission was delicate and equivocal. Strongly worded comments from the pen of virtually all the missionaries left no room to doubt their hostility to Catholicism or their desire that it be excluded from the Islands. Hiram Bingham, after avowing his own belief in religious toleration, expressed the wish that the Catholic missionaries "would keep far, far away" and not attempt to ensnare the Hawaiian people with "the delusions & superstitions of Rome."[116] His colleague at Honolulu, the Rev. Lowell Smith, believed that the "plague could not do more mischief among this people" than would be done by Catholicism.[117] The Rev. Artemas Bishop asserted that the introduction of Catholicism would be "the greatest calamity" that could befall thousands of the Hawaiian people,[118] and in 1837 Bingham and the Rev. Reuben Tinker described the Catholic faith as a "standard of idolatry more hostile to pure Christianity" than had been the ancient system of idols and *kapus.*[119]

[113] *Suppliment to the Sandwich Island Mirror,* January 15, 1840, p. 87.

[114] *Sandwich Island Gazette,* August 26, 1837.

[115] Peirce to Hunnewell, August 6, 1837, in Hunnewell MSS.

[116] Bingham to Hunnewell, Honolulu, October 20, 1839, in *ibid.*

[117] Smith to Anderson, Honolulu, December 3, 1836, in Letters to the American Board, LXVIII, No. 117.

[118] Bishop to Anderson, Ewa, October 20, 1837, in *ibid.,* CXXXV, No. 65.

[119] Bingham and Tinker to Anderson, Honolulu, October 16, 1837, in *ibid.,* CXXXIV, No. 5. See also Artemas Bishop, "The Influence of Christianity upon Paganism," in *Hawaiian Spectator,* I (July 1838), 276.

These were not the unauthorized or private views of irresponsible men. They were the views commonly held by the American missionaries and endorsed by their superiors in the United States. A committee of the American Board, in 1840, approved the course of the missionaries, declaring that as "faithful protestant ministers and teachers" it had been their duty to warn their people against "the great and leading errors of the Romish church." The committee admitted that presumably the chiefs thereby would be persuaded of the dangers which would follow if Catholic missionaries were granted free admission to the Hawaiian Islands.[120]

The American missionaries were of one mind as to the character and menace of Catholicism. They appear to have been united in their belief that the rulers had the right to exclude or deport Catholic missionaries, and some of their number so informed the chiefs.[121] They were less united, or less outspoken, in their views on the treatment of native converts to Catholicism. The fact that the government harassed native Catholics did not produce any public protest from the mission, but individual missionaries seem to have been disturbed by this denial of religious freedom. On one occasion the Rev. Artemas Bishop hastened from Ewa to Honolulu to protest against the punishment of a group of Catholics from Waianae—a protest which was made in vain.[122] Spokesmen for the mission categorically denied that they ever had "sanctioned or countenanced the infliction of any pains or penalties for conscience sake," and Samuel N. Castle asserted that when some of the missionaries had been given "painful evidence" that persecution actually existed, the members of the mission who had "access to the chiefs" had admonished the latter upon that subject.[123] Statements by all of the principal chiefs exonerated the missionaries of responsibility for the policy of the government toward its Catholic

[120] *Report of the American Board*, 1840, pp. 35–37.

[121] Bingham and Tinker to Anderson, Honolulu, October 16, 1837, in Letters to the American Board, CXXXIV, No. 5; Dibble, *History of the Sandwich Islands*, p. 345.

[122] Bishop, *Reminiscences of Old Hawaii*, p. 51.

[123] S. N. Castle to the Editor of the *Polynesian*, October 1841, in *Polynesian*, October 30, 1841; Castle to Anderson, Honolulu, September 16, 1839, and February 4, 1840, in Letters to the American Board, CXXXVII, Nos. 136, 137; *Missionary Herald*, XXXVI (March 1840), 99–100; Letter dated Honolulu, October 2, 1833, in *Chinese Repository*, II (March 1834), 525–526; Letter of W. P. Alexander, October 1, 1839, in Alexander, *William Patterson Alexander*, p. 226.

subjects.[124] These statements may have influenced the judgment of Captain Charles Wilkes, who believed that there was no instance in which the punishment of a native Catholic could be charged directly to the American missionaries.[125]

Reflection brought from some of the missionaries the belated confession that they had been too hesitant in their denunciation of persecution. Castle believed that his brethren had erred in not imposing church discipline upon those responsible for the ill treatment of Catholics;[126] and the Rev. Sheldon Dibble wrote that "in the multiplicity of other cares and labors, we were somewhat remiss, and did not endeavor by 'line upon line and precept upon precept' to inform the chiefs so fully on the subject of religious toleration as we ought to have done."[127] The admissions of Castle and Dibble told less than the whole story. David L. Gregg, a devout Catholic who was United States Commissioner to the Hawaiian Islands from 1853 to 1857, presented a different view. The American missionaries, Gregg asserted, had been indirectly responsible for the sufferings of the Hawaiian Catholics because of the manner in which they had attacked Catholicism in their sermons, but he added that he was "satisfied that the Missionaries never . . . . recommended persecution; on the contrary there are ample proofs that they urged the Regent and Chiefs not to punish Catholics on account of their religion."[128] The judgment of Gregg, formed nearly fifteen years after the close of the period of religious intolerance and based in part upon information received from the Rev. Robert A. Walsh, seems to have been in accord with the known facts.

The visits of men-of-war to Honolulu in 1836 and 1837, and the

[124] Virtually every important chief who had been active in the determination of the policy of the government signed at least one account of the efforts to suppress Catholicism in the Islands, but none of the statements accused the American missionaries of having advised or countenanced the persecution of Hawaiian Catholics. Kanehoa to R. C. Wyllie, Lahaina, January 31, 1851, in *Polynesian*, October 11, 1851; Kaahumanu II to Captain R. Elliott, Honolulu, October 1, 1838, in AH, F.O. and Ex.; Kekuanaoa, Ii, *et al.* to Richard Armstrong, Honolulu, September 28, 1841, in *ibid.*;

Kamehameha III to P. A. Brinsmade, Honolulu, October 28, 1839, in *ibid.*

[125] Wilkes, *United States Exploring Expedition*, IV, 12.

[126] Castle to Anderson, Honolulu, February 4, 1840, in Letters to the American Board, CXXXVII, No. 137.

[127] Dibble, *History of the Sandwich Islands*, p. 346.

[128] Gregg to the Rev. John B. Byrne, Honolulu, April 30, 1854, in Gregg MSS, Archives of Hawaii. Typed copy in Hawaiian Mission Children's Society Library.

threatening attitude of at least four of the visiting commanders—
Kennedy, Russell, Belcher, and Du Petit-Thouars—afforded the local
authorities convincing evidence not only of their weakness when confronted by the threat of force, but also of their inability to conduct
the affairs of government so as to avoid conflict with representatives
of the great maritime powers. Their alarm was increased by the unfriendly attitude of the British consul and of the commercial agent
of the United States. The insistence of Charlton and Jones in pressing the complaints and claims of their fellow countrymen may be explained as a zealous exercise of their consular duties. Both men,
however, were lacking in either tact or patience, and they were open
and determined opponents of some of the most cherished policies of
the government. In these conflicts, the American missionaries uniformly sympathized with the chiefs, and they frankly regarded Charlton and Jones as unfit to act as the representatives of great nations.
They did not hesitate, therefore, to use their influence to undermine
the two representatives at home.

Neither Charlton nor Jones enjoyed the unlimited approval of his
own government. In England, such influential men as William Wil-
berforce, Sir Thomas Baring, Lord Byron, and William Ellis were
said to be opposed to the continuance of Charlton as consul at Honolulu,[129] and in 1836 it was reported, confidentially, in the Foreign
Office that Palmerston did not have "entire confidence in Mr. Consul
Charlton." The same report described Charlton as "a person of violent temper," and contained the caution that a naval officer visiting
Honolulu should take no decisive action against the Hawaiian government unless the consul's charges were "corroborated by other
evidence."[130]

The informal character of the Hawaiian government and the willingness of Charlton to make any supposed infringement upon the
privileges of a British subject the occasion of a vigorous protest to
the local authorities brought him into frequent conflict with the

---

[129] C. S. Stewart to Jeremiah Evarts,
Norfolk, Va., February 6, 1829, in Letters
to the American Board, XXXII, No. 148.
In 1833, one London business house, concerned temporarily in mercantile affairs
at Honolulu, described Charlton's conduct
as "so disgraceful" as to merit a protest

to the Hudson's Bay Company which had
employed him as agent. Wildes & Co. to
Hunnewell, London, May 14, 1833, in Hunnewell MSS.

[130] W. Fox Stangways to Wood, September 21, 1836, in *Correspondence Relative
to the Sandwich Islands*, p. 41.

Hawaiian government.[131] Disturbed by his undisguised opposition to their policies and probably annoyed by the threatening tone in which some of his complaints were couched,[132] the chiefs—in November 1836—formally asked that he be recalled.[133] In October 1837, during the visit of a British man-of-war to Honolulu, they again requested that he be removed. In reply, they were informed that Charlton was favorably regarded in London and that their request probably would go unheeded.[134] This news might have discouraged men less determined than the advisers of the King. Before the close of the month, the King sent a second formal communication to the British government, alleging that Charlton's "oppressive proceedings" were notorious in Honolulu and asking that he be replaced by "a good man."[135]

The statement that Charlton was favorably regarded in London was not wholly correct, for the British government had ordered a secret inquiry into his character and conduct. The report was not flattering to Charlton. It conceded that he had obvious faults which had deprived him of the confidence of the Hawaiian rulers, but it suggested that he be allowed to retain his post, as it was probable that his successor would fare no better—a situation which was attributed to the determination of the American missionaries "to maintain a national preponderance and advantage."[136] Further protests from critics of Charlton produced no tangible results until 1843, when, during a crisis in Anglo-Hawaiian relations, he was removed from office in a gesture apparently designed to conciliate the Hawaiian government.

[131] In 1841 Charlton admitted that for seven years he had been "in constant disputes with this Government on account of the claims of British subjects not being attended to." Charlton to Bidwell, Oahu, January 3, 1841, in *Correspondence Relative to the Sandwich Islands*, p. 74.

[132] For example, see Charlton to Kamehameha III, November 2, 1835, January 7, 1836, in AH, F.O. and Ex.

[133] Kamehameha III *et al.* to William IV, Honolulu, November 16, 1836, in *ibid.*
In support of the request that Charlton be recalled, the King asserted that Charlton had insulted the chiefs, that he had been guilty of an unprovoked act of violence against the person of a native, and that frequently he had sought to intimidate the chiefs with the threat that a British man-of-war would visit the Islands to enforce compliance with his demands.

[134] Journal of Lorrin Andrews, October 7, 9, 10, 11, 1837, in *ibid.*; Journal of Levi Chamberlain, October 11, 1837.

[135] Kamehameha III *et al.* to William IV, Honolulu, October 23, 1837, in AH, Richards MSS. A copy of this letter may be found in Letters to the American Board, CXXXIV, No. 45—testimony to the interest with which the American missionaries followed the efforts to secure the removal of Charlton from his post.

[136] Elliott to Rear Admiral Ross, November 13, 1838, in *Correspondence Relative to the Sandwich Islands*, p. 56.

The mission and the chiefs likewise were engaged in efforts to secure the removal of John C. Jones from his post as commercial agent of the United States. As early as 1827 Jones had been regarded by the missionaries as unfriendly to them[137]—a fact which boded ill for Jones. During the closing months of the administration of John Quincy Adams there was a movement to force Jones from office. This move had the support of Secretary of the Navy Southard and of General Stephen Van Rensselaer and it enjoyed at least the passive blessing of the American Board. This could have been a formidable political alliance, but it came to naught because the critics of Jones were unable to suggest a suitable candidate for his post.[138] In 1833 there were rumors in Honolulu that Jones would resign or be removed from office by President Jackson, and Captain William S. Hinckley became an open aspirant for the place. Opinion in the foreign community, as usual, was divided. Hinckley asserted that the missionaries favored his ambitions, but Henry A. Peirce, whose views probably represented the opinions of the conservative merchants, declared that there was no one available who would be better qualified for the position than was Jones.[139]

The final and successful effort to secure the removal of Jones originated either with the American Board or with the missionaries in the Hawaiian Islands, and was begun during the summer of 1837 when William Richards was in the United States as a representative of the mission. Richards had been sent to the United States to present the views of his colleagues upon questions arising from the organization and contemplated expansion of the mission. Political matters were of secondary concern, but he took the opportunity to discuss the commercial agency at Honolulu with men whose influence might be exerted to secure the displacement of Jones and the appointment of someone more acceptable to the missionaries. He had at least one candidate, Peter A. Brinsmade, whose character and experience in the Islands would command the confidence of the missionaries and of owners of vessels touching at Hawaiian ports. Early in July,

---

[137] Chamberlain to Evarts, Honolulu, February 22, 1827, in Letters to the American Board, XXXI, No. 67.

[138] C. S. Stewart to Evarts, Norfolk, Va., February 6, 1829, in *ibid.*, XXXII, No. 148.

[139] Hinckley to Hunnewell, Honolulu, November 26, 1833, in Hunnewell MSS; Thomas Cummins to Hunnewell, Oahu, November 29, 1833, *ibid.*; Peirce to Hunnewell, Honolulu, December 1, 1833, *ibid.*

Richards was able to report that "one of our good friends in Nantucket" would soon forward a petition signed by "a large number of Captains" urging that Jones be replaced by Brinsmade.[140] While in New England, Richards conferred with Dr. Woodbury, "a good pious man" and a brother of the Secretary of the Treasury. With the good doctor Richards discussed the commercial agency at the Islands and from him Richards received a letter of introduction to the Secretary of the Treasury.[141] In September, Richards was in Washington, where he called upon "Mr. Forsyth" and "Mr. Woodbury"—presumably the Secretaries of State and of the Treasury.[142]

The representations of Richards did not produce immediate results. The problem of the commercial agency, however, was not closed. In November 1837 the Hawaiian government forwarded a memorial to the President of the United States requesting the removal of Jones. In this memorial, which was signed by the King, Kinau, and six other chiefs, Jones was accused of having condoned violations of Hawaiian laws and of having used his influence to prejudice visitors against the native authorities. In the same month, six masters of New England-owned whalers then at Honolulu sent a similar memorial to President Van Buren. The failings of Jones, they asserted, had been "the subject of loud & . . . . almost universal complaint" by persons interested in the commerce of Honolulu. Both memorials complained that Jones was frequently absent from the Islands, on which occasions he appointed as acting commercial agent a man whom the second memorial described as "particularly obnoxious in his official intercourse" to citizens of the United States. Both memorials are endorsed as having been received at the State Department on March 30, 1838; the memorial of the chiefs specifically asked that Brinsmade be appointed to succeed Jones.[143] Less than two weeks

[140] Richards to Anderson, New Haven, July 3, 1837, in Letters to the American Board, LXVII, No. 92.

[141] *Ibid.*

[142] Journal of William Richards (MS, Archives of Hawaii), September 18, 19, 1837.

[143] Both memorials may be found in USDS, "Consular Letters," Honolulu, I. A copy of the memorial of the chiefs is in

AH, F.O. and Ex. See also *Polynesian,* February 7, 1846. The chiefs alleged that Jones "is a person who indulges an intriguing disposition and contempt of us, and we cannot depend upon his advice. He opposes us and prejudices the minds of strangers and natives against us, by misrepresentation. He treats our laws with contempt and violates some of them and supports other persons in doing the same. Moreover he very often goes away from

after the receipt of these memorials President Van Buren nominated Brinsmade as commercial agent of the United States at the Hawaiian Islands.[144]

At the time of the appointment, Brinsmade was in the United States, and not until the following autumn did he embark upon the return voyage to the Hawaiian Islands.[145] While he was on the high seas, the Hawaiian authorities forced the issue when they charged Jones with bigamy and informed him that they could no longer recognize him in an official capacity.[146] Four days later, on January 12,

the islands and leaves his business with a deputy who is a man we do not wish to have employed in that office."

During the ten years from 1829 to 1839 Jones either owned or chartered a varying number of vessels, including the "Griffon," the "Volunteer," the "Avon," the "Harriet Blanchard," and the "Louisa." These vessels he employed in trade with California, and the absences of Jones from Honolulu usually could be explained by a voyage to California to direct in person his commercial ventures along that coast. Bancroft, *History of California*, IV, 694; Journal of Stephen Reynolds, October 5, 1829; Letter of John Diell, Honolulu, October 6, 1836, in *Sailor's Magazine*, IX (March 1837), 222; Peirce and Brewer to Hunnewell, Honolulu, August 8, 1837, in Hunnewell MSS; Davis, *Seventy-Five Years in California*, pp. 1, 2, 8.

When Jones was absent from the Islands Stephen Reynolds acted as commercial agent of the United States. The longest continuous period of service by Reynolds was from August 1837 to December 1838. Prior to that, according to Reynolds, he had "sometimes acted for one month, sometimes five months, and so on." Testimony of Stephen Reynolds, December 7, 1846, in *Arbitration between the . . . . Government of the Hawaiian Islands and Messrs. Ladd & Co.*, p. 404.

Against the criticism of Jones should be balanced his obvious popularity in the foreign community. A visitor in 1836 was told that Jones was "a favorite with all parties," and when Jones left the Islands in 1840 to become a resident of California he was honored with "a splendid Dinner" given by the foreign residents. Ruschenberger, *Voyage Round the World*, p. 491; L. H. Anthon to W. H. Davis, Honolulu,

February 9, 1840, in William Heath Davis MSS, California State Library, Sacramento.

[144] *The Globe* (Washington, D.C.), April 13, 1838. Brinsmade was commissioned as Agent for Seamen and Commerce, but like his predecessor he was commonly regarded in the Islands as the American consul. From the day that he assumed office in April 1839, he signed official papers as "U.S. Consul." In explaining to his government his usurpation of this title, he declared that he thought "it expedient and even necessary . . . . in order to maintain . . . . a position with the authorities of the Country equal to that of the Foreign Consuls of Other Governments." Brinsmade to Secretary of State Forsyth, Sandwich Islands, January 1, 1841, in USDS, "Consular Letters," Honolulu, I.

[145] Brinsmade to Secretary of State Forsyth, Boston, September 26, 1838, in *ibid.*

[146] Kamehameha III to Jones, Lahaina, January 8, 1839, in AH, F.O. and Ex. The charge of bigamy was possible because the government insisted that the long cohabitation of Jones with a Hawaiian mistress was the equivalent of marriage, a contention which Jones denied when he returned to the Islands with a wife whom he had married in California. That the charge of bigamy was a serious factor in the decision of the authorities to withdraw their official recognition of Jones is indicated by the emphasis placed upon it in the letter of Kinau to President Van Buren, dated January 12, 1839. The same charge was stressed in the replies of William Richards, Governor Kekuanaoa, and Kanaina, in 1846, to a question as to the reason for the request that Jones be dismissed. Each of

1839, Kinau signed a communication to the President of the United States, again requesting the recall of the offending agent.[147] Jones ignored the charges and the action of the government; until formally relieved by Brinsmade on April 9, 1839, he continued to exercise the duties of the office which he had held for more than eighteen years.[148]

The new commercial agent was a native of Connecticut, a graduate of Bowdoin College, and a former student at Andover Theological Seminary and at the Yale Divinity School.[149] He had early abandoned theology for commerce, and since 1833 he had been a resident of the Hawaiian Islands and the senior partner in the Honolulu firm of Ladd and Company. Almost alone among the merchants of Honolulu, Brinsmade had been friendly with the missionaries, a situation which may be explained either by his own religious background or by a shrewd realization that he and his company might profit from the favor of the mission. After his assumption of office, he continued to maintain cordial relations with the missionaries and the chiefs; and, in striking contrast to the policy of his predecessor, he was disposed to accept the decisions of the native authorities in cases in which the interests of his fellow countrymen were involved. In September 1841, after declining to intervene on behalf of an American citizen convicted by a Hawaiian court of a breach of the law, he stated his position frankly in a letter to the King wherein he asserted his confidence in "the disposition to justice" of the Hawaiian rulers.[150] Many of the foreign residents would have regarded this opinion as incredibly naïve.

In 1846, after Brinsmade had retired from office, William Richards testified that the conduct of Brinsmade while commercial agent

---

these men was familiar with the situation in 1839, and each replied that the action of the government had been prompted by the belief that Jones had been guilty of bigamy. *Investigation by Command of the King and Premier of the Hawaiian Islands in Vindication of the Course Pursued by His Majesty* (Honolulu, 1846), pp. 5, 32, 45, 59.

[147] Kaahumanu II to the President of the United States, Honolulu, January 12, 1839, in AH, F.O. and Ex.

[148] Brinsmade to Forsyth, April 10, 1839, which may be found in USDS, "Consular Letters," Honolulu, I.

[149] *Eighth General Catalogue of the Yale Divinity School*, p. 8.

[150] Brinsmade to Kekauluohi, September 29, 1841, in AH, F.O. and Ex. Another indication of Brinsmade's faith in native character may be found in the haste with which he accepted the statement of one chief that the master of an American vessel had defrauded natives of a substantial sum of money. Brinsmade to John Adams [Kuakini], May 1, 1840 (copy), in USDS, "Consular Letters," Honolulu, I.

had been "uniformly kind and honorable" and that he had enjoyed the confidence of the government.[151] There was tangible evidence of that confidence in January 1843, when Richards, then in the United States on a diplomatic mission, learned that James J. Jarves hoped to supplant Brinsmade in the commercial agency. Richards acted promptly to clarify the position of the Hawaiian government, and, in a letter to a Major Williams, he declared that his government did not desire the removal of Brinsmade.[152] More than three years later he remembered that he had had "a strong wish" that Brinsmade should remain in office.[153] Few persons, in 1843, could have been better acquainted with the views of the missionaries than Richards; fewer could have spoken with equal authority on behalf of the Hawaiian government.

The lessons in diplomacy which the Hawaiian rulers had received from Charlton and Jones and from the successive visits of men-of-war had been more disturbing than enlightening. Through those experiences, the chiefs had become aware of their own weakness and of the need for competent advice in their relations with other nations and with foreigners in the Islands. When William Richards left the Islands, in 1836, to visit the United States, he was requested by the chiefs to seek a man of good character and with some legal training who would be willing to go to the Hawaiian Islands and serve as adviser to the government in matters of public policy.[154]

While Richards was in the United States the weakness of the government was further demonstrated by the rebuffs which it received during the negotiations with Captains Belcher and Du Petit-Thouars in July 1837. James J. Jarves thought that the need for "a responsible, intelligent adviser" had never been more apparent,[155] and

---

[151] Testimony of William Richards, September 1, 1846, in *Arbitration between the . . . . Government of the Hawaiian Islands and Messrs. Ladd & Co.*, p. 106.

[152] Testimony of William Richards, August 29, 1846, in *ibid.*, p. 78. The "Major Williams" to whom Richards wrote may have been Representative Thomas W. Williams of Connecticut. While in Washington a few weeks earlier, Richards had met T. W. Williams, by whom he had been introduced to John Quincy Adams and per-

haps to other influential persons in the capital. Williams was a resident of New London and was prominent in the whaling industry of that city.

[153] *Ibid.*

[154] Jarves, *History of the Hawaiian Islands*, p. 152.

[155] *Ibid.*, p. 157. A somewhat similar opinion had been expressed by an officer of the U.S.S. "Peacock," who, in October 1836, had suggested the desirability of translating "some one of the many excellent

shortly thereafter the chiefs, acting upon a suggestion from Brinsmade, requested the Rev. Lorrin Andrews to enter their service as an instructor in government and law.[156] Andrews was willing to accept the invitation and the missionaries at Honolulu were unanimous in their approval of the proposal.[157] His colleagues on Maui, however, so strongly opposed the move that he felt constrained to withdraw his acceptance of the offer.[158] In October 1837 he accompanied the King from Lahaina to Honolulu to serve as interpreter during the interviews between the King and Captain Bruce of the British naval vessel, "Imogene." He returned promptly to Lahaina, and in November he wrote that he was again occupied with his "appropriate business" as principal of the seminary at Lahainaluna.[159]

The decision of Andrews to remain at the seminary was not wholly satisfactory to himself, to the chiefs, or to all of his brethren. Andrews was restless at Lahainaluna, the chiefs were left without any immediately available candidate for the post refused by Andrews, and some of the missionaries believed that more was at stake than an ordinary political appointment. Any excursion by a missionary into the realm of politics was fraught with peril for the entire mission, but apparently one group of missionaries believed that the situation was sufficiently critical to justify daring measures.

The most effective guaranty of the security of the religious and educational institutions of the mission was an orderly and peaceable development of Hawaiian political and economic life. The chiefs, however, were ignorant of the affairs of the world, and there was always the danger that through some indiscreet action they would

---

compendiums on political economy" as a guide for the chiefs. See communication signed "Politicus," U.S. Ship Peacock, Honolulu, October 1, 1836, in *Sandwich Island Gazette*, October 8, 1836.

[156] Journal of Levi Chamberlain, August 3, 1837. Andrews was principal of the Mission Seminary at Lahainaluna. The suggestion that he be employed for this delicate task may have been prompted by the satisfaction with which he served as interpreter during an interview between Captain Edward Belcher and the King. Belcher, who was not generally friendly to the American missionaries, wrote that

"from what I saw of Mr. Andrews . . . . I had reason to admire him." Belcher, *Voyage Round the World*, I, 66.

[157] Journal of Levi Chamberlain, August 18, 1837; Lorrin Andrews to Anderson, Honolulu, August 20, 1837, in Letters to the American Board, CXXXV, No. 174.

[158] Bingham to Anderson, Charlestown, Massachusetts, August 22, 1845, in *ibid.*, CLXXIII, No. 35; Andrews to Anderson, Lahainaluna, November 13, 1837, in *ibid.*, CXXXV, No. 175.

[159] *Ibid.*; Journal of Levi Chamberlain, October 6, 11, 24, 1837.

afford one of the great powers an excuse to seize the Islands. More even than Hawaiian independence was involved. Appropriately it was Hiram Bingham who saw beyond the threat to Hawaiian independence to more subtle dangers. Writing to the American Board, at the close of 1837, Bingham declared that unless "disinterested men" were found who would advise and instruct the chiefs, *"cunning speculators* will ere long . . . . give employment to the people as day labor, at a low rate, or introduce foreign labor to their exclusion, & put the products of the soil in their own pockets, thus keeping the aborigines poor, or hastening their extinction."[160] If the fears of Bingham were well founded, such a development could be prevented only if means were found whereby the real control of the political and economic institutions of the Islands remained in the hands of the natives. It was a recognition of the complicated nature of the problem and of its bearing upon the spiritual welfare of the Hawaiian people that caused some of the missionaries, in 1832, to feel "a strong inclination" to assist the Hawaiians in the preservation of their independence by teaching them as far as possible to govern themselves.[161] When, five years later, Lorrin Andrews declared that he was "more and more convinced of the necessity of the chiefs being taught a better system of government,"[162] he but echoed the views of many of his colleagues.

The chiefs were disappointed by the decision of Andrews; they could not afford to be dismayed. They were aware that there were "evils" inherent in their system of government, but they were at a loss to know how to make desirable improvements in their own institutions. They relied upon the missionaries for advice in matters of morals and religion, and they turned naturally to the mission to seek advice upon matters of government. During the year ending in the summer of 1838 they "applied repeatedly" to the mission for the services of someone qualified to assist them in the reorganization of the government, only to be rebuffed because political advice did not fall within "the appropriate sphere" of a missionary. The negative

---

[160] Bingham to Anderson, Honolulu, December 13, 1837, in Letters to the American Board, CXXXV, No. 4.

[161] Chamberlain to Hunnewell, Honolulu, November 12, 1832, in Hunnewell MSS.

[162] Andrews to Anderson, Lahainaluna, November 13, 1837, in Letters to the American Board, CXXXV, No. 175. See also Letter of the Mission, June 20, 1838, in *Missionary Herald*, XXXV (April 1839), 147.

attitude of the missionaries did not arise from a lack of sympathy. They informed the American Board that such an adviser as the chiefs desired would be very valuable, and added that "as a post of usefulness for a philanthropic mind, we know of none equal."[163]

In the spring of 1838 William Richards returned from the United States to report that he had been unable to find any competent person willing to go to the Islands to act as instructor to the chiefs. The failure of Richards and the hesitancy of the missionaries seemed to close the door upon the hopes of the chiefs. The latter, however, made one further effort when they invited Richards to fill the post. After some delay, Richards agreed to accept this offer, hoping that "the *spiritual* as well as temporal good of the nation" would be served thereby. The missionaries acquiesced in this solution of the problem, and at their annual meeting, in 1838, they added their official approval to the decision of Richards.[164]

The selection of Richards proved to be a happy choice.[165] Since 1823 he had resided at Lahaina, where he had enjoyed an unusual opportunity to become the intimate friend and spiritual guide of many of the powerful chiefs. No missionary in the Islands, except Hiram Bingham and perhaps Dr. Judd, was better acquainted with the rulers of the nation; and Bingham's pre-eminent position in the mission, his open and repeated disagreements with many of the foreign residents, and the precarious state of Mrs. Bingham's health combined to preclude any possibility that he would enter upon a political career at the Islands.

Richards hoped to retain his formal association with the American Board and to serve the mission whenever possible. When at

[163] General Letter of the Mission, June 20, 1838, in *Missionary Herald*, XXXV (April 1839), 147. In 1839 the American Board rejected a proposal, originating in the Hawaiian Islands, that it should send to the Islands someone qualified to serve the chiefs as adviser in law and government. *Report of the American Board*, 1839, p. 129.

[164] *Minutes of the Delegate Meeting of the Sandwich Island Mission*, 1838, pp. 7, 29; Richards to Anderson, Lahaina, August 1, 1838, in Letters to the American Board, CXXXV, No. 83. In 1839 the general meeting of the mission approved the continuance of Richards in his post as adviser to the chiefs. *Minutes of the General Meeting of the Sandwich Island Mission*, 1839, p. 19.

[165] Captain Wilkes, who met Richards in 1840, was enthusiastic in his praise of the appointment and congratulated "the government and people of Hawaii upon their fortune in obtaining the services of one who has made such exertions in their behalf, and who is so well qualified for the responsible situation he holds." Wilkes, *United States Exploring Expedition*, IV, 8–9.

Lahaina, he continued to do "a large share of the native preaching" in the church which he had served for so many years,[166] and in 1842 he could report that his relations with the mission were much the same as before except in form.[167] The Board, however, was unwilling to retain a nominal jurisdiction over a man who had become so closely identified with the political life of the nation. It therefore released Richards from his missionary obligations with the condition that should he leave the service of the government he might resume his position as a missionary.[168] In releasing Richards, the Board warned his former colleagues that it would require "much heavenly wisdom on the part of Mr. R. & of the mission, to know how fast to urge the government onward in the progress of reform."[169] In March 1841 Rufus Anderson, speaking for the Prudential Committee of the Board, assured the mission that the committee was much interested in the work being done by Richards and was anxious to extend to him any assistance which might be given "with propriety." With the added explanation that the committee was "accustomed to think and speak of him as a member of the mission," Anderson empowered the missionaries to re-establish the formal relationship between Richards and the mission if such action would facilitate the labors in which he was engaged.[170]

Richards entered upon his duties as chaplain, teacher, and translator for the King in July 1838.[171] For a time he was occupied in the translation of works which would be useful to the King and chiefs in the conduct of public business;[172] but more important and exacting duties were ahead. In August he reported that the King had proposed a modification of Hawaiian political institutions "in favor of the people & specially designed for the encouragement of industry."[173] It was a suggestion with revolutionary implications, and one with

[166] Dwight Baldwin to Anderson, Kaluaaha, November 14, 1840, in Letters to the American Board, CXXXVI, No. 21. See also Richards to Anderson, Honolulu, August 29, 1839, in *ibid.*, CXXXV, No. 86.

[167] Richards to Anderson, January 1, 1842, in *ibid.*, CXXXV, No. 92.

[168] *Report of the American Board*, 1839, p. 130.

[169] Anderson to the Sandwich Island Mission, Boston, May 22, 1839, in Letters from the American Board, Foreign, II (1839), 120.

[170] Anderson to the Sandwich Island Mission, Boston, March 8, 1841, in *ibid.*, IV (1841), 29.

[171] Richards to Anderson, Lahaina, August 1, 1838, in Letters to the American Board, CXXXV, No. 83.

[172] Richards to Hunnewell, Lahaina, August 25, 1838, in Hunnewell MSS.

[173] *Ibid.*

which Richards was in thorough sympathy. It was to absorb much of his time and thought during the ensuing two years.

Equally significant were the efforts of Richards to secure the recognition of Hawaiian independence by one of the great powers. He had been in the employ of the chiefs less than two months when he prepared the draft of what he hoped would become a treaty with the United States.[174] He sent a copy of this draft to Benjamin F. Butler of New York, a member of the cabinet of President Van Buren, with authorization to make any "necessary alterations" and a request that it be submitted to the President.[175] In urging the desirability of such a treaty, Richards referred to the importance of the Hawaiian Islands to American commerce and to the "considerable amount of foreign capital" invested at Honolulu. He suggested, also, that the negotiation of a treaty would diminish the danger that the Islands would be seized by Great Britain or Russia—the nations which he believed were "most likely to take possession of these Islands."[176]

Before this communication reached the United States, Butler had retired from the cabinet. He forwarded the treaty to the Secretary of State with the comment that the success of American missionaries at the Islands made it "peculiarly proper" that the government of the United States should respond "in a liberal spirit" to this request.[177] His comment was without effect. The draft of the treaty reached the State Department early in April 1839. It was filed and promptly forgotten.

[174] Copies of the proposed treaty may be found in AH, F.O. and Ex., and as an enclosure in Richards to Benjamin F. Butler, Lahaina, August 21, 1838, in USDS, "Miscellaneous Letters," January–April, 1839. The proposed treaty and the correspondence relating to it are printed in Miller, ed., *Treaties and International Acts of the United States of America*, V (Washington, D.C., 1937), 623–628.

[175] Richards to Butler, Lahaina, August 21, 1838, in USDS, "Miscellaneous Letters," January–April, 1839.

[176] *Ibid.* At the same time, Richards sent to the Secretary of the American Board some important documents with the request that immediately upon receipt they be mailed to the President. Although the documents were not described, it is probable that a draft of the proposed treaty was in-

cluded. Richards to Anderson, Lahaina, August 21, 1838, in Letters to the American Board, CXXXV, No. 84.

[177] Butler to Secretary of State Forsyth, New York, March 29, 1839, in USDS, "Miscellaneous Letters."

In the following September, Lieutenant C. K. Stribling, a naval officer who had recently returned from a cruise which included a visit to Honolulu, urged the State Department to negotiate a treaty with the Hawaiian government. The arguments which he presented were very similar to those which Richards had used, but Stribling added the observation that Honolulu could be utilized as "the most convenient headquarters" of American naval forces in the Pacific. Stribling to Secretary of State Forsyth, New York, September 27, 1839, in *ibid.*

While President Van Buren and his associates pondered problems more vital to the United States than the fate of a remote archipelago, the Hawaiian authorities were confronted with increasing evidence of the precarious position of their little kingdom. The most striking testimony to the weakness of their position was provided during the visit of the French frigate, "L'Artémise," commanded by Captain Cyrille Pierre Théodore Laplace. When, on July 9, 1839,[178] Laplace arrived at Honolulu, he was in the midst of a voyage around the world. The purpose of the visit became apparent when, after an interview with Jules Dudoit, Laplace sent an ultimatum to the local authorities in which he declared that they had repaid the "excessive indulgence" of France by the expulsion of Catholic missionaries, thereby insulting France and violating the treaty negotiated by Du Petit-Thouars in 1837. Assuming the right to protect all Catholics in the Islands, Laplace demanded that they be given all the privileges allowed to Protestants, that native Catholics imprisoned because of their religious beliefs be released, that the Hawaiian authorities sign a treaty which he would propose, and that the government deposit twenty thousand dollars with him as a guaranty that their future conduct would be satisfactory to France. Should this ultimatum be answered unsatisfactorily, Laplace threatened to bombard the town, and as evidence that he was serious he established a blockade of the harbor.[179]

On July 13, Laplace presented to the local authorities a copy of a treaty which was concerned primarily with the guaranty of religious equality for Catholics in the Hawaiian Islands. Despite the absence of the King, who had not yet arrived from Lahaina, the chiefs at Honolulu did not care to risk the further displeasure of Laplace, and on the afternoon of the same day, Governor Kekuanaoa delivered to the French commander a copy of the treaty signed by Kekauluohi

---

[178] Laplace had sailed eastward across the Pacific without allowing for the change in dates. He believed that he had arrived at Honolulu on July 10, and there is a discrepancy of one day in his dates when compared with the dates given by residents of Honolulu in all documents and accounts relating to the visit of "L'Artémise."

[179] Laplace, *Campagne de Circumnavigation*, V, 440; Jarves, *History of the Hawaiian Islands*, p. 162. The original copy of the ultimatum is in AH, F.O. and Ex. It is printed in Laplace, *Campagne de Circumnavigation*, V, 531–533; *Sandwich Island Gazette*, July 13, 1839; *Missionary Herald*, XXXVI (March 1840), 95–96; Bingham, *Sandwich Islands*, pp. 536–538.

and himself.[180] At the same time the Governor delivered the twenty
thousand dollars demanded by Laplace, much of which had been
borrowed from merchants in the community.[181]

The Governor was not the only visitor received that afternoon by
Laplace. A group of prominent foreign residents, including Charlton
and several Americans, went on board "L'Artémise" to congratulate
the commander upon his success in breaking the power which so long
had been enjoyed by the American missionaries.[182] On the following
morning, which was Sunday, Laplace signalized his triumph when he
went ashore to attend a military mass. He was met at the wharf by
"a large number" of foreign residents, and to the strains of martial
music the entire company marched to the place appointed for the
celebration of the mass.[183]

Laplace was not yet satisfied. The King arrived at Honolulu
on Sunday; on Monday he was visited by Laplace, who lost little
time in asking him to accept a second treaty, the eight articles of
which were designed to improve the position of French subjects and
French commerce at the Islands.[184] Several of the articles were of
great importance, and the King and his advisers desired time to consider them carefully; but Laplace was anxious to conclude the negotiations and demanded that the King accept or reject the treaty by
Wednesday morning. Apparently the King was assured that an unfavorable decision on his part would not be followed by any hostile

[180] Laplace, *Campagne de Circumnavigation*, V, 458–459; *Sandwich Island Gazette*,
July 20, 1839. An original copy of the
treaty is in AH, F.O. and Ex. It is printed
in Laplace, *Campagne de Circumnavigation*,
V, 533–534, and in FRUS, 1894, Appendix
II, pp. 37–38.

[181] Journal of John N. Colcord, pp. 82–
83; Brinsmade to Secretary of State Forsyth, Sandwich Islands, July 17, 1839, in
USDS, "Consular Letters," Honolulu, I;
Amos Cooke to Anderson, Honolulu, September 18, 1839, in Letters to the American Board, CXXXVII, No. 145; Jarves,
History of the Hawaiian Islands, p. 163.

[182] Laplace, *Campagne de Circumnavigation*, V, 459–460. Some of the residents,
apparently fearing violence and perhaps
rioting by the natives, formed a company
for their own defense and applied to La-

place for a loan of arms and ammunition.
This conduct was described by Captain
Wilkes as "most extraordinary," and he
added that it was "with regret" that he
learned that "the Americans as a body"
joined other residents in this action. Wilkes,
United States Exploring Expedition, IV, 16.

[183] Journal of Levi Chamberlain, July 14,
1839; *Sandwich Island Gazette*, July 20,
1839; Laplace, *Campagne de Circumnavigation*, V, 460–461.

[184] *Ibid.*, V, 463, 477–478. The Hawaiian
version of the negotiations declared that
Laplace did not present a copy of the treaty
to the King until Tuesday. This is supported by James J. Jarves, who was in
Honolulu at the time. "A History of the
French War-Ship Artemise," in AH, F.O.
and Ex.; Jarves, *History of the Hawaiian
Islands*, p. 163.

action by Laplace. He and his friends later declared, however, that Laplace and Dudoit had clearly intimated that should the proposed treaty be rejected the government would be beset with difficulties and perhaps with actual hostilities.[185] One of the articles provided that French subjects accused of crime should be tried by a jury composed of foreign residents nominated by the French consul; another stipulated that French goods, including wines and brandies, should be admitted at Hawaiian ports without paying a greater tariff than five per cent.[186] No treaty which limited the freedom of his government could be agreeable to the King, while the reform-minded chiefs and missionaries were seriously alarmed by the provision which would compel the government to admit wines and brandies. The King, however, yielded to expediency. On the morning of July 17 he reluctantly signed the treaty and thereby accepted restrictions upon his sovereignty which were to plague him and his government for nearly twenty years. Three days later "L'Artémise" left Honolulu.[187]

The purpose of Laplace in insisting upon the treaty of commerce is not altogether clear, and it is possible that the inspiration for the second treaty developed after he arrived at Honolulu. There were rumors which credited Jules Dudoit with the suggestion that treaty protection be given French wines, and when Dudoit promptly seized the opportunity to import a cargo of wines there appeared to be some foundation for those rumors.[188] Ten years later Robert C. Wyllie asserted that Dudoit had suggested both of the controversial articles

[185] Brinsmade to Forsyth, Sandwich Islands, July 17, 1839, in USDS, "Consular Letters," Honolulu, I; Kamehameha III to Dudoit, Honolulu, August 8, 1839, in AH, F.O. and Ex.; J. F. B. Marshall to Jarves, Koloa, September 9, 1839, in *ibid.*; Kekuanaoa to Guizot, Honolulu, December 10, 1841, in *ibid.*; James J. Jarves, "Visit of the French Frigate l'Artemise," in *Hawaiian Spectator*, II (July 1839), 360; Wilkes, *United States Exploring Expedition*, IV, 17–18; Jarves, *History of the Hawaiian Islands*, p. 163.

In contrast to the statements of the King and his friends was the emphatic denial of John C. Jones that the King had been induced to sign the treaty through fear. Jones asserted that Laplace had "left the negociation of a treaty to the free will of

the King," and that the latter had approved the treaty "freely and willingly, because it suited his Royal pleasure so to do." *Suppliment to the Sandwich Island Mirror*, January 15, 1840, pp. 68–70.

[186] The text of the treaty may be found in Laplace, *Campagne de Circumnavigation*, V, 535–536, and in FRUS, 1894, Appendix II, p. 38.

[187] *Sandwich Island Gazette*, July 27, 1839.

[188] Fitch W. Taylor, *The Flag Ship* (New York, 1840), II, 288; Wilkes, *United States Exploring Expedition*, IV, 17, 19; Bingham, *Sandwich Islands*, p. 550; Jarves, *History of the Hawaiian Islands*, p. 164; Letter of Artemas Bishop, Ewa, [December 7, 1840], in *Report of the American Board*, 1841, p. 167.

of the treaty—the fourth, which provided for the trial of French subjects by a jury chosen by the French consul, and the sixth, which compelled the government to permit the importation of wine and brandy.[189] Whatever may have been the origin of those provisions, the treaty was greeted with satisfaction by that portion of the foreign community which was hostile to the American mission and to the Hawaiian government. The *Gazette*, a reasonably faithful representative of that section of public opinion, declared that the treaty would be approved by "all lovers of justice, and condemned by every friend of teetotalism and every enemy of liberality."[190] Less realistic was the comment of Richard Charlton that "this most unpleasant affair appears to be settled to the satisfaction of both parties."[191]

Laplace believed that he had broken the power of the American mission, and in his account of the voyage of "L'Artémise" he indulged the pious hope that with the influence of the mission destroyed, Hawaiian agriculture and industry would so prosper that the great maritime powers would find it desirable to protect the Islands against aggression by any one nation.[192] The influence of the missionaries, however, had not been seriously damaged, and they were thoroughly aroused by the conduct of Laplace. They cherished a particular grievance because he had specifically excluded them from his offer to grant asylum on "L'Artémise" to foreign residents should he decide to bombard Honolulu. In explaining this discrimination, Laplace added insult to injury by accusing the missionaries, as the alleged advisers of the King, of being "the true authors of the insults given by him to France," and therefore properly subject to "the unhappy consequences of a war which they shall have brought on this country."[193] The missionaries, in turn, feared that they and their

---

[189] Wyllie to Jarves, Honolulu, April 28, 1849, in AH, F.O. and Ex. This view is supported by the statement of Samuel N. Castle that Dudoit was "the real negotiator of the Treaty." *Polynesian*, September 5, 1840.

[190] *Sandwich Island Gazette.* July 20, 1839.

[191] Charlton to Palmerston, Oahu, July 20, 1839, in *Correspondence Relative to the Sandwich Islands*, p. 61.

[192] Laplace, *Campagne de Circumnavigation*, V, 489–490.

[193] Laplace to Brinsmade, July 10 [9], 1839, in *Hawaiian Spectator*, II (October 1839), 448. It is reprinted in Jarves, *History of the Hawaiian Islands*, p. 161, and in Bingham, *Sandwich Islands*, p. 542.

While Laplace was at Honolulu a young woman of mixed Hawaiian and American parentage and clearly reflecting the views of the anti-missionary element in the community wrote that there had been "plenty of trouble here with the infernal missionaries, but . . . . they are all pretty well ashamed of themselves." Harriet C. Ham-

families would be exposed to acts of violence from "the unbridled lust" of the crew of "L'Artémise."[194]

Two days after the arrival of Laplace the missionaries at Honolulu drafted a memorial to be sent to the Congress of the United States protesting against the discrimination shown by the French commander and urging Congress to take such action as might be appropriate to protect them against similar aggression in the future.[195] In May 1840 the memorial was presented to the House of Representatives by Peter D. Vroom, a Representative from New Jersey and a member of the American Board.[196] The House Committee on Foreign Affairs referred the memorial to the State Department, where it rested until the close of the Van Buren administration.[197]

In June 1841 the Board sought to reopen the question, and sent a copy of the memorial to President Tyler;[198] in July Hiram Bingham visited Washington and interviewed Tyler and Secretary of State Webster.[199] In a statement to Webster, Bingham asserted that "the great importance of the entire independency of the Sandwich Islands to the Commercial interests of our country, & the decided ascendency of American influence there at this moment . . . . seem to call for action in this case."[200] Both Tyler and Webster seem to have been reluctant to act; but Webster was from Massachusetts, and he could not afford to be indifferent to the influence of the American Board. In reply to Bingham he conceded that missionaries were entitled to

---

mett to W. H. Davis, Honolulu, July 20, 1839, in Davis MSS.

Opinions similar to that expressed by Miss Hammett may have been common in Honolulu and may have caused Laplace to overestimate the extent to which his actions had weakened the position of the mission.

[194] S. N. Castle to Anderson, Honolulu, September 16, 1839, in Letters to the American Board, CXXXVII, No. 136.

[195] Copies of this memorial, dated Honolulu, July 11, 1839, and signed by thirty-eight members of the mission, may be found in Letters to the American Board, CXXXIV, No. 46 and in AH, F.O. and Ex. See also Castle to Hitchcock, Munn, *et al.*, Honolulu, July 15, 1839, in *ibid.*; Castle to Anderson, Honolulu, September 16, 1839, in

Letters to the American Board, CXXXVII, No. 136.

[196] *House Journal*, 26th Cong., 1st Sess., p. 944 (May 18, 1840).

[197] *Report of the American Board*, 1841, p. 151; The Prudential Committee of the American Board to the President of the United States, Boston, June 15, 1841, in USDS, "Miscellaneous Letters."

[198] *Ibid.*

[199] Bingham to Anderson, New York, July 23, 1841, in Letters to the American Board, CXXXV, No. 23.

[200] Bingham to Webster, Washington, D.C., July 10, 1841, in USDS, "Miscellaneous Letters."

more protection than were other citizens abroad, and he promised to make at least a nominal protest to France.[201]

Considered alone, Bingham's statement would scarcely have affected the policy of the government of the United States. But Tyler and Webster were unable to continue the official indifference of their predecessors to the fate of the Hawaiian Islands, and at the close of 1842—seventeen months after the interviews with Bingham—they were compelled to formulate a definite policy with regard to that important archipelago. It is interesting, although perhaps futile, to speculate as to whether the action of Tyler and Webster in December 1842 was in any way influenced by a memory of Bingham's recital of the aggression by Laplace or by his emphasis upon the "great importance of the entire independency of the Sandwich Islands" to the commercial interests of the United States.

Laplace had not destroyed the influence of the American mission nor even seriously weakened it. By compelling the government to admit Catholicism and French wines, however, he had successfully attacked two policies which the American missionaries had regarded as almost essential to the fullest success of their labors. The results were soon apparent. The laws which had prohibited the importation of intoxicants became obsolete,[202] and the missionaries observed a marked increase in drunkenness, not only in Honolulu but in parts of the Islands where the use and abuse of intoxicants hitherto had been uncommon.[203] Artemas Bishop declared that the once quiet town

[201] Bingham to Anderson, New York, July 23, 1841, in Letters to the American Board, CXXXV, No. 23.

The American Board, in March 1840, addressed an appeal to King Louis Philippe, protesting against the conduct of Laplace and against the treaty protection granted to French wines and brandies. This memorial was sent to the Rev. Robert Baird, who was then in Paris and who subsequently had interviews with the King and with the Foreign Minister, M. Guizot. Baird reinforced the memorial of the Board by making a personal remonstrance against the conduct of Laplace, and particularly against the forced admission to the Islands of French wines. He reported that Guizot was "astonished and grieved" that such a provision had been incorporated in

the treaty, but neither the memorial of the Board nor the personal representations of Baird had any noticeable effect upon French policy. Baird to Hiram Bingham, New York, July 3, 1841, enclosure in Bingham to Webster, Washington, D.C., July 10, 1841, in USDS, "Miscellaneous Letters"; *Report of the American Board*, 1841, p. 151; [Anderson], *Memorial Volume of the First Fifty Years of the American Board*, pp. 203–204. The memorial of the Board, dated March 10, 1840, was printed in *Polynesian*, December 12, 1840.

[202] Brinsmade to Secretary of State Forsyth, Sandwich Islands, July 17, 1839, in USDS, "Consular Letters," Honolulu, I; *Polynesian*, September 19, 1840, May 15, 1841.

[203] Richards to Hunnewell, Lahaina, Feb-

of Honolulu had become "a scene of revelry and noise,"[204] while a visitor from the United States reported that he found intemperance prevalent "among all classes and conditions of men."[205] In the autumn of 1840, the prohibitory legislation was partially revived when the King issued a decree, effective November 30, forbidding the manufacture of intoxicants within his dominions. This decree had but little effect upon the supply of liquors available to foreigners at Honolulu, and apparently it was intended to restrict, if not to prevent, the use of intoxicants by the native population.[206] The decree presumably had the approval of the powerful chiefs. One year later, at the close of 1841, Richard Armstrong asserted that the chiefs "would tomorrow . . . . tabu all intoxicating drinks, were it not for fear of the French government."[207]

Among the missionaries there persisted for some time the belief, evidently shared by some other Americans in the Islands, that the visit of Laplace had been a part of a program of French aggrandizement in the Pacific and that the commander of "L'Artémise" would have welcomed an excuse to take possession of the Islands. Those who held this view were convinced that Laplace had not anticipated that the government would be able to raise the required twenty thousand dollars and that he intended to use its failure to justify a seizure of the archipelago.[208]

The motives of Laplace appear to have been mixed. His voyage was planned by a Ministry of Marine favorable to the expansion of French influence, but there was nothing in his instructions which

ruary 21, 1840, in Hunnewell MSS; Chamberlain to Anderson, Honolulu, November 13, 1840, in Letters to the American Board, CXXXV, No. 129; Armstrong to Anderson, Honolulu, November 28, 1841, in *ibid.*, CXXXVI, No. 83; Letter of Dwight Baldwin, Lahaina, December 17, 1841, in *Sailor's Magazine*, XIV (August 1842), 374; Letter of Artemas Bishop, Ewa, [December 7, 1840], in *Report of the American Board, 1841*, p. 167.

[204] *Ibid.*

[205] Letter of John W. W. Dyes, Honolulu, November 28, 1840, in *Sailor's Magazine*, XIII (July 1841), 331.

[206] Letter of Artemas Bishop, Ewa, [December 7, 1840], in *Report of the Ameri-*

can Board, 1841, p. 167. The decree, dated October 1, 1840, was printed in *Polynesian*, October 3, 1840.

[207] Armstrong to Anderson, Honolulu, November 28, 1841, in Letters to the American Board, CXXXVI, No. 83.

[208] *Report of the American Board, 1840*, p. 444; Wilkes, *United States Exploring Expedition*, IV, 17; S. N. Castle, in *Hawaiian Star* (Honolulu), June 13, 1893; Judd, *Honolulu*, p. 66; J. F. B. Marshall, "An Unpublished Chapter of Hawaiian History," in *Harper's Magazine*, LXVII (September 1883), 511; Luther Severance to Secretary of State Webster, Honolulu, March 11–12, 1851, in FRUS, Appendix II, p. 92.

would have provided the basis for the occupation of the Islands.[209]
At Honolulu, and later at Monterey, Laplace saw evidence of the
growing influence of Americans throughout the eastern Pacific. While
in California, after his visit to Honolulu, he predicted that the Hawaiian Islands would pass ultimately into the possession of the United
States, because the archipelago certainly would be occupied by the
power that controlled California. Although cognizant of the advantages enjoyed by the United States in any rivalry for power in western
North America or the eastern Pacific, Laplace was not wholly reconciled to American dominance in that area. In a report to the Minister
of Marine he recommended that France "afford her protection" to
the government of the Hawaiian Islands,[210] and during his visit to
Monterey he warned Governor Alvarado that California would fall
prey to the aggressive Americans and urged him to seek the protection which France could give but which it could not offer unso-
licited.[211]

If Laplace hoped to postpone the advance of the United States into
California and across the Pacific to Hawaii, these feeble gestures
availed little. Nor did the treaties imposed upon the Hawaiian government materially benefit the political or commercial interests of
France. There were very few French subjects in the Islands,[212] and
nationals of Great Britain and the United States reaped the major
advantages of Laplace's handiwork. By the consent of the Hawaiian
government or by most-favored-nation provisions in subsequent
treaties, they shared the immunities and guaranties gained by subjects
of France. This was ironical, for the conduct of Laplace and particularly his insistence upon the admission of French wines so alienated a
prominent section of public opinion that a well-informed French

[209] George Verne Blue, "The Report of
Captain La Place on His Voyage to the
Northwest Coast and California in 1839,"
in *California Historical Society Quarterly*,
XVIII (December 1939), 315; George
Verne Blue, "The Policy of France toward
the Hawaiian Islands from the Earliest
Times to the Treaty of 1846," in Taylor
and Kuykendall, eds., *Papers Read During
the Captain Cook Sesquicentennial Celebration*, p. 71.

[210] Laplace to the Minister of Marine,

Bodega, August 14, 1839, quoted in *ibid.*,
p. 73; Blue, "The Report of Captain La
Place," in *California Historical Society
Quarterly*, XVIII (December 1939), 315.

[211] Bancroft, *History of California*, IV,
155 n.

[212] Wilkes, *United States Exploring Expedition*, IV, 15; Jarves, *History of the Hawaiian Islands*, p. 161. Wilkes reported
that aside from the members of the Catholic mission there were but four French
subjects at the Islands.

observer was compelled to admit, forty years later, that the effect of the treaties had been to injure rather than to promote the influence of France in the Islands.[213]

The negotiations with Laplace diverted only temporarily the attention of the chiefs from a sweeping program of domestic reform designed to provide the little kingdom with a more formal political organization, a more adequate protection of the temporal interests of the commoners, and a code of laws appropriate to the condition of the nation. The inspiration for these political changes came from the missionaries rather than from the chiefs. Inertia and self-interest combined to keep the majority of the chiefs content with the political institutions which they had inherited from Kamehameha and Kaahumanu. Few missionaries shared that complacency, and the Rev. Lowell Smith predicted that the nation was "rapidly approaching" a time when the people would refuse to support "the present form" of government.[214] Smith was a pessimist. An opinion more commonly held by the missionaries was that of the Rev. Peter J. Gulick, who feared that the temporal condition of the people could not be improved until there were drastic changes in the system of government.[215] So generally was this opinion shared by the missionaries that Dr. Judd reported, apparently with some concern, that there was "much agitation on the public mind," that some of his colleagues were "very decided" in their hostility to the ancient political system, and that there was "a sort of impatience" with the leisurely method with which reforms were considered.[216] Missionaries holding these or similar views could only hope that Richards would succeed in inducing the chiefs to consent to far-reaching modifications in the political institutions of the kingdom.

Shortly after entering the service of the chiefs, Richards prepared a series of lectures dealing with the organization and functions of government in Europe and the United States. These lectures, which may have been based in part upon the Bible and the Declaration of

[213] C. de Varigny, "La France dans l'Océan-Pacifique," in *Revue des Deux Mondes*, XLIV (March 15, 1881), 404–405.

[214] Smith to Anderson, Honolulu, November 20, 1837, in Letters to the American Board, CXXXVII, No. 21.

[215] Gulick to Anderson, Koloa, July 1838 and July 29, 1839, in *ibid.*, CXXXVI, Nos. 4, 6.

[216] Judd to Anderson, Honolulu, October 7, 1838, in *ibid.*, CXXXVII, No. 77. See also Chamberlain to Anderson, Honolulu, February 7, 1839, in *ibid.*, CXXXV, No. 119.

Independence,[217] were delivered to a small group which included the King, the principal chiefs, and a few interested graduates of the seminary at Lahainaluna.[218] Following these lectures, Boaz Mahune, a graduate of the seminary, drafted a civil code which may be regarded as supplementary to the criminal code of 1835. With some modification this code was approved by the chiefs, and was signed by the King on June 7, 1839.[219] It was prefaced by a general statement as to the rights of man. This was followed by thirteen sections, which outlined in more detail the privileges of the commoners and the responsibilities of the chiefs. Included in the code were provisions which secured the tenure of land to those who paid the stipulated rent or tax, permitted the holders of land to bequeath it to their heirs, limited the powers of the local chiefs—including the governors of the several islands, and required the chiefs to meet annually to enact laws and to transact the necessary business of the government.[220]

The code of 1839, variously described as the Hawaiian "Bill of Rights" and as the "Magna Charta" of Hawaiian freedom,[221] was an important advance in Hawaiian jurisprudence. It was based upon earlier written laws, some of which dated to 1822; but so brief a compilation of laws could not include everything that the chiefs and people recognized as having the force of law. The official translator of the later code of 1842, presumably William Richards, declared that in the Islands "as well as in more civilized countries, there is something like a system of common law," based upon such diverse sources as "their ancient taboos . . . . the practices of the celebrated chiefs . . . . and . . . . the principles of the Bible." In addition the "established customs of civilized nations" were recognized as binding in so far as the chiefs were acquainted with those customs.[222]

The code was welcomed by the American missionaries, who saw

[217] Henry E. Chambers, *Constitutional History of Hawaii* (Baltimore, 1896), p. 12.

[218] Bingham, *Sandwich Islands*, p. 530; Jarves, *History of the Hawaiian Islands*, p. 169; G. P. Judd to R. C. Wyllie, Honolulu, February 17, 1860, in Judd, *Honolulu*, p. 192.

[219] Report of William Richards, May 1, 1839, in HHS, *Fifty-First Annual Report* (Honolulu, 1943), pp. 66–69.

[220] "Sandwich Island Laws," in *Hawaiian Spectator*, II (July 1839), 347–352. The author of this article believed that the laws had been written by David Malo.

[221] Alexander, *Brief History of the Hawaiian People*, p. 229; Blackman, *Making of Hawaii*, p. 106; Robert C. Lydecker, comp., *Roster Legislatures of Hawaii* (Honolulu, 1918), p. 4; Hopkins, *Hawaii*, p. 260; Taylor, *Under Hawaiian Skies*, p. 348.

[222] "Preface to the Laws of 1842," translated in Thurston, comp., *Fundamental Law of Hawaii*, p. vii.

in it the first step toward the protection of the property of the commoners;[223] and after the lapse of a year, the editor of the *Polynesian*
believed that where the laws had been put into effect they had "generally been found to operate well."[224] The code had not remedied the
political inequalities of which some of the missionaries had complained, and there was a continuance of the reports that heavy taxes,
oppression by the chiefs, and a "want of personal liberty" contributed to the poverty of the Hawaiian people.[225] It was this belief, in
part, which led Richard Armstrong to observe that the opinion in the
Islands was becoming "more and more common" that the nation
could not long exist.[226] The best hope of the missionaries for a liberalization of the government which would materially benefit the commoners was their confidence that Richards would exert his great
influence to implement the code of 1839 with further reforms.[227]

The political reformation introduced by Richards and accepted
by the chiefs was followed by a real shift in the balance of power
within the kingdom. This was the result in part of the death of three
of the most powerful of the chiefs. Kinau died on April 4, 1839,
mourned by the American missionaries, but not by all of their
critics.[228] Her successor as *kuhina nui* was her half-sister, Kekauluohi, who—according to Hiram Bingham—entered upon her arduous
duties "with much propriety, though to the exposure of her spiritual
prosperity."[229] She never attained the same position of prominence or
power that had been the lot of her predecessor. The death of Kinau
was followed in the next nine months by the passing of Governors

[223] The Mission to Anderson, Honolulu, June 8, 1839, in Letters to the American Board, CXXXIV, No. 11.

[224] *Polynesian*, July 4, 1840.

[225] Titus Coan to Anderson, Hilo, May 1, 1840, in Letters to the American Board, CXXXVII, No. 37.

[226] Armstrong to the American Board, Wailuku, July 7, 1840, in *Missionary Herald*, XXXVII (June 1841), 266–267.

[227] The Mission to Anderson, Honolulu, June 1, 1840, in Letters to the American Board, CXXXIV, No. 13.

[228] Bingham, *Sandwich Islands*, p. 533. Father Reginald Yzendoorn described Kinau as the *"greatest enemy"* of Hawaiian Catholics, while one of the leading merchants at Honolulu commented that she had so taxed her subjects that they had been un-able to purchase merchandise in any con-siderable quantities. He hoped, therefore, that the death of Kinau would be followed by an improvement in business. Yzendoorn, *History of the Catholic Mission in Hawaii*, p. 127; Peirce and Brewer to Hunnewell, Oahu, April 7, 1839, in Hunnewell MSS.

[229] Bingham, *Sandwich Islands*, p. 534. Another missionary, Mrs. G. P. Judd, de-scribed the new *kuhina nui* as "amiable and well disposed" but lacking in "the statesmanlike qualities" of her predeces-sors. Judd, *Honolulu*, p. 72.

Kaikioewa and Hoapili. There was no one among the younger chiefs who was able to wield the same influence in the councils of the nation. The King did not often assume the active direction of public affairs,[230] and the determination of governmental policy passed to Kekauluohi, Governor Kekuanaoa of Oahu, and William Richards.[231]

The government was still so weak as to cause fear in some quarters that it would be unable to protect its own subjects from "the overweaning rapacity of the whites."[232] Its position improved, however, during the months immediately following the visit of Laplace, and in July 1840 Richards was able to report that among influential foreigners there was "a very favorable state of feeling" toward both the government and the American mission.[233] Five months later Peter A. Brinsmade described the situation as "tranquil," and declared that the disposition of the government toward citizens of the United States was "particularly friendly."[234]

The visit of Laplace compelled Richards to consider whether or not he wished to cast his lot permanently in the sphere of politics. He had little choice, for it was only through the counsel of friendly foreigners that the inexperienced chiefs could be saved from errors

[230] Judd, *Honolulu*, p. 72. Mrs. Judd commented that the King was, at that time, "almost a myth," inasmuch as "when he was most wanted he was not to be found."

[231] Charlton to Palmerston, Oahu, November 12, 1839, October 28, 1841, in *Correspondence Relative to the Sandwich Islands*, pp. 68, 89; Charlton to Aberdeen, London, February 11, 1843, *ibid.*, p. 160. Governor Kekuanaoa was born in 1794. Early in life he was attached to the court of Kamehameha as a servant, but he rose in the esteem of his royal master and during the reign of Liholiho he was of sufficient influence to be a member of the party that accompanied the King to England. He was the husband of Kinau, and probably it was through her influence that, in 1834, he became governor of Oahu, a position which he retained until his death in 1868. His official duties brought him into almost daily communication with members of the foreign community, and in general he seems to have retained their respect and good will. A visitor in 1840 thought him as capable as any chief for his high office. He was

described in 1842 as "noble looking" and well acquainted with the English language. Gorham D. Gilman declared that the governor was "possessed of great energy and judgment" and was tactful in his relations with those with whom he was compelled to do business. Two of his sons were elevated to the Hawaiian throne, and during the last twenty years of his life he was probably better known than any other chief with the exception of the reigning monarch. Olmstead, *Incidents of a Whaling Voyage*, p. 197; Wilkes, *United States Exploring Expedition*, III, 409; Journal of Mrs. Gorham Nye, November 23, 1842; Gorham D. Gilman, "Honolulu, As It Is" (MS, Hawaiian Historical Society Library), p. 67; *The Friend*, December 1, 1868, p. 97.

[232] Robert G. Davis to W. H. Davis, Honolulu, November 16, 1839, in Davis MSS.

[233] Richards to Anderson, Honolulu, July 27, 1840, in Letters to the American Board, CXXXV, No. 88.

[234] Brinsmade to Secretary of State Forsyth, Sandwich Islands, December 31, 1840, in USDS, "Consular Letters," Honolulu, I.

which might endanger the safety of the kingdom.[235] Like his former colleagues in the mission, he believed that a reorganization of Hawaiian political institutions was imperative if the nation was to survive. It was soon evident that this conviction would not be without result.

Throughout the early summer of 1840, Richards and the chiefs were engaged in drafting a written constitution.[236] As rumors concerning the document passed from mouth to mouth in Honolulu, there were varying reactions. Richards hoped it would be effective in protecting the rights of the people;[237] the editor of the *Polynesian* predicted it would "in some degree limit the power, and define the duties of the king, governors and other chiefs";[238] while one resident dismissed the rumor that there was to be a bicameral legislature, with a House of Lords and a House of Commons, with the cynical comment, "what a getting upstairs!"[239] The part played by Richards in the framing of the Constitution of 1840 is vague. In an open letter to the *Polynesian* he merely stated that the chiefs had received "many suggestions" from their native subjects and from foreign residents and visitors;[240] but well-informed contemporaries assumed that the major share of the credit belonged to him.[241] The mixed origins of the new constitution appeared to justify the amused comment that the finished product was "a strange compound of old Puritan principles, modern Yankee notions, and the intricate feudalism of the natives."[242]

The constitution was promulgated by the King on October 8, 1840. When, in the following February, an English translation was

[235] Richards to Anderson, Honolulu, August 29, 1839, in Letters to the American Board, CXXXV, No. 86.

[236] *Polynesian*, July 4, 1840; Kekauluohi to Kekuanaoa, Lahaina, June 1, 1840, in AH, F.O. and Ex.; J. Kapena to Paul Kanoa, Lahaina, June 1, 1840, in AH, "Historical and Miscellaneous Documents"; Richards to Hunnewell, Honolulu, July 31, 1840, in Hunnewell MSS.

[237] *Ibid.*

[238] *Polynesian*, July 4, 1840.

[239] L. H. Anthon to W. H. Davis, Honolulu, July 15, 1840, in Davis MSS.

[240] Letter signed "The Translator," in the *Polynesian*, February 6, 1841.

[241] Jarves, *History of the Hawaiian Islands*, p. 169; [R. H. Dana, Jr.], unsigned review, in *North American Review*, LV (July 1842), 195; *Polynesian*, November 13, 1847; *The Friend*, November 18, 1847, p. 173; G. P. Judd to R. C. Wyllie, Honolulu, February 17, 1860, in Judd, *Honolulu*, p. 192; *Quarterly Review*, XCIV (December 1853), 90.

[242] *Ibid.* Cf. Alfred Jacobs, "Les Européens dans l'Océanie," in *Revue des Deux Mondes*, XXIII (September 1, 1859), 162; Simpson, *Sandwich Islands*, p. 104.

published, one admiring missionary characterized it as "the great magna charta of Hawaiian liberty" and predicted that it would be "hailed by every lover of freedom."[243] His enthusiasm may be explained, in part, by the preamble, which affirmed the divine origin of governments, and by the first article which declared that no law should be enacted which was "at variance with the word of the Lord Jehovah, or at variance with the general spirit of His word." This was followed by a recital of the rights of the people, which were said to have been ordained by God.[244]

The new constitution continued the office of *kuhina nui*, although the occupant of that office was designated as the premier. New restrictions upon the power of the monarch included provisions for the establishment of a judiciary, a definition of the powers of the governors of the several islands, and the creation of a legislature.

There were precedents in Hawaiian history for a legislative body. Many of the early kings had permitted a council of chiefs to exercise quasi-legislative powers,[245] and Kamehameha often had sought the advice of a group of trusted chiefs before announcing a new law or deciding upon some change in policy. The power of the chiefs in political matters had increased steadily through the reign of Liholiho and the regency of Kaahumanu until—after 1832—they were the real authors of the policies of the government.[246] The addition of Richards to the little group of advisers around the King introduced a new element into the national councils, for not only was Richards opposed to the ancient absolutism of the monarch but he favored a further diffusion of political power, so that commoners as well as chiefs would share in the government of the nation. The

[243] William P. Alexander to the American Board, February 15, 1841, in *Missionary Herald*, XXXVIII (April 1842), 149.

[244] The text of the Constitution of 1840 may be found in Thurston, comp., *Fundamental Law of Hawaii*, pp. 1–9; *Polynesian*, February 6, 1841; *British and Foreign State Papers*, XXXI (London, 1858), 1256–1263; Bingham, *Sandwich Islands*, pp. 562–568; Wilkes, *United States Exploring Expedition*, IV, 22–30; and, with several paragraphs omitted, in Jarves, *History of the Hawaiian Islands*, pp. 169–171. For an analysis of the origins and content of the constitution, see Ralph S. Kuykendall, *Constitutions of the Hawaiian Kingdom* (HHS, Papers, No. 21, Honolulu, 1940), pp. 7–14.

[245] W. F. Frear, "Hawaiian Statute Law," in HHS, *Thirteenth Annual Report* (Honolulu, 1906), p. 16.

[246] W. D. Alexander, "A Sketch of the Constitutional History of the Hawaiian Kingdom," in *Hawaiian Almanac and Annual*, 1894, p. 46; Lydecker, comp., *Roster Legislatures of Hawaii*, p. 3.

result was the creation of a legislature in which both chiefs and commoners were to have representation.

Following the example of legislative bodies in Great Britain and the United States, the constitution provided that the chiefs and the representatives of the people should meet separately. It named sixteen chiefs, including the King and the *Kuhina Nui*, as entitled to sit as members of the legislature, but it failed to specify the number of representatives or the manner in which they were to be chosen. The details thus were left to future legislative action.

On November 2, 1840, the legislature of the kingdom, still consisting wholly of chiefs, enacted a law establishing the manner in which the representatives were to be elected. According to the provisions of this curious electoral law, letters were to be written to the King naming the representatives the writer or writers desired to have chosen. Possibly to encourage the use of the suffrage thus extended to the mass of the people for the first time, the law added that if many letters were written "it will be well, for the person who has the most names in those letters will be the person chosen."[247] The number of representatives was set at seven,[248] but this quota was not always filled if we may judge from the official journals of successive legislative sessions.[249]

The first constitutional legislature assembled at Lahaina on April 1, 1841. The King, fourteen chiefs, and three popularly elected representatives were included in this little group of pioneer legislators.[250] Friendly missionaries described the session as "very orderly and pleasant,"[251] and the *Polynesian* commended the "zeal and determination to reform all abuses" exhibited by the chiefs.[252] There was danger, as the editor noted, that the legislators might attempt a too rapid reform of existing institutions or find themselves unable to reconcile the conflicting interests of the foreign residents and the native population.[253] The legislature did enact statutes clarifying at

[247] *Ibid.*, p. 4; Thurston, comp., *Fundamental Law of Hawaii*, p. 11; *Polynesian*, August 28, 1841.

[248] Thomas Marshall Spaulding, "Early Years of the Hawaiian Legislature," in HHS, *Thirty-Eighth Annual Report* (Honolulu, 1930), pp. 26–27; Simpson, *Journey Round the World*, II, 86.

[249] Lydecker, comp., *Roster Legislatures of Hawaii*, pp. 4, 16.

[250] *Ibid.*

[251] The Mission to Anderson, Honolulu, June 5, 1841, in Letters to the American Board, CXXXIV, No. 18.

[252] *Polynesian*, May 8, 1841.

[253] *Ibid.*

least two subjects of great interest to foreigners—the selection of juries and the levying of tariffs. It also considered at length the financial condition of the nation and took measures designed to liquidate the debts of the government.[254] With some reason, Peter A. Brinsmade assured the State Department that the King and chiefs had launched "a promising experiment" in constitutional government, with laws which were creditable to a nation so recently emerged from primitive isolation.[255]

A constitutional legislature which included in its membership democratically chosen representatives of the commoners was more than an innovation in the political life of the nation; it was symbolic of the disintegration of the power of the chiefs. The effective control of the government, however, passed not to the commoners but to foreigners. This transfer of power was almost inevitable. The development of important commercial and agricultural interests within the Islands created a demand that the government be prepared to protect property, to facilitate the transaction of business, and to maintain stable relations with the great maritime powers. There is no evidence in the Constitution of 1840 that the men who framed it were aware of the new problems with which they were confronted; but the specific statement of William Richards that the "grand difficulties" faced by the government arose from the scarcity of men competent to serve in administrative or judicial positions suggests that he at least recognized that the new political system must satisfy more than the native subjects of the King.[256] The chiefs faced a painful dilemma. They could ignore the wishes of the foreign residents and thereby incur unknown risks, or they could seek assistance in the foreign community. In terms of practical politics they had but one choice.

The process of inviting friendly foreigners to act in an advisory or subordinate capacity was one which when begun could not easily be stopped. By 1850 the real control of the executive and judicial departments, together with the determination of public policy, had been transferred from the King and chiefs to a small but politically

---

[254] The Mission to Anderson, Honolulu, June 5, 1841, in Letters to the American Board, CXXXIV, No. 18.

[255] Brinsmade to Secretary of State Webster, Washington, April 8, 1842, in USDS, "Consular Letters," Honolulu, I.

[256] Richards to Anderson, Honolulu, July 27, 1840, in Letters to the American Board, CXXXV, No. 88.

conscious group of foreigners. It was not until 1851, however, that any person other than a native Hawaiian was elected to the legislature.[257]

The judicial system established by the constitution was the product of political evolution. From time immemorial, the chiefs had exercised judicial powers. Appeals were possible, although perhaps not common except in cases involving highly placed Hawaiians. From the decisions of an inferior chief an appeal could be taken to a chief of higher rank or to the governor of the island; from the decisions of the governor an influential litigant might carry an appeal to the King. Court procedure and the letter of the law were alike vague, and to some extent each was determined by the individual chiefs.

The advent of foreigners brought to the Islands an aggressive group which did not regard its members as subject to Hawaiian law or to Hawaiian courts. This position was not acceptable to the chiefs, but cases involving property of foreigners commonly were so complicated that the chiefs had no interest in them. There developed, therefore, in the foreign community, an informal procedure for the adjudication of property disputes. By 1840 it had become common practice to refer such cases to a jury of foreigners, the members of which in some instances had been named by the government.[258]

Criminal cases in which the defendant was a foreigner were sometimes decided by members of the foreign community—a practice that by 1832 had developed into the use of juries to determine the guilt or innocence of the defendant.[259] In Honolulu the institution of jury trials was adopted by the chiefs in cases involving natives; and in 1834 an English visitor believed that Hawaiian juries were "impanneled upon the same impartial principles" as in England.[260] In some instances, cases involving foreigners were decided by a mixed jury with an equal number of whites and Hawaiians;[261] but this practice was interrupted by the treaty imposed by Captain Laplace. The second of the Laplace treaties included a stipulation that French

[257] Lydecker, comp., *Roster Legislatures of Hawaii*, pp. 18, 23, 25, 29.

[258] Simpson, *Sandwich Islands*, pp. 47–48. For a brief sketch of the development of Hawaiian courts, see W[alter F.] Frear, *The Evolution of the Hawaiian Judiciary* (HHS, *Papers*, No. 7, Honolulu, 1894).

[259] For examples, see Journal of Levi Chamberlain, December 20, 1827, December 3, 14, 1832; Peirce to Hunnewell, Honolulu, May 1, 1831, in Hunnewell MSS.

[260] Bennett, *Whaling Voyage Round the Globe*, I, 234.

[261] For examples, see Journal of Levi Chamberlain, December 3, 14, 1832, and September 21, 1835.

subjects accused of crime should be tried by a jury selected from a list submitted by the French consul, and to avoid complications the government extended a similar privilege to the nationals of the United States and of Great Britain. This new practice was not altogether satisfactory to the native rulers, who objected to the influence thus acquired by the consuls and who preferred to have juries in such cases chosen from a list which should include the names of all the generally respected foreigners in the community.[262] The issue was not easily settled, and for nearly twenty years it provided one of the principal objectives of Hawaiian diplomacy.

In other ways Hawaiian legal and judicial procedure was becoming standardized. By 1835, foreigners as well as natives were subject to arrest by the native police and to confinement in the prison at the Honolulu Fort.[263] More significant was the nominal abandonment of the ancient distinctions between chiefs and commoners before the law. This shift was dramatized in 1840, when a high chief who had been convicted of murder was hanged at Honolulu following a jury trial said to have been conducted "equitably, and with dignity."[264]

The earliest written provision governing the organization of Hawaiian courts was in the Constitution of 1840. By the constitution, the governor of each island was empowered to appoint two or more judges to preside over local courts. Litigants were allowed an appeal from the decisions of these local courts to a Supreme Court composed of the King, the premier, and four associate justices. For a time the various governors continued to serve as judges, either in cases of original jurisdiction or in hearing appeals from local courts. Their only authority was the ancient custom of their people, for there was no constitutional provision conferring judicial functions upon the governors.[265]

The codes of 1835 and 1839 quickly proved inadequate. They were superseded, in 1842, by a more comprehensive code of fifty-five chapters, dealing with a wide variety of problems including the en-

[262] Kekuanaoa to Charlton, Honolulu, June 17, 1842, in AH, F.O. and Ex.

[263] Bennett, *Whaling Voyage Round the Globe*, I, 234.

[264] Jarves, *Scenes and Scenery in the Sandwich Islands*, pp. 63–64; Wilkes, *United States Exploring Expedition*, IV, 30–31.

[265] Frear, *The Evolution of the Hawaiian Judiciary*, p. 9.

actment of laws, the composition of the national legislature, taxation, local laws, the police force of the kingdom, quarantine restrictions, roads, marriage and divorce, weights and measures, the observance of the Sabbath, slander, the control of servants, animals, debts and usury, vagrancy, apprenticeship, lost and found property, property administered in trust, the duties of parents, partnership, the labor of prisoners, maritime regulations, unnecessary noise at night, forgery, counterfeiting, perjury, sexual irregularities, horse-racing, theft and burglary, murder, drunkenness, sale and manufacture of liquor, the carrying of weapons, escaped prisoners, the creation and organization of a judicial system, and the appointment of a recorder and interpreter for the government.[266]

The code of 1842 contained all previous laws of the kingdom known to the compilers, but many of these early laws were considerably altered or modified by the legislature. Included in the code were measures which had been suggested first by foreign residents, by the representatives of the United States or Great Britain, or by visitors. The "greatest proportion" of the laws were of Hawaiian origin. Some had their basis in ancient traditions or the customs established by famous chiefs of the past; and others, including those concerning taxation, had been drafted by a group of brilliant young Hawaiians, among whom were John Ii and David Malo.[267] The extent to which members of the mission influenced the provisions of the code is not clear; but it seems certain that Alexander Simpson erred when, in 1843, he wrote that the whole of the code, "it is well known, was written by Judd and Richards, aided by Mr. Baldwin."[268] Closer to the truth probably was the anonymous assertion, attributed to William Richards, that all of the laws had been considered by the legislature, where they had been "repeatedly read and discussed, referred to committees or altered by the suggestion of individuals, according to the will of the council."[269] The same anonymous source gave a clue to the extent of missionary influence upon the formulation of the laws in the statement that not only were the lawmakers influenced by past traditions

[266] An English translation of the code may be found in Thurston, comp., *Fundamental Law of Hawaii*, pp. 10–136.

[267] See "Preface to the Laws of 1842," in *ibid.*, pp. vii–viii.

[268] Simpson, *Sandwich Islands*, p. 46.

[269] See "Preface to the Laws of 1842," in Thurston, comp., *Fundamental Law of Hawaii*, p. viii.

and practices, but that "at the present period the principles of the Bible are fully adopted."[270]

It is not surprising, therefore, that the stern moral legislation which had characterized the period of the regency appeared in a modified form in the code of 1842. The law of October 1840 prohibiting the manufacture of intoxicating beverages in the Islands was included in the published laws of 1842.[271] Gambling was forbidden, and the fine imposed upon any who were so irreligious as to engage in games of chance upon the Sabbath was to be doubled.[272] Fines, imprisonment, or temporary banishment awaited the unhappy person convicted of extra-marital intercourse, but the punishment was to be omitted in the case of an unmarried mother who cared for her offspring.[273] With the explanation that "It is a well established fact that a nation cannot enjoy peace nor the people prosper, unless they are taught in morals and religion," the legislature revived the policy of Kaahumanu and Kinau by outlawing worldly amusements, noise, and "all conduct which creates confusion in worshipping assemblies on the Sabbath."[274] Other statutes which appear to have been the product of missionary influence included laws designed to penalize indolence and to reward industry,[275] to relieve large families of an unfair burden of taxation,[276] and to define the rights and obligations of parents and their children.[277]

The influence of New England appears in the provision that extended to the Hawaiian kingdom the standards of weights and measures in force in Massachusetts.[278] A tentative organization of local government was perhaps more typically a product of New England political experience. The compact nature of the kingdom minimized the importance of any political units smaller than a single island, but the laws of 1842 contained a provision which permitted local communities or districts to pass upon their own needs in matters confined to their own region. A statute enacted in November 1840 authorized any chief or government official to call a meeting of "all the people of the place" should he be requested to do so. A meeting thus con-

270 Thurston, comp., *Fundamental Law of Hawaii*, p. vii.

271 *Ibid.*, pp. 108–109.

272 *Ibid.*, pp. 90–91.

273 *Ibid.*, pp. 96–101.

274 *Ibid.*, pp. 51–52.

275 *Ibid.*, pp. 133–135.

276 *Ibid.*, pp. 17–18.

277 *Ibid.*, pp. 72–74.

278 *Ibid.*, pp. 44–45.

vened was empowered to enact laws governing roads, fences, animals, or any other matters not of sufficiently wide interest to merit the attention of the national government, providing that such local laws were not in conflict with the laws of the kingdom.[279]

The code of June 1839 had provided a vague protection to tenants, but the provisions of that code were of little value to foreign merchants or residents who were anxious to secure full title to land for commercial and agricultural enterprises. Although the chiefs were as yet unwilling to permit foreigners or commoners to acquire an actual title to land in the Islands, the legislature of 1841 made an attempt to arrive at a satisfactory compromise by authorizing the governor of each island to lease tracts of land for a period not to exceed fifty years.[280] Further liberalization of the tenure of land was forced to wait until after more pressing problems had been settled.

Because the government as it emerged between 1839 and 1842 was a limited monarchy, with the legislative power vested in an assembly composed of chiefs and representatives of the commoners, a casual observer might easily note at least a superficial resemblance between the Hawaiian government and that of Great Britain. Had he supposed that this resemblance was the result of any British influence active in the Islands, he would have been mistaken. The limited monarchy and the inclusion of the chiefs in the legislature were made necessary by the facts of Hawaiian history as well as by the contemporary situation in the Islands. Such innovations as a written constitution, universal suffrage, and town meetings were more indicative of some outside influence, and clearly were more akin to American than to English political experience.

[279] *Ibid.*, pp. 34–35. See also Frear, "Hawaiian Statute Law," in HHS, *Thirteenth Annual Report*, p. 41.

[280] *Polynesian*, June 19, 1841. As late as December 1838 Richards believed that the "landed property" in the hands of foreigners should be "diminished in value" until the government had recovered possession of all the land in the Islands. The pressure of foreigners to secure land for agricultural purposes continued great. In March 1841 the *Polynesian* noted that they wished "large grants of land for extensive plantations." Under this pressure, the chiefs had modified their views. They were said to be opposed to the establishment of "extensive plantations," preferring to grant limited acreages for small farms, with leases which would "effectually check any great emigration [*sic*]." Although this fell short of meeting the wishes of the more ambitious foreigners, it was a considerable shift from the view that the chiefs had held a few years earlier. Richards to Levi Chamberlain, December 3, 1838, quoted in Kuykendall, *Hawaiian Kingdom*, p. 156 n.; *Polynesian*, March 13, 1841.

A distinguished British visitor attributed the "radical reform" in Hawaiian political institutions to two forces—the extension of commerce and the influence of the American mission.[281] Of the two, the more direct and effective influence seems to have been that of the mission. From the pulpit, in the classroom, and in conversation with the chiefs, these "Protestant republicans" decried the oppressive character of the ancient system of government, propounded a democratic view of the rights of subjects, and emphasized their own lofty concept of the duties of rulers. The friendship between the chiefs and the missionaries was a guaranty that the opinions of the latter would be received with respect by the highest authorities in the nation.[282] The influence of the mission was further enhanced by its control over education, particularly by the part which it had played in the training of such trusted advisers of the King as John Ii and David Malo. The powerful, although indirect, role of the mission in the constitutional and political reforms was recognized by the editor of the *Polynesian*, who described the mission as "a most democratic body of a most democratic nation."[283] More than sixty years later a Hawaiian jurist included the Constitution of 1840 and the codification of the laws among the "grandest monuments" of the missionaries.[284]

The years which were marked by the efforts of Richards and the chiefs to blend the ancient feudalism with the ideals and institutions of modern republican government were also the years in which the supremacy of American interests at the Islands were seriously challenged for the first time since the reign of Kamehameha. The reestablishment of the Catholic mission under the avowed protection

[281] Simpson, *Journey Round the World*, II, 87.

[282] There was no agreement as to the extent of missionary influence in the political life of the nation. Frederick D. Bennett believed, in 1834, that the chiefs consulted the missionaries upon nearly all the "more important political and commercial affairs." Six years later, however, Captain Wilkes was told that the missionaries regarded it as their duty to refrain from interference in affairs of a temporal character, and that they seldom gave advice to the chiefs upon problems of a political nature. In May 1843 Levi Chamberlain recalled that at an earlier period the missionaries often had been asked to assist the chiefs by acting as translators or interpreters. The missionaries performed these tasks because they believed it to be their duty to do so; but none of the missionaries, Chamberlain declared, had given advice in such a manner as to become responsible "in the least" degree for the actions of the chiefs. Bennett, *Whaling Voyage Round the Globe*, I, 220; Wilkes, *United States Exploring Expedition*, IV, 7; Chamberlain to Anderson, Honolulu, May 3, 1843, in Letters to the American Board, CXXXV, No. 161.

[283] *Polynesian*, October 16, 1841.

[284] Frear, "Hawaiian Statute Law," in HHS, *Thirteenth Annual Report*, p. 44.

of France, the restrictions imposed upon the government by the second Laplace treaty, and a sudden increase in the extent of British commerce with the Islands served as reminders that Great Britain and France shared with the United States a concern in the fate of the archipelago. Laplace was a realist, and he observed that the trend of events indicated the ultimate absorption of the Islands by the United States. There were British subjects, however, who hoped to control the tide of destiny. Ambitious and unscrupulous, they were able in the winter of 1842–1843 to create a situation which resulted in the occupation of the Islands by an English naval force. The anticipated addition of the Islands to the British Empire did not follow. The British government appeared to be disinterested in expansion in the Pacific; had it been interested, it would have encountered the opposition of the United States. The forces represented by American missionaries, American whalers, American merchants, and American planters had so firmly established their position in Hawaiian life that nothing short of the use of force could have deprived them of their pre-eminence in the Islands. Nor were they without influence at Washington, for the government there could not permit the most important archipelago of the mid-Pacific to fall prey to some power whose rule might be inimical either to American investments in the Islands or to a possible extension of the territory of the United States to the Pacific.

VII

THE GREAT REVIVAL

THE death of Kaahumanu was a serious blow to the hopes and influence of the American missionaries. Their eulogy of the late Regent as "a distinguished reformer of her nation, a kind friend, and benefactress of the missionaries, a firm supporter of their cause, and faithful comforter of the brethren, and of the infant churches in these isles" was more than the usual empty compliment to the memory of a dead ruler.[1] For nearly seven years she had been a member of the church at Honolulu, and during those years she had employed her great influence to advance the interests of the mission and to secure popular support for its policies. In view of the almost universal anxiety of the Hawaiian people to please their chiefs and to emulate them when possible, it is reasonable to assume that the influence of Kaahumanu was a powerful force in attracting large crowds of natives to the mission churches. Her admonitions were equally important in filling the schools with more or less willing pupils and in prompting hundreds of her subjects to covet the distinction of church membership.

Beguiled by the widespread interest in education and Christianity which was evident in every part of the Islands, many missionaries did not inquire too closely into the causes of this apparent concern with things spiritual. The difficulty of imposing Calvinist theology and Puritan moral standards upon one hundred thousand

[1] Quoted in Bingham, *Sandwich Islands*, p. 434. See also General Letter of the Mis- sion, June 23, 1832, in *Missionary Herald*, XXIX (May 1833), 166.

pagans was obscured by the maze of optimism which enveloped the mission. The confidence of the missionaries was reflected in the reports which they sent to the United States. The most widely circulated and apparently the most exaggerated account of missionary triumphs was written by the Rev. Charles S. Stewart, a former missionary at the Hawaiian Islands who revisited the Pacific in 1829 as chaplain of the U.S.S. "Vincennes." The two volumes in which he told the story of this voyage contained so glowing a description of the progress of the mission that his former colleagues were led to protest that he had done them no service by thus misleading the American public as to the true state of conditions in the Islands.[2] The missionaries themselves were not without guilt. Upon the basis of their reports, the *Missionary Herald* announced, in January 1833, that the Hawaiians could be considered "a Christian people," adding that in the Hawaiian Islands "Christianity has *preceded* civilization, and is leading the way to it."[3]

The confidence of the missionaries was soon shaken. The realization that Kaahumanu would be succeeded by either the inexperienced Kinau or the vacillating Kauikeaouli was a prospect to disturb the most sanguine member of the mission, but the subsequent decline in attention to religion appeared slowly. In October 1832, four months after the death of Kaahumanu, Dr. Gerrit P. Judd could observe no substantial change in the attitude of the people or in their conduct,[4] and his wife noted that the houses of the missionaries at Honolulu were "thronged with inquirers" throughout the day.[5] Somewhat less cheerful was the comment of Levi Chamberlain, who reported "a

[2] Samuel Whitney to Anderson, Oahu, November 23, 1832, in Letters to the American Board, LXVII, No. 59; Bingham to Anderson, Oahu, March 20, 1833, in *ibid.*, LXVII, No. 25; [Sheldon Dibble], "A Review of the letters of the Revd. C. S. Stewart," in *ibid.*, LXVIII, No. 31.

[3] *Missionary Herald*, XXIX (January 1833), 21. Among the American writers who were impressed by the results of missionary labor in the Hawaiian Islands was the noted New York jurist, Chancellor James Kent. In his famous *Commentaries*, Kent declared:

"The rapid transformation of the natives of those islands from being savages and heathens in 1820, to, in 1830, a civilized and Christian people, is very remarkable, and reflects honor, not only on the mild and teachable disposition of the natives, but also on the diligence, discretion, fidelity, and zeal with which the missionaries have devoted themselves to fulfill the purposes of their trust." James Kent, *Commentaries on American Law* (14th ed., Boston, 1896), II, 198 n.

[4] Judd to Hunnewell, Honolulu, October 29, 1832, in Hunnewell MSS.

[5] Judd, *Honolulu*, p. 45.

partial abatement" in attendance at schools and religious services.[6] Chamberlain and Judd agreed that there was "a revival of religion" on the island of Kauai.

The reaction against the mission was more noticeable after the opening of the new year. Late in January, serious-minded missionaries were shocked when a number of the formerly docile Hawaiians amused themselves by the flying of kites—an outburst of youthful spirit that called forth a rebuke from the pulpit at Honolulu.[7] Within a few weeks the ancient games, often accompanied by gambling, were publicly revived in Honolulu. Shocked by the extent of the reaction, one missionary reported that "multitudes, tired of the restraints of the gospel," had lost all interest in religion,[8] and the usually cautious Levi Chamberlain expressed the fear that the return of many of the Hawaiian people to a state of heathenism was imminent.[9] It was evident that a considerable section of the people had thrown off the "ecclesiastical restraint" which had been imposed during the regency,[10] and the King added prestige to the movement when he suspended all moral legislation and informed some of his subjects that they should consult only their own pleasure as to whether to attend religious services.[11] These evidences of frivolity and revolt were condemned by Hiram Bingham in at least two sermons, one of which was described by Stephen Reynolds as "a Brimstone Sermon."[12] The King was not awed by these admonitions, and he is said to have commented that the Islands were full of missionaries.[13]

Throughout 1833 there were indications that the influence of the mission was on the wane. In May, Levi Chamberlain observed that the numbers who attended public worship had decreased.[14] In June the missionaries were disturbed by public exhibitions of the ancient games and dances, which were said to have been accompanied by "intemperance and confusion."[15] In August, Henry A. Peirce as-

[6] Chamberlain to Hill, Honolulu, October 27, 1832, in Letters to the American Board, CXCI.

[7] Journal of Stephen Reynolds, January 25, 26, February 3, 1833.

[8] William P. Alexander to Anderson, Honolulu, March 15, 1833, in Letters to the American Board, LXVIII, No. 47.

[9] Chamberlain to Anderson, Honolulu, March 26, 1833, in *ibid.*, LXVIII, No. 163.

[10] Peirce to Hunnewell, Honolulu, March 11, 1833, in Hunnewell MSS.

[11] Journal of Levi Chamberlain, March 9, 1833; Journal of Stephen Reynolds, March 3, 1833.

[12] *Ibid.*, March 17, 24, 1833.

[13] *Ibid.*, March 20, 1833.

[14] Journal of Levi Chamberlain, May 5, 1833.

[15] *Ibid.*, June 3, 7, 1833.

serted that the once "unbounded influence" of the missionaries had disappeared, and he believed that they had passed the zenith of their power.[16] In September a public announcement that the laws would again be enforced did not apply to the decrees of the regency which had prohibited prostitution, the use of intoxicants, and Sunday recreations.[17] In October, Peirce reported that the Hawaiian people had almost deserted the schools and churches, and added that "poverty, disobedience, drunkenness, & other bad qualities" were prevalent.[18]

With reason the mood of the missionaries shifted from one of optimism to alarm. This was reflected in the tenor of their reports to the American Board and in private correspondence with friends in the United States. In contrast to the recitals of success, which had been the prevailing note in preceding years, the reports written during the closing months of 1832 contained frank confessions that the greater number of the native converts had little comprehension of the true meaning of the faith they had embraced, and warned the Board that the achievements and immediate prospects of the mission must not be overestimated.[19]

The same cautious note dominated the reports sent to the United States during 1833. From widely separated districts missionaries wrote that the people were still "heathen in their desires,"[20] that they continued to yearn for "the former days of darkness,"[21] that "a large portion of the nation" was ready to discard the religious and moral precepts that once had been so readily accepted,[22] or that there was "a general stagnation in . . . . all that is good."[23] In June,

[16] Peirce to Hunnewell, Honolulu, August 10, 1833, in Hunnewell MSS.

[17] Journal of Levi Chamberlain, September 2, 1833; General Letter of the Mission, Honolulu, July 15, 1834, in *Missionary Herald*, XXXI (April 1835), 149.

[18] Peirce to Hunnewell, Honolulu, October 4, 1833, in Hunnewell MSS.

[19] Dibble and Green to the American Board, May 7, 1832, in *Missionary Herald*, XXIX (February 1833), 60; Lorenzo Lyons to Anderson, Waimea, Hawaii, September 28, 1832, September 6, 1833, in Letters to the American Board, LXVIII, Nos. 52, 53; Dibble to Anderson, Hilo, November 9, 1832, in *ibid.*, LXVIII, No. 29; Cochran Forbes to Anderson, Kaawaloa, November

1832, in *ibid.*, LXVIII, No. 100; Samuel Whitney to Anderson, Oahu, November 23, 1832, in *ibid.*, LXVII, No. 59; John S. Emerson to Anderson, Waialua, December 3, 1832, in *ibid.*, LXVIII, No. 35.

[20] Emerson to Anderson, Waialua, November 25, 1833, in *ibid.*, LXVIII, No. 36.

[21] Baldwin and Lyons to the American Board, Waimea, Hawaii, October 26, [1833], in *Missionary Herald*, XXX (October 1834), 370.

[22] Thurston and Bishop to the American Board, Kailua, September 20, 1833, in *ibid.*, XXX (October 1834), 370–371.

[23] The Missionaries at Lahaina to the American Board, November 20, 1833, in *ibid.*, XXX (September 1834), 341.

Sheldon Dibble expressed doubt that the chiefs who long had been the strongest bulwark of missionary influence would continue to be friendly.[24] In September the Rev. Samuel Whitney reported a decline in attention to religion among the people of Kauai,[25] the island which had been least subject to the shifting fortunes of politics; and in March 1834 Dr. Judd found the people of Oahu everywhere indifferent to the exhortations of the missionaries.[26] So disconcerting to friends of the mission was this flow of pessimism that the American Board warned the missionaries that it was not wise to send to private correspondents or to public journals any information which might convey the impression that the mission in the Hawaiian Islands was a failure.[27]

The general depression which characterized all aspects of the missionary program following the death of Kaahumanu revealed more forcefully than before the weaknesses inherent in the mission schools. With thousands of the natives patently indifferent to reading or religious instruction, the missionaries on all of the islands except Kauai were generally agreed, in 1833, that the common schools no longer commanded the respect of the Hawaiian people. Many of the missionaries reported a decrease in the attendance at schools which came under their notice.[28] Others declared that the teachers were inefficient or immoral,[29] that school buildings had fallen into decay,[30] that the acquisition of knowledge had become "an irk-

[24] Dibble to Anderson, Lahaina, June 20, 1833, in Letters to the American Board, LXVIII, No. 32. See also Forbes to the American Board, Kuapehu, November 8, 1834, in *ibid.*, LXVIII, No. 102.

[25] Whitney to the American Board, Waimea, Kauai, September 9, 1833, in *Missionary Herald*, XXX (December 1834), 449.

[26] G. P. Judd, "Journal of a Tour of Oahu" (MS, Bishop Museum, Honolulu), March 27, 28, 1834.

[27] Rufus Anderson to the Sandwich Island Mission, Boston, September 5, 1834; Benjamin Wisner to the Sandwich Island Mission, Boston, September 6, 1834. Copies of these instructions, printed for the use of the missionaries, may be found in the library of the Hawaiian Historical Society, Honolulu.

[28] Journal of Levi Chamberlain, April 20, July 22, October 19, 22, 1833, July 23, 1834; David B. Lyman to Anderson, Hilo, November 20, 1832, in Letters to the American Board, LXVIII, No. 61; The Mission at Lahaina to the American Board, November 20, 1833, in *Missionary Herald*, XXX (September 1834), 341–342; J. S. Green to the American Board, Wailuku, August 14, December 6, 1833, in *ibid.*, XXX (November 1834), 408, 410; General Letter of the Mission, July 1, 1833, in *ibid.*, XXX (August 1834), 284.

[29] *Ibid.*; Forbes to the American Board, in *ibid.*, XXX (October 1834), 367; Baldwin and Lyons to the American Board, Waimea, Hawaii, October 26, [1833], in *ibid.*, XXX (October 1834), 369.

[30] Judd to Anderson, Wailuku, October 23, 1833, in Letters to the American Board, LXVIII, No. 130.

some business" to the mass of the people,[31] or that little in the way of constructive achievement could be expected from the schools in the near future.[32] During the following year, 1834, there was a further decline in the strength of the schools, and in some districts efforts to maintain them were temporarily abandoned.[33] Only on Kauai did they retain any considerable hold on the interest of the people, and even there it was reported that there was "a lamentable indifference to learning in many parts of the island."[34]

The collapse of the school system compelled the missionaries to reappraise their educational program with some care. For ten years the common schools had served the mission well. Thousands of Hawaiians had learned to read, and many of those humble scholars cherished religious tracts or translations of portions of the Scriptures which had been published by the Mission Press. The schools had been a useful adjunct in the dissemination of religious instruction, and to an uncertain extent they had inculcated the rigid moral standards of Puritan New England. In remote districts, they had occupied a position of peculiar interest, for there the poorly equipped and faltering native teacher was the sole representative of the educational and religious program of the mission.

No missionary entertained a thought that the schools could be permanently surrendered. New England standards of value dominated the thinking of the missionaries, and the almost universal respect for learning which was to be found in New England was shared in full measure by the missionaries in the Hawaiian Islands. The only division of opinion as to the future of the schools concerned the character of the measures which should be adopted to revive and strengthen them.

[31] Journal of Levi Chamberlain, September 21, 1833.

[32] Joseph Goodrich, David B. Lyman, and Sheldon Dibble to the American Board, Hilo, March 28, 1834, in *Missionary Herald*, XXX (October 1834), 373.

[33] General Letter of the Mission, Honolulu, July 15, 1834, in *ibid.*, XXXI (April 1835), 148; Report of the Mission at Kailua, November 5, 1834, in *ibid.*, XXXI (October 1835), 376; Harvey Hitchcock to the American Board, Kaluaaha, September 1834, in *ibid.*, XXXI (July 1835), 258; Emerson to Anderson, Waialua, December 23, 1834, in Letters to the American Board, LXVIII, No. 38.

[34] Whitney to the American Board, Waimea, Kauai, September 9, 1833, in *Missionary Herald*, XXX (December 1834), 448; General Letter of the Mission, Honolulu, July 15, 1834, in *ibid.*, XXXI (April 1835), 148; Alexander to the American Board, Waioli, October 17, 1835, in Letters to the American Board, LXVIII, No. 50.

The most serious weakness of the common schools had been the incompetence of the teachers. It was appropriate, therefore, that any consideration of the plight of the schools after 1832 should include a discussion of possible means of improving the quality of instruction. At least one missionary was convinced that only the payment of regular and adequate salaries to the teachers could save the school system;[35] but in general the missionaries based their hopes on a more adequate preparation of prospective teachers. The annual meeting in 1833 recommended, in rather general terms, that special attention to the training of teachers should be given at each station.[36] A more specific proposal was suggested by Dr. Judd, who urged his colleagues to establish in each district a select school to be taught by a missionary. The superior methods of instruction in these schools, he believed, would serve as a model for the teachers of the district.[37] Despite these proposals, which were received with some favor by the mission and were actually attempted at some of the stations, the majority of the missionaries hoped that the seminary at Lahainaluna would provide the solution for the problem of training future teachers.

The Mission Seminary was founded in 1831, with the primary and specific purpose of preparing teachers for the common schools.[38] Because it was expected that the most important product of the seminary would be teachers, the first class to enter the school consisted of adult men who already had had some experience in teaching. For the same reason, the curriculum was restricted to reading, geography, arithmetic, and writing—subjects taught in the common

[35] Emerson to Anderson, Waialua, December 23, 1834, in *ibid.*, LXVIII, No. 38.

[36] Minutes of the General Meeting of the Missionaries, June 1833, in *Missionary Herald*, XXX (July 1834), 257–258. During the months following this meeting, some of the missionaries devoted a part of their time to actual teaching in the schools, usually in select schools established for that purpose. Although the conduct of these schools varied in detail, all were designed to serve the dual purpose of reviving the common schools and providing additional training and stimulus to the native teachers. Sheldon Dibble later commented that "no small amount of time" had been expended in this type of instruction. Dibble, *History of the Sandwich Islands*, p. 295. For a description of the system employed to train teachers on Kauai, see Whitney to the American Board, Waimea, September 9, 1833, in *Missionary Herald*, XXX (December 1834), 448–449; Alexander, *William Patterson Alexander*, pp. 197–198.

[37] Judd to Anderson, October 23, 1833, October 13, 1835, in Letters to the American Board, LXVIII, Nos. 130, 134.

[38] Chamberlain to Hunnewell, Honolulu, November 12, 1832, in Hunnewell MSS; Lorrin Andrews, "An Account of the Rise of the High School at Lahainaluna," in *Report of the American Board*, 1835, pp. 135–147.

schools and therefore both appropriate and necessary in a course of study designed for prospective teachers.[39] The class which entered the seminary in the autumn of 1831 numbered twenty-five; by the following June the enrollment had increased to sixty-seven.[40] Three years later there were one hundred and eighteen pupils in the seminary and the original faculty of one had been increased to three.[41] Until 1836 the student body was composed of adults preparing to teach, although some of the missionaries hoped that a few of the graduates would serve in other useful capacities, either in the government or as assistants to the missionaries.

Life at Lahainaluna was not easy. The funds available for the establishment and maintenance of the seminary were limited, and from the beginning the pupils were expected to devote a part of their time to various types of manual labor which would contribute to the support of the school. These included the erection of buildings, the improvement of the grounds, and the cultivation of vegetables for the table.[42] More than grim necessity dictated this policy. The missionaries were appalled by the universal poverty and the absence of economic opportunity open to the Hawaiian people. They hoped to ameliorate this evil by inculcating habits of industry and thrift and by providing students in the boarding schools with some training in agriculture or trades. The program of compulsory labor, therefore, was closely allied to the ambition of the missionaries to create a real interest in agriculture and the mechanical arts.

When the seminary was established, in 1832, it was proposed to include instruction in mechanics in the curriculum.[43] This was not done; but when a secular assistant was employed the faculty chose a man who could direct the manual-labor projects and who was willing

[39] Dibble, *History of the Sandwich Islands*, pp. 271–272.

[40] General Letter of the Mission, June 23, 1832, in *Missionary Herald*, XXIX (May 1833), 162.

[41] *Ibid.*, XXXII (August 1836), 307. The original member of the faculty was the Rev. Lorrin Andrews. In 1833, the Rev. E. W. Clark was added to the staff, and two years later the Rev. Sheldon Dibble was assigned to the seminary. These three men constituted the faculty until 1841, when Andrews was replaced by the Rev. John S. Emerson. *He Papainoa o na Kumu, na Kahu a me na Haumanu a Pau o ke Kulanui o Lahainaluna* (Honolulu, 1846), p. 3.

[42] Bingham, *Sandwich Islands*, pp. 423, 425; *Laws of the High School*, June 1835, p. 14; Report of the Mission Seminary, May 1842, in Letters to the American Board, CXXXIV, No. 26; Lieut. [Henry Augustus] Wise, *Los Gringos* (New York, 1849), pp. 355–356.

[43] Chamberlain to Hunnewell, Honolulu, November 12, 1832, in Hunnewell MSS.

to teach some of the pupils the use of carpenter's tools.[44] In 1837 the faculty recommended that a separate department of manual labor be established at the seminary; but this suggestion was urged in vain. The American Board was harassed by the financial crisis which was then enveloping the United States, and it was unwilling to assume the responsibility for any project which would contribute only indirectly to the more immediate object of spreading the gospel.[45] The faculty at Lahainaluna, however, were not easily rebuffed. They attempted to achieve the same end by indirection, and in 1839 they encouraged "a pious blacksmith" to open a shop at Lahaina by promising him such patronage as they could offer in return for an agreement that he would employ a few pupils from the seminary during the vacations. They hoped to conclude a similar agreement with some pious carpenter.[46]

Five years of experience with the seminary convinced the missionaries that they had erred in limiting the student body to adults. Mature men did not yield readily to discipline, and frequently they appeared to be more concerned with the welfare of their families than with the mysteries of arithmetic and geography.[47] There was reason to expect that the younger men could be retained at the seminary for a longer period and that they would prove more adaptable to the routine of the school. At least one of the instructors believed that younger students could be trained more successfully in the habits and customs of civilized society. The mission, therefore, at the annual meeting in 1836 converted the seminary into a school for boys and young men between the ages of ten and twenty.[48] This did not imply any fundamental modification of the role of the seminary. In the thinking of the missionaries, it continued to be the apex of the

[44] Andrews, Clark, and Dibble to Anderson, Lahainaluna, November 11, 1837, in Letters to the American Board, CXXXIV, No. 24. The assistant was Charles Burnham, a carpenter by trade, who had come to the Islands in 1833 with a commission from the American Seamen's Friend Society to superintend the building of the Seamen's Chapel at Honolulu. Alexander, *Koloa Plantation*, p. 25.

[45] Andrews, Clark, and Dibble to Anderson, Lahainaluna, November 11, 1837, in Letters to the American Board, CXXXIV, No. 24; Anderson to the Sandwich Island Mission, Boston, November 1, 1837, in Letters from the American Board, Foreign, II (1836–1837), 506–507.

[46] Clark to Anderson, Lahainaluna, December 28, 1839, in Letters to the American Board, CXXXV, No. 190.

[47] General Letter of the Mission, [July 7, 1836], in *ibid.*, CXXXIV, No. 4.

[48] Dibble, *History of the Sandwich Islands*, pp. 275–276.

educational system, bearing the heavy responsibility of providing teachers and educated workers for both the mission and the government.[49]

Despite the recurrent emphasis upon manual labor and the mechanical arts, the faculty and the missionaries were generally agreed that the seminary should provide primarily a literary and professional education. The ostensible purpose of the mission in founding the school was to train teachers; but the missionaries anticipated that it would do far more than that. In reporting the decision to establish the seminary they expressed the hope that the new school would "disseminate sound knowledge throughout these islands, embracing literature and the sciences, and whatever may tend eventually to elevate the whole mass of the people from their present ignorance; that they may become a thinking, enlightened and virtuous people."[50] As the seminary became more firmly established, the hope of the missionaries that it would provide professional education and serve to raise the level of culture became more specific. In 1839 the mission recommended that a few of the most promising students be encouraged to remain at Lahainaluna for additional study in the hope that those so favored would be prepared to enter a profession or to make some contribution to the slender store of Hawaiian literature.[51] More significant was the conviction, held by an increasing number of missionaries, that the seminary should train young men for a variety of religious positions associated with the mission, including the responsibility for small or remote churches for which missionary pastors could not be provided.[52]

One measure of the aspirations entertained by the faculty and the mission is suggested by the curriculum after 1836. The young

[49] *Missionary Herald*, XLI (January 1845), 28; General Letter of the Mission, 1844, in *ibid.*, XLI (March 1845), 76; Richards and Andrews to Anderson, Lahaina, December 6, 1841, in Letters to the American Board, CXXXIV, No. 25; E. W. Clark, "The Origin, Progress and Importance of the Mission Seminary at Lahainaluna, Maui," in *Hawaiian Spectator*, I (October 1838), 347–350.

[50] *Missionary Herald*, XXVIII (June 1832), 189.

[51] Report of the Sandwich Island Mission, May 1839, in *ibid.*, XXXVI (June 1840), 226.

[52] See, for example, the report of Richards and Lorrin Andrews that there were at least one hundred small villages that could not be supplied with missionaries and which were, therefore, without religious instruction. That instruction, they believed, could be provided by young men trained for that purpose at Lahainaluna. Richards and Andrews to Anderson, Lahaina, December 6, 1841, in Letters to the American Board, CXXXIV, No. 25.

men who were admitted to the seminary were confronted by a truly impressive array of studies, including arithmetic, geometry, trigonometry, composition, sacred geography, navigation, surveying, astronomy, chemistry, natural and moral philosophy, and secular and church history. A few advanced students received some instruction in Greek.[53] A better clue to the academic attainments of the students, however, is furnished by the requirements for admission. From 1831 through 1836 the candidates for the seminary were selected by missionaries in various parts of the Islands and apparently were accepted as students without further qualification. At the close of 1836 the faculty at the seminary sought to establish some more satisfactory standard—a change in policy made imperative by the decision to limit the student body to boys and young men. They therefore decided to require all candidates for admission to pass written examinations in reading, writing, mental arithmetic, and geography. This brief list of prerequisites was supplemented by the stipulation that the candidate should have "some character, or should be as little polluted as possible."[54]

In common with other institutions of the mission, the seminary suffered from illness among the men assigned to it. On several occasions between 1837 and 1843, the nominal faculty of three was reduced to an effective faculty of one.[55] With the staff thus weakened, and with the American Board indifferent to industrial education, the effort to combine a mechanical with a liberal education was impossible of achievement. The resulting concentration upon liberal arts was displeasing to some visitors, who believed that the Hawaiian people would derive a greater profit from a more practical curriculum. This view was vigorously expressed by Captain Charles Wilkes.

---

[53] *Laws of the High School*, June 1835, p. 18; *Missionary Herald*, XXXII (August 1836), 307; General Letters of the Mission, [July 7, 1836], June 20, 1838, in Letters to the American Board, CXXXIV, Nos. 4, 10; Report of the Mission Seminary, May 1842, in *ibid.*, CXXXIV, No. 26; Dibble, *History of the Sandwich Islands*, p. 278.

[54] Andrews, Clark, and Dibble to the Sandwich Island Mission, Lahainaluna, December 26, 1836. This letter was printed for the use of the mission, and a copy may be found in the library of the Hawaiian Historical Society.

[55] Dibble, *History of the Sandwich Islands*, pp. 277–278; Clark to Anderson, Lahainaluna, November 20, 1841, in Letters to the American Board, CXXXV, No. 193; Emerson to Anderson, Lahainaluna, August 30–September 3, 1842, in *ibid.*, CXXXVI, No. 112; Report of the Lahainaluna Seminary, [September 1843], in *ibid.*, CXXXIV, No. 22.

He praised the good intentions of the instructors, though regretting that they were not practical men. The program of the seminary he described as "wholly impracticable and unsuitable" to the condition of the people. For that reason, he believed that the usefulness of the seminary was virtually at an end, and he predicted that it had passed "its meridian" and was rapidly "going to decay." Discipline, he declared, was "loose and irregular," because the students made and enforced their own laws, and, apparently with more sarcasm than approval, he conceded that the seminary could be regarded as "a republican school."[56]

In franker moments, the missionaries admitted that the seminary had fallen short of their more sanguine hopes, although readers of the *Missionary Herald* were informed, in January 1845, that the school had fulfilled "every reasonable anticipation."[57] More than a year later the missionaries assured the American Board that the seminary had accomplished "perhaps all we should have expected" in improving the political, spiritual, and intellectual interests of the people.[58] The most severe test of the seminary was the later career of its graduates; and there the missionaries found no grounds for discouragement or apology. Of two hundred and fifty living graduates, there were, in 1845, one hundred and eight teachers, forty-three in the service of the government, and thirty-one who were said by the missionaries to be usefully employed. The other graduates had failed to measure up to the hopes of their teachers, although even among that group there were some who the missionaries conceded were engaged in honorable occupations.[59] Schools taught by men trained at Lahainaluna were said to be "almost uniformly prosperous,"[60] but the number of teachers produced annually at the seminary

---

[56] Wilkes, *United States Exploring Expedition*, IV, 262–266.

[57] *Missionary Herald*, XLI (January 1845), 28.

[58] The Mission to Anderson, Honolulu, June 1846, in Letters to the American Board, CLXXIII, No. 6.

[59] Alexander and Emerson to the American Board, May 13, 1846, in *Missionary Herald*, XLII (December 1846), 419.

[60] General Letter of the Mission, Honolulu, June 8, 1839, in Letters to the American Board, CXXXIV, No. 11. See also Thurston to the American Board, Kailua, April 24, 1837, in *Missionary Herald*, XXXIV (June 1838), 234; Lyons to the American Board, September 18, 1837, in *ibid.*, XXXIV (July 1838), 256; Armstrong to the American Board, Wailuku, August 4, 1838, in *ibid.*, XXXV (May 1839), 162; Charles McDonald to Anderson, Lahaina, October 10, 1836, in Letters to the American Board, CXXXVII, No. 164; Gulick to Anderson, Koloa, January 12, 1837, in *ibid.*, CXXXVI, No. 1; Edward Johnson to Ander-

fell short of the needs of the common schools throughout the Islands.[61]
Some graduates rendered "great assistance" to the mission as deacons or elders in well-established churches, while others had informal
commissions from individual missionaries which permitted them "to
watch over the fold of Christ" or to preach the gospel with whatever
success their talents might allow.[62] With what may have been greater
satisfaction than reason, the faculty of the seminary reported, in 1846,
that graduates of Lahainaluna were "everywhere the leading members of society, in matters civil, religious and literary."[63]

The students and graduates of the seminary made one notable
contribution to the literature of their native country. Under the direction of their teachers, they studied the early history of the Islands,
gathering together and sifting the numerous oral traditions which
were current in all parts of the archipelago. With the aid of one of
their instructors, the Rev. Sheldon Dibble, a group of students prepared *Ka Mooolelo Hawaii*, the first written history of the Hawaiian
Islands and the basis for the early chapters of Dibble's well-known
History of the Sandwich Islands. The leading spirit in this work
seems to have been David Malo, one of the best-informed of the
natives as to the early history of his people. It probably was through
his influence that, in 1841, a group of graduates of the seminary
organized a historical society to stimulate interest in the study of
Hawaiian history.[64]

The collapse of the common school system after 1832 confronted
the missionaries with the problem of finding some method by which
the schools could be revived. After the lapse of more than three
years, there was a "pretty general" opinion in the mission that the
best solution would be the establishment of boarding schools in which
a select group of boys or girls would be brought directly and continuously under the influence of the mission.[65] This opinion represented

son, Waioli, October 27, 1838, in *ibid.*, CXXXVII, No. 149.

[61] Johnson to Anderson, Waioli, September 8, 1843, in *ibid.*, CXXXVII, No. 151.

[62] The Mission to Anderson, Honolulu,
June 1846, in *ibid.*, CLXXIII, No. 6.

[63] Alexander and Emerson to the Ameri-

can Board, May 13, 1846, in *Missionary
Herald*, XLII (December 1846), 419. See
also *Report of the American Board*, 1847,
p. 181.

[64] *Polynesian*, May 8, 1841.

[65] H. R. Hitchcock to Anderson, Kaluaaha, April 1836, in Letters to the American
Board, LXVIII, No. 56.

an important step in the development of missionary policy, for in contrast to the democracy of the common schools it was frankly hoped that boarding schools would train the future leaders of the Hawaiian churches and the nation. This did not mean any lessening interest in the common schools. It was rather a tacit recognition that they could not produce a well-prepared leadership. The strength of opinion in support of boarding schools was demonstrated at the annual meeting of the mission in 1836, when the missionaries appropriated five hundred dollars toward the support of a boarding school for boys at Hilo and authorized the establishment of a seminary for girls at Wailuku.[66]

In October 1837 the Central Female Seminary at Wailuku was ready to receive its first pupils. Three months later there were at the school thirty-six "little Hawaiian misses" ranging in age from four to ten years.[67] Thereafter the number of students at Wailuku slowly but steadily increased until 1843, when there were sixty-five girls enrolled in the seminary.[68]

The missionaries did not propose to duplicate at Wailuku the curriculum available at Lahainaluna. The Female Seminary was not the product of any feminist sentiment, and the girls who were educated at Wailuku were expected to assume stations in life appropriate to persons of their sex. The mission hoped that their experience at Wailuku would enable them to set an example of piety and morality, which in turn would "raise the character" of the women of the nation. More important, as well as more tangible, was the expectation that some of the girls from the Female Seminary would become wives of graduates of the seminary at Lahainaluna.[69] To train them for their important position in society these prospective wives and mothers were given instruction in "Christianity . . . . geography . . . . moral philosophy, natural theology . . . . and various arts adapted to the station of Hawaiian females."[70] Included among these

[66] David B. Lyman to the American Board, Hilo, November 12, 1840, in *ibid.*, CXXXVI, No. 139.

[67] Green to Anderson, Wailuku, October 19, 1837, in *ibid.*, CXXXV, No. 198.

[68] Green to Anderson, Wailuku, January 24, 1839, in *ibid.*, CXXXV, No. 206; Dibble, *History of the Sandwich Islands*, p. 285.

[69] *Ibid.*, p. 282; J. S. Green, "Female Education at the Sandwich Islands," in *Hawaiian Spectator*, I, No. 1 (January 1838), p. 40; Green and Armstrong to Anderson, Wailuku, November 16, 1836, in Letters to the American Board, Sandwich Islands, 1831–1837, Part I, No. 116.

[70] Bingham, *Sandwich Islands*, p. 582.

various arts were sewing, knitting, braiding, spinning, and "Exhibition of Popery."[71] It is apparent that there was a conscious effort to supply the young ladies with at least the veneer of social accomplishment, and the wife of a missionary recorded that she had watched with pleasure "the little girls spreading the table and eating with plates, knives, forks, and spoons, or neatly dressed and at work in the flower garden . . . . or . . . . in the work-room, learning to sew, knit, spin, and plait straw."[72] Captain Wilkes believed, however, that the habits of the girls were so strongly formed before they arrived at the school that no sooner did they leave the supervision of their teachers at Wailuku than they reverted to "their savage state," which they found more congenial than the "partially civilized habits" they had learned at the seminary.[73]

While at Wailuku the girls had few idle moments between sunrise and sunset. Their day was carefully planned to provide time for study, recitation, labor, and religious exercises.[74] More emphasis was placed upon the formation of character than upon the training of the intellect, and the instructors sought eagerly for evidence that their young charges were conscious of the necessity for salvation. Occasionally they were rewarded with indications of more than casual interest in religious problems among the students; and at one time, in 1843, some of the girls were so alarmed about the state of their religious life that they lost all interest in play and arose each morning before sunrise to engage in prayer.[75] This show of piety may have contributed to their spiritual welfare, but it was not conducive to either health or physical vigor—two assets greatly to be desired in women who were being educated to become wives and mothers.

It is probable, on the contrary, that this unusual absorption in the psychological problems of conversion and salvation increased the tendency to illness and debility which was so common among the girls at Wailuku. This tendency was recognized by missionaries and out-

[71] *Minutes of the General Meeting of the Sandwich Island Mission,* 1841, p. 7; *Polynesian,* January 30, 1841.

[72] Judd, *Honolulu,* p. 70.

[73] Wilkes, *United States Exploring Expedition,* IV, 258.

[74] Anderson, *History of the Mission to the Sandwich Islands,* pp. 180–181; Dibble, *History of the Sandwich Islands,* p. 285; Green to Anderson, January 24, 1839, in Letters to the American Board, CXXXV, No. 206.

[75] Bingham, *Sandwich Islands,* p. 583.

siders alike; but there was no agreement as to the proper remedy. Sheldon Dibble seems to have expressed the views of many of his colleagues when he lamented the fact that efforts to prevent "rude and romping behavior" and to restrict the girls to exercises suitable for females of their station resulted in serious injury to their health. The instructors at the seminary, therefore, were faced with the dilemma of sacrificing either the health or the morals of their students. The answer was suggested by Dr. Judd, who prescribed less restraint and a greater opportunity for play and exercise.[76]

The missionaries generally regarded the progress of the Female Seminary as satisfactory.[77] In one important particular they were disappointed. The graduates of the seminary at Lahainaluna did not commonly seek wives at Wailuku but, like their less educated brethren, they preferred to select their own wives rather than to be guided by the wishes of the missionaries.[78]

The second of the boarding schools authorized by the mission in 1836—the school for boys—was opened at Hilo in October 1836, with seven pupils.[79] This number was soon increased. In the summer of 1837 there were thirty-one boys in the school, and after the completion of the necessary buildings the number of students fluctuated between fifty and sixty-five.[80] The Rev. David B. Lyman, who was in charge of the school, originally proposed to take boys between the ages of seven and twelve. Experience indicated, however, that the instruction at Hilo was better adapted to boys over ten, and Lyman abandoned his earlier intention of concentrating upon younger boys.[81] The formal curriculum of the school included reading, writing, geography, arithmetic, history, singing, and the Bible, with considerable emphasis upon the latter.[82]

[76] Dibble, *History of the Sandwich Islands*, p. 284; Judd, *Honolulu*, pp. 70–71.

[77] Jarves, *Scenes and Scenery in the Sandwich Islands*, p. 175; General Letter of the Mission, 1844, in *Missionary Herald*, XLI (March 1845), 76.

[78] Teggart, ed., *Around the Horn to the Sandwich Islands and California* (Journal of Chester S. Lyman, May 26, December 18, 1846), pp. 69, 153.

[79] Lyman to Anderson, Hilo, December 6, 1836, in Letters to the American Board, LXVIII, No. 66.

[80] Lyman to Anderson, Hilo, November 12, 1840, and November 5, 1842, in *ibid.*, CXXXVI, Nos. 139, 142; *Missionary Herald*, XLV (March 1849), 77–78; Lyman to the American Board, September 3, 1847, in *ibid.*, XLIV (May 1848), 175; *Polynesian*, August 22, 1840.

[81] Lyman to the American Board, Hilo, November 12, 1840, in Letters to the American Board, CXXXVI, No. 139.

[82] Lyman and Coan to Anderson, Hilo, May 1, 1837, in *ibid.*, CXXXIV, No. 28; Lyman to the American Board, Hilo, No-

To an even greater extent than at Lahainaluna, the school at Hilo emphasized manual labor as an indispensable part of the daily program, and Lyman informed the American Board that the training of his young pupils in "industrious moral habits, based on the principles of the gospel" had been his primary objective.[83] The results presumably were as pleasing to Lyman as they were to Captain Wilkes, commonly a severe critic of the boarding schools, who declared that the boys at the Hilo school were more cheerful and appeared in better health than any others he had seen at the Islands. He likewise praised their apparent progress with their studies, writing that during an examination in arithmetic their performance "would have done credit" to a comparable group in the United States.[84] The school which Lyman conducted with such skill was to have influences more far-reaching than he could have anticipated. The combination of formal education with regular periods of manual labor which were blended so carefully at Hilo provided Samuel Chapman Armstrong with the model for Hampton Institute in Virginia.[85]

The seminaries at Lahainaluna and Wailuku and the boarding school at Hilo were formally authorized by the mission to meet specific needs of its educational program. Two other boarding schools were the result of the initiative of individual missionaries. In 1838 Mrs. Titus Coan, the wife of the missionary at Hilo, opened a school for girls between the ages of seven and ten.[86] She made no pretense of offering a literary education to her pupils, being content to teach them "the rudiments of necessary book knowledge, and of singing, sewing, washing and ironing, gardening, and other things."[87] Nearly all of the comment concerning this school is from the pens of persons disposed to be friendly to the institution, and it may be that an unduly

---

vember 12, 1840, in *ibid.*, CXXXVI, No. 139; Lyons to Greene, Waimea, Hawaii, March 7, 1845, in *ibid.*, CLXXIII, No. 106; Wood, *Wandering Sketches*, pp. 159–160; Cheever, *Island World of the Pacific*, p. 260; Hill, *Travels in the Sandwich and Society Islands*, pp. 295, 298.

[83] Lyman to Anderson, Hilo, December 6, 1836, November 12, 1840, in Letters to the American Board, LXVIII, No. 66, CXXXVI, No. 139; Lyman to the American Board, September 3, 1847, in *Missionary Herald*, XLIV (May 1848), 175.

[84] Wilkes, *United States Exploring Expedition*, IV, 225.

[85] Edith Armstrong Talbot, *Samuel Chapman Armstrong* (New York, 1904), p. 155; S. A. E[liot], "Samuel Chapman Armstrong," in *Dictionary of American Biography*, I, 360.

[86] Coan to the American Board, Honolulu, June 6, 1839, in *Missionary Herald*, XXXVI (July 1840), 251–252.

[87] Coan, *Life in Hawaii*, p. 62.

favorable picture of it has been passed on to later generations. It is easy to conjure up a scene of domestic and educational bliss from the comment of Captain Wilkes that upon a visit to the school he found Mrs. Coan "with all her scholars seated around, some hard at work with the needle, and some reading."[88] More significant, perhaps, was the judgment of Sheldon Dibble that the little girls were "interesting, docile, and promising."[89] Docility in young ladies apparently was regarded as a virtue by the stern Calvinists who dominated the mission. From another prejudiced source, the husband of the teacher, came the statement that after leaving the school many former pupils were "distinguished among their companions for neatness, skill, industry, and piety."[90] The number of girls who received the benefits of Mrs. Coan's instructions was quite small, although it was reported that many coveted the privilege of being enrolled in her school. Lack of accommodations compelled her to limit the number of students at any one time to twenty-six, and ill health forced her to discontinue the school after only eight years.[91]

The second boarding school established through the efforts of a single missionary family was a unique experiment in industrial education. It was the result of the conviction of Edwin Locke that the emphasis in the education of Hawaiian boys should be placed upon manual labor and the learning of some useful trade, "even if they were obliged to labour the 4/5th or even 5/6th of their time for their support."[92] Shortly after being assigned by the mission to the station at Waialua, he determined to open a school in which labor would be the central feature and which might become self-supporting. He inaugurated this experiment in 1840 with nine pupils. A year later, there were nineteen boys working and studying under the supervision of Locke—a number approximately equal to the capacity of the school. Thereafter, despite the skepticism of a few of the missionaries and of some of the parents, the number of boys in Locke's school remained almost constant.[93]

---

[88] Wilkes, *United States Exploring Expedition*, IV, 226.

[89] Dibble, *History of the Sandwich Islands*, p. 289.

[90] Coan, *Life in Hawaii*, p. 62.

[91] *Ibid.*, pp. 62–63; Coan to the American Board, May 3, 1844, in *Missionary Herald*, XLI (March 1845), 86.

[92] Locke to Anderson, Waialua, April 11, 1838, in Letters to the American Board, CXXXVI, No. 104.

[93] Dibble, *History of the Sandwich Is-*

The students were required to work in the fields for five hours each day, partly to assist in the support of the school, but primarily to accustom them to habits of industry. Locke worked with them, and improved the occasion by conversing with them on subjects "of such a character as would be useful to them." This program was planned not so much to give the pupils "a knowledge of books as to make them useful and valuable members of society."[94] These efforts met with some success. Captain Wilkes, who visited the school during the first year of its existence, found the boys neatly dressed and looking well, and he observed that some of them were able to yoke oxen or guide a plow "with adroitness."[95] Not less significant was the fact that through the cultivation and sale of sugar the school became entirely self-supporting and at one time had a surplus of several hundred dollars.[96] Thus, at no expense to the mission, Locke was giving a small group of Hawaiians that training in industry and agriculture which many of his colleagues believed essential to the temporal prosperity of the Hawaiian people.

Despite these evidences of usefulness the school did not receive the approbation of all of the missionaries, for there were some who questioned the propriety of a missionary devoting his entire time to an enterprise which was so secular in character.[97] Defenders of Locke, however, included some of the most influential members of the mission, and a committee of the mission, in 1842, reported favorably upon the continuance of his school. In defense of this type of education, friends of the school declared that Locke was providing his pupils with an experience similar to that of boys in Christian homes in the United States.[98] Representative of this point of view was the obituary of Locke, in the *Friend*, which declared that he had taught his pupils "industrious habits, sound morals and religion," and that

lands, p. 289; Wilkes, *United States Exploring Expedition*, IV, 80; Artemas Bishop, A. B. Smith, and Benjamin Parker to Anderson, Waialua, February 14, 1843, in Letters to the American Board, CXXXV, No. 77.

[94] *Ibid.*; Locke to Anderson, Waialua, March 1841, in *ibid.*, CXXXVII, No. 159; Mrs. Locke to G. B. Rowell, July 2, 1841, MS in possession of Miss Dorothy C. Rowell, New Haven, Connecticut.

[95] Wilkes, *United States Exploring Expedition*, IV, 79–80.

[96] Cheever, *Life in the Sandwich Islands*, p. 273.

[97] Chamberlain to Anderson, Honolulu, November 24, 1842, in Letters to the American Board, CXXXV, No. 155.

[98] Armstrong to Anderson, Honolulu, January 14, 1842, in *ibid.*, CXXXVI, No. 84; Alexander to Anderson, Honolulu, January 19, 1843, in *ibid.*, CXXXVI, No. 68; Bishop, Smith, and Parker to Anderson, Waialua, February 14, 1843, in *ibid.*, CXXXV, No. 77.

those who had visited his school could testify to his "indefatigable efforts" to benefit the future generation of Hawaiians.[99] These efforts were brought to a premature close. The school at Waialua was suspended after the death of Mrs. Locke in 1842; it was abandoned after the death of the founder in October 1843.

From the beginning the mission in the Hawaiian Islands enjoyed the particular favor of the American Board. During the critical years from November 1822 to November 1832, the Board sent to the Islands five reinforcements, with an aggregate of twenty clergymen and ten laymen. A sixth reinforcement left Boston in December 1834;[100] the seventh and largest, including four clergymen and eleven laymen, sailed from the same port in December 1836. These additions to the numerical strength of the mission were somewhat offset by the removal from the Islands of some missionaries and the illness of others.[101] As a consequence of these changes, the mission was able

---

[99] *The Friend*, November 4, 1843, p. 65.

[100] The one clergyman who went to the Islands with the fifth reinforcement was the Rev. Titus Coan. Coan, who previously had been sent by the American Board to Patagonia as one of the founders of the short-lived mission in that region, became one of the most active and widely known missionaries in the Hawaiian Islands. For nearly fifty years he was stationed at Hilo, the most populous community on the island of Hawaii. His influence extended beyond the narrow bounds of Hilo, for he regarded all the southeastern part of the island as his parish and he regularly visited the small villages of that area. Everywhere he was welcomed by the natives, who came to regard him as pastor, friend, and counselor. Henry Lyman, who accompanied Coan on a tour of Hilo and Puna, recalled that his "remarkable personality rendered his influence irresistible." Throughout the day, according to Lyman, "the people thronged around him; and as we walked from station to station, they swarmed out from their little homes along the path, to exchange greetings with the beloved pastor, so that our progress was necessarily very slow." Lyman, *Hawaiian Yesterdays*, p. 166. An extended account of this tour may be found in *ibid.*, pp. 157-167.

Coan became much interested in the great volcanoes near Hilo, and his accounts of important lava flows were of interest to students of volcanic action. Some of his letters on this subject appeared in religious publications; others were published in secular journals. See *Daily National Intelligencer*, January 31, 1844; *American Journal of Science and Arts*, LXIII (1852), 395-397, LXV (1853), 63-65, LXVIII (1854), 96-98, LXXI (1856), 100-102, LXXII (1856), 240-243, XCVII (1869), 89-98, CII (1871), 454-456.

For more detailed accounts of the career of Coan, see Coan, *Life in Hawaii: An Autobiographical Sketch of Mission Life and Labors*; Lydia Bingham Coan, *Titus Coan. A Memorial* (Chicago, 1884); S. J. Humphrey, *Titus Coan* (New York, n.d.); J[ohn] C. A[rcher], "Titus Coan," in *Dictionary of American Biography*, IV, 236-237.

[101] The correspondence and journals of the missionaries contain many references to the illness of individual missionaries or to the prevalence of sickness in the mission. For examples see the Rev. and Mrs. David B. Lyman to H. Lyman, Hilo, December 29, 1834, in Letters to the American Board, LXVIII, No. 64; Chamberlain to Hill, Honolulu, November 4, 1834, in *ibid.*, CXCI; The Mission to Anderson, [July 7, 1836], in *ibid.*, CXXXIV, No. 4; Richard Armstrong

to muster, in the summer of 1837, twenty-six clergymen, sixteen laymen, and four unmarried women who were serving as teachers. This increase in personnel permitted a considerable expansion of the activities of the mission, and by the close of 1837, missionaries were regularly stationed in seventeen communities scattered throughout the five major islands. In ten of these communities, there had been no resident missionary prior to the summer of 1832.[102]

The missionaries were not yet satisfied, and they continued to hope for further additions to their number. In June 1837—less than two months after the arrival at Honolulu of the seventh reinforcement —the mission formally requested the Board to send forty-six men and women to the Islands, unless there were other mission fields with "obviously paramount claims."[103] This request was doomed to an unfavorable answer. By the summer of 1837 the disturbed financial conditions in the United States had compelled the Board to restrict its activities;[104] instead of sending new companies of missionaries to the Hawaiian Islands, the Board was urging the mission to carry on its program with less extensive assistance than it had previously received from the United States.

The seventh reinforcement, which arrived at Honolulu in April 1837, included eight men specifically designated as teachers. The mission was therefore encouraged to embark upon a program which some of its members had long regarded as very desirable—the establishment of "select schools" at various mission stations throughout the Islands. Superficially, a select school was merely a school conducted by a missionary rather than by a native. It was expected, however, that the select school would be maintained with regular-

---

to Reuben Chapman, Wailuku, February 18, 1840, in Armstrong MSS; Journal of Mrs. G. P. Judd, April 22, 1828, in Judd, *Honolulu*, p. 16.

[102] The seventeen communities, with the date of the first settlement there of a missionary family, were: Honolulu (1820), Waialua (1832), Ewa (1834), and Kaneohe (1834) on Oahu; Waimea (1820), Waioli (1834), and Koloa (1834) on Kauai; Kailua (1820), Hilo (1824), Kaawaloa (1824), Waimea (1832), and Kohala (1837) on Hawaii; Lahaina (1823), Lahainaluna (1831), Wailuku (1832), and Hana (1837) on

Maui; and Kaluaaha (1832) on Molokai. *Missionary Herald*, XXXVI (January 1840), 25–26.

[103] Bingham and Tinker to Anderson, Honolulu, June 1, 1837, in Letters to the American Board, CXXXIV, No. 5.

[104] Journal of William Richards, May 26, 1837; Anderson to the Sandwich Island Mission, Boston, December 5, 1836, July 21, 1837, May 22, December 14, 1839, in Letters from the American Board, Foreign, II (1836–1837), 231–232, 435–436, and in *ibid.*, II (1839), 113–114, 276–277.

ity, that it would be marked by more careful discipline, and that it would exhibit methods of instruction which might provide a model for the teachers of the common schools. This type of school was not entirely novel, and prior to 1837 there had been schools under the direct supervision of a missionary or the wife of a missionary. Hitherto such schools had been subject to interruption when the burdens of church or family bore too heavily upon the teacher. The addition of a substantial number of teachers to the personnel of the mission seemed to insure greater permanence and usefulness to the station or select schools.

School sessions of six hours a day for five days a week were not considered too great a burden upon the patience of the pupils who attended the select schools. The curriculum was equally formidable, being "nearly as extensive as the limits of Hawaiian science and literature would allow," and including the range of learning from the memorization of the alphabet to elementary astronomy and philosophy.[105] This was a severe test of the will and ability of the students; but the missionaries were pleased by the earliest results. In 1838, less than a year after the establishment of the select schools, they solemnly informed the American Board that "such a charm [had been] thrown around the machinery of instruction, as to create an attachment to the place, and a relish for the employment."[106]

More than the example of select schools, however successful or popular, was needed to restore the prosperity which the common schools once had enjoyed. On the island of Kauai, where they had weathered the reaction in 1833 and 1834 better than on other islands, it was evident by 1837 that the common schools generally were in a feeble state. From Koloa the Rev. Peter J. Gulick wrote that the schools were of "small value, as to their intellectual character";[107] and his neighbor, the Rev. William P. Alexander, reported

---

[105] General Letter of the Mission, June 20, 1838, in *Missionary Herald*, XXXV (April 1839), 144. For other accounts of select schools, see H. R. Hitchcock to Anderson, Kaluaaha, November 7, 1837, in Letters to the American Board, CXXXVI, No. 124; Charles McDonald to Anderson, Lahaina, October 10, 1836, and November 25, 1837, in *ibid.*, CXXXVII, Nos. 164, 165; H. O. Knapp to Anderson, Honolulu, February 4, 1840, in *ibid.*, CXXXVII, No. 153; Edward Johnson to Anderson, Waioli, October 27, 1838, and September 8, 1843, in *ibid.*, CXXXVII, Nos. 149, 151.

[106] General Letter of the Mission, June 20, 1838, in *Missionary Herald*, XXXV (April 1839), 144.

[107] Gulick to Anderson, Koloa, November 29, 1837, in Letters to the American Board, CXXXVI, No. 3.

that not more than five of the schools in his district deserved the name.[108] A year later, in 1838, Alexander declared that the schools for adults virtually had ceased to exist at Waioli, although those for children were generally prosperous. The principal weakness of the schools, he believed, was the absence of adequate means of support for the native teachers.[109] His diagnosis of the situation at Waioli apparently could have been applied in many parts of the Islands.

On the basis of incomplete statistics, the mission reported, in 1838, that about eight thousand children were "more or less under the influence of the common schools."[110] The marked decline in the number of students may be explained primarily by the disappearance of adults from the schools. The problem of the mission, in 1838, was not to increase the number of students nominally enrolled but to keep regularly at their books and slates those who were enrolled and to improve the character of the instruction given those who attended faithfully.

The condition of the schools did not improve during 1839. On the island of Maui friendly chiefs ordered all children of appropriate age to attend school, with the result that the children of that island were said to be "very much under the influence and control of the mission."[111] Elsewhere the attendance at the common schools decreased, although the mission reported that the select schools had held their own. The continued disintegration of the educational system was explained, in part, by the repeal on some of the islands of laws requiring children to attend school. More ominous was the growing dissatisfaction among the teachers, some of whom openly demanded more adequate compensation, while others deserted their students to take positions under the government.[112] By the spring of 1840 it was apparent that some drastic reorganization was necessary if the schools were to be saved from eventual extinction.

The schools, even in their weakened condition, were a valuable adjunct to the mission. They were designed to facilitate the spread

[108] Quoted in Alexander, *William Patterson Alexander*, p. 199.

[109] Quoted in *ibid.*, pp. 199–200.

[110] General Letter of the Mission, June 20, 1838, in *Missionary Herald*, XXXV (April 1839), 143.

[111] Letter of Richard Armstrong, in *ibid.*, XXXVI (February 1840), 74–75.

[112] General Letter of the Mission, Honolulu, June 1, 1840, in Letters to the American Board, CXXXIV, No. 13; *Report of the American Board*, 1840, pp. 154–155.

of religious ideas; and one critic commented, in 1836, that they were "so entirely appropriated to the performance of Calvinistic worship" that they were of less advantage to the nation than could be desired.[113] With this opinion, the missionaries certainly would have disagreed. The collective judgment of the missionaries as to the value of their schools, formed after fifteen years of experience which included prosperity and adversity, may be found in their report to the American Board in 1838, in which they declared:

> Through the instrumentality of common schools, imperfect as they are, thousands on these islands have been taught to read and hundreds have been made more or less acquainted with the elements of writing, calculation, and geography; and hence are the better prepared for the business of life. Such a degree of moral influence has been exerted over the minds of the pupils, as has resulted in the prevention of much evil. Children are taught to love one another, respect their parents, obey God, etc. Such instructions have not been in vain. . . . .

> . . . .

> The influence of the teachers is more or less extensive, according to their qualifications for their office. Teachers from the mission seminary command, as a general thing, the respect of the people among whom they move . . . . they carry their knowledge with them, and use it as an instrument for gathering around them an influence, and in raising their pupils and countrymen from the sink of filth and pollution.[114]

---

[113] Ruschenberger, *Voyage Round the World*, p. 466.

[114] General Letter of the Mission, June 20, 1838, in *Missionary Herald*, XXXV (April 1839), 143.

A similar summary of the influence of the schools may be found in the report of the Rev. Lorenzo Lyons for the year 1839–1840. Commenting upon an examination of the schools at Waimea, Hawaii, Lyons wrote:

"I have held many examinations—some partial & some general; some for children & some for adults—some restricted to a few things, & some extending to the whole range of Hawaiian literature, or rather to every thing that had been taught or learned since the introduction of the gospel. In the examinations of the latter class I have been rather surprised to find that many would begin with the first book printed in Hawaiian, & repeat it all from memory—the first catechism—the ten commandments—Christ's sermon on the mount, a good por-

tion of scripture history &c. To make it go well however they found it convenient to repeat in concert. Beside scripture history they were examined as to their knowledge of scripture miracles—prophecies—doctrines—commandments—prohibitions &c. . . . . I found in many a woful degree of ignorance—even in those from whom I expected better things. Some who had been readers for a long time & had some portions of scripture in their possession, yet could not repeat a single scripture fact or doctrine. Many however could give a pretty good account of what the scriptures contained. Some few could repeat whole chapters, committed to memory. It was particularly interesting to hear the children recite various hymns & portions of scripture & childrens catechisms.

"Nor have the scriptures only received attention in the examinations. All the writers brought their slates & were requested to give a specimen of their penmanship. I

The missionaries were certain to regard the preservation of such an influence as eminently worth while. Meanwhile the establishment of religious toleration in 1839 confronted them with a formidable and aggressive rival in the form of a revived Catholic mission. The maintenance of the common schools seemed more than ever imperative, for should they disappear there was danger that the education of future generations of Hawaiians would pass into control of the Catholic mission. By the summer of 1840 the missionaries were agreed that the only means of saving the common schools was the payment of salaries to the teachers.[115] The mission had no funds for such a purpose, and only the government could guarantee sufficient revenue to assure the teachers of regular salaries. There was but one solution for the problem, and it was a paradox. To save the schools, the mission must surrender them to the government.

Apparently the proposal that the government should finance the common schools was first presented to the chiefs some time in 1839.[116] It was not until the following year, however, that either the chiefs or the mission took definite action to bring this project to realization. The missionaries, at their annual meeting in 1840, appointed a committee to confer with the chiefs concerning the future of the schools.[117]

---

was surprised to find so great a number of writers. Many had taught themselves, by looking on the written characters they had seen. The names they had learned from inquiry, but the manner of forming them was not so clear—whether to begin in the middle, top or bottom, on the right hand or on the left. Yet the greater part could so form them or put them together, as to render their writing intelligible, & some could write a good, fair—if not an elegant hand.

"Among other branches were, Natural history, Arithmetic—geography & astronomy. To wake up the mental powers of the people & excite an interest in the study of the sciences, it has been found a good way to unfold some things new and wonderful to them; take in an orrery & show them the solar system—tell them there are more worlds—more suns, more moons than one. There is of course great ignorance in the above branches—yet there is some light especially among the children and adults

taught at the station, & those at other places taught by graduates from the Seminary." Report of Waimea Station on Hawaii, from April 1839 to April 1840, in Letters to the American Board, CXXXVI, No. 158.

[115] Abner Wilcox to Anderson, Hilo, October 4, 1839, in *ibid.*, CXXXVII, No. 177; General Letters of the Mission, Honolulu, June 8, 1839, June 1, 1840, in *ibid.*, CXXXIV, Nos. 11, 13; Edward Bailey to Anderson, Wailuku, September 10, 1840, in *ibid.*, CXXXVII, No. 129.

[116] This supposition is based upon the statement of the missionaries that for more than a year the chiefs "had before them the project of a law for the encouragement of education." General Letter of the Mission, June 1841, in *Report of the American Board*, 1842, p. 172.

[117] *Minutes of the General Meeting of the Sandwich Island Mission*, 1840, p. 20.

They had chosen an appropriate time, for the chiefs were then occupied with plans for a more systematic organization of their government. Early in October 1840 the chiefs finished the draft of a constitution; one week later, on October 15, they adopted a statute creating a government-supported educational system. This statute declared that attendance at school was to be compulsory for all children between the ages of four and fourteen, and it provided that local committees should be formed to co-operate with the resident missionaries in the selection and support of the teachers.[118] The effect of this law was soon apparent. Within a few weeks, missionaries who were in close touch with the condition of the schools reported an increase in interest in education among the people.[119]

The term missionary as used in the statute clearly referred to members of the American mission. Thus, it appeared possible that they would be able to retain control over the schools while shifting the burden of support to the government. Such a solution naturally was pleasing to the missionaries, and Richard Armstrong asserted that the new law reflected much credit upon the chiefs and that it would "do more for the nation if properly administered, than any other measure they have ever adopted."[120] The Catholic missionaries took quite a different view. With some reason, they regarded the statute as one which had been "dictated" by their Protestant rivals and which would concentrate the control of Hawaiian education in the hands of the American mission.[121] Believing that such partiality was a violation of the first Laplace treaty, they ignored the law. Confronted by this unyielding opposition, the chiefs sought to conciliate the priests. In May 1841 they modified the school law by eliminating the provision making attendance at school compulsory for children,

---

[118] Conde to the American Board, Hana, December 15, 1840, in *Missionary Herald*, XXXVII (December 1841), 496–497; Armstrong to the American Board, Honolulu, November 25, 1840, in *ibid.*, XXXVII (June 1841), 268. The law is printed in part in Yzendoorn, *History of the Catholic Mission in Hawaii*, pp. 156–157.

[119] Knapp to Anderson, Honolulu, November 18, 1840, in Letters to the American Board, CXXXVII, No. 154; Locke to Anderson, Waialua, March 1841, in *ibid.*, CXXXVII, No. 159; Wilcox to Anderson,

Hilo, March 25, 1841, in *ibid.*, CXXXVII, No. 178; Chamberlain to Anderson, Honolulu, December 21, 1840—January 1, 1841, in *ibid.*, CXXXV, No. 132; Cooke to A. F. Waller, Honolulu, March 15–16, 1841, MS, Oregon Historical Society Library.

[120] Armstrong to Reuben Chapman, Honolulu, December 3, 1840, in Armstrong MSS.

[121] Maigret to the Archbishop of Chalcedon, Oahu, January 15, 1841, in *Annals of the Propagation of the Faith*, III (1842), 278.

although they included a provision which imposed severe penalties upon parents of children between the ages of four and eight who failed to send their children to school. At the same time, they created the office of local school agent for each district and assigned to that official the powers and duties given to the resident missionary by the original law.[122] The American missionaries were thereby removed from direct control over the common schools.

The diminution of missionary influence in the conduct of the schools was more apparent than real, and whatever satisfaction the Catholic priests may have found in the removal of their rivals from a privileged position was offset by the tendency of the chiefs to name as school agents men who were known to be friendly to the American mission and who could be expected to look to the mission for inspiration and counsel. This was notably true in the appointment of John Ii and David Malo to the most responsible administrative posts in the newly organized school system.[123] It would have been difficult for the chiefs to find two Hawaiians more closely associated with the mission or more thoroughly imbued with its teachings.

Although the mission had been eliminated as a direct force in the formulation of school policy, representative missionaries expressed satisfaction with the manner in which the government assumed its new responsibility, and reported that the intervention of the government had restored a measure of prosperity to the schools. From some of their number came statements which appear to have bordered upon extravagance. Dwight Baldwin believed that the schools had never been in a "more flourishing" condition, and the usually conservative Levi Chamberlain declared that they had become "the most cheering objects of contemplation in the Sandwich Islands."[124]

[122] Yzendoorn, *History of the Catholic Mission in Hawaii*, pp. 157–164. The amended law is printed in Thurston, comp., *Fundamental Law of Hawaii*, pp. 38–43, and may be found in part in Blackman, *Making of Hawaii*, pp. 170–173.

[123] Malo, who was superintendent of schools for the island of Maui, was also given general supervision of all school administration in the Islands. Ii was named superintendent of schools on the island of Oahu. George Allen Odgers, "Education in

Hawaii, 1820–1893" (unpublished thesis, Stanford University), pp. 73–74; Lowell Smith to the American Board, Honolulu, November 24, 1841, in *Missionary Herald*, XXXVIII (June 1842), 250–251.

[124] Baldwin to Anderson, Lahaina, January 13, 1842, in Letters to the American Board, CXXXVI, No. 25; Chamberlain to Hunnewell, Honolulu, December 1, 1841, Hunnewell MSS. See also Lowell Smith to Anderson, Honolulu, November 24, 1841, in Letters to the American Board, CXXXVII,

A single dissent came from Harvey Hitchcock, who believed that the elimination of compulsory attendance had seriously limited the effectiveness of the school law.[125]

The energy with which the missionaries established schools and sought to diffuse religious and moral instruction was evident to all observers. The hope of many of the missionaries that they might make some substantial contribution to the material prosperity of the Hawaiian people was not so well advertised. More than one critic was deceived by the apparent preoccupation of the missionaries with the schools and churches and accused them of indifference to the temporal welfare of the natives or of failure to impress upon their converts the value of industry as well as of prayer.[126] The comment of the *Polynesian*, in January 1841, that too little credit had been given the missionaries for their efforts "to teach the mechanical arts, and introduce agricultural improvements" was justified by the facts.[127]

Instruction in agriculture had been included in the original program of the mission. It had been abandoned only after experience had indicated that a farmer trained in Massachusetts was not necessarily well qualified to give advice or instruction to farmers faced with the peculiar problems of Hawaiian agriculture. The rapid expansion of churches and schools, after 1824, diverted the attention of the missionaries from the economic problems of the natives, and to an increasing extent their energies were absorbed in a multitude of tasks directly connected with instruction in religion and morals. They could not be oblivious, however, to the fact that they were surrounded by a people living in poverty and without incentives to either thrift or industry. This was a situation which would not be

No. 25; Seth L. Andrews to Anderson, Kailua, December 6, 1841, in *ibid.*, CXXXVII, No. 101; Richards and Lorrin Andrews to Anderson, Lahaina, December 6, 1841, in *ibid.*, CXXXIV, No. 25.

[125] Hitchcock to Anderson, Kaluaaha, October 15, 1841, in *ibid.*, CXXXVI, No. 130.

[126] Newburgh, "A Narrative of Voyage &c.," in AH, F.O. and Ex.; Ruschenberger, *Voyage Round the World*, p. 471; Belcher, *Voyage Round the World*, I, 62; de Mofras, *Exploration*, II, 85–86; Laplace, *Campagne de Circumnavigation*, V, 435, 452; Wilkes,

United States Exploring Expedition, IV, 224. Newburgh asserted that the hostility of Kinau and "the anathemas of the Church thunder'd from the pulpit" had been a barrier to any advance in Hawaiian agriculture or to a development of industry among the natives. Laplace and Wilkes accused the Rev. Titus Coan of having destroyed coffee plants at Hilo because he believed that the cultivation of coffee interfered with the religious duties of his parishioners. This charge was denied by Coan.

[127] *Polynesian*, January 30, 1841.

viewed with complacency by men and women educated in the ideals
and traditions of New England.

Occasionally, in the midst of their other anxieties, they made
some effort to direct the attention of their converts to the material and
moral advantages of thrift and kindred qualities. Thus, in 1828,
when compelled to find occupations for four Hawaiians recently returned from the United States, they requested one of the four to work
at his trade of shoemaker in order to provide "a good example of
useful industry" to his countrymen. Two years later it was reported
that some of the missionaries had commended to their parishioners
"the duty of diligence in business" as a Christian virtue.[128] At the
close of the same year, 1830, Asa Thurston and Artemas Bishop
sent to the United States a description of the material condition of
the Hawaiian people which the *Missionary Herald* characterized as
"a very good representation of the legitimate influence of missionary
exertions upon the domestic habits and the secular affairs of a rude
and heathen people." In the course of this report, Thurston and
Bishop declared:

The peculiar situation of a mission family in the midst of an uncultivated people has always rendered it necessary to devote a large portion of
time to procure the daily necessaries conducive to their comfort; and we
have always justified ourselves in so doing, by setting it as an example of
industry, and a motive to improvement in the people whom we came to teach.
. . . . With the mass of the inhabitants it [life] is literally a round of indolence, with barely sufficient labor to keep them from starvation . . . . Their
houses are mere hovels . . . . Their furniture consists of a few calabashes
for food and water. . . . . Their beds are a mat and tapa; and in the place
where they sit, and eat, and lounge by day, there they repose at night. In
order to excite the desire of improvement among such a people, a proper
example must be placed before them, and when the desire is excited, they
must be taught how to work. . . . . Those employed in our families have
been taught to work, to wash and iron clothes, and to perform all the branches
of domestic labor, according to the usages of civilized life. . . . . Whatever
they see about our persons, or in our houses, that it is in their power to imi-
tate, they endeavor to make for themselves; and though the first attempt at

---

[128] Minutes of the General Meeting of
the Sandwich Island Mission, May 3, 1828
(MS, Hawaiian Mission Children's Society
Library); *Missionary Herald*, XXVI (May
1830), 153. See also Bishop to Anderson,
Ewa, July 8, 1839, in Letters to the American Board, CXXXV, No. 69; W. D. Alexander, "Early Industrial Teaching of Hawaiians," in *Hawaiian Almanac and Annual*, 1895, p. 94.

imitation is commonly a rude one, they usually persevere till they accomplish it . . . . This people need only the example, the motive, and the means properly before them, and they will rapidly overcome their idle and sluggish habits, and become a virtuous and industrious people.[129]

Nearly a year later Thurston and Bishop advanced a specific proposal for converting the Hawaiians into a virtuous and industrious people. They were frankly distressed by the fact that the majority of the people wore only a minimum of clothing, a situation which they described as painful to the eye and injurious to morals. The remedy clearly was to persuade the natives to wear more clothing. They did not favor, however, the free distribution of ready-made clothing among the natives, for that would eliminate one evil by encouraging other evils of idleness and inordinate pride. They suggested that the people should be taught to manufacture their own cloth from the cotton which grew indigenously in many parts of the Islands.[130] This proposal, which combined the clothing of the nearly naked and an incentive to industry on the part of the natives, received support from other missionaries, including William Richards and Lorrin Andrews.[131] It was adopted by the American Board, which, in 1834, employed Miss Lydia Brown as an assistant missionary and assigned her to the Hawaiian Islands for the specific purpose of instructing the Hawaiians "in the art of manufacturing cloth, and in other similar arts."[132] In announcing this decision to the mission, the secretary of the Board suggested that for a time only a small group of women known to be industrious and ambitious should receive instruction directly from Miss Brown. By this means the Board hoped to assure the experiment every opportunity for success.[133]

Upon her arrival at the Islands Miss Brown was assigned by the mission to the station at Wailuku. There, with the tacit approbation of the King and of many of the chiefs, she gathered a small group of

[129] Thurston and Bishop to the American Board, Kailua, December 25, 1830, in *Missionary Herald*, XXVIII (May 1832), 155.

[130] Thurston and Bishop to the American Board, Kailua, October 15, 1831, and November 3, 1832, in *ibid.*, XXVIII (July 1832), 221–222, and XXIX (October 1833), 364.

[131] Richards, Lorrin Andrews, *et al.* to the American Board, Lahaina, November 15, 1832, in *ibid.*, XXIX (August 1833), 268.

[132] *Ibid.*, XXXII (October 1836), 389.

[133] Benjamin Wisner to the Sandwich Island Mission, Boston, June 23, 1834, in Letters from the American Board, Foreign, XV, 66–67.

women to whom she gave instruction in spinning and weaving.[134] The interest aroused by this experiment was not confined to Wailuku; but the high hopes of some of the missionaries that a substantial number of Hawaiian women would find pleasant and profitable employment at the spinning wheel and loom were not to be realized. After ten years in the Islands Miss Brown was compelled to report that cloth imported from abroad could be bought so cheaply that there was no incentive for the native women to weave. At the same time she defended her own labors with the assertion that she had taught some of the women that they could do something more useful than reclining in idleness on their mats.[135]

Perhaps the most tangible result of this experiment had been to stimulate the cupidity of Governor Kuakini. The governor was always anxious to exploit anything which promised a profit for himself, and he invited Miss Brown to move to Kailua to give instruction to some of the women of his entourage. This she was unwilling to do, but Kuakini was able to employ a few women who had studied with Miss Brown. With their assistance he assumed a role unfamiliar to the native chiefs—that of proprietor of a cotton factory.[136]

In a more limited sphere the mission provided either employment or instruction to from forty to fifty young men in the kindred arts of printing, engraving, and book-binding. Some thirty pupils received instruction in these subjects at the seminary at Lahainaluna, and fifteen Hawaiian men were employed as bookbinders in the Mission Press at Honolulu. Henry Dimond, who was in charge of the work at Honolulu, declared that the young Hawaiians in his shop were sober and thrifty and that their work would compare favorably with that done in the United States.[137] There was a division of opinion as to the quality of the engraving at Lahainaluna. Captain Edward

[134] J. S. Green and Richard Armstrong to the American Board, Wailuku, December 17, 1835, in *Missionary Herald*, XXXII, (October 1836), 389.

[135] Miss Brown to Anderson, Kaluaaha, February 21, 1845, in Letters to the American Board, CLXXIII, No. 47.

[136] Miss Brown to Anderson, Wailuku, November 23, 1837, in *ibid.*, CXXXVII, No. 206; Seth L. Andrews to the American Board, Kailua, May 12, 1838, in *Missionary*

Herald, XXXV (May 1839), 167; Wilkes, *United States Exploring Expedition*, IV, 103–104; *Polynesian*, July 25, 1840.

[137] *Missionary Herald*, XXXII (September 1836), 354; Dimond to the American Board, May 10, [1836], in *ibid.*, XXXIII (February 1837), 73; Dimond to Anderson, Honolulu, July 29, 1840, in Letters to the American Board, CXXXVII, No. 112; *Minutes of the General Meeting of the Sandwich Island Mission*, 1836, p. 5.

Belcher, who commonly found little in the mission to commend, praised the engraving done by the students at the seminary as "very creditable"; and James J. Jarves, who was destined to become a distinguished art critic, declared that it indicated a "strong native talent for the art."[138] In contrast was the judgment of Captain Wilkes, who thought the engraving of "a very rude and inferior description."[139] A recent commentator, probably making due allowance for the limited opportunities at Lahainaluna, has suggested that the engraving at the seminary was "mute evidence of the marked adaptability" of the native students as well as of the patience and talent of the instructors.[140]

The reinforcements of the mission between 1830 and 1837 added to its number a small but highly vocal group of men who observed with horror the subjection of the people to their chiefs and who hoped to destroy the flagrant discrimination among classes by assisting the commoners to enjoy a measure of economic security. More than sweeping political reform was required if the mass of the people were to rise above the level of a peasant class. Many of the newcomers therefore looked with favor upon any program which would offer the natives instruction in agriculture and trades. Their arguments gained added significance from the growing power of foreigners at the Islands and the likelihood that the control of the economic and political life of the nation would soon pass into the hands of foreign merchants and speculators. Any effort to stay the rising tide of alien influences at the Islands might well have appeared futile, but many of the missionaries believed that it was imperative to exhaust all possible means of preserving Hawaii for the Hawaiian people.

The crux of the problem was the ultimate control of the resources of the Islands, and especially of the soil. So long as the chiefs refused to relinquish their nominal title to all land in the archipelago, there could be only a limited and precarious participation of foreigners in Hawaiian agriculture. It was clear, however, that a variety of circumstances would compel the chiefs to modify their position; whether the resulting transfer of title would leave the control of the land in

[138] Belcher, *Voyage Round the World*, I, 66; *Polynesian*, June 6, 1840.

[139] Wilkes, *United States Exploring Expedition*, IV, 264.

[140] Nathan van Patten, "Early Native Engravers of Hawaii," in *Papers of the Bibliographical Society of America*, XX (1926), 94.

the hands of foreigners or of the Hawaiian people remained to be determined. One thing was certain: Unless the people generally could be trained to exploit their own land more effectively than they had done hitherto, the real control of Hawaiian agriculture—and hence of the economic life of the nation—would pass into the hands of aliens. The missionaries could not be indifferent to the dangers inherent in such a development.

In 1834, when the American Board employed Miss Brown, it seems to have contemplated a further expansion of its interests to include some support for a program of agricultural or industrial education in the Islands. The letter which announced to the mission the appointment of Miss Brown gave more than a hint of this larger program. In it the missionaries were asked to consider whether their appropriate duties should include efforts to promote the well-being of the Hawaiian people by "introducing and encouraging among them such agriculture as is suited to their climate." With frankness and wisdom the Board disavowed any hope that the easy-going natives, accustomed to their fields of kalo and living amidst tropical surroundings, either could or should be converted into farmers upon the New England model.[141] The assistance which the Board contemplated was not described, and apparently this communication was intended to do little more than raise questions and make tentative suggestions as to policy. It did not commit the Board to any program for the agricultural or industrial education of the Hawaiian people.

The modest questions raised by the Board received careful attention among the missionaries. Their first response was a resolution, adopted in 1835, to encourage the cultivation of "cotton, coffee, sugar cane, etc., that the people may . . . . increase their temporal comforts."[142] A more ambitious answer was given in a memorial, dated July 1836, in which the missionaries urged the Board to send to the Islands a group of laymen who were prepared to take a leading part in the political and agricultural development of the nation. They recommended that this company include someone "thoroughly acquainted" with law and able to advise the chiefs upon matters of

[141] Wisner to the Sandwich Island Mission, Boston, June 23, 1834, in Letters from the American Board, Foreign, XV, 68.

[142] *Minutes of the General Meeting of the Sandwich Island Mission*, 1835, p. 19. Cf. Bingham, *Sandwich Islands*, pp. 489–490.

government, four farmers to supervise the cultivation of cotton and sugar on each of the four principal islands, a merchant who could transact the business thus established and market the products, someone familiar with the manufacture of cotton, and a number of artisans who could give instruction to promising natives in the various arts and trades. The profits from this enterprise, the memorial continued, "must be devoted to the support of schools, or churches, charitable institutions or internal improvements in the nation." Such an enterprise would furnish an example of industry which the missionaries believed would have a salutary influence upon the natives; if successful, it would produce funds for the support of missionary enterprises and provide steady employment with a regular income for a considerable number of Hawaiians.[143]

The program outlined in the memorial suggested a departure from the general policies of the Board. Under the most favorable circumstances there was little possibility that it would be adopted. It was certain to be rejected when, as in 1837, the Board was committed to a program of financial retrenchment. Vital issues, however, were at stake; and the missionaries were not easily discouraged. Some practical members of the mission argued that it would be wise to encourage improvements in agricultural methods, as thereby the natives would be enabled to make more generous contributions to the support of the churches.[144] At the other extreme were a few idealists, who believed that only through instruction in agriculture and the arts could the natives develop "a balanced character" which would guarantee "usefulness in after life."[145] The views of the majority appear to have been those expressed in the general letter of 1838, in which the missionaries asserted that they had an "intense interest" in the development of the largely neglected agricultural possibilities of the Islands, believing that it was a problem intimately connected with "the future destinies" of the people and the nation.[146]

[143] Memorial of the Mission, signed by Hiram Bingham, William Richards, Lorrin Andrews, and Levi Chamberlain, July 1836, in Letters to the American Board, CXXXIV, No. 3.

[144] Alexander to Anderson, Waioli, November 1, 1837, in *ibid.*, CXXXVI, No. 61; Emerson to Anderson, Waialua, August 20, 1838, in *ibid.*, CXXXVI, No. 105; Bishop to Anderson, Ewa, July 8, 1839, in *ibid.*, CXXXV, No. 69.

[145] Thomas Lafon to Anderson, North Fairhaven, April 10, 1843, in Letters to the American Board, CXXXVII, No. 74.

[146] General Letter of the Mission, June 20, 1838, in *Missionary Herald*, XXXV (April 1839), 146–147.

In harmony with these convictions, the mission approved the proposal of some of its number to give instruction to the natives in methods of farming,[147] while individual missionaries carried this general policy even farther. Thus the Rev. Lorenzo Lyons included in the requirements for church membership at Waimea, Hawaii, the qualification that the candidates must "attend to the cultivation of the soil, build themselves good native houses & . . . . contribute to other benevolent objects according to their abilities."[148] The missionaries recognized that their own unaided efforts would scarcely bring the reforms they desired, and they continued to hope that American philanthropists could be persuaded to take an interest in the development of Hawaiian agriculture. It was this hope which led them to welcome the establishment of plantations on Kauai as "auxiliaries in the work of civilizing the people,"[149] and to endorse with particular approval the activities of Ladd and Company at Koloa.[150] They recognized that before the Hawaiian people could be converted into a prosperous nation there were certain difficulties which must be overcome. Chief among these barriers to Hawaiian prosperity were the indolence and poverty of the people and the "old system of despotic government" in which everything of value was liable to seizure by the chiefs and which permitted the rulers to levy oppressive taxes upon the produce of the poor.[151]

---

[147] *Minutes of the Delegate Meeting of the Sandwich Island Mission,* 1838, pp. 28–29.

[148] Lyons to Anderson, Waimea, Hawaii, August 27, 1838, in Letters to the American Board, CXXXVI, No. 148.

[149] General Letter of the Mission, June 20, 1838, in *Missionary Herald,* XXXV (April 1839), 147.

[150] Bingham, Chamberlain, Castle, *et al.* to Ladd & Co., Honolulu, January 11, 1840, in *Arbitration between the . . . . Government of the Hawaiian Islands and Messrs. Ladd & Co.,* Appendix, pp. 43–44; Reuben Tinker, Thomas Lafon, and Peter J. Gulick to Ladd & Co., Koloa, January 10, 1840, in *ibid.,* Appendix, p. 43.

Not all of the missionaries were so confident that benefits would accrue to the native population. In the summer of 1840, the Rev. J. S. Emerson visited Kauai and saw "no better native houses & no better apparel & apparently no better habits among the people in the vicinity of the plantations than on Oahu or Maui or places far remote from such plantations." Emerson also feared that such mills as that of Ladd and Company produced sugar so efficiently and rapidly that no native could hope to compete. Emerson to Anderson, Waialua, July 27, 1840, in Letters to the American Board, CXXXVI, No. 108.

[151] Thurston and Bishop to the American Board, Kailua, September 20, 1833, in *Missionary Herald,* XXX (October 1834), 371–372; General Letter of the Mission, June 20, 1838, in *ibid.,* XXXV (April 1839), 147; Richards to Anderson, Lahaina, August 7, 1835, in Letters to the American Board, LXVII, No. 87; Alexander to An-

The interest of the missionaries in the temporal welfare of the Hawaiian people was genuine. In some instances, it was so intense as to be almost passionate. With few exceptions, however, the active attention of the missionaries, after 1836, was absorbed by a dramatic resurgence of religious interest among the mass of the people. This resurgence became so extensive in 1838 and 1839 that it was known to the missionaries as the "Great Revival"; it brought to a close the period of uncertainty through which the mission had passed in the years immediately following the death of Kaahumanu.

It is doubtful if the position of the mission or its hold upon the confidence of its converts had been as precarious as might have been inferred from some of the reports sent to the United States during 1832 and 1833. Attendance at public worship had declined; and, in the summer of 1834, Levi Chamberlain believed that the majority of the people in Honolulu had "cast off entirely the fear of God."[152] Honolulu was the center of hostility to the mission; but even there the mission retained a considerable measure of influence, and the congregations which gathered each Sunday to listen to the exhortations of Hiram Bingham numbered about two thousand, one-half of whom were said to be daily engaged in the study of a verse of Scripture.[153] The missionaries could have found comfort also in the fact that, during the twelve months ending in June 1834, they had admitted 124 converts to their churches.[154] This was a larger number than had been added to the Hawaiian churches during any year prior to 1832.

At the annual meeting in 1834, the mission added to the means by which it hoped to influence opinion when it voted to publish a religious newspaper. Such a paper could serve the dual purpose of providing reading material for the schools and presenting in an effective manner the views of the missionaries upon religious and moral questions. The editor was a member of the mission, the Rev. Reuben Tinker. He undertook his new duties with some skepticism as to

derson, Waioli, November 1, 1837, in *ibid.*, CXXXVI, No. 61; Gulick to Anderson, Koloa, July 29, 1839, in *ibid.*, CXXXVI, No. 6; Letter of John Diell, Honolulu, January 1, 1836, in *Sailor's Magazine*, VIII (July 1836), 339; Bingham to Levi Chamberlain, Brooklyn, January 31, 1846, MS, in Hawaiian Historical Society Library.

[152] Chamberlain to Greene, Honolulu, August 26, 1834, in Letters to the American Board, LXVIII, No. 170.

[153] Bingham, *Sandwich Islands*, p. 450.

[154] General Letter of the Mission, Honolulu, July 15, 1834, in *Missionary Herald*, XXXI (April 1835), 148.

whether such a paper could interest the mass of the people.[155] Its popularity surpassed all his expectations, and within a short time he found it expedient to double the number of fifteen hundred copies to which the earlier editions had been limited.[156] The seven hundred natives in the district of Waioli, Kauai, who subscribed to the *Kumu Hawaii* were said to have looked forward "with eagerness" to the arrival of each issue.[157] A visitor to Honolulu noted that the little paper consisted of "a single sheet, containing subjects for moral and general instruction, local intelligence, and traditional songs of the islands . . . . with wood-cuts, illustrative of public buildings in Europe, foreign animals, and other objects calculated to excite curiosity in the native mind."[158] In its varied interests the *Kumu Hawaii* represented the broad aim of the mission to create a nation that was not only Christian in name and spirit but also intelligent and industrious.

The success of the *Kumu Hawaii* reflected the reviving prestige and influence of the mission. That, in turn, was reflected in the tone of the reports sent by the missionaries to their superiors in Boston. In those reports friends of missions could read of increased congregations at the Hawaiian churches and of the success of protracted meetings similar to the religious revivals so common in many parts of the United States. Nowhere did there appear to be a danger that the churches would relapse into the religious stupor which had so shocked the missionaries throughout 1833.[159] By the summer of 1836 the position of the mission had been greatly strengthened. Levi Chamberlain reported cautiously that it was "very much altered for the better,"[160] and Dr. Ruschenberger, after a visit to Honolulu, concluded

[155] Tinker to the American Board, Honolulu, August 29, 1834, in Letters to the American Board, LXVIII, No. 21.

[156] *Missionary Herald*, XXXII (September 1836), 353.

[157] Alexander to the American Board, Waioli, October 17, 1835, in Letters to the American Board, LXVIII, No. 50; James M. Alexander, *Mission Life in Hawaii: Memoir of Rev. William P. Alexander* (Oakland, Calif., 1888), p. 92.

[158] Bennett, *Narrative of a Whaling Voyage Round the Globe*, I, 225–226.

[159] Hitchcock to the American Board,

Kaluaaha, September 1834, in *Missionary Herald*, XXXI (July 1835), 258–259; Report of Asa Thurston and Artemas Bishop, May 1834, in *ibid.*, XXXI (September 1835), 338; General Letter of the Mission, [July 7, 1836], in *ibid.*, XXXIII (July 1837), 275–276; Journal of Richard Armstrong, July 20, August 3, November 1, 1837, in *ibid.*, XXXIV (July 1838), 245, 248, 249; Journal of Levi Chamberlain, February 1, 1836; Armstrong to Reuben Chapman, Maui, November 8, 1836, in Armstrong MSS.

[160] Chamberlain to Anderson, Honolulu, March 22, 1836, in Letters to the American Board, LXVIII, No. 177. Cf. Benja-

that the Hawaiian people had become "a christian nation."[161] From one of Chamberlain's colleagues, however, came a warning that pride rather than piety was the motivating force behind the apparent interest in affairs of the spirit. Membership in the church, he observed, gave a degree of social distinction; and on Kauai, at least, there was reason to suspect that some of the natives who professed to desire salvation were more anxious "to get into the church than to get into heaven."[162] The missionaries, nevertheless, were on the threshold of a Hawaiian "Great Awakening" destined to be one of the most remarkable demonstrations of religious fervor ever aroused by a missionary enterprise.

The Great Revival affected all parts of the Islands.[163] Even at Honolulu there were evidences of unusual religious excitement. A protracted meeting in January 1838 was attended by "greater numbers" than had ever before attended a similar meeting in that community,[164] and within a few weeks the congregations had become so large that the missionaries thought it desirable to establish a second church in Honolulu. The division of the original church had no apparent effect upon the number of Hawaiians who worshiped there. From the most important pulpit in the mid-Pacific Hiram Bingham continued to preach to congregations said to have included from three thousand to four thousand Hawaiians. Somewhat smaller

min Parker to Anderson, Kaneohe, May 4, 1836, in *ibid.*, LXVIII, No. 123; Armstrong to Anderson, May 5, [1836], in *Missionary Herald*, XXXIII (February 1837), 73.

161 Ruschenberger, *Voyage Round the World*, p. 474.

162 Letter of the Rev. W. P. Alexander, January 23, 1835, in Alexander, *William Patterson Alexander*, pp. 191–192.

163 S. N. Castle to Anderson, Honolulu, November 20, 1838, in Letters to the American Board, CXXXVII, No. 135; Alexander to Anderson, Waioli, November 1, 1837, August 25, 1838, in *ibid.*, CXXXVI, Nos. 61, 62; Richard Armstrong to Reuben Chapman, Wailuku, February 1, 1838, in Armstrong MSS; Armstrong to Samuel Chapman, Wailuku, December 13, 1838, in *ibid.*; Emerson, *Pioneer Days in Hawaii*, pp. 122–125; Whitney to the American Board, Waimea, Kauai, July 28, [1838], in *Mis-*

sionary Herald, XXXV (April 1839), 151; Journal of Richard Armstrong, June 10, November 1, 1837, in *ibid.*, XXXIV (July 1838), 244–245, 250; Armstrong to the American Board, Wailuku, February 1, 1838, in *ibid.*, XXXIV (December 1838), 478–479; Baldwin to the American Board, Lahaina, August 17, November 13, 1838, January 7, 1839, in *ibid.*, XXXV (April, August, October, 1839), 152–156, 305, 391–392; Thurston to the American Board, Kailua, [April 12, 1838], October 12, 1838, in *ibid.*, XXXV (April, June, 1839), 148–149, 196; Bishop to the American Board, Ewa, September 1, 1838, in *ibid.*, XXXV (April 1839), 149–150; Benjamin Parker to the American Board, Kaneohe, October 10, 1838, in *ibid.*, XXXV (July 1839), 258–259.

164 Journal of Levi Chamberlain, January 8, 1838.

congregations, variously estimated to have numbered from one thousand to twenty-five hundred, gathered each week at the Second Church to listen to the Rev. Lowell Smith.[165] In both churches visitors noticed that these large congregations behaved with decorum and propriety and gave "grave and careful attention" to the services.[166]

Emotionally and statistically the Great Revival reached its greatest extent in the districts of Waimea and Hilo, on the island of Hawaii. Late in 1837 the Rev. Titus Coan reported that there was "a glorious work of grace" at Hilo, in which hundreds claimed to have become converted. In the following January he undertook an evangelical tour of the neighboring district of Puna; when he returned to Hilo he was followed by scores of natives who had heard his preaching and who wished to hear more. The excitement thus engendered was contagious, and soon a religious revival of extraordinary proportions was in progress at Hilo. On the first Sunday in July, Coan administered the sacrament of baptism to 1,705 hopeful converts, and during the year ending in December 1838 he admitted more than five thousand persons to membership in the church.[167] Three years later the number of communicants in the church at Hilo had increased to more than seven thousand. This was a number equal to three-fourths of the adult population within Coan's parish, and it gave him the distinction of presiding over a church which was numerically the largest Protestant church in the world.[168]

The course of the revival at Waimea was similar to that at Hilo.

[165] Bingham to the American Board, March 3, April 26, 1838, in *Missionary Herald*, XXXIV (November, December, 1838), 444–445, 484; Chamberlain to the American Board, March 1, [1838], in *ibid.*, XXXIV (November 1838), 444; Lowell Smith to the American Board, in *ibid.*, XXXV (April 1839), 152; Journal of Henry Bridgman Brewer, April 12, 1840, in *Oregon Historical Quarterly*, XXIX (December 1928), 347.

[166] [J. H. Belcher], *Around the World*, II, 308; Olmstead, *Incidents of a Whaling Voyage*, p. 256; Allen, comp., *Ten Years in Oregon*, p. 45; Townshend, *Sporting Excursions in the Rocky Mountains*, II, 40; Parker, *Exploring Tour Beyond the Rocky Mountains*, pp. 360–361; Journal of Joseph Frost (MS, Oregon Historical Society Library), April 12, 1840.

[167] For accounts of the "Great Revival" at Hilo, see Titus Coan to the American Board, Hilo, November 20, 1837, September 26, 1838, January 21, 1839, in *Missionary Herald*, XXXIV (December 1838), 476–477, XXXV (June, December, 1839), 197–198, 462–463. See also Coan, *Titus Coan. A Memorial*, pp. 41–50; Coan, *Life in Hawaii*, pp. 53–57. During the twelve months ending in June 1837, twenty-three persons were admitted to the church at Hilo. During the following twelve months the number of new members was 639, and in the year ending in June 1839, it reached the astonishing total of 5,244. *Report of the American Board*, 1840, p. 38.

[168] S. J. H[umphrey], in Coan, *Titus Coan. A Memorial*, p. ii.

In the winter of 1837–1838 the Rev. Lorenzo Lyons believed that God was "doing great things" in Waimea. A few months later the revival there reached its climax with much of the excitement which marked its counterpart at Hilo. Hiram Bingham and others were disturbed lest Lyons was acting too hastily in admitting professed converts to his church, but Lyons was not moved by the fears of his colleagues. The statistical results were less impressive than at Hilo; but during the two years ending in June 1839 nearly five thousand Hawaiians were added to the membership of the church at Waimea.[169]

By the summer of 1839 the excitement—amounting in some districts almost to hysteria—had so far subsided that the Great Revival could be regarded as having come to a close.[170] The mission and its friends were in a position to evaluate the events of the preceding months. Not all of the missionaries had been equally willing to admit self-styled converts to the privileges and responsibilities of church membership. Although some of the pastors had carried their caution to an extreme,[171] more than fifteen thousand converts became members of the Hawaiian churches during the period of the revival; and Mrs. Judd declared that few persons could be found who did not regard themselves as Christians.[172]

The wholesale additions to the membership of the churches was observed with disapproval by conservative missionaries and by officers of the American Board.[173] In May 1839 the secretary of the Board declared that all "friends of missions" were following the progress of the revival with great interest but that they were waiting "in some suspense to see what will be the result of the extraordinary numbers admitted to the fellowship of the church."[174] Five months

[169] Lyons to Anderson, Waimea, January 15, August 27, 1838, in Letters to the American Board, CXXXVI, Nos. 147, 148; Bingham to Anderson, Honolulu, April 26, 1838, in *ibid.*, CXXXV, No. 6; *Report of the American Board*, 1840, p. 38.

[170] Bishop to Anderson, Ewa, July 8, 1839, in Letters to the American Board, CXXXV, No. 69.

[171] Jarves, *Scenes and Scenery in the Sandwich Islands*, pp. 187–188; Cheever, *Life in the Sandwich Islands*, p. 248. Statistics relative to the number added to each of the churches during the three years ending in June 1839 may be found in *Report of the American Board*, 1840, p. 38.

[172] *Ibid.*; Judd, *Honolulu*, p. 62.

[173] Bingham to Anderson, Honolulu, April 26, 1838, in Letters to the American Board, CXXXV, No. 6; Armstrong to Anderson, Wailuku, January 23, 1839, in *ibid.*, CXXXVI, No. 74; *Report of the American Board*, 1839, p. 128.

[174] Anderson to the Sandwich Island Mission, Boston, May 22, 1839, in Letters from the American Board, Foreign, II (1839), 119–120.

later this same fear was again expressed by the Board, whose members believed that it had been unwise to admit converts after "so short a probation"; and the mission was informed that news of the revival had exerted "far less influence among us than it would have done, had there been no precipitancy in admitting members into some of the churches, even had the number of admissions been not half as great as it was."[175]

Apparently Coan was not disturbed by the doubts of his colleagues. He vigorously defended his policy, declaring that "neither Scripture nor philosophy, nor prudence" dictated excessive caution.[176] In June 1839 he insisted that he had been neither hasty nor careless in the admission of converts to membership in the church and suggested that those among his colleagues who believed otherwise had been "vastly misinformed."[177] Two years later he admitted that the revival at Hilo had been accompanied by "too much physical agitation—too much weeping & wailing & crying out for mercy . . . . to suit the calm & sober philosophy of some." Such emotional excesses, he believed, were to be regarded as the "nearly indispensable" means by which a rude and ignorant people gave expression to their religious convictions.[178]

Few of the Hawaiian churches were entirely free from the emotionalism which had been so prevalent at Hilo and Waimea. In every part of the Islands the missionaries had stimulated interest in religious concerns by the use of "protracted meetings"[179]—the very epitome of mass emotion. It is reasonable to suppose that the protracted meeting held at Lahaina during March 1838 was typical of those held elsewhere. The Rev. Dwight Baldwin described the week during which the meeting was held as a period of "awful solemnity," during which he preached in a church which was "almost always crowded to excess." Continuing his description, he wrote:

---

[175] Instructions of the American Board to the Rev. Sheldon Dibble, October 6, 1839, in *Missionary Herald*, XXXV (December 1839), 484.

[176] Coan to Lyons, January 29, [1838], in Coan, *Titus Coan. A Memorial*, p. 44.

[177] Coan to Anderson, Honolulu, June 6, 1839, in Letters to the American Board, CXXXVII, No. 34. This letter was printed,

in part, in *Missionary Herald*, XXXVI (July 1840), 246–255.

[178] Coan to Anderson, Hilo, December 7, 1841, in Letters to the American Board, CXXXVII, No. 41; Coan to Anderson, Hilo, May 25, 1842, in *Missionary Herald*, XXXIX (May 1843), 195–196.

[179] General Letter of the Mission, June 20, 1838, in *ibid.*, XXXV (April 1839), 142.

Feeling among the people evidently deepened every day from that time; and every day we were hearing of new and interesting cases of sinners awakened. Though I have seen many revivals in the United States, I was never before in a place where the Spirit of God seemed so ready to follow up every truth exhibited before the people. Every sermon seemed to do thorough execution. If terror was preached, the people were terrified; if love was the theme, they were melted; and those who had before been the most set against the gospel, were in many cases, the first to fall under its power. . . . .

. . . . Besides public preaching, conversation was used as a means of converting sinners. Our house was thronged, from morning till night . . . . Our time, at the house was almost wholly employed in conversation and personal application of the truth, not always excepting the time when we were taking our meals. Generally those who came exhibited marks of feeling and often of deep feeling. Often they could not refrain from weeping. Tears rolled freely. There were times, when the threshold of my study, where many stood to converse was wet so often and so profusely with their weeping, as scarcely to be dry for the whole day together. They exhibit much of the simplicity and many of the other traits of children; and doubtless their profuse weeping is sometimes to be ascribed to that cause, rather than to the depth of their feeling.[180]

Every influential chief, with the single exception of the young King, was a communicant of some mission church, and with varying degrees of enthusiasm each was friendly to the missionaries.[181] At

---

[180] Baldwin to the American Board, Lahaina, August 17, 1838, in *ibid.*, XXXV (April 1839), 153–154.

[181] Among the chiefs who were consistently friendly to the mission were Kinau and the governors of Oahu, Maui, Hawaii, and Kauai. Except in the rare instances when the King took an active part in public affairs, this quintet constituted the effective government of the Islands. The friendship of Kinau for the mission and especially for some of the missionaries in Honolulu was apparent to every well-informed person in Honolulu during her tenure of high office. Her husband was Governor Kekuanaoa of Oahu, whose attachment to the mission may have depended in part upon the influence of his wife. It was none the less useful to the mission, and continued long after the death of Kinau.

Governor Hoapili of Maui was one of the few surviving associates of the first Kamehameha. He early became interested in the teachings of the missionaries and after 1824 he was consistently sympathetic with the program of the mission. He was notable for the tenacity with which he sought to enforce the moral legislation, even after the abrogation of those laws in 1833. He occupied a prominent place in the councils of the chiefs, and on more than one occasion he used that influence to advocate some measure or to promote some policy favored by the missionaries. With reason, the official historian of the mission declared that Hoapili was "a striking monument of the grace of God," who surpassed most of his associates in "his humble faith, his attachment to the word and house of God, and his patriotic devotion to the interests of his country." Anderson, *History of the Mission to the Sandwich Islands*, p. 175. See also the Mission to Anderson, Hono-

least two of the less powerful chiefs—Liliha and Paki—were so influenced by the emotional excitement of the revival that they abandoned their former hostility to the mission and sought membership in the church. In like manner, some of the King's retinue, said by William Richards to have included many of "the vilest persons" associated with the King, demonstrated an unexpected interest in religion.[182] The unwillingness of the King to become a church member was therefore the more noticeable. His failure to follow the other

lulu, June 1, 1840, in Letters to the American Board, CXXXIV, No. 13.

Governor Kaikioewa was less notable and less consistent in his devotion to the interests of the mission. He commonly used his great influence, however, to advance policies favored by the missionaries. In 1825, he ordered the natives of Kauai to give attention to instruction and to refrain from work or pleasure upon the Sabbath. In the following spring, he accompanied the Rev. Samuel Whitney on a tour of Kauai, during which he often assured his people of the great benefits conferred upon them by the missionaries. In 1829, he became a member of the church on Kauai, and in the same year it was reported that he was using his position to enforce such reforms as a strict observance of the first day of the week and a prohibition of the use of intoxicants. Journal of Levi Chamberlain, September 8, 1825; Journal of Samuel Whitney, April 12–30, 1826, in *Missionary Herald*, XXIII (June 1827), 183–186; General Letter of the Mission, February 20, 1830, in *ibid.*, XXVI (October 1830), 312; P. J. Gulick to the American Board, May 13, 1829, in *ibid.*, XXVI (April 1830), 107–108; Townshend, *Sporting Excursions in the Rocky Mountains*, II, 61.

Governor Kuakini of Hawaii was less directly associated with the work of the missionaries than were Hoapili and Kaikioewa. In 1823 he welcomed the missionaries when they resumed their work at Kailua, and he seems to have taken the lead in directing the work of building the first two church edifices at that place. In 1829 he became a member of the church at Kailua, and he remained a professed Christian until his death in 1845. He was a regular attendant at public worship, and during a brief term as governor of Oahu he was unusually active in enforcing the moral

legislation favored by the missionaries. They never regarded him, however, as a truly pious man, and some observers thought him more interested in wealth than was becoming in a good Christian. Ethel M. Damon, ed., *Early Hawaiian Churches and Their Manner of Building* (Honolulu, 1924), pp. 8–10, 22; Thurston and Bishop to the American Board, October 1, 1829, in *Missionary Herald*, XXVI (May 1830), 152; *Life and Times of Lucy G. Thurston*, pp. 211–213; Jarves, *Scenes and Scenery in the Sandwich Islands*, p. 212; *Polynesian*, January 4, 1845.

Kapiolani was less powerful in the councils of the nation, but among the chiefs she was the most devoted adherent of the mission. In 1826, James Ely described her as "indeed a mother in Israel." Six years later, the Rev. Cochran Forbes declared that she was "an exemplary Christian & probably the most advanced in civilized manners of any native on the Islands." These comments were confirmed by the statements of virtually every missionary at the Islands. Following her death in May 1841, the *Polynesian* commented that as magistrate of the district of South Kona she had exerted "a most salutary influence in favor of pure religion, good order and civilization." See *Missionary Herald*, XXIV (April 1828), 97–98; Anderson, *History of the Mission to the Sandwich Islands*, pp. 184–195; Ely to Evarts, Kaawaloa, November 23, 1826, in Letters to the American Board, XXXI, No. 115; Forbes to Anderson, Kaawaloa, November 1832, in *ibid.*, LXVIII, No. 100; Forbes to the American Board, Kealakekua, July 22, 1841, in *Missionary Herald*, XXXVIII (April 1842), 156; *Polynesian*, June 5, 1841.

[182] Richards to Hunnewell, Lahaina, August 25, 1838, in Hunnewell MSS.

great chiefs into the church was explained by some of the missionaries as the result of the influence of his associates,[183] while others
believed that he hesitated because he did not care to submit to the
restrictions upon his personal freedom which invariably would accompany membership in the church.[184] After the Great Revival,
however, the missionaries could take some comfort in the fact that
he was "apparently friendly" to them and was "disposed to favor
improvements."[185]

The mission thus seemed assured of at least the friendly interest
of all the powerful chiefs. This was less important in 1840 than it
had been fifteen years earlier, when the mission had relied to so considerable an extent upon the co-operation of Kalanimoku and Kaahumanu. It was with a strong sense of personal loss rather than as any
weakening of their own position in the Islands that the missionaries
mourned the death of Kinau, Kaikioewa, Hoapili, and Kapiolani
between April 1839 and May 1841. Few of the remaining chiefs
were as devout or as dependable as the members of that quartet. They
were, in general, friendly with the missionaries, and none of their
number openly opposed the policies advocated by the mission. At
the close of 1841, however, Richard Armstrong lamented that the
chiefs were "far from what they should be,"[186] and not one of the
chiefs who survived 1841 had escaped the censure of the church during the preceding two years.[187] This was not an unmixed evil. As the
influence of the chiefs declined, the churches became more truly representative of all classes of the Hawaiian people.

For some years the missionaries at Honolulu included among

[183] Coan, *Life in Hawaii*, p. 129; E. Bailey, "Historical Notes," in HHS, *Fourth Annual Report* (Honolulu, 1896), p. 14.

[184] General Letter of the Mission [July 7, 1836], in Letters to the American Board, CXXXIV, No. 4; Chamberlain to Anderson, Honolulu, February 7, 1839, in *ibid.*, CXXXV, No. 119.

[185] Bingham to Anderson, Honolulu, April 26, 1838 and April 19, 1839, in *ibid.*, CXXXV, Nos. 6, 8; Dwight Baldwin to Anderson, Lahaina, August 17, 1839, in *ibid.*, CXXXVI, No. 13; Daniel Conde to Anderson, Hana, December 15, 1840, in *Missionary Herald*, XXXVII (December

1841), 497; Anderson, *History of the Mission to the Sandwich Islands*, p. 262; Judd, Honolulu, p. 229; Coan, *Life in Hawaii*, pp. 128–129.

[186] Armstrong to Anderson, September 23–October 18, 1841, in Letters to the American Board, CXXXVI, Nos. 80, 81.

[187] *Ibid.* Armstrong declared that one chief had escaped the censure of the church, but in this he erred. The one chief whom he named had been suspended from the privileges of church membership in the spring of 1840. See J. S. Emerson to Anderson, Waialua, March 17, 1840, in *ibid.*, CXXXVI, No. 107.

their numerous responsibilities the spiritual care of any seamen or foreign residents who were concerned with religious problems. Only a small minority of the thousands of officers and seamen who annually visited Honolulu called at the mission or sought religious counsel; those who did were certain to be welcomed by the missionaries and to receive advice and religious literature. Occasionally one of the missionaries preached by invitation on board a vessel in the harbor; and with considerable regularity the missionaries provided religious services in English for the benefit of foreigners.[188] These services were often so poorly attended that they could be held in the home of a missionary family. Frequently they were conducted by a missionary who was a visitor at Honolulu or by one who had not yet mastered the Hawaiian language and who therefore was unable to preach to the natives.[189] By these means the missionaries at Honolulu hoped to offer at least a minimum of spiritual guidance to foreign residents and seamen without causing any diminution of the time or energy which they were able to devote to missionary labors among the Hawaiian people.

The mission was relieved of this burden by the arrival at Honolulu, on May 1, 1833, of the Rev. John Diell. Diell had been sent to the Islands by the American Seamen's Friend Society for the specific purpose of ministering to the religious needs of visiting seamen. He was welcomed by "the principal residents," who received him "very kindly" and offered to give "any assistance in their power."[190] He entered immediately upon his labors, which included conferences with seamen, the distribution of religious tracts, and services of public worship at stated times. In June he declared that his preaching services were "fully attended by the resident population, and by the seamen in port."[191] He regarded the entire foreign community at Honolulu as his parish. He therefore organized a Bible class for the foreign residents;[192] and, with the assistance of Peter A. Brinsmade,

[188] Bingham to the Rev. Joseph Brown, Oahu, May 8, 1833, in *Sailor's Magazine*, VI (February 1834), 187.

[189] Tinker to Anderson, Honolulu, July 9, December 6, 1832, in Letters to the American Board, LXVIII, Nos. 13, 14; Baldwin to Anderson, Waimea, Hawaii, August 10, 1832, in *ibid.*, LXVIII, No. 4.

[190] Letter of John Diell, Honolulu, May 7, 1833, in *Missionary Herald*, XXX (March 1834), 109; Peirce to Hunnewell, Honolulu, May 6, 1833, in Hunnewell MSS.

[191] Letter of John Diell, June 1, 1833, in *Missionary Herald*, XXX (March 1834), 109, and in *Sailor's Magazine*, VI (February 1834), 185.

[192] *Ibid.*

he commenced a Sunday school and Bible class for Negroes, of whom there were between twenty and thirty living in or near Honolulu.[193]

These early evidences of personal popularity and professional success were not fully borne out by subsequent events. By October it was reported that he had incurred the dislike of some of the residents because he was too rigid in his insistence upon standards of conduct and because he was "hand & hand with the Missionaries." The latter was sufficient to lessen his popularity with "many people of influence."[194] If Diell was aware that his popularity was on the wane, his labors were not slackened and his correspondence betrayed no alarm.[195] It was also apparent that there was no open breach between Diell and the majority of the influential members of the foreign community. In November 1833, he dedicated a newly erected Seamen's Chapel in the presence of a congregation said to have included nearly all of "the Big Folks" in Honolulu;[196] and among his parishioners he included such consistent critics of the mission as Henry Peirce, John C. Jones, William French, and Eliab Grimes.[197]

Fifty years later Peirce recalled that Diell, whom he described as "a mild and pleasant gentleman," had been compelled to contend with great difficulties.[198] This was no exaggeration, but Diell was not easily discouraged. He visited ships in the harbor and saloons in the city in search of seamen whose confidence and interest he might win; and it was reported that some sailors acquired so great an affection for Diell that they would willingly leave a saloon to accompany him to church.[199] It is improbable that such instances of

[193] Letter of John Diell, Oahu, October 8, 1833, in *Sailor's Magazine*, VI (March 1834), 221.

[194] Peirce to Hunnewell, Honolulu, October 4–8, 1833 (P.S.), in Hunnewell MSS. W. S. Hinckley reported that Diell was "a good sort of man," but that he had incurred the hostility of Stephen Reynolds, who insisted that all who attended the Seamen's Chapel should be ostracized from Honolulu society. Hinckley to Hunnewell, Honolulu, November 26, 1833, in *ibid.*

[195] See Diell to Hunnewell, Honolulu, October 8, December 11, 1833, in *ibid.*

[196] Journal of Stephen Reynolds, November 28, 1833.

[197] Bingham to Anderson, Honolulu,

March 27, 1836, in Letters to the American Board, LXVII, No. 43.

[198] Peirce to Samuel C. Damon, San Francisco, February 12, 1884, in *The Friend*, March 1884, p. 17.

[199] Parker, *Exploring Tour Beyond the Rocky Mountains*, p. 376; Journal of John N. Colcord, pp. 85–86; Letter of B. F. B., September 9, 1836, in *Sailor's Magazine*, IX (November 1836), 100. Some years later, Colcord recalled that Diell had "visited the rum houses to invite the sailormen to leave the cup and go to the evening meetings." In this, Diell had some success "till a hue and cry was shouted among the venders, and some began to abuse, and even ordered, Mr. Diell

personal influence were numerous; but apparently they sustained Diell in his conviction that his labors were not in vain. A friendly observer who preached from Diell's pulpit in the autumn of 1836 noted that often there were "very few attendants" at services at the Chapel,[200] but, perhaps with a thought of the obstacles he daily encountered, Diell declared that attendance at his church was "pretty good."[201] Although not universally popular among the foreign residents, he retained the confidence and support of a small group of foreigners who had been known for their sympathy with the American mission. With this group as a basis, Diell, in May 1837, organized the Oahu Bethel Church—the first church for foreigners in the Hawaiian Islands. Among the eight communicants of the new church were Peter A. Brinsmade, William Ladd, Andrew Johnstone, John N. Colcord, and Peter Anderson.[202]

Diell was not able to prosecute his labors much longer. Because of the precarious state of his health he was absent from Honolulu from October 1838 to June 1840. He left Honolulu again in December 1840 to return to the United States, and died at sea during the following month.[203] The five years of active labor among the diverse elements which constituted his strange parish closed with few tangible results. The single visible monument to his ministry was a feeble church which had been without an active pastor during the greater part of its corporate existence; and one of the most faithful members of Diell's congregation believed that little could have been accomplished toward a reformation of seamen or foreign residents "while ardent spirits were so prevalent among all classes."[204] In 1836, however, Levi Chamberlain reported that Diell's influence had contributed to the formation of a public sentiment "more favorable to morality" than hitherto had existed in Honolulu.[205] After the final de-

---

out of the house, and threatened him with a whipping if he did not desist."

[200] Parker, *Exploring Tour Beyond the Rocky Mountains*, p. 376.

[201] Diell to Hunnewell, Oahu, April 13, 1835, in Hunnewell MSS.

[202] Letter of John Diell, Oahu, May 25, 1837, in *Sailor's Magazine*, X (February 1838), 188; Diell to Hunnewell, Honolulu, May 29, 1837, in Hunnewell MSS. Brinsmade and Ladd were members of the firm

of Ladd and Company. Anderson and Colcord were former sailors, and both had been in the Islands for many years. Since 1834 they had been members of Bingham's church at Honolulu. Johnstone, a former missionary, was the teacher of a school supported by a group of foreign residents.

[203] *The Friend*, September 16, 1843, p. 44.

[204] Journal of John N. Colcord, p. 85.

[205] Chamberlain to Hunnewell, Honolulu. January 25, 1836, in Hunnewell MSS.

parture of Diell from Honolulu a visitor was told that he had arrested "the course of vice" in that community and that through his influence there had been a decrease in the ill will which had divided the foreign residents into embittered factions.[206] All that the historian may safely assume is that, within the limits of his opportunity and strength, Diell had supported the efforts of the American missionaries to transform a Polynesian seaport into a Christian community where the ideals of faith and conduct prevalent in New England would become the standards of thought and action.

At Lahaina, where in some years nearly as many seamen were ashore as at Honolulu, the only religious counsel available to English-speaking visitors was provided by the resident missionaries. When there were two or more missionaries at Lahaina, one of them often devoted a part of his time to the care of the spiritual interests of visiting seamen. When there was but a single missionary there the religious problems of visitors received only casual attention. The missionaries tried to maintain regular weekly preaching services in English whenever there was any considerable number of seamen in port. This work they supplemented by personal conferences with interested seamen or by the distribution of religious tracts on board visiting vessels.[207] To this formal but somewhat sporadic instruction was added the influence of a reading room for seamen which was maintained by the mission at Lahaina as early as 1834. In 1839 this reading room owned approximately six hundred volumes, consisting chiefly of religious literature. These volumes circulated to sailors on whaling vessels cruising in the Pacific, and a friendly visitor expressed the opinion that the reading room had been "instrumental in doing much good" among seamen.[208]

Not all of the philanthropic enterprises at the Islands were to be

[206] Wilkes, *United States Exploring Expedition*, IV, 6–7.

[207] Letter of Mrs. William Richards, Lahaina, November 1, 1832, in *Sailor's Magazine*, VI (April 1834), 251; Reuben Tinker to Anderson, Honolulu, July 9, 1832, in Letters to the American Board, LXVIII, No. 13; The Mission to Anderson, [July 7, 1836], in *ibid.*, CXXXIV, No. 4; Letter of John Diell, Honolulu, December 6, [1836], in *Sailor's Magazine*, IX (June 1837), 324;

Dwight Baldwin to Anderson, Kaluaaha, November 14, 1840, in Letters to the American Board, CXXXVI, No. 21; Cheever, *Life in the Sandwich Islands*, pp. 63–64.

[208] Letter of Dwight Baldwin, Lahaina, January 4, 1839, in *Sailor's Magazine*, XI (July 1839), 354; Letter of Charles Macdonald (no date) in *ibid.*, p. 355; *Scraps from the Log Book of George Lightcraft* (Syracuse, 1847), p. 78.

traced to the activity of missionary organizations. The most important exception was the Oahu Charity School, established at Honolulu
by a small group of residents who wished to provide the rudiments
of an education for the children of foreigners at that place. It was
the outgrowth of the interest shown in some of those children by
Andrew Johnstone, a member of the American mission. He had gathered a group of children of mixed or foreign parentage, to whom
he had given informal and rather elementary instruction. Within a
short time a few interested foreigners were collecting funds and making plans for the establishment of a school for a class of children
which hitherto had been neglected by parents and missionaries alike.
Early in September seven prominent residents, including Henry A.
Peirce, Richard Charlton, and John C. Jones, were chosen officers
and trustees of the Oahu Charity School. The King donated a site for
the school building, and Peirce reported that the project was universally popular in Honolulu.[209] The extent to which the missionaries
shared in this general approval is not wholly clear. The committee of
seven included men who were notoriously hostile to the American
mission, and they frankly sought to limit any possible influence of the
missionaries in the conduct of the school by a ruling that no religious
literature other than the Bible could be read in the school and that the
reading of the Bible must be without explanatory comment.[210]

If the secular character of the school and the hostility to the mission on the part of some of the trustees caused any uneasiness among
the missionaries it was not apparent when, on January 10, 1833, the
school was formally opened with an appropriate ceremony. Among
those present at the opening exercises were the King, many of his

[209] Journal of Stephen Reynolds, August
9, 20, September 6, 1832; John Diell, "Oahu
Charity School," in *Hawaiian Spectator*,
I, No. 1 (January 1838), p. 26; W. D.
Alexander, "The Oahu Charity School," in
HHS, *Sixteenth Annual Report* (Honolulu,
1909), pp. 20–21; Peirce to Hunnewell,
Oahu, November 13, 1832, in Hunnewell
MSS. Among the contributors to funds for
the school were officers of the U.S.S. "Potomac," the masters and officers of vessels
in port, and a considerable number of the
foreign residents. *Polynesian*, April 10,
1841.

[210] Journal of Stephen Reynolds, September 6, 1832; Journal of Levi Chamberlain, September 7, 1832. The seven officers and trustees were Richard Charlton,
John C. Jones, Henry A. Peirce, Alexander Adams, James Robinson, George W.
Cole, and Eliab Grimes.
Frederick D. Bennett, who was at Honolulu in 1834, was told that the school was
established "at the suggestion" of Richard
Charlton, but there seems to be no other
evidence to support this statement. Bennett, *Whaling Voyage Round the Globe*,
I, 207.

chiefs, some of the missionaries, a group of foreign residents, and several masters of visiting vessels. Hiram Bingham offered the opening prayer; John C. Jones delivered "an able address" in which he paid a tribute to the good accomplished by the missionaries; and the ceremony was concluded with a prayer by the Rev. Reuben Tinker. Levi Chamberlain and Stephen Reynolds agreed that the exercises gave "general satisfaction" to all elements in the community.[211]

The first teachers in the school were Mr. and Mrs. Andrew Johnstone. The willingness of the Johnstones to accept the offer to become teachers in the Oahu Charity School raised a serious problem as to the future relations between Johnstone and his missionary colleagues. Johnstone had been sent to the Islands by the American Board to act as an assistant to the secular agent of the mission. The time which he had given to the instruction of children had been apart from the regular course of his missionary duties, and it was not to be expected that the missionaries would view with equanimity the association of one of their number with an institution controlled by men known to be out of sympathy with the general program of the mission. In May 1833 this issue was directly raised when the trustees of the school offered the Johnstones a salary of five hundred dollars a year if they would sever all connection with the mission.[212] The result was a compromise by which the Johnstones were to give all their time to the school while retaining a formal membership in the mission until the attitude of the American Board could be ascertained. The missionaries, at their annual meetings in 1833 and 1834, approved this arrangement and agreed to require of the Johnstones only the annual report which was received from all members of the mission.[213] This was not a permanent solution of the problem, and Levi Chamberlain shrewdly observed that it had been adopted only as a matter of expediency.[214] At least two missionaries expressed doubts as to the wisdom of the agreement. They contended that the school was not under the control of the mission, that the primary duty of a mission was to provide for the religious and educational needs of the

[211] Journal of Levi Chamberlain, January 10, 1833; Journal of Stephen Reynolds, January 10, 1833.

[212] *Ibid.*, May 20, 1833.

[213] *Minutes of the General Meeting of* the Sandwich Island Mission, 1833, pp. 20–21; *ibid.*, 1834, p. 32.

[214] Chamberlain to Anderson, Honolulu, December 3, 1833, in Letters to the American Board, LXVIII, No. 166.

native population, and that there were at least one thousand Hawaiian children in Honolulu who were as much entitled to an education as were the few children of foreign or mixed parentage.[215]

The precarious relationship between Johnstone and the mission continued until June 1835, when he and the missionaries received the official information that the American Board did not approve his course and that he must leave the school if he wished to remain a member of the mission.[216] The receipt of these instructions was followed by a series of conferences between some of the missionaries and friends of the school.[217] The mission was in a delicate position. It could not defy the Board, and it would be impolitic to appear to be unsympathetic with a project designed to add to the educational opportunities in Honolulu. Dr. Judd expressed the opinion that the school "would do good,"[218] and Levi Chamberlain believed that none of his colleagues wished to have Johnstone leave the school.[219] Certainly the missionaries would have been pleased to avoid an open break between Johnstone and themselves. They therefore were willing to postpone any positive action until Johnstone could communicate again with the Board.[220] Johnstone, however, believed that some of the missionaries were responsible for the dilemma which he faced, and he refused to associate with his former colleagues.[221] When it was apparent that he would persist in this attitude, the missionaries had no recourse but to dismiss him from the mission.[222]

With ample justification Levi Chamberlain anticipated that the breach between Johnstone and the mission would be "the occasion of much evil speaking"—a fear which evidently was shared by Hiram Bingham.[223] There was some basis for this fear, and Dr. Judd re-

[215] Emerson to Anderson, Waialua, November 25, 1833, in *ibid.*, LXVIII, No. 36; Judd to Anderson, Wailuku, October 23, 1833, and Honolulu, August 3, 1835, in *ibid.*, LXVIII, Nos. 130, 133.

[216] Letter of Mrs. Bingham, August 5, 1835, in *ibid.*, LXVII, No. 37; Journal of Stephen Reynolds, June 9, 1835.

[217] *Ibid.*, June 16, 17, 18, 19, 23, 1835.

[218] Judd to Anderson, Honolulu, August 3, 1835, in Letters to the American Board, LXVIII, No. 133.

[219] Chamberlain to Anderson, Honolulu, June 27, 1835, in *ibid.*, LXVIII, No. 172.

[220] *Ibid.*; Bingham to Anderson, Honolulu, August 5, 1835, in *ibid.*, LXVII, No. 35.

[221] Letter of Mrs. Bingham, August 5, 1835, in *ibid.*, LXVII, No. 37; Bingham to Anderson, Honolulu, August 7, 8, 1835, in *ibid.*, LXVII, Nos. 38, 39.

[222] Chamberlain to Anderson, Honolulu, August 3–5, 1835, in *ibid.*, LXVIII, No. 173.

[223] *Ibid.*; Bingham to Anderson, Honolulu, August 7, 1835, in *ibid.*, LXVII, No. 38.

ported that he "could perceive an unusual clamor against the mission . . . . whenever there was a subscription to be filled for the school."[224] None of the patrons of the school could be regarded as entirely sympathetic with the purposes and ideals of the mission; some of them were ranked among its most outspoken opponents. By 1838 the original group of seven trustees had been supplanted by a new group which was equally unsympathetic with the policies of the mission.[225] The editor of the *Sandwich Island Gazette* was a trustee of the school; the British consul occasionally used his official influence on its behalf;[226] and its most persistent and faithful supporter was the generous, erratic, and bitterly antimissionary merchant, Stephen Reynolds. So obvious was the hostility toward the mission of the men who directed the policies of the school that Alexander Simpson, who was intimately acquainted with several of the trustees, believed that the institution owed its existence to that fact.[227]

Numerous observers, including some of the missionaries, testified to the services rendered by the school or to the progress of the pupils.[228] The comment of Stephen Reynolds that the school was "much more useful & important, than all those *Bigots* put together"— evidently a reference to the missionaries—may be dismissed as the crabbed views of an embittered man.[229] More impressive was the comment of James J. Jarves that the school was an "exceedingly

[224] Judd to Anderson, August 3, 1835, in *ibid.*, LXVIII, No. 133.

Friends of the school believed that the missionaries were hostile to the institution. This view was expressed by the publishers of the *Gazette*, who asserted that the missionaries entertained "a sort of feeling *versus* the foreigners, their children, and their doings," and had expressed "opinions unfavorable to the Charity School." The same editorial stressed the fact that Johnstone was not then a member of the mission. *Sandwich Island Gazette*, April 29, 1837.

[225] The new group of trustees included S. D. Mackintosh, John Meek, William French, Stephen Reynolds, George Pelly, T. C. B. Rooke, and Francis J. Greenway. *Ibid.*, May 19, 1838.

[226] See, for example, Charlton to Kamehameha III, Honolulu, March 24, 1834, in AH, F.O. and Ex.

[227] Simpson, *Sandwich Islands*, pp. 17–18.

[228] Newburgh, "A Narrative of Voyage &c.," in AH, F.O. and Ex.; Journal of Stephen Reynolds, April 9, 1834, November 25, 1835, December 25, 1844; Diell to Hunnewell, Honolulu, December 11, 1833, in Hunnewell MSS; Letters of John Diell, Oahu, October 8, 1833, January 1835, January 1, 1836, January 1, 1838, in *Sailor's Magazine*, VI (March 1834), 222, VIII (September 1835), 26, VIII (July 1836), 343, and XI (May 1839), 267; Chamberlain to Anderson, Honolulu, June 27, 1835, in Letters to the American Board, LXVIII, No. 172; Bingham, *Sandwich Islands*, p. 453; Belcher, *Voyage Round the World*, I, 65, 270–271; Laplace, *Campagne de Circumnavigation*, V, 467–468; *Polynesian*, November 14, 1840.

[229] Reynolds to Hunnewell, Oahu, October 4, 1839, in Hunnewell MSS.

beneficial institution," in which children who had been "exposed to more than ordinary temptations" were being trained to occupy useful and respectable positions in society.[230] An English visitor noted that the pupils were given instruction in "all the branches of British charity education,"[231] and the Rev. Richard Armstrong reported that the schoolroom was "well furnished with cards, maps, books, slates, &c., of an excellent character and in sufficient variety."[232] The number of students did not vary greatly during the first few years. In his annual reports to the mission at the close of 1834 and 1835 Johnstone declared that some seventy children had attended the school, although fewer than sixty had attended with regularity.[233] Five years later, the number of students had increased to eighty.[234] So well and favorably known was the school among the English-speaking population of the region bordering upon the northeastern Pacific that the student body occasionally included pupils who had come from Kamchatka or California.[235]

The Oahu Charity School was not in direct competition with any school maintained by the mission. It did represent the first successful invasion of a field that had been monopolized by the mission prior to 1833. A more direct competition for control of Hawaiian religious and educational institutions followed the re-establishment of the Catholic mission in 1839. When, in 1840, the American mission surrendered the administration of the common schools to the government, the major share of the responsibility for the education of Hawaiian youth passed into the control of organizations independent of the mission or even hostile to it. The old order, established soon after 1820, was passing away.

If further evidence were required to indicate the shifting tide of events, it was furnished by the departure from the Islands of Hiram Bingham, who for twenty years had dominated every important deci-

[230] Jarves, *Scenes and Scenery in the Sandwich Islands*, pp. 35–36.

[231] Belcher, *Voyage Round the World*, I, 65.

[232] Letter of R. Armstrong, in *Polynesian*, November 14, 1840.

[233] First and Second Annual Reports of Andrew Johnstone on the Oahu Charity School, in Letters to the American Board, LXVIII, Nos. 198, 199.

[234] *Polynesian*, November 14, 1840.

[235] Bingham to Anderson, Honolulu, August 5, 1835, in Letters to the American Board, LXVII, No. 35; *Polynesian*, April 10, 1841; R. C. Wylie, in *The Friend*, August 1, 1844, p. 71; Jarves, *Scenes and Scenery in the Sandwich Islands*, p. 36; Dibble, *History of the Sandwich Islands*, pp. 294–295.

sion made by the mission and who was universally recognized as the counselor and confidant of royalty and chiefs. The slowly failing health of Mrs. Bingham compelled her to relinquish her missionary duties; in the hope of restoring her health, she and her husband planned a visit to the United States. On August 3, 1840, they left Honolulu after bidding farewell to a large congregation of friends, many of whom had come, as Bingham declared, to express "the mutual desire and hope of meeting there again."[236] Five days later a modest notice in the *Polynesian* carried the news that the Binghams expected to be absent "about eighteen months."[237]

The hope of the Binghams that they could return to the scene of their missionary labors was never realized. For about four years the health of Mrs. Bingham continued to be so uncertain that they postponed from time to time the date of their departure from the United States.[238] In 1844 the mission anticipated the ultimate decision of the Binghams when it named the Rev. Richard Armstrong permanent pastor of the First Church at Honolulu. Armstrong believed that this action would cause Bingham to decide against a return to the Islands,[239] and it seems probable that it had some weight in prompting Bingham to leave the service of the American Board. Whatever may have been the factors which led Bingham to his fateful decision, the health of Mrs. Bingham was too feeble to allow any hope that she might be able to resume her work at Honolulu. At the close of December 1845 Bingham requested a formal dismissal from the service of the Board. This was promptly granted, and a long and fruitful missionary career had come to its formal conclusion.[240]

---

[236] Bingham, *Sandwich Islands*, p. 578.

[237] *Polynesian*, August 8, 1840. The expectation that the Binghams would return to the Islands was shared by their missionary associates. See Judd, *Honolulu*, p. 74; Lowell Smith [for the mission] to the Methodist Episcopal Mission in Oregon, August 29, 1840 (MS, Oregon Historical Society Library); Chamberlain to David Leslie, Honolulu, March 31, 1841, *ibid.* On one occasion it was believed in Honolulu that the Binghams were actually on their way to the Islands. See J. F. B. Marshall to Thomas O. Larkin, Honolulu, January 15, 1842, in Larkin MSS, I, No. 207.

[238] Bingham to Anderson, Charlestown, October 6, 1842, in Letters to the American Board, CXXXV, No. 27; Bingham to W. J. Armstrong, Springfield, August 16, 1843, in *ibid.*, CXXXV, No. 35; Anderson to the Sandwich Island Mission, Boston, October 28, 1842, in Letters from the American Board, Foreign, V (1842), 234; Greene to the Sandwich Island Mission, Boston, November 11, 1844, in *ibid.*, VII (1844), 264.

[239] Armstrong to Reuben Chapman, Honolulu, July 18, 1844, in Armstrong MSS.

[240] Bingham to Anderson, Brooklyn, December 26, 1845, in Letters to the Ameri-

It is difficult to estimate the influence of Bingham upon the development of ideas or institutions in the Hawaiian Islands. Few would deny that he was able, active, and interested in all the varying phenomena of Hawaiian social and institutional life. Like many of the missionaries, he hoped to create not only churches but a Christian nation. This forced him to turn his attention beyond the strictly religious and educational institutions established by the mission. The instructions by which he and his colleagues were to be governed forbade them to interfere in the political life of the nation. Bingham may have believed that he observed the letter of these instructions; it is an open question how far he deemed it necessary to ignore their spirit. He was frankly the adviser of the chiefs, and it was not always possible to draw a fine distinction between problems of morals and questions of public policy. He gave his advice freely and doubtless with a profound conviction that he was providing the chiefs, as individuals and as rulers, with a safe guide to personal and national salvation. So implicit was the confidence of some of the chiefs that Bingham's advice had for them almost the force of revelation. He occupied a position which was powerful in its potential influence upon

---

can Board, CLXXIII, No. 36; Anderson to the Sandwich Island Mission, Boston, January 22, 1846, in Letters from the American Board, Foreign, IX (1846), 7.

Several times during the ensuing years the possibility that Bingham would return to the Islands was raised. In January 1846, less than a month after he had been released by the American Board, Bingham wrote to Levi Chamberlain that it was possible though not probable that he would resume his missionary post. During and after the visit of Dr. Judd to the United States, in the spring of 1850, the possible return of Bingham to the Islands was discussed. The Board appeared ready to furnish financial assistance to Bingham if he would return as a missionary pastor without thought of entering the employ of the government and if he were willing to accept certain new arrangements in the administration of the mission which had been introduced since 1840. In communicating this information to Bingham, Rufus

Anderson conceded that Bingham had the spirit of a pioneer and that it was not easy for him "to enter into plans formed by others." Although Anderson expressed the opinion that Bingham's "natural home" was at the Islands, he probably was not surprised when the veteran missionary decided that it would be too difficult to make the necessary adjustments to the new conditions that existed at Honolulu. Bingham never returned to the Islands, remaining in the United States until his death in 1869. Bingham to Chamberlain, Brooklyn, January 31, 1846 (MS, Hawaiian Historical Society Library); Private Journal of Alexander Liholiho, 1849–1850 (MS, *ibid.*), May 29, 1850; Anderson to the Sandwich Island Mission, Boston, May 3, June 21, 1850, in Letters from the American Board, Foreign, XIII (1850), 115, 173; Anderson to Bingham, Boston, April 2, 1851, in *ibid.*, XIV (1851), 201–203; Anderson, *History of the Mission to the Sandwich Islands*, pp. 234–235.

the course of Hawaiian history and vulnerable to the criticism of all who disliked the policies of either the mission or the government.

There were some who professed to believe that Bingham's zeal was mingled with an ambition to control Hawaiian politics;[241] but following his departure from the Islands the doubt and suspicion which once had surrounded his every act gave way to a sense of admiration for the ability and devotion with which he had performed his duties as a pioneer missionary. Alexander Simpson declared that Bingham had been a "disinterested, if not always judicious, counsellor" of the chiefs;[242] the *Quarterly Review*, which never had been friendly to the mission in the Hawaiian Islands, conceded that he "possessed the most organizing head of all the men whom the missionary institutions have sent to the South Seas, except perhaps John Williams";[243] and Charles Gordon Hopkins, the editor of the *Polynesian* at a time when it had become critical of the American missionaries, ascribed the remarkable development of the Hawaiian nation and its recognized position among the civilized nations of the world largely to the influence of seven advisers of the chiefs, among whom he named Hiram Bingham.[244]

The residence of Bingham at Honolulu and his own aggressive personality caused him to become identified in the minds of many contemporary or later writers with the political policies of Kaahumanu and Kinau. His principal interest during his score of years in the Hawaiian Islands was always the advancement of the religious and moral program of the American mission, and it is probable that he considered any influence he enjoyed with the chiefs as nothing more than an effective agency in promoting the one great cause of his presence in the Islands—the conversion of the Hawaiian people to Protestant Christianity. His colleague and successor at Honolulu, Richard Armstrong, described Bingham as a shrewd man who would have made "a good Jesuit" but who erred *"in not keeping his management out of sight."* Many of Bingham's colleagues in the mission had often found themselves in disagreement with him or restless under

---

241 [Graham, comp.], *Voyage of H.M.S. Blonde*, p. 147; Kotzebue, *New Voyage Round the World*, II, 254–256.

242 Simpson, *Sandwich Islands*, p. 49.

243 *Quarterly Review*, XCIV (December 1853), 90.

244 *Polynesian*, September 3, 1859.

his efforts to direct the policy of the mission; few, if any, would have disagreed with Armstrong's further statement that Bingham "is a good old man & has done much good."[245] It is the memory of the benefits conferred upon thousands of Hawaiian converts by Bingham's ministry at Honolulu which has been treasured by members of the Honolulu church which he founded and which he served for a score of years. They have recorded a summary of his achievements on a marble slab on the wall of the Kawaiahao Church in the heart of the present city of Honolulu. Paying tribute to the founder of the church and a pioneer member of the mission, it reads:

This slab is placed here in grateful remembrance of a pioneer missionary by descendants of Hawaiians . . . . among whom he preached Christ for more than twenty years. He preached the first sermon ever delivered in this city April 25, 1820 from "Fear not for I bring you glad tidings of great joy." Here he taught confiding kings, queens and chiefs, faced danger, bore calumny from abroad, aided in reducing the language to writing, translated much of the Bible, composed hymns and tunes, here he baptized a thousand converts, planted a church, planned this edifice and with his loving people on June 8, 1839 laid this adjoining cornerstone. . . . .

No other member of the mission could hope to attain the position of pre-eminence which Bingham's long service at Honolulu and his stubborn defense of the policies of the mission had given him in the opinion both of foreigners and of natives. It would be no disparagement of his contributions to the establishment of the mission and to its prosperity, culminating in the Great Revival, to note that the loss of his leadership was less serious to the mission than would have been his departure from the Islands ten years earlier. With the Great Revival, the reintroduction of Catholicism, and the organization of the Hawaiian government, the problems facing the mission had been materially modified. As a result of the revival, the influence of the mission had been extended to the most remote sections of the Islands, and there were few, if any, natives who had not come into contact with its ideas and doctrines. The missionaries likewise could have found some comfort in the realization that the thousands of hopeful

[245] Armstrong to Reuben Chapman, Honolulu, September 27, 1842, in Armstrong   MSS. Cf. Anderson, *History of the Mission to the Sandwich Islands*, pp. 233–234.

converts produced by the Great Revival had been moved by some force other than the wishes or example of their chiefs. This realization, however, could not give a sense of complete security, for the revival had been marred in many of the districts by evidences of mob hysteria. A reaction from the extraordinary religious interest manifested during the months of the revival was inevitable; this unpleasant fact, combined with the dangers of inroads from Catholicism, provided ample reason for anxiety on the part of the American missionaries.

VIII

INTERNATIONAL RIVALRIES AND HAWAIIAN INDEPENDENCE

THE expansion of American interests into the region bordering the northeastern Pacific was a by-product of the trans-Pacific trade in furs and sandalwood. Later there developed within that area a small but important commerce by which manufactured goods destined for California and Oregon were distributed from Honolulu and exports from those territories were sent to Honolulu for transshipment to Europe or to the United States. The Hudson's Bay Company enjoyed a share of that commerce by virtue of its monopoly of the produce of Oregon. Otherwise the trade which linked Honolulu, Monterey, and the mouth of the Columbia in an economic interdependence was carried almost exclusively in American vessels and was controlled by American merchants, many of whom resided either at Honolulu or in California.

The community of interests thus established was strengthened by other and less tangible bonds. Ideas and opinions as well as goods were interchanged among the American settlers in Oregon, California, and the Hawaiian Islands. Far from home, those American pioneers were closer to each other than to friends in the eastern part of the United States. To some extent they were also united by the spiritual ties of a common pride in the institutions and growing power of their native land and by a common hope that those institutions would soon be extended to the shores of the Pacific. The American colony at

Honolulu was the oldest in the area; it was likewise the most accessible to travelers who visited the region by sea. English-speaking residents of California read newspapers published at Honolulu, and a few of their number sent their children to Honolulu to be educated. The American missionaries at the Islands had a peculiar interest in Oregon. They had been the first to suggest the establishment of Protestant missions there, and they watched with friendly solicitude the labors and trials of their Presbyterian and Methodist brethren in that territory.

American residents of the region around the northeastern Pacific lived under different political jurisdictions. Few of them could have failed to recognize, by 1840, that a far-reaching shift in political power within that area was imminent; nor could they have been blind to the probability that their own country would play the leading role in the new order. Alaska and Oregon were under the control of great powers, although the division of the vast region then known as Oregon remained to be determined by negotiations between the United States and Great Britain. California and the Hawaiian Islands were ruled by feeble governments and were prospective prey for an adventure in imperialism. This was particularly true of California. The weakness of Mexican rule in that province was notorious and the control of the economic life of California was obviously passing into the hands of aliens, the majority of whom were from the United States. Nowhere was this trend of events better understood or followed with greater interest than at Honolulu. The comments of Peter A. Brinsmade, in the first number of the *Hawaiian Spectator*, reflected the views of both missionaries and non-missionaries in the Islands. In an introductory editorial Brinsmade announced that a vast area, including "the whole extent of coast that borders the Pacific on the north and east" would fall within the scope of the magazine, and added:

The western coast of North America, which has for years been the scene of active commercial enterprise, is now rapidly opening its facilities and inducements to civilized colonists and Christian philanthropists. The value of its hitherto unappreciated agricultural interests, is beginning to revive and push to a definite termination the questions of territorial limits, both on the north and south, between the governments concerned. Interests peculiarly weighty and lasting are involved in the adjustment of existing adverse claims —interests made more and more prominent by every movement in furtherance of Christianity and civilization in the Pacific. The civil and moral destiny of every portion of the vast territory between the Rocky Mountains and this Western Ocean, must of necessity be shaped by the government under whose jurisdiction it shall fall. That whole region . . . . cannot fail soon to be the theatre of measures and events, whose consequences upon the world will be as enduring as time.[1]

Four majors powers—Russia, France, Great Britain, and the United States—had some stake in the fate of the territory around the northeastern Pacific. Russia, however, was little more than a passive observer of events south of Alaska. In 1841, the Russian American Company sold its post at Bodega Bay to John Sutter, and the retreat of Russia from North America had begun.[2]

The government of Great Britain had no colonial aspirations in the North Pacific and was concerned only with the protection of British interests already established there. This involved diplomatic moves designed to prevent or to postpone any disturbance of the political equilibrium in Oregon, Mexico, and the islands of the Pacific if such a shift in power might threaten the interests of British subjects in that area. The government at London could not be indifferent to the advance of its greatest maritime rivals, France and the United States, into the region bordering upon the northeastern Pacific; but it did not propose to use other than peaceful measures to block that ad-

---

[1] [Peter A. Brinsmade], "Introductory Observations," in *Hawaiian Spectator*, I, No. 1 (January 1838), pp. 1–2.
Two years later, in an editorial in the first issue of the *Polynesian*, James J. Jarves noted that the Hawaiian Islands and the Pacific area generally were "rapidly drawing the attention of the older countries," and added that whatever tended "to develope their greatness or throw light upon their condition and history" was certain to attract "general notice." In May 1841 he asserted that the attention of the government of the United States could not be "too often or too forcibly directed towards the rapidly increasing interests of its citizens in the North Pacific." *Polynesian*, June 6, 1840, May 22, 1841.

[2] The indifference of Russia to the fate of the region south of Alaska may be explained by the declining profits from the investments of the Russian American Company in Alaska. If the company had been as prosperous in 1840 as it had been a quarter of a century earlier, it is unlikely that Russia would have been content to remain a passive spectator of the struggle for the dominance in the northeastern Pacific. Sitka, in 1840, was no less dependent upon the outside world for supplies than it had been at the opening of the century. This was recognized by Sir George Simpson, who admitted, in 1846, that "if expediency could justify aggression, the czar might . . . . excusably have seized this archipelago [the Hawaiian Islands] . . . . Even now, France, and America, and England, might be more willing to let the Sandwich Islands fall into the hands of Russia than to see them continue liable to be seized, on some pretext or other, by any one of themselves." Simpson, *Journey Round the World*, II, 136.

vance.[3] Individual British subjects resident in Oregon, Mexico, and the Hawaiian Islands did not share the apparent complacency of their government. Recognizing, as did their American contemporaries, that much of the region would soon pass under the jurisdiction of one or another of the great maritime powers, they frankly hoped that Great Britain would be the beneficiary of impending events, and some of them apparently believed that they might bring about the addition of California or the Hawaiian Islands to the British Empire.[4]

Unlike Great Britain, France under Louis Philippe was definitely committed to a program of expansion in the Pacific.[5] The first fruits of this policy were the seizure of the Marquesas Islands and the establishment of a protectorate over Tahiti, the latter at the risk of a breach of relations with Great Britain. How much more France coveted in the Pacific was uncertain. The energy of the French navy in that ocean and the willingness of the French government to identify the cause of Catholic missions with its own interests furnished ample reason for the fear, shared by many American and English residents

[3] A useful survey of the political interests and ambitions of the great maritime powers in the island groups of the Pacific may be found in Jean Ingram Brookes, *International Rivalry in the Pacific Islands, 1800–1875* (Berkeley, California, 1941).

For accounts of British interests in this region, see *ibid.*, chapters iv, vi, and Ephraim Douglass Adams, *British Interests and Activities in Texas 1838–1846* (Baltimore, 1910), pp. 234–264. In the pages cited, Professor Adams discussed the policy of the British Foreign Office with respect to California.

When, in March 1840, the question was directly asked in the House of Commons as to whether the government still regarded the Hawaiian Islands as being under the protection of Great Britain, Viscount Palmerston, then Foreign Secretary, avoided an answer to the question. *Hansard's Parliamentary Debates*, 3d ser., LIII (March 27, 1840), 171. The evasiveness of Palmerston appeared more ominous when, later in the same year, British sovereignty was formally extended to New Zealand—an action which was regarded by many as indicating that Great Britain was again interested in colonial expansion.

[4] See, for example, Forbes, *California: A History of Upper and Lower California*, pp. 309–325; Alexander Simpson to Sir John Barrow, February 3, 1844, in Alexander Simpson, *The Life and Travels of Thomas Simpson, the Arctic Explorer* (London, 1845), pp. 385–387. See also Bancroft, *History of California*, IV, 382–384, 451–452; Lester G. Engelson, "Proposals for the Colonization of California by England, 1837–1846," in *California Historical Society Quarterly*, XVIII (June 1939), 136–148.

[5] A detailed account of the expansion of French interests in the South Pacific may be found in A. C. Eugène Caillot, *Histoire de la Polynésie Orientale* (Paris, 1910). Brief accounts of French ambitions and of the expansion of French power in that part of the world may be found in Louis de Carné, "Des Intérêts Français dans l'Océanie," in *Revue des Deux Mondes*, n.s., II (April 15, 1843), 288–301; Christian Schefer, "La Monarchie Julliet et l'Expansion Coloniale," in *ibid.*, 6th ser., XI, (September 1, 1912), 152–184; Brookes, *International Rivalry in the Pacific Islands*, chapters iii, v–vii.

of the Hawaiian Islands, that French aggression would not be confined to the region south of the equator.

Among the great maritime powers, the United States was in the most favorable position to profit from any modification of the status quo in the northeastern Pacific. The claim of the United States to a share of Oregon had been recognized in the Anglo-American convention of 1818 and by the treaty with Spain in 1819. During the ensuing twenty years American interests on the shores of the Pacific had been concentrated at the Hawaiian Islands rather than on the mainland; but after 1835 the expansion of whaling in the North Pacific, the establishment of Protestant missions in Oregon, and the beginning of the migration of pioneers across the continent had given more than a hint of what was to come. By 1842 there were nuclei of American settlements in California and in the Willamette Valley as well as in the Hawaiian Islands; and the most influential French visitor to the region, Captain C. P. T. Laplace, had conceded that in Oregon and California the future belonged to the United States.[6] It was this inexorable course of events, rather than any territorial ambitions on the part of the administration at Washington, that prompted President Tyler to appoint a resident Indian agent for Oregon and to authorize the American minister to Mexico to negotiate for the purchase of California.

During the quarter-century from 1815 to 1840, there was a steady decline in British prestige and influence at the Hawaiian Islands. The commerce which centered at Honolulu passed almost exclusively into the control of American citizens, many of whom were resident at the Islands. With the exception of the agency of the Hudson's Bay Company, there was no English-owned firm at Honolulu which offered serious competition to Peirce and Brewer or to Ladd and Company. No British subjects had been so active in attempting to develop great plantations as had a small group of American citizens. In the interest of harmony and good will, British missionary societies had made no effort to invade a field already occupied by American Protestants. The influence of the United States, on the contrary, was strengthened not only by missionaries and merchants but also by the

[6] Quoted in Blue, "The Report of Captain La Place on His Voyage to the Northwest Coast and California," in *California Historical Society Quarterly*, XVIII (December 1939), 322–323.

sympathetic attitude of visiting naval officers, several of whom—notably Captain Jones in 1826 and Captain Finch in 1829—had gone beyond the limits of ordinary courtesy to indicate their friendly feeling for the native rulers. By 1830 the United States had replaced Great Britain as the accepted friend and most likely protector of the little kingdom. Commercially and spiritually the Hawaiian Islands were as much a part of the American frontier as were Oregon and California, but the two thousand miles of ocean which separated them from the continent were a formidable barrier to the tide of manifest destiny.

There was a temporary revival of British trade at the Hawaiian Islands in 1840 and 1841. The value of goods imported at Honolulu from England rose from $15,600 in the two years 1838–1839 to $94,000 in the eighteen months from January 1840 through July 1841. The value of imports from the northwest coast, where the Hudson's Bay Company had gained an almost complete monopoly of the trade, more than doubled during the same period.[7] Late in 1841 Henry Skinner estimated that the annual value of British trade at the Hawaiian Islands had increased, within a period of three years, from $20,000 to $150,000.[8] The social and political repercussions threatened the very existence of the native monarchy. The former division of the foreign community into missionary and mercantile factions receded into the background; in its place appeared a no less bitter schism which followed national lines and which arrayed American and British residents on opposing sides. The new division was quite as apparent to visitors as the old had been. Captain Wilkes declared that it afforded "ample room for the tongue of scandal to indulge itself"; and Sir George Simpson, who visited Honolulu in 1842, found discord rampant, with English and American residents opposed to each other "as desperately, as if the dignity and power of their respective countries could be enhanced or diminished by the rancour of a few traders in the middle of the North Pacific."[9]

---

[7] Jarves, "The Sandwich or Hawaiian Islands," in *Merchants' Magazine*, IX (August 1843), 116–117.

[8] Henry Skinner to Captain Jenkin Jones, Honolulu, October 11, 1841, in *Correspondence Relative to the Sandwich Islands*, p. 120.

[9] Wilkes, *United States Exploring Expedition*, III, 415; Simpson, *Journey Round the World*, II, 157. See also J. F. B. Marshall to Hunnewell, Honolulu, March 11, 1841, in Hunnewell MSS; Chamberlain to Anderson, Honolulu, February 21, 1843, in Letters to the American Board, CXXXV,

In the new feud, as in the old, the British consul played a leading role. In October 1839 he warned the King not to decide any issue which involved the interests of a British subject without referring the matter to the British consulate;[10] and during the ensuing three years there was an almost interminable series of disputes to place a further strain upon the relations between Charlton and the local authorities.[11] In at least two of these disputes, Charlton had a personal interest. Neither was settled to his satisfaction. Early in 1840 he presented a claim to a large tract of land in the heart of the commercial district of Honolulu. The government agreed that a part of the land was the property of Charlton; but it refused to recognize his claim to all of it, contending that the most valuable section of the land was the property of the infant princess, Victoria Kamamalu. A year later Charlton became involved in a personal altercation with the American-born editor of the *Polynesian*, James J. Jarves. As an aftermath of this affair, Charlton was convicted in a local court of a breach of the peace, was fined six dollars, and was compelled to listen to a public rebuke delivered by Governor Kekuanaoa. Among Americans at Honolulu feeling ran high, and some of the most influential of their number signed a statement expressing confidence in Jarves and condemning the action of Charlton.[12]

Indignation seems to have been mixed with alarm in the minds of British residents. One British subject, commenting upon the fail-

No. 157; Gilman, "Streets of Honolulu in the Early Forties," in *Hawaiian Almanac and Annual*, 1904, p. 78.

The complaint of British residents that they were the victims of a preference on the part of the Hawaiian government for the interests of American citizens appeared so frequently in the correspondence of British subjects at the Islands as to be almost commonplace. American residents, in contrast, believed that their British rivals were busily engaged in creating anti-American sentiment in Honolulu. This charge was openly made by the editor of the *Polynesian*, in February 1841, when he asserted that "a strong prejudice against Americans, and their institutions exists at these islands." All who visited the Islands, he added, noticed and commented upon

this prejudice. *Polynesian*, February 27, 1841.

[10] Charlton to Kamehameha III, Oahu, October 17, 1839, in AH, F.O. and Ex.

[11] For example, see Charlton to Kamehameha III, Oahu, September 28, October 15, 1839, March 11, April 18, 1840, July 26, 1841, in *ibid.*; Charlton to Kekuanaoa, Oahu, September 18, 1840 and March 5, 1841, in *ibid.*; "Account of an Interview with Charlton at the Honolulu Fort," August 18, 1841, in *ibid.*; Jarves, *History of the Hawaiian Islands*, p. 172.

[12] Marshall to Hunnewell, Honolulu, March 11, 1841, in Hunnewell MSS; *Polynesian*, March 13, 1841. Among the signers were Peter A. Brinsmade, Stephen Reynolds, Henry A. Peirce, Dr. R. W. Wood, John Meek, and William Paty.

ure of the government to admit the validity of Charlton's claim to land, accused the chiefs of entertaining "a hostile attitude . . . . toward all Britishers" while regarding Americans with greater sympathy.[13] Charlton asserted that the policy of the government was determined by William Richards, whom he accused of being prejudiced against nationals of Great Britain;[14] and in March 1841 he informed the Foreign Office that Americans at Honolulu, disturbed by the growth of English trade at the Islands, were exerting "all their influence" to persuade the native authorities to annoy British residents.[15]

The growing breach between American and British residents of Honolulu was widened, in the autumn of 1841, as the result of a commercial dispute between Henry Skinner and John Dominis. Skinner was a British subject; Dominis was a naturalized citizen of the United States. When they were unable to agree upon the interpretation of a contract, each appealed to the local representative of his own country. Charlton thereupon insisted that the case be referred to a jury for trial; but, with a curious indifference to the possibly adverse views of the future jurors, he added a demand that at the conclusion of the trial, the sum demanded by Skinner should be promptly paid.[16] The government and Dominis readily agreed to a jury trial. Serious complications, however, arose when it proved impossible to empanel a jury consisting of an equal number of British and American residents. Governor Kekuanaoa ordered the trial to proceed with a jury in which American citizens outnumbered the nationals of Great Britain; and when Skinner withdrew from the court in protest the governor dismissed the case. Although the commander of a British man-of-war suggested that the case be reopened,

---

[13] Manuscript account of an interview between Charlton, T. C. B. Rooke, Kekauluohi, and Kekuanaoa, April 16, 1840, in AH, F.O. and Ex.

[14] Charlton to Bidwell, Oahu, January 3, 1841, in *Correspondence Relative to the Sandwich Islands*, p. 74.

[15] Charlton to Palmerston, Oahu, March 11, 1841, in *ibid.*, p. 75. For expressions of similar views see Alexander Simpson and Henry Skinner to Aberdeen, Honolulu, September 24, 1842, in *ibid.*, pp. 141–142; Charlton to Aberdeen, London, February 11, 1843, in *ibid.*, pp. 159–161, and a memorial addressed to Queen Victoria, dated Honolulu, September 24, 1841, and signed by thirty-five British subjects, in *ibid.*, pp. 131–132. In the summer of 1841 Charlton reproached the King with the scarcely veiled accusation that British subjects could expect less sympathetic treatment from the Hawaiian government than could the nationals of more favored countries. Charlton to Kamehameha III, Oahu, August 28, 1841, in AH, F.O. and Ex.

[16] Charlton to Kamehameha III, Oahu, October 7, 1841, in *ibid.*

Brinsmade and Dominis persuaded the governor to consider his dismissal of the case as the final disposition of the issue.[17]

In reporting this affair to the Foreign Office, Charlton advised his superiors that "great good would arise, and much trouble saved" if naval officers were authorized to investigate disputes in which British subjects were involved and to enforce what should appear to them to be just.[18] Skinner was equally alarmed. He declared that his countrymen were in constant danger of suffering annoyance at the hands of the government, and he professed to fear that "the few enterprising British subjects who have, within the last three years, increased British trade in these islands . . . . must abandon the field and fair prospects of this capable group of islands, to others."[19] Charlton assured Captain Jones that the native rulers were governed only "by principles of avarice or fear,"[20] but Jones does not seem to have shared the misgivings of either Charlton or Skinner. To Rear Admiral Ross, he reported that he was not convinced that Skinner had been the victim of injustice or that the complaints of Charlton had been well founded.[21]

While Charlton and his associates feared that British interests at the Islands were menaced by an anti-English bias on the part of the native rulers, the American residents seemed to have been generally satisfied with the policies of the government. The American missionaries were not parties to the newer division of opinion and society along national lines,[22] and they had no reason to suppose that the

---

[17] There is a general lack of agreement as to what occurred at different stages of the hearings. The situation as viewed by several of the participants may be found in Charlton to Rear Admiral Ross, Oahu, October 27, 1841, in *Correspondence Relative to the Sandwich Islands*, p. 90; Captain Jenkin Jones to Rear Admiral Ross, Monterey, November 6, 1841, in *ibid.*, pp. 97–99; Skinner to Captain Jones, Oahu, November 30, 1841, in *ibid.*, pp. 127–128; Charlton to Kamehameha III, Oahu, October 22, 1841, in AH, F.O. and Ex.; Brinsmade to Kamehameha III, Sandwich Islands, October 19, 1841, in *ibid.*; Kamehameha III to Charlton, Honolulu, October 25, 1841, in *ibid.*; Kamehameha III to Captain Jones, Honolulu, October 28, 1841, in *ibid.*, and printed in *Correspondence Relative to the Sandwich Islands*, pp. 126–127. See also Miscellaneous MSS, dated October 14, 1841, in AH, F.O. and Ex.

[18] Charlton to Palmerston, Oahu, October 28, 1841, in *Correspondence Relative to the Sandwich Islands*, p. 89.

[19] Skinner to Captain Jenkin Jones, Honolulu, October 11, 1841, in *ibid.*, p. 120.

[20] Charlton to Jones, Oahu, October 27, 1841, in *ibid.*, p. 126.

[21] Jones to Rear Admiral Ross, Monterey, November 6, 1841, in *ibid.*, pp. 97–99.

[22] Wilkes, *United States Exploring Expedition*, III, 415; Chamberlain to Anderson, Honolulu, February 21, 1843, in Letters to the American Board, CXXXV, No. 157.

government would be less friendly to them in the future than it had been in the past. In July 1839 the American commercial agent assured the Secretary of State that the "kind and honorable conduct" of American citizens at the Islands, reinforced by the "mild and conciliating demeanour" of American naval officers who called at Honolulu, had been successful in securing "the partialities of the King and his chiefs towards Americans."[23] Two years later he praised the "disposition to justice" which he thought was "the controlling principle" of the government.[24] Lieutenant George Colvocoresses, an officer of the United States Exploring Expedition, believed that the King entertained "a high opinion of Americans," whom he frequently consulted "upon matters of state."[25] If the judgment of Colvocoresses was correct it is not strange that Brinsmade was well content with the policies of the government nor that nationally conscious British subjects were restive in the face of the mounting evidence of American influence in Hawaiian politics.

The scene of this intra-community rivalry for political position and influence was a small Polynesian seaport, located far from the great centers of the commercial world. The government which offered its services to maintain peace, to protect property, and to dispense justice was a feeble monarchy, whose policies were determined by men of little experience in the broader world of politics and diplomacy and who could not be indifferent to the fact that the Islands they governed constituted one of the great prizes in any struggle for colonial empire in the Pacific. In no archipelago in that ocean was there so considerable an investment of foreign capital or so numerous a colony of American and European residents. No government in the entire region of the eastern Pacific had more cause to fear that aliens living within its jurisdiction might precipitate some incident which would lead to bloodshed, intervention, or the loss of independence. One obvious means of forestalling a seizure of the Islands was to persuade the great maritime powers to recognize the independent

[23] Brinsmade to Secretary of State Forsyth, Sandwich Islands, July 17, 1839, in USDS, "Consular Letters," Honolulu, I. See also Wilkes, *United States Exploring Expedition*, IV, 20.

[24] Brinsmade to Kekauluohi, Sandwich Islands, September 29, 1841, in AH, F.O. and Ex., and printed in Jarves, *History of the Hawaiian Islands*, p. 172.

[25] Colvocoresses, *Four Years in the Government Exploring Expedition*, p. 216.

sovereignty of the Hawaiian kingdom. The early official efforts to secure such a recognition were the by-products of the commercial ambitions of individual American speculators in the Islands rather than the result of any anxiety upon the part of either William Richards or the native rulers.[26]

The central figure in the first formal attempt to secure an acknowledgment of Hawaiian independence was Thomas Jefferson Farnham, an Illinois lawyer who had led a small band of adventurers from Peoria to Oregon in 1839.[27] Disappointed by the unfavorable prospects for settlement in Oregon, and deserted by his followers,[28] Farnham sailed for Honolulu, where he arrived in December 1839.[29] He remained in the Islands for about three months. While there he became acquainted with the King, chiefs, missionaries, and foreign residents, from whom he gleaned some information concerning the legends, customs, and history of the Hawaiian people.[30] His judgments were not infallible, but it is significant that he described the government as "more paternal, and administered more kindly than any other known to civilized man."[31]

While at Honolulu, Farnham became acquainted with Milo Calkin, an American who had been in the employ of Ladd and Company since June 1837.[32] Calkin expected to obtain from the government the lease of a large tract of land on Kauai, five miles wide and extending inland for a distance of about five miles. He hoped to interest American capitalists in the development of this land. He discussed his plans with Farnham, who agreed to do what he could to create interest among possible investors in the United States. Both men

---

[26] Richards was not greatly alarmed about the immediate future, for, in July 1840, he believed that the Hawaiian government was more generally respected than it had been at any previous period. He did add, however, that its relations with other nations could not be placed "on an equable basis" until Great Britain and France were represented at Honolulu by men more sympathetic with the native government than were Charlton and Jules Dudoit. Richards to Anderson, Honolulu, July 27, 1840, in Letters to the American Board, CXXXV, No. 88.

[27] R. G. Thwaites, in *Early Western Travels* (Cleveland, 1904–1906), XXVIII,

10–12; J[oseph] S[chafer], "Thomas Jefferson Farnham," in *Dictionary of American Biography*, VI, 283.

[28] *Peoria Register*, quoted in *Niles' Register*, LVIII (June 20, 1840), 242.

[29] Testimony of Milo Calkin, October 5, 1846, in *Arbitration between the . . . . Government of the Hawaiian Islands and Messrs. Ladd & Co.*, p. 183.

[30] T. J. Farnham, *Life, Adventures, and Travels in California* (New York, 1849), p. 41.

[31] *Ibid.*, p. 45.

[32] Testimony of Milo Calkin, *loc. cit.*, p. 183.

anticipated that the "delicate state" of the Hawaiian government would prove an obstacle to the realization of Calkin's hopes, and Peter Brinsmade advanced the opinion that they could accomplish nothing until the independence of the Islands had been formally recognized by the great maritime powers.[33] From Brinsmade, Farnham received a letter of introduction to the King in which there was the suggestion that Farnham's "influence at Washington" might be utilized by the Hawaiian government.[34] Thus armed, Farnham went to Lahaina to lay Calkin's plan before the King and, if possible, to interest him in a project for securing the acknowledgment of Hawaiian independence.

The influence of Farnham at Washington was almost wholly the product of his own imagination. If Richards suspected as much, the suspicion was offset by his approval of the plans of Calkin and by his belief that the visit of Farnham had been "instrumental of some good."[35] He was willing to enlist the services of the visitor in the cause of Hawaiian independence, and apparently he joined with Brinsmade and others in persuading the King to designate Farnham as Minister to the United States, Great Britain, and France. The King and Richards shrewdly withheld a formal commission from their envoy; instead, they sent it to Benjamin F. Butler, of New York, with the request that he investigate the character and qualifications of Farnham. If the investigation indicated that Farnham was well fitted for the mission, Butler was to deliver the commission to him and to draw bills upon the Hawaiian government to meet his expenses while in the service of the King.[36]

[33] *Ibid.*, pp. 184–185.

[34] Brinsmade to Kamehameha III, Oahu, January 8, 1840, in AH, Farnham MSS.
Farnham had gained some publicity as a result of his organization, in 1839, of a group to go to Oregon. From Honolulu he sent a letter to Secretary of War Joel Poinsett, with some information concerning Oregon. This letter was published by the Senate (*Senate Documents*, 27th Cong., 3d Sess., No. 102, pp. 2–4), but there is no indication that either Congress or the War Department was impressed by its contents. In 1843 a Washington newspaper described Farnham as a person "favorably known in

our public archives" because of a report on Oregon which it alleged he had been commissioned by Poinsett to prepare. *Daily National Intelligencer*, April 5, 1843. The only published report by Farnham is the letter noted above. The original copy of the report, dated Oahu, January 4, 1840, is in USDS, "Miscellaneous Letters."

[35] Richards to Hunnewell, Honolulu, March 22, 1840, in Hunnewell MSS.

[36] Kamehameha III and Kekauluohi to Butler, Lahaina, March 17, 1840, in AH, Farnham MSS. Apparently this communication was sent to Rufus Anderson, Secretary of the American Board, with the re-

The instructions by which Farnham was to be guided were given directly to him. They commanded him to visit the United States, Great Britain, and France, to "leave no honorable means untried to secure from each of these nations" an acknowledgment of Hawaiian independence and a guaranty of the future security of the kingdom, to seek a revision of the treaties negotiated by Laplace, to request the removal of Charlton, to provide means of securing a just and amicable settlement of disputes between the Hawaiian government and the principal foreign powers, and to explain to the ministers of the various governments the Hawaiian viewpoint concerning certain past difficulties which had threatened to involve the Kamehameha dynasty in serious international complications.[37] Leaving Honolulu in March 1840, Farnham went directly to the California coast. From there he went to his home in Illinois, and in the summer of 1840 he was again in Peoria.[38]

Around the diplomatic career of Farnham there remains a veil of mystery. It is apparent that he made little effort to press the cause of the sovereign who had entrusted him with so important a task, and any hope the King may have entertained with respect to the mission was doomed to disappointment. Farnham did not visit either of the European courts to which he was accredited,[39] and there is no evidence that his alleged influence at Washington was ever exerted on behalf of the Hawaiian government. In the summer of 1841 he explained his failure to act by asserting that Butler, who was to secure the funds necessary for the success of the mission, had been criminally negligent of that duty.[40] More than two years later Farnham

quest that it be forwarded to Butler. Should Butler be unable to attend to these matters, Anderson was asked to send the enclosed papers to Theodore Frelinghuysen, the vice-president of the Board and a prominent New Jersey Whig. Richards to Anderson, Honolulu, March 23, 1840, in Letters to the American Board, CXXXV, No. 87.

[37] Kamehameha III and Kekauluohi to Farnham, no date, in AH, Farnham MSS. An extract from the instructions to Farnham is printed in *Appendix to the Report of the Minister of Foreign Relations*, 1855, p. 3. Farnham was empowered to act as attorney for the King to collect certain debts said to be owed to the King by various American traders and masters of vessels. Testimony of William Richards, August 29, 1846, in *Arbitration between the . . . . Government of the Hawaiian Islands and Messrs. Ladd & Co.*, p. 88.

[38] J. S[chafer], "Thomas Jefferson Farnham," in *Dictionary of American Biography*, VI, 283.

[39] Farnham to Kamehameha III, New York, November 25, 1843, in AH, Farnham MSS.

[40] Farnham to Richards, New York, June 17, 1841, in *ibid.*

reasserted his great love for the Hawaiian rulers and deplored his failure to accomplish anything. Explaining this failure by his inability to cash the drafts sent to him by the Hawaiian government, he declared that he had waited in vain for more than two years for a reply to the "many dispatches" which he had sent to the King.[41]

At the close of 1841, another project for large-scale speculation in agriculture provided the motive for the second formal effort to secure a recognition of Hawaiian independence. On November 24, 1841, representatives of the government and of Ladd and Company signed an agreement whereby the company was given permission to lease all unoccupied land in the archipelago and to use that land for agricultural development. On the same day, Peter Brinsmade, as senior partner of the company, signed an additional agreement which contained the stipulation that the lease was not to become effective until the independence of the Islands had been recognized by the United States, Great Britain, and France.[42] Clearly the government was prepared to pay a high price for whatever assistance Ladd and Company could furnish in securing the continued independence of the native dynasty. This, in large measure, was the result of an increasing realization of the precarious situation in which the government had been placed by recent events. The rejection of Charlton's claims to valuable land, followed by the abortive trial of the case of Skinner *v.* Dominis, had created problems which were almost certain to reappear to embarrass the native rulers.[43]

For the difficult task of presenting the Hawaiian version of these

---

[41] Farnham to Kamehameha III, New York, November 25, 1843, in *ibid.* Despite the lack of success which attended his adventures in diplomacy, Farnham embarrassed the Hawaiian government by demands for full compensation for the period from his departure from Honolulu until 1843, at the rate of $6,400 a year. In 1844 Richards, who was then in the United States, agreed to add one thousand dollars to the eight hundred which Farnham had already received. This amount Farnham accepted under protest. *Ibid.*; Journal of William Richards, September 11, 12, 14, 28, 1844. The receipt, signed by Farnham and dated September 27, 1844, is in AH, Farnham MSS.

[42] The contract is printed in Jarves, *History of the Hawaiian Islands*, p. 218 n., and, with the additional agreement of the same date, in *Arbitration between the . . . . Government of the Hawaiian Islands and Messrs. Ladd & Co.*, Appendix, pp. 30–32.

[43] Five years later, Richards recalled that there had been urgent political motives for the desire of the King to have the independence of his kingdom acknowledged. Among these motives were the fears aroused by the "threats and intimidations" of Charlton and the rise of "important conflicting interests, suits of many thousand dollars, &c." Testimony of William Richards, September 1, 1846, in *ibid.*, p. 96.

episodes at foreign capitals, Brinsmade was an obvious candidate. He enjoyed the confidence of Richards and of the Hawaiian government. He was the official agent of the United States and was presumed to have the respect and confidence of his own government. He had a personal stake in the continued independence of the Hawaiian kingdom, and he had boasted of his influence in the United States.[44] Following the signing of the two agreements of November 24, 1841, the King twice asked Brinsmade to undertake a mission abroad for the express purpose of urging the great powers to recognize the Islands as an independent nation.[45] Shortly thereafter Brinsmade left Honolulu for a visit to the United States and Europe. In Honolulu it was reported that he had gone abroad "on special business, supposed to be for the Sand. Is. Gov't," as well as to interest capitalists and prospective settlers in the development of the land on Kauai.[46]

Brinsmade contributed little to the cause of Hawaiian independence. While in Washington, in April 1842, he addressed to Secretary of State Webster a lengthy communication, in which he proposed that the three great maritime powers recognize the independence of the Hawaiian kingdom and unite in a tripartite agreement to guarantee that independence. He also declared that the King desired "to be released from the obligations of his engagements with the commanders of War Ships" in order to be able to raise revenue by higher customs duties than the five per cent allowed by the Laplace treaty. In support of the King's proposals, Brinsmade listed the commercial importance of the Islands, the phenomenal emergence of the nation from barbarism toward orderly government, the interest already shown in education and industry, the possibility of an agricultural development of the Islands, and the willingness of the King and his government to submit any dispute with a foreign power to some form of peaceful mediation. Continuing, Brinsmade declared that Americans in the Islands would receive "numerous and obvious" benefits if the proposed tripartite guaranty were concluded, including greater

[44] Testimony of Richards, August 27, September 1, 1846, in *ibid.*, pp. 73, 96.

[45] *Ibid.*, p. 100.

[46] Journal of Stephen Reynolds, September 2, 1842.

Richard Charlton later declared that when Brinsmade left the Islands it was "currently reported" that he proposed to organize a company and a party of settlers "to purchase the island of Atooi [Kauai], the most fertile of the group." Charlton to Aberdeen, July 18, 1843, in *Correspondence Relative to the Sandwich Islands*, p. 252.

security of property and the unhampered access of American whalers to Hawaiian ports.[47] Brinsmade reported that his business in Washington was "as agreeably disposed of as I could wish" and that the King's proposals were "very favourably entertained by the Govt";[48] but eight months later, when Richards visited Washington, he found that the Secretary of State "appeared to know little about the Islands or Mr. Brinsmade."[49]

From the United States, Brinsmade went to England. In London he sought the advice and assistance of Edward Everett, the American Minister.[50] Everett introduced him to the Under Secretary of State for Foreign Affairs, who was reported to be interested in the proposals suggested by Brinsmade.[51] Brinsmade was also the bearer of a letter from Kamehameha III to Queen Victoria; but because he failed to present it in the proper manner, the Foreign Office ruled that the letter could not be received. In instructions to Charlton, the Earl of Aberdeen explained that the refusal was not to be interpreted as an intentional lack of courtesy, and that the British government, although unwilling to participate in the proposed tripartite guaranty of Hawaiian independence, was ready to offer its good offices at any time.[52] Brinsmade crossed the Channel to France, where he had an interview with Guizot and left a letter signed by Kamehameha III and addressed to the King of the French.[53] Four years later a prominent American resident of Honolulu ventured the opinion that Brinsmade had been "chiefly instrumental" in securing the acknowledgment of Hawaiian independence by the great powers.[54] None of the nations

[47] Brinsmade to Secretary of State Webster, Washington, April 8, 1842, in USDS, "Consular Letters," Honolulu, I.

[48] Brinsmade to Milo Calkin, Boston, May 15, 1842, in USDS, "Hawaii, U.S. Legation, Miscellaneous Letters Received," II.

[49] Journal of William Richards, December 7, 1842.

[50] Brinsmade to Everett, London, June 3, 1842, in *Correspondence Relative to the Sandwich Islands*, pp. 91–92.

[51] Everett to Webster, London, July 1, 1842, in FRUS, 1894, Appendix II, p. 108.

[52] Aberdeen to Charlton, [London], December 1, 1842, in *Correspondence Relative to the Sandwich Islands*, p. 129.

[53] Blue, "Policy of France Toward the Hawaiian Islands," in *Papers Read During the Captain Cook Sesquicentennial Celebration*, p. 81; Testimony of William Richards, September 1, 1846, in *Arbitration between the . . . . Government of the Hawaiian Islands and Messrs. Ladd & Co.*, p. 96; Journal of Stephen Reynolds, October 27, 1842.

Richards testified that he knew of the visit of Brinsmade to Guizot only from the former and that he had never heard Guizot mention any conversation with Brinsmade.

[54] Gorham D. Gilman to S. K. Gilman, Honolulu, May 5, 1846, MS in Hawaiian Historical Society Library.

which Brinsmade visited, however, showed any inclination to recognize the independent status of the Islands until after his efforts had been reinforced by a formal Hawaiian diplomatic mission which visited the United States and Europe from 1842 to 1844.

On February 11, 1842, shortly after Brinsmade had left the Islands, Sir George Simpson, Governor of the Hudson's Bay Company's territories in North America, arrived at Honolulu.[55] For nearly a month Simpson remained on Oahu, apparently interested in the commercial possibilities of the island and imbibing the prejudices of a section of the foreign community. While there he was informed that the American missionaries were "in a certain degree, a political Engine in the hands of the Government of the United States," that the principal adviser of the King was "a narrow minded, illiterate American," and that the missionaries had been guilty of diverting "the stream of justice from the proper course, in order to favor their own friends and countrymen." From conversations with residents of Honolulu, Simpson believed that the missionaries had used "their best judgment" in their efforts to promote the welfare of the Hawaiian people; but he accused them of having sponsored "some very strange and unusual laws," which had caused great annoyance to the residents.[56] In an interview with Governor Kekuanaoa, he suggested the advisability of replacing Richards with some "more enlightened" person.[57] Despite this pessimistic report, Simpson believed that British prestige at the Islands had not been seriously impaired, for it appeared to him that the chiefs wished "to stand well" with the governments of both the United States and Great Britain. More encouraging to him was the persistence of a belief among the chiefs that the Islands were "in a certain degree under the protection of Great

[55] Journal of William Paty, February 11, 1842.

[56] Simpson to Sir John Pelly, Honolulu, March 10, 1842, in *American Historical Review*, XIV (October 1908), 91. The "narrow minded, illiterate American" to whom Simpson referred was William Richards.

While Simpson was gathering such uncomplimentary impressions of the influence of the missionaries, the latter were pleased by what Richard Armstrong called his

"very respectable and friendly" attitude toward the mission. Armstrong also reported that on "all points of difference between the chiefs and resident foreigners," Simpson took "good ground . . . . to the no small annoyance of some who heard him." Armstrong to the American Board, Honolulu, March 21, 1842, in *Missionary Herald*, XXXVIII (December 1842), 481.

[57] Simpson to Pelly, Honolulu, March 10, 1842, in *American Historical Review*, XIV (October 1908), 91–92.

Britain."[58] With these judgments already formed, Simpson proceeded to Lahaina, the residence of the royal family and of Richards.

While Simpson was at Lahaina his views on the personalities and problems of Hawaiian politics underwent a major modification. Within a few days he was engaged in discussion of various political issues with the King, Richards, and the chiefs; and he was able to write that he had acquired "a great degree of influence over these good people."[59] In the course of those discussions Simpson expressed doubt that Brinsmade would be able to persuade the great powers to recognize the independence of the Islands, and he volunteered to carry to London any communications which the King might wish to send.[60] More important was his suggestion that Richards be sent to the United States and Europe on a formal diplomatic mission in order to present the case for the recognition of Hawaiian independence and if possible to negotiate treaties with the United States, Great Britain, and France.[61]

The spectacle of an influential official of the Hudson's Bay Company actively interested in the preservation of Hawaiian independence was one calculated to surprise those Americans who feared that the company had political as well as commercial ambitions in the eastern Pacific. The motives which led Simpson to adopt the unexpected role of friend and adviser of the Hawaiian rulers are not entirely clear. Apparently he was satisfied that the interests of the company would not suffer in an independent Hawaii, and it is probable that he was sufficiently well informed to realize that the British government would be reluctant to assume new imperial burdens in the Pacific. A recognition of Hawaiian independence, therefore, would not involve a reversal of British policy; it might become a barrier to territorial ambitions of the United States and France in that part of the world. Such a recognition, if secured through the good offices of the

<hr />

[58] *Ibid.*

[59] Simpson to Pelly, Maui, March 24, 1842, in *ibid.*, p. 93.

[60] Simpson, *Journey Round the World*, II, 171–172; Testimony of William Richards, August 29, 1846, in *Arbitration between the . . . . Government of the Hawaiian Islands and Messrs. Ladd & Co.*, p. 76.

[61] *Ibid.*; Simpson to Pelly, Maui, March 24, 1842, in *American Historical Review*, XIV (October 1908), 93. Simpson suggested that in the letters of credence given to Richards his own name and that of two of the high officials of the Hudson's Bay Company should be added, so that they might assist Richards if that should seem desirable.

Hudson's Bay Company, might pay tangible dividends in the form of good will and political favors for the company's post at Honolulu.

Such practical considerations were reinforced by personal factors. At Honolulu, Simpson had found an estranged nephew, Alexander Simpson. The latter had recently left the service of the Hudson's Bay Company, embittered by the conviction that neither he nor his brother, Thomas, had been justly treated by their distinguished uncle. More than fourteen years earlier, lured by his uncle's "highly coloured descriptions" of the opportunities in North America, Alexander Simpson had entered the employment of the company in Canada; but after a considerable experience with the "cares and crosses" of life there he had severed all connections with the company. Unrealized hopes of promotion and a feeling that his uncle had been indifferent to the valuable services of Thomas Simpson bred in the mind of Alexander Simpson a resentment that had not subsided in 1842.[62] This is indicated by a letter which he addressed to his uncle while the latter was at Lahaina.[63] The letter, which was filled with accusations of bad faith, probably did not reach Sir George until after he left the Islands. It is difficult to believe, however, that he was ignorant of the sentiments of his nephew.

Alexander Simpson was without permanent occupation in the Islands. He was free therefore to participate in public or semipublic affairs. It soon became apparent that he approved the domineering diplomacy of Charlton, and his hostility toward the Hudson's Bay Company threatened to cause a division among British residents of Honolulu. He became a leader of a small group of British nationalists who were generally in opposition to the Hawaiian government— a contrast to the company's agents, who were more interested in trade

[62] Simpson, *Life and Travels of Thomas Simpson*, pp. 47, 78–81, 183–184.

Alexander Simpson wrote that he and Sir George were cousins (*ibid.*, p. 44), but later writers believed that they were uncle and nephew. C. A[lexander] H[arris], "Sir George Simpson," in *Dictionary of National Biography*, LII, 269; J. K. L[aughton], "Thomas Simpson," in *ibid.*, LII, 279.

[63] A. Simpson to G. Simpson, Oahu, March 23, 1842, in AH, F.O. and Ex. See

also A. Simpson to Ross, Kauai, July 13, 1842, in *ibid.*

In November 1842 the Honolulu agent of the company informed Sir George Simpson that he had secured a copy of "the infamous and cowardly libel" which Alexander Simpson had "industriously circulated through this community, and a copy of which Charlton has taken home with him to do what mischief he can there." George Pelly to George Simpson, Honolulu, November 2, 1842, in *Correspondence Relative to the Sandwich Islands*, p. 163.

than in politics. The danger that Alexander Simpson might become a dominant factor in Hawaiian political life was remote; should unexpected developments favor him, his rise to power might prove embarrassing to the company. The mere existence of such a possibility may well have been sufficient to prompt his uncle to assist the Hawaiian government.[64]

On March 24 Sir George Simpson left Lahaina for Sitka,[65] with the intention of returning to London before the Hawaiian representatives should arrive there. Before leaving the Islands he insured the financial support of this diplomatic venture when he ordered George Pelly, the agent at Honolulu of the Hudson's Bay Company, to give the Hawaiian government a letter of credit, to be drawn upon the company, for the sum of ten thousand pounds.[66] A week later, while at sea, he wrote to Richards, emphasizing again his desire to be of assistance to the Hawaiian commission when it should reach London and naming two officials of the Hudson's Bay Company who would be able to give valuable aid in the event of his own absence.[67]

Following the departure of Simpson, the King and his advisers lost little time in making the necessary arrangements for the dispatch of a diplomatic mission to the United States, Great Britain, and France. In this, the King seems to have been guided largely by the advice of Simpson, who, with William Richards, was appointed as envoy to the three countries. The instructions by which Simpson and Richards were to be governed informed them that the "grand, ultimate object" of their mission was to secure from the governments of the three great powers a recognition of the independence of the Islands. Scarcely less important was the instruction that they were to seek

[64] This was the belief of J. F. B. Marshall, a Honolulu merchant who was acquainted with both of the Simpsons. Marshall, "An Unpublished Chapter of Hawaiian History," in *Harper's Magazine*, LXVII (September 1883), 511–512. Five years later one of the Honolulu agents of the Hudson's Bay Company declared that he had been called upon to defend Sir George against "the most unjust attack," apparently caused by resentment among British subjects at Honolulu who remembered the part that Simpson had played in securing the independence of the Islands. G. T. Allan to Donald Ross, Honolulu, December 22, 1847, MS, Provincial Library and Archives, Victoria.

[65] Simpson, *Journey Round the World*, II, 173–174.

[66] Simpson to George Pelly, March 24, 1842, in AH, F.O. and Ex. In May, Pelly loaned the Hawaiian government the sum of ten thousand pounds.

[67] Simpson to Richards, April 1, 1842, in *ibid.* The two officials of the company named by Simpson were Sir John Pelly and Andrew Colville.

the annulment of certain treaties which were "very embarrassing" to the Hawaiian government and which it was hoped would be replaced by "formal treaties, which shall be honorable to our nation and beneficial to all concerned."[68]

The mission committed to Richards and Simpson was one which promised to be of the utmost importance in the life of the kingdom. Should success attend their efforts, Hawaii could take a modest place among the nations of the world; should their mission fail, the kingdom of the Kamehamehas could scarcely hope for a better fate than to be included in the colonial empire of some ambitious and expanding power. Recognizing this unenviable alternative, the King provided Richards with extraordinary powers, including blank papers bearing the seal and signature of the monarch, and additional instructions giving the conscientious but inexperienced envoy unlimited authority in negotiating with the diplomats of Europe and the United States.[69]

While at the Islands Simpson had discussed with the Hawaiian rulers the advisability of including one native Hawaiian in the proposed commission. At that time, the name of Keoni Ana—a son of the famous John Young—was suggested for this honor;[70] but later it was determined to send Timothy Haalilio, the King's secretary. Preparations necessary for so momentous a mission delayed its departure until summer. In July the commissioners, in company with the King, left Lahaina, presumably for Oahu; but instead of proceeding to Honolulu, Richards and Haalilio were transferred at sea to a vessel bound for the American coast. They had departed on an errand the nature of which was known only to the most intimate advisers of the King.[71] William Hooper, acting commercial agent of the United States, learned in advance that the King would send Richards abroad

[68] Instructions to G. Simpson and Richards, April 8, 1842, in AH, F.O. and Ex. They are printed in *Appendix to the Report of the Minister of Foreign Relations*, 1855, pp. 3–4; and in *Arbitration between the . . . . Government of the Hawaiian Islands and Messrs. Ladd & Co.*, Appendix, pp. 41–42. The power of attorney given Richards, also dated April 8, 1842, is in *ibid.*, pp. 53–54.

[69] Kamehameha III and Kekauluohi to Richards, Lahaina, July 9, 1842, in AH, F.O. and Ex.

[70] Simpson to Richards, April 1, 1842, in *ibid.*; Richards to Brinsmade, Honolulu, March 31, 1842, in *Arbitration between the . . . . Government of the Hawaiian Islands and Messrs. Ladd & Co.*, Appendix, p. 44.

[71] Journal of Alexander Liholiho, 1843–1845 (MS, Bernice Pauahi Bishop Museum), April 14, 1845.

as a "special agent"; but he reported that as to the purposes of the King he thought it not "necessary to conjecture."[72] Others in Honolulu evinced more curiosity, and before the end of July the departure of Richards and Haalilio, their destination, the purpose of their mission, and their prospects for success had become "the topic of conversation in every group among the foreigners."[73]

The departure of Richards brought into prominence another former missionary, Dr. Gerrit Parmele Judd, who became the successor of Richards as the most trusted counselor of the King and chiefs. Judd was born in Paris, New York, in April 1803, at a time when that region was still distinctly a part of the frontier. He was educated in the schools of his native state and studied medicine at Fairfield, New York. Being anxious to participate actively in the spread of Christian principles, he volunteered to serve under the American Board, and was sent to the Hawaiian Islands as a medical missionary.[74] From 1828 to 1842 he continued to serve the mission as its physician. During those fourteen years he resided at Honolulu; but the duties of his profession frequently called him to other islands, and he was familiar with nearly every part of the archipelago. By 1832, he had become the accepted medical adviser of "most of the chiefs and their families."[75] Kinau was a frequent visitor at his home, and after 1835 Judd was often consulted by her and by other chiefs upon matters of state.[76] After the death of Kinau, Governor Kekuanaoa continued to rely upon the counsel and assistance of Judd, who advised the governor on matters of private business, translated official documents, and was "usually . . . . present at all important trials" as well as during "the adjustment of difficulties between the government and the foreigners."[77]

[72] Hooper to Secretary of State Webster, Sandwich Islands, June 30, 1842, in USDS, "Consular Letters," Honolulu, I.

[73] Journal of Stephen Reynolds, July 20, 1842.

[74] Anderson, *History of the Mission to the Sandwich Islands*, p. 379; R. S. K[uykendall], "Gerrit Parmele Judd," in *Dictionary of American Biography*, X, 229.

[75] Journal of Dr. and Mrs. Alonzo Chapin, II, 32 (May 20, 1832).

[76] Judd to R. C. Wyllie, Honolulu, February 17, 1860, in Judd, *Honolulu*, pp. 190–192. In October 1837 Judd assisted Lorrin Andrews in "instructing the King and chiefs" concerning communications to be sent to England, presenting the Hawaiian version of the events which led to the seizure of the "Clementine" and the subsequent intervention of Captain Edward Belcher. Journal of Lorrin Andrews, October 12, 1837, in AH, F.O. and Ex.

[77] Report of G. P. Judd, 1840–1841, in Letters to the American Board, CXXXVII,

The formal entrance of Judd into the service of the Hawaiian government occurred in May 1842. Early in that month the Legislature—apparently adopting proposals of Sir George Simpson[78]—provided for the creation of a treasury board of three members. Shortly thereafter it approved a statute authorizing the selection of "some foreigner as Recorder and Interpreter for the Government." In addition to clerical duties the new official was charged with the care of public documents and was expected to provide information concerning the conduct of business in other countries.[79] For the treasury board, the King, on May 10, chose Timothy Haalilio, John Ii, and Dr. Judd.[80] Five days later, Judd was informed that he was to fill also the position of Recorder and Interpreter, and in July his duties were further increased when he was ordered to gather and forward information to Richards and Haalilio.[81]

The influence of Judd was not to be measured by official titles or duties. After the departure of Richards he was the only foreigner who was available for advice and assistance, and who possessed the entire confidence of the King and of the principal chiefs. The power of his associates on the treasury board was only nominal; for Haalilio left the Islands in July in company with Richards, and Ii had such confidence in the ability and integrity of Judd that he was not disposed to question the views or actions of his ex-missionary associate. By the late summer of 1842 Judd was the dominant figure in the Hawaiian government, and virtually in complete control of the formulation of domestic and foreign policy.[82]

The section of the foreign community which continued to harbor an antipathy for the mission learned of the appointment of Judd with frank misgivings. Before Judd had been in office two weeks, Stephen

No. 91. Many years later Mrs. Judd recalled that her husband had taught clerks in the service of the government "to keep . . . . records of all important business, and to preserve all receipts on payment of debts, in order to prevent being compelled to pay them twice, which had not unfrequently happened." Judd, *Honolulu*, pp. 63–64.

[78] Simpson to Kamehameha III, Honolulu, March 12, 1842, in AH, F.O. and Ex.

[79] Thurston, comp., *Fundamental Law of Hawaii*, p. 125.

[80] The commissions of Haalilio, Ii, and Judd, dated May 10, 1842, are in the Archives of Hawaii.

[81] Kamehameha III and Kekauluohi to Judd, May 15, July 18, 1842, in AH, F.O. and Ex. See also Judd, *Honolulu*, pp. 84–86.

[82] Testimony of J. F. B. Marshall, November 23, 1846, in *Arbitration between the . . . . Government of the Hawaiian Islands and Messrs. Ladd & Co.*, pp. 259–260.

Reynolds feared that the missionaries had "everything in their own hands";[83] and in July he accused Richards and Judd of being "determined to make all feel their weight."[84] Robert G. Davis, long hostile to the mission, declared that Judd had become "a greater man than any chief on the island" and was able to do as he pleased. Davis added that new laws were being promulgated which were designed "to oppress as much as possible the foreign interest."[85] These judgments obviously were biased; but the fear in the foreign community that Judd, like Richards, had carried into office a reverence for the rigid tenets of his missionary brethren was not without foundation.

The decision of Judd to leave the mission and to enter the service of the government came as an unpleasant surprise to the American Board and to many of his friends. In April 1842, Judd informed the Board that he had been invited by the King to take the position in the government soon to be vacated by Richards. He admitted that no member of the mission was yet aware of his intention to accept the offer, but he declared that he planned to submit the matter to the next annual meeting of the mission.[86] Before that meeting convened, however, the King had become impatient and Judd had yielded to pressure. Without consulting his brethren, either individually or as a group, he accepted a position in the government. In this he had the approval of Richards.[87] Among the missionaries, however, the haste

[83] Journal of Stephen Reynolds, May 21, 1842. See also R. G. Davis to W. H. Davis, Oahu, January 14, 1843, in William Heath Davis MSS.

[84] Reynolds to Larkin, Oahu, July 3, 1842, in Larkin MSS, I, No. 285. Reynolds further complained that Judd "rides us down to the dust—we have no mercy to expect from him! !" Reynolds to Larkin, Oahu, July 31, 1842, in *ibid.*, I, No. 299. Levi Chamberlain reported that some persons unfriendly to the mission had said that Judd's entrance into official life would soon be followed by similar action by other missionaries, and he feared that such critics would "make use of these cases to our injury." Chamberlain to Anderson, Honolulu, July 8, 1842, in Letters to the American Board, CXXXV, No. 149. Nearly a year later, Richard Armstrong wrote that there were rumors in Honolulu that Judd's action was "in reality the work of the mis-

sion; that to save appearances we had nothing to do with his engaging in the service of government, and yet every thing was well understood." Armstrong to Anderson, Honolulu, March 2–6, 1843, in *ibid.*, CXXXVI, No. 96.

[85] R. G. Davis to W. H. Davis, Oahu, July 8, 1842, in Davis MSS.

[86] Judd to Anderson, Honolulu, April 19, 1842, in Letters to the American Board, CXXXVII, No. 84.

[87] Judd to Anderson, Honolulu, June 11, September 26, 1842, in *ibid.*, CXXXVII, Nos. 85, 86; Armstrong to Anderson, Honolulu, June 8, 1842, in *ibid.*, CXXXVI, No. 86; Lowell Smith to Anderson, Honolulu, June 8, 1842, in *ibid.*, CXXXVII, No. 26. Upon announcing to the mission his intention to leave the service of the Board, Judd promised to give as much attention to the

with which Judd accepted political preferment "produced a very unpleasant sensation," although with some of his colleagues it was the secrecy surrounding his move rather than the action itself which was the subject of censure. Richard Armstrong believed that if Judd had presented his case tactfully to the mission it would have been generally approved, and Levi Chamberlain reported that "the highest good of the mission and of the nation" would be secured through the participation in politics of men of the character of Richards and Judd.[88]

The officers of the American Board likewise were displeased by the action of Judd. When the news reached Boston the Secretary of the Board expressed the hope that Judd would reconsider his decision and would be willing to return to the mission.[89] The missionaries seem to have been less anxious for Judd to resume his former duties, fearing that such action might seem an open approval of his course and thus appear to substantiate rumors in Honolulu that his employment by the government was part of a political intrigue planned and directed by the mission.[90] There was no danger that the mission would be thus embarrassed. Judd was convinced that the Hawaiian rulers needed the advice and assistance of a sympathetic foreigner, and he believed that no person could be found who would serve them faithfully and satisfactorily except some member or former member of the mission.[91] He was strong-willed to the point of stubbornness, conscientious, more endowed with ability than with tact, and certain of the confidence of his royal master and of the principal chiefs.[92] In

---

medical needs of the missionaries as was possible in view of his new duties. *Minutes of the General Meeting of the Sandwich Island Mission,* 1842, p. 30.

[88] Armstrong to Anderson, Honolulu, June 8, 1842, in Letters to the American Board, CXXXVI, No. 86; Chamberlain to Anderson, Honolulu, July 8, 1842, in *ibid.,* CXXXV, No. 149.

[89] Anderson to the Sandwich Island Mission, Boston, October 28, 1842, in Letters from the American Board, Foreign, V (1842), 235–239.

[90] Armstrong to Anderson, Honolulu, March 2–6, 1843, in Letters to the American Board, CXXXVI, No. 96; Samuel C.

Damon to Anderson, Honolulu, April 5, 1843, in *ibid.,* CXXXVII, No. 209.

[91] Judd to Anderson, Honolulu, March 20, 1843, in *ibid.,* CXXXVII, No. 88. A defense of Judd's motives, the more convincing because by a man who was known to be hostile to him, may be found in Alexander Simpson, *Sandwich Islands,* p. 72.

[92] James F. B. Marshall, who knew Judd well during the ten years in which the latter was active in Hawaiian political life, described him as "a man of indomitable courage, unusual ability, and unflinching devotion to his sovereign." Marshall, "An Unpublished Chapter of Hawaiian History," in *Harper's Magazine,* LXVII (September 1883), 513.

spite of his inexperience in the difficult profession of statecraft, he was on the threshold of one of the most important, but stormy, political careers in the entire history of the Islands.

The first problem which faced Judd after his entrance into public life was the creation of an adequate financial system for the government. A complete lack of organization had hitherto prevailed; no accounts had been kept; debts had been carelessly contracted without any thought of providing for their ultimate payment; and there was no systematized control of the expenditure of the money received from taxation.[93] There was a large national debt, the amount of which has been variously estimated at from $45,000 to $160,000.[94] The introduction of an orderly routine in the nation's fiscal affairs and strenuous efforts to wipe out the national debt were the first problems to absorb the attention of the new Treasury Board. In September 1842 Judd believed that if the French government returned the $20,000 taken by Laplace the debt could be discharged within two years without the necessity of resorting to further loans.[95] Additional taxes, however, were deemed necessary. Judd had been in office less than ten days when it was announced that a three per cent duty would be charged upon all imports and that a similar tax would be levied upon all money exported from the Islands.[96] Within nine months, according to Judd, the new Treasury Board had "so far arranged the finances as to have regular books of accounts, a regular system of receiving the taxes in produce, and converting them into money; . . . . paid the most pressing debts, and had cash enough in the chest to establish

[93] *Report of the Minister of Finance,* 1851, p. 12; Jarves, *History of the Hawaiian Islands,* p. 174. The principal tax levied in the Islands prior to the advent of Judd was a poll tax, payable either in money or in certain acceptable products of the soil. Port charges and fines added to the income of the government. Newburgh, "A Narrative of Voyage &c," in AH, F.O. & Ex. Frederick D. Bennett (*Narrative of a Whaling Voyage Round the Globe,* I, 397–398) noted that the American and English residents of the Islands hesitated about complying with the requirement that they pay a poll tax but that after some complaint they paid the required amount.

[94] In September 1842 Judd estimated that the total debt was about $45,000; but three

years later he recalled that at the time he had taken office there had been a public debt of $60,000, with public credit "at a low ebb." J. J. Jarves, who had access to many sources of information, placed the total debt, in 1842, at $160,000, although it is possible that this large figure may have been a printer's error. Judd to Richards, Honolulu, September 16, 1842, in AH, F.O. and Ex.; *Report of the Minister of Finance,* 1845; Jarves, *History of the Hawaiian Islands,* p. 203.

[95] Judd to Richards, Honolulu, September 16, 1842, in AH, F.O. and Ex.

[96] Journal of Stephen Reynolds, May 20, 1842; Robert G. Davis to Larkin, Oahu, May 27, 1842, in Larkin MSS, I, No. 277.

a pretty good credit for the Government."[97] That the achievements of Judd in reorganizing the confused finances of the little kingdom had been substantial and valuable was conceded by men who in other respects were among the bitterest critics of his policies.[98]

Judd had been invited to enter the government to assist in the reorganization of the national finances. The principal part of his energies soon were diverted from the problems of finance to those of diplomacy. This situation arose in part from the activities of French naval commanders in the Pacific. The occupation of the Marquesas Islands by France, in July 1842, was an event which could be regarded only with alarm by friends of the Hawaiian government, for it was tangible evidence that France had colonial ambitions in the Pacific and an unpleasant reminder that relations between France and the Hawaiian government were less than cordial.

The chief source of embarrassment in Franco-Hawaiian relations arose from the belief of Catholics that the Hawaiian authorities had not observed in good faith the treaty stipulations that Catholic missionaries should be accorded privileges equal to those granted to the American missionaries. To Catholics the equality of treatment guaranteed by the Laplace treaty involved more than the unrestricted right to propagate their faith; it meant that they must be granted all favors given to their Protestant rivals, and especially that their schools must be placed upon a basis of real equality with the schools established by the American mission.

Following the enactment of the school law of October 1840, there were complaints from the priests that the new system gave an undue advantage to the American missionaries,[99] and the French consular agent protested that the law constituted a violation of the treaty negotiated by Laplace.[100] Two months later, in February 1841, Dudoit was still "calling frequently" upon Governor Kekuanaoa, reiterating these protests and warning the governor that a failure to adjust the

[97] Judd to Wyllie, Honolulu, February 17, 1860, in Judd, *Honolulu*, p. 193.

[98] For example, see *Sandwich Island News*, December 23, 1846.

[99] Yzendoorn, *History of the Catholic Mission in Hawaii*, pp. 157–160.

Apparently the principal source of contention was the selection of teachers, in which the American mission had a distinct advantage, inasmuch as it had trained nearly all of the natives likely to be judged eligible for the necessary license.

[100] Journal of Levi Chamberlain, December 15, 1840.

grievances of the Catholic mission would result in another visit to the Islands by a French man-of-war.[101] Although the school law was revised in the hope of conciliating the Catholic missionaries, there continued to be reports that they and their converts were openly boasting of their indifference to the Hawaiian authorities and of their expectation that they would be supported in this stand by the French government.[102]

It was with reason, therefore, that Governor Kekuanaoa was worried when the report reached Honolulu, early in August 1842, that the commander of a French man-of-war had taken possession of the Marquesas Islands.[103] He had additional cause for concern, later in the same month, when the French sloop, "Embuscade," dropped anchor at Honolulu without firing the usual salute of courtesy. The commander of the "Embuscade," Captain Mallet, quickly called upon Kekuanaoa and informed him that he proposed to investigate alleged violations by the government of the Laplace treaties.[104] The governor denied that there had been any such violations, but Mallet was not convinced. A week later he addressed a letter to the King submitting seven demands which, if accepted, were expected to improve the position of the Catholic mission and to prevent attempts to limit the importation or sale in the Islands of French wines.[105] Three days later, on September 4, the King and the *Kuhina Nui* replied that they were sincere in their efforts to treat the rival faiths impartially, that they had not sought to circumvent the liquor clause of the Laplace treaty, and that they had sent a commission to France to adjust the pending

[101] *Ibid.*, February 10, 1841. In these complaints, Dudoit was joined by Charlton, although it is not apparent that any British interests were menaced by the school law.

[102] Lorenzo Lyons to the American Board, September 13, 1841, in *Missionary Herald*, XXXVIII (June 1842), 245; John D. Paris to the American Board, April 28, 1843, in *ibid.*, XL (February 1844), 47–48; J. S. Emerson to the American Board, June 15, 1841, in *ibid.*, XXXVIII (June 1842), 246; Armstrong to Anderson, Honolulu, September 23, 1841, in Letters to the American Board, CXXXVI, No. 80; Lowell Smith to Anderson, Honolulu, November 24, 1841, in *ibid.*, CXXXVII, No. 25.

[103] Journal of Stephen Reynolds, August 8, 1842.

[104] Haalilio and Richards to Guizot, Paris, January 10, 1844 (copy), in AH, F.O. and Ex.; Yzendoorn, *History of the Catholic Mission in Hawaii*, p. 165.

[105] Mallet to Kamehameha III, Honolulu, September 1, 1842, in AH, F.O. and Ex. This note may also be found in Jarves, *History of the Hawaiian Islands*, pp. 165–166, and in Bingham, *Sandwich Islands*, pp. 590–591. Levi Chamberlain described Mallet's demands as being principally "of a frivolous nature." Journal of Levi Chamberlain, September 2, 1842.

difficulties. Having received these assurances, Mallet decided not to press his demands further, and shortly thereafter he left Honolulu.[106] In this manner the visit of the "Embuscade," which for a few days had appeared to menace the continued independence of the Islands, ended without serious incident. There were persons in Honolulu and in France, however, who believed that had the occasion been more propitious, Mallet would have taken possession of the Islands. Only the fact that the King already had sent a commission to Europe to settle outstanding difficulties, they believed, prevented Mallet from making an effort to add the Hawaiian Islands to the colonial empire of France.[107] The little kingdom had survived one threat to its continued independence; whether it would be equally fortunate in the future was far from certain. The dangers which beset the government in its foreign relations were recognized by residents and visitors, and two well-informed missionaries in Honolulu believed that only forbearance or even the active support of the great powers could perpetuate an independent Hawaiian kingdom.[108]

Mallet sailed from Honolulu on September 8, 1842. Before the close of the month the mysterious departure from Honolulu of Richard Charlton added to the growing feeling of tension and insecurity in the community. It had been generally known that Alexander Simpson had engaged passage to Mexico on the "Maryland." When Charlton and Simpson boarded that vessel, on September 26, those who observed the event assumed that the British consul had accompanied

106 Kamehameha III and Kekauluohi to Mallet, Honolulu, September 4, 1842, in AH, F.O. and Ex., and printed in Jarves, *History of the Hawaiian Islands*, p. 166; Bingham, *Sandwich Islands*, pp. 591–592. Friction between Protestants and Catholics in the Islands was not eliminated by the visit of Mallet. Less than two weeks after the departure of the "Embuscade" Father Hurlet wrote that church and school buildings belonging to the Catholic mission had been burned, that native Catholics had been attacked and driven from their land, presumably by Protestants, and that local magistrates had failed to extend to them a reasonable protection. Father Desvault reported that "the ship having once departed, the arbitrary conduct recommenced . . . . at the end of the year 1842, the scholars of Mr. Maigret were put in irons . . . . and to release themselves from prison, they had to pay double tax." Desvault also complained that it was impossible for a native Catholic to secure the diploma required of teachers. Hurlet to Kamehameha III, Kailua, September 20, 1842, in AH, F.O. and Ex.; Letter of the Rev. Father Desvault, Oahu, December 29, 1843, in *Annals of the Propagation of the Faith*, VI (1845), 104.

107 Richards to Judd, Paris, December 28, 1843, in AH, F.O. and Ex.; Judd, *Honolulu*, p. 91; S. N. Castle in *Hawaiian Star*, June 13, 1893.

108 Chamberlain to Anderson, Honolulu, February 21–March 7, 1843, in Letters to the American Board, CXXXV, No. 157; Armstrong to Reuben Chapman, Honolulu, September 22, 1842, in Armstrong MSS.

his friend only to bid him farewell. To their surprise, it was Simpson rather than Charlton who returned to shore after the "Maryland" sailed from the harbor.[109] The secrecy with which Charlton had cloaked his plans boded ill for the Hawaiian government. The chiefs found further cause for concern in the tone of the letter in which Charlton explained to the King his purposes in leaving the Islands. In that letter Charlton declared that "the insults" he had received at the hands of the Hawaiian government, together with "other weighty causes affecting the Interests" of British subjects at the Islands, had prompted him to return to England. To this was appended the ominous warning that the British government would not be indifferent to the ill-treatment which had been accorded its consul, and that justice, although tardy, would ultimately redress those grievances.[110] So belligerent was the tenor of this communication, that the Earl of Aberdeen rebuked Charlton, asserting that the letter was intemperate, improper, and deserving of "severe censure."[111]

The manner of Charlton's departure gave rise to rumors and speculations as to his purpose. Explanations came from various sources and were numerous. None could be regarded as authoritative; more than one was plausible. There was a report, attributed to Charlton, that he was going home to inform his government of the danger that the Hawaiian Islands would be seized by France.[112] Alexander Simpson explained the decision of his friend with the simple statement that the situation in the Islands had become so unfavorable to British interests that it was imperative for Charlton to present in person to the Foreign Office his version of recent events at Honolulu.[113] Simpson added that Charlton hoped to counteract the possible influence in London of the mission of Richards and Haalilio.[114] Others

[109] Jarves, "The Sandwich or Hawaiian Islands," in *Merchants' Magazine*, IX, (August 1843), 127.

Charlton later defended the secrecy of his departure by asserting that he had been unable to secure passage on the "Maryland" in his own name. This, he thought, resulted from the desire of Americans at Honolulu to prevent him from going to London, where he would be certain to promote British interests in the Islands. Charlton to Aberdeen, London, March 13, 1843, in *Correspondence Relative to the Sandwich Islands*, pp. 173–174.

[110] Charlton to Kamehameha III, Oahu, September 26, 1842, in AH, F.O. and Ex., and printed in *Correspondence Relative to the Sandwich Islands*, p. 158.

[111] Aberdeen to Charlton, [London], March 9, 1843, in *ibid.*, p. 173.

[112] Letter of Lieutenant L. M. Powell, U.S.N., Havana, January 2, 1843, quoted in W. M. Crane to Secretary of the Navy Upshur, January 19, 1843, in USDS, "Miscellaneous Letters."

[113] Simpson, *Sandwich Islands*, p. 7.

[114] *Ibid.*, p. 58.

in Honolulu shared a widely held suspicion that the true motive of Charlton was to urge his government to take possession of the Islands.[115] In any event, the Hawaiian authorities had no reason to anticipate that the results of his visit to England would be favorable to them.

The last official act of Charlton before leaving the Islands was the designation of Alexander Simpson as acting British consul. Simpson was no stranger in the Islands. He had been in Honolulu for brief visits, varying in length from two weeks to two months, in 1839, in the summer of 1840, and in January 1841.[116] He returned to the Islands for a fourth time early in 1842, and he had been in Honolulu for more than six months at the time of his appointment to the consulate. The Hawaiian authorities were officially apprised of the appointment of Simpson in a letter written by the latter two days after Charlton left Honolulu.[117] Although Simpson later asserted that he had established "the most friendly" relations with the King and chiefs,[118] the government refused to recognize him in an official capacity.[119] Simpson believed that Dr. Judd had been responsible for this decision[120]—a reasonable assumption in view of the undoubted influence of Judd in the councils of the chiefs. Simpson, however, was not without blame in this unpleasant affair, and Judd explained that it was impossible to accept him as acting consul because of his known hostility to the government and because of his "difficulties" with other foreigners at Honolulu.[121]

[115] Journal of Stephen Reynolds, September 27, 1842; R. G. Davis to W. H. Davis, Oahu, October 31–November 3, 1842, in Davis MSS; Judd to George Simpson and William Richards, Honolulu, October 18, 1842, in *Correspondence Relative to the Sandwich Islands*, p. 161; Marshall, "An Unpublished Chapter of Hawaiian History," in *Harper's Magazine*, LXVII (September 1883), 511; William Hooper to Secretary of State Webster, Oahu, October 10, 1842, in USDS, "Consular Letters," Honolulu, I. Hooper, who was acting commercial agent of the United States, wrote, "If the British Government act on the representations of its Consul . . . . it may be reasonably expected that these Islands will soon be under British rule."

[116] Simpson, *Sandwich Islands*, p. 50;

Simpson, *Life of Thomas Simpson*, pp. 352–353; *Polynesian*, June 27, July 18, 1840, January 9, 23, 1841.

[117] Simpson to Kamehameha III, Oahu, September 28, 1842, in AH, F.O. and Ex.

[118] Simpson, *Sandwich Islands*, p. 58.

[119] Kekuanaoa to Simpson, Honolulu, September 30, 1842, in AH, F.O. and Ex.

[120] Simpson to Aberdeen, Oahu, October 1, 1842, in *Correspondence Relative to the Sandwich Islands*, p. 157; Simpson, *Sandwich Islands*, p. 59.

[121] Judd to Richards, Honolulu, October 27, 1842, in Letters to the American Board, CXXXVII, No. 87. See also Chamberlain to Anderson, Honolulu, February 21, 1843, in *ibid.*, CXXXV, No. 157; George Pelly to Sir George Simpson, Hono-

If the Hawaiian rulers had been able to fathom the thoughts of Simpson they would have found added cause to fear his influence. At the time he was appointed acting consul he already had come to the conclusion that the King and chiefs were "quite unfit to decide upon any case of importance" and that the real powers of government were lodged in men who were inimical to British subjects and to British interests at the Islands. At the same time he asserted that only the presence at Honolulu of a British man-of-war could make the protests of a British consul really effective.[122] Six weeks later he described the King as "quite a cypher," and declared that Governor Kekuanaoa was "a man of violent passions" who was under the influence of Dr. Judd, "an American of bad character and strong anti-English prejudices."[123] More dangerous to the Hawaiian government, however, were the political ambitions harbored by Simpson. Thomas J. Farnham, who became acquainted with Simpson during a voyage from Oregon to Honolulu in 1839, described him as a young man of considerable energy, who was well informed and, "like most other British subjects abroad, troubled with an irrepressible anxiety at the growing power of the States, and an overwhelming loyalty toward the mother country."[124] His devotion to his country soon manifested itself in a desire to enlarge the British empire through the addition to it of the most valuable archipelago in the mid-Pacific.[125] Early in 1844, when it was evident that this ambition was not to be realized, Simpson frankly confessed that he was "somewhat crossed, by the failure of a measure to accomplish which I had made large

lulu, March 13, 1843, in *Correspondence Relative to the Sandwich Islands*, p. 236.

An official statement of the position of the government, written in March 1843, contained an elaboration of this explanation. In it Simpson was described as "a known and declared enemy of our Government, who had openly insulted the chief magistrate of this island [Governor Kekuanaoa of Oahu] and other high officers of our appointment, who had publicly threatened to involve us in difficulties, and whose recognition as consular agent was protested against by two British subjects who represented the chief commercial interests in these islands." Kamehameha III to President Tyler, Honolulu, March 10, 1843, in

FRUS, 1894, Appendix II, p. 53. The two prominent British subjects were the agents of the Hudson's Bay Company. See George Pelly and George Allan to Kekuanaoa, Honolulu, September 30, 1842, in AH, F.O. and Ex.

[122] Simpson and Henry Skinner to Aberdeen, Honolulu, September 24, 1842, in *Correspondence Relative to the Sandwich Islands*, pp. 141–142.

[123] Simpson to Sir John Barrow, Oahu, November 1, 1842, in *ibid.*, pp. 200–201.

[124] Farnham, *Life, Adventures, and Travels in California*, p. 8.

[125] Simpson, *Sandwich Islands*, p. 51.

sacrifices, and devoted much time and labour—the annexation of the Sandwich Islands to the British Crown."[126]

Simpson may have been surprised by the refusal of the King to recognize him as British consul, but he had no intention of retreating. On October 1 he informed the authorities that they had no alternative other than a recognition of his position;[127] when this failed to produce results, he issued a formal protest against all actions of the government which might involve the interests of British subjects.[128] For four months Simpson continued to exercise such consular functions as did not require the active co-operation or approval of the Hawaiian government; but there is no indication that the King's advisers abandoned their position long enough to give respectful attention to the notes in which Simpson complained of real or imagined grievances suffered by British subjects.

New complications had been injected meanwhile into the conflict between British residents and the government. Soon after Charlton departed for London, the government permitted George Pelly to prosecute a suit against the absent consul for the recovery of a debt alleged to be due a firm in Valparaiso. Despite the protests of Mrs. Charlton, a jury composed largely of American residents decided in favor of Pelly, and the government seized Charlton's property in order to assure the enforcement of the judgment. No sale was made, but Simpson was supplied with an issue which neither the government in London nor the commander of a British man-of-war was likely to ignore.[129] Two months later, early in December, the long and acri-

[126] Simpson to Barrow, February 3, 1844, in Simpson, *Life of Thomas Simpson*, p. 386.

[127] Simpson to Kekuanaoa, Oahu, October 1, 1842, in AH, F.O. and Ex.

[128] A copy of this protest, dated October 10, 1842, may be found in *ibid*.

[129] The documents relating to the trial and subsequent attachment of Charlton's property may be found in *Correspondence Relative to the Sandwich Islands*, pp. 214–218, 280–297.

Shortly after the conclusion of the trial, Simpson called a meeting of British subjects at Honolulu. Approximately fifty of his countrymen responded to this call. In

a series of resolutions they expressed their confidence in Simpson, declared that the Hawaiian courts had no right to adjudicate the question of Charlton's alleged indebtedness to a firm in Valparaiso, and asserted that the attachment of his property constituted an insult to Great Britain and its sovereign. A manuscript copy of these resolutions may be found in AH, F.O. and Ex. Simpson later declared that the only dissenters at the meeting had been persons sent by the agents of the Hudson's Bay Company, who, he asserted, "made common cause" with friends of the Hawaiian government. Simpson, *Sandwich Islands*, p. 61.

It was not strange that Pelly, one of the

monious litigation which had followed the bankruptcy of Francis J. Greenway, a British subject, was climaxed by the seizure and sale of Greenway's property in order to satisfy the insistent creditors, most of whom were American merchants resident in Honolulu.[130] This action was protested vigorously by Simpson;[131] and Simpson and Henry Skinner, who once had been the co-assignees of Greenway's

agents of the company, should have dissented from resolutions attacking his suit against Charlton. He and his associate, George Allan, were already on record as disapproving the manner in which Charlton left Honolulu and the appointment of Simpson as acting British consul. Pelly and Allan to Kekuanaoa, Honolulu, September 30, 1842, in AH, F.O. and Ex.

[130] Greenway announced his bankrupt condition in April 1842. At a meeting of the creditors, marked by "much wrangling and harsh language," Simpson, Henry Skinner, and Stephen Reynolds were chosen as assignees of Greenway's property. The situation became more complicated when William French, who was believed to be indebted to Greenway, announced that he had been a silent partner of Greenway and was prepared to assume the latter's obligations. When this offer was refused, French declared himself bankrupt and assigned his property to Reynolds and William Ladd. Simpson and Skinner thereupon ejected Reynolds from further participation in the settlement of Greenway's difficulties, and then brought suit to collect the amount which they claimed was owed Greenway by French. They refused to submit their case to a jury trial, presumably fearing that the jury would be composed largely of Americans; and when Governor Kekuanaoa insisted that a jury trial was required by Hawaiian law, they withdrew the suit. After a threat to appeal to the British government and other efforts at intimidation had failed to move the governor, Simpson and Skinner proceeded to divide Greenway's remaining assets among the creditors. Uncharitable critics believed that the apportionment of the assets unduly favored friends of the assignees at the expense of some of the most influential of the American merchants.

The case again appeared in court when Reynolds sued to recover a share of Greenway's property. Skinner and Simpson declined to appear, and a decision against them was rendered in default. The governor then invited the litigants to meet him privately, assuring them that the conference would be "conducted with good feeling" and with "protection to all parties." Neither Simpson nor Skinner attended. Other merchants, including the French consul, joined Reynolds in declaring that they had been the victims of discrimination in the distribution of Greenway's assets. To satisfy those insistent creditors Governor Kekuanaoa finally ordered the estate of Greenway seized and sold at auction. Journal of William Paty, April 7, 22, 23, 29, 1842; Pelly to George Simpson, Honolulu, March 13, 1843, in *Correspondence Relative to the Sandwich Islands*, p. 236; Simpson and Skinner to Kekuanaoa, Honolulu, August 29, 1842, in AH, F.O. and Ex.; Statement of G. P. Judd, September 20, 1842, in *ibid.*; Statement of William Paty, in *ibid.*; Statement of Kekuanaoa, November 20, 1842, in *ibid.*; Statement of Jules Dudoit, March 8, 1843, in *ibid.*; Simpson and Skinner to Grimes and Paty, Honolulu, September 15, 1842, in *ibid.*; Kekuanaoa to Simpson and Skinner, Honolulu, September 22, 1842, in *ibid.*; E. and H. Grimes to Kekuanaoa, Honolulu, November 24, 1842, in *ibid.*; Dudoit to Kekuanaoa, Honolulu, November 28, 1842, in *ibid.*; Journal of Stephen Reynolds, November 26, December 2, 1842. Pelly reported that Simpson and Skinner had treated the local officials "with every mark of obloquy and contempt."

[131] Simpson and Skinner to Kekuanaoa, Honolulu, November 26, 1842, in AH, F.O. and Ex.; Simpson to Kekuanaoa, Honolulu, November 26, 1842, in *ibid.*

property, were reported to have used force in an effort to prevent the seizure of the estate.[132]

The decisions of the Hawaiian court in the case of Pelly *v.* Charlton and in the suit brought by the creditors of Greenway widened still further the breach between American citizens and British subjects at the Islands. They seemed to confirm the belief of British residents that the Hawaiian courts would deal more generously with American litigants than with nationals of Great Britain—a belief which was shared by Charlton and Alexander Simpson. In London, Charlton informed the Foreign Office that the conduct of the Hawaiian government in the settlement of Greenway's affairs had been "so unjust and flagrant" as to leave little doubt that there was "a deep-laid scheme on the part of the Americans, through the aid of the Sandwich Islands Government, not only to deprive the British residents of their property, but also to annihilate our infant, but growing commerce."[133] The seizure of Charlton's property, in October 1842, precipitated a more serious chain of events; and Pelly reported that Simpson had gathered some of "the dregs of the community" in an effort to prevent the attachment of the property.[134] More significant was the appeal of Simpson to the commander of the British fleet in the Pacific. With this appeal, Simpson forwarded documents designed to prove "the urgent necessity" of a visit to Honolulu by a British man-of-war, not only to secure "full recompense for past injuries and insults" but to remain at Honolulu as long as might be required to protect British interests at the Islands.[135] In quite a different vein, the acting commercial agent of the United States assured his government that the Hawaiian rulers had exhibited "the most friendly feeling" toward citizens of the United States.[136]

On January 17, 1843, Admiral Richard Thomas responded to the appeal from Simpson by ordering Lord George Paulet, the commander of the "Carysfort," to proceed at once to Honolulu, where he was to communicate with Simpson and to assist him "in watching

[132] Statement of Joseph Slater, Honolulu, November 29, 1842, in *ibid.*

[133] Charlton to Aberdeen, London, February 10, 1843, in *Correspondence Relative to the Sandwich Islands*, pp. 133–136.

[134] Pelly to George Simpson, Honolulu, November 2, 1842, in *ibid.*, pp. 163–164.

[135] Simpson to Admiral Richard Thomas, Oahu, October 29, 1842, in *ibid.*, pp. 167–168.

[136] William Hooper to Secretary of State Webster, Oahu, December 31, 1842, in USDS, "Consular Letters," Honolulu, I.

over and protecting the interests of British subjects."[137] On the following day Thomas forwarded to Paulet a letter describing the proceedings and result of the suit of Pelly *v.* Charlton, with the comment that the action of the court had been without justification. Paulet was therefore instructed to make a peremptory demand for the immediate restitution of Charlton's property.[138] In sending a naval officer to Honolulu, Thomas was belatedly carrying out instructions from the Admiralty to dispatch one of his vessels to the Islands to inquire into grievances reported by Charlton and if need be to protect British nationals there.[139] The policy outlined in these instructions represented the views of the Foreign Office as well as of the Admiralty. The concern of the Foreign Office was confined to the protection of the property of British nationals at the Hawaiian Islands; it did not involve political ambitions. This was indicated in October 1842 when the Foreign Office recommended that British men-of-war maintain "a more frequent intercourse" with those islands. By this means, Aberdeen hoped "to maintain the just influence of Great Britain" in the Pacific and to counteract the efforts of other powers to gain "a dominant authority" in that ocean. This suggestion was accompanied by the admonition that British naval officers should treat the rulers "with great forbearance and courtesy" and should not "interfere harshly or unnecessarily with the laws and customs" of the native government. Finally the instructions declared that the Foreign Office harbored no territorial ambitions in that part of the world and wished only that no other power "should exercise a greater degree of influence" than that enjoyed by Great Britain.[140] This statement of policy

---

[137] Thomas to Paulet, San Blas, January 17, 1843, in *Correspondence Relative to the Sandwich Islands*, p. 199.

[138] Thomas to Paulet, San Blas, January 18, 1843, in *ibid.*, p. 200.

[139] Sir John Barrow to Thomas, [London], August 21, 1841, in *ibid.*, p. 81. On his way to London, Charlton had stopped for about two weeks at Mazatlan, where he talked with Admiral Thomas and other officers of the British squadron. It is unlikely that he lost that opportunity to criticize the Hawaiian government or to charge it with discriminating against British subjects. Judd to Richards, Honolulu, February 27, 1843, in AH, "British Commission Documents"; Marshall, "An Unpublished Chapter of Hawaiian History," in *Harper's Magazine*, LXVII (September 1883), 512; *The Friend*, January 1, 1858, p. 5.

[140] Viscount Canning to Sir John Barrow, October 4, 1842, in Hawaiian Historical Commission, *Publications*, I, No. 2, pp. 34–36, and in *Correspondence Relative to the Sandwich Islands*, pp. 128–129. A similar policy is indicated in the instructions of Aberdeen to Charlton, December 1, 1842, in *ibid.*, p. 130.

was unknown to Thomas and Paulet when the latter left the coast of Mexico for the Hawaiian Islands.[141]

The "Carysfort" arrived at Honolulu on February 10, 1843. It did not fire the usual salute upon arrival, and the only visitor to the vessel that day was Alexander Simpson.[142] On the following day Paulet was visited by the local representatives of the United States and France, by Dr. Judd, and by "many of the residents." They met with "a very cool if not insulting reception,"[143] and Dr. Judd was informed that no representatives of the Hawaiian government would be received until the grievances of British subjects had been redressed.[144] That section of the foreign community which had sympathized with Charlton and Simpson hoped that the visit of the "Carysfort" would bring an end to the domination of the Hawaiian government by Americans.[145] This enthusiasm was temporarily dimmed by the arrival, on February 13, of the U.S.S. "Boston." Americans on Oahu hailed the visit of the "Boston" as most opportune;[146] and, on February 14, "upwards of thirty of the most respectable residents," principally Americans, visited the vessel and were greeted by Captain Long with "the utmost cordiality and kindness."[147] On the same day, Paulet went ashore. In what may have been an effort to conciliate Americans at Honolulu, he called upon two prominent merchants, J. O. Carter and Charles Brewer. Carter was not at home, and Brewer was reported to have received Paulet with only scant courtesy.[148] On the following day, February 15, Paulet again went ashore. He made "a long call" at the home of one of the missionary families, and visited the mission press and the school for

[141] Kuykendall, *The Hawaiian Kingdom*, p. 212.

[142] Simpson, *Sandwich Islands*, pp. 74–75; "History of the Provisional Cession of the Hawaiian Islands and Their Restoration," in *Hawaiian Almanac and Annual*, 1893, p. 46; Letter signed R. D. G., Honolulu, February 27, 1843, in *Niles' Register*, LXIV (June 24, 1843), 258.

[143] Journal of William Paty, February 11, 1843; Journal of Stephen Reynolds, February 11, 1843; Journal of Levi Chamberlain, February 11, 1843. Chamberlain noted that because of the cool reception accorded to the representatives of France and the United States, American and French vessels at Ho-

nolulu lowered the flags which they had raised earlier as a mark of courtesy to the "Carysfort."

[144] Judd to Richards, Honolulu, February 27, 1843, in AH, "British Commission Documents."

[145] Journal of Stephen Reynolds, February 12, 1843.

[146] Journal of William Paty, February 13, 1843; Journal of Mrs. Gorham Nye, February 15, 1843.

[147] Journal of William Paty, February 14, 1843.

[148] *Ibid.*; Journal of Stephen Reynolds, February 14, 1843.

young chiefs conducted by Mr. and Mrs. Amos Cooke.[149] Other American families were slighted by Paulet, with the result that the feeling between American and British residents of Honolulu could be conservatively described as "far from agreeable."[150]

Further evidence of the sympathies of American residents was provided when "nearly all the respectable Americans" in Honolulu gathered at the wharf, on February 16, to greet the King upon his return from Lahaina.[151] Paulet was not present, and he confined his welcome to a brusque note in which he demanded a private interview with the King.[152] In reply, the latter declined to receive Paulet privately and suggested that Paulet either submit his communication in writing or confer with Dr. Judd.[153] This rebuff brought an immediate response from Paulet, who forwarded to the King a list of six specific proposals for the redress of injuries suffered by British subjects or for the better protection of British interests in the future. Accompanying this list was a threat to take "immediate coercive steps" if the proposals were not accepted by four o'clock on the following afternoon.[154] In a note to Captain Long, Paulet defined these coercive measures as "an immediate attack" upon Honolulu.[155]

[149] Armstrong to Anderson, Honolulu, February 14–16, 1843, in Letters to the American Board, CXXXVI, No. 95. The missionaries had already called upon Paulet on board the "Carysfort," where they had been politely received. Journal of Levi Chamberlain, February 14, 1843.

[150] Chamberlain to Anderson, Honolulu, February 21, 1843, in Letters to the American Board, CXXXV, No. 157.

[151] Journal of William Paty, February 17, 1843.

[152] Paulet to Kamehameha III, Honolulu, February 16, 1843, in AH, "British Commission Documents." The documents which passed between Paulet and the Hawaiian government may be found in *British and Foreign State Papers*, XXXI, 1023–1029; *Merchants' Magazine*, IX (August 1843), 128–131; *Niles' Register*, LXIV (June 10, 1843), 238–239; Bingham, *Sandwich Islands*, pp. 593–597; Jarves, *History of the Hawaiian Islands*, pp. 176–177, 181–182; *Missionary Herald*, XXXIX (July 1843), 291–294; Dibble, *History of the Sandwich Islands*, pp. 388–396; FRUS, 1894, Appendix II, pp. 47–52.

[153] Kamehameha III and Kekauluohi to Paulet, Honolulu, February 17, 1843, in AH, "British Commission Documents." Simpson believed that the refusal to grant an interview to Paulet was the result of advice given by "some half dozen American shopkeepers." Simpson, *Sandwich Islands*, p. 78.

[154] Paulet to Kamehameha III, Oahu, February 17, 1843, in AH, "British Commission Documents." Prominent Americans at Honolulu professed to believe that Paulet's demands were without justification. See Hooper to Webster, Oahu, March 7, 1843, in FRUS, 1894, Appendix II, pp. 45–46; Journal of William Paty, February 18, 1843; Letter from a Young Gentleman in the United States Naval Service, Oahu, March 6, 1843, in *New Orleans Bulletin*, May 24, 1843, and quoted in *Niles' Register*, LXIV (June 10, 1843), 237–238.

[155] Paulet to Long, Oahu, February 17, 1843, in FRUS, 1894, Appendix II, p. 50. Alexander Simpson (*Sandwich Islands*, p. 82) justified the threat to bombard Honolulu on the ground that the firing of a single shot from the "Carysfort" would

Throughout the morning of February 18 the foreign community was gripped with excitement and alarm,[156] which was relieved only when it became known that the King had accepted the proposals submitted by Paulet.[157] An outward semblance of good will was thereby restored,[158] but one well-informed observer shrewdly predicted that the concessions would lead to "an endless succession of difficulties and sacrifices, many of them deeply interesting to Americans and other foreign residents" in the Islands.[159]

The sequel followed quickly. With the King and his advisers obviously overawed by the presence of the "Carysfort," Simpson took advantage of the opportunity to present further demands involving a variety of grievances alleged to have been suffered by British subjects at the Islands.[160] In some instances these demands were so exacting as to imperil the solvency of the government or to furnish cause for protests from the United States or France. In this crisis several interested observers, including the representatives of the United States and France, suggested a joint Franco-American protectorate of the Islands as an alternative to further concessions to Paulet and Simpson. On the evening of February 23, Judd, Captain Long, Jules Dudoit, and William Hooper met to discuss this proposal. Before adjourning, they had agreed in principle and had prepared the necessary documents. By the following morning, however, Judd had lost enthusiasm for the proposed protectorate, and he refused to advise the King to sign the documents which a few hours earlier he had helped to prepare. In thus shifting his position, Judd may have been influenced by the known views of his former colleagues in the mission.

---

have sufficed to disperse any force which might have attempted to prevent the landing of troops from the vessel.

[156] Journal of William Paty, February 18, 1843; Journal of Stephen Reynolds, February 18, 1843; Journal of Levi Chamberlain, February 20, 1843; Letter signed R. D. G., Honolulu, February 27, 1843, in *Niles' Register*, LXIV (June 24, 1843), 258–259.

[157] Kamehameha III and Kekauluohi to Paulet, Honolulu, February 18, 1843, in AH, "British Commission Documents"; William Hooper to Captain Lawrence Kearny, Oahu, July 11, 1843 (copy), in

NRL, "China Station, Commodore Kearny," enclosure in No. 56.

[158] Judd to Richards, Honolulu, February 27, 1843, in AH, "British Commission Documents."

[159] Journal of William Paty, February 18, 1843.

[160] Simpson to Aberdeen, Oahu, February 25, 1843, in *Correspondence Relative to the Sandwich Islands*, pp. 211–213; Judd to Richards, Honolulu, February 27, 1843, in AH, "British Commission Documents"; Kekuanaoa to Haalilio, Honolulu, March 6, 1843, in AH, F.O. and Ex.

Like them, presumably, he realized that it was improbable that the United States would be willing to become a party to a joint protectorate and that a request for intervention by France and the United States might result in the dominance of France in the Hawaiian Islands. Such an eventuality, the missionaries believed, would be "disasterous in the extreme" to the influence and program of the American mission.[161] To that possibility Judd could not be indifferent.

The menace of French control was avoided by a measure which could be explained only by the desperate situation of the native monarchy. On the morning of February 24, after the proposal to seek a Franco-American protectorate had been rejected, the King and Judd informed Paulet that they had determined to avoid further controversy by making a provisional cession of the Islands to Great Britain. In reply, Paulet protested that he had not come to Honolulu to take possession of the Islands; but he did not refuse to accept the cession. Twenty-four hours later the temporary transfer of sovereignty to Great Britain was announced, and the Union Jack replaced the Hawaiian flag on public buildings in Honolulu.[162] By a curious

[161] Journal of Levi Chamberlain, February 24–25, 1843; Journal of Stephen Reynolds, February 24, 1843; Armstrong to Reuben Chapman, Honolulu, March 3, 1843, in Armstrong MSS; Chamberlain to Anderson, Honolulu, February 21–March 7, 1843, in Letters to the American Board, CXXXV, No. 157; Judd to Richards, Honolulu, February 27, 1843, in AH, "British Commission Documents"; Letter signed R. D. G., Honolulu, February 27, 1843, in *Niles' Register*, LXIV (June 24, 1843), 258–259.

A copy of the uncompleted deed, ceding the Islands to the United States and France, dated February 23, 1843, but unsigned, is in AH, F.O. and Ex. Stephen Reynolds thought that the King was prepared to sign the deed, but both Chamberlain and Armstrong implied that the King would have been unwilling to take an action which would result in French control of the Islands.

The missionaries were not alone in realizing that there was little chance the United States would participate in a joint protectorate and that the ultimate result of a request for a protectorate might be the establishment of French rule in the Islands. Nevertheless, the bitterness which had developed between British and American residents of Honolulu was so intense that many Americans in Honolulu would have preferred to see the Islands under the control of France if that were the only alternative to British rule. Judd to Richards, Honolulu, February 27, 1843, in AH, "British Commission Documents"; Letter signed R. D. G., Honolulu, February 27, 1843, in *Niles' Register*, LXIV (June 24, 1843), 258–259; Simpson, *Sandwich Islands*, p. 87.

[162] Judd to Richards, Honolulu, February 27, 1843, in AH, "British Commission Documents"; Kekuanaoa to Haalilio, March 6, 1843, in AH, F.O. and Ex.

The deed of cession and the accompanying documents are printed in many places, including FRUS, 1894, Appendix II, pp. 51–52; Bingham, *Sandwich Islands*, pp. 596–598, and Jarves, *History of the Hawaiian Islands*, pp. 181–182. That the King was not wholly subdued was indicated by a proclamation addressed to his former subjects on the day of the cession. In this proclamation, he declared: ". . . . I am in perplexity by reason of difficulties into

coincidence, this occurred on the forty-ninth anniversary of the cession of Hawaii by Kamehameha to Vancouver.

Alexander Simpson later asserted that it had been "the studied intention" of Judd to effect a permanent transfer of the Islands to Great Britain if France could not be persuaded to guarantee the independence of the Hawaiian kingdom.[163] It appears that Simpson took too simple a view of a complicated situation. Certainly a guaranty of Hawaiian independence by one or more of the great powers would have been welcomed by all friends of the native government, and it is probable that a majority of the advisers of the King would have preferred either American or British rule to that of France. Judd was seeking a solution of an immediate problem, and he hoped that the government of Great Britain would disavow the conduct of Paulet and would restore the full independence of the Islands.[164] This hope was implicit in the terms of the cession; for, in accepting a temporary sovereignty over the Islands, Paulet acknowledged that the future of the archipelago would be determined by the government in London, either unilaterally or in consultation with Richards and Haalilio. The apparent optimism of Judd was not shared by all Americans in the community, and Richard Armstrong reported that there seemed to be "very little hope" that Great Britain would relinquish control of the Islands.[165]

In reports to the government in London, Paulet and Simpson sought to explain the cession of the Islands as the product of Hawaiian

---

which I have been brought without cause; therefore, I have given away the life of our land . . . . But my rule over you, my people, and your privileges, will continue, for I have hope that the life of the land will be restored when my conduct is justified." Paulet was displeased by the tenor of the proclamation, displeasure which was increased when the proclamation was included in the printed copy of the correspondence leading to the cession. "British Commission Minute Book" (MS, Archives of Hawaii), p. 25 (March 3, 1843). The phrase "the life of the land" (*ke ea o ka aina*), used twice by the King at this time and repeated by him in a speech at the time of his restoration to power at the close of July 1843, became the foundation of the national motto: "The life of the land is preserved by righteousness" (*Ua mau ke ea o ka aina i ka pono*).

[163] Simpson to Aberdeen, London, August 11, 1843, in *Correspondence Relative to the Sandwich Islands*, p. 307.

[164] Judd to Richards, Honolulu, February 27, 1843, in AH, "British Commission Documents." After events had justified Judd's optimism and Hawaiian sovereignty had been restored by the British authorities, the provisional cession was hailed by both friend and critic as having been a brilliant stroke of statesmanship. *Polynesian*, April 12, 1845; R. C. Wyllie to John Ricord, Honolulu, May 13, 1859, in AH, "Miscellaneous Local and Foreign Correspondence."

[165] Armstrong to Reuben Chapman, Honolulu, March 3, 1843, in Armstrong MSS.

fears of French aggression. Paulet declared that the expectation that a French man-of-war would soon arrive to take forcible possession of the Islands was "the moving cause" in the decision of the King.[166] Simpson was less definite, being content with the observation that the King wished the protection afforded by a British naval vessel in order to thwart any hostile move by France.[167] To critics of Paulet and Simpson these post facto explanations were less than convincing.[168] There were well-informed persons in Honolulu, however, who did believe that the activity of French naval commanders south of the equator was the prelude to an effort to add the Hawaiian Islands to the growing colonial empire of France.[169] Similar fears disturbed British naval officers in the Pacific, if we may judge from their reports to the Admiralty.[170] At least two American missionaries gave some credence to the explanation that Paulet had accepted the cession of the Islands in order to forestall possible French aggression;[171] and during the following May, when it was reported that a French man-of-war would soon arrive at Honolulu, Levi Chamberlain noted that Paulet anticipated trouble and was making preparations "to meet

[166] Paulet to the Secretary of the Admiralty, Honolulu, March 9, 1843, in *Correspondence Relative to the Sandwich Islands*, p. 184.

[167] Simpson to Aberdeen, Oahu, February 25, 1843, in *ibid.*, p. 212.

[168] For example, see a communication to the *Boston Atlas*, reprinted in the *Globe* (Washington, D.C.), June 12, 1843. This letter evidently was written by someone who had been at Honolulu at the time of the cession; it may have been written by James F. B. Marshall, who left Honolulu in March and who was in Boston in June. The anonymous author declared that Paulet and Simpson "desired to have the impression go abroad . . . . that the King had petitioned Lord Paulet to take possession of the islands as he was in fear of France, and in trouble with his own subjects and with foreigners. This was a most barefaced falsehood."

[169] Journal of Levi Chamberlain, November 10, 1842; Hooper to Secretary of State Webster, Oahu, October 10, 1842, in USDS, "Consular Letters," Honolulu, I; Armstrong to David Greene, Honolulu, November 3–24, 1842, in Letters to the American Board,

CXXXVI, No. 92; Armstrong to Anderson, Honolulu, February 14–21, 1843, in *ibid.*, CXXXVI, No. 95; Horton Knapp to Anderson, Honolulu, March 10, 1843, in *ibid.*, CXXXVII, No. 157; Armstrong to Reuben Chapman, Honolulu, March 3, 1843, in Armstrong MSS; Letter signed R. D. G., Honolulu, February 27, 1843, in *Niles' Register*, LXIV (June 24, 1843), 258; Reynolds to Larkin, Oahu, December 5, 1842, in Larkin MSS, I, No. 383; R. G. Davis to W. H. Davis, Oahu, January 14, 1843, in Davis MSS.

[170] For permission to use copies of these reports, the present writer is indebted to the late Professor Ephraim Douglass Adams of Stanford University.

[171] Chamberlain to Anderson, Honolulu, February 21–March 7, 1843, in Letters to the American Board, CXXXV, No. 157; Castle to Anderson, Honolulu, April 17, 1843, in *ibid.*, CXXXVII, No. 142. For later statements of the same theory, see S. N. Castle, in *Hawaiian Star*, June 13, 1893; Taylor, *Under Hawaiian Skies*, pp. 339–340; Henry B. Restarick, in *Honolulu Star-Bulletin*, February 23, 1929, and January 18, 1930.

it."[172] The menace of French aggrandizement seemed to be real; it is probable that it provided Paulet and Simpson with an excuse rather than with a cause for accepting a provisional sovereignty over the Hawaiian Islands.

After the government of the Islands had been restored to the native rulers, Alexander Simpson recalled that an "overwhelming majority of the white residents" had been pleased by the accession of Paulet to power.[173] This judgment is open to serious question. Four days before the cession occurred, Richard Armstrong believed that the interests of American residents were "deeply involved" in the issue of the conflict between Paulet and the Hawaiian government.[174] Stephen Reynolds noted that many Americans had been "ignorant and foolish enough" to express openly and without reservation their disapproval of the new regime;[175] Levi Chamberlain reported that "the American party" was critical of Judd because he had declined to use his influence to secure the establishment of a Franco-American protectorate;[176] George Pelly declared that among the foreign residents there was "but one feeling of indignation and disgust" with the conduct of Paulet and Simpson;[177] and Richard Armstrong observed that many of his fellow countrymen feared that "American interests" at the Islands had been "ruined."[178] The agents of the Hudson's Bay Company expressed regret at the political change which had taken place, predicting that, should the Islands remain in the possession of Great Britain, "most, if not all the respectable American merchants and shipping" would abandon the Islands and thus inflict upon Hawaiian commerce a shock from which it could not soon recover.[179]

[172] Chamberlain to Anderson, Honolulu, May 3, 1843, in Letters to the American Board, CXXXV, No. 161.

[173] Simpson, *Sandwich Islands*, p. 105.

[174] Armstrong to Anderson, Honolulu, February 14–21, 1843, in Letters to the American Board, CXXXVI, No. 95.

[175] Journal of Stephen Reynolds, February 25, 1843.

[176] Journal of Levi Chamberlain, February 25, 1843. Simpson asserted that several American residents had urged the King to resist forcibly the demands made by Paulet. Simpson to Aberdeen, Oahu, February 25, 1843, in *Correspondence Relative to the Sandwich Islands*, p. 211.

[177] Pelly to Sir George Simpson, Honolulu, March 13, 1843, in *ibid.*, p. 238.

[178] Armstrong to Reuben Chapman, Honolulu, March 3, 1843, in Armstrong MSS. Cf. Letter signed R. D. G., Honolulu, February 27, 1843, in *Niles' Register*, LXIV (June 24, 1843), 259; Letter of Richard Armstrong, in *ibid.*, LXIV (July 1, 1843), 273; Armstrong to Anderson, Honolulu, March 2, 1843, in Letters to the American Board, CXXXVI, No. 96.

[179] Pelly and George Allan to Sir George Simpson, Honolulu, March 12, 1843, in *Correspondence Relative to the Sandwich Islands*, pp. 233–236.

The acting commercial agent of the United States, William Hooper, avoided an open break with Paulet, but he advised the King to have no official communication with the British commander or with any of the officers of the provisional government.[180] From Honolulu a petition, said to have been "numerously signed by American residents and other Americans," was sent to President Tyler, urging him to use the influence of the United States in an effort to persuade Great Britain to disavow Paulet's occupation of the Islands.[181] With the sense of national rivalry within the foreign community heightened by the transfer of sovereignty, the misgivings and fears of the American residents were scarcely allayed by the report that Paulet had characterized the former government as essentially American whereas his rule was to be truly British.[182]

The American missionaries accepted the change in government with mixed feelings. Some were apprehensive lest the prominence of Dr. Judd in the previous regime react against the entire mission when the administration passed into the control of men hostile to the doctor.[183] The missionaries had faith in the integrity and good intentions of the native rulers, and they would have preferred the continuance of the native government. At least one of their number, however, conceded that the chiefs were not competent in the government of "a commercial community, where national jealousy, cupidity, and conflicting interests" were rampant. It was with sentimental regret, tempered by resignation, that the missionaries saw the flag of the Hawaiian kingdom replaced by that of Great Britain.[184] They were reconciled, "in a degree," by the confidence that the mission would be no less prosperous under British rule than it had been under the former government, while they were frankly relieved that the danger of French aggression was over.[185] Secure in that important satisfaction,

[180] Hooper to Kamehameha III, Oahu, no date, in AH, "British Commission Documents."

[181] A printed copy of the memorial, undated and with the endorsement cited above in the handwriting of R. C. Wyllie, may be found in *ibid.*

[182] Journal of Gerrit P. Judd (copy), in *ibid.*

[183] Lowell Smith to Anderson, Honolulu, March 10, 1843, in Letters to the American Board, CXXXVII, No. 28.

[184] The Mission to Anderson, Honolulu, May 30, 1843, in *ibid.*, CXXXIV, No. 19; Armstrong to Reuben Chapman, Honolulu, March 3, 1843, in Armstrong MSS.

[185] Knapp to Anderson, Honolulu, March 10, 1843, in Letters to the American Board, CXXXVII, No. 157; Armstrong to Anderson, Honolulu, March 2, 1843, in *ibid.*, CXXXVI, No. 96.

they contemplated life and labor in a British colony with greater
equanimity than could be mustered by the American merchants, who
anticipated that British rule meant a favored position for British
commerce.

This political revolution produced more excitement and ill will
in the foreign community than it did among the natives. The King and
chiefs were said to be "very desponding"; and, early in March, the
King and the *Kuhina Nui* addressed an appeal to the President of the
United States, soliciting his influence to secure the restoration of
Hawaiian sovereignty.[186] If the King's subjects were equally distressed, they did not give evidence of it. Paulet and Simpson asserted that the natives seemed "much pleased" by the change, and
Herman Melville declared that by his "firm and benignant spirit"
Paulet "soon endeared himself to nearly all orders of the islanders."[187] Less biased and probably more reliable was the comment
of Richard Armstrong that the transfer of political control had
aroused "but little excitement" among the Hawaiian people.[188]

The career of Paulet as administrator and virtual dictator of the
Hawaiian government was beset with difficulty and controversy. He
reserved for himself the final decision upon all important questions,
but to assist him in the problems of policy-making he organized a
commission whose functions were both legislative and advisory. It
was scarcely an independent body; for the four persons who composed the commission were Paulet, two other officers of the "Carysfort," and Dr. Judd—the latter serving as the personal representative
of the King. Governor Kekuanaoa and other native officials retained
a degree of power in local affairs; but their position was that of

[186] Pelly to Sir George Simpson, Honolulu, March 13, 1843, in *Correspondence
Relative to the Sandwich Islands*, p. 238;
Kamehameha III and Kekauluohi to President John Tyler, Honolulu, March 10, 1843,
in FRUS, 1894, Appendix II, pp. 53–55. A
copy of this appeal, taken from a Boston
newspaper, was forwarded to London by
the British minister to the United States,
who commented that it was "not intemperate or offensive towards Great Britain; less
so, perhaps, than, under the circumstances,
might have been apprehended." Fox to
Aberdeen, Washington, D.C., September 5,
1843, in *Further Papers Relative to the
Sandwich Islands* [London, 1843], p. 27.

[187] Paulet to the Secretary of the Admiralty, Honolulu, March 9, 1843, in *Correspondence Relative to the Sandwich Islands*, p. 184; Simpson, *Sandwich Islands*,
p. 42; Herman Melville, *Narrative of a Four
Months' Residence Among the Natives of a
Valley of the Marquesas Islands* (London,
1846), p. 282.

[188] Armstrong to Reuben Chapman, Honolulu, March 3, 1843, in Armstrong MSS.

subordinates, and it is evident that Kekuanaoa was in frequent conflict with Paulet and the British Commission.[189]

The most distinguished defender of Paulet, Herman Melville, asserted that the commander of the "Carysfort" undertook "the task of reconciling the differences among the foreign residents, remedying their grievances, promoting their mercantile interests, and ameliorating as far as lay in his power the condition of the degraded natives."[190] Paulet began his administration of the government with an influential part of both the foreign and native population suspicious of his motives; he did little to conciliate that section of public opinion. The commission reversed the decisions of the Hawaiian court in the case of the estate of F. J. Greenway;[191] and this and other policies of Paulet were said to have aroused "the indignation of . . . . every American resident" of the Islands.[192] The American missionaries, who had once regarded Paulet as a "very condescending mild and amiable man,"[193] were alienated by the modification or repeal of the laws prohibiting prostitution and restricting the sale of intoxicants.[194] The minutes of

[189] For example, see Kekuanaoa to Judd, no date, in AH, "British Commission Documents."

[190] Melville, *Narrative of a Residence Among the Natives of the Marquesas Islands*, p. 283.

[191] "British Commission Minute Book," pp. 67–69 (March 22, 1843) ; Henry Sea to Kekuanaoa, Honolulu, March 22, 1843, in AH, "British Commission Documents."

[192] Hooper to the Secretary of State, Sandwich Islands, June 30, 1843, in USDS, "Consular Letters," Honolulu, I. An anonymous correspondent of the *Boston Atlas* reported that business at Honolulu had been interrupted and that the "doors of the residents" were closed to Paulet and his officers. This correspondent added that Paulet had made an effort to conciliate the foreign residents but had been "repulsed with a manly indignation." Quoted in the *Globe* (Washington, D.C.), June 12, 1843.

[193] Armstrong to Reuben Chapman, Honolulu, March 3, 1843, in Armstrong MSS.

[194] "British Commission Minute Book," pp. 77–78, 142–143 (March 27, April 27, 1843) ; Kekuanaoa to Haalilio and Richards, Honolulu, May 6, 1843, in AH, F.O. and Ex.; Chamberlain to the American Board, August 1, 1843, in *Missionary Her-*

ald, XL (January 1844), 20–21; Coan to the American Board, Hilo, August 12, 1843, in *ibid.*, XL (June 1844), 187; Armstrong to Reuben Chapman, Honolulu, July 21, 1843, in Armstrong MSS. Armstrong wrote that the modification of the moral legislation had resulted in such "scenes of pollution" as had not been seen in Honolulu since "the days of darkness."

Apparently the repeal of these laws caused some division of opinion among natives in Honolulu. Gorham D. Gilman thought that the only native partisans of Paulet were "a few of the baser sort"; and Richard Armstrong declared that the British rule was favorably regarded by "the wicked," while the "steady, sober class" were opposed to it. Gilman, "Honolulu As It Is," p. 59; Armstrong to the American Board, Honolulu, November 7, 1843, in *Missionary Herald*, XL (June 1844), 191. In contrast, Herman Melville, writing in 1846, declared that Paulet's policies had been approved by "the great body of the Hawaiian people," who recalled "with gratitude . . . . the time when his liberal and paternal sway diffused peace and happiness among them." Melville, *Narrative of a Residence Among the Natives of the Marquesas Islands*, p. 285.

the meetings of the British Commission are mute evidence that Dr. Judd was often in disagreement with his colleagues, by whom he was suspected of unduly favoring the interests of American citizens.[195] Finally, on May 8, he resigned from the Commission in a move which was intended partly as a protest against the relaxation of the moral legislation.[196] The action of Judd received the approval of the King.

A new factor entered the situation, on July 7, when the U.S.S. "Constellation," commanded by Captain Lawrence Kearny, arrived at Honolulu.[197] Kearny found "much excitement" at Honolulu, and he believed it to be his duty to remain there to protect the interests of American residents.[198] Four days later he indicated his position by the publication of a general protest against any action of the British Commission which might affect adversely the interests of an American citizen.[199] There were reports, apparently unfounded, that Kearny would advise Americans not to recognize the government established by Paulet;[200] but no hint of such a purpose is to be found in a note to Paulet of the same date as the public protest. In that note Kearny observed that the political future of the Islands was a question which "may perhaps more appropriately belong to our respective Governments" than to naval officers. He declared that he would, therefore, "withhold all further comment upon questions so grave and important."[201]

One week later, a memorial signed by nearly all the influential American residents of Honolulu, except the missionaries, was pre-

[195] Journal of G. P. Judd, May 8, 1843 (copy), in AH, "British Commission Documents."

[196] "British Commission Minute Book," pp. 156–160 (May 11, 1843). The protest filed with the Commission by Judd at the time of his resignation may be found in FRUS, 1894, Appendix II, pp. 55–57.

[197] For a brief account of the visit of Kearny to Honolulu, see Carroll Storrs Alden, *Lawrence Kearny, Sailor Diplomat* (Princeton, N.J., 1936), pp. 187–203.
Kearny reported that he had arrived on July 6, but other accounts gave the date of his arrival as July 7. Kearny to the Secretary of the Navy, Sandwich Islands, August 2, 6, 1843, in NRL, "China Station, Commodore Kearny," Nos. 58, 59; T. ap C.

Jones to the Secretary of the Navy, Oahu, August 5, 1843, in NRL, "Pacific Squadron Letters, 1841–1845," No. 68; Chamberlain to Anderson, Honolulu, July 21, 1843, in Letters to the American Board, CXXXV, No. 162.

[198] Kearny to the Secretary of the Navy, Honolulu, August 2, 1843, in NRL, "China Station, Commodore Kearny," No. 58.

[199] The protest is printed in FRUS, 1894, Appendix II, pp. 57–58; *Missionary Herald*, XL (January 1844), 22; *Niles' Register*, LXV (December 2, 1843), 211.

[200] Journal of Stephen Reynolds, July 12, 1843.

[201] Kearny to Paulet, Honolulu, July 11, 1843 (copy), in NRL, "China Station, Commodore Kearney," enclosure in No. 56.

sented to Kearny. In this memorial the signers urged him to remain at Honolulu to afford them protection and to secure "the just & honourable preservation of American interest in this Ocean."[202] By this protest against possible future actions of the Commission and by the cordial entertainment of members of the royal family on board the "Constellation," Kearny had indicated his sympathy for the views of his countrymen. He was anxious, however, to avoid an open break with Paulet. In acknowledging the receipt of the memorial, he informed the memorialists that he was "not disposed to do anything to excite disturbance," but that he would limit his actions to efforts to prevent "any unjust exercise of power against American citizens" by the King or by the British Commission.[203] A more belligerent attitude might have produced some serious incident.

Rear Admiral Thomas was at Valparaiso when he learned that Paulet had taken possession of the Hawaiian Islands. He immediately proceeded to Honolulu "to remedy, if possible, whatever might prove prejudicial to British interests."[204] Shortly after his arrival at Honolulu, he sought and obtained an audience with the King, following which it became known that he proposed to restore the government of the Islands to the native rulers.[205] The formal ceremony by which

[202] The memorial, dated Honolulu, July 18, 1843, may be found as an enclosure in NRL, "China Station, Commodore Kearny," No. 56. See also Hooper to Kearny, Honolulu, July 19, 1843 (copy), enclosure in *ibid.*, No. 56; Journal of William Paty, July 18, 1843. The memorial and Kearny's reply are printed in Alden, *Lawrence Kearny*, pp. 199–202.

[203] Kearny to Hooper, Honolulu, July 20, 1843 (copy), in NRL, "China Station, Commodore Kearny," enclosure in No. 56.

[204] Thomas to the Secretary of the Admiralty, Honolulu, August 2, 1843, in *Further Papers Relative to the Sandwich Islands*, p. 36. See also "Declaration of Rear Admiral Richard Thomas," Honolulu, July 31, 1843, in *The Friend*, August 11, 1843, p. 41.

[205] Thomas to Henry Sea, Honolulu, July 26, 1843, in *Further Papers Relative to the Sandwich Islands*, p. 37; Thomas to Kekuanaoa, Honolulu, July 26, 1843, in FRUS, 1894, Appendix II, p. 58; "Declaration of Rear Admiral Thomas," July 31, 1843, in *ibid.*, pp. 58–60, and in *The Friend*, August 11, 1843, pp. 40–41. The official communications which preceded the restoration of Hawaiian sovereignty may be found in *ibid.*, pp. 40–42, and in *British and Foreign State Papers*, XXXI, 1029–1035.

It was reported in Honolulu that Thomas assured the King that no instructions had been given Paulet which would justify the demands that had been made upon the King or the acceptance of the provisional cession. Three months later Thomas was said to have spoken of Paulet's action "in terms of high disapprobation." R. G. Davis to W. H. Davis, Honolulu, July 8–August 4, 1843, in Davis MSS; George Brown to Secretary of State Upshur, Honolulu, November 4, 1843 (No. 6), in USDS, "Despatches," Sandwich Islands, I.

Before the actual restoration of the Hawaiian government occurred, Thomas persuaded the King to sign an Anglo-Hawaiian convention, designed to govern the relations of the Hawaiian government with British

political power was transferred from the British Commission to the King was held on an open plain east of Honolulu on the morning of July 31.[206] There was no immediate assurance that the authorities in London would approve the action of Thomas,[207] but the pleasure of the chiefs and of their friends was too intense to be disturbed by doubts as to their future security.

Contrary to the expectation of many of their number, American residents of Honolulu suffered little or no inconvenience during the five months that the Islands were governed by Paulet.[208] They greeted with almost universal satisfaction, however, the restoration to power of the native government.[209] From this general approval Stephen Reynolds as usual dissented, apparently in the belief that the missionaries would again enjoy a considerable influence in the making of

---

consular officials and to facilitate the adjudication of disputes in which subjects of Great Britain were involved. Under the circumstances neither the King nor Judd could refuse to accept the terms suggested by Thomas, but Judd was not wholly satisfied and he declared that the King signed the convention only because it would have been impossible to secure better terms. Judd to Richards, Honolulu, August 1, 1843, in AH, "British Commission Documents"; Judd to Thomas (private), Honolulu, February 6, 1844, in AH, F.O. and Ex.

[206] Chamberlain to Anderson, Honolulu, August 1, 1843, in Letters to the American Board, CXXXIV, No. 20; "British Commission Minute Book," p. 254 (July 31, 1843); Jarves, *History of the Hawaiian Islands*, pp. 183–184.

[207] Early in August, news reached Honolulu that the governments of Great Britain and France had determined to recognize the independence of the Hawaiian Islands. They had reached this decision before the news of the cession of the Islands to Paulet had arrived in either London or Paris. The question as to how the British government would react to the cession, therefore, remained unanswered. Lowell Smith to David Leslie, Honolulu, August 12, 1843, MS, Oregon Historical Society Library.

[208] William Hooper to the Secretary of State, Sandwich Islands, September 30,

1843, in USDS, "Consular Letters," Honolulu, II.

[209] Hooper to the Secretary of State, Sandwich Islands, August 15, 1843, in *ibid.*, and in FRUS, 1894, Appendix II, p. 55. Kearny wrote that the action of Thomas had "tranquilized the public mind"; and Commodore Thomas ap C. Jones—who arrived at Honolulu on August 3—declared that it brought "universal joy" to all except "the instigators of Lord Paulet's movements." One of the American missionaries, in reporting the restoration of the native government, referred to "the *recent, joyful political* movements" which had occurred, and declared that July 31 had been a "great & joyful day for the King & chiefs —American residents & missionaries & some of the English residents." Kearny to the Secretary of the Navy, Sandwich Islands, August 6, 1843, in NRL, "China Station, Commodore Kearny," No. 59; Jones to the Secretary of the Navy, Oahu, August 5, 1843, in NRL, "Pacific Squadron Letters, 1841–1845," No. 68; Lowell Smith to David Leslie, Honolulu, August 12, 1843, MS, Oregon Historical Society Library.

When Thomas left Honolulu, a farewell reception in his honor "was crowded with *Americans*," but only one English resident appeared to pay his respects to the commander of Her Majesty's squadron in the Pacific. Honolulu Correspondence in *Boston Mercantile Journal*, quoted in *Sailor's Magazine*, XVI (July 1844), 333–334.

Hawaiian policy.[210] To Reynolds and to the group of foreigners who shared his suspicion of the mission this was a prospect more terrifying than the continuance of British rule.

Thirteen months had elapsed since Richards and Haalilio had left the Islands. They had intended to go directly to London, where they were to meet Sir George Simpson. They modified these plans during the voyage from Vera Cruz to New Orleans, after being advised to present their case first to the government at Washington.[211] This was a reasonable suggestion, for the United States could not be indifferent to the future of the Hawaiian Islands. Few ports in any part of the world gave shelter to as many New England–owned vessels as did Honolulu and Lahaina, and New England statesmen were prominent at Washington. Daniel Webster was Secretary of State, Caleb Cushing was an intimate friend and adviser of the President, and former President John Quincy Adams was a respected and influential member of the House of Representatives. Should personal predilections or sectional interests prove insufficient to move the Tyler administration to favorable action, the proximity of the Islands to the American coast added to the probability that American recognition of Hawaiian independence could be secured by a judicious representation of the danger that the archipelago might be seized by some powerful European nation.

Richards and Haalilio arrived in Washington on December 5, 1842;[212] within three days they had met Secretary Webster, Lewis Cass, Caleb Cushing, ex-President Adams, and several less influential members of Congress.[213] Their first meeting with Webster was on the morning of December 7. The results were far from satisfactory to Richards, who later recalled that his fears had been "considerably awakened by the coldness" with which they had been received.[214]

[210] Journal of Stephen Reynolds, July 28, 1843; Reynolds to W. H. Davis, Oahu, August 9, 1843, in Davis MSS. See also R. G. Davis to W. H. Davis, Honolulu, July 8–August 9, 1843, in *ibid.*

[211] Journal of Alexander Liholiho, April 14, 1845. The account recorded in this journal was based upon a lecture given by Richards to the students of the school for young chiefs.

[212] Journal of William Richards, December 5, 1842.

[213] *Ibid.*, December 5, 6, 1842; Charles Francis Adams, ed., *Memoirs of John Quincy Adams*, XI, 274 (December 8, 1842); Cushing to Hunnewell, Washington, D.C., December 8, 1842, in Hunnewell MSS.

[214] Journal of William Richards, December 7, 1842; Testimony of William Richards, September 1, 1846, in *Arbitration between the . . . . Government of the Hawaiian Islands and Messrs. Ladd & Co.*, p. 97.

During this first interview, Webster—apparently seeking to evade the issue thus raised—advised the commissioners to go immediately to England and seek a British recognition of Hawaiian independence.[215] On the following day they visited Adams, who promised to assist them by all means at his disposal. He could not accept Webster's view that the United States should await the action of Great Britain in the matter; and, in his famous journal, he expressed the belief that the hesitancy of the Secretary was caused by the dark complexion of Haalilio.[216] The effort of Webster to avoid a consideration of the wishes of the Hawaiian envoys was a harbinger of hesitation and evasion to come. On December 9 Richards and Haalilio called unofficially at Webster's home and Richards had a "free talk" with his host. During the conversation Webster made many inquiries about the conditions and commerce of the Islands; finally he requested Richards to state the position and wishes of the Hawaiian government in a formal note.[217] Five days later the communication was ready for transmission to the State Department.[218]

During the week following the dispatch of this note Richards was occupied with the preparation of the draft of a treaty which he hoped would be acceptable to Webster.[219] On December 23 he called at the State Department, where he learned that his note of the 14th had not yet been read with care. Webster promised that a reply would soon be prepared and he agreed to furnish Richards and Haalilio with a letter of introduction to the American Minister in London. It appeared, however, that he wished to avoid fulfilling an earlier promise to introduce them to the President; when Richards specifically raised that point, Webster replied that some friendly member of Congress would accompany the commissioners to the White House.[220] Richards thereupon visited a Congressional friend, with whom he discussed the Hawaiian situation. He declined an offer of an introduction to the President; and declared that should efforts to secure a recognition of Hawaiian independence prove fruitless he was prepared to place the Islands under the formal protection of Great Britain.[221]

[215] *Memoirs of John Quincy Adams*, XI, 274–275 (December 8, 1842).   [216] *Ibid.*

[217] Journal of William Richards, December 9, 1842; Testimony of William Richards, September 1, 1846, *loc. cit.*

[218] Journal of William Richards, December 12, 13, 14, 1842.

[219] *Ibid.*, December 21, 22, 1842.

[220] *Ibid.*, December 23, 1842.

[221] *Ibid.*

Apparently reports of this conversation soon reached the State Department.[222] When Richards and Haalilio next called upon Webster they were received with greater cordiality and attention, and the Secretary instructed his son to accompany them to the White House and to introduce them to the President and to the heads of the executive departments, who were scheduled to assemble that day for a cabinet meeting.[223] The ensuing interview was as satisfactory as Richards could have wished. The President and the members of his cabinet appeared to be particularly interested in the relations of the Islands to Great Britain and in the intentions of Richards should he fail to persuade the great powers to acknowledge the independence of the Hawaiian government. In reply to questions, Richards explained the purposes of his mission, and reiterated his statement that if there were no recognition of Hawaiian independence he would seek the establishment of a formal protectorate by Great Britain.[224] Following this interview, which Richards described as "pleasant free and full,"[225] events moved rapidly.

That evening, Richards and Haalilio again met Webster, with whom they had a "long talk in the presence of Mr. Cushing."[226] The following day another conference with the Secretary of State brought the first official intimation that the United States would recognize Hawaiian independence, and Richards agreed that the note submitted on December 14 should be modified.[227] On December 29 Richards and Haalilio carried the rewritten note to Webster and listened to the reply of the United States, a copy of which was sent to them the following day.[228]

The long-awaited reply of the government of the United States was characterized by Richards as "Not quite what I want," but he added that "others think it is well."[229] Former President Adams noted that the language was "not very explicit," and he believed that Webster had evaded "a direct acknowledgment."[230] This judgment appears to

---

[222] *Ibid.*, December 26, 1842.
[223] *Ibid.*, December 27, 1842.
[224] *Ibid.*; Testimony of William Richards, September 1, 1846, *loc. cit.*
[225] Journal of William Richards, December 27, 1842.
[226] *Ibid.*
[227] *Ibid.*, December 28, 1842.

[228] *Ibid.*, December 29, 30, 1842. The modified note, with the original date, December 14, 1842, may be found in FRUS, 1894, Appendix II, pp. 41–44.
[229] Journal of William Richards, December 30, 1842.
[230] *Memoirs of John Quincy Adams*, XI, 283–284 (December 31, 1842).

have been fair. Webster was not yet willing to negotiate a treaty with the Hawaiian government, and he was vague as to future representation of the United States at the Islands, being content to observe that a "consul or agent" would continue to reside at Honolulu. In the enunciation of more general principles, however, the note was a milestone in the development of American policy in the eastern Pacific. In thus defining the American position, Webster declared:

> The United States have regarded the existing authorities in the Sandwich Islands as a Government suited to the condition of the people, and resting on their own choice; and the President is of opinion that the interests of all the commercial nations require that that Government should not be interfered with by foreign powers. . . . . The United States . . . . are more interested in the fate of the islands, and of their Government, than any other nation can be; and this consideration induces the President to be quite willing to declare, as the sense of the Government of the United States, that the Government of the Sandwich Islands ought to be respected; that no power ought either to take possession of the islands as a conquest, or for the purpose of colonization, and that no power ought to seek for any undue control over the existing Government, or any exclusive privileges or preferences in matters of commerce.[231]

The position of the United States was stated publicly in a special message which President Tyler sent to Congress on December 30. This message, believed to have been written by Webster,[232] was concerned with the wider problem of American interests in the central and western Pacific, and with specific treatment of the defense of those interests in China and the Hawaiian Islands. In the section of the message which dealt with Hawaii, Tyler disavowed any desire on the part of the United States for possession of the Islands or for any exclusive privileges there. He declared, however, that the commercial value of the Islands and their "near approach" to the American continent would cause the United States to view with "dissatisfaction" any threat by another power "to take possession of the islands, colonize them, and subvert the native Government."[233] This was, in effect,

---

[231] Webster to Haalilio and Richards, Washington, D.C., December 19[29], 1842, in FRUS, 1894, Appendix II, pp. 44–45.

[232] *Memoirs of John Quincy Adams*, XI, 284 (December 31, 1842) ; Claude M. Fuess,

The Life of Caleb Cushing (New York, 1923), I, 408.

[233] This message may be found in: *House Executive Documents*, 27th Cong., 3d Sess., No. 35, pp. 1–4; FRUS, 1894, Appendix II, pp. 39–41; [J. W. McIntyre, comp.], *The*

an extension to the mid-Pacific of the famous dictum of President Monroe.

In the course of this message, the President urged Congress to appropriate funds for the establishment of a consulate at the Hawaiian Islands in order that "in a Government so new and a country so remote" citizens of the United States might have "respectable authority" to which they could apply for redress of injury and to which the native government could refer acts of Americans of which it wished to complain. The Senate promptly referred this message to the Committee on Printing,[234] whence it never returned. It received more respectful attention in the House, where Caleb Cushing interpreted the portion of the message which related to Hawaii as a proposal to Congress that the independence of the Islands should be recognized rather than as an announcement of a recognition already extended. With this explanation from a man who was acknowledged to be a spokesman for the administration, the House referred the message to the Committee on Foreign Affairs.[235] That committee, in turn, delegated the task of preparing a report on the subjects of the message to its chairman, former President John Quincy Adams.[236]

Adams was committed in advance by his known sympathy for the aspirations of the Hawaiian government. Although politically hostile to Tyler and suspicious of Webster, he regarded the message as "an elaborate and able argument" for the recognition of Hawaiian independence.[237] With the co-operation of Webster he undertook the preparation of a bill designed to place the relations of the United States with the Hawaiian government upon a more permanent basis. This bill, which appropriated $3,000 as compensation for an American representative at the Islands, was unanimously approved by the committee and was introduced in the House by Adams on January 24, 1843. With it was a report in which Adams asserted that the dominance at the Islands of American interests, both missionary and

Writings and Speeches of Daniel Webster (Boston, 1903), XII, 137–141; Richardson, comp., *Messages and Papers of the Presidents*, IV, 211–214.

[234] *Senate Journal*, 27th Cong., 3d Sess. (January 4, 1843) p. 72.

[235] *Daily National Intelligencer*, January

2, 1843; *Madisonian* (Washington, D.C.), January 2, 1843; *Congressional Globe*, XII, 103; *House Journal*, 27th Cong., 3d Sess. (December 31, 1842) p. 124.

[236] *Memoirs of John Quincy Adams*, XI, 290 (January 9, 1843).

[237] *Ibid.*, XI, 284 (December 31, 1842).

mercantile, together with the peaceable methods by which that dominance had been won, constituted important arguments in favor of the establishment of formal diplomatic relations with the Hawaiian government.[238] Only six weeks remained before the date for adjournment, and inertia and an unusually virulent partisan feeling were major obstacles to the success of any measure proposed by the administration and supported by Adams. The appropriation was included, however, in the general appropriation bill which was signed by Tyler on March 3, the last day of the session.[239] The sum of $3,000 had been suggested by Webster as one adequate for "a salaried Consul, like those maintained at the Barbary States,"[240] but the bill in its final form provided for a commissioner who was to have diplomatic status. On the same day that he signed the bill President Tyler nominated George Brown of Massachusetts to be Commissioner to the Sandwich Islands. The Senate, without a record vote, promptly confirmed the nomination.[241]

While these events were occurring in the United States, the problem of Hawaiian independence had been called to the attention of the British government. Late in January, Sir John Pelly, the Governor of the Hudson's Bay Company, informed the Earl of Aberdeen of the impending arrival in England of the Hawaiian commissioners. With some significance, he commented that, in opening negotiations with the Foreign Office, Richards would "in all probability be regulated by the opinion and advice of Mr. Colville, Sir G. Simpson and myself," and he requested Aberdeen for advice concerning the proper

[238] *Memoirs of John Quincy Adams*, XI, 290, 297, 299–300 (January 9, 19, 24, 1843); *House Journal*, 27th Cong., 3d Sess. (January 24, 1843) p. 250; *House Reports*, 27th Cong., 3d Sess., No. 93, pp. 1–2.

[239] *Public Statutes at Large*, V, 643 (27th Cong., 3d Sess., Chap. 100).

[240] *Memoirs of John Quincy Adams*, XI, 290 (January 9, 1843).

[241] *Senate Executive Journal*, VI, 190–191 (March 3, 1843). This would appear to be indisputable evidence that the government of the United States had formally acknowledged the independence of the Hawaiian kingdom. Some

doubts were later expressed, nevertheless, by officials in the foreign offices of Great Britain and France. To remove all doubt, Richards and Haalilio returned to Washington in the summer of 1844 and secured from Secretary of State Calhoun specific assurances that the United States had recognized without reservation the independent sovereignty of the Hawaiian government. Journal of William Richards, June 29, 1844; Haalilio and Richards to Calhoun, Washington, D.C., July 1, 1844 (copy), in AH, F.O. and Ex.; Calhoun to Haalilio and Richards, Washington, D.C., July 6, 1844, in *ibid.* This correspondence was printed in the *Polynesian*, March 29, 1845.

procedure.[242] On February 18 Richards and Haalilio arrived in London; two days later they called upon Sir George Simpson.[243] During the ensuing two weeks they were occupied in framing a note to the Foreign Office and in conferences with friends and advisers, among whom was the Minister of the United States, Edward Everett.[244]

Charlton was already in London, actively engaged in presenting to the Foreign Office his version of events in the Islands. He was particularly anxious to thwart a possible recognition of Hawaiian independence by the government of Great Britain. In a note to Aberdeen, dated February 11, he asserted that the Hawaiian people would welcome British protection, including the control of their government by "a person of rank and talent" selected by the British government. There were, he added, so many Americans at the Islands, some of whom had secured "large and valuable tracts of lands," that the Islands were "in fact . . . . colonies of the United States." If the independent sovereignty of the native rulers were to be recognized, Charlton feared that the dominance of the United States in the Islands would be strengthened, with the result that "that beautiful and interesting group" would be lost "for commercial purposes" to Great Britain.[245] At the close of February, Charlton sent a more alarming note to the Foreign Office. Although he described the young King as friendly to British interests, he asserted that the real control of the Hawaiian government was in the hands of American residents, with the result that, in an archipelago which offered "great advantages for honest and industrious emigrants," no British subject could secure land except "on ruinous terms."[246]

Richards was soon aware that efforts were being made to have the Foreign Office prejudge the case against the Hawaiian commissioners, and before his first visit to Aberdeen he admitted that these efforts had been partially successful. His apprehensions appeared to be confirmed when, on March 6, he and Sir George Simpson called

[242] J. H. Pelly to Aberdeen, January 23, 1843, in *American Historical Review*, XIV (October 1908), 71–73.

[243] Journal of William Richards, February 18, 20, 1843.

[244] *Ibid.*, February 21, 22, 25, 27, March 2, 3, 6, 1843.

[245] Charlton to Aberdeen, London, February 11, 1843, in *Correspondence Relative to the Sandwich Islands*, pp. 159–161. This fear apparently was shared by many of Charlton's compatriots at Honolulu.

[246] Charlton to Aberdeen, London, February 28, 1843, in *ibid.*, pp. 165–166.

at the Foreign Office. In the course of the ensuing interview, Aberdeen expressed the belief that the government of the Islands was so under the influence of American missionaries as to make a recognition of independence undesirable.[247] In reply, Richards and Simpson left at the Foreign Office a note which they had previously prepared. In it they attributed the failures of the Hawaiian government to the interference in Hawaiian politics by visiting naval officers, and they asserted that only through a recognition of the sovereignty of the native rulers could the government command the respect which was necessary if it was to protect the interests of all foreigners within its jurisdiction.[248] This interview strengthened the fears of Richards. He was not without hope, however, for he was assured of the assistance of the American legation, of the Hudson's Bay Company, and of "several of the first men in England." To this material support he was confident there would be added "the sympathy and the prayers of all the Pious and Philanthropic parties of the community." Thus fortified by friends and by hope, Richards declared that he would remain in England long enough "to opperate on the Ministry through the People."[249]

The apparent hope of Richards that he could arouse public sentiment powerful enough to modify the position of the cabinet was little short of fantastic. The situation, nevertheless, was not so desperate as appeared on the surface. The British government did not covet the possession of the Islands, although it would have taken advantage of an opportunity to diminish American or French influence there. In view of general British policy it was very unlikely that Great Britain would withhold a recognition of Hawaiian independence after it had become known that the government of the United States had established formal diplomatic relations with the Islands. Charlton had presented serious charges against the Hawaiian government, but the weight of those charges was offset by the fact that the conduct of Charlton had not received the approval

[247] Richards to Anderson, London, February 25, 1843, in Letters to the American Board, CXXXV, No. 95; Journal of William Richards, March 6, 1843; Testimony of William Richards, September 1, 2, 1846, *loc. cit.*, pp. 97, 124.

[248] Simpson and Richards to Aberdeen, London, March 6, 1843 (copy), in AH, F.O. and Ex.

[249] Richards to Anderson, London, February 25, 1843, in Letters to the American Board, CXXXV, No. 95.

of his government. The probable line of British policy was indicated when, on March 9, Aberdeen informed Charlton that it would be "highly inexpedient" for him to return to the Hawaiian Islands in an official capacity.[250]

On March 8, Richards, Haalilio, and Sir George Simpson left London for a hurried visit to the Continent. Less than two weeks later they were again in England. During that brief interval they had met and presented their case to King Leopold in Brussels and to M. Guizot, the French Minister of Foreign Affairs, in Paris. Leopold appeared friendly. He expressed the opinion that the independence of the Hawaiian Islands should be recognized, and he promised to use his influence to hasten such a recognition by the governments of Great Britain and France.[251] In Paris the visitors were received cordially by Guizot. To him they explained that the objectives of their mission included the recognition of Hawaiian independence by the great powers, the negotiation of a treaty to replace or modify the treaties negotiated by Laplace, and the removal of Jules Dudoit from the French consulate at Honolulu. In reply Guizot stated "positively and strongly" that the Hawaiian government should not be compelled to admit intoxicants into the Islands. He also conceded that there was no reason to withhold a recognition of Hawaiian independence, but he was unwilling to give any hope that France would assent to a modification of the Laplace treaties.[252]

Soon after the return of the commissioners to London, Sir George Simpson had a series of conferences with Aberdeen.[253] Apparently the arguments and assurances which Simpson presented to the Foreign Office were effective. On the morning of March 25 the London

[250] Aberdeen to Charlton, [London], March 9, 1843, in *Correspondence Relative to the Sandwich Islands*, p. 173.

[251] Journal of William Richards, March 13, 1843; George Simpson and Richards to Kamehameha III, London, April 1, 1843, in AH, F.O. and Ex.

[252] Richards to Anderson, London, April 3, 1843, in Letters to the American Board, CXXXV, No. 96; Journal of William Richards, March 17, 1843; Testimony of William Richards, September 1, 1846, *loc. cit.*, pp. 97–98; "History of the Hawaiian Foreign Embassy during the Years 1842, 1843, 1844" (MS in AH), pp. 20–22. Upon leaving Guizot, the commissioners left with him a memorandum outlining the concessions which they hoped France would be willing to make. A copy of this memorandum may be found in AH, F.O. and Ex.

[253] Journal of William Richards, March 25, 1843; Testimony of William Richards, September 1, 1846, *loc. cit.*, p. 98.

press prepared the way for a statement of the government's policy by announcing that France was ready to acknowledge the independence of the Hawaiian kingdom.[254] Three days later Edward Everett reported that he had learned from Aberdeen that Great Britain would extend a formal recognition of Hawaiian independence.[255] The official statement of this policy was contained in a note from Aberdeen to the Hawaiian commissioners, dated April 1, 1843. The statement that the British government had decided "to recognize the independence of the Sandwich Islands under their present sovereign" was sufficiently explicit to remove any doubt as to British policy. The note contained the added warning that Great Britain would insist upon redress in all cases where its nationals had been the victims of injustice.[256]

This was a major victory for the Hawaiian commission, and the last in which Sir George Simpson had a share. He left for Canada on April 3 to resume his duties as director of the Hudson's Bay Company's far-flung interests in North America.[257] Immediately thereafter Richards and Haalilio returned to Paris. On April 13, Richards sought to open formal negotiations with the French Foreign Office, when he sent a note to Guizot, but no answer was immediately forthcoming.[258] On May 1, Richards called at the Foreign Office and talked with Guizot, who again assured him that France would recognize the independence of the Islands. Guizot also appeared willing to consider the negotiation of a new treaty, but he mentioned two specific provisions which must be included in such a treaty. The first was a demand that France be placed upon a basis of

254 *Morning Herald* (London), March 25, 1843.

255 Everett to Secretary of State Webster, London, March 28, 1843, in FRUS, 1894, Appendix II, p. 111. Apparently Aberdeen was still uneasy concerning the possible influence of the American missionaries, for he told Everett that he hoped they would abstain from any interference in Hawaiian politics.

256 Aberdeen to Simpson and Richards, London, April 1, 1843, in AH, F.O. and Ex., and printed in *Correspondence Relative to the Sandwich Islands*, pp. 175–176. The information that Great Britain had recognized Hawaiian independence appeared in news-papers in the United States late in April. *Daily National Intelligencer*, April 25, 1843; *Niles' Register*, LXIV (April 29, 1843), 130.

257 With justice, Richards reported that the services and advice of Simpson had been "of invaluable benefit" to the Hawaiian Commission. To this testimony, Richards added, "No zeal, or diligence, or disinterestedness could have exceeded that which he has manifested for the last six weeks." Richards to Anderson, London, April 3, 1843, in Letters to the American Board, CXXXV, No. 96.

258 Journal of William Richards, April 13, 19, 1843.

equality with the most-favored nation. This was promptly approved by Richards. The second indispensable provision was a guaranty that Catholic institutions in the Islands should be placed on a basis of equality with Protestant schools and churches. This was rejected by Richards.[259] The negotiations had reached an apparent impasse.

If Richards continued to hold any hope that his mission could be brought to an early termination, that illusion was dispelled at the close of May by the news that the Hawaiian Islands had been ceded provisionally to Great Britain. The first report of the cession to reach Richards was contained in an item in a Paris newspaper.[260] For some days thereafter there were contradictory reports and rumors. The distress of the Hawaiian commissioners was somewhat allayed when twice, during the first week in June, Guizot assured them that the government of France was still determined to acknowledge the independence of the Hawaiian kingdom.[261] Thus assured, they reopened negotiations with Guizot by submitting to him, on June 5, the draft of a proposed treaty which they hoped would be an acceptable substitute for the Laplace treaties. The draft contained fourteen articles, but conspicuously avoided any provisions which would permit consular participation in the selection of juries or which would limit the power of the Hawaiian government over imports.[262] Through June, Richards and Haalilio lingered in Paris, hoping in vain that Guizot would consent to negotiations on the basis of their draft. Meanwhile, they learned that the reports of a cession of the Islands to Great Britain were authentic and that a special envoy from Kamehameha III had arrived in London to present the King's version of events leading up to the cession. In response to the urgent request of this envoy, Richards and Haalilio left Paris for London during the second week in July.[263]

The new addition to the company of Hawaiian diplomats was James F. B. Marshall, a youthful American merchant who had been a resident of the Islands for less than four years.[264] He had been

[259] *Ibid.*, May 1, 1843.

[260] *Ibid.*, May 31, 1843.

[261] *Ibid.*, June 3, 5, 1843.

[262] *Ibid.*, June 5, 1843.

[263] Richards to Guizot, Paris, July 13, 1843 (copy), in AH, F.O. and Ex.; Marshall, "An Unpublished Chapter of Hawaiian History," in *Harper's Magazine*, LXVII (September 1883), 516–517.

[264] For a brief summary of Marshall's career see W. L. W[right], Jr., "James

selected for the mission by Dr. Judd, after the chiefs had expressed
a desire to be represented in England by someone who was familiar
with the most recent events in the Islands.[265] Marshall was able to
leave the Islands only by resort to a ruse, for Paulet was determined
to prevent the King from sending an agent abroad. When, on March
11, Marshall sailed from Honolulu, he went ostensibly as an agent
of Ladd and Company on a vessel which that company had chartered to Paulet.[266]

Marshall arrived in New Orleans on May 22. Apparently he
brought to the United States the earliest report of the occupation of
the Hawaiian Islands. He arrived at a time when public opinion
was centered upon a variety of pressing problems, including the
recovery from the recent commercial depression and the vigorous
political maneuvering which preceded a presidential election. Commerce, the tariff, banking, Texas, Oregon, and party schisms vied
for public attention and left little time for concern over the fate of
a distant archipelago. There was, however, a body of public sentiment already hostile to Great Britain because of the belief that the
British government was seeking to thwart the legitimate expansion
of the United States into Texas and Oregon. At the same time, those
elements in American society which wished to have American jurisdiction firmly established in Oregon or extended to California could
not be indifferent to the possibility that the Hawaiian Islands might
pass into the possession of an unfriendly power.

At New Orleans, according to Marshall, the news of the cession
of the Islands caused "great excitement," particularly because the
public there was already sensitive on the subject of British inter-

Fowle Baldwin Marshall," in *Dictionary of
American Biography*, XII, 312–313.

[265] Testimony of Governor Kekuanaoa,
November 25, 1846, in *Arbitration between
the . . . . Government of the Hawaiian Islands and Messrs. Ladd & Co.*, p. 295.

[266] Marshall, *loc. cit.*, pp. 512–514; Journal of Stephen Reynolds, March 11, 1843;
Journal of William Paty, March 11, 1843.
Reynolds declared that Marshall's destination and mission were known to "only a
few favorites." Paty, who had been associated with Judd in the government prior
to the time of the cession, was aware of

the objectives of Marshall's trip; but how
Reynolds, who scarcely could be regarded
as a friend of Judd or as being in sympathy
with the King, learned the secret which he
said was revealed only to a few trusted
persons is uncertain and raises the question as to how generally it may have been
known among Americans in Honolulu.

A copy of Marshall's credentials may be
found in AH, F.O. and Ex. Funds to meet
the expenses of the mission were advanced
by Charles Brewer, a prominent American
merchant of Honolulu. Sullivan, *History of
C. Brewer and Company, Ltd.*, p. 64.

ference in the affairs of Texas.[267] From New Orleans, Marshall and the news of events at Honolulu traveled northward. On June 1 newspapers in Washington, quoting from New Orleans papers, announced the British occupation of the Hawaiian Islands. The *Madisonian,* the Washington organ of the Tyler administration, failed to comment editorially upon the cession. Its rival, the *Globe,* assailed England, predicted that if the propensity of the British government for colonial expansion remained unchecked Oregon would become the scene of British aggression, and expressed the hope that editorial indignation in various parts of the nation would "produce a prompt and decisive protest from our government."[268] Influential newspapers in the principal seaports of the nation joined the *Globe* in condemning Paulet and Great Britain and in expressing the belief that the government of the United States should take such measures as would compel Great Britain to disavow the occupation of the Hawaiian Islands.[269]

In Boston, where American commercial and religious interests in the Islands were centered, the *Post* stressed the importance of the Hawaiian Islands to the United States and declared: "No occasion has ever presented itself where the claim for action, on the part of this country, has been so urgent."[270] At least two editors favored an extension of the traditional American opposition to European aggression on the American continents to include the maintenance of Hawaiian independence, and the *New Orleans Bulletin* asserted that not only the Hawaiian Islands but also the island archipelagoes south of the equator, recently seized by France, "belong to the coast of this continent, and therefore upon the principle laid down by Mr. Monroe, in 1823 . . . . ought to be sacred, at our peril, from European aggressions."[271]

[267] Marshall, *loc. cit.,* p. 515.

[268] *Globe,* June 1, 7, 9, 1843; *Madisonian,* June 1, 1843.

[269] *New Orleans Bulletin,* quoted in *Niles' Register,* LXIV (June 10, 1843), 229; *New Orleans Bee,* quoted in the *Globe,* June 2, 1843; *New York Evening Post,* quoted in *ibid.,* June 5, 1843; *New York Plebeian,* quoted in *ibid.,* June 13, 1843; *Boston Atlas,* quoted in *ibid.,* June 12, 1843; *Phila-*

delphia Ledger, quoted in *ibid.,* June 9, 1843; *Boston Post,* quoted in the *Madisonian,* June 10, 1843.

[270] *Ibid.*

[271] *New Orleans Bulletin,* quoted in *Niles' Register,* LXIV, (June 10, 1843) 229; *New York Plebeian,* quoted in the *Globe,* June 13, 1843.

Several editors and correspondents emphasized the geographical proximity and

The British minister to the United States reported that the news of the cession of the Hawaiian Islands "is occasioning a good deal of excitement in the United States; and the American newspapers, with very few exceptions, are filled . . . . with vehemently abusive articles against Great Britain."[272] Merchants in Boston and New York sent memorials to President Tyler, protesting against the British occupation of the Hawaiian Islands and suggesting in the words of the Boston memorial that it would be expedient and proper for the United States to make "a decided remonstrance against a measure so destructive of its best interests."[273]

On June 2, Marshall arrived in Boston. While there he called upon former Secretary of State Webster, who appeared to be disturbed by the news that the Hawaiian Islands had passed into the control of Great Britain. Webster could no longer speak with authority as to the policy of the United States. He did express the opinion that the administration would use its influence to secure a restoration of Hawaiian sovereignty, and he provided at least minor assistance to Marshall in the form of a letter of introduction to Edward Everett.[274]

The administration moved deliberately, but emphatically. After

economic interdependence of the Hawaiian Islands and the west coast of North America. This theme was developed at length by a correspondent who signed his letters "M" in two communications to the *Baltimore American*, which were reprinted in the *Globe*, June 26, 29, 1843. A contributor to the *New York Plebeian* stated the extreme fears of this group when he wrote that the British acquisition of the Hawaiian Islands, together with the British claim to the mouth of the Columbia, gave Great Britain a position in which it could, if it were so disposed, "put an end to our whale fisheries, and deprive us of the 20,000 able seamen that they support." It was the aim of Great Britain, this writer feared, "to destroy the American preponderance" in the commerce of the Pacific. He concluded, therefore, that "the same policy which forced us to announce many years ago, in our feeble state, that we would endure no European interference in the affairs of the western hemisphere, would justify us in abating the evil of which we now complain."

[272] Fox to Aberdeen, Washington, D.C., June 13, 1843, in *Correspondence Relative to the Sandwich Islands*, p. 230.

[273] The memorial from Boston was printed in the *Madisonian*, June 10, 1843, and in *Niles' Register*, LXIV (July 1, 1843), 273. The memorial of the New York merchants, dated New York, June 14, 1843, may be found in USDS, "Miscellaneous Letters." It was transmitted to the President by P. J. Farnham & Co. in a letter dated New York, July 8, 1843, in *ibid.* From three residents of Warren County, Illinois, there came another memorial, expressing regret at the seizure of the Islands and asking the President to exert "all the power of your station, to ensure the restoration of the independence of those isles." A. C. Harding *et al.* to President Tyler, [June 26, 1843], in *ibid.*

[274] Marshall, *loc. cit.*, pp. 515–516. Henry A. Peirce and James J. Jarves accompanied Marshall when the latter called upon Webster.

a lapse of ten days, acting Secretary of State Hugh S. Legaré informed Everett that the anticipated opening of China to foreign commerce made it "impossible to overrate the importance of the Hawaiian group as a stage in the long voyage between Asia and America." Moreover, added Legaré, Hawaiian ports were so essential to the prosperity of the whaling fleets that it was doubtful "whether even the undisputed possession of the Oregon Territory and the use of the Columbia River, or indeed anything short of the acquisition of California . . . . would be sufficient indemnity to us for the loss of these harbors." Everett was instructed, therefore, to exert every effort to forestall a permanent British occupation of the Islands.[275]

There was little probability that the British government would make any effort to retain permanent possession of the Hawaiian Islands. At the close of May, two weeks before Legaré prepared the instructions to Everett, the latter had conferred with Aberdeen concerning the British occupation of the Islands. On that occasion, Aberdeen declared that the action of Paulet in taking possession of the Islands was wholly unauthorized, and he added that the pecuniary claims of British subjects were not a sufficient pretext for the occupation of the archipelago. He declined to promise that Great Britain would withdraw from the Islands; but Everett gained the impression that the British government was already so far committed to a recognition of Hawaiian independence that it would not reverse that policy.[276] On June 3 Aberdeen sent instructions to the British minister in Washington which contained the assurance that the government, while requiring adequate redress for the injustices suffered by its nationals, would adhere to its earlier promise to recognize the independent status of the Islands and would, "with the least practicable delay, ... call on Lord George Paulet to render an account of his conduct."[277] A more explicit statement of policy was contained in instructions to the minister in Paris, in which Aberdeen

[275] Acting Secretary of State Legaré to Everett, Washington, D.C., June 13, 1843, in FRUS, 1894, Appendix II, pp. 113–114.
[276] Everett to Legaré, London, June 1, 3, 1843, in *ibid.*, pp. 111–113; Everett to Daniel Webster, London, May 31, 1843 (private), in Edward Everett MSS, Massachusetts Historical Society Library.

[277] Aberdeen to Fox, June 3, 1843, in *Correspondence Relative to the Sandwich Islands*, pp. 180–181.

stated definitely that Great Britain would not retain possession of the Islands and would acknowledge the independence of the little kingdom.[278] This was repeated, in substance, in a note to Richards and Haalilio.[279]

On June 25 the British minister in Washington conveyed to the State Department the assurances from Aberdeen, and early in July, his note was published in newspapers in Washington. Observers in Washington were pleased, although perhaps not convinced. The *Globe* commented briefly that its readers would be "much gratified"; and President Tyler regarded the information as "very gratifying," but his suspicion of British diplomacy was too strong to overcome a fear that the apparent determination of Great Britain to protect its nationals might cover some "ambiguous or hidden intent."[280] In view of his concern lest Great Britain was engaged in an intrigue designed to deprive the United States of Texas and perhaps California, his skepticism with respect to British policy in Hawaii was not unnatural.

Apparently a considerable section of influential opinion in Great Britain was prepared to support the self-denying policy of the government. The influential *Times* declared that Great Britain would derive as much advantage from an independent Hawaii as from actual possession of the Islands.[281] For a time the *Spectator* dissented, but by the first of July it was ready to admit that its earlier judgment had been based upon a misapprehension as to conditions at the Islands and it advocated a policy of dealing justly with the Hawaiian rulers.[282] Six months later, after the episode had become history, the *Edinburgh Review* characterized Paulet's action as "imprudent," and praised the recognition of Hawaiian independence as "sound

[278] Aberdeen to Cowley, June 6, 1843, in *Correspondence Relative to the Sandwich Islands*, p. 181.

[279] Aberdeen to Haalilio and Richards, London, June 15, 1843, in AH, "British Commission Documents."

[280] Fox to Acting Secretary of State Upshur, Washington, D.C., June 25, 1843, in FRUS, 1894, Appendix II, p. 115; *Globe*, July 6, 1843; *Madisonian*, July 3, 1843; Tyler to Webster, Washington, July 8, 1843, in Lyon G. Tyler, *The Letters and Times of the Tylers* (Richmond, 1884–1885), II, 272.

[281] *The Times* (London), June 15, 1843. This editorial was described by Edward Everett as having "the appearance . . . . of being semiofficial, and from its having remained for two or three days uncontradicted in any quarter I am inclined to think that it was at least founded on good information." Everett to Legaré, London, June 14–19, 1843, in FRUS, 1894, Appendix II, p. 114.

[282] *The Spectator*, XVI (June 17, July 1, 1843), 554, 602.

doctrine, moral as well as political."[283] At the same time, Richards was assured by a Judge of the Admiralty Court that the upper classes in England generally had disapproved the occupation of the Islands.[284]

When Marshall reached London he found the government ready to give him a sympathetic hearing, while alert to protect British interests in the mid-Pacific. Shortly after his arrival he called upon Edward Everett, by whom he was advised to communicate with Richards and Haalilio, who were then on the Continent.[285] Two weeks later, after having awaited in vain the return of the commissioners, Marshall called at the Foreign Office. He had a lengthy and friendly interview with Addington, the Under Secretary of State—an interview which Richards later believed had strengthened the Hawaiian case.[286] British policy, however, had been clearly stated in a note from the Foreign Office to the Admiralty written three days before Marshall called upon Addington. That note contained nothing that could have surprised anyone familiar with the situation. In it Addington repeated the determination of the government to withdraw from the Hawaiian Islands, while discounting the fear that some other power would seize the archipelago. He stated that the government would not order Paulet to discontinue the occupation until certain grievances of British subjects at the Islands had been "finally and formally redressed." To this he added that the Foreign Office hoped to conclude an Anglo-French agreement for a joint recognition of Hawaiian independence, and that efforts would be made to negotiate such an agreement before Great Britain surrendered the diplomatic advantage which she enjoyed through the temporary occupation of the Islands.[287] This, apparently, was the policy which Addington outlined to Marshall during their first interview.

On July 14, the day of the interview between Addington and Marshall, Richards and Haalilio returned to London. They were disturbed by the reports from Honolulu and disappointed by the

[283] *Edinburgh Review*, LXXIX (January 1844), 44–45.

[284] Richards to Judd, London, February 28, 1844, in AH, Richards MSS.

[285] Marshall, *loc. cit.*, p. 516.

[286] *Ibid.*, pp. 516–517; Richards to Judd, London, July 29, 1843, in AH, F.O. and Ex.

[287] Addington to Barrow, July 11, 1843, in *Correspondence Relative to the Sandwich Islands*, pp. 239–240. This may be found also in Hawaiian Historical Commission, *Publications*, I, No. 2, pp. 36–37.

apparent unwillingness of Guizot to extend a formal recognition of Hawaiian independence until the British had withdrawn from the Islands. The hint by Addington that there were grievances which must be redressed contained the possibility of almost limitless disagreement, and Richards was further depressed by the jealousy which was aroused in London by the obvious dominance of American citizens in Hawaiian trade and politics. Despite the assurances which Marshall had received from Addington, Richards frankly was worried; and in a letter to Rufus Anderson he expressed the fear that the obstacles to be overcome were so serious that only the influence of the Hudson's Bay Company could save his mission from failure.[288]

This pessimism presumably was caused by the uncertainties which followed the occupation of the Islands by Paulet. Not the least of these uncertainties was the extent to which the British government would be influenced by the views of Alexander Simpson. Simpson had been in London for about one month. He had made good use of his time, if we may believe his own statement that he had been "engaged in daily communication on the affairs of Polynesia" with representatives of the government.[289] His arguments had not been wholly in vain. On July 22 the Queen's Advocate reported that a "great injustice" had been done to Simpson and Henry Skinner in the disposition of Greenway's estate and that the British government "would be justified in interfering" on their behalf.[290]

Some time passed before Richards and his associates learned of this opinion; but they had not been idle. Among the correspondence which Richards received from Honolulu was a statement of the charges which the Hawaiian government wished to prefer against Alexander Simpson.[291] In view of Simpson's obvious efforts to prejudice the British officials, this exposition of the case against Simpson came at an opportune time. For several weeks the Ha-

[288] Richards to Anderson, London, July 18, 1843, in Letters to the American Board, CXXXV, No. 97.

[289] Simpson, *Life of Thomas Simpson*, pp. 376–377.

[290] J. Dodson to Aberdeen, July 22, 1843, in *Correspondence Relative to the Sandwich Islands*, p. 254.

[291] Journal of William Richards, July 24, 1843. The charges against Simpson were that he had been abusive in his attitude toward officers of the Hawaiian government, that he had been contemptuous of Hawaiian legal procedure and laws, and that his conduct as a trustee of the estate of F. J. Greenway indicated that he was unfriendly to the native authorities. A copy of these charges, dated September 8, 1843, is in AH, F.O. and Ex.

waiian commissioners, assisted by officers of the Hudson's Bay Company, were occupied with the preparation of a note to be transmitted to the Foreign Office. Upon this note and the accompanying documents rested the hope of Richards and his associates that the influence of Alexander Simpson could be nullified; when, on August 7, note and documents were sent to Aberdeen, the Hawaiian case was materially strengthened by the fact that it had the approval of the great company whose agency at Honolulu constituted the most important British investment at the Islands.[292] These communications were not without effect at the Foreign Office. Aberdeen admitted that they contained "a good deal worthy of consideration,"[293] and, on August 9, Alexander Simpson was informed that because of conflicting reports of what had occurred at the Islands the government was experiencing "the greatest difficulty" in determining what policy would be consistent with justice.[294]

On August 14 Marshall called again at the Foreign Office. He was received by Addington, who was particularly solicitous to learn the details of the contract whereby Ladd and Company had been granted extensive privileges in the exploitation of Hawaiian land. During the interview Addington stated that he had been told that the King had surrendered all his land and even his sovereignty to an American. If this were true, he declared, the King was not fit to rule the Islands. Marshall seems to have been taken by surprise; but on the following day he returned to the Foreign Office accompanied by Peter A. Brinsmade. During the ensuing conversation, Addington admitted that he was convinced that the lease did not endanger the independent sovereignty of the Hawaiian government. As a result of these interviews Richards believed that the outlook for a decision favorable to the Hawaiian government had become "a little brighter."[295] In this he was correct, and, on August 17, the

[292] Richards to Judd, London, July 29, 1843, in *ibid.;* Journal of William Richards, August 2, 4, 7, 1843.

[293] Everett to Upshur, London, August 15, 1843, in FRUS, 1894, Appendix II, pp. 117–118.

[294] Canning to Simpson, August 9, 1843, in *Correspondence Relative to the Sandwich Islands,* pp. 306–307.

[295] Journal of William Richards, August 14, 15, 1843; Marshall, *loc. cit.,* pp. 518–520; Testimony of J. F. B. Marshall, November 23, 1846, in *Arbitration between the . . . . Government of the Hawaiian Islands and Messrs. Ladd & Co.,* pp. 253–254; Haalilio, Richards, and Marshall to Kamehameha III, London, August 18, 1843, in *ibid.,* Appendix, pp. 118–120.

Hawaiian commissioners learned that it was probable that the British government would accept their views upon the several matters in dispute.[296] The pessimism which had gripped Richards one month before largely disappeared, and he reported to Rufus Anderson that his communications to the Foreign Office had been well received and that they appeared to have produced "a very considerable effect on the mind of Lord Aberdeen."[297] Marshall likewise was satisfied. Believing that the objects of his special mission had been accomplished, he left London on August 18 to begin the long return journey to Honolulu.[298]

The general outline of British policy had been formulated, and it was evident that ultimately Great Britain would withdraw its forces from the Islands. There remained the consideration of specific complaints which had been submitted on behalf of British subjects at Honolulu. These complaints were referred to the legal advisers of the Crown, who, after several weeks of deliberation, sent their report to the Foreign Office on September 7. Five days later Aberdeen transmitted a summary of this report to Richards and Haalilio. It constituted a major diplomatic victory for the Hawaiian commission. Of the four cases of alleged grievance which had been submitted to the Queen's Advocate, three were dismissed either by the acceptance of the arguments of the commission or by an acquiescence in a settlement already reached at Honolulu. Only in the fourth case, the claim of Richard Charlton to a large tract of land in Honolulu, were the arguments of the commissioners rejected and a decision given in favor of a British subject.[299]

[296] Marshall, "An Unpublished Chapter in Hawaiian History," in *Harper's Magazine*, LXVII (September 1883), 520.

[297] Richards to Anderson, London, August 18, 1843, in Letters to the American Board, CXXXV, No. 98.

[298] Journal of William Richards, August 18, 1843. Richards wrote that Marshall was "an honor to Oahu" and that he had "done much good" in London.

[299] Dodson to Aberdeen, September 7, 1843, in *Further Papers Relative to the Sandwich Islands*, pp. 1–9; Aberdeen to Haalilio and Richards, September 12, 1843,

in AH, F.O. and Ex. and printed in *Further Papers Relative to the Sandwich Islands*, pp. 9–16. In July, Aberdeen had referred to the case of Pelly v. Charlton as one in which there had been "every appearance of personal animosity on the part of the prosecutors, and gross partiality on the part of the Government." Aberdeen to Cowley, July 21, 1843, in *Correspondence Relative to the Sandwich Islands*, pp. 252–253. The decision of the Hawaiian courts in Pelly v. Charlton was not questioned by the Law Officers of the Crown, but the belief that Charlton had been the victim of injustice may have prompted the Queen's Advocate

These decisions were received by Richards with mixed sentiments. He recognized that they represented, in general, a triumph for his government.[300] He was disappointed, however, by the award of the land to Charlton, believing it to involve a greater injustice than would have been caused by an adverse decision in any of the other cases.[301] He hoped to secure a reversal of this opinion; and, on September 20, he and Haalilio submitted to the Foreign Office additional evidence designed to clarify the position of the Hawaiian government with respect to Charlton's claims.[302] This new evidence had the approval of an officer of the Hudson's Bay Company, and Richards described the note in which it was embodied as "a strong document." It failed to produce any modification of the decision rendered by the Queen's Advocate and endorsed by Aberdeen.[303] Although the authorities at Honolulu appear to have been no less disappointed than Richards by the award of the land to Charlton, they had no alternative but to accept the decision with as much grace as possible. In the following February, therefore, the Hawaiian government formally ratified the decisions of the British government.[304]

The decision announced by Aberdeen on September 12 was the final step in the evolution of British policy toward the Hawaiian Islands. There remained the problem of securing from France some guaranty to respect the independence and integrity of the native monarchy. This was an integral part of Aberdeen's policy in the eastern and central Pacific. During July he had suggested that the United States, Great Britain, and France join in a pledge not to encroach upon the sovereignty of the Hawaiian government.[305] The United States was traditionally unwilling to become a party to a

or the Foreign Office to hope that he could be given compensation through the validation of his claim to the disputed land in Honolulu.

[300] Journal of William Richards, September 16, 1843.

[301] Richards to Anderson, London, September 18, 1843, in Letters to the American Board, CXXXV, No. 100.

[302] Haalilio and Richards to Aberdeen, London, September 20, 1843, in *Further Papers Relative to the Sandwich Islands,* pp. 16–23.

[303] Journal of William Richards, September 23, 1843; Aberdeen to Haalilio and Richards, London, September 30, 1843, in AH, F.O. and Ex.; Aberdeen to Haalilio and Richards, November 9, 1843, in *Further Papers Relative to the Sandwich Islands,* p. 34.

[304] Judd to Miller, Lahaina, February 12, 1844, in *The Friend,* February 20, 1844, p. 22.

[305] Aberdeen to Cowley, July 21, 1843, in *Correspondence Relative to the Sandwich Islands,* pp. 252–253.

multilateral commitment, and presumably Aberdeen had no real hope that it could be induced to abandon this policy of aloofness. France was more responsive. Guizot promptly expressed approval, but he suggested that the negotiations be postponed until Great Britain was ready to withdraw from the Islands.[306] This was a concession which Aberdeen was not then prepared to make.

The governments of Great Britain and France were in agreement upon fundamental policy, but they were divided as to procedure. Aberdeen therefore dropped temporarily the negotiations with France and concentrated upon the adjustment of the issues in dispute with the Hawaiian government. The larger problem of guaranteeing the future safety of the Hawaiian Islands was not forgotten. By the middle of August the Hawaiian commissioners and the minister of the United States were aware that no order for the evacuation of the Islands would be issued so long as the occupation by Paulet might serve as a weapon in the negotiations with France. A hint of this policy appeared in the *Times* late in August, and the determination of the British government upon this point was reaffirmed by Addington in conversations with Richards in September.[307] With this policy Richards had no quarrel. He and Everett feared that France, if given an opportunity, would seize the archipelago; and both men believed that the continuation of the British occupation pending a recognition of Hawaiian independence by France would be "for the interest of the islands." That recognition, Everett predicted, would not long be withheld.[308]

Early in October, Aberdeen instructed the British ambassador in Paris to inform Guizot that Great Britain was prepared to evacuate the Hawaiian Islands as soon as an Anglo-French agreement to re-

[306] Cowley to Aberdeen, Paris, July 28, 1843, in *Correspondence Relative to the Sandwich Islands*, pp. 273–274, and in *Report of the* [Hawaiian] *Minister of Foreign Relations*, 1855, Appendix, p. 19.

[307] Everett to Upshur, London, August 15, 1843, in FRUS, 1894, Appendix II, pp. 117–118; Marshall, *loc. cit.*, p. 520; *The Times* (London), August 26, 1843; Journal of William Richards, September 18, 30, October 2, 11, 1843. When, early in November, the news reached Europe that Admiral Thomas had restored the native government,

Aberdeen assured the Hawaiian commissioners that Great Britain would not be "disposed to disapprove . . . . a step which has given so much satisfaction to the King of the Sandwich Islands." Aberdeen to Haalilio and Richards, November 13, 1843, in AH, "British Commission Documents," and in *Further Papers Relative to the Sandwich Islands*, p. 35.

[308] Everett to Upshur, London, September 28, 1843, in FRUS, 1894, Appendix II, pp. 118–119.

spect the future independence of the Islands had been signed.[309] Guizot promptly agreed to resume the negotiations which had been first proposed during the preceding July;[310] and, on November 28, 1843, Aberdeen and the French ambassador to Great Britain signed a convention in which the two nations agreed to respect the independence and territorial integrity of the Hawaiian kingdom.[311] Richards, of course, was pleased. He wrote that the pact was "written strongly" and that it was well designed to serve its purpose. The chief source of his satisfaction was to be found in the added comment that it was believed in Paris that as a result of this agreement the "designs of the French government" had been "completely baffled."[312]

Aberdeen was not yet satisfied. He continued to hope that the Anglo-French agreement might be converted into a tripartite pact. Such a hope was in harmony with the general policy of Great Britain; for if the United States could be persuaded to join in this self-denying move, a bulwark would be erected around the status quo in one important section of the eastern Pacific. In May 1844 the ministers of Great Britain and France at Washington joined in inviting the government of the United States to become a party to the convention of November 28, 1843. This invitation was declined by President Tyler on the ground that acceptance would be a violation of the traditional policy of the United States, and Aberdeen was compelled to be content with a reaffirmation by Secretary of State Calhoun of the intention of the United States to respect the sovereignty of the Hawaiian government.[313] Meanwhile, in March 1844, Belgium had followed the lead of its powerful neighbors by formally acknowledging the independence of the little Pacific kingdom.[314]

[309] Aberdeen to Cowley, October 9, 1843, in *Further Papers Relative to the Sandwich Islands*, p. 31.

[310] Cowley to Aberdeen, Paris, October 13, 1843, in *ibid.*, p. 32.

[311] The text of the treaty has been published in many places. It may be found in FRUS, 1894, Appendix II, p. 64; *The Friend*, May 1, 1844, p. 45; Bingham, *Sandwich Islands*, pp. 606–607; Jarves, *History of the Hawaiian Islands*, p. 189.

[312] Richards to Judd, Paris, December 28, 1843, in AH, F.O. and Ex.

[313] Aberdeen to Pakenham, December 26, 1843, July 3, 1844, in *Additional Papers Relative to the Sandwich Islands* [London, 1844], pp. 1, 3; Pakenham to Aberdeen, Washington, D.C., May 29, June 3, 1844, in *ibid.*, pp. 2–3.

[314] Goblet to Haalilio and Richards, Brussels, March 26, 1844, in *Polynesian*, November 9, 1844; *Report of the Minister of Foreign Relations*, May 21, 1845, p. 17.

One object of the Hawaiian commission remained to be realized. It was an object in which Richards had a particularly strong interest. As a former missionary he shared the hope of the entire missionary group that the government of France could be persuaded to modify the commercial treaty negotiated by Laplace. Richards and Haalilio therefore returned to Paris late in October 1843.[315] It was quickly apparent that Guizot was still unwilling to consider any change in the Laplace treaty.[316] Richards, however, did not abandon hope. Twice during December the Hawaiian commissioners urged Guizot to consider favorably the draft of a proposed treaty which they had submitted in June.[317] Guizot was adamant. Finally, in apparent exasperation, he declared that further negotiations must await the settlement of certain complaints made by Dudoit; and he informed the persistent commissioners that "from this time, Gentlemen, you will without doubt judge that nothing further prevents you to quit Europe, and return to your country."[318] This pointed suggestion did not deter Richards. He addressed a lengthy dispatch to Guizot on January 10, 1844, and this was followed by an interview with Desages, an Under Secretary of State,[319] but the French government did not alter its announced policy of refusing to consider the modification of the obnoxious treaty. Convinced at last that Guizot was immovable, Richards and Haalilio left Europe to return to the Hawaiian Islands by way of the United States.

It is evident that Richards was greatly disappointed by the refusal of Guizot to negotiate a new treaty. He had reason, however, to recall the results of his mission with satisfaction. Neither he nor any of his associates had been experienced in the devious arts of diplomacy, and only Sir George Simpson had been familiar with the problems of politics and government in a great capital. Throughout the mission, Haalilio had been a silent partner, whose principal contribution was to provide tangible expression of the fiction that the

[315] Journal of William Richards, October 24, 26, 1843.

[316] Guizot to Richards, Paris, November 8, 1843, in AH, F.O. and Ex.

[317] Richards to Guizot, Paris, December 11, 1843, in *ibid.*; Haalilio and Richards to Guizot, Paris, December 21, 1843, in *ibid.*

[318] Guizot to Richards and Haalilio, Paris, January 4, 1844, in *ibid.*

[319] Haalilio and Richards to Guizot, Paris, January 10, 1844, in *ibid.*; Journal of William Richards, January 30, 1844.

quest for Hawaiian independence was managed in part by natives of the Islands. Richards had received invaluable assistance from Simpson and from James F. B. Marshall, and he had been favored by the influence of powerful friends in Washington and in London. Without that assistance his mission might have been a failure. Withal it was Richards who carried the principal burden of the organization of the mission, of determining its itinerary, of the negotiations in Washington and Paris, and of preparing the substantial mass of correspondence by which the commissioners presented their case to the several foreign offices. The results were an impressive tribute to the skill and patience of Richards, and it was with justification that Sir George Simpson described him as a man who was "as shrewd and intelligent as he was pious and humble."[320]

The recognition of Hawaiian independence was the climax of sixty-five years of Hawaiian history. During that period the Islands emerged from the obscurity of an unknown Polynesian archipelago to gain a position, however humble, among the nations of the world. The little kingdom had already acquired many of the outward aspects of Western civilization. It catered to the trade of a great ocean, and it was the center from which the manufactures and influence of the United States radiated to all parts of the northeastern Pacific. It could boast of a written constitution, a code of civil and criminal law, a score of flourishing churches, and a system of public education. Few among "the younger people" were unable to read and write, and these thousands of literate Hawaiians had, in their own language, "a library, embracing a considerable variety of books on a variety of subjects, including the Holy Scriptures, works on natural history, civil history, church history, geography, political economy, mathematics, and statute law, besides a number of elementary books."[321]

This development of a Polynesian kingdom with Western institutions was, in part, the result of the location of the Hawaiian Islands astride the principal trade routes of the northern and central Pacific. It had been possible only because of the ready amiability with which

---

[320] Simpson, *Journey Round the World*, II, 162.

[321] Haalilio and Richards to Secretary of State Webster, Washington, D.C., December 14, 1842, in FRUS, 1894, Appendix II, p. 42.

Hawaiian chiefs and commoners had welcomed all classes of foreigners to the Islands. The principal forces in the creation of the
new Hawaiian kingdom, however, had been the few score of American traders and missionaries who had made the Islands their home
and whose energy in the introduction of the political, religious, and
economic ideals of their native land had established an American
frontier in Hawaii.

INDEX

Aberdeen, Earl of, negotiations concerning Hawaiian independence, 407, 448, 450, 459–463; rebukes Charlton, 421, 449; disavowal of Paulet, 455–456; guaranty of Hawaiian independence, 461–463; approves restoration of Hawaiian government, 462 n.
"Account Book of Ship Sultan," 56 n.
"Acteon," visit to Honolulu, 1836, 281
"Active," 101 n.
Adams, Alexander: 38, 57, 94 n., 382 n.; "Log of the Kaahumanu," 57 n.
Adams, C. F., *Memoirs of John Quincy Adams*, 90 n.
Adams, E. D., *British Interests and Activities in Texas*, 395 n.
Adams, John Quincy, 90, 194, 441; favors Hawaiian independence, 442, 445–446
Addington, H. U., statement of British policy, 457; skeptical of lease to Ladd and Company, 459
Additional Papers Relative to the Sandwich Islands, 463 n.
Adultery, laws prohibiting, 174, 176, 190, 330
Agriculture, 7; early plantations, 239–250; interest of American missionaries in, 250; speculative character of, 251–252
Alaska, discovery of sea otter trade, 11; American trade with, 19–20, 78–79, 220–221
"Albatross," 29, 31, 56 n.
Alden, C. S., *Lawrence Kearny*, 438 n.
Alexander, A. C., *Koloa Plantation 1835–1935*, 236 n.
Alexander, J. M., *Mission Life in Hawaii*, 370 n.

Alexander, M. C., *William Patterson Alexander*, 146 n.
Alexander, W. D., *Brief History of the Hawaiian People*, 141 n.; "Early Industrial Teaching of Hawaiians," 362 n.; "Early Trading in Hawaii," 56 n.; "Oahu Charity School," 382 n.; "Origin of the Polynesian Race," 3 n.; "Overthrow of the Ancient Tabu System," 125 n.; "Russians on Kauai," 47 n.; "Sketch of the Constitutional History of the Hawaiian Kingdom," 324 n.; "Story of the Cleopatra's Barge," 62 n.
Alexander, Rev. William P., quoted, 248 n., 324, 336, 356
Allan, G. T., quoted, 411 n.
Allen, A. J., *Ten Years in Oregon*, 234 n.
Allen, Anthony, 38–39
Allen, Captain Joseph, commander of the "Maro," 80
Allen, R. H., "Hawaii's Pioneers in Journalism," 263 n.
Alphabet, Hawaiian, creation of, 134
Americans, at the Hawaiian Islands, 94–95, 266–268, 400–401, 466; fear of possible aggression by, 95–96; predominance in Hawaiian economy, 265–267; property at Honolulu, 267; alleged hostility to British subjects, 398 n., 399, 426, 447; dislike of Paulet, 428–429, 431 n., 435, 437; memorial to Captain Kearny, 438–439; pleasure at restoration of King, 440. *See also* Missionaries, American
American Board of Commissioners for Foreign Missions, organized, 122; early interest in Hawaiian Islands, 122–124; instructions to missionaries, 124, 137–138,

467

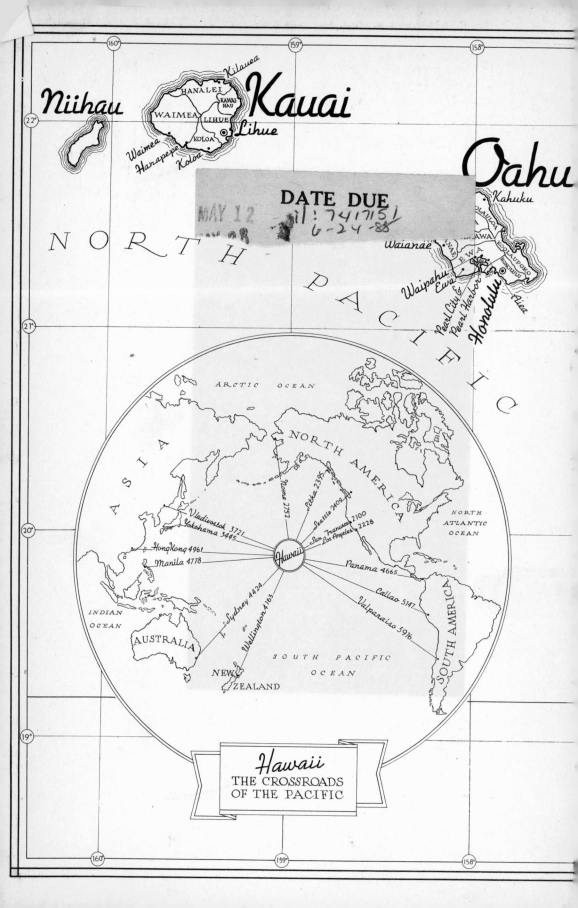

Niihau

Kilauea
HANALEI
WAIMEA
KAWAI
HAU
LIHUE
KOLOA
Kauai
○ Lihue
Waimea
Hanapepe
Koloa

Oahu
Kahuku

N O R T H   P A C I F I C

Waianae
NAE
KOOLAULOA
EWA
AWA
KOOLAUPOKO
Waipahu
Ewa
Pearl City &
Pearl Harbor
Honolulu
Aiea

ARCTIC   OCEAN

A S I A

NORTH AMERICA

Rome 7752
Sitka 2396
Seattle 2409
San Francisco 2100
Los Angeles 2228

Vladivostok 3721
Yokohama 3445
HongKong 4961
Manila 4778

Hawaii

Panama 4665
Callao 5147
Valparaiso 5916

NORTH
ATLANTIC
OCEAN

INDIAN
OCEAN

Sydney 4424
Wellington 4163

AUSTRALIA

NEW
ZEALAND

SOUTH   PACIFIC
OCEAN

SOUTH AMERICA

Hawaii
THE CROSSROADS
OF THE PACIFIC